Date Due
FEB 21 1972
DEC 12 1973
APR 23 2005
W/D
Demco 38-297

D1256798

THE ART OF DISCRIMINATION

The Art of Discrimination

THOMSON'S *THE SEASONS*
AND THE LANGUAGE
OF CRITICISM

Ralph Cohen

UNIVERSITY OF CALIFORNIA PRESS
Berkeley and Los Angeles
1964

Published in the United States of America
by the University of California Press
Berkeley and Los Angeles, California

Published in Great Britain by
Routledge & Kegan Paul Ltd
London

Printed in Great Britain

To
Rose and Sam Cohen

CONTENTS

ILLUSTRATIONS

(between pages 276 and 277)

FIGURES

ACKNOWLEDGEMENTS

DURING THE PREPARATION OF THIS MANUSCRIPT I have received many helpful suggestions from John Espey, Earl L. Griggs, Judd Hubert, William Matthews, Blake Nevius, Marjorie H. Nicolson, Charles Peake, and Abraham Rothberg. I have tried to write a book that these readers would find valuable; I hope they will not be disappointed.

To Edna Davis and William Conway of the William Andrews Clark Memorial Library, to Esther Euler and Edward Mignon of the UCLA Library, to David Foxon and Ian Willison of the British Museum, and to the staffs of the Huntington Library, the Library of Congress, the Columbia University Library, the New York Public Library, and the National Library of Scotland, I am indebted for kind assistance in a long and provoking search for materials.

In preparing the manuscript for publication I have received valuable help from Diana Azar (typing), Constance Bullock (check list), and Toni Mennell (proofreading). The errors that remain are, I regret, my own.

I was assisted in completing the manuscript by generous grants from the American Council of Learned Societies and from the Research Committee of UCLA. I thank them for their help, and I thank Routledge & Kegan Paul and Columbia University Press for permission to reprint a portion of Chapter V which originally appeared in *Reason and the Imagination*, ed. Joseph Mazzeo (1962).

To my wife who has patiently aided in the preparation of this manuscript, hoping for me to follow it with an explication of *The Seasons*, I promise the rewards of patience, soon.

R. C.

Minute discrimination is not accidental. All sublimity is founded on minute discrimination.

BLAKE

INTRODUCTION

This art [of criticism], like every other, must have its science to analyse and improve it . . .

JOHN BRUCE,
First Principles of Philosophy, 1780

(a) ON THE CHOICE OF SUBJECT

The 'technique', or treatment, of a problem begins with its first expression as a question. The way a question is asked limits and disposes the ways in which any answer to it—right or wrong—may be given.

SUZANNE LANGER

THIS IS A BOOK ABOUT CRITICISM: it explores the principles and practice of criticism applied to a single poem, James Thomson's *The Seasons* (1730–46). Within the past two hundred years this poem has been a model for other poems, the butt of satire, the occasion for fine printing and extensive engravings, the subject of books, essays, letters, paintings, even the legal document in a copyright precedent. Of these uses of the poem I have focused on the ones called 'criticism'; I have sought to analyse the diverse meanings attributed to 'criticism', the boundaries extending or confining each meaning, the method and evidence provided for maintaining such boundaries.

I deal with the relation between 'practical' and 'philosophical' criticism, although the term 'practical' criticism was not used in the eighteenth century—the common term being 'particular'. ('Particular' criticism was applied to explanation of specific works or passages; 'philosophic' to exposition of principles governing such works or passages. For example, John Scott, in his essay 'On Thomson's Seasons' (1785), distinguished between 'general criticism', dealing with principles governing the poem as a whole and 'particular criticism', which referred to the examination of specific passages.[1])

I have distinguished three eighteenth-century applications of the term 'criticism': (1) process, (2) product, (3) by-product. As 'process', criticism is the activity of the poet in making aesthetic decisions in the composition of his work; as 'product', criticism is the formal discipline of explaining or evaluating (or theorizing about) literary works; as 'by-product', criticism appears as explanations, interpretations, or evaluations incidental to other artistic activities. The sources of the first are letters, manuscripts, and revisions of the poet; of the second, critical essays and books; of the third, parodies,[2] illustrations, and poems that become models for other poems.

The first two uses are self-evident; the third requires an explanation in as much as I have assumed that illustrations are non-verbal interpretations. I have devoted Chapter V to demonstrating this assumption although many eighteenth-century critics took it for granted. Illustrations not only explain a passage, but, when put into words, support, contradict, and in some cases even test, verbal comments.

Of criticisms made on *The Seasons*, many were fragmentary, others incomplete, and still others systematic (systematization includes illustrations) though limited to specific subjects such as diction or

[1] John Scott, *Critical Essays* (London, 1785), p. 1. For eighteenth-century distinctions between 'philosophical', 'historical', and 'corrective' criticism, see James Harris, *Upon the Rise and Progress of Criticism* (County of W., 1752), pp. 6–23. See also Ephraim Chambers, *Cyclopaedia* (London, 1741), I: '*Literary Criticism* is of great extent, as it takes in the art of judging of facts: a branch of *criticism*, which regards not only history, but also the discernment of the real works of an author, the real author of a work, the genuine reading of a text, and the art of discovering supposititious monuments, charters, interpolated passages, etc. The other parts of *literary criticism*, are, the art of judging of works of genius, their excellencies and defects. We have also *Grammatical Criticism*, or the art of interpreting and discovering the words and meanings of an author.'

Chambers defined 'philosophical criticism' as 'the art of judging of opinions and hypotheses in philosophy'.

For 'the science of rational criticism', see 'Criticism', *Encyclopaedia Britannica* (Edinburgh, 1771), II, 292–3.

For a study of Thomson's reputation, see Ann I. Mellard, *English Critical Opinions of James Thomson from 1726 to 1942* (unpublished M.A. thesis, U. of Colorado, 1945).

[2] For a parody of Thomson's style, see Isaac H. Browne, *Pipe of Tobacco* (London, 1736).

unity. Critics often consider that their criticism refers to the 'whole' poem, but criticism, no matter how systematic, always explains only some parts or procedures, and although no criticism attempts to explain everything, this has not prevented critics from claiming that everything has been explained.

This book analyses claims and comments that English critics have made about *The Seasons*. It is not an explication of the poem —I hope in the not-too-distant future to publish such a study—but of interpretations of the poem. Although this book includes a history of English criticisms of *The Seasons* and refers to changes in Thomson's reputation and in literary taste from 1750 to 1960,[1] it is not a history of criticism or a study of Thomson's reputation or his receptions. It is an analysis of critical statements and critical activity, spanning more than two hundred years, with regard to a single poem; it seeks to formulate and evaluate these criticisms and to consider their applicability to a general theory of criticism. Such a study is exploratory, and may, perhaps, encourage similar metacritical enterprises leading to systematic statements about criticism more reliable than many now available.

In selecting a descriptive poem as the object of criticism, I have had to neglect critical issues raised in other genres, and my findings have relevance to these only when the issues overlap. This study, moreover, takes its start from eighteenth-century critical theory, and for such an initiation *The Seasons* has immense advantages. Being, as Johnson said, a poem 'of a new kind', it made specific demands upon the inherited critical tradition. It was the model for other nature poems that were later used to discriminate its 'style'. It repeatedly led critics to compare it with works in painting, and it became the most illustrated poem in the English language. For long periods of time critics agreed in approving its subject and disapproving of its diction. Critics praised it for precise natural description and accurate scientific knowledge, yet it described some places imprecisely, and it relied upon the findings of contemporary science that were not always accurate. For more than a hundred years,

[1] *The Seasons* was published in 1730, *Winter* having been issued in 1726, *Summer* in 1727, *Spring* in 1728, and *Autumn* with the whole in 1730. From 1730 to 1746 the poem was revised twice, exclusive of the revisions of individual seasons prior to 1730. In 1748 Thomson died, and the posthumous English critical commentaries on the poem began in 1753 with Robert Shiels's life of Thomson.

common readers joined critics in making *The Seasons* a popular success.

These facts have served to make it the focus of critical activity for two centuries so that, in addition to reflecting changes in interpretation and evaluation, commentaries disclose the techniques used in arriving at interpretations and evaluations. To study these techniques, I have selected a number of issues, each of which, while derived from criticisms of *The Seasons*, possesses relevance for theory of criticism. Each chapter poses a problem or a cluster of problems and traces its ramifications from the eighteenth century to the present. I have analysed the poet's process and its expression in revisions; the critical neglect of relevant and available evidence and the means by which this neglect is overcome; the conditions for 'attention' and the significance of attending; the role of the exception challenging critical hypotheses to trust perceptions rather than principles; the self-correcting function of criticism in relying upon later works to provide verification of earlier judgements; the limits of comparison and the need for speculation; the functions of analogy in critical language; the significance of non-verbal criticism in interpretation; the consequences of critical agreements and disagreements and the criteria for their examination.

In this book, these issues fall into three main groups in rough chronological order in which they develop in the criticism of the poem: the composition of the poem, discriminations made about it by critics other than the poet, and the implications of settled judgements based on these discriminations: (1) Chapters I and II—the study of 'process' and its absorption into criticism as 'product'; (2) Chapters III, IV, and V—the functions and implications of comparative discriminations; (3) Chapters VI and VII—the analysis of critical agreements and disagreements. Chapter VIII, the last chapter, draws some inferences for general critical theory from the particular instances in the preceding chapters.

There are two appendices in the book. The first is a checklist of all the English and foreign editions of *The Seasons*, the purpose of which is to determine the number of editions and to specify the years in which it was most frequently reprinted. I have used this checklist to substantiate assumptions about popularity and interpretations discussed in Chapters V and VII. It represents a tool for criticism and thus has a place in this book. The second appendix is an example of bibliographic identity that has been important in my critical approach because, by identifying John More, I have been able to expound his critical views with some assurance that I understand his use of critical ideas and terms (Chapter IV). At the same time I have been able to track down the history of a bibliographical blunder, a modern analogy to the textual steeplechase which I pursue in Chapter I.

(b) ON METHODS

> In every systematic treatise two things are required. The first is a statement of the subject; the other, which although second in order ranks higher in importance, is an indication of the methods by which we may attain our ends.
>
> LONGINUS

> Among the best critics of late, there is a decided tendency toward a more careful and discriminative use of critical terms.
>
> J. BRAY, 1898

This essay both uses and describes the language of criticism; and although problems are analysed by the evidence to which they refer, the language guides us to the attitude as well as to the evidence of the critic. But critical language, especially eighteenth-century uses of it, is very slippery. Regarding 'taste', for example, David Hume wrote (1757), 'Every voice is united in applauding elegance, propriety, simplicity, spirit in writing; and in blaming fustian, affectation, coldness, and a false brilliancy. But when critics come to particulars, this seeming unanimity vanishes, and it is found that they had affixed a very different meaning to their expressions.'[1] I have had, therefore, to prepare a reader's handbook as I proceeded, noting and explaining the changes in critical usage reflected by the interactions described in the following chapters.

I have found it necessary to use current terms like 'method', 'insight', 'speculation', 'judgement', 'limitations', combating their imprecision by examples, definitions, and careful usage. I know that 'method' and 'insight', for example, can conceal absence of knowledge as readily as did 'genius' and 'delicacy' in the eighteenth century. In not shying away from critical dilemmas by assuming they

[1] 'Of the Standard of Taste', *Essays Moral Political and Literary*, ed. T. H. Green and T. H. Grose (London, 1875), I, 266.

do not exist or can be hidden in a hazy or systematic explanation, I have had to venture alternative explanations with the acknowledgement that information is meagre and the inference tentative. But I am prepared to take the risk of distinguishing between useful and useless speculation, between 'hunches' that are provocative, and those that are made in and lead to the dark.[1]

[1] Limitations appear not only in explorations of problems but also in the very language of criticism, which, having a past, cannot, even in context, disregard the social, religious, scientific, and later, industrial attitudes attached to it, especially in a term like 'discrimination'. For this term, which originally was restricted (Phillips, *The New World of English Words*, 1658) to a 'putting a difference between one thing and another', was applied in the latter part of the eighteenth century to the making of appropriate and intelligent critical distinctions. John More, in 1777, used the term with approbation when he referred to 'classical firmness of discrimination' (John More, *Strictures Critical and Sentimental on Thomson's Seasons* (London, 1777), p. 73) which could be exercised in explaining *The Seasons*. John Gregory, however, in 1765 argued that 'discrimination' implied the capacity of some critics to observe qualities which were trivial, and thus identified discrimination with tendencies towards over-refinement in critical analysis. By the mid-nineteenth century discrimination was identified by some as a wise, anti-democratic critical process in which sensitive critics were opposed to popular but unrefined approval, and by other critics, who supported theories of general approbation and the taste of the mass readers, as a process of over-refinement and the creation of undeserved distinctions. Our contemporary social meanings of discrimination are bound up with 'unfair or injurious distinctions' against groups or classes, in contrast to the earlier uses referring to discerning, penetrating, and appropriate distinctions, and exist side by side with them.

In addition to eighteenth-century usages of 'discrimination' identified with taste or value, with refinement and progress, distinctions attributed to the sensibility of the writer and critic, modern uses of 'discrimination' identify it with types of problems or with distinctions within them. Ronald S. Crane declares that 'there can thus be no good "literary" criticism, in this language, that does not presuppose a constant making of moral and psychological discriminations and a constant concern with nuances of thought' (Ronald S. Crane, *The Languages of Criticism and the Structure of Poetry* (Toronto, 1953), p. 189). For eighteenth-century critics, the opposite of discrimination was either over-refinement, no refinement (absence of taste), or the imposition of a 'systematic' refinement. For modern critics, the opposite of discrimination can, in addition, be a wrong selection of problems.

I have sought to make my uses clear by context and I have tried to illustrate the 'discrimination' I trace by aligning myself with the critics who use it to make precise and revelant distinctions, not those who identify it with social preferences. Yet I cannot escape a self-conscious recognition

INTRODUCTION

In the criticism of *The Seasons*, certain problems persist while others change. Critics pursued reasons for Thomson's skill as nature poet through two centuries; his flattering eulogies, his love passages, his historical catalogues led to no continuing inquiries. I have sought to explain why criticism selects problems, why it pursues, abandons, or resumes them.

Although I focus upon 'problems', the identification of 'problems' with critical inquiry was found in no eighteenth-century synonymy. 'Inquiry' was a synonym for 'search', but 'problem' was identified with mathematical propositions for which solutions were available by rule or with dark or concealed wisdom. Its application to literature and to life in our contemporary sense as 'a matter which needs thinking about in order to find the solution; a difficulty; something to which an answer must be found . . . any difficult situation in life' was due to the realization that, even in mathematics, rules did not always solve the 'problem'.

When Cleanth Brooks writes that criticism needs 'to discriminate more closely among the various problems with which criticism in the large is concerned' he uses 'problem' to mean a carefully bounded inquiry.[1] Yet when Dewey uses the term, the 'bounds' of the inquiry become clear only as the inquiry proceeds. The very conceptions of what a 'problem' is, what 'evidence' is, are historical: thus Dacier's view of 'evidence', Hume's view, and John Wilson's view presented three different versions of the 'exception' to rules. But these were not equally valid. In the largest possible sense, the value of criticism is measured by the exclusion which its inquiries entail, the limitations they impose.

Although use and definition of 'problem' are tied to what the critic considers relevant, the conception of 'problems' in contrast to 'propositions', of questions in contrast to answers, marks an important shift within critical issues. This very shift, while giving 'scientific' weight to method, sets limits with regard to knowledge and subjectivity. The exploration of problems, when such takes place, is dependent upon the subjective insight of the critic and his need for speculative ventures on one hand, and on evidence, data, and logic on the other. The issues of criticism tend to be resolved within these limitations, with insight and speculation expanding or

[1] Cleanth Brooks, *The Well-Wrought Urn* (New York, 1947), p. xxi.

---

that a somewhat sceptical attitude to critical language inhibits my minting new coinages, while distrusting the old.

contracting as the power of the critic or the knowledge of the issues increases or decreases.

Methodologically, the single poem identified what elements constituted the critic's problem. Thus for the poet, additions and revisions implied areas of new interest, dissatisfaction or amplification. For the explanatory critics who directed their comments at an audience (Thomson or others), such criticism could discuss unity, digression, diction, sentence structure, subject matter, period, poet and considerable variations of these. In illustrative (non-verbal) criticism, only some of the problems could be handled—unity and digression, subject matter, relation of language to sight. Obviously, the verbal criticism carried the bulk of the commentary, but its usefulness and limitations are, to a considerable extent, defined by the other type.

All criticism operates with possible choices—of language, subject matter, sequence—and within choices: the poles of tradition-innovation, unity-variety, obscurity-clarity. Each critical problem implies a range beyond which it ceases to be applicable—thus *The Seasons* can be considered a poem of great variety, but when it is defined as a series of poems, it can no longer be treated as a single entity. It is important, therefore, that 'unity' should be altered to include more choices than 'unity' of plot or action, without violating the whole. When 'unity' is an 'assemblage of poetical ideas', however, it implies a series of poems without one whole.

I am aware that modern critics often refer to problems as governed by 'frameworks',[1] but I find it unwarranted to identify every critical remark with an implied or constructed critical theory. The critics of Thomson's poem were not often concerned with placing their analysis within system and such systems should not be forced upon them. Indeed, writers like John More (1777) and John Pinkerton (1785) both denied critical systems and dealt only with inferences about specific passages, though More did rely upon 'system', whereas Pinkerton did not. Such writers begin with assumptions as do all human beings, but they do not seek and often do not possess a consistent theory to explain inconsistencies or gaps in knowledge.

[1] See Stephen C. Pepper, *The Basis of Criticism in the Arts* (Cambridge, Mass., 1945). See also Meyer H. Abrams, *The Mirror and the Lamp* (Oxford, 1953); Walter J. Hipple, Jr., *The Beautiful, the Sublime, and the Picturesque in Eighteenth-Century British Aesthetic Theory* (Carbondale, 1957).

Where frameworks have seemed to form a coherent body of assumptions on which the critic based his conclusions, I have discussed them as such; but I have avoided reducing every problem to part of a non-existent 'framework'.

I seek in this work to provide a statement about criticism without accepting the view that criticism represents one unified system or that critical contributions are necessarily generalizations about all literature rather than particular poems; therefore, I have attended to problems, to diverse methods, to specific comments because I find that critical continuity exists in particulars which, like water, can at one time flow, and, at others, solidify or completely evaporate. I have tried to make clear at all times the 'evidence' presented and its relevance. Thus the statement of the problem or the area of analysis which I have chosen, as well as the evidence presented and the inferences drawn, make available the grounds which can be used to refute my position. Like most critics I have tried to move with care so that I can avoid rather than encourage refutation.

(c) AN APOLOGY FOR RESEARCH

> As historian, the scholar has the task of rendering our knowledge more and more exact and thorough; as critic, he has the task of rendering our standards of worth more and more authoritative and serviceable.
>
> N. FOERSTER, 1929

In examining this book, readers will find that many of the critics quoted have long disappeared from view, and it may seem that some never came into it. Some justification is necessary for recalling minor figures rather than major writers, especially since the time of man is too short to rehearse others' ignorance, considering how much one commands by himself. The obvious answer, of course, is that one knows the major critics clearly only as one understands the distinctions which they made and others didn't. But it is not always clear that one has understood their distinctions; the obvious answer is not quite so obvious, and perhaps a more devious one is necessary.

Survival among literary critics is not always due to the principle of the 'fittest', and some defence should be made for those critics whose works, though familiar to some, are not well known and who belong to the realm of silent, or, in Percival Stockdale's case, the unhonoured, dead. In order to make our past meaningful, it is necessary to create in it a recognition of the choices men had. Recovery and scholarship do that. I have recovered one critic, John More, lost because of time and blunders, and I have tried to make clear the critical intelligence of others like Robert Heron and John Aikin, who, the *Monthly Magazine* declared, was best fitted to take the place of Johnson in English letters.

Since I am analysing the criticisms of *The Seasons*, the poem dictated the critics to be discussed. Robert Shiels, John Gregory, Sir Harris Nicolas, Allan Cunningham and many others were intelligent, but not the most significant, critical interpreters of their time. They do, however, make possible a clearer comparative picture of criticism than a study only of the major critics because they often express views, discuss problems, use methods of such critics; and the relation between Robert Shiels and Samuel Johnson, for example, is a comparative procedure necessary for the analysis of critical values. By this procedure, research constructs the kind of alternatives critics had in the concepts and practices of criticism, creates revised conceptions of the past and validates insights into the present.

Coleridge wrote in one of his letters that the life of any man, no matter how insignificant, would, if truthfully told, be of interest. And with regard to research one might note that the recovery from oblivion of one single human being is an act of respect men pay to human dignity and intelligence. Scholarship, when undertaken as an inquiry with awareness of its danger and limitations, is an act of liberty and a resistance to the restraints imposed upon it by the scholarship of the past. Johnson recognized that a poet's text should be printed as the poet left it, because the act of respect is an act of freedom; it accepts man for what he has done and permits him to speak in his own voice. In the recovery of human voices, scholarship can represent a model of the scrupulous exercise of human energy.

In a study of critics it is unnecessary to affirm that the history of their statements like any other history is the story of wisdom and folly. *The Seasons* has ceased to be a seminal poem to our poets, although it still lives for selected readers and critics. It ought to be of importance to us which of its once accepted values have become irrelevant to our society, which survive, and why. If one of the important issues for criticism is how to use its resources, then it can be studied in the critical history of *The Seasons*, which includes careful use of critical knowledge, prolonged abuse of critical potentialities, questions long unasked, blind inquiries and critical blunders.

The Seasons has qualities which critics have often overlooked, and its very experimentalism and playfulness, so long neglected, are instances of the need to ask the right questions and the consequences of not asking them. And in pursuing criticism, is it not important to inquire why some men do not and others cannot ask the releasing questions?

Not all critical data are available or serviceable; research involves decisions to recover (to cover again) as well as uncover materials. For such decisions every critic is responsible exactly as he is responsible for deciding to omit some of the research he has canvassed. It is this type of decision which offers a challenge to further study, and which makes research not only an inquiry in itself, but an imperative to further inquiry. Sometimes such research is prevented by lack of data, as sources of Thomson's poem had to wait for Alan D. McKillop to track them down; but scholars frequently build upon the results of others. They may sometimes appear to be (and at other times they actually are) examining each other's flatulencies, but reliable scholarship is based on knowledge and study and care, and counting streaks on a tulip may be a necessary part of a proper classification system.

The amount of effort which research involves often seems incommensurate with the results, and Waller's couplet about poets may perhaps be equally relevant to scholars:

> Poets lose half the Praise they should have got
> Could it be known what they discreetly blot.

Perhaps the scholarly enterprise might be more impressive if one measured the discard rather than the discovery. For scholarship, the great danger is not the futility of failure but the futility of success, the dread that what has been preserved is unworthy. Every subject is potentially worthy of study, but the study is not always worthy of its potential. The analysis of criticism is a study of studies. If Emerson's definition of a scholar as a 'man thinking' is admissible, then the study of criticism, even in so limited an area as that of a single poem, is the study of how men think about poetry, how they discover, express, defend and justify facts and ideas. And to what man is this alien?

I

CRITICISM AND PROCESS: THE PROBLEMS OF THOMSON'S REVISIONS

Every poet is a critic, though the reverse is not true.

SHENSTONE

But, though concealed, to every purer eye
The informing Author in his work appears.

THOMSON

THERE HAVE BEEN AMPLE REASONS for abandoning a study of Thomson's critical process in the creation of *The Seasons:* for more than a hundred and fifty years after his death in 1748 no collated edition existed. During the first fifty years of that time, criticism tactfully refrained from examining the early efforts of the poet, and for the next fifty, it assumed that the significant revisions of *The Seasons* were made by Pope; finally, in 1908, a collated edition was published and the Pope theory refuted, but there developed conflicting theories on the value of revisions for criticism so that this 'process', although available, had to establish its justification as 'criticism'.

In the 'process' of criticism, most of Thomson's articulate decisions have been lost, if they ever existed in any such form. What remains is fragmentary and inferential. Like most poets, Thomson in *Winter* (1726) was using forms that had been initiated by other poets, and although he gives some reasons for his choice, they are very meagre, and much of the explanation remained, perhaps, not clearly formulated, even to himself. The purpose of reconstructing the process, therefore, is not to speculate about 'reasons' which may be private and not even relevant to literature, but (1) to study those choices accepted and rejected which made the poem what it became; (2) to discover how and why such choices were recognized or ignored by critics; (3) to analyse the place of this 'process' in interpretation of the poem.

(a) THE IMPLICATIONS OF 'PROCESS'

He does not . . . regard the Turn of my Genius enough.

J. THOMSON

The importance of 'process' as a critical procedure was taken for granted at the beginning of the eighteenth century in the sense that the poet was to learn from poems and from critics. The definitions of criticism, as Pope's *Essay on Criticism* makes clear, included references to the poet's art and wisdom in writing his poem as well as in judging the poems of others. William Wimsatt, Jr. has pointed to some of these distinctions by remarking that 'a literary theory which operates as an influence upon a poem ought to be distinguished more often than perhaps it is from a literary theory which manages to appear in the poem itself. And both of these ought to be distinguished from yet a third thing, the theory which is unified with a work by being really exemplified or carried out in that work.'[1]

In the early eighteenth century, the definitions of 'criticism' included interpretation and evaluation. *The New World of English Words* (1658) defined 'criticisme' as 'a playing the critick, a learning which consists in the nice examining of Authors'. Blount's *Glossographia* (1674) defined it as, 'The art of judging or censuring men's words, writings or action; also a quillet or nicety in judgment'. *Glossographia Anglicana Nova* (1707) defined 'critical' as, 'Of a Nice Judgment, Censorious', and 'criticism', 'the Art of Judging or Censuring Men's words, Writings or Actions'. *A General English Dictionary* (1715), defined 'criticism' as, 'nice Judgment,

[1] William K. Wimsatt, Jr. and Cleanth Brooks, *Literary Criticism* (New York, 1957), p. 234; see also Edward Cook, 'Poets as Critics', *More Literary Recreations* (London, 1919), pp. 201–3; Henry James, Preface to *The Golden Bowl*; René Wellek, 'Literary Theory, Criticism, and History', *SR*, LXVIII (1960), 4.

critical Discourse, or Reflection'.[1] Bailey's definition of 'criticism' in 1724 was a combination of Blount's definition followed by Kersey's. 'Nice judgment' applied to the poet's own work as well as to his judgement of the work of others. Poets took it for granted that the process of making poems required acts of judgement in the choice of models to follow and in how to follow or not follow them. When James Thomson proposed in the second edition of *Winter* (1726) to have poetry return to serious subjects, he was suggesting the kind of 'end' he saw for his poem.

The 'process' of criticism, in so far as it is available to modern critics, exists in the form of revisions and in examples which friends and critics suggest as revisions—those taken and agreed with or those rejected by the poet as inconsistent with his 'turn' of genius or the needs of the poem. 'In three letters to David Mallet in August 1726 . . .', writes Alan Dugald McKillop, 'Thomson discusses installments of Mallet's *Excursion* and in turn sends Mallet installments of *Summer*. . . The passage on light in precious stones, *Summer*, ll. 132–44 of the first edition, was evidently added or expanded at Mallet's suggestion.'[2] 'Your Hint,' wrote Thomson to Mallet, 'of the Saphire, Emerald, Ruby, etc., strike[s] my Imagination with a pleasing Lustre; and shall not be neglected . . .'[3]

Other critics, however, who did not make such precise suggestions or whose recommendations have disappeared, have left puzzling fragments to tease the future. Somerville wrote, upon Thomson's publication of *Winter* (1726):

[1] Edward Phillips, *The New World of English Words* (London, 1658); Thomas Blount, *Glossographia* (London, 1674); Thomas Blount, *Glossographia Anglicana Nova* (London, 1707); John Kersey, *A General English Dictionary* (London, 1715).

[2] Alan Dugald McKillop, *James Thomson (1700–1748) Letters and Documents* (Lawrence, 1958), pp. 41–42.

[3] McKillop, *Letters*, p. 40. Horace E. Hamilton, 'James Thomson's Seasons: Shifts in the Treatment of Popular Subject Matter', *ELH* (1948), 111, comments as follows upon the shared subject matter of Thomson and his friends: 'In a manner strikingly similar to that of Thomson and Mallet, Savage filled his poem, *The Wanderer*, with pictures of the wholesale destruction of cities and the icy tumult of arctic seas. The indebtedness of these . . . contemporaries to each other alone provides a tangle of sources to challenge the literary detective.' For a misstatement of the facts about Thomson's friends, see Isaac Disraeli, *An Essay on the Manners and Genius of the Literary Character* (London, 1795), p. 48.

> I read thee over as a friend should read,
> Griev'd when you fail, o'erjoyed when you succeed.
> Why should thy muse, born so divinely fair,
> Want the reforming toilet's daily care.[1]

Joseph Mitchell wrote of the mixed beauties and faults, and after the publication of *Liberty*, Isaac H. Browne parodied Thomson's extravagant imagery and feigned intensity:

> O Thou, matur'd by glad Hesperian suns,
> Tobacco, fountain pure of *limpid truth*,
> *That looks the very soul*; whence pouring thought
> *Swarms all the mind*; absorpt is yellow care,
> And at each puff imagination burns.[2]

The smoke that poured from the fountain and looked 'the very soul' was an example of Thomson's 'puffy' language and inflation of the trivial. And the awkward expression—'swarming all the mind'—parodied the insect image of 'swarming thoughts'. The pun in the last line 'at each puff imagination burns', points to an occasional ambiguity of image.

> Half in a blush of clustering roses lost,
> Dew-dropping Coolness to the shade retires;
> There, on the verdant turf or flowery bed,
> By gelid founts or careless rills to muse,
> [*Summer*, ll. 205–8]

Of this image John Scott was to write in 1785: 'Little master *coolness* "lost" among his *blush* of *roses*, "dropping his dews", and musing on the *turf*, or by the *rill*, is a very curious figure.'[3]

This conception of 'process' as revision and supervision was sanctioned by Horace and Longinus, and it has been a continuing kind of criticism. Pope corrected Wycherley's poems, Akenside corrected Dyer's *The Fleece*, and the Scriblerus group criticized and commented on each other's work. When the classical critics urged the poet's use of models, of friendly criticism and advice, they did

[1] William Somerville, 'Epistle to Mr. Thomson on the First Edition of his Seasons', *The Poetical Works of William Somerville Esq.*, *A Complete Edition of the Poets of Great Britain*, ed. Robert Anderson (Edinburgh, 1794), VIII, 504.

[2] *A Pipe of Tobacco* (London, 1736), pp. 13–14.

[3] John Scott, 'On Thomson's Seasons', *Critical Essays* (London, 1785), p. 355.

so on the grounds that 'process' was a social enterprise, a 'handmaid' to poetry, and the critics were often poets themselves. But at the turn of the seventeenth century the enterprise of criticism had begun to be competitive. In 1693, Dryden declared that formerly critics

> were defenders of poets and commentators on their works; to illustrate obscure beauties; to place some passages in a better light; to redeem others from malicious interpretations; to help out an author's modesty, who is not ostentatious of his wit . . . Are our auxiliary forces turned our enemies?[1]

That the social community of poet and critic had begun to decay in Thomson's time can be seen from the fewness of 'critics' whom the poet trusted and the growing hostility between poets and critics. 'Me-thinks all tolerable Authors in this Age,' wrote Thomson to Mallet in 1729, 'all who can give Honour and Entertainment to it, should in Opposition to this and the General Discouragement they labour under, enter into an Association not to write at all; or, if they do write for their own Pleasure and that of their particular Friends, yet never to publish.'[2]

The growing conflict between critics as a class and poets stemmed from the competition for authority and the new reading public. The critic claimed a dual allegiance: to the education of the audience and to the analysis and evaluation of the work of art. Instead of assisting poetry he became its competitor. Thus the poet who was a critic in his own poetry and, up to the eighteenth century, a frequent commentator upon the poetry of others, found himself in competition with men who began to consider criticism as a profession.

That the separation of creation and criticism evolved simultaneously with nature poetry as a genre was not purely accidental. The larger and sympathetic audience which Thomson sought, he found in 'courting nature'—'I solitary court / Th' inspiring breeze, and meditate the book of Nature, ever open.' Nature gave to the poet the

[1] John Dryden, 'Dedication to Examen Poeticum (1693),' *Essays of John Dryden*, ed. W. P. Ker (Oxford, 1900), II, 3. See T. Noon Talfourd, *Critical and Miscellaneous Writings, The Modern British Essayists*, VIII (Phil. 1850), 38: 'In the first critical days of England those of the Rymers and the Dennises—commenced the arrogance on the side of the supervisors, and the impatience and resentment of that of their subjects.' See 'Letter on Criticism', *Literary Magazine* (1756–7).

[2] McKillop, *Letters*, p. 65.

sense of sympathy which he found only in his limited friendships, and although he was unable to match the vividness and variety of nature, he found security in its comfort and power. The poet who hastened 'into the midwood shade' established once again that reciprocal relation between poet and 'critic' which the competition had undermined.

For Thomson, as for many of his contemporaries, selection of a form for poetry, of 'epithets', versification, and subjects was a matter of conscious choice in which the poet discovered his particular abilities and originality. To this extent the poem was the product of a critical process and a cultural situation.

In his *Reflections on Aristotle's Treatise of Poesie* (1694) René Rapin wrote:

> 'Tis therefore by reflecting a long time on a man's self, and by continued study of his Nature, join'd with the care and exercise of Composing, that he dare accomplish his Genius, and arrives to perfection.[1]

The 'care and exercise of Composing' was accomplished by revisions, by attempts in different forms, by a process of literary self-discovery. This criticism developed, for the poet, by a knowledge of other literary works, by a knowledge of explanatory criticism, by response to and assistance from his friends, acting as critics. It is self-evident that this 'process' of criticism applied only to the poet's lifetime, and to that part of his life in which he composed a specific poem. *The Seasons* was, in this instance, characteristic of eighteenth-century poems, although it had more revisions than most, and its 'process' extended from 1726, the publication of *Winter*, to 1746, the last revision published during Thomson's lifetime. Otto Zippel in 1908 collated these revisions as shown below.[2]

[1] René Rapin, *Reflections on Aristotle's Treatise of Poesie* (London, 1694), p. 23. See also S. Dunster, tr. *Satires and Epistles of Horace* (London, 1712, 2nd ed.), p. 423; Thomas Rymer, *Critical Essays*, ed. Curt Zimansky (New Haven, 1956), pp. 22–23; Mme. de Scudéry, *Conversations upon Several Subjects*, tr. F. Spence (London, 1683), pp. 77–78.

[2] Otto Zippel, *Thomson's Seasons Critical Edition, Palaestra*, LXVI (Berlin, 1908), XI: *Winter A* (first edition, published March 1726), *Winter B* (second edition, published June 1726), *Winter C* (published in 1730, in quarto, part of first collected edition of *The Seasons*), *Winter D* (published in 1730, in octavo, part of *The Seasons*). For other editions see Appendix I. The number of lines in each edition of *The Seasons* is as shown overleaf.

This concept of 'process' as a form of criticism, identified 'criticism' with the poet's literary self-knowledge; he not only found a place within the great tradition of poetry by discovering the form which best suited him, but he also discovered his individuality within this form. 'To have right Thoughts of Things,' wrote John Petvin (1750), 'we must study ourselves, and other Men; and the Knowledge of ourselves, and other Men, furnishes us not only with *Matter* for our Thoughts, but with the *Method* of *communicating* them: For we must proceed from their *present* to *that* Sense of Things to which we would bring them.'[1] This individuality, moreover, was not only the consequence of conscious choice; the skilled poet found that he was able to 'snatch a grace beyond the reach of art'. Thomson, when he first composed his *Winter*, was developing a form which he identified in his preface to the second edition of *Winter* (1726) as related to *Job* and Virgil's *Georgics*.

[1] John Petvin, *Letters Concerning Mind* (London, 1750), p. 1. See Charles Gildon, *Letters* (London, 1694), p. 26: 'a poet through his whole performance, both whilst he contrives, converts and puts his thoughts into Metre, is still at the same time contemplating, so that he's compos'd of Speculation and Action'. I regret the ambiguity of a term like 'process', but it does derive from the eighteenth-century use of 'proceeding' and is more pertinent than such terms as 'exercise' or 'practice'. For a similar use, see Phyllis Bartlett, *Poems in Process* (New York, 1951), and for a text-book constructed on the process assumption, A. F. Scott, *The Poets' Craft* (Cambridge, 1957). George Sherburn, in a review of Alan Dugald McKillop's 'James Thomson: Letters and Documents', *JEGP*, LVII (1958), 815, writes: 'In his letters we see Thomson as the projector of poems in process.' For analysis of this process as pertinent to modern criticism, see Donald Stauffer, 'Genesis, or the Poet as Maker', and Rudolf Arnheim, 'Psychological Notes on the Critical Process', in *Poets at Work*, ed. Charles D. Abbott (New York, 1948), pp. 39–82, 125–62.

(Footnote 2—*contd.*)

	1726	1727	1728	1730	1744	1746
Spring			A 1082	B 1087	C 1173	D 1176
Summer		A 1146		B 1206	C 1796	D 1805
Autumn				A 1269	B 1375	C 1373
Winter	VA 405			C 781 (4e)C	E 1069	
	CB 463			D 787 (8e)V	F 1069	
Hymn				A 121	B 118	C 118
Totals				4464 (4470)	5531	5541

> The best, both ancient, and modern, Poets have been passionately fond of retirement, and solitude. The wild romantic country was their delight. And they seem never to have been more happy, than when, lost in unfrequented fields, far from the little busy world, they were at leisure, to meditate, and sing the Works of Nature.
>
> The book of Job, that noble and ancient poem, which, even now, strikes so forcibly through a mangling translation, is crowned with a description of the grand works of Nature; and that, too, from the mouth of their Almighty Author.
>
> It was this devotion to the works of Nature that, in his Georgics, inspired the rural Virgil to write so inimitably.[1]

Yet Thomson's publicly stated conception of the nature tradition did not include some recent poems which he had seen and which formed the more immediate models of his *Winter*. In a letter he made an oblique reference to his friend and teacher, Robert Riccaltoun, who had written a poem on winter; he had seen the manuscript of John Armstrong's *Winter*,[2] and Cecil Moore (1916) suggested and Dwight Durling (1935) annotated correspondences between William Hinchliffe's *Seasons* (1718) and Thomson's poem.

> Both poets repeat details of Vergil's picture of the Golden Age of eternal spring; both seem to echo his description of summer's noonday heat, in which languish nature and mankind. With the latter passages are connected in both poets lines *not* from the *Georgics*, expressing desire for solitary poetic inspiration in the

[1] Preface to *Winter*, 2nd ed. 1726, as reprinted in James Logie Robertson, *The Complete Poetical Works of James Thomson* (Oxford, 1908), p. 241. This edition of Thomson's poems is referred to unless otherwise noted.

[2] Robert Riccaltoun, 'A Winter's Day', reprinted in Robert Bell, ed. *Poetical Works of James Thomson* (London, 1855), II, 7–9; John Armstrong, 'Imitation of Shakespeare', *The Poetical Works of John Armstrong, M.D.* (Perth, 1792), pp. 92–98. The 'Advertisement from the Publisher' declares that the poem 'was just finished when Mr. Thomson's celebrated poem upon the same subject appeared. Mr. Thomson, soon hearing of it, had the curiosity to procure a copy by the means of a common acquaintance. He shewed it to his poetical friends Mr. Mallet, Mr. Aaron Hill, and Dr. Young, who it seems did great honour to it, and the first mentioned gentleman wrote to one of his friends at Edinburgh, desiring the Author's leave to publish it, a request too flattering to youthful vanity to be resisted: but Mr. Mallet altered his mind, and this little piece has hitherto remained unpublished.' The imitation was first published in 1770.

solemn scenes of nature. These are very similar in imagery. In his *Autumn,* Hinchliffe seems to echo Vergil's

> Libra die somnique pares ubi fecerit horas
> et medium luci atque umbris iam dividit orbem

in these lines:

> Soon as the radiant balance *weighs*
> *In equal scales* the nights and days.

Thomson uses exactly the same phrase, perhaps recalling the same lines of Vergil:

> When the bright Virgin gives the beauteous days,
> And Libra *weighs in equal scales* the year,
> [*Autumn*, ll. 23–4]

Both adapt Vergil's striking figure of the war of the winds, and in similar phrases. Both borrow the picture from the Aeneid, of the flood bearing away the fruits of the year while the peasant watches from a near-by hill. Each includes the georgic theme of plagre and pestilence, though Hinchliffe's use of it is limited to fourteen lines. They have points in common also which are not Vergilian: tableaus personifying all the seasons; a similar kind of pleasure in the grandeur of winter, its more violent, stormy aspects; prominence given to the gloom of autumn and winter storms; and humanitarian sentiment. In each poet's *Winter* is a description of the formation of ice upon a river—of a clear, starry night and a keen eastern breeze which seizes and fixes the stream, of the shining prospect revealed by the light of morning. These descriptions follow the same outlines and include phrases which seem to be echoes of Vergil's *Concrescunt subitae currenti in flumine crustae*', Hinchliffe's 'sudden th'arrested waters creep', and Thomson's 'in its mid career, arrests the bickering stream'. Both poets express a wish for a sheltered retreat where friends, 'a chosen few', may help them pass gloomier days joyfully. Sometimes the phraseology has a very striking similarity. Hinchliffe exclaims

> Bear me, O Muse, to Pindus' shades!
> To sacred groves! Pierian glades!
> To grottos crown'd with sylvan pride,
> Under th'Aonian mountain's side!

And Thomson says

> Oh! bear me then to vast embowering shades,
> To twilight groves, and visionary vales,
> To weeping grottoes, and prophetic glooms;[1]
> [*Autumn*, ll. 1030–2]

The poet's acknowledgement of a tradition must be considered as an explanatory comment; his critical processes are unstated and need to be reconstructed. It has been possible to confirm in detail Thomson's borrowings from Virgil,[2] but his reliance upon *Job* is more in the sublime intent than in actual borrowing. The term 'borrowing' is misleading: the reconstruction of 'process' is both more difficult and less mechanical than the 'borrowing' transaction implies. The poet writes his poem from a knowledge of other poems and from other kinds of knowledge and makes choices for reasons often obscure to him, if indeed he seeks to express them at all. But the later critic who probes particular usages or meanings finds them tied to public techniques made private by the special hand of the poet. The discovery of this 'special hand', this 'signature' demands a knowledge of 'process'.

The critic who has before him an anonymous 'poem' does not know whether he is analysing a part or a whole. And in discovering unity of language or action, he has, by whatever methods he can, to distinguish the distinctive from the traditional qualities. Still, the critic who is aware of the poet's 'process'—his revisions and letters—is in danger, if he is the poet's contemporary, of converting his own preferences into his friend's 'process'. And if he is a much later critic, he is in danger of converting the poet's 'process' into a philosophical framework. 'Process', however, can be a clue which leads to a guess on the part of the critic—whether the guess becomes an

[1] Dwight L. Durling, *Georgic Tradition in English Poetry* (New York, 1935), pp. 43–44. For Hinchliffe, see also Cecil Moore, 'A Predecessor of Thomson's *Seasons*', *MLN*, XXXIV (1919), 278–81. Apparently unaware of Dwight Durling's book, Arthur L. Cooke repeated the attribution of influence, 'James Thomson and William Hinchliffe', *JEGP*, LVII (1958), 755–61.

[2] Durling, pp. 45–53. Durling notes and incorporates borrowings listed by earlier critics: *The Northern Star* or *Yorkshire Magazine* (London, 1817), I, 343–7, 432–8, 505–8, II, 9–16, 118–22, J. Logie Robertson, *The Seasons* (Oxford, 1891), Zippel (1908), W. P. Mustard, 'Virgil's Georgics and the British Poets', *AJP*, XXIX (1908), 1–32, Elizabeth Nitchie, *Virgil and the English Poets* (New York, 1919).

insight is determined by later discoveries or by the evidence of more poems trying to do what the poet was doing.

As a critical tool, 'process' describes the kind of innovation the poem develops; it describes the relation of the poem 'in creation' to the ideas of the poet's friends and their current critical assumptions; it displays the willingness or unwillingness of the poet to accept particular critical positions; it reveals the materials of the poet (his readings) and the command of this material in the finished product; it can be, as it is in Thomson, an attitude to language and unity which is itself experimental and tentative, and the frequent revisions indicate that in *The Seasons* he was dissatisfied with and unable to withdraw from the published work.

Whatever fragments of the 'process' exist, they throw light on the poem as belonging to a continuum of poetry—its relation to Virgil, Cowley, and others—and they provide data about interpretation of the language and structure of the poem. Upon publication of *Winter* Thomson received a letter, now lost, from William Aikman about his use of epithets in it. And he wrote to David Mallet (11 August 1726): 'His Reflections on My Writings are very good; but He does not, in Them, regard the Turn of my Genius enough; Should I alter my Way, I would write poorly. I must chuse what appears to me the most significant Epithet or I cannot, with any Heart, proceed.'[1]

The defence of his 'epithets' was a defence of certain adjectives and their 'significance', their applicability in Thomson's sense. Thus those retained and those revised in his 1730 *Winter* provide some grounds for conclusions about his poetic usage. At the same time they prove how sceptically the critic must handle the poet's comments on himself. Thomson's revisions 'altered' his way of writing, yet he obviously felt that they improved his work. If it be claimed that what he meant was a 'style', not a series of 'epithets', then it still must be conceded that he was not happy with some of the epithets he chose, and he was not always himself sure of the 'turn' of his genius. Some of the changes in epithets between the second edition (June 1726) and the 1730 edition are as follows:

2nd edition (1726)	*1730*
Welcome kindred Glooms! Wish'd, wint'ry, Horrors, hail! (ll. 5–6)	Welcome, kindred glooms! Cogenial horrors, hail! (ll. 5–6)

[1] McKillop, *Letters*, p. 46.

2nd edition (*1726*)	*1730*
Thus pass'd the Time, Till, thro' the opening Chambers of / the South, Look'd out the joyous Spring, look'd / out, and smil'd. (ll. 14–16)	Till thro' the lucid chambers . . . (l. 15)
First Rains obscure Drive thro' the mingling Skies, with / Tempest foul; Beat on the Mountain's Brow and / shake the Woods, That, sounding, wave below. (ll. 113–16)	First rains obscure Drive thro' the mingling skies, with / vapour vile; Dash on the mountain's brow, and / shake the woods, That grumbling wave below. (ll. 74–7)
At last the muddy Deluge pours / along, Resistless, roaring; (ll. 133–4)	At last the rouz'd-up river pours / along, Resistless, roaring; (ll. 97–8)
In what untravel'd Country of / the Air, Hush'd in deep Silence, sleep you, / when 'tis calm? (ll. 153–4)	In what far-distant region of / the sky, Hush'd in dead silence, sleep you / when 'tis calm? (ll. 117–18)
And the Sky saddens with th'impend-ing / Storm. (l. 220)	And the sky saddens with the gather'd / storm. (l. 210)
Earth's universal Face, deep-hid, / and chill, Is all one, dazzling, Waste. (ll. 227–8)	Earth's universal face, deep-hid, / and chill, Is one wild, dazzling waste.[1] (ll. 220–1)

Whatever reasons Thomson had for his revisions of these 'epithets', the changes predominantly created a personified nature, possessing the qualities of nature and man—mild and violent. 'Wish'd, wint'ry, Horrors, hail!' contained the irony of wished-for 'horrors' and the 'kindred' originally suggested that the glooms of winter were kin to the narrator. The change to 'cogenial horrors' carried on the kinship and, while retaining the irony, removed the 'wish' by assuming cogeniality as a fact. In this revision consonantal repetition was abandoned for the familial closeness of idea; the revision of 'at last the muddy Deluge pours along', to 'at last the rouz'd-up river pours along', introduced the repetition, but with it came the personified, angered river and its natural description 'pours along'. In the famous revision of 'is all one, dazzling, Waste' to 'is one wild, dazzling waste', the face which was 'all one' became an increased personification in 'one wild' waste.

[1] Zippel, *Winter*, Text A and Text C.

We do not know what epithets William Aikman referred to, but the justification for these epithets lay, for Thomson, in what he called their 'significance'. It can, of course, be argued that the critic who has 'one wild, dazzling waste' before him can discover this without comparing it to 'all one, dazzling, Waste', but this is not only to reject information that is available, it is to assume that the alternatives which critics construct are equally appropriate with those of the author. When Thomson changed 'Tempest foul' for 'vapour vile' he may have been seeking to avoid the repetition of idea in driving 'rains obscure', but 'vapour vile', despite its implications of ugly smells, included in its meaning 'vain imaginations' and, therefore, reduced the force of the description. Here, even the scientific description—'a watery Exhalation raised up either by the Heat of the Sun or any other Heat'[1]— seems inappropriate to a winter storm. Yet the change from 'sounding' woods to 'grumbling' woods was a successful personification of mere 'sound' to a sullen, angry, particularized human sound.

More puzzling than the successful revisions are lines now considered successful—and which seemed originally successful—which were converted into new contrasts and placed in different contexts. In the 1726, 2nd edition, ll. 272–4 read:

> the Bear,
> Rough Tenant of these Shades! shaggy with Ice,
> And dangling Snow, stalks thro' the Woods, forlorn.

In 1730, ll. 370–80 read:

> There thro' the ragged woods absorpt in snow,
> Sole tenant of the shades, the shaggy bear,
> With dangling ice all horrid, stalks forlorn;
> Slow-pac'd and, sowrer as the storms increase,
> He makes his bed beneath the drifted snow;
> And scorning the complainings of distress,
> Hardens his heart against assailing want.
> While tempted vigorous o'er the marble waste,
> On sleds reclin'd, the furry Russian sits;
> And, by his rain-deer drawn, behind him throws
> A shining kingdom in a winter's day.

In 1744, ll. 799–832 read:

> There, thro' the Prison of unbounded Wilds,
> Barr'd by the Hand of Nature from Escape,

[1] 'Vapour', Kersey.

Wide-roams the Russian Exile. Nought around
Strikes his sad Eye, but Desarts lost in Snow;
And heavy-loaded Groves; and solid Floods,
That stretch, athwart the solitary Vast,
Their icy Horrors to the frozen Main;
And chearless Towns far-distant, never bless'd,
Save when it's annual Course the Caravan
Bends to the golden Coast of rich Cathay,
With News of Human-kind. Yet there Life glows;
Yet cherish'd there, beneath the shining Waste,
The furry Nations harbour: tipt with Jet,
Fair Ermines, spotless as the Snows they press;
Sables, of glossy Black; and, dark-embrown'd,
Or beauteous freakt with many a mingled Hue,
Thousands besides, the costly Pride of Courts.
There, warm together press'd, the trooping Deer
Sleep on the new fallen Snows; and, scarce his Head
Rais'd o'er the heapy Wreath, the branching Elk
Lies slumbering sullen in the white Abyss.
Nor Dogs, nor Toils, he wants; nor with the Dread
Of sounding Bows the ruthless Hunter drives
The fearful-flying Race; with ponderous Clubs,
As weak against the Mountain-Heaps they push
Their beating Breast in vain, and piteous bray,
He lays them quivering on th'ensanguin'd Snows,
And with loud Shouts rejoicing bears them home.
There thro' the piny Forest half-absorpt,
Rough Tenant of these Shades, the shapeless Bear,
With dangling Ice all horrid, stalks forlorn;
Slow-pac'd, and sourer as the Storms increase,
He makes his Bed beneath th'inclement Drift,
And, with stern Patience, scorning weak Complaint,
Hardens his Heart against assailing Want.[1]

In 1744 he removed the last three lines and combined 'marble waste' with 'shining kingdom' into 'shining waste' and contrasted the lonely exile with the teeming life of nature, the ruthless hunter with the stoic bear. In the 1730 passage the uncomplaining bear was contrasted with the ease and gaiety of the Russian. The altered conceptions of man and nature seemed to imply, in 1744, a change of philosophy; yet the alterations do not support this. The revision established a clearer point of view between the 'Russian exile' and the Russian

[1] Zippel, *Winter*, Texts *B* (1726), *C* (1730) and *E* (1744).

bear, the solitariness of both. The original contrast between motion and motionlessness, man and bear, joy and isolation, was developed by the considerably increased contrasts of colour, attitude, man and animal. In this passage, too, the accretion of meaning is clear. When Thomson refers to the bear who 'makes his bed beneath th' inclement Drift', he now implies the acceptance of hardship in contrast to other animals who live

> Cherish'd there, beneath the shining Waste,
> The furry nations harbour.

'Beneath' thus becomes a posture or attitude which can be a social or a forlorn condition just as the 'shining Waste' can be an 'inclement drift', 'solitary Vast' or 'new fallen Snows'.

The revisions, therefore, provide a clue to the interpretation of language as posture and attitude indicating the conception of man and nature as part of complex and mysterious 'wild'. The prepositions and conjunctions which carry the idea of posture are spotted far more readily through analysis of revisions than through consultation only of the final text. The concept of 'posture' language is important because it provides a formalized version of nature despite Thomson's realism, and implies a conception of its force and power expressed in Augustan postures. Such implications of 'process' are not discoverable very readily without analysis of what has not been changed in contrast to what has. Moreover, revisions indicate how meaning accrues by the development of alternatives. In addition to alternatives and accretion of meanings, revisions provide an artistic conception of experience in contrast to the stated theories of benevolence. Thomson as didactic poet must be no more credited than as articulate critic. His overt comments upon religion must be weighed with the implicit view of man and nature as part of an objective world seen through the postures of both—thus the constant passage between personification and nature and the repeated consciousness of posture or attitude.

Bonamy Dobrée declares that in 'a shining kingdom in a winter's day', there is 'a connotative glimpse which easily makes up for the bear shaggy with ice having become "the shaggy bear with dangling ice all horrid". But, and this is why we suspect his unawareness, in the 1744 version the bear becomes merely "shapeless", and the "furry Russian" is extinguished, in the interests of "accuracy".'[1] One can

[1] Bonamy Dobrée, *English Literature in the Early Eighteenth Century, 1700–1740* (London, 1959), p. 491.

agree that the lost lines are 'connotative', without in any way accepting the 'unawareness'. For one point of these revisions is that the poet should be able to throw off fine lines, to have more than he can use, because such demonstration was proof of poetic fertility. But more significant for the purposes of criticism is the 'concept' of revisions: revisions were a form of poetic experimentalism. Dobrée assumes the context of the bear passage remains the same, whereas the range is extended and the bear, seen in 1726 by a 'wilder'd Traveller' as a corresponding sufferer, was in 1744 compared with the happy animals, the exiled Russian and the joyful killers of the reindeer. The extension of range implied a world more complexly and puzzlingly formed than the correspondence of the original. The bear 'shaggy with ice' was originally compared with barren nature, the 'Yew-clad, stony, Wastes', but the 'shapeless' bear—a reference to the myth of the bear's origin—was now part of the drifts and 'deserts lost in snow'. The fine precise passage of the group of animals—'tipt with jet'—is here contrasted with the single, lone, cheerless and shapeless bear.

Revision was not merely a form of experimentation necessary to grasp the extending variety and complexity of the contexts; revision illustrates specifically how Thomson built meaning into terms like 'shapeless' and into passages like that of the 'furry nations'. Such knowledge clarifies the implication even of an overt passage like the one in *Winter*, 1726 (and repeated with slight variations throughout the editions):

> Now, fond Man!
> Behold thy pictur'd Life: Pass some few Years,
> Thy flow'ring Spring, Thy short-liv'd Summer's Strength,
> Thy sober Autumn, fading into Age,
> And pale, concluding Winter shuts thy scene.[1]

This passage, comparing man's life to the seasons, led critics like John Aikin (1778) and Allan Cunningham (1841)[2] to assume that the poem reflected nature as analogous to the life of man. But not only was *The Seasons* not analogous to the life of man or that of man analogous to *The Seasons*, its application was to the postures of nature—'pictur'd life'—which by taking on human attitudes as well as natural

[1] Zippel, *Winter*, Text A, ll. 363–7.

[2] John Aikin, 'An Essay on the Plan and Character of Thomson's Seasons' (1778). *The Seasons* (London, 1792), pp. xii–xiii. Allan Cunningham, ed., *The Seasons* (London, 1841), p. xlvii.

ones indicated the objective interrelation of man and nature, not the dramatic unfolding of human life. Thus the revisions implied which elements in an image were related implicitly rather than overtly by pointing to the characteristics compared—as in the last line revised with more complete personification to read:

> And pale concluding Winter comes at last
> And shuts the scene.

As a study of 'position' words that provide the implicit meanings of an important revision there are the last six lines of *Winter*, originally published in 1726, revised in the first edition of *The Seasons* in 1730, and again in 1744. The original read:

> Ye good Distrest!
> Ye Noble Few! that, here, unbending, stand
> Beneath Life's Pressures—yet a little while,
> And all your Woes are past. Time swiftly fleets,
> And wish'd Eternity, approaching, brings
> Life undecaying, Love without Allay,
> Pure flowing Joy, and Happiness sincere.
> [ll. 399–405]

The revisions with the dates of the revised passages are as follows:

> Ye good distressed!
> Ye noble few! who here unbending stand
> Beneath life's pressure [1730], yet bear up a while [1744],
> *And what your bounded view, which only saw
> A little part, deemed evil is no more;
> The storms of wintry time will quickly pass, [1730]
> And one unbounded Spring encircle all.[1]

Both versions make clear that the good who suffer, but endure, in this life find a life without suffering in eternity. A study of the 1746 edition reveals the fact that Thomson is restating Pope's 'partial evil, universal good'—the noble few have in life only a limited, a 'bounded' view, whereas in eternal spring the view is unlimited, 'unbounded'.

* 1730–8. These two lines were compressed into one: 'And what you reckon evil is no more'.

[1] Zippel, *Winter*, Text A, ll. 399–405, Text E, ll. 1063–9. The passage is quoted from the standard edition edited by James Logie Robertson, *The Complete Poetical Works of James Thomson* (London, 1908), *Winter*, ll. 1063–69.

One might indeed say that the 'spring of eternity', by ending the seasons, concludes the poem by bringing a time when seasons shall cease to exist. One could then indicate that the terms 'bounded' and 'unbounded', 'part' and 'all', form the basis for the limited cyclical view of change in limited human understanding, and the realization that in the religious and eternal view the changes of nature become continual bliss.

These analyses are possible without cognizance of revisions though revisions certainly assist in making them, and not merely assist in making them: the revisions suggest the implication toward which the poem is aiming. There are other clues, however, which seem little likely to be grasped without knowledge of the revisions. The 'unbending', for example, which is retained in all revisions, is gradually supported by 'bear *up*', by 'view', and 'saw', all of which join with the 1730 version of 'unbounded Spring encircle all'. The insight which this gives is that the unbending, the bearing 'up' of the good men who suffer, creates a courage in pain that binds them, while they accept their limited view; yet by being upright, they see more than those who are bent or who do not 'bear up'. The revision insists upon the metaphor of morals and position—of 'uprightness'. In the secular world, virtue is not free from limitations, that is, it demands endurance in accepting God's mysterious ways; only in eternity can virtue become encircling—for where the virtuous man looks or bends in heaven 'one unbounded Spring encircles all'. This interpretation is readily 'clued' from the revising. Thomson is moving toward a far more subtle poetic statement about virtue than his early comparison between life's pressures and eternal peace.

In these revisions Thomson acted as a critic: he made subtle changes in transition, in language, in organization. Because of such processes, it was self-evident to a poet like Dryden (1678) that 'Poets themselves are the most proper, though I conclude not the only critics. But till some genius, as universal as Aristotle, shall arise, one who can penetrate into all the arts and sciences, without the practice of them, I shall think it reasonable that the judgement of an artificer in his own art should be preferable to the opinion of another man; at least where he is not bribed by interest or prejudiced by malice.'[1] Although Leonard Welsted (1713) pointed out that he knew

[1] Dryden, 'Preface to All for Love' (1678), *Essays*, ed. W. P. Ker (Oxford, 1900), I, 195. Henry Felton, *A Dissertation on Reading the Classics and Forming a Just Style* (London, 1713), pp. xvi–xvii, Ambrose Philips,

a poet who could not articulate comments on poetry, even though he understood criticism, and Dryden and others recognized that good critics like Aristotle and Quintilian were not poets; it was assumed that the poet as artificer could be a subtle and accurate responder to formal achievements, and a sympathetic responder to the difficult decisions involved in creativity. As commentator upon his own work, he was assumed to possess a consciousness of its references and aims. 'This poet', said Joseph Spence of Pope, 'is the best commentator on himself.' In 1763, B. Newburgh suggested that if poems required notes and comments, the poets ought to be their own critics. 'It were to be wish'd', he wrote, 'that Authors of this Class, would condescend, where necessary, to be their own interpreters.'

As articulate commentator, the poet, because of his own knowledge of 'process', could suggest alternatives to other poets or even write them in. He was, therefore, free to revise or to recommend revisions in public. Because of his creation of 'beauties' in poetry, it was assumed he could recognize and account for those of others. Yet there were disagreements between poets, and since the poet himself was unable often to explain the 'graces' he snatched beyond the reach of art, the assumption was that at least he would recognize them.

The poet was considered—as Horace pointed out in the 'si vis me flere' passage—to be capable of sympathy with poems of other poets because in his own process he had to make himself feel in order to convince others of his feeling. Thus he was assumed to be capable of a properly responsive reading, if his prejudices were not aroused. But there was as yet no clear procedure to eliminate these prejudices, especially the investment in a particular kind of poetry.

The exercise of 'process', it was assumed, made it possible for the poet-critic to recognize particulars and to read the poem in the author's spirit. But as some critics realized, Aristotle and Quintilian could accomplish this feat without practice in poetry. The claims for 'process' were practical rather than theoretical and until there arose with them a respect for revisions and data as actual examples of a poet's procedures, there was no proper ground by which a poet's assumptions could be more reliably discovered by another poet than by another critic.

A Collection of Old Ballads (London, 1721), pp. i–ii. See Leonard Welsted, *Epistles, Odes*, etc. (London, 1724), p. lix; George Stubbes, *A Dialogue in the Manner of Plato on the Superiority of the Pleasures of the Understanding to the Pleasures of the Senses* (London, 1734), p. 63.

THE PROBLEMS OF THOMSON'S REVISIONS

(b) 'PROCESS': CONTINUITY AND DISCONTINUITY

Conformably to the intention and will of the author.

G. LYTTELTON

It was possible for the author to respond to criticism, to revise, add to or otherwise change his poem so long as he lived, but after his death, the concept of 'process' became increasingly disengaged from the kind of evidence that might be used to construct it. Each attempt to explain what the revisions implied revealed certain characteristic assumptions about criticism. (1) 'Process', especially in the revisions, was considered a form of comparative improvement, and the obligation of the critic as editor and friend was to continue these improvements in the alleged 'intention' of the author. (2) 'Process' was considered a form of the poet's search for himself, and his friends, therefore, identified the 'style' with certain traits of character. (3) 'Process' was considered a form of experimentation by the poet, and the critic, therefore continued the experimentation by rewriting the same subject in a different poetic form—the blank verse of the 'Hymn', for example, was rhymed. (4) 'Process' was a detailed comparison by which the critic indicated the alternatives the poet might have taken but didn't.

These eighteenth-century views shared an acceptance of criticism as a comparative procedure in the creation or interpretation of a poem, as a shared effort between the poet and critic involving judgement and imagination, as a procedure which was conscious and which demonstrated respect for the poem by making it conform to what was considered the proper type of communication. What opposed such views was the belief in the latter part of the century that creation and criticism involved different faculties, or that the 'best' parts of the poem were the result of unconscious expressions.

Thus simultaneously with removing the revisions made by the editor of *The Seasons* and the establishment of Thomson's own text, there developed an area of random speculation about the 'unconscious' elements, some of which, it turned out, were not unconscious at all. And those critics who explained 'intention' in terms of Thomson's character without an awareness of the letters to Mallet and the extent of Thomson's revisions, reduced the range of 'process' to Thomson's conscious statements about God's benevolence. And it was not until the middle of the nineteenth century that letters became available suggesting a few of the revisions involved in 'process'.

Immediately after Thomson's death George Lyttelton, Thomson's literary executor, prepared *The Seasons* and the poet's other work for the press. He issued *The Seasons* with his own revisions in 1750, and then undertook further revisions in order to make the poem conform to what 'good' judges desired:

> In this Edition, conformably to the intention and will of the Author, some Expressions in the Seasons which have been justly thought (by good Judges) too harsh, or obscure, or not strictly grammatical, have been corrected, some Lines transposed, and a few others left out. The Hymn, which was printed at the end of the Seasons in some of the last Editions, is likewise omitted; because it appears to good Judges that all the Matter and Thoughts in that Hymn are much better exprest in the Seasons themselves.[1]

It was self-evident that Lyttelton's view of 'good judges' differed from Thomson's although he was acting out of friendship, and it was self-evident that 'process' was governed here by much more rigid principles than Thomson practised. To certain critics, this conception of criticism implied a share in the poem that showed disrespect for the poem and for the poet. Of Lyttelton's revisions of Thomson's *Liberty*, Johnson (1781) declared:

> The poem of *Liberty* . . . was shortened by Sir George Lyttelton, with a liberty which, as it has a manifest tendency to lessen the confidence of society, and to confound the characters of authors, by making one man write by the judgement of another, cannot be justified by any supposed propriety of the alteration or kindness of the friend.—I wish to see it exhibited as its author left it.[2]

[1] Quoted by Zippel, p. xxiii. See George Lyttelton, ed., Preface to *The Works of James Thomson* (London, 1750), I, for the first preface: 'This edition of Mr. Thomson's works was designed by him and must be considered by the reader as a collection of such of his works as he thought worth preserving, corrected and amended. If therefore any detached poems of his have appeared in other collections, or are to be found in manuscript in private hands, they are such as his judgment rejected; and the publication of them in any future edition of his works or otherwise, would be contrary to his will and prejudicial to his memory.' 'It is hoped that all his writings will appear much more advantageously in their present form (many redundancies being pruned away, and many faults of diction corrected) than they did on their first publication.'

[2] Samuel Johnson, *Lives of the Poets*, ed. G. Birkbeck Hill (Oxford, 1905), III, 289–90. As late as 1779, a reviewer of John Aikin's 1778 edition of *The Seasons* still urged excision of the burlesque episode: 'Should this

Lyttelton's continuation of the poet's 'process' was a debasement of the author's text, an attack upon his 'character' as an author, and a disrespect for independence. There was, moreover, no justification, aside from the critic's arbitrary assumptions, for this meddling with the text. Resistance to such a continuing process was frequently voiced by Shakespeare critics; William Dodd, for example, wrote in 1752 that 'the text of an author is a sacred Thing: 'tis dangerous to meddle with it, nor should it ever be done, but in the most dangerous cases. The best of critics will acknowledge how frequently they have found their most plausible conjectures erroneous; and readings, which once appeared to them in the darkest and most unintelligible light, afterwards clear, just and genuine.'[1]

The view which Dodd took was that the usage of a poet did not always conform to what the critic assumed the usage to be, and that time and knowledge often made clear the principles or practice of the poet. Such a view began by granting the poet the right to his form of expression. The attempt to understand the poem involved not only accepting its form, but, for Thomson's friend, Patrick Murdoch (1762), the creation of a sympathy or rapport with the faculties of the poet: these had to be in '*a certain consonance* to those of the poet'.[2]

[1] William Dodd, *The Beauties of Shakespeare* (London, 1752), I, vii.

[2] Patrick Murdoch, 'An Account of the Life and Writings of Mr. James Thomson', *The Works of James Thomson* (London, 1762), I, 29. Murdoch refused to accept Lord Lyttelton's alterations, even those he thought improved for the better, unless published by Thomson. In a letter to Millar he wrote: 'A detail of my reasons would be needless, it being agreed that an author's works should be presented genuine and entire. If he has written well, well: if not the sin lieth, and ought to lye, at *his* door. It is pity indeed

elegant edition be reprinted, we would recommend it to the editor, to consider whether it might not be adviseable, to omit, as is done in other editions, the burlesque episode of *The Return from the Fox-Chase*, which he has inserted as it originally stood in the third book. Though not without its merit, yet, by being incorporated into a serious and philosophical poem, it evidently offends against that uniformity which is expected in any regular performance', *Monthly Review*, LXI (August, 1779), 117–19. The nationalistic defence of combining the 'grave with the low' was made by Edward Bulwer in 1835, who identified this procedure as characteristically English: 'These are passages which (mixing the serious with the burlesque) would be rarely found in the same poem in any other language than ours—and the spirit which pervades blank verse, such as this, is altogether different from that which reigned over the contemporaneous rhymes of the day.' Edward Bulwer, 'The New Phaedo', *The Student* (London, 1835), II, 296.

The aim of this sympathy was to avoid misunderstanding the individuality of the poet and his innovations of subject matter or language. But in a poem so frequently revised as *The Seasons*, 'consonance' with the faculties of the poet was either impossible to achieve, or it meant nothing more than a willingness to accept the awkwardness of style in order to respond to the sentiments. Murdoch found in the poem a benevolent feeling for nature and a kindness of temper that formed the key to the work; his view of the poet's

---

that Mr. T. aided by my Lord L. did not correct and alter many things himself; but as that went no farther than a bare intention, 'tis too late to think of it now, and we can only say,

Emendaturus, si licuisset, erat . . .

Let us suppose there is an edition such as his Lordship proposes, and that one asks, would I have adopted this variation, or not; and if he had, whether it would have been from a conviction of its being preferable, or out of modesty, and deference to my Lord's judgement, and taste? We could not answer such questions, nor could my Lord himself. And what if, after all, some of my Lord's alterations should prove bad, ought not his Lordship to avoid that unnecessary risque? and to forsee that this must produce a second edition by some other critic, and perhaps *that* a third, which would end either in a total contempt of Mr. T.'s works, or in a restitution of them from the copies published by himself (and with so much deliberation and care, that his printers were tir'd to death, as you will remember) . . .

'The reasons I formerly gave for restoring the conclusion to the Fox-chace still seem to hold good notwithstanding my Lord's scruples. Nor is there any necessity to be so very grave and solemn throughout. The very comparisons my Lord draws from painting make against him—as we see in the best masters the foreground stor'd with nurses and children, boys playing, etc. which have nothing to do with the principal subject, and yet have their natural and proper place in the composition, because they belong to the scene that is represented. And for authorities; his Lordship will scarce shew any thing more burlesque and Hogarthian in Thomson than the monk's cowls, etc. flying about in Milton's Limbo of Vanity . . .

'There remain two things to be mentioned relative in general to the caution with which original writings should be touched. One from the life of Virgil as given us by Donatus, who, when he found it would be impossible to suppress his unfinish'd Aeneis, ordered that at least nothing should be added to it—which injunction his friends so religiously observed, that the blank hemisticks remain unfill'd up. Yet those friends were men of taste, whose assistance, had he lived to use it, he would probably have been very glad of. The other remark I would make, is on the bad success our commentators and editors have had, either in improving their authors, or advancing their own reputation as critics—witness Bentley's Milton, and the late editions of Shakespeare. Those men being able grammarians, were 'process', therefore, reduced poetic decisions to moral attitudes, and the difficulties of expression were concealed under the appeal to 'consonance'. Such a considerable abandonment of elements within 'process' permitted an easy conversion of the poet's 'intention' to the moral preferences of the reader. Although such preferences may have coincided with the poet's own expressed views in his life and his poetry, they did not reflect the implications of his poetry. Such views of 'process', which had as a check upon them direct friendship with the poet and served, as did Murdoch's 'account', to persuade his audience to read Thomson, became in the hands of later critics not searches into 'process' but almost religious indulgences for the poem's faults.

The 'fire' and 'enthusiasm' of the poet could be grasped only by those who, according to Percival Stockdale, could first respond with

---

tempted to deal in criticism; which requires what they wanted, a feeling of poetical beauty. Whence it happens that an image or phraze which they cannot convert into very intelligible prose, is declared faulty, and to need their correction . . .

'As to Mr. T.'s *diction*, of which my Lord's acquaintances so much complain, I would recommend to those gentlemen to read Milton with care, and the greatest part of their objections would vanish; for the rest Thomson himself is answerable; and I believe would answer tolerably well, if he were alive to speak for himself. Certain it is that T.'s language has been well receiv'd by the publick, excepting perhaps those my Lord speaks of, who are more *dispos'd to find blemishes* than *capable of feeling beauties*; and who I think do not much deserve his Lordship's regard. His numbers and manner have been adopted by good authors; and since he began to write, our poetry is become more nervous and rich.

'Grammars and dictionaries will always have their due place and consideration: but no man of genius ever found himself distress'd and fetter'd by them. He could always use the liberty that belonged to and became him, without falling into solecisms, or into obscurity; and indeed without this liberty, no language could be enrich'd or improv'd, but must soon be reduc'd to a dead stand, like the stile of law-writings. For particulars I refer you to my remarks at the end of the copy-book.'

'From Dr. Murdoch to Mr. Millar' [1760–1 ?], *Biographical Memoirs of the Late Revd. Joseph Warton, D.D.*, ed. Rev. John Wooll (London, 1806), pp. 253–7. See also Rose M. Davis, *The Good Lord Lyttelton* (Bethlehem, Pa., 1939), p. 214; John Edwin Wells, 'Thomson's *Seasons* Corrected and Amended', *JEGP*, XLII (1943), 104–14, who points out that Murdoch introduced some new readings as compared with the 1746 ed. (111); Alan Dugald McKillop, ed., *James Thomson (1700–1748) Letters and Documents* (Lawrence, 1958), p. 215. Murdoch's 'Account' was reviewed favourably in *The Monthly Review*, XXVI (1762), 298–305.

feeling to the poetry. In his sermon 'On Self-Knowledge' published in 1784, Stockdale explained that an accurate and impartial examination and knowledge of ourselves would produce in us a 'most amiable temper of mind, in our intercourse with others; it would produce in us a christian candour, and indulgence to their frailties and their faults'. Stockdale, by assuming that the individual could know himself and thus become the successful imitator 'of our mild and merciful Master', indicated that the religious basis of his literary 'sympathy' involved allowances for the faults of a poet who was himself religious. Self-knowledge for Stockdale involved relation to others and was analogous to critical sympathy in advocating freedom from prejudice. 'Before we presume to examine and know ourselves, we must resolve to clear our minds from all partiality to ourselves; to our own habits, persuits and pleasures'.[1] The sympathetic critic sought to identify himself with the feelings of the poet by removing his own prejudices and partialities. And a contemporary (1783) of Stockdale explained that insincerity was the only drawback to self-knowledge. 'Know Thyself, was a wise precept but generally ranked among the number of those easier laid down than followed. True it is, that it seldom is so; but as I have said, the task is not attended with difficulty from the inscrutableness of our natures, but the insincerity of our hearts in the work.'[2] If the poet was sincere, the critic could by means of his sincerity and impartiality grasp the meaning of the poet by understanding his feelings. Stockdale's view of sympathy was directed at the poet and he tended to identify the poem with what he assumed were the feelings of the poet.

In so far as 'consonance' implied an initial suspension of judgement it was possible to develop from it a theory of the separation of the poet's process from critical procedure. For 'criticism' could then be interpreted as that act which differed from the poet's creation, and since judgement and interpretation were not 'spontaneous' but reasoned activities, the act of criticism was defined only by its differentia from the poet's process. This was the position defended by Thomas Twining in 1789 in his essay prefixed to his translation of Aristotle's *Treatise on Poetry*.

He praised Aristotle because 'he never lost sight of the difference between that spontaneous operation of genius and feeling in the Poet,

[1] Percival Stockdale, *Sermons* (London, 1784), pp. 64, 73.

[2] *Essays and Letters on the Most Important and Interesting Subjects* (London, 1783), p. 19.

which *produces* poetic beauty, and the slow and cautious process of calm examination and inquiry in the Critic, whose business it is to discover its *principles*'.[1] Twining's distinction between the spontaneity of creation and the detachment of criticism denied to poet and critic any similarities in practice. To Twining there was no doubt that the poem was based on 'principles', but the poet's awareness of them was not articulated. There were, too, passages in the poem which were not consciously selected.

Twining's position was an attack upon critical 'consonance' or 'sympathy' as a substitute for analysis, and he distinguished between the end of criticism and the end of poetry. Such a view was a corrective to the belief that the critic could place his faculties in consonance with those of the creator. Critics who accepted the 'sympathy' premise, however, did not deny judgement but sometimes preceded it by a spontaneous response: 'The general idea of the scene makes an impression', wrote William Gilpin (1793), 'before any appeal is made to the judgment, we rather feel than convey it'. And Percival Stockdale (1806) wrote: 'How can he presume to admire, and distinguish burning pages, who never caught a spark from the fire of his author?'

But this 'spark' could only be caught if one had some understanding of the kind of poem one was reading, and the 'spark' was, after all, some response to a word, passage, idea, or feeling expressed. The critics, who were 'sparked', caught Thomson's religious fervour, or claimed to catch his spontaneous passages. In 1818 William Hazlitt, operating within a theory of imagination, declared that Thomson 'takes no pains, uses no self-correction; or if he seems to labour it is worse than labour lost'. Yet in the passage which he selected as 'profound and striking', he was quoting a revised passage, not inserted into the poem until 1744. And in 1830 Sir Harris Nicolas claimed to discover the 'spark' in certain passages which seemed digressive but which contained the 'charm' of poetry:

> If it were possible to strip The Seasons of every passage not strictly relevant, they would lose their chief attractions, and soon be thrown aside.
>
> One charm of poetry is, that it often presents a vivid picture of

[1] Thomas Twining, *Aristotle's Treatise on Poetry* (London, 1789), p. 269, n. 66. For a memoir of Twining and a selection of his correspondence, see *Recreations and Studies of a Country Clergyman of the Eighteenth Century* (London, 1882).

the idiosyncrasy of an author's mind, and this is most conspicuous in the episodes to the immediate subject of his labours. The chain of thought which led him astray may not unfrequently be discovered, and it is on such occasions, chiefly, that those splendid emanations which become aphorisms to future ages are produced. Genius seems then to cast aside all the fetters which art imposes, and individual feeling usurping for the moment entire dominion, the mistress who has cheered his hopes, or the coquette who has abandoned him, his friend, or his enemy, as either may occur to his imagination, is sure to be commemorated in words glowing with the fervour of inspiration. Whilst he pursues the thread of his tale, we are reminded of the Poet alone, and though we may admire his skill, it is only when he breaks upon us in some spontaneous burst of passion that we sympathize with the man, and are excited to kindred enthusiasm.[1]

Hazlitt and Nicolas both agreed on the value of 'spontaneity' as opposed to 'artificiality', but in specific examples—like the narrative digressions—they disagreed. Hazlitt called the narratives of Palemon and Lavinia, Damon and Musidora, Celadon and Amelia 'framed and glazed', and wrote, 'those parts of any author which are most liable to be stitched in worsted, and framed and glazed, are not by any means always the best'.[2] But Nicolas found the digressions resulted from 'some spontaneous burst of passion'. Neither critic analysed a digression but Hazlitt's conception of 'process' or spontaneity was derivable from his quotations. He interpreted 'spontaneity' in the poem to refer to passages in which man and nature were seen in their vivid growth or effects. Thus static passages or those which did not build to a single impression were considered 'artificial'. In this respect, Hazlitt noticed valuable qualities in *The Seasons*—the personifying, changing shape of nature—though he attributed them to the '*minutiae* of a landscape' or to a single, imagined transfer of the poet's impression to the reader. But Nicolas attributed 'spontaneity' to the author's release of his personal experiences in poetry, and although this might, hypothetically, be reasonable, the digressions in Thomson were not then and have not yet been identified with such experiences. His assumption of passion, therefore, in an episode like that of Palemon and Lavinia,

[1] Sir Harris Nicolas, ed., *The Poetical Works of James Thomson* (London, 1830), I, lxxxiii–lxxxiv.

[2] William Hazlitt, *Lectures on English Poets* (London, 1841, issued 1818), p. 174.

or Musidora, seemed a justification of Thomson by reference to a general rule which had no applicability in his case.

The critical process in creation, therefore, came to be questioned on grounds of 'artificiality', although there seemed no proper evidence to assume that the revision of a passage drained it of its passion. But there were critics who defended the independence of the writer and identified it with his freedom of expression. For such critics revision formed an interesting account of literary self-knowledge. The critic who first called attention to revisions as a characteristic of *The Seasons* was Johnson, who interpreted revisions as a possibility for, not necessarily an accomplishment of improvement. In commenting upon Milton's early projects for *Paradise Lost* Johnson wrote:

> These are very imperfect rudiments of *Paradise Lost*, but it is pleasant to see great works in their seminal state pregnant with latent possibilities of excellence; nor could there be any more delightful entertainment than to trace their gradual growth and expansion, and to observe how they are sometimes suddenly advanced by accidental hints, and sometimes slowly improved by steady meditation.[1]

Johnson found Milton's poem improved by meditation and craft, and he wrote of Pope's revisions that he 'examined lines and words with minute and punctilious observation, and retouched every part with indefatigable diligence, till he had nothing left to be forgiven'. But Johnson did not consider this 'process' a necessary progress: 'It was remarked by Pope, that the *Dispensary* had been corrected in every edition, and that every change was an improvement', he wrote in his life of Garth. 'It appears, however, to want something of poetical ardour, and something of general delectation'. And in his life of Akenside, he declared, 'I know not whether he has gained in closeness what he has lost in splendour'.

The tentativeness with which Johnson made his recommendation suggested the unsureness of his observation, and the paucity of evidence by which to guide himself. Yet the characteristic awareness

[1] Johnson, 'Milton', *Lives of the Poets*, ed. G. Birkbeck Hill (Oxford, 1905), I, 124. For Johnson's comments on Pope, see III, 221; on Garth II, 64; on Akenside, III, 418. For earlier comments on the critical process as connected with 'polish' 'smoothness', 'ease', and 'improvement', see 'Preface to the Second Part of Mr. Waller's Poems' (1690), Elijah Fenton, ed. *Observations on the Poetry of Edmund Waller* (London, 1729), p. 442, and Joseph Warton, *Essay on the Genius and Writings of Pope* (London, 1756), I, 150–2.

of proportion guided his statement even in this area, whether it was the improvement of details which neglected the creation of ardour, the development of closeness at the sacrifice of splendour, the widening of range with consequent loss of detail. For although he found that the revisions improved *The Seasons* in general, he felt that they had lost part of their 'race'.

> These poems, with which I was acquainted at their first appearance, I have since found altered and enlarged by subsequent revisals, as the author supposed his judgement to grow more exact, and as books or conversation extended his knowledge and opened his prospects. They are, I think, improved in general; yet I know not whether they have not lost part of what Temple calls their *race*; a word which, applied to wines in its primitive sense, means the flavour of the soil.[1]

Johnson pointed to revisions as allegedly reflecting a more exact judgement, an extension of book knowledge and actual experience. What the poem lost was apparently a directness and immediacy of impression in the composition. Johnson's view summed up the doubts which students of revision had begun to have about the poet's process reflecting the intelligent practice earlier critics had ascribed to the poet. In 1779, in his *Column*, Boswell wrote, 'Warburton has obliged us with several variations in Pope's poetry; and while we are entertained by comparing them with the text, we have an opportunity of being at the same time convinced that correction is not always for the better'.[2]

The earlier views had considered 'process' (including revisions) as an example of the good poet's wisdom in making choices—what Dryden called 'the maturest digestion from judgment'—and in the fertility and energy presented by many equally good possibilities. But Waller's couplet which offered a key passage reflecting these views had come by Johnson's time to be interpreted with sceptical reservations. Waller had written:

> Poets lose half the Praise they should have got,
> Could it be known what they discreetly blot.

[1] Johnson, 'Thomson', *Lives*, III, 300–1.

[2] James Boswell, 'On Authorship and Revision' (Dec. 1779), *Boswell's Column*, ed. Margery Bailey (London, 1961), p. 159. A similar comment had been made in a letter by William Walsh to Pope (Sept. 9, 1706) in which over-refinement was attributed to undue submission to 'mechanical' rules and comments governed by them.

And Henry Felton (1713) had explained that delicate and lively wits were obliged 'to retrench more Wit, than others have to lavish: The Chippings and Filings of these Jewels, could they be preserved, are of more Value, than the whole Mass of ordinary Authors; and it is a *Maxim* with me, that *He hath not Wit enough, who hath not a great deal to spare*'.[1] What poets omitted was often as valuable, if not more so, than what they included. Johnson also interpreted this couplet to mean that poets would have received twice the praise they got if the readers knew the value of what they had blotted. But this view considered revisions an example of the poet's productiveness, not his improved or extended skill.

A second interpretation was that poets would have only half the praise they now had if readers knew how badly they could write. Both interpretations agreed, however, in recognizing the importance of a 'finished' as against an 'unfinished' work. Boswell in 1780 commented on Waller's couplet with considerable irony on authors as critics of their own works, explaining that if such interpretations were accepted, they paradoxically underrated or overrated the poet's critical ability. Boswell's position was that the poet's self-criticism often involved unnecessary polishing or unusual refining and that such labour was not worth the sacrifices involved: 'No doubt a certain attention in revising and correcting afterwards is right; and this Pliny allows, though he also very properly observes that too much polishing weakens a performance, and that an excessive delicacy at once prevents us from finishing our works, and from entering upon other attempts.' He did not deny writers this role of self-criticism, but sought to question what he considered a commonplace. 'I am not sure', he wrote, referring to the Waller couplet,

> that this is a just remark, though its quaintness has a decisive appearance. If it is meant they lose half the praise they would have got, had they preserved what they have blotted, their blotting was not discreet. And if it is meant that their additional praise would have arisen from their discretion in blotting being known, I think it is rated too high, if it is to have half as much praise as excellent composition.[2]

Boswell, therefore, discounted the importance of discarded revisions on the grounds that if well revised, the finished product was far more

[1] Henry Felton, *A Dissertation on Reading the Classics* (London, 1713), p. 91.

[2] Boswell, 'On Criticism' (Jan. 1780), *Boswell's Column*, p. 162.

important than the discard. And if poets should not have revised, the process demonstrated their lack of taste.

In order to defend Thomson's revisions against the attack on his 'refinement', the Edinburgh editor of *The Seasons* in 1789 sought to provide a basis for evaluating Johnson's view by publishing the passages from the first edition of *The Seasons* in 1730:

> By way of Appendix to the present edition, those lines and passages which have suffered any alteration are exhibited as they appeared in the 4to edition of 1730. Dr. Johnson has taken notice of the alterations as producing no favourable effect on the general merits of the poem [a misinterpretation of Johnson]. We are not altogether of the same opinion.[1]

Thus were published, for the first time, some of Thomson's revisions which could provide evidence for his 'process' now that all who had had direct contact with the poet had ceased to publish. Two years later (1791) a complete collation of the 1730 with the 1744 edition was under way—though never completed—by Thomson's nephew, Dr. Bell, if his letter to Lord Buchan is to be trusted.

> I have begun to collate the Seasons—the edition 1730 with that of 1744. . . . A great many beautiful passages in the edition of 1730 are entirely struck out of all subsequent editions, and the other alterations made are considerable, far more than I had any conception of previous to collating them with accuracy. The improvements made on the edition of 1744 will be taken notice of; they are highly important.[2]

In 1798, the letters of Anna Seward to Thomas Park contained critical comments on comparisons of the first and last editions, later reprinted (1824) as 'A Comparative View of the First and Finished Editions of The Seasons'. And in 1806 Sir Egerton Brydges reprinted the second edition of *Winter* 'for the gratification of those who have a pleasure in tracing the progress of cultivated intellect'.[3]

The controversy over revisions became merged with and then altered the inquiry into the poet's self-knowledge. The poles of this

[1] *The Seasons* (Edinburgh, 1789), published by Sibbald.

[2] Nicolas, I, cxv–cxvi.

[3] Sir Egerton Brydges, *Censura Literaria* (London, 1806), II, 67. The letters pertaining to *The Seasons* were reprinted in John D. Williams, *The Seasons* (London, 1824), pp. xxxviii–l, as 'A Comparative View of the First and Finished Editions of the Seasons'.

controversy included 'refinement'—'over-refinement', 'spontaneity' —'reason' (later 'artificiality'), 'finished'—'unfinished', 'control' or 'reject'—'uncontrolled' or 'indiscriminate', 'polished'—'rough', 'sketch'—'painting', 'perfect'—'imperfect'. Revisions were defended or attacked in terms of these opposites, but they were not as irreconcilable as they appeared.

In criticizing the spontaneity of Thomson, his close friend and editor George Lyttelton wrote: 'Nor did he always know when to *stop* or what to *reject*'.[1] Knowing 'when to stop' and 'what to reject' constituted practical examples of self-knowledge (though these procedures were bound up with decisions of critical taste and not at all as clear as the statement implied). But criteria for such awareness had puzzled critics throughout the period. Hildebrand Jacob wrote (1734), referring to diction: '*Poets* and *Painters* never gratify more the Observers of their Works, than when they express themselves not so fully, but that these may find Matter enough to exercise their own *Imaginations* upon . . . and it is for this Reason, that the *Sketches*, or, unfinished *Designs* of some great *Masters*, which are but lightly *touched*, seem sometimes to have more *Spirit*, and often *please* more than such as are perfected'.[2] And after Lyttelton, Boswell explained the classical concern with polishing and over-refinement. The problem, in Lyttelton's statement, was based on the conscious control of the fertile imagination. Conditions for such control were, of course, catalogued in rules, but such rules applied to traditional (and general) rather than original or particular efforts. In so far as the imagination required conscious control, the fiction of knowing when to abandon spontaneity was trusted. But knowing when to leave off had other interpretations which considered not the relation between uncontrolled and controlled imagination, but between poem and reader. Burke (1756) argued that a drawing 'stopped' at a 'sketch' left the reader 'with the promise of something more'.[3] To complete a work

[1] George Lyttelton, 'Dialogue XIV', *Dialogues of the Dead, Works*, ed. George E. Ayscough (London, 1776), II, 202. See John Young's comment on the nineteenth stanza of Gray's 'Elegy': 'Gray never could be brought to see when he had said enough', [John Young], *A Criticism on the Elegy Written in a Country Church Yard* (London, 1783), p. 47.

[2] Hildebrand Jacob, *Of the Sister Arts: An Essay* (London, 1735), p. 25.

[3] Edmund Burke, *An Enquiry into the Sublime and the Beautiful* (1756), ed. J. T. Boulton (London, 1958), p. 77. See also Beattie, *Essays*, pp. 100–1. The preservation of the 'sketch' or 'draught' was defended by reference to classical fragments and belief in the value of anything said by

in every detail was to deny the reader a sense of imaginative participation. For him, knowing when to stop was not so much a matter of conscious control of imagination, as conscious use of the norms of behaviour. A work ought not to be too unfinished for perception or too complete for imaginative participation.

These views, of course, took for granted some types of spontaneity and some types of control, but 'stopping', 'completeness' or the 'unfinished' implied either antecedently regularized responses or responses which were associative rather than aesthetic. The 'sketch' in Burke was based on normal imaginative 'promise' rather than associations controlled by the structure of the work dependent, as James Beattie and Frank Sayers argued, on the type of transition and the interrelatedness of part and whole.[1]

A quite different view of 'where to leave off' was argued by Boswell (1779). His criterion was, as noted above, the appearance of ease and spontaneity. Refinement was distinguished from over-refinement by the smoothness and ease of the work. But smoothness and ease were not, of course, always agreed upon. Boswell looked upon 'finishing' as a conscious process the advantages of which had to be weighed against the disadvantages of spending time and energy on trivial corrections instead of engaging in new works. His argument was directed against excessive correction or refinement, but neither Boswell nor any of the other critics cited was prepared to deny that

[1] James Beattie, *Essays*, pp. 106–7 ff. Frank Sayers, 'Of Beauty', *Disquisitions* (London, 1793), pp. 37–43, argued for a theory of associated norms of response rather than interrelatedness and referred to unfinished sentences, in the hands of 'most polished poets' as 'sufficient to call up the emotions and ideas intended' (p. 34). See also *Disquisitions* (Norwich, 1808), pp. 412–15. The norms for the ode required a single subject and end and 'whatever is unconnected with the end is idle'. 'Of the Poetical Character of Horace', 1793, p. 142. For a modern discussion of literary associationism see Walter J. Bate, *From Classic to Romantic* (Cambridge, 1946). For critics who opposed associationism, see Martin Kallich, 'The Argument Against the Association of Ideas', *MLQ*, XV (1954), 125–36.

---

a great poet, see e.g. 'Preface to Second Part of Mr. Waller's Poems' (1690), Fenton, ed. *Waller's Works*, p. 447: 'care has been taken by the learned, to preserve the fragments of the ancient *Greek* and *Latin* Poets: there has been thought to be a Divinity in what they said; and therefore the least pieces of it have been kept up, and reverenc'd like religious reliques'. The denial of the 'poet's divinity' disposed of this argument. See also Tamworth Reresby, *A Miscellany* (London, 1721), p. 366.

some type of finishing was an essential characteristic of the poetic process.[1]

On the other hand, the Earl of Buchan (1792), Walter Whiter (1794), Sir Harris Nicolas (1830), and other defenders of spontaneity, did not deny the role of skill, but offered as a theory of imagination, certain bursts of feeling which seemed to ignore the order of events and expression imposed upon the poem. One assumption of spontaneity and force was that the poet underwent serious childhood experiences—probably in rural areas—and that these were unconsciously expressed in his poetry, as the Earl of Buchan (1792) claimed. 'Spontaneous' or 'difficult' passages were also considered the result of idiosyncratic associations which had taken hold of the poet unawares: 'I define therefore the power of this *association* over the genius of the poet', wrote Walter Whiter (1794), 'to consist in supplying him with words and with ideas, which have been suggested to the mind by a principle of union unperceived by himself, and independent of the subject, to which they are applied.'[2]

These theories were not antithetical to Lyttelton's need for conscious control, for some control was granted as necessary even to types of disorder and feeling that he neglected. In 1830 Nicolas explained that the digressions of a poem were often the areas in which the poem rose to its greatest heights. Far from being irrelevant, they were moments in which the poet burst forth as man as well as poet.

> The chain of thought which led him astray may not unfrequently be discovered, and it is on such occasions, chiefly, that those splendid emanations which become aphorisms to future ages are produced. Genius seems to cast aside all the fetters which art imposes, and individual feeling usurping for the moment entire dominion, the mistress who has cheered his hopes, or the coquette who has abandoned him . . . is sure to be commemorated in words glowing with the fervour of inspiration. Whilst he pursues the thread of his tale, we are reminded of the Poet alone, and though we may admire his skill, it is only when he breaks upon us in some

[1] Boswell, p. 160,

[2] Walter Whiter, *A Specimen of a Commentary on Shakespeare* (London, 1794), p. 68. See also Robert Burrowes, 'On Style in Writing' (read May 11, 1793, and also April 19, 1794), *Transactions of the Royal Irish Academy* (Dublin, 1795), V, 51–52. So far as I know, M. H. Abrams was the first to draw attention to this essay.

spontaneous burst of passion that we sympathise with the man, and are excited to kindred enthusiasm.[1]

The criterion of spontaneity was welcomed by Nicolas precisely because it transformed the anonymous narrator into the man, the poet as poet into the poet as man. For the 'feeling' created by the poem served to evoke deep responses to a human being rather than mere respect for his skill. This spontaneity, therefore, minimized the role of poetic skill, and in doing so it served to attack that criticism based on attention to particulars and parts. Archibald Alison (1790) explained that in criticism, the mind 'is either fettered to the consideration of some of its minute and solitary parts; or pauses, amid the rapidity of its conceptions, to make them the objects of its attention and review. In these operations, accordingly, the emotion, whether of beauty or sublimity, is lost; and if it is wished to be recalled, it can only be done by relaxing this vigour of attention, and resigning ourselves again to the natural stream of our thoughts.'[2] Spontaneity, in so far as it enforced a separation between skill and inspiration, craft or art and nature, could be used to explain Thomson's faults. 'Thomson's ideas spring up so naturally and unforced', wrote Henry Neele (1826), 'that he seems to think himself bound to clothe them in a cumbrous and elaborate versification, before he ventures to exhibit them to the world.'[3]

What literary explanations were there for the forty years' neglect of Thomson's revisions, and why did there occur a burst of collation activity? And why, despite this activity, did the full collation have to wait another hundred years until Otto Zippel published it in 1908?

The neglect of a comparison between early and late editions of *The Seasons* despite the fact that critics knew of such editions was a form of criticism by rejection. Critics chose not to discuss this problem, and their reasons for this have to be pieced together by inferences. In theories of 'process' which found the practitioner the best critic, practice was compared with its absence so that exercise of craft gave more knowledge than absence of exercise. Yet as evidence was accumulated of Pope's and others' revisions it became clear that 'exercise' was not a sufficient criterion for discrimination, and,

[1] Nicolas, 'Memoir' (1830), I, lxxxiii–iv.

[2] Archibald Alison, *Essays on the Nature and Principles of Taste* (London, 1790), pp. 8–9.

[3] Henry Neele, *The Literary Remains of Henry Neele* (London, 1829), p. 181. The lectures were delivered in 1826.

as the philosophers made plain, not even necessary for proper perception.

Moreover, so long as poetry was considered a social art, it was tactless to analyse the early rather than the mature efforts of one's 'artifice'. If the poet undertook the 'reforming toilet's daily care' it was bad manners to refer to times prior to 'toilet training'. Such comparison was futile in comparing a poet's work with the best models, because early performances were obviously supplanted by later works, and comparing a poet with himself could provide information about his progress, but not about the best poetry.

Yet critics who obviously were interested in the poet's progress but who claimed to find the poet in the poem by means of sympathy, also resisted study of revisions because these indicated the multiple 'personae' of the poet. Revisions showed that the author sought different expressions for the same feelings, and that not his faculties were the harmony, but his medium—the expressive language. 'What is said of the Nightengle's singing with her Breast against a Thorn, may be justly apply'd to the Poets', wrote a perceptive critic. 'Their Harmony gives Pleasure to Others, but is compos'd with Pain to Themselves'.[1] But the persistence of a critical explanation in the face of contrary data—Horace had written that 'when a good and just Choice of subject is made, Eloquence and Method will never fail'—indicated the disregard for 'evidence' in the reliance on 'ideal' assumptions. Five years before Murdoch wrote, David Hume (1757) had argued that 'consonance' was not an act of natural taste or harmony; it was an empirical method of observing a work of art, requiring impartiality, diverse perspectives and repeated examinations. Proper examination of a work of art depended upon the knowledge of the audience and conditions of observation: 'We may observe, that every work of art, in order to produce its due effect on the mind, must be surveyed in a certain point of view, and cannot be fully relished by persons, whose situation, real or imaginary, is not conformable to that which is required by the performance.'[2]

Even those who implied a theory of the poet's increased knowledge and skill did not test this hypothesis by comparative examination of editions, because such comparison would have been disrespectful to the poet, tactlessly reminding the audience of the poet's failures. Yet

[1] Elizabeth Cooper, ed. *Muses' Library* (London, 1737), p. vii.

[2] David Hume, 'Of the Standard of Taste', *The Philosophical Works*, ed. T. H. Green and T. H. Grose, I, 276.

when Johnson in 1781 declared of *Liberty* that he wished to see it as Thomson left it, he argued in defence of individual freedom.

By the last quarter of the eighteenth century there existed comparisons of the published poem with possible revisions the poet might have made, based on the critic's literary criteria, such as 'appropriateness', 'decorum', 'simplicity', 'correctness', etc. John More (1777) and John Scott (1785) both revised passages of *The Seasons* in terms of such hypotheses. But they were not considering Thomson's own revisions, comparing his early with his late work; they practised criticism as a comparative endeavour, and all critics shared this view. But they did not compare the poet with himself. When critics like Robert Shiels (1753) offered such comparisons, it was in terms of different genres, not of revisions. 'As a dramatic writer . . .' wrote Shiels, 'he [Thomson] is not so excellent as in other species of poetry.'[1]

Revisions continued in the late eighteenth century to be something of a game, and the sober Christian clergyman Daniel Turner 'translated' Thomson's 'Hymn to the Seasons' into rhymed 'lyric verse'—in quatrains of alternating tetrameter and trimeter, with the second and fourth lines rhyming. The grounds he gave for his practice were: (1) the creation of variety by adding to the same sentiments an experimental playfulness in poetry; (2) the conversion to lyric poetry would particularly please 'lovers of lyric poetry'; (3) the change would provide 'some amusement for the critic'; (4) it would 'be the means of spreading still further abroad the moral and divine sentiments of this *excellent Hymn*; as it is possible these lines may fall under some eye, that has never seen Mr. Thomson's SEASONS'.[2]

The critical grounds of experimental playfulness, intellectual variety and moral evangelism were coupled with a belief that such rewriting did not involve 'too much defacing any essential ornament of the original poem'. It merely meant 'putting off the solemn majestic dress of heroic blank verse, and putting on the more easy, gay, and lively one of the lyric, and yet preserving all the leading sentiments'. In assuming that preservation of sentiments meant preservation of essential ornaments as in a translation, Turner misconstrued what types of value a poem had. The flatness of his version reduced rather than enhanced the interest of *The Seasons*, and if he had succeeded

[1] Robert Shiels, *Lives of the Poets*, ed. T. Cibber (London, 1753), V, 203.

[2] Daniel Turner, 'The Seasons Being a Version of Mr. Thomson's Hymn on that Subject', *Poems Devotional and Moral* (Henley, 1794), p. 71.

he would have produced a 'good' but still a different poem. What he did compose was a flat and ineffective 'ode'.

Thomson had written:

> These, as they change, Almighty Father! these
> Are but the varied God. The rolling year
> Is full of thee. Forth in the pleasing Spring
> Thy Beauty walks, thy Tenderness and Love,
> Wide-flush the fields; the softening air is balm;
> Echo the mountains round; the forests live;
> And every sense, and every heart, is joy.
> [ll. 1–7]

In Turner this became:

> The Seasons, as they circling roll,
> Almighty Father! shew
> The *varied Godhead* still the same
> In every changing view.
>
> Forth in the gay enlivening *Spring*,
> Thy beauty walks abroad,
> The flushing fields and balmy air,
> Confess th'indulgent *GOD*.
>
> The grassy hills to sound thy praise,
> Their echoing tongues employ;
> The forests smile; and every sense,
> And every heart is joy.

Turner's revisions showed a misunderstanding of Thomson's sentence structure and blank verse. He did not recognize that 'these' and 'these' were forms of repetition to enclose a statement of change and that 'and every sense, and every heart' was a structural repetition bringing to a close a series of short and varied sentences. And the God who was varied, creating nature and personifying it, was transposed by Turner into an 'indulgent God' with two assertions—'still the same' and 'confess'—which eliminated the deliberate vagueness of Thomson's God and insisted upon 'The varied Godhead still the same'.

If these were the reasons for neglect derived from varied critical premises, what accounted for the interest in revisions as critical (in contrast to textual) procedures? Johnson's inquiry—based as it was upon a faint recollection—arose from a desire to comment upon Thomson's total work, from a wish for comprehensiveness. Other reasons were based on the respect for personal freedom, granting the poet the right to be understood on his own terms or assuming that growth equalled progress. Critics seized upon 'self-correcting' as a synonym for revision so that some identified second sight (re-vision) with wiser views; still others, by attributing self-correcting powers to the poet, saw him as functioning critically independent of other critics and poets, and they thus emphasized the separation of the artistic and critical community which Pope decried. In praising the poet for his self-help, they denied the need for criticism to serve him. The very method of comparing versions reflected the reliance upon particulars and the use of the past to illustrate the refinement and delicacy of later times.

The comparison of the poet with himself was from the first related to theories of personal freedom and politics. Indeed, the very language of this criticism suggested social attitudes and behaviour: 'refinement', 'delicacy', 'cultivation', 'progress'. When Anna Seward in 1798 compared the first editions of each season with the last she considered this procedure an 'interesting proof of the progressive powers of the fancy and the judgment in so fine a writer' and of his 'self-correcting powers'.[1] In 1806 Sir Egerton Brydges wrote that reprinting the second edition of *Winter* made it possible for 'any poetical reader to observe how much it was afterwards dilated and embellished by the refining hand of its original artificer'. In the same year, however, Mrs. Anna Barbauld wrote of Akenside's revisions: 'The flowers of fancy are apt to lose their odour by much handling, the glow is gone, and the ear itself after a certain time loses its tact amid repeated alterations, as the taste becomes confounded by the successive trial of different flavours.'[2]

[1] Anna Seward, *The Letters of Anna Seward*, ed. A. Constable (Edinburgh, 1811), V, 80–81. According to Joel E. Spingarn, 'Introduction', *Critical Essays of the Seventeenth Century* (Oxford, 1908), I, lxv, 'prior to 1674, scarcely a line of English verse had been quoted for the purpose of critical analysis and discussion . . . except for the sake of ornament or argument, or to illustrate the rules of language or versification'.

[2] Sir Egerton Brydges, II, 67; for other representative discussions of eighteenth-century revisions of poetry, see 'Alterations in the *Pleasures of Imagination* from the Author's MS. Remarks on a Copy in his own Possession', John Pinkerton, *Letters of Literature* (London, 1785); Charles Burke, *On the Life, Writings and Genius of Akenside* (London, 1832),

Anna Seward's comments on selected passages from the four seasons were, methodologically, a study of particulars. Thus, although she brought 'proof' of Thomson's 'progressive powers' it was possible to deny that Thomson always did improve because 'improve' became defined by the examples quoted and by her revision of these examples. To the critic 'improvement' equalled precision, factual truth, visual pictures. In comparing the eagle passage in *Spring* in the first and last editions, she wrote:

> I miss, with regret, some lines which highly animated the passage in the earlier composition. The circumstance, whether true or fabulous, of the old eagle teaching the young ones to soar to the sun, forms a sublime picture in motion, which I am sorry to lose. Some expressions are finer in the altered passage of the last edition, and the local situation is more ascertained,—'but O! but O! the picture is forgot'. Compare the two passages.

FIRST EDITION

'High from the summit of a craggy cliff,
Hung o'er the green sea grudging at its base,
The royal eagle draws his young, resolv'd
To try them at the sun. Strong pounc'd and bright,
As burnish'd day, they up the blue sky wind,
Leaving dull sight below, and with fix'd gaze
Drink in their native noon. The father king
Claps his glad pinions, and approves their birth.'

[ll. 702–9]

LAST EDITION

'High from the summit of a craggy cliff,
Hung o'er the deep, such as amazing frowns
On utmost Kilda's shore, whose lonely race
Resign the setting sun to Indian worlds,
The royal eagle draws his vigorous young,
Strong pounc'd and ardent with paternal fire,
Now fit to raise a kingdom of their own.
He drives them from his fort, the towering seat
Through ages of his empire, which in peace
Unstain'd he holds, while many a league to sea
He wings his course, and preys in distant isles.'

[ll. 755–65]

---

pp. 228–9; Robert Schmitz, *Pope's Windsor Forest 1912* (Washington, 1952); Jeffrey Hart, 'Akenside's Revision of *The Pleasures of Imagination*', *PMLA*, 74 (1959), 67–74.

I do not like the expression, 'amazing frowns', and the mention of the Indian world is superfluous. I think the passages might be blended by the introduction of a few connecting half lines, so as to retain the excellencies of both—thus:

> 'High from the summit of a craggy cliff.
> Hung o'er the ocean, such as sternly frowns
> On utmost Kilda's shore, his vigorous young
> The royal eagle draws, resolving straight
> To try them at the sun. He marks their form,
> Strong pounc'd and ardent with paternal fire,
> Now fit to raise a kingdom of their own.
> He drives them from his fort, the towering seat,
> Through ages, of his empire, See they rise,
> Wind up the clear blue sky, and with fix'd gaze
> Drink in their native noon! The father king
> Claps his glad pinions, and approves their birth.
> Behold him then resume, in lonely state,
> His promontory throne, whence many a league
> He wings his course, and preys in distant isles.'[1]

The original passage was characterized by the motion of flight and the sentimental, approving parent, but the revision abandoned the grace and the sentiment and replaced it by independence enforced by rejection, and the sense of isolation in place and flight. The loss of educative procedures was supplanted by a consistent point of view. The reference to the Indian world—'resign' and 'setting'—the distant isles in contrast to the 'summit of a craggy cliff'—stressed the loss of earthly qualities in acceptance of wild ones: ('lead me through the maze; / Embowering endless, of the Indian fig', *Summer*, ll. 670–1).

Referring to *Summer*, Seward declared: 'Alterations crowd upon us in the poem Summer, and with fine general effect, though there are expressions, and even successive lines expunged in the last edition which I grieve to part with.' The critic was aware of word changes, omissions, alterations, transpositions and additions, but noting these in passing, she explained them in terms of 'strengthened fancy' or 'happy chisel'.

> In the poem Autumn, instead of the strengthened fancy of the bard expanding his descriptions, and exploring a wider range of country, to add new scenery in his finished edition of Summer,

[1] Seward, *Letters*, V, 85–87.

> we perceive here his matured judgement removing, with happy chisel, the incrustations of obscurity, and brilliantly polishing, by little touches, as it passes through the first 500 lines.[1]

The 'self-correcting' powers attributed to Thomson in *Autumn* related the revisions to the poet's private development, yet, in fact, 'the pretty simile of the myrtle in the desert' was not Thomson's but Lyttelton's. And a number of other revisions in this season resulted from suggestions made to Thomson. The theory of personal revision ignored the group participation in poetic criticism and mistakenly attributed powers to the poet which in his own time were obviously not his alone. But the revisions made the artistic process appear a private affair, although, in Seward, privately conscious, with obvious reservations about progressive improvement. In 1830, Sir Harris Nicolas declared, without such reservations: 'From time to time Thomson polished this work with great assiduity and success, perhaps from the anticipation that by it he would be best known to posterity.'[2]

Whatever Nicolas meant by 'polish', what others called improved 'delicacy of thought and language', neither he nor any other critic in the first half of the nineteenth century studied the revisions systematically. The 'delicacy', therefore, was a random view of preferences, reflecting the alliance of critical terms with extrinsic philosophic assumptions. Seward's comparative passages permitted a refutation of steady progress, but her interpretation of 'process' tended to make conscious and judgemental what earlier critics had attributed to instinctive creation. At the beginning of the eighteenth century, 'delicacy' together with 'elegance' were used to specify the *je ne sais quoi* of taste. In Shaftesbury's explanation, 'delicacy' of response in author or critic might be considered the result of an 'inward Sense common to Mankind, which operates with the same Efficiency upon the Generality of the Species'. According to Nathaniel Lancaster (1748), 'delicacy' was inborn, but it could be refined and cultivated.

> The criterion then of *Delicacy* in any action or composition, is the sure feeling and consciousness of its conformity to a like natural sensation within us, operating necessarily on the mind, the very instant that the kindred forms or ideas are exhibited to us. This sense and taste of beauty may, indeed, like all our other faculties, be greatly improved by discipline and exercise; as on the contrary,

[1] Seward, *Letters*, V, 93.

[2] Nicolas, I, xxv.

> for want of them it may be very much impaired. But still, it is evident, that this discerning power is born within us, and is as certain a principle, as any belonging to our nature.[1]

Edmund Burke, using a different hypothesis, related 'delicacy' to fragility (1756): 'An air of robustness and strength is very prejudicial to beauty. An appearance of delicacy, and even of fragility, is essential to it.'

The definition of 'delicacy' which Nathaniel Lancaster offered in 1748 and described as a human 'faculty' was only one of several versions of 'delicacy'. Lord Kames (1762) defined 'delicacy of taste' as a human potentiality which required cultivation rather than any initial 'sure Feeling'. He identified it with a calm sedateness and opposed it to the warmth of genius. 'Genius is allied to a warm and inflammable constitution; delicacy of taste to calmness and sedateness. Hence it is common to find genius in one who is a prey to every passion; but seldom delicacy of taste.' To Lancaster, delicacy was identified with 'cultivation of refined sentiment' (elegance of sentiment) and opposed to 'Inelegance and Coarseness'.[2]

Other critics saw the same problem in social rather than merely individual terms. Mrs. Montagu, for example, in her essay on Shakespeare (1769), explained that 'if perfect and faultless composition is ever to be expected, it must be at some happy period, when a noble and graceful simplicity . . . reigns through the general manners'. William Jackson in 1795 explained that though taste and refinement could not be acquired without 'much attention and application', yet it was 'certain that all these circumstances united, will not alone confer taste—there must be an aptitude to receive the impression, which does not more depend on ourselves, than on the period in which we live. The English writers and artists a hundred and fifty years since, tho'

[1] Nathaniel Lancaster, *The Plan of an Essay Upon Delicacy* (London, 1748), p. 60.

[2] In *Glossographia Anglicana Nova* (1707) and Kersey's *Dictionary* (1718), 'delicate', 'delicacy', 'refine upon', 'elegancy' were terms of praise and approbation—'fine,' 'nice', 'curious', 'excellent', 'to handle nicely', 'to purify'. By mid-century, 'delicacy' and 'refinement' had both positive and negative meanings in Johnson's *Dictionary* (1755). 'Delicacy' had also come to be used as 'softness, elegance of feminine beauty', 'weakness of constitution', 'smallness'; and 'refinement' included 'artificial practice', 'affectation of elegant improvement'. For the connection of 'elegance', 'refinement', 'polish' with the term 'Augustan', see James W. Johnson, 'The Meaning of "Augustan" ', *JHI*, XIX (1958), 507–22.

they had the same classic authors to read, and the same ancient works of art to study as we have, yet were as deficient in taste as if those models of perfection had not existed.'[1]

The conversion of 'delicacy' from a generalized, inborn to a social or self-developed quality, reduced the puzzle of 'genius' while oversimplifying the explanation; as long as such theories did not demand particular analysis of all revisions, they selected those—if they selected any at all—which served their hypothesis. In the second half of the century, 'delicacy' and 'refinement' developed social, antipopular implications, and in 1762 John Gregory pointed out the dangers of such terms.

> Delicacy or refinement of taste is an acquisition both dangerous and deceitful. It flatters our pride by giving us a consciousness of superiority, and by specious promises of conferring upon us enjoyments of which the common herd of mankind are totally ignorant, not infrequently deprives us of those pleasures which are attainable to the Whole Species.[2]

In 1770 William Baker wrote, 'delicacy is a principal ingredient in the composition of that being we stile a *gentleman*'.

Gregory found the value of *The Seasons* in the extensiveness of its prospects and the innumerable views it offered, but it was clear that he did not look upon increased 'refinement' as a virtue. The freedom of the poet was discoverable in the range he offered to the reader, not in the limits he set upon this range. Yet the spurt of collation activity was the attempt to provide a factual method for arriving at artistic judgements. The meaning of 'delicacy' could be checked in the kinds of examples *The Seasons* offered.

The procedure of reducing an 'instinctive' term to one defined by literary evidence and analysis, checked the divergence of interpretation and led to a concentration on particular aspects of the problem, like 'delicacy' and 'progress' of revisions, and on particular terms and contexts. This concentration produced changes in critical terminology drawn from practices originally overlooked or assumed to be beyond analysis.

The study of a poet's revisions arose as a development of 'self',

[1] William Jackson, *Thirty Letters* (London, 1795), pp. 167–8; Elizabeth Montagu, *An Essay on the Writings and Genius of Shakespeare* (London, 1777), 4th ed., p. 8.

[2] John Gregory, *A Comparative View of the State and Faculties of Man* (London, 1765), p. 152.

a search for the poet's self-knowledge within a tradition. Imitation of classical models gave room for independence, but independence within tradition. As 'genius', 'delicacy', 'self-knowledge' made inroads on how tradition was used, criticism as a discipline offered to readers the possibility of acting as their own critics because they could compare the first and 'finished' editions. As Brydges wrote (1806), 'the early and late editions could be compared for the gratification of those who have a pleasure in tracing the progress of cultivated intellect'. But study of revisions also destroyed the belief in 'finished' models because critics preferred the provocative imagination of the imperfect work to perfection which did not stimulate the beholder's imagination or to imperfection resulting from human limitation rather than artistic deliberation. Other critics, however, rejected 'models' because they defined 'finished' as homogeneousness of impression; for them, 'models' were inconsistent with originality.

In 1710 'model' meant a pattern 'which an Workman proposes to imitate'; in the second half of the century it became involved with the cultural milieu, the writer's self, the difference rather than the similarity between poetic styles. Finally in 1816, in a preface to *The Seasons*, a critic declared that no original work could ever be a model:

> There is in the human frame a perfect but indefinable correspondence which extends to every joint, to the very hair of the head: The artificial isolation of this harmony is immediately perceptible. Something of this kind exists with respect to the productions of real genius. As models, they will be found exceedingly defective. They would mislead, as much as they defy imitation. But there is in them, as a whole, a certain homogeneousness of expression, which rescues even their faults from impropriety.[1]

[1] 'Critical Observations', *The Seasons* (London, 1816), p. vi. These 'Observations' quote from Wordsworth's 1815 preface and incorporate some of his conclusions on *The Seasons*. 'Imitation' and 'originality' were opposed only if critics defined the first as mere 'copying' and the second as completely free from 'copying'. But without such false distinctions, critics acknowledged that 'originality' (independence of tradition) developed from 'imitation' (personal interpretation of tradition). Sir Joshua Reynolds was quoted by T. Wright, *Some Account of the Life of Richard Wilson, Esq., R.A.* (London, 1824), p. 46, as follows: 'I am, on the contrary, persuaded that by imitation only, variety and even originality of invention is produced. I will go further; even genius, at least what is so called, is the child of imitation. Invention is one of the great marks of genius; but if we consult experience, we shall find, that it is by being conversant with the inventions of others, that we learn to invent, as by reading the thoughts of others, we

Critics who analysed revisions could at least consider, even if they did not pursue, the resistance of the poet to certain changes as well as his 'delicacy' in making others. Such analysis called forth new puzzles as it began to solve others. For the preferences of the poet, as Anna Seward remarked, were 'odd'—and the meaning of the unchanged, of the stable elements needed both to be identified and explained: 'Thomson never lost his odd partiality for the inharmonious words *thick* and *things*; they occur perpetually in all the editions, and might generally have been exchanged to advantage.' But in 1816, there occurred an accident that turned collation in another direction, and created a puzzle which seriously questioned that 'process' was a personal, conscious development: a body of manuscript revisions of *The Seasons* (1738) was discovered written by Thomson and someone alleged to be Pope, and many of these were included in the extensively revised 1744 edition. The argument for self-correction was confronted by evidence that refuted the individualist assumption.

(c) JOHN MITFORD: THE TEXTUAL STEEPLECHASE

> One of the most extraordinary 'mare's-nests' to be found in English literature . . . is the assumption that Pope assisted Thomson in revising *The Seasons* . . .
>
> JOHN CHURTON COLLINS

Although a stable text is necessary for explication to proceed, the search for such a text can sometimes point to other inquiries which undermine it. In 1842 Bolton Corney published the 1746 text of *The Seasons* as Thomson's last revised version, but there were already outlined two major problems which made explication difficult, if not impossible. The first was the failure to develop a variorum edition of revisions. The second was the discovery, announced in 1816 by John Mitford in his notes to an edition of Thomas Gray, that he had discovered Pope's corrections of the 1738 edition of *The Seasons*. *The Seasons*, he remarked, 'improved very much and very rapidly in the course of the second and third edition; so much so, that I have often been struck, in reading them in the difficult stages of their improvement, with the uncommon *taste* of the author during so short a

---

learn to think. It is in vain for painters or poets to endeavour to invent without materials on which the mind may work, and from which invention must originate. Nothing can come of nothing.'

period. For this change, in some degree, I can now account satisfactorily; as I possess an interleaved copy of The Seasons (of the edition of 1738) which belonged to Thomson, with his own alterations; and, with numerous alterations and additions by *Pope*, in his own writing. Almost all the amendments made by Pope, were adopted by Thomson in his last edition; and many lines in The Seasons, as they now stand are Pope's own composition.'[1]

The assurance of the remark, 'For this change, in some degree, I can now account satisfactorily,' announced the respect for 'facts' that characterized the investigative procedures of nineteenth-century critics. Indeed the critical purpose of examining this textual steeplechase is to demonstrate the need to attend to the methods by which 'facts' are determined as well as the 'facts' themselves, and to insist on the speculative nature of some factual disputes. For the solution to the 'Pope' revisions came not from further information about the revisions themselves, but from examining a quite different but related body of evidence.

The identification of interleaved revisions was a problem of considerable subtlety, and its solution was significant for criticism, because as Mitford remarked somewhat unbelievingly, Thomson's revisions 'improved very much and very rapidly in the course of the second and third edition'. If Pope revised *The Seasons*, the latest edition had significant changes which were not Thomson's and which were an improvement upon his work. Such facts, if accepted, would alter the judgement of Thomson's quality as a poet as they would alter the belief that Pope didn't write blank verse. Analyses, moreover, of the direction of improvement (of Thomson's possibilities as reviser) would also be changed.

But before one accepted Mitford's judgement, the revisions had to be identified, although the identification of revisions would not in themselves have settled the issue. For even if Pope wrote them down, the possibility of ideas being exchanged before such writing was not excluded. What Mitford needed, therefore, before he could 'account satisfactorily' for the revisions, was a knowledge of how they were composed. The submission of a manuscript to a friend who sought to revise or recommend revisions in accordance with the practice of the poet did not preclude the poet as author. Such determinations required quantitative measurements. When Mitford wrote that *The*

[1] John Mitford, ed. *The Poems of Thomas Gray* (London, 1814), pp. cxiv–cxv *n*. See also *Gentleman's Magazine* (1841), Part II, 563 ff.

Seasons 'improved very much and very rapidly in the course of the second and third edition', such judgement depended upon the number of revisions made, the grounds for considering changes to be improvements; and comparison of the kind of revisions made in the 'second edition' with those in the 'third'. Since the 1738 edition (the 'second') was identical with the text of the quarto edition of 1730, except *Winter* which had the same number of lines as the 1730 octavo, Mitford probably referred to the 1744 edition.

Mitford did not publish selections from his edition of the 'Pope' revisions until 1841 [*Gentleman's Magazine*, Pt. 2, 563 ff.]. That the revisions were by Pope, Mitford took for granted, judging apparently by what he called Pope's 'small and beautiful writing' and Warton's undocumented mention that Thomson took the first idea of *The Seasons* from the title of Pope's four pastorals, though Thomson himself had declared that he had decided to write *Winter* because of a winter poem by Riccaltoun.

But in a review of Nicolas's edition of Thomson's *Works* in 1847, Peter Cunningham cast doubt upon the handwriting attributed to Pope. The volume, he explained, 'contained numerous corrections in Thomson's own handwriting, and still more numerous alterations in a smaller and neater handwriting,—not unlike Pope's, but still to our thinking (as we remarked at the time) a good deal more like Lord Lyttelton's. The point is worth settling. Pope is not known to have corrected "The Seasons"—but Lord Lyttleton corrected them in the poet's lifetime, and actually published a corrected and altered edition of his own after the poet's death.'[1]

In the face of Mitford's handwriting experts, it was difficult to accept Cunningham's attribution of the revisions to Lord Lyttelton; nor did his suggestion at once lead to a proper solution. For the problem of the hand was obviously unresolvable at this point, and a comparison of the 1750 Lyttelton edition with the Mitford volume might have indicated whether Lyttelton inserted revisions omitted by Thomson. It would thus have been possible to resolve a matter-of-fact difference by a related and non-controversial body of data. But this was not the direction the inquiry took.

In 1860 Bolton Corney accepted Mitford's claim: 'The edition of

[1] Peter Cunningham, 'Review of the Critical Works of James Thomson', *The Athenaeum* (July 24, 1847), 784–5. Edward E. Morris supported Cunningham; see *Thomson's Seasons*, ed. Edward E. Morris (London, 1869), I, 127, note to line 906.

1744 was improved by the suggestions of Pope; and the interleaved volume which received his emendations has become the property of John Mitford.' In 1861 Robert Bell in his edition of *The Seasons* sought to base the allegations upon adequate evidence. In explaining why the revisions were Pope's he gave the following reasons: (1) Thomson set about revising *The Seasons* two years after he went to reside at Richmond; (2) Pope was his frequent visitor during this period; (3) The hand was 'not likely to be mistaken by any one familiar with Pope's hand'; (4) 'If they were not Pope's, whose were they?'[1]

It can be seen that only one of Bell's arguments was crucial in determining the author: the 'hand' of the revisions. The other arguments were highly speculative or irrelevant. But to the study of the handwriting no further evidence was brought. The result was that by refusing to cast doubt upon this type of inquiry, the participants were deadlocked. The complexities of authorship and the immense task of establishing a variorum edition resulted in a note of despair by Peter Cunningham in 1862. Sir Harris Nicolas had declared that Dr. Johnson's nephew Dr. Bell 'intended to publish an edition of "The Seasons" with all variations', but never completed his task; Cunningham added: 'An intention which no one can carry out. Wordsworth tried it—Mr. Dyce tried it—I have tried it.'[2]

But in 1883 Karl Borchard published in *Anglia* the *Textgeschichte von Thomson's Seasons*, VI (1883), 375–424, identifying two editions of *Winter* in 1726 as 'A' and 'B', editions which, as Borchard recognized, were first noted by Sir Egerton Brydges in 1806. The third and fourth editions in 1726 were identical with the second. The noting of revisions was begun in 1789 (Sibbald's edition) and the attempt to determine differences was carried on in part by Brydges for the first two editions of *Winter*, by Bolton Corney in publishing a chart of numbered revisions, by Mitford who published a large sampling of his interleaved revisions, by Cunningham, by Nichols and now systematically for each edition of *The Seasons* by Borchard.

Borchard confirmed the presence of a 1744 edition ('C')—Corney had not found one—and he counted the differences between it and

[1] Robert Bell, ed., *Poetical Works of James Thomson* (London, 1855), II, 40–41 n.

[2] P. Cunningham, ed., *Poetical Works of James Thomson* (London, 1862), I, liii n.

the 1738 edition ('B'). Borchard repeated Cunningham's comment about the difficulty of publishing all the revisions:

> Es ist daher unmöglich, im folgenden die ganze masse der textunterschiede im einzelnen zu berücksichtigen, sondern wir werden uns darauf beschränken müssen, die veränderung und entwickelung des textes im allgemeinen durch die einzelnen ausgaben hindurch zu verfolgen, dabei gelegentlich zu einer stelle die varianten mehrerer texte anzuführen und so die art und weise, wie Thomson bei der überarbeitung verfuhr, näher zu beleuchten.[1]

By his investigative procedures Borchard brought new evidence to bear on the Pope theory. He relied upon Lyttelton's correspondence (published in 1845) to show that Thomson brought Lyttelton a revised poem in 1743, and that at that time, when the poem was being revised, Pope was ill, nearing his last days. He urged a comparison of the handwriting of Lyttelton with that of the revisions and supported Cunningham's view of the reviser.

In 1895 Duncan C. Tovey edited a new edition of Thomson's poems, and in his 'Critical Notes on "The Seasons",' he wrote that 'if the best authorities at the [British] Museum many years ago were positive that this handwriting is Pope's, their successors at the present time are equally positive that it is not'. But although the critics denied Pope as the writer, Tovey had no other poet as alternative, rejecting Lyttelton on the grounds that 'Lyttelton's is neat and scholarly, but quite unlike the Unknown's manuscript'. The revisions, he declared, 'were written by a man of finer taste than Thomson himself, but perhaps not sufficiently tolerant of some rough felicities which marked the earlier editions of "The Seasons". But within the critical dates to which we are limited we know no one but Pope who would have at once the capacity and the opportunity to improve Thomson's work, except perhaps Young. But this was not Young's handwriting.'[2] The most significant contribution of Tovey to the controversy was the reprinting of all the emendations to the 1738 edition—'except what, for want of space, I have been compelled to reject as microscopic'—indicating the attributions to Pope and Thomson. Thus for the first time the revisions became publicly available.

In his review of this edition, John Churton Collins rebuked Tovey

[1] Karl Borchard, *Textgeschichte von Thomson's Seasons*, *Anglia*, VI (1883), 390.

[2] Duncan C. Tovey, ed., *The Poetical Works of James Thomson* (London, 1897), I, 194–5.

for attributing the corrections to Pope after admitting that the handwriting was not Pope's. He provided no adequate alternative, but he underlined the fact that the Pope theory rested 'on a mere assumption of Mitford'.

In 1904 George Macaulay, upon examination of the handwriting, agreed that the hand was not Pope's: 'The next step was to endeavour to find out whose hand it actually was.' Macaulay's candidate was George Lyttelton on the grounds of (1) handwriting; (2) circumstances —Thomson was at Hagley in 1743, 'the period when this revision was made,'[1] and Lyttelton was Thomson's executor and editor; (3) the style of the passages contributed to *The Seasons* and that of Lyttelton's poems were similar.

The argument from handwriting was untenable because the experts disagreed and because no one presented the grounds for their decision. Such deadlock was not to be broken by gathering more disagreements. The argument for circumstantial evidence could be read both ways, and since Lyttelton outlived Thomson, but Pope did not, the executor argument was not reliable. And the argument from 'style' was self-evidently without sufficient discrimination of stylistic traits.

In 1908 Otto Zippel published his variorum edition. Working from the premises of Macaulay, he made one further and convincing contribution to the controversy; he attempted 'to establish a connection between the contributions in the copy of 1738 and the later emendations of Lord Lyttelton. It seems an interesting task to discover instances in which suggestions of the collaborator that had not been accepted by Thomson were repeated by Lyttelton. And such instances actually occur.'[2]

But the new data did not immediately erase the old inconsistency, and Otto Zippel himself, having supplied sufficient circumstantial evidence about the 'collaborator' 'to remove any remaining doubts as to his identification with Lyttelton',[3] declared in his headnotes to

[1] George Macaulay, *Athenaeum* (Oct. 1904), p. 446. See also George Macaulay, 'Appendix', *James Thomson* (London, 1908), pp. 243–5. For summaries of the textual controversy which support Macaulay, see Amanda V. Rau, *A Minor Augustan* (Calcutta, 1934), pp. 127–33; Rose M. Davis, *The Good Lord Lyttelton* (Bethlehem, Pa., 1939), pp. 211–15.

[2] Zippel, p. viii.

[3] Zippel, p. ix. The most extensive textual study of editions of *The Seasons* has been that of John Edwin Wells. See 'Thomson's *Seasons*, 1744 —An Unnoticed Edition', *Englische Studien*, LXX (1938), 221–6; 'Variants

Spring that in his reproduction of the manuscript notes, 'T stands for Thomson, P for Pope', although in his 'corrigenda' he corrected his error, replacing Pope 'by "L" (= Lyttelton)'. As late as 1920, J. W. Mackail repeated what was now an error of fact: 'Pope not merely subscribed to the sumptuous first edition of the complete *Seasons*; he helped largely, with advice and suggestion, in the minute revision through which the poem repeatedly went for subsequent editions.'[1]

(d) JAMES L. ROBERTSON, GEORGE C. MACAULAY, ALAN D. McKILLOP: THE EXTENSION OF 'PROCESS'

> A detailed examination of the successive versions may be commended to students of English literature in the eighteenth century; it is instructive and full of interest.
>
> J. W. MACKAIL, 1920

Even before there was a variorum text, critics recognized that the revisions might provide some clues to Thomson's limits and capabilities. In her theory of progressive refinement, Anna Seward had implied that the revisions were not all for the best, and Johnson had, of course, suggested this in his remarks. But without complete examination, without some attempt to separate the kinds of revisions, all remarks about them were bound to be fragmentary and preferential. 'Few who have examined Thomson's work very critically will much regret, even if they suspect, with Johnson, that the "Seasons" lost part of what Temple calls "race" in enlargement and revision. On the contrary, we should rejoice . . . that he submitted the "Seasons" to the skilful hands of Pope.' Tovey declared that words came readily to Thomson, 'but they were not always well-chosen words'.

Tovey's preferential grounds for approving the revisions were that Thomson was representative of his age in that he was neither intense

[1] John W. Mackail, 'The Poet of the Seasons' (1920), *Studies in English Poets* (London, 1926), p. 92.

in the 1746 Edition of Thomson's *Seasons*', *The Library* (Sept. 1936), pp. 214–20; 'Note on a Poem to the Memory of Mr. Congreve', *TLS*, 1936, p. 791; 'Manuscripts of Thomson's Poems to Amanda and Elegy on Aikman', *PQ*, XV (1936), 405–8; 'James Thomson's Poem "On the Death of his Mother" ', *MLR*, XXXIII (1938), 46–50; 'Thomson's *Spring*; Early Editions True and False', *The Library* (March 1942), pp. 223–43.

nor rebellious as a poet, and every correction of technique, especially by a technical master like Pope, was bound to improve the looseness of structure. That the revisions were not by Pope and showed an awareness of extended knowledge and point of view was a refutation of Tovey's position. But Tovey did not respect Thomson as a poet, and the kind of 'process' he guessed at had little to do with the possibilities of the kind of poem Thomson was writing.

The conception of 'process' at the end of the nineteenth century began to include a reconstruction of the period as well as of the development of the poet's taste. This meant that the poem reflected the poet's absorption of his environment and his differences from it; but the analysis of such characteristics seemed to be a defence of or attack upon the concept of the artist. Tovey found that Thomson was considered a 'poet' by his contemporaries, but poetry was 'scarcely in the real convictions of most of them, a divine gift, scarcely an enthusiasm'. The true poet, for Tovey, was the 'divine', a view which eliminated Pope as it did Shakespeare in the sonnets. Edmund Gosse, on the other hand, found that in his revisions Thomson 'worked in the true spirit of the artist'.

The true spirit of the artist depended no more upon the revisions than upon the lack of them in Byron's famous boast about not rewriting. The test of the artist is in the result, not the process. Even Gosse conceded that the revisions were not always improvements and that Thomson's tone was sometimes 'downright ludicrous'. In an analysis of a passage from *Summer*, he found the 'pedantry' removed but the sharpness blunted. The pedantry referred to 'watery mirrors', a scientific image, and the 'gorgeousness' to the Amphitrité passage.

The sunset scene in *Summer* now reads thus:

> Low walks the sun, and broadens by degrees,
> Just o'er the verge of day. The *shifting* clouds
> *Assembled gay, a richly glorious* train,
> *In all their pomp attend his setting throne*;
> *Air, earth and ocean smile immense. And now,*
> *As if his weary chariot sought the bowers*
> *Of Amphitrité and her tending nymphs*
> (*So Grecian fable sung*), he dips his orb;
> Now half immersed; and now a golden curve
> Gives one *bright glance*, then *total* disappears.
> [ll. 1620–9]

The words printed in italics are those not found in the original text, which now follows; it will be noticed that nearly two-thirds of the passage suffered revision:

> Low walks the sun, and broadens by degrees,
> Just o'er the verge of day. The rising clouds,
> That shift perpetual in his vivid train,
> Their watery mirrors, numberless, opposed,
> Unfold the hidden riches of his ray;
> And chase a change of colours round the sky.
> 'Tis all one blush from east to west! and now
> Behind the dusky earth, he dips his orb;
> Now half-immers'd; and now a golden curve
> Gives one faint glimmer, and then disappears.
> [ll. 939–48]

On the whole, the alterations here are, as Johnson says, an improvement; we are glad to lose the clumsy pedantry about the cloud's 'watery mirrors'. But the sharp presentation of the scene is blunted with gorgeousness, and Amphitrité is a poor exchange for the 'one blush from east to west'.[1]

This very same passage had earlier been treated in detail by John Scott (1785) who found the imagery inconsistent: 'the mention of the "*setting throne*", again indicates a prosopopoeia, and the "*dipping*" of "*the orb*", again implies a reference to the natural object'. Scott found the 'immense smile of air' 'bombastic' and the setting of the sun unnecessarily impeded by the Amphitrité image. The difference between the two interpretations of the passage was in the standards applied, yet whether one used those of consistent imagery and 'simplicity', or precision and a somewhat different definition of 'simplicity', the basis for judgement rested on imposed standards.

Yet the changes obviously had pertinence for the author, and the contexts implied what this pertinence was. It would, in fact, have seemed reasonable to predict that the study of revisions would develop a contextual theory. If a passage, rewritten by the poet, possessed implications somewhat different from the original, the critical analysis of these implications (and how they were expressed)

[1] Edmund Gosse, 'A Critical Study of James Thomson', *The Seasons*, ed. Henry D. Roberts (London, 1906), pp. xxvii–xxix. An earlier statement recognizing the critical possibilities of drafts and revisions was made by Edward Dowden, 'The Interpretation of Literature', *Transcripts and Studies* (London, 1888), p. 265.

might have led to the importance of poetic contexts. Such analyses, too, would have made possible distinctions between proper and improper, successful or unsuccessful rewritings. In the revised passage, the sun was seen as a gay, commanding power, who leaves the heavens surrounded by his 'train'. But the gaiety and joy seem inappropriate to the weariness; and the tone of weariness—called up by reference to allegorical figures—could enforce a sense of the past inconsistent with the joy and brightness of the present, just as 'he dips his orb' conveys false tonal implications for regal behaviour.

With the development of a variorum edition in 1908, there began to be developed a recognition of the different contexts within which changes were to be examined. The concept of the poet did not create an interpretative basis for revisions, which had continued to be explained as stages in the poet's taste. But with the disagreements over the value of specific revisions, there began to develop exchanges between critics which, by explaining the purpose of changes, saw revisions as interpretatively significant alterations.

In the Oxford, 1908, edition of *The Complete Poetical Works of James Thomson*, James Logie Robertson, the editor, explained in the preface that the

> various readings show that kind of development in which refinement and repose are gained, but not without some expense of vitality and vigour. There is sound criticism in the judgement of Johnson that in the process of improvement *The Seasons* lost somewhat of their original race or flavour. The Scotticisms, too, were expressive. And the keenness of his colour-sense, which he had inherited from his country's ballads, became dulled in deference to the taste of Pope and Lyttelton. But the loss of raciness is chiefly seen in the substitution, for example, of so comparatively tame a line as—
>
> Then scale the mountains to their woody tops
> (*Autumn*, l. 483)
>
> for
>
> Then snatch the mountains by their woody tops
> (*Autumn A*, l. 480)
>
> in the description of the fox-hunt; or in the exchange of 'Shook from the corn' for 'Scared from the corn', in the hare-hunt.[1]

[1] James Logie Robertson, ed., *The Complete Poetical Works of James Thomson* (Oxford, 1908), p. vi.

In answer to these objections, George Macaulay in the same year wrote:

> Examples have sometimes been cited of alterations, in which it is supposed that picturesqueness or vigour has been sacrificed without any sufficient compensation; but in most cases it will be found that these are concerned with exaggerated or tasteless forms of expression, which no sound critic would desire to preserve . . the idea of scaling mountains rapidly is rather absurdly expressed by the line,—
>
> Then snatch the mountains by their woody tops,
>
> and with reference to the startled hare, 'Shook from the corn' is not more expressive than 'Scared from the corn', and it is less grammatical . . . Much the same account may be given of a supposed toning down of colour effects in revision . . . Thomson inherited little from the Scottish school of poetry, and when we come to examine the instances in which vivid colouring is actually less prominent in the later than in the earlier texts, we shall find that there are excellent reasons for the changes apart from the mere question of colour.[1]

Despite the differences in conclusion to which Robertson and Macaulay came, only some of their disagreement was located in aesthetic taste, that is, only some of their disagreement was preferential. The difference in expressiveness between 'scale' and 'snatch' or between 'shook' and 'scared' depends upon the context of pertinence which is considered. For example, 'shook' referred to the action of the hunters, implying their elementary efforts, not even requiring force or resistance. 'Scared' referred to the behaviour of the hare and emphasized his timidity, creating a feeling of sympathy for him instead of disrespect for the hunters. The difference attributed to 'expressiveness', therefore, was a difference in expressive implication, not a difference between vigour and its absence.

With regard to the generalizations about the revisions as a whole, the difference between Robertson and Macaulay depended upon the number of representative instances examined and the criteria used as guides. Improvement, by Macaulay, was measured by 'expression', by 'balance of clauses', by removal of 'unfortunate Latinisms', by providing 'better sound and better sense'. Such assumptions did not

[1] Macaulay, *Thomson*, pp. 247–8.

always consider the relevant contexts, but they were clear guides. Macaulay admitted that some changes were regrettable—'the alteration in *Spring*, 65 1, is no doubt unfortunate'—but in terms of number of changes, he concluded, 'in general, there can be no doubt that the alterations are for the better'. And in 1913, A. Hamilton Thompson declared, 'in the successive revisions to which *The Seasons* was subjected, the poem gained in arrangement and in variety of surface'.[1]

The judgements upon Thomson's revisions offered the following alternatives: they were 'better' or 'improved' if they: (1) were more precise than the original; (2) more 'vivid'; (3) included more information—historical, geographical, scientific; (4) simplified the language; (5) made the point of view consistent; (6) displayed greater technical (verse) facility. But a number of matters of fact hindered the validity of such judgements if they claimed to be 'in general'. The revisions were not analysed as a group, and they were not analysed in the order of their publication. Thus the revisions from 1726 to 1730 of *Winter* proved considerably different from those of 1730 to 1744. Agreements or disagreements about the function of revisions that did not consider distinctions were unreliable as interpretations.

If, therefore, during the lifetime of the poet he made a series of decisions about usage, about subject, versification, syntax, diction and other matters, and if some of these decisions were the result of non-conscious and conscious choices made by himself or in consultation with others, the attempt to explain these decisions after his death was a form of reconstruction. Such reconstruction was obviously limited by the knowledge involved in such decisions, and by the actual changes themselves. But the totality of these changes was not collected until 1908. Previous critics, therefore, generalized about their meaning from whatever fragments they collected, and, even in this respect, they found that the revisions did not readily fit the theories they applied to them. The progressive improvement was tied to a theory of refinement, but the loss of 'race' implied a loss of immediacy and individuality. These studies considered revisions in terms of 'taste' and 'skill', but 'taste' and 'skill' were determined by the ends which the critic considered desirable.

Now this procedure appears hopelessly redundant, but it is not so

[1] A. Hamilton Thompson, 'Thomson and Natural Description in Poetry', (1913), *The Cambridge History of English Literature*, ed. Sir A. W. Ward and A. R. Waller (Cambridge, 1937), X, 109.

in practice. The determination of 'skill' was for More and Scott and Seward combined with demonstrations of alternative revisions, of what they meant by skill or taste. In so far as knowledge permitted, it was possible to distinguish arguments which seemed appropriate to the end sought and those which were inappropriate to the purpose of the revisions. Scott repeatedly objected to the mixing of personification and natural traits, but this was characteristic of Thomson's descriptions and would eliminate the work as a poem if Scott's comments were to be taken seriously. If, on the other hand, Thomson was granted the right to mix such traits, then there were mixtures more or less adequate. One to which Scott and Gosse pointed was a failure, even though they did not give similar reasons.

In considering revisions as matters of 'improvement', critics did not always define 'improve' in the same way, but this did not imply that any definition was as adequate or as testable as any other. To define 'improve' as meaning to extend the geographical or scientific range was perfectly satisfactory so long as 'adding' did not mean 'adding well'. But 'improve' implied a value statement, and unless adding could be shown to be literarily necessary or desirable, it was not a value. As for 'simplicity' or 'vividness' or 'facility', it was important to discover whether these were indeed the values sought. Such a search meant the location of passages affected by and pertinent to the revisions. This was no arbitrary matter, but there was no reason to assume that if 'snatch' was changed, the grounds for this change were located in the meaning of the word, not the passage or verse paragraph in which it occurred.

It was possible to argue that analysing the revisions and understanding the purposes to which they were put (for example, personification in the 'setting sun' passage) did not provide a proper basis for evaluation. But this would be to confuse the apparent aim with the implications of the achievement. What such implications were was demonstrable so long as the critic kept the text before him. Such implications, in Thomson, made possible a study of his organization by an analysis of transpositions, or it made possible a study of his work in *The Seasons* as compared with his other works written simultaneously with it. It made these possible, but no critic immediately undertook them.

The analysis of revisions could function critically in several ways. One was the codification of types: in his essay on 'The Second Thoughts of Poets' (1919), Sir Edward Cook analysed the different kinds of revisions undertaken by the poets he discussed. Such comments were far more careful than the later generalization of T. R. Henn (1934) that in 'a second draft of any poem we may expect, in theory, to find two things: a greater artistry of technique, and a dulling of the original image, or the substitution of a fresh one'.[1] Such a generalization was not only factually incorrect when applied to *The Seasons*—see 'all one dazzling waste' to 'one wild dazzling waste'—but it reduced the variety of revisions (transpositions, extended knowledge, heightening of original image, tighter contrasts, etc.).

The conception of revisions was, however, only one aspect of 'process', for 'process' included the poet's use of other works—his reworking of them in the poem. Thus in 1935 Dwight L. Durling analysed Thomson's use of the *Georgics*, its actual text and conventions. This view of Thomson as influenced by or influencing other poets constituted a series of notes for the study of the poem; but while implying that the poet came, in some way, to use these materials, this commentary never reached the analysis of the finished product. Thus there developed in the concept of 'process' a kind of overdetermination. Whatever in some way affected the poet was considered pertinent without demonstrating such pertinence in the finished product. In thus expanding the concept of the artist to include all other roles, this criticism could not discriminate between the adequate and inadequate poetic uses of data. As early as 1908 Otto Zippel had published a list of 'Models and Sources' for the different versions of *The Seasons*, but he did not use them to analyse or interpret the poem.[2] And the great critical danger of these models and sources was the disregard of the poem's individuality. The paradox of the attempt to reconstruct 'process' was that in the search for the inimitable poem, all that was found related to other works and ideas.

Some critics, however, were more careful than others in relating sources to poetry, the most careful being Alan D. McKillop in *The Background of Thomson's Seasons* (1942), although even for his work the caution was uttered that 'perhaps because so much scholarship has been devoted to Thomson's sources, he is made to appear more derivative and "literary" than he was'.[3] McKillop was cognizant of

[1] Edward Cook, *Literary Recreations* (London, 1918), pp. 246–317; T. R. Henn, *Longinus and English Criticism*, p. 34.

[2] Zippel, 'Models and Sources', pp. xxxii–xl.

[3] Marjorie H. Nicolson, *Mountain Gloom and Mountain Glory* (Cornell U. Press, 1959), pp. 351–2.

this possibility and modestly suggested that a more accurate title might be '*Studies and Notes in the Background of "The Seasons"*'.[1] In tracing the history of some of Thomson's ideas in poetry, McKillop quoted the sources and their reworking in the poem. Material thus became available illustrating the scientific language of the poem and refuting the view that it was an artificially constructed poetic diction. It was possible through the transpositions to detect the kind of organization the work possessed, and it was possible to note that some passages had no sources other than the poet's mind.

Even McKillop, however, admitted that many sources remained to be found, and there were many not to be found. The search for sources and models belonged to a theory of the poet in which poet and poem turned into a search for the poet's self. Even in a poet like Thomson there remained repeated comparisons between the 'indolence' ascribed to him by John Armstrong in *The Castle of Indolence* and his actual 'indolence' as a poet. The study of revisions was particularly tempting as a study of the poet's laziness or failure 'to find himself'. Some modern critics, therefore, denying the critical validity of such extension, deliberately limited the concept of criticism to interpretative statements about the work as a whole, thus excising 'process' as a form of criticism, while creating a false assurance of the consistency of this discipline.

Such critics argued that explication was the function of criticism, and assuming a work to be an imaginative organic entity, they attacked the use of work sheets and revisions because, as René Wellek and Austin Warren declared in *Theory of Literature* (1949), they 'are not necessary to an understanding of the finished work or to a judgment upon it'.[2] But this assumption ignored the fact that revisions provided contexts of meaning and that these functioned as controls upon interpretation. 'Understanding' is a matter of greater or lesser probability, and the study of revisions is 'necessary' because it decreases probability of error in 'understanding' and increases the probability of careful interpretation. Even if analysis of literary works were the only function of criticism—a historically naïve assumption—revisions indicate parts in which expression is not quite adequate for the author and thus direct the critic to passages in which the manner of expression is being altered without being readily recognizable.

[1] McKillop, *Background*, p. 1.

[2] *Theory of Literature* (New York, 1949), p. 86.

Such alterations, when spotted, are not always understood. Dobrée and other modern critics have pointed to what they claim is Thomson's failure to discriminate. 'Thomson's fundamental weakness, both in content and in style,' writes A. M. Oliver, 'is his inability to discriminate. A true Augustan, he is alive to the poet's responsibility to teach, to exhort, to be actively a man of his time. Thus he loads his Muse with luggage so heavy and so awkward that movement is difficult and soaring impossible.'[1]

If 'discriminate' here is to mean more than that Thomson might have been Milton if he could have lived in a different time and written in a more precise way, it should imply that the poet considered and rejected better choices than he made. In the making of available choices, Thomson seldom chose wrongly. The decisions he made had sound sensibility behind them if one grants the kind of poem he was writing. In contrast to his decisions, were his limits. He seemed unable to make good poetry of moral declamation, of eulogies,[2] of historical catalogues, of narratives. Here his choices all seemed bad from the beginning; he seemed unable to see and interpret history and human motivation as he could nature. Here his experiments most often failed, but every experiment that does not work out is not a failure of discrimination unless one is prepared to argue that not to have certain abilities is to be indiscriminate in one's character. An analysis of revisions seems to confirm that Thomson had justifiable artistic reasons for most of his revisions.

In so far as this study attempts to return 'process' to criticism, by applying the study of the poet at work or his increase or decrease of poetic powers, to the interpretation of the poem, it has shown that revision provides a clue to the poet's verbal usages, to his philosophical views (his 'posture' language), to his organization. For all critics who pursue 'understanding', such supports seem essential.

[1] A. H. Oliver, 'The Scottish Augustans', *Scottish Poetry, A Critical Survey*, ed. James Kinsley (London, 1955), p. 28. See also Oliver Elton, *A Survey of English Literature 1730–1780* (London, 1928), I., 359–61.

[2] According to Smollett, Thomson intended to withdraw all his dedications in prose and verse. See Peter Cunningham, ed., *A Poem to the Memory of William Congreve by James Thomson* (London, 1843), p. 29, n. 1.

II

HYPOTHESES AND THEIR TRANSFORMATION: CRITICAL TRADITION AND THE PRESSURE OF THE POEM

> I suspect this objection to be the cant of those who judge by principles rather than perceptions.
>
> S. JOHNSON, 'Pope', *Lives*

CRITICISM, like all thinking, involves assumptions and hypotheses; this chapter deals with the reshaping of such assumptions and hypotheses resulting from contact with particular literary works. 'Assumptions' ('presuppositions') is the general term expressing attitudes, conscious or unconscious, which are taken for granted; it reflects the religious implications of such grounds as well as the occasional ascent into groundless belief. A 'hypothesis', however, is a conscious assumption, tentatively held, which is subjected to the tests of further investigation. The readiness to investigate is a necessary methodological step in the handling of hypotheses, for not all are willing to test data or willing to test their tests. This chapter analyses how inquiries into the 'unity' of *The Seasons* were initiated, what 'unity' was, what it became, how it altered theories of character and diction, and finally, what caused the abandonment then resurgence of interest in 'unity'.

In order for a 'law' to be made inapplicable, there must exist a readiness to question it, a cultural preparation for and a theoretical hospitality to proof or disproof, or to what Isaac Watts called (1741) 'enlarging the Capacity of the Mind'. Such readiness existed in the accumulation of nature poems in the latter half of the eighteenth century, in the 'particular' analysis of poetry, and in the sympathy for the exception to rules, but such exceptions became meaningful only to critics who welcomed empirical evidence. Such critics appealed to perceptions which led them to justify the exception and to reconsider their hypotheses.

The alterations in hypotheses were often speculative because there did not exist sufficient examples upon which to proceed, and the critics who accepted the issue often disagreed upon the inferences from it. Yet, looking back upon such speculations, it is possible to grant that some were more firmly based than others. Some speculations have been retrospectively validated or invalidated and have ceased to be speculations; others continue as guesses until they are forgotten.

Hypotheses that are transformed do not involve rejection of all previous assumptions, but permit recognition of the continuity of problems. Continuity exists in terms of particulars; by revising unity to include emotive as well as dramatic unity, critics did not abandon wholeness, the relations between thought and feeling, part and whole, or the concept of a poem as an order of some kind. But the extension of unity created analytical difficulties: one type of unity was substituted for all and the value of 'unity' was taken to include all other literary values or to dominate them.

(a) R. STEELE, D. HUME: THE APPEAL TO PERCEPTION

> There never yet arose a distinguished genius, who had not an air peculiarly his own.
>
> R. SHIELS

At the beginning of the eighteenth century, poetic unity was tied to the drama and epic; still, it was necessary for critics to defend originality of plot or to attack it as an artistic failure. The arguments for what might be called 'exceptions' to the rules were proposed by William Davenant in 1650 when he defended his epic *Gondibert* by calling it a drama and arguing that it was a 'new design', 'no more answerable for disobedience to Predecessors than *Law makers* are liable to those old *Laws* which themselves have repealed'.[1] *Gondibert* was not an imitation of the *Iliad* or the *Aeneid* and, therefore, was to be judged by the unity of 'design', a unity like that in art in which the different actions served a common purpose rather than the tracing of a single action. Written during the Commonwealth, and appealing in

[1] William Davenant, 'Preface' to *Gondibert* reprinted in *Critical Essays of the Seventeenth Century*, ed. Joel E. Spingarn (Oxford, 1908), II, 20.

terms of liberty for the initiation of a new version of epic, Davenant's justification could easily justify unity in genres for which no traditional principles existed.

The clue to the shift in definition of unity of plot was contained in 'design', and John Hughes (1715) explained that the rules for epic poetry were not applicable to allegory, and he offered principles which he considered appropriate to this species.

> The whole Frame of it wou'd appear monstrous if it were to be examin'd by the Rules of Epick Poetry, as they have been drawn from the Practice of *Homer* and *Virgil*. But as it is plain the Author never design'd it by those Rules, I think it ought rather to be consider'd as a poem of a particular kind, describing in a Series of Allegorical Adventures or Episodes the most noted Virtues and Vices: to compare it therefore with the Models of Antiquity, wou'd be like drawing a Parallel between the *Roman* and Gothick Architecture.[1]

Bishop Hurd, continuing the image of Gothic architecture, stated (1762) that the unity of the Faerie Queene 'is not the classic Unity, which consists in the representation of one entire action: but it is an Unity of another sort, an Unity resulting from the respect which a number of related actions have to one common purpose. In other words, it is an unity of *design*, and not of action'.[2]

This argument of irrelevance was based on an implied nationalistic appeal and it did not come to terms with the differences within the accepted form which would make one poem possess faulty unity and another appropriate unity substantially different from the models. One traditional opinion, expressed by Le Bossu (1695), for example, assumed that the fundamentals of epic poetry had been set by the ancients, and he urged applications of models, not re-examination of principles, and René Rapin (1694)[3] pointed out that the exception was

[1] John Hughes, 'An Essay on Allegorical Poetry' (1715) as quoted in Willard H. Durham, *Critical Essays of the Eighteenth Century 1760–1725* (New Haven, 1915), p. 106.

[2] Richard Hurd, *Letters on Chivalry and Romance* (1762), reprinted in *Hurd's Letters on Chivalry and Romance*, ed. Edith J. Morley (London, 1911), p. 122. For an analysis of Hurd's criticism, see Edith Morley's introduction and Hoyt Trowbridge, 'Bishop Hurd: A Reinterpretation', *PMLA*, LVIII (1943), 450–65.

[3] René Le Bossu, *Treatise of the Epick Poem*, tr. W. J. (London, 1695), p. 2; René Rapin, *Reflections on Aristotle's Poesie*, tr. Thomas Rymer (London, 1694), pp. 17–18, 69–70.

irrelevant in critical theory because the theory was governed by the customary achievements and responses, not the uncommon. The critical issue was to justify certain 'uncommon' kinds of unity as 'common' or appropriate.

For this decision to be confirmed in theory, the loophole of originality within tradition had to be extended to an arch which opened into a new form. Extensions of the theory of models were made by particular analogies of poetic devices with nature or with politics or with religion. Davenant (1650) considered the poet a legislator in his poetry; William Walsh argued that pastorals ought to be free from exact connections and transitions by analogy with ancient Eastern writings and because such freedom was analogous to the religious beneficence of a Christian deity.

> Thus a meadow, where the beauties of the spring are properly blended together, makes a more delightful prospect, than a curious pasture of sorted flowers in our garden, and we are much more transported with the beauty of the heavens, and admiration of their Creator, in a clear night, when we behold stars of all magnitudes promiscuously moving together, than if those glorious lights were ranked in their several orders, or reduced into the finest geometrical figures.[1]

The handiwork of God was the varied and unsymmetrical model for the poet; moreover, the 'beauties of the spring' made a 'more delightful prospect' than arranged flowers to the beholder, and the freedom of connections and transitions in the poem was analogous to the freedom, the ungeometrical 'system' of the universe. 'Poetical Reason', wrote Leonard Welsted (1713), 'is not the same as mathematical Reason.'[2] The poet was, therefore, in this respect, a creator like God, blending apparent disorder into a new kind of order. Longinus in discussing anaphora and asyndeton provided a source for this poetical order by declaring that so long as the orator everywhere 'preserves the native character of anaphora and asyndeton by

[1] William Walsh, 'Preface to the Pastorals', Virgil, *Works*, ed. John Dryden (London, 1695), I, 104. For early use of geometrical or regular and anti-geometrical or irregular figures in nature, see William Temple, 'Upon the Garden of Epicurus' (1685), *Works* (London, 1720), I, 18. For a discussion of this subject, see Nikolaus Pevsner, 'The Genesis of the Picturesque', *Architectural Review*, 96 (1944), 139–76. Christopher Hussey, *The Picturesque* (London, 1927), Chap. 2, and H. F. Clark, *The English Landscape Garden* (London, 1948), pp. 4–16.

[2] Leonard Welsted, *Epistles, Odes, etc.* (London, 1728), p. xxii.

his unbroken variation; to such a degree in him is order disordered, and conversely, does disorder include a certain order.'[1] Joseph Addison (1712) pointed out that God provided man with the pleasures of the senses, the primary pleasures of the imagination, by creating the world, and the poet sought to create an analogous world in his poetry.[2] In 'To Mr. Thomson on his Seasons' (1734), James Delacour declared:

> Thy works a little world new found appear,
> And thou the Phoebus of a heav'n so fair;
> Thee their bright sov'reign all the signs allow,
> And Thomson is another name for nature now.[3]

The arguments from analogy were applied to critics as well as to poets; thus Richard Steele (1713) urged critical independence as an analogy to political independence: 'The cautious ("regular") Critics are like the Subjects of an arbitrary Prince: the Licentious ("Natural") are in a State of barbarous Anarchy; but the free Critick, like a free *Briton* is governed by the Laws which he himself votes for; whose Liberty is checked by the Restraints of Truth, and the Monarchy of right Reason.'[4] The monarchy of 'right reason' was a limited monarchy because the divergence from the customary assumptions of

[1] *Longinus: On the Sublime and Sir Joshua Reynolds: Discourses on Art*, tr. and ed. Benedict Einarson and Elder Olson (Chicago, 1945), pp. 42–43.

[2] Joseph Addison, *Spectator*, pp. 411–21. For a discussion of Addison's criticism, see the following essays by C. D. Thorpe: 'Addison and Hutcheson on the Imagination', *ELH*, II (1935), 215–34; 'Addison's Theory of the Imagination as "Perceptive Response" ', *Papers of the Michigan Academy of Arts and Sciences*, XXI (1936), 509–30; 'Addison and Some of his Predecessors on "Novelty" ', *PMLA*, LII (1937), 1114–29; 'Addison's Contribution to Criticism', *The Seventeenth Century* (Stanford, 1951), pp. 316–19; Wimsatt and Brooks, *Literary Criticism*, pp. 254–61. Addison's *The Pleasures of the Imagination* is reprinted with notes and bibliographical materials in *Eighteenth Century Critical Essays*, ed. Scott Elledge (Ithaca, 1961), I, 41–76, 498–507.

[3] James Delacour, *A Prospect of Poetry and Other Poems* (Cork, 1807), p. 82.

[4] Richard Steele, *The Englishman* (Oct. 20, 1713); see also Ambrose Philips, *A Collection of Old Ballads* (London, 1723), I, 66–67; Samuel Cobb, 'Discourse on Criticism and of Poetry', *Poems on Several Occasions* (London, 1707), reprinted in *ARS* (Los Angeles, 1946); Richard Fiddes, *A Prefatory Epistle Concerning Some Remarks to be Publish'd on Homer's Iliad* (London, 1714). Pevsner, 'Picturesque', p. 146, declares that the landscape garden, conceived between 1710 and 1730, is 'the garden of liberalism'. Quoting from Thomson's *Liberty*, he adds that the 'free growth of the

unity meant, in the writings of Davenant, Walsh, Hughes, Welsted and Steele a defence for their own variations from regularity. Thus there were available not only theoretical statements, but examples to which such statements referred.

The readiness to investigate new principles was encouraged by and tied to Locke's theory of particular impressions. 'We should make greater progress in the discovery of rational and contemplative knowledge', wrote Locke (1690), 'if we sought it in the fountain, *in the consideration of things themselves;* and made use rather of our own thoughts than other men's to find it.'[1] The reliance upon individual 'perceptions'—'the state of being affected by something'—meant that principles or generalizations resulted from accumulations of perceptions. 'Perceptions', therefore, became a key term in philosophy and criticism, and it had begun to have the weight of philosophic authority behind it when Johnson wrote in 1781: 'I suspect this objection to be the cant of those who judge by principles rather than perceptions.'[2]

'Perception', 'conception', 'sensation', 'reflection' formed a cluster of terms used to describe the apprehension and response to sense experience or recalled experience. Thus, though Isaac Watts (1725) distinguished between 'perception' and 'conception' he acknowledged that 'they are often used promiscuously'—or interchangeably. William Jameson (1749) distinguished between perceptions that resulted from absent objects (Watts's 'conception') and 'sensations' which arose from external impressions. Perceptions, pleasant or unpleasant, were 'if the Term may be allowed, *internal Sensations*'.[3]

[1] John Locke, *An Essay Concerning Human Understanding*, ed. 1690; A. C. Fraser (Oxford, 1894), I, 115; see also pp. 345–55.

[2] Johnson, 'Pope', *Lives*, III, 248. See William Jackson, 'Letter IV', *Thirty Letters* (London, 1795), p. 27: 'Our greatest mistake in the pursuit of happiness as well as of science, is to judge by the perceptions of others, and not by our own.' See also Ezekiel Sanford, ed., 'Thomson', *The Works of the British Poets* (Philadelphia, 1819), XXII, 2: 'Men hazard their reputation for judgment, when they praise a work written in a style, for which no canons of criticism have yet been established.'

[3] Isaac Watts, *Logick* (London, 1725), pp. 12–13; and William Jameson, *An Essay on Virtue and Harmony* (Edinburgh, 1749), p. 37. The determina-

---

tree is obviously taken to symbolize the free growth of the individual, the serpentine path and rivulet the Englishman's freedom of thought, creed and action and the adherence to nature in the grounds, the adherence to nature in ethics and politics'.

Richard Steele in *The Conscious Lovers* (1721) distinguished between 'sensation' and 'reflection' in the response to literature, identifying the first with mere feeling, and the second with the operation of thought upon feeling. The meaning of these terms, therefore, was dependent upon the contrasting functions that were being discussed. Lord Kames (1762) found that 'perception' and 'sensation' 'are commonly reckoned synonymous terms, signifying consciousness we have of objects'.[1] But he insisted that they should be distinguished by confining 'perception' to knowledge of external objects and 'sensation' to pleasure or pain felt in perception. And William Duff (1762), returning to Steele's distinctions, opposed 'reflection' to 'sensation' and defined 'perception' as an internal artistic sense; a highly refined sensitivity to works of imagination, like Shaftesbury's internal sense.[2]

As applied to literary works, 'perception' set the conditions under which adequate observation could be exercised. All such applications recognized the effective quality of literary perception and the particularized or individual consciousness which resulted from it. When, therefore, Johnson (1781) opposed 'perceptions' to 'principles' in his comment on some of Pope's critics, he was opposing individual affective responses to prescribed or generalized ones. He was opposing the power or art of perceiving, the state of being affected by something to a 'settled rule for action'.

Henry Felton had, in 1713, denied the need for particular examples in any but 'minute Matters' because 'we have natural Notions of these Things, and can only set them off by showing several Ways of offending against them'[3] and because such rules were ideals not present in any particular examples. But these 'natural Notions' and rules were themselves explained as the result of a series of particular impressions and as Johnson later declared, Aristotle's

[1] Henry Home, Lord Kames, *Elements of Criticism* (Edinburgh, 1762), III, 378.

[2] William Duff, *An Essay on Original Genius* (London, 1767), 2nd ed., p. 16.

[3] Henry Felton, *A Dissertation on Reading the Classics* (London, 1713), p. vii.

tion to act in accordance with 'good' is called by Jameson 'mental gravitation or attraction' (p. 10). Herbert J. Drennon, 'James Thomson's Ethical Theory and Scientific Rationalism', *PQ*, XIV (1935), traced Thomson's use of 'moral' gravitation to earlier writers. See also his 'James Thomson and John Norris', *PMLA*, LII (1938), 1904 n., for further reference to 'moral gravitation' in John Norris (1688).

rules were derived from the study of particular works. The trust, therefore, in particular impressions was necessary even to arrive at general principles.

Literary criticism, especially, had to rely upon particular impressions, for as David Hume explained (1741): 'No criticism can be instructive, which descends not to particulars, and is not full of examples and illustrations.' And in another essay (1757) Hume declared:

> Did our pleasure really arise from those parts of his [Ariosto's] poem, which we denominate faults, this would be no objection to criticism in general: It would only be an objection to those particular rules of criticism, which would represent such circumstances to be faults, and would represent them as universally blameable.[1]

This reliance upon a trained response (governed by specific conditions of perception) had, by the 1750's, become well known and it had superseded the dependence upon traditional responses as expressed, for example, by John Bancks (1738) in a quotation almost identical with Hume's in subject but contradictory in approach: 'But if now, or at any other Time, I should not exactly conform to my own Rules, let it rather be imputed to me as a Fault, than brought as an Objection against the Justice of those Rules; which, if I am not deceived, will be all founded in the Nature of Things, or on the Observations of those Masters, who have been allow'd the most Excellent in the Art of Oratory.'[2]

Hume distinguished between particular perceptions of rules and the generalizations based on such perceptions. Given the stringencies involved in particular responses, the objections would, therefore, be to particulars: for example, repeated readings can make a passage which appears obscure at first, quite clear after careful scrutiny. Thus the particular rules about obscurity would have to be revised; such revisions would not be an attack on criticism in general; it would merely mean that criticism was, by careful analysis, subject to alteration based upon particular responses. But Bancks provided no method by which the rules could be changed. Thus where individual perception clashed with the customary assumptions about responding, Bancks assumed the particular perception was always wrong, and the rules always right—because founded on 'the Nature of Things'.

[1] 'Of the Standard of Taste', *Essays Moral Political and Literary*, ed. T. H. Green and T. H. Grose (London, 1785), I, 270.

[2] John Bancks, 'A Discourse Concerning Language', *Miscellaneous Works* (London, 1738), II, 292.

But could it not be argued that the observations of the nature of things and the observations of the masters were both observations, and that within such limitations, observation permitted different perceptions of the same work? The function of rules is to methodize perceptual response and to make room for differences without destroying the principles; to guide, not to rule.

This was the point made by Walsh to Pope, by Samuel Cobb, by Richard Fiddes. The 'rules' were to control the immense energy of imagination, not to stimulate mechanical responses. They constituted a series of limits which might be broken but which prevented writers from beginning without any sense of what had previously been done.

In creating the philosophical grounds for reliance upon independent perception, critics had to distinguish responses to nature from those to art. To distinguish between these, conditions were set up. In regard to art, theories of immediacy were invoked—immediate sympathy or of sympathetic response to impassioned moments—as Horace had explained—or of 'consonance' with the author as Murdoch and More proposed. Horace had indicated that there were certain limitations with regard to perception, by analogy with painting. Each work had a particular 'light' by which it was to be observed, but the manner in which this 'light' was to be achieved was not explained. Hume (1757) suggested a method for viewing works of art from many 'lights' and thus offered a methodological resolution of the dilemma. The work required a response which was to be checked by frequent perspectives, although he realized that perception often involved deep-rooted prejudices, culturally conditioned—such as his own religious prejudice—which prevented the critic from responding to the work as a work of art.[1]

The appeal to individual perception was also justified—paradoxically—by an appeal to authority: Aristotle developed his theory by examining particular works and by drawing inferences from these. He was the model, so that the argument used by Thomas Rymer (1694) to defend authority was used by John Landseer (1806) to overturn it. The appeal was also defended—as immediate pleasure or pain—on the grounds of taste: the critic had to exercise 'that instantaneous Glow of Pleasure which thrills thro' our whole Frame, and seizes upon the Applause of the Heart, before the intellectual Power, Reason, can descend from the Throne of the Mind to ratify its

[1] Hume, 'Of the Standard of Taste', *Essays*, I, 283.

Approbation' (1752). But despite the 'Glow of Pleasure' which John G. Cooper defined as 'taste', he assumed that there were certain universal responses to scenes and works.[1]

To confront the poem with a readiness to accept its differentness was to be forced to decide, or at least to recognize, the important role of the exception in critical theory. The 'pleasure' which a particular part of Ariosto's poem or *The Seasons* gave, although denominated faulty, could be an indication of inadequate 'particular rules'. But the importance of the exception was not its mere justification as an attack on authority but its use by Hume as a test of judgement. The exception, therefore, raised questions about the conditions under which artistic observation took place. Was the work seen in its proper light? Was it seen with impartiality? Was it seen from different perspectives? Such questions led in Hume's 'Essay on the Standard of Taste' (1757) to a series of conditions governing the perceptual process, a summary of ideas developed by Addison and Jonathan Richardson now placed within the context of Hume's experimental or hypothetical method. The conditions were not always agreed upon, for Murdoch and Stockdale insisted on sincerity, consonance and personal criteria.[2] But there was agreement on the need for perceptual criteria in contrast to non-criterial conditions.

The appeal to perceptions was an appeal to a consciousness of certain qualities, despite some literary claims that such qualities were not to be expected. It turned upon problems that theories of imitation or of inspiration found it necessary to avoid. Particular confronta-

[1] John G. Cooper, *Letters on Taste* (London, 1752), pp. 2–3. For Rymer, see *The Critical Works of Thomas Rymer*, ed. Curt Zimansky (New Haven, 1956), p. 3.

[2] For an analysis of Hume's essay, see Teddy Brunius, *David Hume on Taste* (Uppsala, 1952), pp. 75–87; Martin Kallich, 'The Associationist Criticism of Francis Hutcheson and David Hume', *SP*, XLIII (1946), 664–67; Ralph Cohen, 'David Hume's Experimental Method and the Theory of Taste', *ELH* (1958), 270–89. The substitution of the term 'tact' for 'taste', common in our time to suggest an innate sensitivity which is inexplicable, began at the end of the eighteenth century. See Dugald Stewart, *Philosophical Essays* (London, 1810), pp. 497–8, who distinguished 'tact' from 'taste' as follows: 'Taste presupposes a certain degree of original susceptibility, and a certain degree of relish, stronger or weaker, for the beauties of nature; whereas the word *tact* is appropriated to things in which the power of judging is wholly acquired.' Stewart noted, however, that in some instances 'tact' superseded 'upon the subjects with which it is conversant, the exercise of reasoning'.

tion sought to explain the 'niceties' and 'refinements' and 'delicacies' which earlier critics acknowledged but attributed to genius or inspiration; it provided individual explanations for those qualities which general criticism could not handle because they were individual with each work. The individual explanations therefore began to form a new body of generalizations drawn from particular responses. Earlier in the century it was argued that some poetical excellencies could not be explained: 'Some of these, I have said, may be discoursed of with Accuracy and Clearness enough, that is, so as to be understood by those who understand them already; but there are others of that exquisite Nicety, that will not fall under any Descriptions, nor yield to the Torture of Explanation.' And even Johnson himself was not prepared to generalize from particulars when he referred to the 'nameless and inexplicable elegancies which appeal wholly to the fancy'.[1]

With regard to a new work like *The Seasons*, the critic was involved in a venture. The principles of criticism, in so far as they were based on particular poems, were principles derived from past works. Confronted with a new poem, the critic had to be sensitive not merely to traditions within the poem—the dependence of *The Seasons* upon Virgil's *Georgics* or *Cooper's Hill*—but to those elements which altered inherited critical principles or presented new ones. The precise recognition of newness in a poem depended upon poems unwritten at the moment of criticism, and the appeal to 'perceptions' was an appeal to become conscious of qualities which had no literary traditions or formulations.

Even where the poem operated within conventions, the critic was challenged to discover the uses of conventions. In appealing to 'perceptions' critics were defending the reliance upon sensibility, arguing not the value of sameness, but the value of differences. It would therefore be inaccurate to suggest that earlier critics had no 'perceptions'; rather they neglected to explore differences or exceptions to the rules. But because critics trusted 'perceptions' did not imply that they distrusted hypotheses. If one examines the operation of perceptions with regard to unity in *The Seasons*, it will be apparent that the activity of the critic was intimately bound up with assumptions and hypotheses about literature.

Granting the fact that by mid-century there existed a readiness to

[1] Johnson, *Rambler*, p. 92.

perceive differences in unity and in other elements of poetry, the adequacy and validity of any particular perception was, according to Hume, governed by specific criteria. Yet these criteria applied to the critic's perception; even if the critic perceived according to the given conditions, he had to operate with the poems already published and make distinctions by comparison with them. He might venture into statements about unity of association, because such theories had been developed in philosophy, but to see the unity of *The Seasons* as a love poem, or as a world in which diverse types of natural and human love were explored, would have implied a theory of action (or plot) for which only guesses existed. Speculation existed, in other words, within the conventions or by opposition to aspects of the conventions, but no attempt was made to speculate about conventions themselves.

Thus the interpretations of unity in *The Seasons* began in 1726, by assuming that in *Winter* the new kind of unity was merely 'the *new* and *masterly* manner in which he had introduced his Reflections, and made them to succeed his several Descriptions throughout the whole Performance'.[1] But *Cooper's Hill* and *Windsor Forest* had illustrated the difficulties of uniting a loosely descriptive poem. When Robert Shiels (1753) discussed the unity of *The Seasons*, he had to face this problem.

(b) R. SHIELS, J. AIKIN, S. JOHNSON, R. HERON: THE TRANSFORMATION OF UNITY

> In nova fert animus mutatas dicere formas——
> Of transformations new and strange I tell.
>
> OVID.

> There appears no particular design; the parts are not subservient to one another; nor is there any dependence or connection throughout.
>
> R. SHIELS

The unity of *The Seasons* constituted a serious puzzle for critics because it lacked the types of dramatic or epic unity which they had traditionally associated with poetry. Critical analysis of the unity of *The Seasons* moved in two major directions: unity which resulted from formal properties, such as diction and character, and unity

[1] *London Journal* (1726), as quoted in McKillop, *Backgrounds*, p. 176.

which resulted from the author's handling of the subject (associationism). Both types of unity were emotive, that is, they assumed a unity of feeling; yet because they were both dependent upon current doctrines, though not the same, and because they were innovations, they necessitated areas of speculation. Yet some types of speculation, like Johnson's, became key statements, while others disappeared from critical discussion.

(1) *R. Shiels, J. Aikin, R. Heron: Unity, Poetic Ideas, and Natural Science*

> His mode of thinking and of expressing his thoughts is original.
>
> S. JOHNSON

Thomson's four seasons were written as detached pieces; even *Winter* itself, according to Shiels, 'was first wrote in detached pieces, or occasional descriptions; it was by the advice of Mr. Mallet they were collected and made into one connected piece . . . By the farther advice, and at the earnest request, of Mr. Mallet, he wrote the other three seasons.'[1] *The Seasons* was a poem which, in origin, presented a problem of unity, defined as beginning, middle and end when applied to the drama. Confronted with this problem of a poem without a story, Shiels undertook to defend the poem, although retaining the formulation of dramatic unity. That this was his conception of the unity of *The Seasons* was apparent from his comparing it with *The Castle of Indolence* and preferring the latter: 'We cannot here complain of want of plan, for it is artfully laid, naturally conducted, and the descriptions rise in a beautiful succession.' But of *The Seasons* this type of art could not be premised.

> The Four Seasons considered separately, each Season as a distinct poem has been judged defective in point of plan. There appears no particular design; the parts are not subservient to one another; nor is there any dependance or connection throughout;

[1] Shiels, *Lives*, V, 195. William Willis in his introduction to *Thomson's Winter* (London, 1900), p. 18, argued that 'before the first edition of "Winter" appeared, he (Thomson) is thinking of three of the Seasons, has written of one ("Winter") and promises to write of "Autumn". I cannot doubt that before "Winter" appeared he intended to write of "Summer"; and if he intended to write of three, it is not an unfair inference that he included "Spring" within the range of his vision.'

> but this perhaps is a fault almost inseparable from a subject in itself so diversified, as not to admit of such limitation. He had not indeed been guilty of any incongruity; the scenes described in spring, are all peculiar to that season, and the digressions, which make up a fourth part of the poem, flow naturally. He has observed the same regard to the appearances of nature in the other seasons; but then what he has described in the beginning of any of the seasons, might as well be placed in the middle, and that in the middle, as naturally towards the close. So that each season may rather be called an assemblage of poetical ideas, than a poem, as it seems written without a plan.[1]

Shiels accepted the arguments against the poem's 'design'. The seasons did not lead to a whole, though each season was emotively congruous. Yet within each season, the parts were not subservient; the beginning, middle and end could be interchanged without loss. Shiels argued that this fault was inseparable from so diversified a subject; at least within each season there was complete consistency. The poem was to be understood as a group of four parts each consistent in subject and tone.

Shiels was struggling to attain a more adequate statement of poetic unity, but he was trapped by his own assumptions. For not only was his assumption of congruity inaccurate—neither the single line description of the town (l. 102) nor the description of the farmer burning straw to check the insect plague (ll. 127–8) were 'peculiar' to spring—but at the end of his explanation he contradicted his conception of a poem by declaring that *The Seasons* was not really a poem, but 'may rather be called an assemblage of poetical ideas'. And this 'jumble' of verses was defined in Brightland's early textbook on poetry (1714, 3rd ed.) as an essential failing of poetry: 'If a Design be necessary in the shortest and least of our Poems, it is vastly more necessary in those of greater length; which without this will infallibly prove intolerably tedious, and a rude indigested Heap.'[2]

This position had also been taken by Swift when, in a letter to Sir Charles Wogan in 1732, he declared: 'One Thomson, a Scotchman, has succeeded the best in that way [blank verse], in four poems he

[1] Shiels, *Lives*, V, 202. For a discussion of Thomson's unity and that of other eighteenth-century poets, see F. W. Bateson, *English Poetry and the English Language* (Oxford, 1934), pp. 78–85. Bateson overlooks the types of contrast, repetition, shifts in voices essential to Thomson's organization.

[2] John Brightland, *A Grammar of the English Tongue* (London, 1714), p. 138.

has writ on the four seasons: yet I am not over fond of them, because they are all description, and nothing is doing; whereas Milton engages me in actions of the highest importance . . .'[1] Shiels sought to provide an alternative to Brightland's traditional conception, and the tonal unity was, therefore, a possible escape from the dilemma of disunity. Shenstone parenthetically suggested another type of unity. 'Might not the poem on the Seasons', he wrote, 'have been rendered more uni[fied], by giving out the design of nature in the beginning of winter, and afterwards, considering all the varieties of seasons as aiming at one end?'[2] Shenstone's suggestions would surely have improved the unity of a poem on the seasons, but it assumed the very issue it was to answer. Was *The Seasons* indicative of this kind of unity, and did it fail because of it, or was this criticism —as indeed it was—irrelevant to the repetitive and loose organization of the poem?

However, Shiels's alternative of an 'assemblage of poetical ideas' was an abandonment of Aristotelian unity rather than a successful re-consideration of it. It offered a concept not of holism, but of disparate yet emotively related 'ideas'. There is not sufficient information available to trace the implications of Shiels' 'assemblage of poetical ideas', but Joseph Warton, his contemporary, explained that poetry was identified with certain qualities of vigour and energy of language, and although a poem could be rephrased in prose, the poetical elements would creep out in particular expressions.[3] And Shelley in his 'Defence' identified poetry with the linguistic expression of 'inextinguishable thought', and declared: 'The parts of a composition may be poetical, without the composition as a whole being a poem.'[4] The 'assemblage of poetical ideas' was for Shiels a highly tentative and vague effort at explaining unity in the poem, but Warton and Shelley divorced 'poetical ideas' from a theory of unity and joined them to a theory of poetic essences of thought or feeling.

[1] Swift, *Letters* (to Sir Charles Wogan, 1732).

[2] William Shenstone, 'Essays on Men Manners and Things', *Works* (London, 1764), II, 192. For a French theory of nature poetry which sought to relate ruler of decorum and propriety to emotional unity, see a summary of St. Lambert's preface to *Les Saisons, Poëme*, *The Monthly Review*, XLI (1769), 489–503.

[3] Joseph Warton, *An Essay on the Writings and Genius of Pope* (London, 1756), I, vii, ix.

[4] John Shawcross, ed., *Shelley's Literary and Philosophical Criticism* (London, 1909), pp. 153–4.

The second major effort to convert Thomson's poem to unity of a new kind was made by John Aikin in 1778, based on the assumption that the poem began a new genre, descriptive poetry. The groundwork of the poem was its truth to natural history. Its unity was the description of nature in all its vicissitudes throughout the year.

> To paint the face of nature as changing through the changing seasons; to mark the approaches and trace the progress of these vicissitudes, in a series of landscapes all formed upon images of grandeur or beauty; and to give animation and variety to the whole by interspersing manners and incidents suitable to the scenery; appears to be the general design of this Poem . . .
>
> It is an attention to this leading idea, that in this piece there is a progressive series of descriptions, all tending to a certain point, and all parts of a general plan, which alone can enable us to range through the vast variety and quick succession of objects presented in it, with any clear conception of the writer's method, or true judgment concerning what may be regarded as forwarding his main purpose, or as merely ornamental deviation.[1]

Aikin's view of unity, which attempted a 'clear conception of the writer's method', was free from epic preconceptions, but in imposing a unity of progressive descriptions, he was compelled to find an order that did not exist. The order of progression was the life of man—spring, summer, autumn, winter—and within each season he implied a development which 'forwarded' the purpose, despite the fact that Shiels could find no such unity. The disagreement on unity was not as complete as it seemed, for Shiels did find a consistent emotive tone for each season; the disagreement was on the forwarding of the main purpose or general plan.

Aikin saw a series of changes in the poem due to the changes in the '*oeconomy of nature*', and the characteristic progression meant the characteristic changes of the season. Thus the selectivity of details and the transitions from one change to another became the basis for approving or disapproving unity. Yet even in this definition there was the analogy of human life which the poem did not present,[2] and

[1] John Aikin, 'Essay on the Plan and Character of Thomson's Seasons', *The Seasons* (London, 1792), first published, 1778, pp. ix-xi. For biographical and bibliographical information on Aikin, consult Lucy Aikin, *Memoir of John Aikin* (London, 1823), I, 1–275; Betsy Rodgers, *Georgian Chronicle, Mrs. Barbauld and her Family* (London, 1958), is a study of the Aikin family with extensive bibliographical materials. See also pp. 175–181, 388–95 below.

[2] Aikin, p. xii.

there were storms, sunrises and sunsets in each season which were contrasted with activities in other seasons. Within each season—*Summer* excepted—Thomson's own summary belied a 'normal' progression' and although Aikin was the first to understand the unity as indicative of a view of man and nature—an economy of nature—he did not see the contrasting parts within each season; he did not consider unity as a structural device but as a variant of a dramatic unfolding of life. His analysis even of the unity of *Summer*, for example, illustrated this procedure.

> The period of Summer is marked by fewer and less striking changes in the face of Nature. A soft and pleasing languor, interrupted only by the gradual progression of the vegetable and animal tribes towards their state of maturity, forms the leading character of this Season. The active fermentation of the juices, which the first access of genial warmth had excited, now subsides; and the increasing heats rather inspire faintness and inaction than lively exertions. The insect race alone seem animated with peculiar vigour under the more direct influence of the sun; and are therefore with equal truth and advantage introduced by the poet to enliven the silent and drooping scenes presented by the other forms of animal nature. As this source, however, together with whatever else our summers afford, is insufficient to furnish novelty and business enough for this act of the drama of the year, the poet judiciously opens a new field, profusely fertile in objects suited to the glowing colours of descriptive poetry. By an easy and natural transition, he quits the chastened summer of our temperate clime for those regions where a perpetual Summer reigns, exalted by such superior degrees of solar heat as to give an entirely new face to almost every part of nature. The terrific grandeur prevalent in some of these, the exquisite richness and beauty in others, and the novelty in all, afford such a happy variety for the poet's selection, that we need not wonder if some of his noblest pieces are the product of this delightful excursion. He returns, however, with apparent satisfaction, to take a last survey of the softer summer of our island; and after closing the prospect of terrestrial beauties, artfully shifts the scene to celestial splendors, which, though perhaps not more striking in this season than in some of the others, are now alone agreeable objects of contemplation in a northern climate.[1]

Robert Shiels found his theories of poetry challenged by the 'unity' of *The Seasons*, but John Aikin declared that the poem was

[1] Aikin, pp. xxv–xxvi.

'the original poem whence our modern descriptive poets have derived that more elegant and correct style of painting natural objects'. He stripped 'unity' of its beginning—the invocation and dedication—of its narratives or digressions—of its moralizing reflections—of its didactic addresses to Britain, to industry—of its references to urban life. The unity of the poem for Aikin resided in the descriptions of nature; everything else was related to this 'plan' by transition or association. Of the two kinds of unity that were discussed, the unity of *The Seasons* as a whole and the unity of each part, Aikin had to construct a human analogy for the 'whole', while in each part he was compelled to relate the non-natural elements to the natural economy.

Yet Aikin, despite his construction of a theory to fit the poem, considered unity as a type of progression, as a form of drama: 'In all the temperate climates of the globe, the four seasons are so many progressive stages in this circuit, which, like the acts in a well-constructed drama, gradually disclose, ripen, and bring to an end and the various business transacted on the great theatre of Nature.'[1] Despite his wish to attend to the 'writer's method', Aikin saw the poem as accurate natural history, not as a loosely constructed entity often illustrating contrasting views of man and nature.

In 1730, in the 'argument' to *Summer* Thomson had described the season as 'a progress': 'As the face of nature in this season is almost uniform, the progression of the poem is a description of a Summer's day.' But the order of this 'progress' was changed in 1744 from what it was in 1730. The latter part of the day was originally described as follows:

> Noon-day. A woodland retreat. A groupe of flocks and herds. A solemn grove. How it affects a contemplative mind. Transition to the prospect of a well-cultivated country; which introduces a panegyric on Great Britain. A digression on foreign summers. Storm of thunder and lightning. A tale. The storm over; a serene afternoon. Bathing. Sunset. Evening. The whole concluding with the Praise of Philosophy.[2]

In 1744 this was revised to indicate an altered order:

> Noon-day. A woodland retreat. Groupe of Herds and Flocks. A solemn grove. How it affects a contemplative Mind. A Cataract, and

[1] Aikin, 'Essay', p. xii.

[2] Zippel, *Thomson's Seasons Critical Edition*, p. 59.

rude Scene. View of Summer in the torrid Zone. Storm of Thunder and Lightning. A Tale. The Storm over, a serene Afternoon. Bathing. Hour of walking. Transition to the Prospect of a well-cultivated country; which introduces a panegyric on Great Britain. Sun-set. Evening. Night. Summer Meteors. The whole concluding with the Praise of Philosophy.[1]

Thomson himself made two types of changes regarding unity: he added material as contrast or amplification, and he altered the order. Thus, at least, consideration of these two characteristics was necessary in order to discuss 'the writer's method', and Aikin disregarded as sentiment what Thomson included—digressions, reflections, invocations and panegyrics. But still more limiting was the failure to study the 'economy of nature' to which Aikin pointed. For Thomson shifted to *Summer* a portion of *Spring* and to *Autumn* sections from *Winter*. The implications for unity did not require this knowledge; editions had, of course, not yet been collated in 1778. But what was important was the kind of unity the 'economy of nature' implied. Regarding Thomson's description of insects Aikin declared: 'The insect race alone seem animated with peculiar vigour under the more direct influence of the sun; and are therefore with equal truth and advantage introduced by the Poet to enliven the silent and drooping scenes presented by the other forms of animal nature.[2] But the insect passage was enlarged [ll. 287–317] in 1744 with a transfer from *Spring*, and the purpose may or may not have been scientific truth. The purposes for unity, however, were to establish contrasts in nature: its parching heat and refreshing shade, the playfulness and death in which insects participated, the drowsy shepherd and the active insects, the multitudes of unseen insects which inhabit the so-called 'lucid air' and which would, if seen and heard by man, stun him.

This doubleness of nature, its puzzling order, was the 'economy' that Thomson described, but which Aikin ignored because he was reality-centred and because he could not disengage unity from progression. Thus the 'transitions' which were, in his theory, the very basis of unity were passed over by putting praise words in front of Thomson's laconic 'view of Summer in the torrid zone': 'By an easy and natural transition, he quits the chastened summer of our temperate zone.' But the reason for quitting it at one moment in the

[1] Zippel, p. 59.

[2] Aikin, p. xxv.

poem rather than another was not clear, and this was, after all, the objection of Shiels.

Summer was a test-case for unity; Thomson made a single day characteristic of the season. The precise characteristic of *Summer* was not, however, a special variation of the doubleness of nature, but of a soft and pleasing languor leading, in insects, to maturity. The most violent storms, however, in which lovers died, sailors drowned and Africans were buried in sand, could hardly be identified with soft and pleasing languor. Yet this languor did characterize some elements of nature, though the assumptions of natural history created serious distortions: 'A Summer's day', wrote Aikin, 'is, in reality, a just model of the entire season. Its beginning is moist and temperate; its middle sultry and parching; its close soft and refreshing.'

Attempts to explain 'unity' involve a reduction of the poem to a principle of organization; such a principle may be loose or open, as in Shiels' suggestion, or tight and limited as it was for Aikin. But the principle must confront the order ('progress' or 'succession') of the poem and make some generalization about its end. The speculative element in this generalization is that based on knowledge of other poems or, as in Aikin's essay, on assumptions about nature. The value of an assumption depends, however, not only upon confirmation—Thomson's science was, for the most part, accurate—but upon recognition of what the poem presents. 'What the poem presents' means an analysis of similarities and differences of action, events, language, sequence—especially in a poem like *The Seasons* which is essentially cyclical.

Such analysis is limited not only by available information and literary hypotheses, but by the critic's location of similarities and differences and his attribution of dominance to some and subordination to others. Dominance was given to natural history by Aikin, to vividness of the sublime by Shiels. To Aikin, the cause for dominance—which is a form of evaluation or significance given to an element or group of elements—was the assumption that scientific reality was more vivid than fiction. To Shiels, 'vividness' was a criterion of proper imitation. The standard for Aikin's view of unity, therefore, was a more accurate poem, with fewer 'digressions'; the standard for Shiels' was a poem equally vivid but more dramatically unified. The objection to such alternatives is that they neglect the order and types of relationships within each season, although each alternative might produce a more 'unified' poem on its own principles. The kind of errors discovered in 'unity' would not, if corrected, read like the types of correction Thomson himself made. Whatever errors the poem had as a unity—and Shiels was correct in recognizing the aggregate quality of the work—such errors stemmed from a misuse of its 'kind'. But what the 'kind' was—this was the pursuit in all studies of its unity. It is possible to argue that to join the head of a horse with the body of a man creates a picture of a preposterous 'kind'. But this would mean that we dislike this 'kind', or that we do not know what could be 'good' of its 'kind', or that we do not understand how a subject matter could be made interesting by any changes of art.

Therefore, when Robert Heron (1793) disagreed with John Aikin about the unity of *Summer*—'This poem has less unity of design than Spring'—he was considering unity of design from premises of 'images and sentiments'. Assuming that each season was organized by a series of images and sentiments appropriate to it, Heron argued that 'luxuriance' enfeebling men and nature, was characteristic of *Summer*. Thus what Aikin considered the accessory, Heron considered the essential, relationship between man and nature.

> The tenderness and delicacy of Spring are insensibly matured into the vigorous luxuriance of *Summer*. The beauties of the vegetable world became more garish and splendid. Light streams on the face of nature with such fullness; heat, with such force, as to overpower, at times, both animals and vegetables, with what might otherwise, only tend to nourish and invigorate them. Animals become more languid in their exertions. The temperate assume somewhat of the character of the torrid. This is the season, when nature seeming to offer to man, to the full, every sensual joy that she has to bestow, tells him, at the same time, that sensual joy destroys the organs, enfeebles the faculties, and disappoints the wishes which it is sought to gratify.[1]

Because Heron defined poetry as an assemblage of sentiments and images joined to operate directly on the imagination and feelings,

[1] Robert Heron, 'A Critical Essay on the Seasons', *The Seasons* [Perth, 1793), p. 16. For an analysis of Heron's theory, see A. A. Mendilow, 'Robert Heron and Wordsworth's Critical Essays', *MLR*, LII (1957), 329–338, who draws interesting parallels between the critical essays of Wordsworth and Heron, and provides a bibliography of Heron. For the historical context of Heron's theory, see Chapter III.

he pursued these more deliberately and systematically through the season, thus avoiding Aikin's exclusiveness. In addition, he related man and nature as equal parts of Thomson's universe and was not tied to the assumption of a new genre demanding a separation, since images and sentiments operated in all poetry. Aikin identified the soft and pleasing languor of *Summer* and noted that a 'universal benevolence extending to every part of the animal creation, manifests itself in almost every scene he draws', but Heron observed the contradictory qualities of splendour and enfeeblement.

The more precisely the critic descended to the particulars, the less did his own generalizations distort the poem. Heron did not discuss the recurrence of storms and sunrises, and thus did not observe the kind of precise differences the poem was developing, but this was due to the assumption that comparisons with other poems rather than comparison with Thomson's own images, where possible, discriminated the quality of images. Heron's theory also caused him to assume that the unity would have been more impressive if Thomson had chosen some other kinds of images. But it must be observed that the season's unity remained the progression of a day, that it encompassed man as well as nature, and that it created a sense of the contrast characteristic of Thomson's view. But the assumption that the image (and its associated sentiment) formed the elements for unity neglected the larger contrasting elements: the buzzing insect life in its profusion and conflict compared with the swarming rural activity of man and animal which formed part of 'social glee' (ll. 352–431), the terrors of the torrid zone (amid 'this gay profusion of luxurious bliss', l. 861) hurled upon guilty, savage man and those hurled upon the innocent Amelia (ll. 860–1222) or the comparison between the 'pure' exercise of swimming and the prurient spying upon bathing Musidora (ll. 1259–1370). It was possible, of course, to group and contrast images, but Heron saw poetry as an accumulation of them.

(2). *S. Johnson: Imagination and Unity*

The great defect of *The Seasons* is want of method.

S. JOHNSON

When Johnson (1781) came to consider the unity of *The Seasons*, he saw it in the tradition of descriptive poems aiming at a spatial unity. The poem sought to present many scenes which had a simultaneous existence; by definition this did not require any tightly knit order, but rather a vividness of detail. To Johnson this unity was endemic to this genre of poetry, although it would seem possible to argue that within a genre more or less success could be achieved. This was what Johnson meant when he said that the attention 'must be excited by diversity' in this kind of poem, and in this concept of loose unity was located a readiness for difference. He had first discussed the want of design in description as early as 1744 in Savage's *The Wanderer* (in the *Life*), then in *Windsor Forest*, and had minimized this argument in his life of Thomson. Of *Windsor Forest* he had written:

> The objection made by Dennis is the want of plan, of a regular subordination of parts terminating in the principal and original design. There is this want in most descriptive poems, because as the scenes, which they must exhibit successively, are all subsisting at the same time, the order in which they are shown must by necessity be arbitrary, and more is not expected from the last part than from the first. The attention, therefore, which cannot be detained by suspense, must be excited by diversity, such as this poem offers to its reader.[1]

Of *The Seasons* Johnson wrote:

> The great defect of *The Seasons* is want of method; but for this I know not that there was any remedy. Of many appearances subsisting all at once, no rule can be given why one should be mentioned before another; yet the memory wants the help of order, and the curiosity is not excited by suspense or expectation.[2]

Johnson refused to judge the poem by rules which were obviously inappropriate, yet he recognized that certain psychological qualities which were normally attributed to unity—'the curiosity is not excited by suspense or expectation'—were absent from the poem. And in one of his conversations with Shiels, Johnson 'took down Thomson, and read aloud a large portion of him, and then asked,—Is not this fine? Shiels having expressed the highest admiration. Well, Sir . . . I have omitted every other line.'[3] This demonstration was,

[1] Johnson, 'Pope', *Lives*, II, 225.

[2] Johnson, 'Thomson', *Lives*, III, 299–300.

[3] Boswell, *The Life of Johnson*, III, 37. See John Nicols, ed., *The Seasons* (London, 1849), p. lxxv: 'Now, had any one, on the strength of this random assertion, tried the absurd experiment of omitting every other line in Thomson's poetry, no one sooner than Johnson would have ridiculed the insane attempt.'

for Johnson, a conclusive 'proof' of Thomson's occasional 'cloud of words' as well as his lack of unity. But the inferences to be drawn from this are perhaps not precisely those of Johnson. For the emotional coherence of Thomson, though not his successive unity of sense, was revealed by the diverse passages conveyed. Johnson's 'demonstrations' were not always reliable, and the 'portion' he read to Shiels might very well have yielded the 'highest admiration' for its emotive tone. For it is possible, as Kenneth Burke has shown, to select first lines from Whitman's poems and to make some coherence of continuity and a great deal of coherence of feeling from them. The shift in the kind of unity developed in *The Seasons* was indicated by the increased looseness of connection between parts in contrast to the need for a dominant successive plot unity in a drama or epic.

Another pressure which *The Seasons* represented as a poem—especially with regard to unity—was the fact that each season was printed separately and had an independent identity. The problem, therefore, was to discover the independence of the parts while yoking them together. The dilemma of part-whole relationships which puzzled Shiels and Johnson has been equally puzzling to at least one critic in our own time. 'I do not know . . .' writes William Wimsatt, 'to what extent a loosely constructed whole may be redeemed by the energy of individual chapters or scenes.'[1]

Percival Stockdale in the 1793 edition of *The Seasons* and in his *Lectures on the Truly Eminent English Poets* (1807) correctly understood the kind of unity which Johnson demanded, but could not accept it and could provide no critical concept in its stead. He wrote: 'To excite that eager, and anxious curiosity, suspense and expectation, which it is incumbent on the writer of a novel, or of a drama to raise, did not enter into the plan of the Seasons.'[2] Stockdale's definition of unity in *The Seasons* was equivalent to 'attention', and thus it indicated that *The Seasons*, like any interesting poem, engaged the attention. But Johnson, too, had pointed out that Thomson interested the reader, he 'leads us through the appearances of things as they are successively varied by the vicissitudes of the year, and imparts to us so much of his own enthusiasm that our thoughts expand with his imagery and kindle with his sentiments.'

'Attention' would not have become a much-debated idea in literary

[1] William Wimsatt, 'Explication as Criticism', *The Verbal Icon* (Lexington, 1954), p. 239.

[2] Stockdale, *Lectures*, II, 114.

theory if readers had not reconsidered their relation to the reading of poems. In order to perceive the poem, a due intentness was requisite, and as Goldsmith said of the reader of *The Deserted Village*, 'I want his unfatigued attention.' The concept of 'attention' was not solely the result of the appeal to perception, but it was sharply focussed by it. Whereas Felton had explained that a poem had to have force and spirit to be interesting and Addison had written that the role of the reader was to complete the poem, the appeal to perceptions was an appeal to attention without which the response to the particularities of the poem was not forthcoming.

'Attention' was defined by Locke as a procedure in which 'the ideas . . . that offer themselves . . . are taken notice of, and, as it were, registered in the memory,' and he indicated 'that the mind employs itself about them with several degrees of attention'.[1] Lord Kames (1762) explained that 'attention is that state of mind which prepares a man to receive impressions. According to the degree of attention, objects make a stronger or weaker impression',[2] though it was also true that 'an interesting object seizes and fixes the attention beyond the possibility of control'. Thus with regard to the poem, attention as a critical concept involving consciousness led to careful discrimination of particulars, but as an involuntary force it compelled response to one area of a work rather than another. Conscious attention was focussed on discriminations within the poem, but unconscious attention—a synonym for the poet's sincerity rather than awareness—urged 'sympathy' as a substitute for discrimination. As John More explained (1777), defending Thomson's lack of harmony: 'he [Thomson] uniformly writes from a full heart, and in that temper could hardly be supposed sufficiently attentive on all occasions, to the smoothness of his verse'.[3] And James Beattie (1776), explaining that a long poem required prosaic passages to maintain the attention, that is, alertness, declared: 'the high lyric style continued through many pages would fatigue the attention, confound the judgement, and bewilder the fancy'.[4]

[1] Locke, *Essay*, I, 298–9.

[2] Henry Home, Lord Kames, *Elements of Criticism* (Edinburgh, 1762), III, 396. For a study of Kames's critical theory, see Helen Whitcomb Randall, *The Critical Theory of Lord Kames, Smith College Studies in Language and Literature*, XXII (October, 1940; July, 1941).

[3] John More, *Strictures Critical and Sentimental on Thomson's Seasons* (London, 1777), p. 80.

[4] James Beattie, 'An Essay on Poetry and Music as they Affect the

The issue here was the use of 'attention'—a relation between poet and materials or reader and finished poem—to explain the need for prosaic passages. Beattie argued for an organic view in which 'prosaic' passages were essential to psychological perception. John More argued that the poet made choices in terms of his own 'temper' preferring to create an emotive response even at the cost of traditional 'smoothness'. The development of attention as an authorial function was, according to More, partly unconscious, thus the argument that the critic did not clearly 'see' the meaning of the poem but felt it and sought to convey it. But both defenders of Thomson recognized difficulties in the poem while arguing that such difficulties were proportionately insignificant.

The concern for 'attention' developed in the criticism of *The Seasons* from the concept of unity because once the dramatic unity was denied, and a loose connection between parts granted, the reader became obligated to maintain his interest by supplanting with 'attention' and its proper conditions, the intensity found in plot. Johnson had noted that common criticism of *The Wanderer* referred to it as a 'heap of shining materials . . . which strikes rather with the solemn magnificence of a stupendous ruin'; Shiels thought *The Seasons* might be considered an assemblage of poetical ideas and Johnson indicated that it contained 'many appearances subsisting all at once'. In criticizing *Windsor Forest* Johnson had suggested that the attention must be 'excited by diversity', and in criticizing *The Seasons* as well, he had posited a spatial unity in which the poem as a whole was associatively rather than dramatically interrelated. The unity referred to the whole poem, and it posited the values of extensive 'appearances' or incidents.

The concept of a poem as a whole preserving a consistency and coherence, was an accepted hypothesis, regardless whether the unity was to be completed by the author—as Aristotle indicated of tragedy—or by the reader, as Burke indicated of sublime poetry. The reformulation of unity in poetry, therefore, was undertaken by Shiels and all subsequent writers on *The Seasons*.

Mind', *Essays* (Edinburgh, 1776), p. 292. For discussions of 'attention' or controls upon perception, see Isaac Watts, 'Of Fixing the Attention', *The Improvement of the Mind* (London, 1741), pp. 211–17; Elizabeth Hamilton, 'Essay II' and 'Essay III', *A Series of Popular Essays* (Edinburgh, 1813), I, 51–260.

> Mr. Thomson's poetical diction in the Seasons [wrote Shiels] is very peculiar to him: His manner of writing is entirely his own: He has introduced a number of compound words; converted substantives into verbs, and in short has created a kind of new language for himself. His stile has been blamed for its singularity and stiffness; but with submission to superior judges, we cannot but be of opinion, that though this observation is true, yet it is admirably fitted for description. The object he paints stands full before the eye, we admire it in all its lustre . . . Thomson has a stiffness in his manner, but then his manner is new; and there never yet arose a distinguished genius, who had not an air peculiarly his own.[1]

The discussion of unity was transformed here into a discussion of Thomson's 'air peculiarly his own'. This 'air' was a manner of writing, a poetical diction and a poetical structure. But this manner of writing gave *The Seasons* an identity which it would otherwise not have had. Shiels found the locus of Thomson's originality in the descriptions, but he was not very clear about how Thomson accomplished this feat. 'The object he paints stands full before the eye',

[1] Shiels, 'Thomson', *Lives*, V., 202–3. For a discussion of authorship of Cibber's *Lives*, see Walter Raleigh, 'Early Lives of the Poets', *Six Essays on Johnson* (Oxford, 1910), pp. 119–26. Shiels 'life' was translated into German by Lessing and formed the basis for the life of Thomson in Thomas Flloyd, 'James Thomson', *Bibliotheca Biographica* (London, 1760), III, unnumbered. Johnson's view of Thomson as poet was considered undistinguished by the reviewer of *Lives*, *Monthly Review*, LXV (Dec. 1781), 408: 'In characterizing Thomson's merit as a poet his Biographer nearly coincides with general opinion. As a man, however, the representation of his character is not so favourable.' Shiels's life and Murdoch's life formed the basis for three other English 'lives' of Thomson published anonymously before Johnson's: 'An Account of the Life and Writings of Mr. James Thomson', dated Edin., July 15, 1768, *The Works of James Thomson* (Edinburgh, 1772, R. Clark), I, 5–23, and 'An Account of the Life and Writings of Mr. James Thomson', dated Edin., July 28, 1768, *The Seasons* (Edinburgh, 1768, A Kincaid), pp. iii–xxxiv, and 'The Life and Literary Character of James Thomson', *The Seasons* (Dublin, 1773), pp. i–vii. For Johnson's dependence upon and analysis of other critics in the *Lives*, see Benjamin Boyce, 'Samuel Johnson's Criticism of Pope in *The Life of Pope*', *RES*, N.S. V (1954), 37–46. Immediately after Johnson's life, a comprehensive life appeared which included material from Warton, Flloyd, Murdoch, and Johnson, 'The Life of James Thomson', *British Biography* (London, 1780), X, 321–32. An account of Thomson's life based on Johnson is also to be found in Alexander Campbell, *An Introduction to the History of Poetry in Scotland* (Edinburgh, 1797), pp. 214–20.

but Thomson's manner in painting it was not very comely. Thomson compounded words, made substantives out of verbs and created a new kind of language, but this 'air peculiarly his own' was a necessary concomitant of his minute description. This criticism therefore described the newness in ambiguous terms: 'peculiar' and 'peculiarly' were terms which had their origin in law and the social order. They suggested exclusiveness and were obviously related to 'genius' and 'originality', yet Shiels used the terms without complete approval.

He described Thomson's manner as entirely his own, but even Shiels knew that it was not 'entirely' his own. Compound epithets were to be found in Spenser, as Shiels himself indicated, and Thomson's use of Virgilian passages and Miltonic references was noted by his contemporaries. Thomson paraphrased passages from the *Georgics* and at least one translator of the *Georgics* paraphrased Thomson.[1] However, the use of 'peculiar' could be interpreted as a tautology—Thomson's diction was peculiar to him because no one ever wrote exactly like Thomson. It is not unlikely that Shiels was trying to define Thomson's 'manner of writing'—he also referred to it as a 'stile'—but the complicated data necessary for this task were unavailable to him. How a writer's diction can be distinguished from that of his followers, Thomson's from John G. Cooper's or William Cowper's for instance, or (still more perplexing) how the diction of the mature Thomson can be distinguished from the diction of youthful works such as 'On the Hoop'—in heroic couplets—or even the later 'To the Nightingale'—these were questions not to be resolved without analysis of vocabulary, imagery, sound and rhythm patterns, sentence structure, word order and the role of the narrator. Such tentative efforts as Shiels made in explaining Thomson's diction were not pursued by Murdoch, Johnson or Stockdale.

Johnson declared that Thomson was entitled to 'one praise of the highest kind':

> His mode of thinking and of expressing his thoughts is original. His blank verse is no more the blank verse of Milton or any other poet than the rhymes of Prior are the rhymes of Cowley. His numbers, his pauses, his diction, are of his own growth, without transcription, without imitation. He thinks in a peculiar train, and

[1] William Mills, Jr., *The Georgics of Virgil* (London, 1780), preface: 'The translator having taken Thomson and Phillips for his models, has borrowed a few lines from those justly-admired poets.' See also James Grahame, 'Preface,' *Rural Poems* or *British Georgics* (Edinburgh, 1821), p. viii.

he thinks always as a man of genius; he looks round on Nature, and on Life with the eye which Nature bestows only on a poet, the eye that distinguishes in every thing presented to its view whatever there is on which imagination can delight to be detained, and with a mind that at once comprehends the vast, and attends to the minute.[1]

Johnson's discussion of Thomson's originality sought to identify originality with thinking and the expression of thoughts. Thomson thought in an associative train that was particular—'peculiar'—rather than general and it was a particularity that conveyed insights which the reader had not possessed: 'The reader of *The Seasons* wonders that he never saw before what Thomson shews him, and that he never yet has felt what Thomson impresses.'

The reconsideration of his own principles applied to *The Seasons* led Johnson to defend blank verse in that poem. 'Poetry may subsist without rhyme,' he wrote in his life of Milton, 'but English poetry will not often please; nor can rhyme ever be safely spared but when the subject is able to support itself.' In *The Seasons* Johnson found blank verse 'properly used'. 'His is one of the works in which blank verse seems properly used; Thomson's wide expansion of general views, and his enumeration of circumstantial varieties, would have been obstructed and embarrassed by the frequent intersections of the sense, which are the necessary effects of rhyme.' The use of general views and particular views created a necessary continuity which the intersection of the sense would have interrupted. But Johnson did not analyse the relation of general to particular views although John More had noted in 1777 that the narrator always mounted a high place to take a general view. Johnson did not, in fact, suggest why enumerations of such views could not have avoided intersection of the sense in rhyme.

Johnson's ventures in *The Seasons*—the praise of its blank verse, the realization of inherent difficulties in the unity, the praise of its diction and the recognition of its originality—were frequently attacked by his contemporaries and by some nineteenth-century critics to whom Johnson's tentative speculations appeared as conservative versions of their 'demonstrated' hypotheses, Thus Stockdale (1793) attacked Johnson's statement about 'want of method' by calling it one 'among the many futile, absurd, and ungenerous

[1] Johnson, 'Thomson', *Lives*, III, 298–9.

passages in Johnson's Lives of the Poets'. And Anna Seward (1798) attacked Johnson's speculation that the revisions lost part of the 'race' of the original, declaring that Johnson's taste was corrupted by age and envy—though her own comments indicated that she sometimes preferred the original to the revisions. It was not until the mid-century that Cunningham discriminated among Johnson's different evaluations.[1] And it should, of course, be noted that Johnson's *Life* continued to be printed with editions of Thomson's poetry during the first half of the nineteenth century.

The attacks on Johnson's remarks revealed two factors about criticism of *The Seasons*: those critics who had no methodological procedure for reading the poem could use 'sympathy' or 'consonance' as a basis for attacking all critical inferences different from their own; and the critics made no distinction between Johnson's language of hypothetical conjecture or venture and the assertion of fact. Neglect of discriminations between critical language [the manner of asserting] and critical data [that which is asserted] led to disagreements based on misunderstandings of facts or expressions. Thus Sir Harris Nicolas [1831] found that Johnson's biography was hostile to Thomson whereas a method of collecting critical evidence would have been revealed, as G. B. Hill has shown, that Johnson's biography was almost entirely a compilation from Shiels's and Murdoch's early and favourable biographies. And although Johnson disliked *Liberty*, he praised Thomson's originality of thought and expression.

Despite attacks on Johnson's anti-liberal views, critics of the nineteenth century who attacked his comments on unity often quoted his praise of Thomson's genius. Stockdale, for example, in his edition of 1793 and again in his *Lectures* (1807) quoted with approval the famous passages on Thomson's mode of thinking and expressing his thoughts. Shiels had made a similar statement, but it was never quoted. The passage by Johnson rather than that of Shiels or More endured because Johnson was recognized as an important critic, and the strategic weight which his statement had was the result of his critical practice in other areas. This procedure of selection is understandable, and until a different method in selecting was developed, Johnson's quotation gave authoritative stature to interpretations of Thomson's originality. As Stockdale said, 'I am the more inclined to

[1] A. Cunningham, *Seasons*, pp. xliii–xlvi, for Stockdale, see *Lectures*, II, 110; for Seward, *Letters*, V, 89–90.

think favourably of some of my own sentiments on the poetry of Thomson, that they coincide with those of that great man'.[1]

Johnson's passage was quoted in whole or part by Hugh Blair (1783), the Earl of Buchan (1792), by Stockdale (1793), by Robert Anderson (1794), by John Evans (1802), by the 1816 editor, by the 1822 editor of *Scottish Lives*, by John D. Williams (1832), by Cunningham (1842), by the editor of the 1849 *Sketches of British Poets*, by James R. Boyd in 1852, and by the editor of the 1864 text edition of *Winter*. The persistence of a *locus criticus* in which the total view of a critic is disregarded and a passage endures as an independent judgement is a practice which could be continued only on the grounds that particular conclusions do not involve the total context of a man's thinking. And, indeed, Johnson's expression, 'he thinks in a peculiar train' required explanation, but the passage is noteworthy precisely because it contains within it the definition of its terms.

It persisted in criticism not only because it was self-contained, but because the ideas it expressed continued to prove hospitable to critics and the language in which it was expressed, 'original', 'without imitation', 'genius', 'imagination', remained key terms in Thomson criticism, even though they did not always possess the same meanings. But criticism, especially practical criticism, in so far as it became historically conscious of Thomsonian biography and study, required continuity of language and problems in some areas in order to undertake innovations in others. The *locus criticus* indicated that the critical past was not wholly dispensable.

Johnson's statement represented a comprehensive description of Thomson's talent, and in that respect it had durability as an isolated statement capable of being detached from the undistinguished and occasionally erroneous biography. It speculated how Thomson observed and composed. It suggested that the medium used was distinct and original, containing inimitable values but not without shortcomings. Thomson's view of nature was compared with that of his audience, and the relation between them was noted in terms of sight, insight, and sympathetic expressiveness: 'The reader of the "Seasons" wonders that he never saw before what Thomson shows him, and that he never yet had felt what Thomson impresses.' This passage depended for its self-contained quality upon a scope of reference sufficiently broad to apply to critical theories—for example,

[1] Stockdale, *Lectures*, II, 98.

those of the Earl of Buchan and Stockdale—based on moral impressionism rather than on Johnson's own analytical comparisons. Without sharing Johnson's method, these critics could accept his explanation of originality. And the use of quotation was, in itself, a method by which evidence was presented to the reader.

Allan Cunningham (1841) quoted Johnson on 'lack of method' in *The Seasons*, but found the unity more tightly related to a religious aim.

> The poet seems not to have erred as the critic imagines: he has truly observed the great order of the Seasons, and followed the footsteps of nature, without ascribing to one period of the year what belongs to another; while he has regarded storms and tempests, earthquake and plagues, as common to all seasons and employed them accordingly.[1]

Cunningham found the aim of *The Seasons* to be 'to raise men's thoughts to God' by the contemplation of the beauties of nature. He summarized the unity of each season as a series of representative pictures, all of which suggested the variety of the universe and the presence of God.

> Thomson perceived order, unity and high meaning in the lowliest as well as the loftiest things: he loved to observe the connexion of the animate with the inanimate; the speechless with the eloquent and all with God: he saw the testimony of heavenly intelligence in the swelling sea, the dropping cloud, and the rolling thunder; in earthquake and eclipse, as well as in the presence of Spring on the fields, of Summer on the flowers, of Autumn in her golden harvest, and of Winter in her frosty breath and her purifying tempests.[2]

'Unity' applied to the poem as a whole rather than to each season. The seasons were seen melting into each other, dominated by the imaginative force of nature. Aikin and Heron had descended to particulars because they sought to analyse each season; Cunningham interpreted 'unity' as a series of progressive characteristics based on the analogy of man. For him, 'unity' ceased to be a series of relational contrasts.

[1] A. Cunningham, *Seasons*, p. lxvi.
[2] *Ibid.*, pp. xlv–xlvi.

(3) *P. Murdoch, J. Beattie, P. Stockdale: Character and Unity*

> It is commonly said, the life of a good writer is best read in his works . . . the distinguishing character of his mind, his ruling passion, at least, will there appear undisguised.
>
> P. MURDOCH

Johnson defended Thomson's originality in general, but he accepted his own perceptions in finding that Thomson's language occasionally was less original than empty. In other words, Johnson's qualifications formed part of his analysis of Thomson's originality. But whereas Johnson and Shiels sought to analyse the diction as the area of originality, as an example either of Thomson's manner of writing or manner of thinking or both, Patrick Murdoch found Thomson's unity to be his 'distinguishing qualities of *mind* and *heart*'.

> They are better represented in his writings, than they can be by the pen of any biographer. There, his love of mankind, of his country and his friends; his devotion to the *Supreme Being*, founded in the most elevated and just conceptions of his operations and providence, shine out in every page.[1]

Robert Shiels and later Johnson had concentrated on the work as the locus of the poet's originality; Murdoch found this originality in the biography of the poet. He identified Thomson's personal goodness with his expression of goodness in his poetry, Thomson as man with Thomson as poet. The distinction between these was almost unidentifiable: 'His digressions, too, the overflowings of a tender benevolent heart, charmed the reader no less; leaving him in doubt whether he should more admire the *Poet*; or love the *Man*'.[2]

In the distinguishing traits of the biography, Murdoch also found the distinguishing traits of the poet. In the attitude of the poet, rather than in the expression of these attitudes, he found the key qualities of the poem, imitating Longinus who had declared, 'the truly eloquent must possess an exalted and noble mind'. This sympathetic view of life and work gave an identity to the whole poem, to the digressions as well as to the descriptions and moral reflections. But by making them equally distinctive, it made them equally undistinctive. The lustre of

[1] Patrick Murdoch, 'An account of the Life and Writings of Thomson' (London, 1762), I, xix.

[2] *Ibid.*, p. vii.

the writer was shown forth 'in every page', but Murdoch could provide no explanation for the more as against the less successful pages which occurred in *The Seasons*.

The view of 'character' which this unity displaced was that of appropriateness; Aristotle had declared that the manners and diction of the dramatic character were to be appropriate to the profession and age and sex of the speaker; and Richard Steele (1713), applying the concept to the author's writings, found that in each genre the author assumed a different 'character'. 'Whether they write in the Dramatick, Lyrick or Epick Manner, they seldom fail to keep up to the several characteristicks, which distinguish those various Kinds from one another.'[1] The terms 'character' and 'characteristics' meant roles, or traits which identified the poet in his different manners. Each manner was judged by consistency and appropriateness within its own kind so that the poet was himself 'so many different Persons' or personae. In 'The Character of a Truly Accomplished Poet' (1733), Bezaleel Morrice explained that Virgil appeared 'in the Mirror of his Works', but the mirror was a reflection of the understanding, fancy, judgment, memory and the other faculties involved in the writing of poetry.[2] It was not a reflection of the 'distinguishing character' of mind, nor of the ruling passion. Murdoch's conception of 'character', however, rested on the enduring poetic identity of the author rather than all reflections. Such attempts were not without their difficulties and ironies and as Arthur Murphy once remarked (1753): 'No Rules that I know of, have been yet laid down, nor is there any certain Standard which should fix the Degree of Elevation to which the ruling Passion must necessarily rise, before it can have Strength sufficient to determine the Character'.[3]

John Baillie (1746) wrote: 'As every different Manner of Writing has its peculiar *Character*, it must likewise have its different *Principles* . . .' Aristotle had explained that in all parts of a work, except the descriptive, studied and artificial language intruded upon the

[1] Richard Steele, *The Englishman* (Oct. 20, 1713). For the sources of this view in Shaftesbury, see 'Advice to an Author' (1710), *Characteristics of Men, Manners, Opinions and Times*, ed. J. M. Robertson (London, 1900), I, 131, 157, 168–9; also *The Polite Arts* (London, 1748), p. 26.

[2] Bezaleel Morrice, 'The Character of a Truly Accomplished Poet', *On the English Translations of Homer* (London, 1721).

[3] Arthur Murphy, 'On the Standards of Modern Criticism' (1753), *The Gray's Inn Journal* (London, 1756), I, 174. In trying to lay down these standards, Murphy derided the immodesty of critics.

action; in the drama and epic, plot was central and the author's invasion of the narrative—either to explain or embellish—detracted from the relationship established between the work and the reader. Such invasions were not considered part of the imitation, and Henry Pemberton (1738)—in the tradition of Fenelon and Dryden—urged the poet to maintain his anonymity. 'A poet should write entirely for the benefit of his readers without any appearance of setting off himself. To make a work truly excellent it is necessary, that the author should so forget himself, that the reader may forget him likewise, and have his attention engaged only on the subject.'[1] But loco-descriptive poetry which was marked by an absence of plot and by a series of meditations and reflections, altered the proportion between plot and embellishment. The intrusion of the author—or the narrator as author—into the poem called forth a reformulation of character. But together with character, it raised the question of belief. Not until reflective poetry made assertions about religious and social issues did the problem of belief become associated with 'character' and 'description' as against 'plot' and 'imitation'. Poetry as plot or imitation was considered 'feigning' by Plato and critics frequently referred to the 'fable' as a lie. But the problem of belief as related to reflective-descriptive poetry was posed in terms of the poet's honesty or sincerity. 'Not only in his plays', wrote Sir George Lyttelton of Thomson, 'but all his other works, there is the purest *morality*, animated by *piety*, and rendered more touching by the fine and delicate sentiments of a most *tender* and *benevolent* heart'.[2]

Murdoch made no artistic distinctions between the conscious moralizing 'founded on the most elevated and just conceptions' of the Supreme Being, and 'the overflowings of a tender benevolent heart', between the moral reflections and the digressions. It was a formulation, therefore, which was without adequate discrimination for poetry, and Johnson [1781] attacked it for confusing poetic with literary 'character' in his biography of Thomson:

> The biographer of Thomson has remarked that an author's life is best read in his works: his observation was not well-timed. Savage, who lived much with Thomson, once told me how he heard a lady remarking that she could gather from his works three parts of his

[1] John Baillie, *An Essay on the Sublime* (London, 1747), p. 2; Henry Pemberton, *Observations on Poetry* (London, 1738), p. 102.

[2] George Lyttelton, 'Dialogue XIV', *Dialogues of the Dead, Works* (London, 1776), II, 203.

character, that he was 'a great lover, a great swimmer, and rigorously abstinent'; but, said Savage, he knows not any love but that of the sex; he was perhaps never in cold water in his life; and he indulges himself in all the luxury that comes within his reach.[1]

Murdoch sought to explain Thomson's sublime in *The Seasons* by tentatively attributing it to his early religious education and 'his early acquaintance with the sacred writings'. He readily assumed that conscious impressions, such as knowledge of sacred writings, became absorbed into Thomson's style. This type of inference was also made by Shiels, who assumed that because young Thomson used to converse with 'Mr. Rickerton' who knew natural and moral philosophy, his later poems exhibited that knowledge. Murdoch was, however, seeking to explain the origins of the sublime conceptions which 'shine out in every page' and of the digressions which were the 'overflowings' of a tender heart, of the conscious statements and the spontaneous overflow: 'The Muse unprompted warm'd his gentle mind.' Such language implied that 'overflowings' were to be distinguished from 'shining forths' or 'lustres' which were religious terms traditionally applied to literary qualities although Murdoch provided no means to make these discriminations.

The reliance upon the author's beliefs and honesty which shone on every page resulted from several causes. The reflective descriptive poem could be lyrical, didactic, and narrative—could, in fact, contain many of the quite diverse characteristics of other poetry. Thomson's poem was, in fact, called 'pastoral', 'didactic', 'picturesque' and 'descriptive'.[2] The beliefs, therefore, provided one way for finding a unity which had been attacked on traditional grounds. Another was

[1] Johnson, 'Thomson', *Lives*, III, 297–8. See Robert Bell's comments upon Savage and Thomson in *Poetical Works of James Thomson, The Annotated Edition of the English Poets* (London, 1855), II, 262–3. For additional comments on Savage's remarks see Bolton Corney, ed., 'An Account of the Life and Writings of Mr. James Thomson by Patrick Murdoch', *The Seasons* (London, 1842), p. xxxix, n. 88; and Peter Cunningham, ed., 'Preface', *A Poem to the Memory of William Congreve by James Thomson* (London, The Percy Society, 1843), pp. xii–xvii.

[2] Hussey, *Picturesque*, p. 18: 'Thomson, Dyer and their immediate followers are usually designated the Landscape Poets. I call them the Picturesque Poets.' For the use of 'picturesque' applied to Thomson, see Dugald Stewart, 'On the Beautiful', *Philosophical Essays* (Edinburgh, 1810), pp. 271–3. For the classification of *The Seasons* as 'didactic', see Rev. J. Huskisson Robertson, *A Catechism of Criticism* (London, 1825), p. 43.

that this type of poetry was dominated by a narrator, a single character who served as a focus for the diverse views and incidents in the poem. Because of his function as 'spectator', his reliability depended upon his accurate, that is, his honest views. An identity was made, therefore, between the honest reflections which the character exhibited in his observations and the author whose reflection the character could be. 'Those writings in which the author gives his detail in person', wrote Robert Burrowes (1793), 'and particularly oratory and lyric poetry, where he speaks from the fulness and force of his own mind, must bear the strongest marks of his peculiar habits of thinking.'[1]

What Murdoch and critics who agreed with him did, was to interpret character in terms not of different roles but of the same role, to insist on the enduring trait rather than diverse characteristics. What Murdoch sought was 'the distinguishing character of his [Thomson's] mind', a ruling passion which survived all temporal changes. James Beattie (1776) reformulated Murdoch's view suggesting that the character of the poetic *narrator* created a unity of language; 'in the Epic poem (and in all serious poetry, narrative or didactic, wherein the poet is the speaker), language, in order to be natural, must be suited to the assumed or supposed character of the poet, as well as to the occasion and subject'. But Beattie was involved in a contradiction between the 'nature' of the man and the assumed character of the poet. The latter was governed by the demands of the epic or didactic poem, yet 'persons of different characters . . . contemplating the same thing, . . . feel different emotions, and turn their view to different objects'.[2]

[1] Robert Burrowes 'On Style in Writing' (read 1 May 1793 and 19 April 1794), *Transactions of the Royal Irish Academy* (Dublin, 1795), V, 50. See also pp. 50–51. For an example of this shift applied to another 'descriptive' poet, see Robert Southey's preface to Cowper's *Works* (London, 1835–7): 'Cowper himself, perhaps, was not aware of what it was that supplied the place of plan, and with happier effect than the most skilful plan could have produced . . . In *The Task* . . . *the reader feels that the poet is continually present; he becomes intimately acquainted with him, and this it is which gives to this delightful poem its unity and its particular charm.*'

These views sought to avoid the earlier theories of direct correspondence ridiculed by Johnson and frequently assumed by critics at the beginning of the century. See Jonathan Richardson, *Theory of Painting* (London, 1715), p. 205.

[2] James Beattie, 'On Poetry and Music' (written in 1762), *Essays* (Edinburgh, 1776), p. 221.

Beattie attributed an assumed character to the author and yet found the author's own character in his work. 'We often see an author's character in his works; and if every author were in earnest when he writes, we should oftener see it. Thomson was a man of piety and benevolence, and a warm admirer of the beauties of nature; and every description in his delightful poem on the Seasons tends to raise the same laudable affections in his reader.' The criterion was his 'earnestness' and his subject matter—the parts of nature which would not affect an impious man. But Beattie's attack on Swift indicated that he interpreted 'earnestness' not as a literary quality inducing belief but as an indication of the author's belief. Thus Swift's irony was not 'serious' and the confusion of literary qualities with biographical qualities remained. Nevertheless Beattie correctly assumed that descriptive and didactic works welcomed a greater closeness of author to work than the drama.

In trying to account for the new kind of unity, Beattie pointed to stylistic characteristics which 'unified' the work. One was the importance of transitions which kept the work a 'whole' despite its associative pattern, and the other provided the basis for interpreting these transitions—the 'style' of the author. 'Style' controlled unity because it represented the vivacity of the author's own thinking. As Percival Stockdale (1809) declared: 'Style is the copy of thought; therefore, as our substance, and manner of thinking *are*, such will our words, and such will their order *be*. The language, like the sentiments of Thomson, has an essence, and a structure, by which it is predominantly discriminated from the styles of other poets. The style of *his* poetry is almost constantly impressive; and his epithets are often as happily applied to their objects as they are few.'[1]

But the difficulty with Beattie's view of style as unity was that as soon as it descended to particulars, it ceased to win any agreement. For Lord Kames (1762) before Beattie and John Scott (1785) and others after him disagreed that the epithets were happily applied or that these were characteristic of his 'style'. The unity which Beattie saw was that of a poem marked by proper transitions. As John Aikin (1778) explained, the proper introduction of a passage depended upon the kind of transition made, and this position was echoed by Dugald Stewart who explained that the passage on 'Industry' in

[1] Percival Stockdale, 'Thomson', *Lectures on the Truly Eminent English Poets* (London, 1807), II, 96. For preceding quotations, see Beattie, pp. 54–55.

Autumn was properly introduced in *The Seasons* but would be inappropriate in prose.[1] The conditions for this unity operating were that of a 'sympathetic' reader, but it also assumed that characteristics of the poet dominated the poem. Thus the burlesque fox hunt and the Musidora digressions were not considered proper either to Thomson's 'style' or his unity, which thus merely assumed a wholeness which was highly selective rather than literal. The need for a proper measure of identity between poet and poem existed, but the speculative grounds chosen by Beattie depended upon a religious sympathy with Thomson rather than an artistic insight. In 1793 Robert Burrowes sought to provide such distinctions, while answering Johnson's attack on the confusion of literary and biographical 'character'.

> The lady who from Thomson's poems found reasons to persuade herself that he was much addicted to swimming attempted a species of mental physiognomy for which she was not qualified. It is not every description, made necessary to an author by his subject, which is to be considered as giving certain information of his habits and propensities: a man who has chosen for his topic the pleasures of the country, may be said to have a general fondness for rural life or rural situation, but he will be obliged sometimes to depict scenes of which he has not felt the pleasure, and sometimes to describe sports of which he has not partaken. The indolence and benevolence of Thomson appear in many parts of his writings; but unless he had gone out of his way to treat of swimming, or had treated of it more frequently or more fully than was proportioned to its importance towards his general scheme, there was no reason for supposing it an amusement in which he took particular delight.[2]

Burrowes argued that the character of an author was expressed in his choice of subject, and on his concentrated or unusual emphasis on particular subjects. He repeated the commonplace of Thomson's biographers that the poet lived a life of 'indolence and benevolence', though there was considerable reason to doubt that indolence was exercised in his writing however it may have been in his rising. The critics who sought to identify unity with character were aware of the submerged value of many elements in a literary work, and they were

[1] Dugald Stewart, *Elements of the Philosophy of the Human Mind, The Collected Works of Dugald Stewart*, ed. William Hamilton (Edinburgh, 1854), II, 267.

[2] Burrowes, 'On Style in Writing', 47.

seeking some explanation for the personal quality which descriptive poems possessed.

The objection to the unity found by these critics was that they imposed a consistency upon poets in excess of the facts. Human nature was far from consistent, and Sir Egerton Brydges (1808) wrote in *The Ruminator* on the character of Thomas Gray, 'can we judge of a man's actions by the hues of his mind? I am afraid that we cannot with any reasonable certainty. They who are bold in intellect are often timid in conduct; and imbecility, or, at least, a morbid delicacy, marks the personal character of many, whose abstract sentiments are constantly distinguished by vigour and energy. Instead of withdrawing on this account our admiration from individuals, we must only lament the inconsistencies of our weak and imperfect nature!'[1]

For these critics, the character of the poet which they read into the poem made the unity of every element of little importance. Percival Stockdale's formulation of 'character' revealed also a marked circularity in relating the poet and the man to the work. Because the work revealed God-like virtues. Thomson had them. And because he had them, the work revealed them.

> I know, we are every day told, that we must not presume to determine what the author is, from his book; and the remark, if it is limited to general validity, is true. . . . But both the substance, and the colouring of Thomson's poetry show that his life was animated, and directed, by those amiable, and God-like virtues which adorned, and dignified his verse. The heart; the Soul is poured forth, in every line. You see an anxiety; a tenderness; an interest for the cause which he pleads; which absorbs the whole man; and which are wanting in those literary works that are produced merely by the exertion of the understanding, and the imagination.[2]

[1] Sir Egerton Brydges, 'Traits in the Character of Gray the Poet', *The Ruminator* (first printed 1808) (London, 1813), p. 177. See E. L. Bulwer (Bulwer Lytton), 'On the Difference Between Authors, and the Impression Conveyed of them by their Works', *The Student* (London, 1835), I, 2–26. Bulwer suggests (following an unnamed critic) that a work reflects two conflicting characters of the author—the ideal belonging to his imagination and the cynical copied from experience, a view that creates serious contradictions in unity. See also Isaac Disraeli, *An Essay on the Manners and Genius of the Literary Character* (London, 1795), pp. 145–9; Edward Mangin, *A View of the Pleasures Arising from a Love of Books* (London, 1814), pp. 173–7; and Leigh Hunt, 'Cowley and Thomson', *Men, Women and Books* (London, 1847), II, 51–64.

[2] Stockdale, *Lectures*, II, 82, 84–85.

Thomson's soul was 'poured forth' in every line, and because the soul was overflowing, it was sincere; this sincerity could only be exhibited by one who was completely absorbed by it. The 'colouring', or diction, by its images and force, demonstrated that Thomson meant what he said, and was not functioning as a persona or 'person' in Steele's sense. In any work in which the man and poet were at odds, 'there are wanting those impressive, and indelible marks, those infallible criteria, by which the moral and practical sincerity of the writer are ascertained'. These were 'the sincere, tender, and ardent affections, which moved, and guided the hand of the writer'. In 1777, John More had written: 'I much doubt if any real Poet can write with success, in a counterfeit character.'[1]

'Character' in the eighteenth century moved from a series of consistent and appropriate 'persons', to a 'character' which maintained in diverse situations a series of distinguishing qualities, not necessarily consistent, belonging to the author or the author as narrator. For this reason the criteria for *The Seasons* became 'earnestness', 'sincerity', 'honesty', 'spontaneity' and their synonyms. 'All that is admirable in the Seasons', wrote William Hazlitt (1818), 'is the emanation of a fine natural genius, and sincere love of his subject, unforced, unstudied, that comes uncalled for, and departs unbidden.'[2]

But it must not be assumed the qualities of 'sincerity', 'spontaneity' and 'ardour' were not found by earlier critics than Beattie and Stockdale and Hazlitt. Shiels found in Thomson's style a 'tow'ring sublimity', and the sublime was a quality praised by Longinus. Horace had explained that 'Force, and Dignity, and Loftiness of Spirit . . . constitute a true Poem', and Plato in the *Ion* interpreted poetry as inspired. The 'fire' and 'ardour' were characteristics of poetry in the seventeenth as in the eighteenth century, for Meric Casaubon, John Dennis, for Henry Felton as for Percy Shelley. If the poet 'hath not Life and Fire to give his Work some Force and Spirit', wrote Felton (1713), "tis nothing but a meer Corps, and a lumpish unwieldly Mass of Matter'.[3]

These critical terms functioned differently because they were applied to different areas. For Felton, as for Horace, 'Force' and 'Spirit' served as essential qualities of poetry as against prose, whereas

[1] John More, *Strictures, Critical and Sentimental, on Thomson's Seasons* (London, 1777), p. 10.

[2] William Hazlitt, *Lectures on the English Poets* (London, 1941), p. 165.

[3] Felton, *A Dissertation on Reading the Classics*, p. 141.

for Beattie 'sincerity' or 'earnestness' was to be distinguished from insincerity and falsehood. For the former these were essential to a definition of a poem, for the latter to a definition of 'good' poetry. The narrowing of the categories for these qualities revealed that for Beattie a poem was not defined by 'Fire' or 'Force' but by what was called 'poetry' by common usage.

The emphasis on spontaneity as a value—on the flame and the fountain as images of spontaneity and on the 'unforced, unstudied' and 'uncalled-for' presence of poetic fire and inspiration which the poet possessed—persisted for centuries. 'By natural *Enthusiasme*', wrote Meric Casaubon, 'I understand an extraordinary, transcendent, but natural fervency, a pregnancy of the soul, spirits or brain, producing strange effects, apt to be mistaken for supernatural.' The 'poetical Enthusiasme' to which Casaubon referred was the result of the expression of the passions; it was, in the language of Longinus, controlled disorder; and it was discovered by tropes and figures as well as by ardour. 'If through exuberance of wit and good language, he happen, without affectation, to ravish everywhere; he is not an Orator, but a Poet.'[1]

The critics of *The Seasons*, however, applied the concept of poetic fire and inspiration to a theory of mechanical or artificial diction as against spontaneous eruptions of poetic depth. The determination of the spontaneous area of the poem became for them an act of critical sympathy. Since the confrontation of the poem had made possible the defence of individual perceptions, these were, by means of the notion of spontaneity, transferred from the poem to the poet. Thus recognition of ardour or spontaneity meant that the critic could 'not infrequently' trace in the poet 'the chain of thought which led him astray', and the critic's perceptions pierced the poem to the mind of the poet. To these critics sympathy formed a necessary adjunct for spontaneity; it was the means by which it could be recognized. But there were other critical positions based on the awareness of poetic language as a skill. These referred to the *appearance* of spontaneity resulting from great care and artifice. Morrice, in 1732, had referred to 'that graceful, neat and most admirable seeming Negligence; where the finest Art is conceall'd under the Resemblance of a familiar Ease and in *Reality* is the highest Pitch of Human

[1] Meric Casaubon, *A Treatise Concerning Enthusiasme* (London, 1656), p. 207.

Skill'.[1] In 1738, Dr. Rundle, Thomson's friend, stated this position in a letter to Mrs. Sandys, referring to Thomson's forthcoming play *Agamemnon*: 'He wants that neatness and simplicity of diction which is so natural in dialogue. He cannot throw the light of an elegant ease on his thoughts, which will make the sublimest turns of art appear the genuine unpremeditated dictates of the heart of the speaker'.[2] And Daniel Webb (1763), using the terms 'accidental' and 'unstudied', terms later used by Hazlitt to characterize poetic force and value, explained that 'unstudied eloquence' was the result of artificiality and what appeared most accidental in versification was 'most artificial', and that 'it passes along unheeded, as the casual flow of an unstudied eloquence'.[3] Making a similar point, Hannah More wrote: 'a writer of real taste will take great pains in the perfection of his style, to make the reader believe he took none at all'.[4]

But although the critical terms were used with diverse meanings, this usage implied less disagreement than appeared. The techniques by which verse was carefully formed and the words, the passages, and terms to which the critics might point, could very well be identical passages. The area of disagreement then became the intention of the author: were the passages planned or spontaneous? As a problem this could be resolved in several directions—by direct inquiry, by consultation of notes and letters, by internal hypotheses. Or it could be resolved by inquiring whether any poetic expression could take place without spontaneity or whether spontaneous expression did or did not involve some contemplation and language selection.

The conversion of *The Seasons* into a poem the unity of which was related to the character of the poet was expressed by certain key terms: 'spontaneous', 'sincere', 'ease', 'natural'. For Murdoch, these terms were aesthetic as well as moral. But when Sir Harris Nicolas

[1] Bezaleel Morrice, 'The Preface', *An Essay on the Poets* (London, n.d.), p. 21.

[2] Thomas Rundle, 'Letter XXVII' (1730), *Letters of the Late Thomas Rundle to Mrs. Barbara Sandys* (Gloucester, 1789), II, 196–7. For Rundle's comments on *The Seasons*, see 'Letter IX' (March, 1729), II, 76–78, and 'Letter XVI' (July 16, 1730), II, 132–5.

[3] Daniel Webb, *Remarks on the Beauties of Poetry* (London, 1762), pp. 36–37.

[4] Hannah More, *Works* (New York, 1835), II, 576. William Gilpin, *Three Essays* (London, 1794), distinguished two uses of 'free' strokes in art—'free' that was 'bold' (a stroke that led to an image of the whole) and 'free' that was 'impudent' (a stroke done for play) so that 'free' was divided into directed and undirected 'ease'.

in 1831 discussed Thomson's skill as a nature poet he disengaged 'style' from passages which were 'spontaneous', recognizing the role of skill in poetry, but finding that the spontaneous passages were those in which the reader sympathized with the man rather than the skilled poet.

The distinction between skill and feeling was interpreted by Neele in 1826 as the conflict between artificiality and naturalness. Because Neele separated diction from feeling, he sought to return Thomson to that pristine childhood of particular impressions with which in 1792 the Earl of Buchan had identified him. 'Thomson', wrote Neele, 'is the genuine child of nature'. This attempt to praise Thomson by reducing him to an uninhibited child was made clearly and unfortunately by George Gilfillan in 1853: 'His great power lay in his deep, glowing, childlike enthusiasm for nature, and in the fullness with which he retained this on to mature manhood; so that, while in understanding he was thirty, in freshness of feeling he was only thirteen.'[1]

Gilfillan did not investigate why this freshness of feeling did not apply to *Liberty* or to Thomson's dramas, and he saw this freshness opposed to any 'high ideal of art'. Another critic applied this interpretation to the characterological view of unity. He inferred Thomson's 'childish' traits of style from his innocence of feeling. Thomson's character, he wrote,

> is discernible in his writings. His simplicity is seen in the purity and warmth of his sentiments, sometimes even childish; his indolence in the slovenliness of his versification, and the inappropriateness of so many of his epithets; he never seems to have thought anything worth the toil of polishing, and hence the perpetual use of pompous, glittering diction, substituted for thought or description; his sincerity appears in the gusto with which he describes all luxuries of the senses, and the horrors of deprivation. Amidst much that is truly exquisite, both in feeling and in expression, he mingles the absurdities of a schoolboy's trite commonplaces, and mechanical contrivances to piece out his verse.[2]

The critic drew direct analogies between social and literary attitudes without even ascertaining the validity of the social traits. To identify

[1] George Gilfillan, ed., *Thomson's Poetical Works* (Edinburgh, 1853), p. xvi.

[2] Quoted in *Thomson's Seasons*, '*Spring*', ed. C. P. Mason (London, 1862) pp. vi–vii. In his 1864 edition of 'Winter', Mason hedged this state-

'indolence' with 'slovenliness' of versification was to overlook the regularity of Thomson's scansion and to be persuaded by critical imagery rather than accuracy.

Somewhat later, another interpretation was given to 'artificiality' and 'spontaneity' based on the Arnoldian assumption (insufficiently informed or extensive) that eighteenth-century poetry was a reflection of an age of prose and reason. In 1911, Sir George Douglas, defining 'artificiality' to mean conventions and traditions of art fashioned by society and 'spontaneity' as freedom from restraints other than those accepted by oneself, related Thomson's stylistic 'artificiality to his society: It was an age of reason, of mild enlightenment. . . . It was an age of prose rather than of poetry'.[1] But the passages occasionally identified as 'spontaneous' often turned out to be those reworked and revised.

The antitheses between 'spontaneity' and 'artificiality', 'ardour'

[1] George Douglas, *Scottish Poetry* (Glasgow, 1911), p. 71.

---

ment with expressions of Thomson's 'purity of feeling'. This view was reflected in another textbook, 'Introduction', *Thomson's Seasons*, *Winter* (English School Classics), ed. J. Franck Bright (London, 1874), p. xviii, which transmitted the errors and assumptions of the original. 'Both the beauties and the faults of his poetry are characteristic, his simplicity and childlike goodness of heart is visible in the religious and didactic tone which pervades his works, the sensuousness of his nature in his descriptions of the miseries of hardship; while the marks of indolence are only too obvious in the use of idle epithets, of lines of incongruous roughness or sweetness introduced where the contrary feeling is required, and in the want of polish that marks all his work.'

Compare Dennis's view of Thomson, J. D. (John Dennis), 'To Mr. Thomson on his Generous Concern for Mr. Dennis's Last Benefit', *Gentleman's Magazine*, III (1733), 656, with that of the above critics.

> While I reflect thee o'er, methinks, I find
> Thy various Seasons, in their author's mind!
> *Spring* in thy flow'ry *fancy*, spreads her hues;
> And like thy soft compassion sheds her dews.
> *Summer's* hot strength in thy expression glows;
> And o'er thy page a beamy ripeness throws.
> *Autumn's* rich *fruits* th'instructed reader gains,
> Who tastes the meaning *purpose* of thy strains,
> *Winter*—but that no resemblance takes from thee!

For an important distinction between personal and literary indolence, see Anna Barbauld, 'On the Poetical Works of Mr. William Collins', *The Poetical Works of Mr. William Collins* (London, 1797), pp. vii-viii.

and 'coolness', 'unforced' and 'forced' that discriminated good from bad revisions in accordance with social, psychological, or literary theories, also formed the basis for identifying the kind of unity. Theories which exclusively argued for one type of unity, in practice, made allowance for some aspect of antithetical positions. Whereas for Dr. Rundle, Daniel Webb, Hannah More and others the first term included its opposite by concealing the 'art' or 'effort', for Murdoch, Stockdale, and Sir Harris Nicolas the two terms represented antithetic types of value. For the latter, therefore, the conception of unity was qualitatively different from Johnson's; for, to them, the value was housed in fragments that were 'spontaneous' whereas, for Johnson, the value lay in its originality of expression and subject, not inconsistent with loose unity. There were grounds for recognizing in *The Seasons* the personal note, but the equation of spontaneity with it was a speculative procedure at this time almost wholly idiosyncratic.

The conception of unity as a series of fragments was recognized in the nineteenth as in the eighteenth century, but the relation between fragments—the associative transitions, the acceptance of traditional conventions—was assumed to represent psychological wholeness. Nineteenth-century critics conceived of a fragmentary unity in which the parts lost touch with the digressions or the moral didacticism. The grounds for deciding upon the pertinence of fragments were a knowledge of the poet's childhood experiences—the psychological recollections which impressed themselves upon his work or the personal affairs which unconsciously commanded his attention. Each of these demanded a somewhat different kind of 'sympathy' in terms of the knowledge which the critic brought to the poem. In these views a great part of the poem, considered as a unity with a loose spatial structure, disappeared from discussion. Moreover the poem was assumed to have a unity which was worth defending only by denying value to the digressions. But even within the fragments, John C. Shairp did not find the religious and moral tension necessary for the highest view of nature.[1] And the 1864 critic who found

[1] John C. Shairp, *On Poetic Interpretation of Nature* (Edinburgh, 1877), p. 193. For an application of this concept to the poetry of Edward Young, see George Eliot, 'Worldliness and Otherworldliness' (originally published in *Westminster Review*, 1857), *Essays* (Edinburgh, 1889), pp. 1–78, and for the defence of difficulty as an aesthetic value, see Bernard Bosanquet, *Three Lectures on Aesthetics* (London, 1915), pp. 87–97. The importance of

Thomson's revisions a basis for his 'style' was unable to indicate the qualities which defined a style.

The interesting paradox with regard to unity discovered through fragments was that the physical 'whole' was reduced to psychologically significant parts and that the historic grounds for seeing the poem in its own time reduced the 'time' to tiny recapturable moments. And Thomson, who Murdoch in 1762 had claimed was to be found in his work, was likewise reduced in these theories to a sum of few speculative characteristics.

(c) THE RELAXATION OF THE PRESSURE

> His Seasons, and his Castle of Indolence, have taken a permanent place in literature. He is one of those minor poets who are read by each successive generation with about equal favor.
>
> JOHN S. HART, 1882

When *The Seasons* was first published, it demanded a reinterpretation of unity; critics placed it within the contexts of the drama and epic or Virgil's *Georgics*. But after a hundred years of criticism the context of *The Seasons* was neither the drama, the epic, Virgil or Cowper, but Wordsworth and Tennyson. In the second half of the nineteenth century the poets no longer sought the unity of Thomson, and the critics no longer felt unity as a pressure. In 1864 the editor of *The Seasons* declared, 'Thomson's place in English literature has long ago been fixed, and criticism of his poems must in great degree be mere reflection of what others have written'.[1]

The poem which had created a reliance upon individual perceptions was now seen by poets and critics within a body of assumptions almost as rigid as the 'rules' which had to be rejected. For this poem and for this period the 'unity' assumptions were not re-examined, though at the beginning of the twentieth century the Victorian interpretation of 'nature' no longer satisfied critics of Thomson. It took a century for the appeal to perceptions to become a critical 'given'; but by the time of John Veitch's *The Feeling for Nature in Scottish Poetry*

[1] Preface to *The Seasons* (Edinburgh, 1864).

Eliot's essay in the Victorian decline of *Night Thoughts* is discussed by Henry Pettit, 'The English Rejection of Young's *Night Thoughts*', *University of Colorado Studies*, Series in Language and Literature, No. 6 (Boulder, 1957), pp. 23–38.

(1887), 'imagination' and 'history' had converted a hypothesis to a principle.[1]

Thomson was still considered an uneven writer—praised for description, attacked for diction—but the reasons had changed and his function in literature had changed. He had represented to Collins the 'sweet bard', to Wordsworth the poet who brought back nature to English poetry, and to Tennyson the poet who taught him first how to look at nature. But in the late nineteenth century no poet found in Thomson the voice he sought. The critics who reserved for him a place in English literature did so not because he challenged them, but because they respected tradition.

The very appeal to perceptions which originally represented an attack on tradition could now become not only a justification for this exception but a recognition that all poetry was 'exceptional'. In his essay on 'Poetry and Criticism' (1855), George Brimley explained that poetry must represent a particular object and 'include and contain at least all the qualities or properties of an object necessary to constitute it a possible phenomenal objective whole'.[2] Every poem was an imaginative activity which constituted a whole different from other poetic wholes. Thus every poem was an 'exception' and all poetry was distinguished from science by the imagination which made it poetry.

This view of imagination, therefore, replaced the conception of unity defined by Johnson as a 'regular subordination of parts terminating in the principal and original design', but the unifying concept of the imagination did not create a relativity of ends. Whatever types of imagination were created, whether primary or secondary, physical or intellectual, pictorial (representative), idealizing or symbolic, *The Seasons* was seen as transitory to or initiating the highest types. In 1860, Thomas Shaw wrote that the 'new era' was 'first seen to glimmer . . . in the poetry of Thomson', but in 1877 John C. Shairp wrote that Thomson's 'way of handling Nature stands to that of Wordsworth or Tennyson much as Claude's landscapes do to those of Turner or some of the other modern painters'.[3]

The absorption of the appeal to perceptions into the assumptions of literary theory made them a part of a more general theory of organic or imaginative wholeness which attributed the awkward or

[1] John Veitch, *The Feeling for Nature in Scottish Poetry* (Edinburgh, 1887), I, Chap. II.

[2] George Brimley, *Essays* (London, 1882), p. 176.

[3] Shairp, *On Poetic Interpretation of Nature*, pp. 189–90.

artificial parts of the poem to Thomson's indolence or his affections, personal or social. But this absorption did not serve to question the theory itself.

Summarizing the definitions of 'unity' by Coleridge, Lamb, Dowden, Moulton, and Pater, Bray (1898) declared:

> Occasionally during the latter portion of the eighteenth century, and during all the present century, the term 'unity' has represented an activity in the mind either of the author or the reader; if in the mind of the author, the unifying principle is the imagination; if in the mind of the reader, the unity is one of mental impression, of emotional effect. But whether referring to the active creation of literature, or to its more passive appreciation, unity is never regarded as depending upon formal regularity within the composition itself. Unity represents an imaginative blending of the different parts of a composition with one another,—a continuity of thought and feeling.[1]

This description of the shift in unity is accurate only in the most general terms, for the unifying principle of imagination did see formal properties of association as responsible for 'one' impression of the whole. Association, Heron illustrated (1793), worked by contrast, by suggestion, and Cunningham's examples were governed by assumptions of representative instances in the poem. Moreover the reprinting of Aikin's essay and its description of the details of each season as late as 1852 made more than one unifying principle available throughout the first half of the nineteenth century. And Johnson's view of spatial unity was held up as sufficiently important to be answered by some theories of imaginative unity. All theories of unity were, in terms of 'progress', placed within a context of evolutionary literary history in the second half of the century.

But more important than this diversity of unity was the continuity of the analogy with man's life in unifying *The Seasons*, with the consequent neglect of the cyclical pattern of the poem. Unity continued, in Cunningham, to be seen as a 'progress' rather than as recurrent or cyclical phenomena with variations of life and death, action and inaction. The theory of imagination, therefore, tended to reduce the variation and to stress the similarities within the poem. The theory of imagination included the descriptions, digressions and didactic passages, but a critic like William Bayne who argued that the 'plan' in each season included all that Thomson proposed, had to

[1] J. Bray, *A History of English Critical Terms* (Boston, 1898).

make excuses for the tenuous connection of the digressions with 'the natural development of each of the year's divisions'. Thus 'relevance' or 'connection' was of two types: one type was artistic, i.e. structurally interesting, and the other was psychological, i.e. structurally irrelevant but inserted to prevent monotony. The more comprehensive the unity, the more it was necessary to rely upon non-literary justification.

In 1898 William Bayne wrote:

> The plan of *The Seasons* is exceedingly uniform. *Autumn*, the last to be composed, differed in no important point of form from *Winter*, the original of the series. The plan adopted was that of the natural development of each of the year's divisions. Considerable objection has sometimes been taken as to the introduction of the didactic passages which appear in all. These, it is true, embody the poet's philosophy of Nature, but are by no means of the best illustrations of his art. But apart from their philosophical bearing they have in their place a distinct literary utility, creating as they do an appropriate sequence of pauses in the general narrative. The same may be said on behalf of his idyllic stories. None of them, with the exception of that on Lavinia, can count for more than a necessary variation in the treatment of the subject at large. Without these endeavours at diversity, the purely descriptive discourse would have incurred undoubted risks of monotony; and, howsoever serious their faults, the discretion that originated their introduction was a sound one. The usage, in short, is not more than an ordinary necessity of any continued literary composition. Any teller of a story who wishes his narrative to be engrossing must do the same.[1]

Two years later (1900), however, Bayne conceded that 'Johnson showed 'greater accuracy than he generally exhibited with reference to Thomson as a poet and as a man, [when he] declared that the glaring defect of *The Seasons* was "its want of method". And yet this, too, is not the whole truth.'[2] The truth was that distinctive aspects of nature, episodes, and reflections while pertinent to each season did not quite 'dove-tail'. But if they were to dove-tail in the 'natural development of each season', such 'natural' development presupposed a series of discriminated transitions, distinguishing those which did from those which did not dove-tail. Such formal distinctions, however, Bayne assumed but did not make.

[1] William Bayne, *James Thomson* (Edinburgh, 1898), pp. 113–14.

[2] William Bayne, ed. *Poems by James Thomson* (London, 1900), p. xxvi.

Imaginative associationism saw the poem as a whole with a single speaker; it therefore had difficulty with the several styles or 'voices' in the poem. The burlesque fox-hunter, the references to the innocent speaker—

> Pleased have I, in my cheerful morn of life,
> When nursed by careless solitude I lived
> And sung of nature with unceasing joy,
> Pleased have I wandered through your rough domain;
> [*Winter*, ll. 7–10]

the narrator of idealized stories, the nationalistic poet, were all 'voices' and the 'transition' was interpreted in terms of subject rather than of narrator or point of view. For this reason the digressions seemed not to belong.

The analysis of 'not belonging' or of lack of coherence arose from a number of alternatives. In so far as *The Seasons* was placed within the Augustan period it was seen as being freed from the 'incurable habit of reposing on mechanical helps' and thus was searching for an adequate form. Again, in terms of the evolutionary theory, the poem was seen as resulting from a series of revisions so that, as Edmund Gosse wrote (1906), 'though so successful in essence' it was not 'without incoherencies in execution'.[1] But the attempt to specify types of incoherence arose also from a theory of character or unity of man and work in which Thomson's character was seen as creative but indolent, or as that of an uncomfortable Augustan. The hypothesis of imaginative unity led to a more stringent and formal analysis of transitions and parts—of Thomson's philosophy, diction, and nature—and placed each of these elements within the unfolding of romantic poetry, not of Thomson's own unity. Thus the unity itself was 'transitional': incoherence and lack of unity was due to conflicting artistic ends. This view was expressed by Gosse as follows:

> It was not a small difficulty connected with the composition of this poem, that the subject was necessarily of a desultory character. No thread of narrative runs through, it has no distinct evolution. The poet watches the year revolve, describes what he sees, and sums up his reflections in a hymn to the spirit which pervades the whole. A certain air of indecision hangs about the entire central

[1] Edmund Gosse, 'A Critical Study of James Thomson', *The Seasons*, ed. Henry D. Roberts (London, 1906), p. xxvii.

plan of *The Seasons*, an air which we need not regret, since some of the most beautiful touches which the poem contains are due to this intellectual vacillation. The author is never certain whether to remain at home or to fly abroad. Now his reveries seem to be those of a man whose experience has never passed outside his mountain home at Southdean, who has scarcely crossed the ford of the sweeping Jed, and to whom all that lies beyond the scalp of Carter Fell is unknown ground. Now he writes as one to whom both hemispheres are familiar, from China to Peru. More inconsistently still, he sometimes languishes for the age of innocence to come again, for

> Those white unblemished minutes, whence
> The fabling poets took their golden age,

to free him from 'these iron times, these dregs of life', and then, immediately afterwards, he pities the barbarian, and congratulates himself on the regular march of modern civilisation, casting off the inexperience of infancy, 'and ever rising with the rising mind'.

This absence of coherency, in the execution no less than in the plot of *The Seasons*, is by no means such a disadvantage to it as we might be prepared to suppose. The existence of an iron framework, especially in the eighteenth century with its incurable habit of reposing on mechanical helps, might have injured the poem far more than it improved it. As it is, the individuality of Thomson has to come every instant to the aid of his conception; the poet is forced to carry on the thread of his languidly constructed poem by a repeated effort of character, and the consequence is that we are charmed and startled by the incessant interposition of a living mind, where we might have been abandoned to a system or a plot. The inconsistencies do not trouble us, for they are those of a natural man, and our sympathies are gratified even when we smile at the wavering judgment of our charming interlocutor. His didactic intentions, moreover, are not, in our eyes, his main claim to our respect. We hang upon his lips not to hear what he has to say about providence and civilization, but to enjoy the rich stores of his observation, to look out at nature with his keen and brilliant vision.[1]

The perceptive comments on the speaker were made within the context of a 'character' theory of unity, governed by vagaries of the subject. Yet Gosse implied that the subject did not need to be disunified despite the fact that it 'was of a desultory character'. Gosse's criticism took as the 'end' or purpose of the poem the speaker's

[1] Gosse, 'A Critical Study', pp. xxv–xxvii.

observations and reflections upon the changes in nature. This view placed the 'charm' of the poem's unity upon the 'charm' of the speaker, disengaging imagination as a way of conceiving experience from his 'brilliant vision'. The alleged 'indolence' of Thomson found its way into the unity because the poem was 'languidly constructed' despite the fact that it was carefully and precisely revised (as Gosse confirmed).

The narrator's indecision in treating his experience as an innocent or as a man of knowledge and experience, his 'intellectual vacillation', provided some of the most beautiful touches which the poem contained. But such a causal relationship was in no way demonstrable, and the philosophic implications of the poem were ignored in order to defend a looseness and freedom attributed to the natural man. Thus the recognition of incoherence in the speaker was excusable on the grounds that the alternatives available were to become mechanical or 'unnatural'—alternatives which did not seriously consider the meaning of 'charm'.

Two years later (1908) in his biography, *James Thomson*, George Macaulay continued the pursuit of the unity of *The Seasons* and began with Johnson's statement about 'want of method'. 'It is true, no doubt', wrote Macaulay,

> that the poems are of a somewhat rambling character, but it would be unjust to say they are without plan. *Winter* describes the gradual progress of the season, from wind and rain to snow-storms, from snow to frost and from frost to thaw; *Summer* sets before us the process of a day from sunrise to midnight; and *Spring* displays the influence of the season upon the natural world, in regular ascent from the lower to the higher spheres: *Autumn* alone can, with any justice, be said to be incoherent. But the advantage of regularity is to a great extent lost in all these poems by diffuseness and digressions; and in so far as each poem produces an impression of unity, this is chiefly by virtue of the accumulation of scenes harmonized to a particular tone, and representing in various forms the same characteristics of external nature. The total impression would undoubtedly be more satisfactory, if there were not an element of confusion and disorder in the materials by which it is produced.[1]

Macaulay was cognizant of two types of unity: unity of season and unity of *The Seasons*. The unity of each season was determined by

[1] Macaulay, pp. 106–7.

the holistic view of a single 'tone' and this could only be achieved by a harmony of particular scenes. Although he wrote in the language of 'impression' upon the reader, it was clear he assumed that this harmony was attainable by certain formal transitions which prevented diffuseness and digressions. Each season was 'unified' by a dominant set of nature scenes the regular tone of which was broken by digressions. Thus the fishing scene in *Spring* did not display the influence of the season upon the natural world and was, therefore, a disunifying influence.

Since the critic wished to proceed empirically, the question was how intimate a unity to demand. The poem was composed of words, phrases, clauses, sentences, verse paragraphs, and groups of stanzas. The determination of what was to be unified was answerable not in a specific way by the poem itself but by some determination of the kind of genre it fitted. Johnson had assumed the spatial unity of the poem and Gosse had granted it a desultory character. Granting, however, the 'desultory character' of the subject, the critic had to determine whether its desultoriness was determined by key passages—dominant tone—or by all passages. For if the latter was granted then that quality which was held in common by all actions, events, invocations, provided the basis for unity. Such a statement, therefore, that '*Autumn* alone can, with any justice, be said to be incoherent', would be an admission that no possible organizing principle underlay this section. Such a poem is possible, but highly unlikely; it surely is not Thomson's *Autumn* which deals with the pleasurable as well as ironic surfeit of life and nature, and of which Macaulay wrote: 'In *Autumn* there is less appearance of a systematic plan than in the other poems, but on the whole the natural course of the season is followed from harvest-time to the fall of the leaf, and so to the fogs and frosts of the later season.'[1]

The description of 'unity' of each season, in Macaulay's criticism, presupposed that unity was a value by which other values in the poem were to be judged. Thus whatever hindered the order seriously hindered the grasp of the 'whole', and the assumption of holism was a 'given'. Yet in this poem there was no reason to assume such authority for unity; rather it was one possible source of value. Referring to the fishing scene in *Spring*, he wrote:

The orderly development of the poem is here rather seriously

[1] Macaulay, *James Thomson*, p. 122.

> interrupted by a passage, inserted in the later editions, which describes some of the occupations of the morning and noon-day hours in spring. The passage in itself is valuable, but there is no proper connection here: it is, perhaps, the most glaring instance in *The Seasons* of this kind of interpolation of picturesque or poetical passages without sufficient regard to the general sequence. What we have here is a scene of fly-fishing for trout, described with an accuracy and a fulness of detail which betrays the enthusiastic angler.[1]

There are two comments to be made about this criticism. One is that this passage can be fitted into the unity of *Spring* if one assumes that this season presents the joy, peace and violence of love. Then fishing, which represents a joy that involves killing, is a contrast to the ideal man of the golden age who did not harm living things but loved them. The other point—that the passage 'in itself is valuable'—assumes that value in a poem can be completely divorced from any connection with it. A passage may be knit in many ways to the 'end' of a poem or it may be only loosely connected, but its value in the poem depends upon its music, the extent of its reference and the working of its words and sentences and ideas as well as its unity, which may be, though it is not necessarily, the chief basis for value.

By making unity a normative rather than a descriptive quality, the critic found unifying contexts to be 'good' and those not relevant to be 'bad' for the poem even though 'good in themselves'. But such a position tended for Macaulay, as it did for Aikin, to restrict the poem to a dominant type of value rather than gauging the various value characteristics, unity being only one. The rejection of irrelevant passages created a special unity for the poem rather than working from the total work and urging a more or less stringent unity upon parts. One of the difficulties of this position was that it had to deny that the total poem was a context since only parts of it were relevant to the chosen end: Aikin selected the economy of nature and man, Cunningham the progress of each season as analogy with the life of man, Macaulay the progress of seasonal nature, and the most restrictive form of unity was urged by Patricia Spacks (1959): 'the specific concept of a pattern of natural order as manifesting the glory of God, which is the dominant philosophic theme of *The*

[1] Macaulay, p. 110.

Seasons, gives it what approaches organic unity'. In this latter view the poem did not possess 'total thematic unity' and could, therefore, only be considered by excluding much of its material.[1]

Whether considering the unity of each season or of *The Seasons*, the critics operated by contexts, and the two major differences were between those who excluded passages as 'irrelevant' or 'incoherent' towards an end, and those who accepted all passages and, like Johnson or Gosse, tried to arrive at a common ground—such as spatial unity or unity of speaker. This meant that the exclusionists considered unity as the chief value and treated it as the basis for judgement and the inclusionists treated it descriptively and considered it as one of several possible grounds for value.

But these two positions, and the particular disagreements about unity, cannot be easily accepted as 'perspectives'—as taking different but equally adequate views of unity. For if the guide for analysis of unity is indeed the published poem, then the theory which explains its parts rather than a selection of its parts is more adequate—putting aside the issues of inept or wrong explanations. Determining the 'end', setting up a hypothesis toward which to work, is not only a factual matter—establishing the text, determining relations between parts—it also rests upon individual judgement in order to arrive at a context (words, sentences, etc.) pertinent to unity. For the pertinent context is defined by lines, rhythmic patterns, verse paragraphs, actions, which rest upon insights that need to be validated. The selection of associated passages by Aikin, Heron, Cunningham were only sometimes identical, and the definition of unity depended upon the accumulated relations among such passages.

When, in the eighteenth century, the unity of *The Seasons* challenged its critics, the efforts to defend it by redefining unity also involved, for Aikin, a defence of a new kind of descriptive poem. Unity became, therefore, defined by a valued end, and unity became the chief value. Instances of unity were identified as valued passages, at the same time that other passages possessed lesser value. For Shiels, and for Johnson, however, unity remained a descriptive term which made the new poem acceptable, i.e. granted it a hearing, and its values were placed on traits which included unity among others. Unity as an end, therefore, has been entangled in theories of holism with valued rather than descriptive contexts. And the determination

[1] Patricia Spacks, *The Varied God* (Berkeley and Los Angeles, 1959), p. 43.

of the appropriateness of one or the other depended on what held *The Seasons* together.

Shiels's view of unity as an assemblage of poetical ideas, Johnson's 'many appearances subsisting all at once', Cunningham's unifying fervour of the imagination have identified 'unity' with emotional tone, subject matter, order of development. In descending to particular examples, the critics agree on the variety of subjects, but some assume that they ought to be tightly knit, others accept its looseness. The very naming of unity implies the critics' attitude to a tight or loose structure—'assemblage of poetical ideas', 'miscellany', 'loose plan'.[1]

But the choice of unity is not a matter of preference: more than subject unifies a poem, and the critics who assume that unity in *The Seasons* is—or ought to be—organic as in *Oedipus Rex* demand of the poem a structure inconsistent with its development. For it contains repetitions, contrasts, stated and implied visions of nature. In accepting the poem as a special kind of unity, critics have sometimes substituted names rather than descriptions. All critics accept the fact that some parts of *The Seasons* are 'better' than others, but there is no reason to believe that this is due to a tighter relation to the 'end' of the poem. *The Seasons* is unified by a narrator with different 'voices', by subjects which are repeated because reflective of nature's pattern, by certain didactic affirmations of belief in God's power. What critics have begun to do, therefore, is to discriminate the kinds of unity, the sections which hang together and the techniques used. Only a beginning has been made in outlining these procedures; some, like the metaphoric descriptions in natural and human postures, creating a stylized 'family' of nature, have yet to be investigated.

But in order to do this certain critical assumptions of 'unity' need to be divested of authority. In *The Seasons* unity is not organic, and all values do not stem from it. Moreover, it is not very rewarding to assume that *The Seasons* might have been a much more unified poem

[1] For 'miscellany' see Oliver Elton, *A Survey of English Literature, 1730–1780* (London, 1928), I, 357. See also A. M. Oliver, 'The Scottish Augustans', *Scottish Poetry: A Critical Survey*, ed. James Kinsley (London, 1955), p. 124. 'The "embellishments" are added with a hand so ungrudging that the poem becomes a miscellany—and the eighteenth century loved miscellanies.' Douglas Grant, *Thomson*, p. 115: '*The Seasons* is in fact a collection of many poems.' In 1724 Allan Ramsay declared that the 'best Works are but a kind of Miscellany', Durham, p. 401. For 'loose plan', see McKillop, p. 129.

if Thomson had attended to this aim. On the contrary, the aim of Thomson seemed in no way likely to create that kind of unity; in his dramas, when he wished it, he achieved it. What he presented in *The Seasons* was experimental and exploratory, parts held together in a loose type of unity. At no point in his revisions did he seek to reduce all passages to a common language or a single voice.

The critics who have recognized this have tried to indicate the varieties of unifying techniques. They have also accepted the fact that once such techniques are described, some reasons can be given for passages which are analogous (like the storms or sunsets) but which are not equally forceful or expressive. Alan D. McKillop's summary (1942) can be seen as representative of this view of unity.

> The loose plan on which Thomson laid out *The Seasons* makes possible the coexistence of a number of patterns. There is a long ascent up the philosophic ladder that admits of an account of various levels of being. There is also the drama of the forces of nature within the extensive prospect: obscure impulsions and instincts, vibrations and echoes in earth and air, the ceaseless, shifting play of light and color. All this has philosophical and religious implications, but it may at times be accepted without analysis. Sometimes it is not seen vividly and breaks down into lists and catalogues. Sometimes there is delicate notation of detail that is all the more striking because of its position in a larger scheme. Throughout there is likely to be a loose employment of the principle of contrast—the beautiful over against the ugly, the delightful against the terrible, the generative forces of nature over against violence and destruction.[1]

Although not all critics recognize this 'loose plan', it seems the best definition available of what Thomson meant when he wrote

> These, as they change, Almighty Father! these
> Are but the varied God.
>
> [*Hymn*, ll. 1–2]

[1] McKillop, pp. 129–30.

III

THINGS, IMAGES AND IMAGINATION: THE RECONSIDERATION OF DESCRIPTION

> Poetry consists much more in description than is generally imagined.
>
> J. TRAPP, *Lectures on Poetry*

EVEN BEFORE THE PUBLICATION of Thomson's *Winter* (1726), description as a poetic technique had become a controversial issue, owing to its extension from a traditional rhetorical device to the whole or a considerable part of a poem. The initial disagreement arose over the value of this extension. The justification of description was grounded first in new theories of imitation, then in theories of imaginative composition and perception. The critical issue was to justify the reproportioning of the areas of poetry so that description—regardless of how defined—would be defended.

The reproportioning of poetic values moved in two directions: the naturalistic grounds of description led to discussion of details of nature and their expression in language; the other was the imaginative recreation of nature by the poet and its apprehension by the reader. Here, again, certain views of the problem disappeared from criticism: 'description' in *The Seasons* could no longer be considered as a traditional poetic device and this conventional view was supplanted by the theory that any kind of details could be used to create moving descriptions. In other words, criticism used diversity of evidence to arrive at an embracing economical generalization.

By the end of the eighteenth century, criticism which became embracing (encyclopedic) in this respect, became restrictive in its analysis of Thomson's precision. With the publication of *The Task* (1785), a poem similar in subject and treatment to *The Seasons*, the descriptive analysis became more particularized yet narrower in range. No critic denied the accuracy and vividness of Thomson's descriptions, only its importance in the total poem. Disagreement, therefore, did not result from disagreement upon the function of description, but upon the importance of its function or its relation to other parts of the poem. Such disagreements, however, were amenable to critical analysis.

(a) THE DEFINITIONS OF 'DESCRIPTION'

> The first capital work in which natural description was professedly the principal object.
>
> J. AIKIN

When James Thomson used the word 'description' in his preface to the second edition of *Winter* (1726), he applied it to the depiction of natural scenes which inspired him with religious feeling, attributing to poetic description the possibility of conveying these same responses: 'I only wish my description of the various appearance of nature in *Winter* (and, as I purpose, in the other Seasons) may have the good fortune to give the reader some of that true pleasure which they, in their agreeable succession, are always sure to inspire into my heart.'[1] Nature, he explained, awakened poetical enthusiasm, philosophical reflection and moral sentiment.

[1] 'Preface' quoted in Robertson, p. 242. Eighteenth-century meanings of the word and concept 'nature' have been explored as history of ideas in the works of Arthur O. Lovejoy, *The Great Chain of Being* (Cambridge, Mass., 1936), and 'Nature as Aesthetic Norm', 'The Parallel of Classicism and Deism', *Essays in the History of Ideas* (Baltimore, 1948), pp. 69–98, and that of his followers: Lois Whitney, *Primitivism and the Idea of Progress* (Baltimore, 1934), and Margaret M. Fitzgerald, *First Follow Nature* (New York, 1947). Other approaches to 'nature' can be found in James R. Sutherland, 'Nature', *A Preface to Eighteenth Century Poetry* (Oxford, 1948), pp. 111–19 and C. S. Lewis, 'Nature', *Studies in Words* (Cambridge, 1960), pp. 24–74, who declares that 'a full account of *nature* as a term in neo-classical criticism would require a whole book' (p. 55). Lewis's comment on the term 'nature' in *The Seasons* seems to me excessively narrow: 'Thomson is actually thinking of British landscapes when he says *Nature*.' See also Joseph W. Beach, *The Concept of Nature in Nineteenth Century Poetry* (New York, 1936), pp. 3–27.

But this explanation of 'description' as conveying religious feelings analogous to those called forth by the objects themselves was but one of several contemporary meanings of 'description'. Thomson dropped the preface in 1730, and, noting the reconsideration of the subject which was going on, he may have preferred to let the poem speak for itself. No one, indeed, spoke for the preface, until Sir Egerton Brydges re-published it in 1806. Literary description was, at the beginning of the eighteenth century, the least recorded in formal dictionaries. The two dominant definitions were the logical and geometrical, and in each of these, the enumeration of details was a characteristic, for in geometrical definition, description referred to drawing a line or circle. Description even in non-literary contexts, was identified with details and with a visual process.

In Kersey (1715) 'to describe' meant 'to write or set down in writing: in *Geometry*, to draw a line, a circle, etc.' Bailey (1722) defined 'description' as 'a setting forth the Natures and Properties of any thing, either by Figures or words'. Dyche and Pardon (1758) defined it as 'an account of the general accidents, shapes, and properties of a thing, in order to know and distinguish it from something else; in Geometry it is the constructing or forming a figure'.[1]

The setting forth the nature of a 'thing' in words, the rhetorical application of 'description', was apparent in such a use as Rapin's in his essay on pastorals: 'Theocritus', he wrote, 'made a long immoderate description of his Cup', whereas Virgil was sparing in his description of Meliboeus' beechen pot. And 'sparing' or brevity was, according to Rapin, the proper procedure for handling description.[2] This use of 'description', as a device for comparing language

[1] John Kersey, *A General English Dictionary* (London, 1715), Nathan Bailey, *An Universal Etymological English Dictionary* (London, 1721), Thomas Dyche and William Pardon, *A New General English Dictionary* (London, 1750), E. Chambers' *Cyclopaedia* (London, 1741), I, defined 'description' as 'an imperfect, or inaccurate definition of a thing' because it distinguished one 'thing' from another by enumerating its particulars without explaining its 'essence'. Johnson defined 'description' under four heads: 1. 'The act of delineating or expressing any person or thing by perceptible properties.' 2. 'Any sentence or passage in which any thing is described.' 3. 'A lax description.' 4. 'The qualities expressed in a description.'

[2] René Rapin, 'A Treatise de Carmine Pastorali', prefixed to Thomas Creech's *Idylliums of Theoritus* (London, 1684), p. 65. See also Pope quoted in Joseph Spence, *Anecdotes*, ed. Samuel W. Singer (London, 1820), pp. 139–40: 'It is a great fault, in descriptive poetry, to describe everything.

with the object referred to, was confined to small objects and views to be used as ornament or embellishment in poetry. 'Views, and little Descriptions of Lawns and Groves,' wrote Joseph Trapp in 1713, 'ought always to be interspersed in these Poems [Pastorals], whatsoever the Subject of them be.' And in 1718, Anthony Blackwall defined 'lively description' as 'a figure of speech' which provided 'such a strong and beautiful Representation of a thing, as gives the Reader a distinct View and satisfactory Notion of it'.[1]

But although Trapp referred to 'description' as a literary device which had been practised by the ancients, he offered to extend the meaning of 'description' so that it referred to rural objects as well as to human actions, and he sought to extend the meaning of poetry to include illustrations [reflection] as well as imitation [description]. This extension was based on the assumption that description of things, like imitations of actions, depended upon the comparison of words with the objects described. 'It is certain', he wrote, 'if by Imitation is meant that which impresses upon the Mind a true and genuine Representation of any Thing, it will be no less repugnant to common Sense than to *Aristotle's*, to affirm that nothing but Actions can be imitated. For besides them, we see Passions, Things, Places, and Men are imitated not only by Poets, but by Painters too.' Imitation was 'that which impresses upon the Mind a true and genuine Representation of any Thing', and 'illustration' referred to 'things that relate to Science and Discipline, such as the Ideas of the Mind, Vertues, Vices, Manners and the like [which] are *illustrated* by being explained; but no one will say that by being explained they are *imitated*'.[2]

[1] Joseph Trapp, *Lectures on Poetry*, tr. anon. [London, 1742,] p. 174. Anthony Blackwall, *A New Introduction to the Classics* (London, 1718), p. 238.

[2] Trapp, pp. 14, 16.

[That is the fault in Thomson's Seasons.] The good artists (but when I named them, I meant Virgil) have no long descriptions: commonly no above ten lines, and scarce ever thirty.' See also Le Bossu, 'Of Descriptions', *Epick Poem*, pp. 239–43; descriptions are properly defined as parts of long recitals; they should be short and appropriate. '*Seneca* is far from this Method. If he has any Recital to make, tho' never so Melancholy and frightful, he begins it with such *Descriptions* as are not only useless, but trifling and foolish' (p. 242). For a modern statement of the functional use of descriptions, see A. Clutton-Brock, 'Description in Poetry', *Essays and Studies* (Oxford, 1911), II, 91–103.

The distinction between 'illustration' and 'imitation' which Trapp made was ineffective because virtues, vices, and manners were nevertheless explained with reference to human actors and could, therefore, be classed as 'true and genuine representations' of behaviour. For it was clear that a 'true' and 'genuine' representation extended not merely to natural description, but to manners, passions, and sentiments. The 'true' and 'genuine' representation indicated that the criterion for description was a specific literal reality, the 'true', rather than the ideal in the mind of the artist.

In the midst of the inquiries about 'description', there appeared *Winter* (1726), *Summer* (1727), *Spring* (1728) and then *The Seasons* (1730). It became a key poem in the developing discussion because it offered a naturalistic view of the external world. The definitions indicated that 'description' was a visual act or words which 'set forth' shapes and properties so that they could be visualized. Description in rhetoric seemed tied to reality and, since the reality was considered one and unchangeable, the words were to represent it 'truely' and 'genuinely'. *The Seasons* therefore provided a basis for analysing the kinds of details necessary to convey 'truly' the 'things' they described, the language in which they were expressed, and the relation of this expressiveness to the reader.

The concept of an external world in which 'things', not words, were to be learned was expressed by Thomas Sprat in 1668. Ornaments of language had once served the uses of knowledge, but now, they made 'the *Fancy* disguise the best things, if they come sound and unadorn'd'. The strategy of the time, therefore, demanded a remedy for this extravagance, and a return to the objects that were prior to language. Cowley in his 'Ode to the Royal Society' stressed the need to return to 'things, the Mind's right Object'.

> From Words, which are but Pictures of the Thought
> (Though we our Thoughts from them perversely drew)
> To Things, the Mind's right Object, be it brought,
>
> . . . . .
>
> The real Object must command
> Each Judgment of his Eye, and Motion of his Hand.[1]

[1] Abraham Cowley, *To the Royal Society* (London, 1667). For discussions of language and the role of the Royal Society, see R. F. Jones, *The Triumph of the English Language* (London, 1953); for 'words' and 'things' before the eighteenth century, see A. O. Howell, '*Res et Verba*; Words and Things', *ELH*, XIII (1946), 131–42.

The ideal of language was to be as plain as possible and to correspond —in number and directness—to the objects described. The ideal which Sprat sought was a 'return back to the primitive purity and shortness, when men deliver'd so many *things* almost in an equal number of *words*'.[1] And in his *Essay*, John Locke warned of the dangerous dissociation of words from things. In contrast to this view of exactness of language—the test of words was the things described—stood the view that things could only be described by evoking their vividness in language. And if the first was identified with scientific discourse, the second was related to Longinian rhetoric. For it was Longinus's view that one function of the orator was to evoke in himself images or pictures which were not only the result of expressions of thought, but 'in a more particular and confined sense' referred to 'Discourses we make, when through any extraordinary Transport of Mind we seem to view the things we speak of, and when we place them in their full Light, before those who hear us'.[2] Another defence of dictional freedom was the model of the Hebrew writings—'in his first pieces, *The Seasons*,' wrote Murdoch of Thomson (1762), 'we see him at once assume the majestic freedom of an Eastern writer'—which rejected the stiffness and economy of formal language. From these two views of description, there arose a series of critical explanations new to poetry and equally new to criticism.

One group of theories stressed vividness rather than action, force rather than economy or brevity, and used scripture to imply a rejection of the dichotomy between the literary values of secular and prophetic writings. The result was a development of theories which attributed to poets—and later to readers—a visual imagination. The external world was reseen in language that was a picture language. The descriptive vigour was attributed to the expression, and the analysis of diction became a significant problem in identifying the 'genuine' description. Joseph Warton (1756) identified actual observation as the basis for precise and original literary description.[3]

[1] Thomas Sprat, *History of the Royal Society of London, Critical Essays of the Seventeenth Century*, ed. J. E. Spingarn (Oxford, 1908), II, 118.

[2] *Longinus*, tr. L. Welsted, *Works* (London, 1724), p. 183.

[3] Joseph Warton, *An Essay on the Genius and Writings of Pope* (London, 1782), 4th ed., I, 42. Part I was published in 1756. Description replaced pastoral as a genre in the late eighteenth century. A bibliography of writings on pastoral poetry in the eighteenth century can be found in J. E. Congleton, *Theories of Pastoral Poetry in England, 1684–1798* (Gainesville, 1952).

The history of descriptive criticism moved from the localization of problems in the visual presentation of external nature to the description of the landscape of the mind,[1] from sight to insight, and the most obvious example of this shift appeared in observation of the 'thing' or 'object'. Such observation indicated the development of psychological meanings attributed to or developed from the literal terms—'image' to 'imagination', 'prospect' (view and anticipation), 'vision' (outer and inner sight), and 'revision', 'landscape', and 'inscape'. Such terms internalized the object and created new series of comparisons, the 'eye of the mind' and the 'external eye', accepted by Allan Ramsay in 1725 as two separate faculties, were joined in the nineteenth century by the unifying imagination.[2]

Simultaneously with the conception of description as 'vividness'—a theory which was identified with the mode of perception of works of art, the theory of imagination and creation—'description' continued for other critics to be limited to inanimate nature rather than human actions or to literal accuracy rather than emotive vividness. The two conceptions were based on complementary views of 'nature', the first dealing with the internal unity of nature and its external expressions and the second with the extent of the representation of nature of which description formed but one element.

Description had, as pointed out above, been consistently tied to a rhetorical and mathematical precision as one of their elements, but the difference between the seventeenth- and nineteenth-century expression of this view was the realization that 'description forms a part of every poem' (Blair) and that it was, because of its prevalence and its objectivity, a test of a writer's imagination. This view maintained, in a naïve way, that imagination exercised itself most on 'objects' rather than on feelings or actions and, in this respect, held common ground with description as 'vivid'.

At the beginning of the nineteenth century, 'description' was defined extensively as subject matter, a device, a genre. George Dyer (1812) declared,

[1] For a perceptive discussion of psychological landscape, see H. M. McLuhan, 'Tennyson and Picturesque Poetry', *Essays in Criticism* (1951), 268–74. See also McLuhan, 'The Aesthetic Moment in Landscape Poetry', *English Institute Essays, 1951* (New York, 1952), pp. 168–81.

[2] Allan Ramsay, 'Preface to the *Ever-Green*' (1724), *Critical Essays of the 18th Century*, ed. Willard H. Durham (New Haven, 1915), p. 24.

> The adjunct *descriptive*, in the present connexion, is not to be confined exclusively to a particular species of poetic composition, called descriptive poetry; such, for instance, as Thomson's Seasons, Denham and Grongar Hill: it applies to subject and matter, rather than to mode, or any thing specific, to description or scenery in general, which may increase the elegance of the ode, improve even the dignity of tragedy, and heighten the majesty of the epic: in short, it may assist any poetry, as well as form the characteristic excellence of what is properly called a descriptive poem.[1]

Werner Heisenberg has pointed out that during the nineteenth century nature became, in science, a collective concept for all those areas of experience which could be entered through science and technology 'regardless of whether or not they appeared as "nature" '.

> The phrase 'description of nature' lost more and more of its original significance of a living and meaningful account of nature. Increasingly it became to mean the mathematical description of nature, i.e. an accurate and concise yet comprehensive collection of data about relations that hold in nature.[2]

The decline of 'description' as a value for Victorian critics of *The Seasons* was due not to a denial of its accuracy but to a distinction between 'description' of nature—'to picture what the eye sees and the ear hears'—and 'interpretation' of nature—when the poet 'enters into the life and movement of Nature by a kind of imaginative sympathy and brings . . . a conviction that he has been allowed for a moment to penetrate into their secret'.[3]

Shairp's distinction (1877) between 'description' and 'interpretation' contrasted the superficiality of Thomson's feelings with the depth of Wordsworth's. Shairp's interpretation of nature stressed awareness of inner strife and stubborn pain which man felt, and this view of nature involved a close interrelation between man and the

[1] George Dyer, 'On the Use of Topography in Poetry', *Poetics* (London, 1812), II, 115. For other discussions of 'topographical' poetry, see Hilda Taylor, *Topographical Poetry during the Renaissance* (unpublished dissertation, Chicago, 1926), and John Aubin, *Topographical Poetry in the Eighteenth Century* (New York, 1936).

[2] Werner Heisenberg, *The Physicist's Conception of Nature* (London, 1958), p. 11.

[3] Shairp, *On Poetic Interpretation of Nature*, p. 110. Shairp quoted Matthew Arnold's essay on Maurice de Guérin to explain what he meant by 'interpretation'—the power to awaken in the reader a sense of the divine in nature.

natural world. But Thomson's feeling was identified with his expressed religious views rather than with the implications of the energetic storms, rains, and beauties of nature. The term 'description' in so far as it referred to a type of poetry written in the eighteenth century reflected an absence of that moral conflict which Shairp identified with 'good' nature poetry. The misinterpretation of 'description' as a definition of what Thomson, for example, was doing, is prevalent in other modern uses which define 'description' as 'discourse whose object is to present a picture' or a use of language which is formal and rhetorical rather than iconic—Leavis' distinction between 'description' and 'enactment'.[1]

All such definitions are based on identifications of 'description' with drawing and mathematics, with precision, with the merely visual, for even the concept of vividness was the result of visual qualities derived from imitation or direct sight. Modern critics who reject this eighteenth-century view usually reject, too, the poetry to which it refers. But there were critics, even in the eighteenth century, who refuted the visual theory in order to provide a more adequate defence of the nature poetry it originally sought to explain. In this respect, the pejorative uses of 'description' continue to propagate misapprehensions, identifying preferred values such as moral strife and complexity with 'interpretation', 'enactment'—and distasteful values, though far from accurately defined, with 'description'.

(b) J. HUGHES, T. RERESBY, J. WARTON: THE LANGUAGE OF THINGS

To every thing there is a season.
Ecclesiastes

Locke had pointed to the need to think upon 'things' rather than 'words', because the latter were treacherous and ambiguous. By thinking of things it was possible to construct a clear and 'distinct' image of the object. 'Another thing', wrote Locke, in a sentence indicating the varied use of 'things', 'which is of great use for the clear conception of Truth is if we can bring ourselves to it, to think

[1] F. R. Leavis, ' "Antony and Cleopatra" and "All for Love": A Critical Exercise', *Scrutiny*, V (1936), 158–69, for the difference between 'enacting' and 'descriptive eloquence'. See also F. R. Leavis, 'English Poetry in the Eighteenth Century', *Scrutiny*, V (1936), 13–31.

upon things abstracted and separate from words.' And the reason for this effort was that words were slippery and treacherous: 'for words are, in their own nature, so doubtful and obscure, their signification for the most part, so uncertain and undetermined which men even designedly have in their use of them increased, that if in our meditation our thoughts busy themselves with words, and stick at the names of things, it is odds but they are misled or confounded.'[1] With regard to this belief in the neutrality of things—that views of them created universal pictures in the mind and that the function of words was to call up these pictures clearly, there existed the Cartesian explanation of animal spirits given by Addison (later quoted with some doubt by Hume) and the picture theory of language. According to Tamworth Reresby (1721), every articulated word was a picture of thought which 'must be immediately painted in the Imagination; because otherwise we could not with Words paint what we had conceiv'd. Our Thoughts then are follow'd by certain Traces in the Imagination; these Traces are followed by those of Speech, and those of Speech by others of Writing, when we have a Mind to record our Conceptions . . . It is therefore manifest, that the exterior Representation of anything by the Mediation of Words, is the same as that first painted in the Brain.'[2]

Locke's argument had its impact upon writers like Henry Felton (1713) who insisted that the writer required not only clear thoughts, 'a clear Perception of the Matters he undertaketh to treat of' but a clear expression, 'a Faculty of easy Writing in plain obvious Expressions'. Yet Hildebrand Jacob (1734) attacked writers who sought the exact expression because they usually neglected great 'things'. Writers who aimed 'at being carefully finish'd in their Style', he wrote, 'are very curious and exact in their Words, [yet] have rarely any Thing *great*, and *solid* in their *Compositions*'.[3]

When Thomson in *Spring* exclaimed that the poet could never

[1] John Locke, 'Of Study', *Thoughts on Education*, ed. Rev. R. H. Quick (Cambridge, 1899), p. 200. For characteristic views of 'words' in the eighteenth century, especially their relation to things, see Samuel Werenfels, *A Discourse of Logomachy* (London, 1711), p. 176:'Let our great concern be, not to teach Words, but Things.' Joel E. Spingarn equates the concern for 'things' over 'words' with the defence of the 'turn' over the 'conceit' in the late seventeenth century; introduction, *Critical Essays of the Seventeenth Century* (Oxford, 1908), I, xlv.

[2] Tamworth Reresby, *A Miscellany* (London, 1721), pp. 20, 21.

[3] Felton, p. 106.

match the vividness of nature for 'who can paint / Like Nature', he clearly did not subscribe to the theories of the neutrality of images. The vividness of nature represented an ideal which he could only approximate, though Delacour in his poem to Thomson insisted that the latter improved upon nature in his *Seasons*.[1] But prior to Thomson, description was defended on traditional grounds; poetic views of the object involved re-creation of the object and Aristotle had explained that a dungheap could be made beautiful in description by artistic language. Addison in his essay on didactic poetry (1693) wrote that in Virgil's *Georgics* 'we receive more strong and lively ideas of things from his words, than we could have done from the objects themselves'.[2]

These two theories of poetic language differed with regard to language and its impression upon the reader. Thomson found reality more vivid than any impression of it; poetry only approximated but never achieved the immediate impact of reality. The actual impression, therefore, created an ideal which poetry could only seek but never approach. The view of Addison was that the artistry of the poet—the artistic exploitation of language—could create in the reader ideas more 'lively' than the sight of things themselves.

The differences among these views stemmed from the relation of the artist to his subject matter. The theories assumed that the poet imitated or reflected reality, but the process by which this took place in poetry was somewhat of a puzzle. For critics who argued that sight operated by pictures and that language was readily found for the pictures, there was no significant difference between vividness of description and vividness of reality. But for those who denied the picture language, vividness either could not be re-created (Thomson) or could be enhanced by artistic processes (Addison). Yet all critics argued that the criterion of poetic language was vividness. The dilemmas were of two types: one was the conversion of direct experience into poetic language. The other was the measurement of 'vividness'. The first therefore resorted to a theory of artistic imagination or skill to explain the artist's transformation of sense into poetry. Such explanations were seriously hampered by physiological explanations of picture language, for they created a poem which was a

[1] Delacour, p. 82.

[2] Joseph Addison, 'An Essay on Virgil's Georgics' (written in 1693), *Works*, ed. G. W. Greene (New York, 1856), II, 384.

direct recall of actual experience. Yet the examples of vividness repeatedly indicated that selectivity and emotional inequality operated in poetry, regardless of the original impression. The concern with artistry was hampered by traditional views of propriety and proportion and a theory of genres, so that instances of artistry were accumulated, but each was explained in terms of its own genre rather than in terms of a context creating vividness.

The other dilemma—the measurement of vividness—was usually stated in terms of the effect upon the spectator of feelings originally felt by the poet. Since such effects varied considerably, there were offered a large number of diverse, sometimes even contradictory, examples, each exhibiting vividness, according to different critics. In this sense, though each critic generalized from his example, the process was an accumulation of critical instances, and the greater the number of instances, the more extensive became the generalization. Thus, by the end of the century, 'intensity' was a quality applicable to any group of details emotively developed rather than to a single process of development.

John Hughes, the most vigorous spokesman of a revised theory of description, argued that precisely because description was based on sense perception, on sight, it was more vivid than sentiment or reflection. Hughes (1713) accepted the picture theory of language, but instead of confining it to a subordinate role in poetry, he lauded it by contrast with sentiments and reflections which, despite the fact that they were spoken by people, were not the consequences of sight.

> The Reason why Descriptions make livelier Impressions on common Readers than any other parts of a Poem, is because they are form'd of Ideas drawn from the Senses, which is sometimes too call'd Imaging, and are thus, in a manner, like Pictures, made Objects of the Sight: whereas moral Thoughts and Discourses, consisting of Ideas abstracted from Sense operate slower and with less Vivacity. Every one immediately perceives the Resemblance of Nature in the Description of a Tempest, a Palace, or a Garden; but the Beauty of proper Sentiments in the Speeches of a Prince, a General or a Counsellor, is more remote, and discern'd by a kind of second Thought or Reflection.[1]

[1] John Hughes, II, 39 (12 Feb. 1713), *The Lay Monastery* (London, 1714) pp. 227–8. This essay is included in *Poems* (London, 1735), 2 vols.; for the following quotation, see 'Charon: or The Ferry Boat', *Poems*, II, 352. For a later view that description is 'the very essential Beauty of Poetry', see

Hughes identified the seeing of rural nature with the expression of this sight, assuming that the distinctness and vividness of the sight would be mechanically translated into language. His language was communicated to the reader by what Hughes called the 'visionary Power' of the imagination. 'Every one may observe upon reading any Story or Description, which strikes his Mind in a very lively manner, that the Imagination exercises for a while, a sort of *Visionary Power*, and we fancy we view the Scene, and see before us the Objects describ'd.'

Hughes's justification of description, based as it was on an inadequate theory of sense perception, ceased to have validity when it was demonstrated that dreams and hallucinations could be more 'vivid' than sense impressions. But the value of Hughes's criticism was its encouragement to what Aristotle had referred to as the non-imitative parts—the 'idle' or descriptive parts—of a poem. Hughes did not argue for the elegance of diction in description, but its vividness. His argument was an implicit attack on the concept of imitation as well as a justification for descriptive 'licence' in poetry. If licence is to be considered a deviation from the accepted norms, Hughes's attitude was to permit licence or play in description. The importance of this justification and its implication for criticism far exceeded the arguments which Hughes used.

The traditional limits of description were defined by Pope who opposed 'pure description' [minute enumeration of particulars] to sense [thought] and who called description 'a feast made up of sauces'.[1] The attacks on description before *The Seasons* were directed against the 'wantonness' and 'chance' of descriptions. In 1720, for example, dramatic descriptions by the moderns were attacked because they did not properly relate natural descriptions to the fable, manners or sentiments, as the ancients did, but emphasized them at the expense of the design: 'They have not taken care to make 'em of some Use to the Design; but right or wrong, with a boyish Wantonness, give us such as are merely idle, and not at all necessary . . . when Fancy and Chance have furnish'd them with an Occasion to describe a Fountain, a rapid Stream, a stormy Sea, they have

[1] Quoted in Warton, *Essay on the Genius and Writings of Pope* (London, 1756), I, 50.

'An Essay on Description in Poetry', *The St. James's Journal*, LII (20 April 1723), 311.

laid out all their Genius upon it.'[1] And in March of the very same year in which *Winter* (1726) was published, a critic for the *Dublin Journal*, explaining that the function of poetry was 'to work on the Passions', declared that the 'descriptive part of Poetry, however agreeable to a well-informed Imagination, raises none of the wonderful Emotions, which are stirred by a Recital of those Actions, which are attended with Dangers, Distresses and Escapes, and the various Sentiments which arose [*sic*] in the Mind on such Occasions'.[2]

For this critic intensity resulted from identification with the narrator, whereas for Hughes intensity resulted from initial sense impressions. The controversy arose over the strength or faintness of sense impressions in contrast to sympathetic identification with the characters. The grounds for affirmation or refutation depended upon the hypothesis accepted, yet it could be argued that both hypotheses provided instances of vividness. Here the critical role of description functioned to extend the kinds of explanation of poetry, and this extension with regard to the reader was paralleled by an extension of the use of details (language and subject matter). Description, in other words, expanded the number of possible explanations characterizing the reader-work relation and the work-subject matter relation. In so doing it created a sufficient variety of instances to permit an adequate generalization.

Shiels pointed out that Thomson's descriptions were governed by minute details, and Johnson found Thomson capable of 'wide expansion of general views, and [his] enumeration of circumstantial varieties'. Longinus had insisted that the sublime required the most exciting details, as in Homer's description of a shipwreck; Addison had urged the selection of the most pleasant details, as in the *Georgics*, and Pemberton (1738) the details which first struck the beholder, as in *Leonidas*. Arthur Murphy (1753) proposed that description selected contrary details and reconciled them: 'It often happens in mere descriptive Poetry, that the Writer observing some surprising Agreement between Things, which in their Natures seems totally inconsistent with each other, from thence takes Occasion to reconcile Contrarieties in such an agreeable Assemblage, that the tasteful

[1] 'A Voyage to the Mountains of the Moon under the Equator: or Parnassus Reformed', *Miscellanea Aurea*: or *The Golden Medley* (London, 1720), pp. 22–23.

[2] James Arbuckle, No. 50, 12 March 1726, *Hibernicus' Letters* (London, 1729), I, 424–5.

Reader is entertained with a picture, which at once amuses his Fancy and satisfies his Judgment.'[1]

Although these critics disagreed about the pertinent details, each of their examples did provide a vivid description, if one defined description, with Anthony Blackwall (1718), as 'lively Description'. But the explanation of this vividness on which they all agreed—such descriptions were vivid because they were visual—was inaccurate and untenable. The methodological basis for this inaccuracy was the process of selection, for visualization involved far more complex issues than the critics realized. They each pointed to different aspects of visual perception of authors and viewers—the immediacy, the emotional excitement, the associated relations upon perceiving, the perceiver's imaginative response—all of which were different elements of a response treated as complete in each example. The descriptive details were tied to observation, and they revealed how close literary description was to the careful and precise sight of objects. But the very explanation of details indicated that mere enumeration was not responsible for the 'liveliness', 'energy', or vividness of description.

The fact, however, that poets 'laid out all their Genius upon it', was obviously not sufficient justification for neglecting the traditional relationship of embellishment to design. Hughes's argument seized upon an important value in the practical defence of description. The justification of description required a defence of the vividness of artistic play at the expense of unity of design. The qualitative vividness of description which roamed over fountain, stream, and sea provided this playful disorder because it did not submit to its minor and proportionate role of embellishment. This playfulness, this disorder, attending to the visual surface of nature, though not merely to this surface, had a possible justification in a world which was 'a wild, where weeds and flowers promiscuous shoot'. According to H. M. McLuhan, the landscape offered a broader and less exacting course 'for those who were preoccupied with the new psychological interests on one hand and with means of evading the new insistence on non-metaphorical and mathematical statement as the mode of poetry, on the other hand'.[2]

[1] Arthur Murphy, 'On the Art of Acting', *The Gray's Inn Journal*, 59, (1 Dec. 1753), II, 41. Murphy identifies the concept with Addison's term 'thwarting ideas'. See also John Newbery, *The Art of Poetry on a New Plan* (London, 1762), I, 128–9.

[2] McLuhan, 'Picturesque Poetry', 269.

If the ordered universe was supported by the expected and the common, then the elements of confusion and disorder required some artistic presence: one view was that description created a vividness and energy and accuracy that made the world interesting; it was a display not only of the sights but of the sounds and smells of nature. Thomson in *Spring* referred to 'the negligence of nature wide and wild'. And, indeed, the defenders of description, offered as justification the interrelation between the 'clear' and the 'surprising'. This was apparent in Shiels's and Johnson's analysis of unity, and even John Aikin (1778), despite his 'plan' of *The Seasons*, acknowledged that 'every grand and beautiful appearance in nature, that distinguishes one portion of the annual circuit from another, is a proper source of materials for the poet of the Seasons'. Comparing the confined plan of the *Georgics* to Thomson's unconfined plan, Aikin wrote: 'I mean . . . only to suggest a comparison between the result of Thomson's unconfined plan, scarcely less extensive than nature itself, and that of some other writers, not inferior in genius, who thought it necessary to shackle themselves with teaching an art, or inculcating a system.'[1]

Thomson's poem expressed the view that movement and change were essential to life, and the erupting energy of nature was illustrative of this force. In a poetry handbook in 1762 John Newbery attributed this verbal and material energy to personifications and images. 'The royal Psalmist tells us, the clouds drop fatness, and the hills rejoice, that the fruitful fields smile, and the valleys laugh and sing. And these short allegories and images, which convey particular circumstances to the reader after an unusual and entertaining manner, have a fine effect in poetry, that delights in imitation, and endeavours to give to almost every thing, life, motion, and sound.'[2] Thomson's poem, as John Gregory said (1765), viewed the 'numberless beauties of Nature in her various and successive forms'.[3]

This defence of description, therefore, involved an attack upon epic or dramatic unity, the propriety of traditional description and

[1] Aikin, *An Essay in the Application of Natural History to Poetry* (Warrington, 1777), p. 59.

[2] John Newbery, *The Art of Poetry on a New Plan* (London, 1762), I, 42.

[3] John Gregory, *A Comparative View of the State and Faculties of Man* (London, 1765), p. 153. For John Gregory's background and a summary of the argument of *A Comparative View*, see William Smellie, 'The Life of John Gregory', *Literary and Characteristical Lives* (Edinburgh, 1800), pp. 1–118.

the standard of 'brevity'. As John More was to write in 1777, the 'fertile imagination' discovers 'a thousand new variations, distinctions and resemblances . . . where novelty wantons in all her charms'.[1] By creating a 'wantonness' of description governed by 'genius' and skill, Thomson's descriptive poetry served to stress the 'discors' of *concordia discors* and to minimize the reconciliation of extremes. H. S. V. Ogden and others have pointed to the inference of harmony in the wantonness of nature, but the harmony expressed itself in subject matter or philosophy, the 'wantonness' in a different conception and unity.[2]

Yet the principle of *concordia discors* which Earl R. Wasserman has described in Pope, for example, as 'a presiding faith in a grand cosmic pattern of harmonious confusion and agreement through difference—a pattern governing "Nature", the physical universe, human society, man and the arts',[3] was even in Pope governed by external and uneven rather than balanced opposition. For the 'lights and shades' involved agreement upon propriety just as the extremes of people and kings involved agreement upon 'serving' and justice, just as in imagination the function of opposites was to control the imagination without inhibiting it. In the practice of *concordia discors*, agreement through difference was not always the same. Descriptive poetry, by referring to nature in its physical and personified aspects, implied that natural characteristics had meaning in so far as their appearances were human and their forces natural. *Concordia discors* stressed the control and resolution of discordant energies whereas descriptive poetry revealed similar energies as the very valuable 'wanton' sources of beauty and nature.

[1] John More, *Strictures Critical and Sentimental on Thomson's Seasons* (London, 1777), p. 179. For an explanation of variety in landscape painting, see Gerard De Lairesse, 'Of Landskips', *The Art of Painting*, tr. John Frederick Fritsch (London, 1738), pp. 265–6.

[2] H. V. S. Ogden, ed., *Theologica Ruris* (1686), reprinted by ARS (Los Angeles, 1956), p. 3. For discussions of this issue, consult Ernest Tuveson, 'Space, Deity and the Natural "Sublime" ', *MLQ*, XII (1951) 20–38, and other references given by Ogden in this work, in his essay, 'The Principles of Variety and Contrast in Seventeenth Century Aesthetics, and Milton's Poetry', *JHI*, X (1949), 159–82, in H. V. S. Ogden and Margaret S. Ogden, *English Taste in Landscape in the Seventeenth Century* (Ann Arbor, 1955), pp. 36–40; and Earl R. Wasserman, 'Nature Moralized: The Divine Analogy in the Eighteenth Century', *ELH*, XXI (1955), 39–76.

[3] Earl R. Wasserman, 'Windsor Forest', *The Subtler Language* (Baltimore, 1959), p. 105.

Critics who objected to natural descriptions which did not embellish the unity and who pointed to the faintness and ineffectiveness of description compared with actions and sentiments, sought to restrict 'description' to its earlier bounds. They refused to acknowledge that descriptions could be qualitatively more significant than other passages: 'when Fancy and Chance have furnish'd them with an Occasion to describe a Fountain, a rapid Stream, a stormy Sea, they have laid out all their Genius about it'. They sought, in other words, to restrict the domain of poetry by offering to accommodate description within the prescribed categories.

The extension of description also converted the reader's response to poetry from a reliance upon sense perception to reliance upon 'visionary imagination'. In the visionary imagination, literary description became vivid. This 'visionary imagination', indebted as it was to Longinus, nevertheless proposed a new mode of perceiving poetry. For the reader did not identify with the poet, but, by imagining, gave the fiction an immediate presence. Hughes's 'visionary imagination' was created to explain descriptive vividness, and it dealt with conscious sights that were recalled with initial intensity. But it failed to explain the fact that some visions were more intense even than actual sights. Moreover, it created a passive theory of imagination so that the spectator did not enhance the object he observed.

Lord Kames (1762) sought to convey this interaction by his concept of 'ideal presence', but he, as well as John Aikin and Erasmus Darwin, sought to distinguish this state of mind as a suspension of normal activity from the state of disbelief proposed by Johnson and Sir Joshua Reynolds, and from the falsehood of hallucinations and delusions. For if poetry could be more intense than reality, if it could through illusion lead to truth, it was necessary to locate a state of mind which would make 'temporary illusion' of truth possible. Aikin explained this 'suspended' dream state as a form of 'sympathy' with characters in novels and dramas; Erasmus Darwin applied it to poetry.[1] This suspension of active disbelief was created by

[1] John Aikin, 'On the Impression of Reality Attending Dramatic Representative', *Memoirs of the Literary and Philosophical Society of Manchester* (Manchester, 1793), IV, Part I, 96–108; Erasmus Darwin, *Loves of the Plants* (London, 1789), Interlude III; Samuel Johnson, 'Preface to Shakespeare' (1765). The theories of Aikin and Darwin were directed against the concept of 'belief' or 'falsehood' developed by Johnson and Sir Joshua Reynolds. Aikin argued that 'temporary illusion' suspended belief or disbelief; it was a sympathy with the characters that could be maintained by

congruity and other structural qualities in the work which permitted the spectator to achieve artistic illusion and the exercise of sympathy.

Prior to Aikin's and Darwin's theories of imaginative suspension Hume urged a careful concentration on the aesthetic object and attention to its content and expression. Though concentration was created most easily by artistic works—it could also be created by nature—the critics who attended to conscious details were concerned with the thought and language of poetry, the artistic devices creating feeling, whereas Darwin and Aikin were concerned with the effects of artistic illusion upon the spectator. Descriptive poetry, in other words, was defended both by a theory of dream analogy or 'temporary illusion' and a theory of attention to details and concentration on the object. Such defences turned to the psychological truth of poetry when it was dispossessed of literal truth.

In the same year that *Winter* was published Bezaleel Morrice issued *The Amour of Venus* (1726) with a preface in which he explained descriptions, natural or allegorical, as embellishments, but found them to contain when well managed, the 'essential *Beauty of Poetry*'. Such a description contained, he explained, the 'truest Resemblance of its Original'. 'In Description (whether natural or allegorical) we ought to make our *Images* so perfect, that the Reader may not have an obscure or confused, but clear and distinct View of Things in his *Mind*; and by Choice of the *Expression*, have his Mind as much surpriz'd as entertain'd.'[1]

Morrice used the language of object-description and of universals —'the essential Beauty'—based on sight. But he overtly distinguished between sight and expression and between types of description. 'Clear' and 'distinct' views did not in themselves involve 'surprize'— this was the result of expression. The problem of expression necessarily included the distinctness of description, its vividness: 'Sentiments which are merely natural, affect not the mind with any pleasure

[1] Morrice, *The Amour of Venus* (London, 1733), pp. 3–4, 5.

congruity and other artistic qualities. But he was not clear about the kind of effects that resulted after the illusion ceased. It was, of course, further developed in Coleridge's 'willing suspension of disbelief'. For a discussion of Darwin's theory, see James V. Logan, *The Poetry and Aesthetics of Erasmus Darwin* (Princeton, 1936), pp. 47–54. For the use of 'temporary description' or 'illusion' with regard to personification, see Joseph Priestley, *A Course of Lectures on Oratory and Criticism* (1777), as quoted in Earl R. Wasserman, 'The Internal Values of 18th Century Personification', *PMLA*, LXV (1950), 442.

. . . productions which are merely surprizing, without being natural, can never give any lasting entertainment to the mind.' Thus the very concern with 'things' developed for him a concern for language.

Universal nature tended to make faithful descriptions alike; similar details, therefore, encouraged the use of imagery in order to avoid triteness and to arouse the imagination of the reader. The traditional explanation for the use of figures of speech was traceable to the *Poetics* in which Aristotle explained that 'the Diction should be most laboured in the *idle* parts of a Poem—those in which neither *manners*, nor *sentiments* prevail'. These passages were the descriptive ones and Sheffield in *An Essay Upon Poetry* (1682) sought to confine figures of speech to them only.

> *Figures of Speech*, which Poets think so fine,
> Art's needless Varnish to make Nature shine
> Are all but Paint upon a beauteous Face
> And in Descriptions only claim a place.

But the shift in the role of figurative language was analogous to the shift in the concept of description as vivid and moving expression of persons, places, and things. George Turnbull (1746) sought to make this a principle in training students in the sublety of languages: 'After young people understand any truth, it would neither be unpleasant nor unprofitable, but on the contrary, a very pleasing and useful exercise, to show them in what different manners or lights different authors have represented it, each according to his own genius, or in order to adapt it to some particular cast of understanding; and then to make them try to find out other ways of expressing the same truth with due force, elegance and perspicuity.'[1] The paradoxical inference to be noted was that if diverse images expressed uniformity of subject it was possible to argue that the subject itself (nature) could be seen diversely. This view had of course developed in Thomson criticism as a justification of varied unity. But there was another inference to be drawn from the use of expressive language: there were required discriminations within the different descriptions, and thus a sensitivity to nuances in expressive language. As Twining (1789) explained, using 'metaphor' as figurative language, 'almost all the Beauty of Poetry, as far as *language*

[1] George Turnbull, *Observations Upon Liberal Education* (London, 1742), pp. 427–8. For the preceding quotations, see Twining, p. 121; Henry J. Pye, *A Commentary Illustrating the Poetics of Aristotle* (London, 1792), p. 75.

is concerned, all that distinguishes the Poet of genius, from the versifier who trusts solely to his ear, and to his memory, arises from the *uncommon* and *original* use of *metaphor*'.[1] Blair (1783) explained that 'figures form the constant language of poetry. To say, that 'the sun rises' is trite and common; but it becomes a magnificent image when expressed, as Mr. Thomson has done

> But yonder comes the powerful king of day
> Rejoicing in the east.[2]
>
> [*Summer*, ll. 81–2]

John Aikin (1777) pointed out that in description a simile might function as explanation, but such functions were insufficient for poetical merit: 'A simile may perfectly answer in the end of *explanation*, without offering anything new or engaging to the mind. Such an one might be excellent for the purpose of instruction, but comes far short of poetical merit.'[3] In other words, the realization by critics that details might be similar in description resulted in careful examination of the expression of such details.

(c) JOSEPH WARTON AND ROBERT ANDREWS: FROM REALITY OF DETAILS TO DETAILS OF REALITY

> 1. Words are signs of natural facts.
> 2. Particular natural facts are symbols of particular spiritual facts.
> 3. Nature is the symbol of spirit.
>
> EMERSON (1836)

(1) *Joseph Warton: The Object of Sight*

> Thomson 'painted from nature itself and from his actual observation'.
>
> J. WARTON

It was not until thirty years after Morrice's preface that *The Seasons* became the extended subject of analysis as a descriptive

[1] Twining, p. 113 n.

[2] Hugh Blair, *Lectures on Belles Lettres* (London, 1783), I, 286. For an analysis of Blair's rhetorical theory, see Herman Cohen, *The Rhetorical Theory of Hugh Blair* (unpublished dissertation, State University of Iowa, 1957).

[3] John Aikin, *An Essay on the Application of Natural History to Poetry* (Warrington, 1777), p. 95.

poem. The poem had, of course, been praised parenthetically between 1726 and 1756, the year of Joseph Warton's first volume of his *Essay on the Genius and Writings of Pope*. Delacour (1734) had praised the poem for improving upon nature; Blackwell had praised it in realistic terms for doing what Homer had neglected to do: '*That* [rural scenery] is a Subject stil remaining to us, if we will quit our Towns and look upon it. We find it accordingly, nobly executed by many of the Moderns, and the most illustrious Instance, of it, within these few Years, doing Honour to the *British* Poetry.'[1] In 1746 Lord Hervey referred to Thomson as 'that Great master of just description and lively painting', and in 1753 Shiels declared, 'Description is Thomson's peculiar genius.'

Joseph Warton's digression on *The Seasons* constituted the first extensive attempt, governed by particular examples, to place Thomson within the context of close observation of 'things'. It is important, therefore, to note that Warton provided contexts of vividness and originality, and that this latter which seemed like a new category was merely a statement of novelty or vividness of sight due to careful observation of the object, for which Warton was, in fact, indebted to Addison.

In his *Essay on the Writings and Genius of Pope*, I, Joseph Warton had written that Thomson 'hath enriched poetry with a variety of new and original images which he painted from nature itself and from his actual observation: his descriptions have therefore a distinctness and truth'.[2] Warton's conception of particular observation was used to contrast with the hereditary images, the clichés of other poets. In his 1753 edition of Virgil, Warton had written that 'a set of hereditary images [derived from Theocritus] has been continued from one poet to another, which have often been made use of without any propriety either as to age or to climate'. Thomson's eye on the object, however, resulted in new, 'original' images and observations; 'who in speaking of a summer evening hath ever mentioned, "the quail that clamours for his running mate"?' Like the 'breeze' and 'trees' that Pope satirized in the *Essay on Criticism*, Warton objected to the

[1] Thomas Blackwell, *An Enquiry into the Life and Writings of Homer* (London, 1735), p. 35. Selections from the *Enquiry* with bibliographical data about Blackwell are included in *Eighteenth Century Critical Essays*, ed. Scott Elledge (Ithaca, 1961), I, 432–47, 561–3.

[2] Warton, *Essay*, I, 42. For a view of *The Seasons* derived from Warton, see Blair, *Lectures*, II, 372–4.

stereotyped descriptions of rivers, 'which are generally said only to wind and to murmur'. Pope ridiculed the triteness of the rhymes; Warton objected to descriptions of rivers because 'their qualities and courses are seldom marked'.

Warton saw in the object the basis for literal truth and though he too was aware that certain types of detail were necessary to create the object with vividness, he acknowledged that poets were bound to see similar aspects of the same object. 'There is a general Similitude', wrote John Hughes in 1713, in all true Descriptions 'of the same Object drawn by several Hands.'[1] Warton, as did Bishop Hurd, came to this same conclusion: 'descriptions, therefore, that are faithful and just must be uniform and alike'. Originality of detail was 'entitled to the praise of priority', but of two writers on the same subject, the criterion was a 'selection of such adjuncts and circumstances upon each subject, as are best calculated to strike the imagination and embellish their descriptions'. What Warton realized was that any group of descriptive details which functioned to create vividness was a proper selection.

The novelty of description was an inadequate criterion of value because if one accepted Warton's interpretation of imitation, novelty of subject could not distinguish one observer of nature from another, nor could it distinguish the historian or geographer from the poet. Methodologically, Warton made three distinctions in considering Thomson's descriptive value: compared with the pastoral poets, Thomson eschewed descriptive commonplaces; compared with nature, Thomson exhibited distinctness and accuracy of imitation; compared with the vision of a painting or picture in the mind, the poem revealed a perfect idea. And all three were, in the tradition of descriptive poetry, common criteria; Hoyt Trowbridge has stressed not only the traditionalism of this position but the fact that Warton's 'delight in and insistence upon the visual image' was the characteristic feature of his poetic theory, and James Allison has explained that although Warton supported 'fidelity of detail' in

[1] John Hughes, 39 (12 Feb. 1713), *The Lay Monastery* (London, 1714), p. 228. See Joseph Warton, *Essay*, I, 90. See also *Adventurer*, p. 23; Bishop Hurd, 'On Poetical Imitation'. For views that found perception of the same object to be different, see Aikin, *Application*, p. 87; More, *Strictures*, p. 178; Egerton Brydges, 'On the Different Taste of Virgil and Horace with Respect to Rural Scenery', *The Ruminator* (London, 1818), I, 21–22.

descriptive poetry, in other forms of poetry, 'such as dramatic and lyric, for example, Warton recognizes the ability of the imagination (seemingly because of its combinative power) to act independently of sensory experience . . . Here, as everywhere, Warton is inconsistent and his theory inconclusive.'[1] Thomson's novelty was not defensible as a literary value of importance—it was merely priority—and when John Aikin (1778) following Warton (1756), also identified novelty as a value, he did so with an awareness of its strategic role for the period: 'It would seem, then, that novelty was the present requisite, more, perhaps, than genius.'

Warton proceeded from novelty to an analysis of Thomson's accuracy and truth to nature. Thomson 'painted from nature itself and from his actual observation: his descriptions have therefore a distinctness and truth'; because Thomson painted from nature, not from other poets, and because Thomson described from his own observations, therefore his descriptions had a distinctness and truth. By 'distinctness' Warton meant precision of details, a particularity of description, and by 'truth' he meant truth to rural nature. Johnson defined 'distinctness' as 'nice observation of the difference between different things' and 'such discrimination of things as makes them easy to be observed'. Warton, for example, objected to some of the epithets in *Windsor Forest*, and wished they had been particular and picturesque, instead of general and indiscriminating. That distinctness and truth were not causally related to a writer's own observations could have been argued from allegory or from Homer's descriptions of the gods. But even in description of rural scenery it was not necessary for the poet to have seen nature in order to particularize it. 'Thomson mostly described what he had really seen,' wrote John Scott in 1785, 'but from the description of others, his imagination often formed very striking and beautiful pictures. Such are his accounts of the vegetable productions of the West-Indies and of the supposed appearance of the internal parts of Abyssinia.'[2]

If it was possible for John Scott (1785) to argue that Thomson sometimes described well what he did not see and for Robert Heron (1793) to argue that he sometimes described poorly what he did see,

[1] James Allison, *The Reputation of Alexander Pope's Early Poems: A Study of Joseph Warton's Essay* (1756) (Unpublished Dissertation, Harvard, 1948). See also Hoyt Trowbridge, 'Joseph Warton on the Imagination', *MP*, XXXV (1937), 73–87.

[2] Scott, *Essays* (London, 1785), p. 380.

then the grounds existed regardless of whether they were used, to argue that observation and vividness of description were not causally related as Warton presented them, although they might be associatively related. But such an argument would not do full justice to the implications of Warton's poetic theory or to his comments on Thomson.

Comparing the poem with the object or location described was a test for the nature aspects of the poem known by the critic, but the poem also dealt with actions, reflections, and digressions. Since vividness was the result of truth to fact, it was necessary to defend other parts of the poem for other reasons, denying, at the same time, that the natural historian or geographer were poets in their natural descriptions. Warton urged the hypothesis of a latent poetic power or force which on the one hand distinguished poetry from prose, and on the other brought the poetic fragments under a general principle. This theory, which had its source for him in Horace's fourth satire (Book I), provided the assumption that the poet's force and vividness were necessary to animate language and make a 'true' poet. Warton explained it as follows: 'It is a creative and glowing Imagination, "acer spiritus ac vis", and that alone, that can stamp a writer with this exalted and very uncommon character, which so few possess, and of which so few can properly judge.'[1]

Warton sought to distinguish the poet from the prose writer, the historian, the didactic or impure poet. The test of poetic quality, he explained, was 'to drop entirely the measures and numbers, and transpose and invert the order of the words: and in this unadorned manner to peruse the passage. If there be really in it a true poetical spirit, all your inversions and transpositions will not disguise or extinguish it; but it will retain its lustre, like a diamond, unset, and thrown back into the rubbish of the mine.'[2] The argument was that poetry was not a form but a quality of spirit or mind, an indestructible 'true poetic spirit'. The adjective 'true' was a clue to the universalist basis of this assumption, and the 'true' spirit was not identified with a specific form, but a quality of language, expressive of spirit or mind. The consequence of this position was that prose could contain poetry and that even history could exhibit 'poetry'—a particular force in language—but that the 'poetic spirit' was essential to poetry, not to other forms of literature.

[1] Warton, *Essay*, I, v–vi.

[2] Ibid., I, viii–ix. Warton ascribes this 'method' to Horace.

Trapp, too, had exhibited this essentializing method of defining poetry, but he had found the 'true' spirit in a form, not a quality. Trapp realized that sometimes the very phrases and words of poetry could be used in prose, yet he felt that when the word order was shuffled, a special quality disappeared from poetry.

> There is not so much as one Phrase, not one Word, but what might with Propriety be used in Prose. It is observable, however, that even these, and the like Expressions, when transposed, and taken out of Metre, lose all their Elegance: For tho' every Word, considered in itself, is agreeable to either Style, yet there is somewhat so distinguishing in the poetical, as throws a Beauty upon Words, which, out of Metre, would appear insipid or absurd; and yet, tho' we are sensible of the Thing, it is impossible to assign a Reason for it.[1]

Trapp faced his inability to explain his position, for he, too, was seeking the 'true spirit' of genres of poetry—'Here, again, the true Spirit of Epigram seems wanting'—the 'true spirit' of Trapp differed from that of Warton because he was concerned with the uniqueness of the poem as a form, whereas Warton was concerned with identifying poetry as a quality in all forms. But both accepted the essentializing method of distinguishing poetry from prose. Trapp found that rhetoric could not possibly exhibit the passion of poetry and Warton found that a 'minute and particular enumeration of circumstances judiciously selected, is what chiefly discriminates poetry from history, and renders the former, for that reason, a more close and faithful representation of nature than the latter'. For Warton, observation of literal reality made vividness possible; he assumed that the more faithful the representation, the more vivid the work. The poetical qualities resided in concepts or expressions which, though sometimes found in the formal properties of poetry, did not necessarily reside there. It was a hypothesis which was especially pertinent to descriptive poetry which had, as Johnson said, 'no particular design'. But it was a theory that, by neglecting the formal order and properties of the poem, judged it by an ideal in the mind of the reader for which no literal reality could be provided.

Such a theory was obviously open to attack for disregarding the given. Stockdale engaged in this attack in 1778, arguing that the poem's uniqueness was the result of its coherence in which all its

[1] Trapp, *Lectures*, p. 43.

elements were mutually interrelated: 'In the productions of the fine arts, nothing is indifferent; the minutest parts have their great importance and influence; they reflect proportion, and expression on the other parts, from which *they* likewise draw those advantages; and all the parts as they are disposed, and compacted by the artist, form a striking whole.'[1] Stockdale saw these interrelations as deriving from traditional distinctions such as the sublime and pathetic, and although he attributed to mankind universal characteristics, he at least focussed attention upon the intrinsic areas of analysis as a whole, rather than upon some details segmented from the entire poem.

Consistent with his theory, Warton appealed to the 'idea' in the mind as an ideal, rather than to the relational elements within *The Seasons* in order to discover its value. Description was for him the communication of pictures to the mind rather than the communication of feelings about pictures, although he recognized the role of feeling when he referred to the digressions dealing with human beings. 'Examine the exactness of the ensuing description, and consider what a perfect idea it communicates to the mind.'

> Around th'adjoining brook, that purls along
> The vocal grove, now fretting o'er a rock,
> Now scarcely moving through a reedy pool,
> Now starting to a sudden stream, and now
> Gently diffus'd into a limpid plain:
> A various groupe of herds and flocks compose
> Rural confusion.[2]
>
> [*Summer*, ll. 480–6]

When Warton described this passage as 'perfect', 'complete', or 'finished', he referred to the visual qualities which the selection exhibited. The periodic sentence structure, however, the repetition of the temporal quality in the spatial scene ('now,' 'now', 'now'), the comparison between the moving stream and the herds and flocks, the

[1] Percival Stockdale, *An Inquiry into the Nature and Genuine Laws of Poetry* (London, 1778), pp. 7–8.

[2] Warton, *Essay*, I, 45. For the use of 'idea' as a visual term, see Kenneth MacLean, *John Locke and English Literature of the Eighteenth Century* (New Haven, 1936), pp. 54–55. Chambers' *Cyclopaedia* (London, 1741), I, gives the first meaning of 'idea' as 'the image, or resemblance of a thing, which, though not seen, is conceived by the mind'. See also Dugald Stewart, 'Of Imagination', *Elements of the Philosophy of the Human Mind* (London, 1792), I,477: 'the very etymology of the word Imagination has a reference to visible objects'.

personification in 'fretting,' 'moving', 'starting', followed by a return to natural characteristics in 'gently diffused'—did not represent to him the 'perfect' idea. Rather, the particular visual details formed the basis for poetic value, but the visual theory of language was under attack at the very time Warton was developing his argument. For in the same year that Warton wrote his comment Burke published his *Inquiry* (1756) in which he objected to the assumption that language operated by pictures: 'Let any body examine himself, and see whether he has had impressed on his imagination any picture of a river, mountain, watery soil, Germany, etc. Indeed, it is impossible, in the rapidity and quick succession of words in conversation, to have ideas both of the sound of the word and of the thing represented.'[1]

Warton's criticism served a strategic purpose: it attacked hereditary images and the poet's neglect of the present by insisting on Thomson's close observation of nature and the objects around him. He accepted the universalist assumption that viewers who would study nature closely would be bound to see it alike, but he explained that a relation of 'adjuncts and circumstances' which struck the imagination 'best', was the best description. Thus, not any single set of circumstances was proper for description. but those which worked 'best'. Regardless of the difficulty of determining the 'best', Warton rejected the prescription of details offered by Longinus, by Pemberton, by Murphy, and others. These advocates of particular details were all correct: they each assumed that a particular set of details explained the vividness of description. And each set did. But they were not the only particulars which created vividness. The critics of Thomson, after Warton, repeatedly asserted the differences in description by different writers, and the vividness possible in all.

In 1777 John More in his essay on *The Seasons* explained that 'nature appears uniformly the same to none of us; that every mind has something distinguishing in its structure and operations, from another, and that we have all our own way of thinking, whenever we do think, and drop it only, in a slavish imitation of others'.[2] In 1785, John Scott wrote:

> Nature is rich in a variety of minute, but striking circumstances, some of which engage the attention of one observer, and some that of another. Thomson and Browne have both described the sun in

[1] Edmund Burke, *A Philosophical Enquiry into the Origin of our Ideas and of the Sublime and the Beautiful*, ed. J. T. Boulton (London, 1958), p. 167.
[2] More, p. 50.

the act of setting. Browne has represented the picturesque effect of its radiance on the clouds of the western horizon, and Thomson has remarked the gradual extinction of that radiance.[1]

Dugald Stewart remarked in 1798 that there were no details which could not be joined together in the imagination to form a whole, and Isaac Disraeli declared, 'There is no subject in nature, and in the history of men, which will not associate with our feelings and our curiosity, whenever genius extends its awakening hand.' And in 1831 John Wilson explained. 'Some poets there are who show a scene all of a sudden by means of a few magical words . . . Others, again, as good and as great, create their world gradually before your eyes.'[2]

These quotations reveal a critical process of considerable interest—the dissolution of a critical problem: some critical problems are not solved, they are dissolved. Fidelity to literal details ceased by the beginning of the nineteenth century to be a serious criterion of descriptive poetry. This issue was dissolved, not in any single-handed way, but by a disengagement of critics from the issue. There was no longer any serious justification for arguing that observations of the object could, without feeling or attitude, be translated into poetry. There was, as Burke claimed, a distinction between a 'clear' expression and a 'strong' expression, 'the former regards the understanding; the latter belongs to the passions. The one describes a thing as it is; the other describes it as it is felt.' 'Thomson's representations', said the editor of the 1779 edition, 'charm and astonish, and engage our attention more than the originals from which they are drawn.' Language was itself capable of being a 'thing', of being surprising and expressive. Observation which had been so intimately tied to sight, what Addison called 'the most noble, pleasant and comprehensive of all the senses', was not what Thomson conveyed, according to Hazlitt (1818): 'he describes not to the eye alone, but to the other senses, and to the whole man'. And when the anonymous critic who supplied a preface to the 1816 edition sought to attack Thomson for lack of 'a devotional recognition of the revealed character of the Divine Being', he wrote: 'He saw, as Johnson remarks, everything

[1] Scott, p. 352.

[2] Dugald Stewart, *Elements of the Philosophy of the Human Mind* quoted in *Philosophical Essays* (Edinburgh, 1870); see also, *Elements* (London, 1792), I, 478, pp. 322–3; John Wilson, *The Recreations of Christopher North* (1842) (London, 1864), II, 263.

with the eye, though he does not appear to have felt everything with the heart of a poet.'[1] But the distinction, even here, was between two types of feeling, not a contrast between feeling and its absence.

To discuss Thomson's literalness without including his feeling toward place would have been to assume that Thomson wrote not poetry, but science, not to the feelings but to the understanding. When he was accused of writing prose, there appeared sometimes the argument that he was writing literal not poetic truth. 'His larger landscape', wrote Francis Palgrave in *Landscape in Poetry* (1897), 'is comparatively rare, and, though minutely accurate, apt to be prosaically tame.'[2]

There was no formal proof available that Thomson's descriptions could not be judged by the pictures they created in the mind, although James Gregory had pointed out in 1793 that 'it is self-evident, that thoughts cannot be arranged in order of place', despite the fact that words fell into succession of place on a page and time in speech. 'I believe it is equally certain, though not actually evident, that *many* of our thoughts are not even arranged in order of time.'[3] But the attack on the picture theory of language did not prevent George Dyer in 1796 from defining descriptive poetry as a picture in the mind.

> Descriptive poetry is then most excellent, when calculated to excite in the mind the clearest and most lively picture of the object imitated; and in proportion as the ideas forming that picture are vivid and the more they answer to the reality of the proto-

[1] *The Seasons* (London, 1816), preface. See also Burke, p. 175; *The Seasons* (Edinburgh, 1779), preface; Hazlitt, *Lectures*, p. 168; R. L. Gerardin [Victe. D'Ermenonville], *An Essay on Landscape*, tr. anon. (London, 1783), pp. 72–3.

[2] Francis Palgrave, *Landscape into Poetry* (London, 1897), p. 169; see also Palgrave's 'The Growth of English Poetry', *The Quarterly Review*, CX (1861), 448. For eighteenth-century poetry in *The Golden Treasury*, see Colin J. Horne, 'Palgrave's Golden Treasury', *Essays and Studies, 1949* (London, 1949), 60–61.

[3] James Gregory, 'Theory of the Moods of Verbs', *Transactions of the Royal Society of Edinburgh* (Edinburgh, 1790), II, 241. For a view that thinking is verbal and that shades of meaning are detected by linguistic (not picture) comparisons, see William Godwin, *The Enquirer* (Dublin, 1797), pp. 43, 53. Frank Sayers, 'Of Beauty', *Disquisitions* (London, 1793), pp. 29 ff. argued that poetical passages with no clear ideas or containing ideas repugnant to sense could 'merely from agreeable associations with the words' be generally received as beautiful.

type or scene, the more complete is the imitation, and the more impressive the resemblance.[1]

Dyer concluded his comments by altering Warton's argument that to see well was essential to write well; one of his chief points was that the poet could learn particulars from the topographical historian without seeing what he described: Milton, Sir William Jones, and Collins wrote 'happy imitations, as well of place as of character and manner, when yet the writers possessed no ocular proof of the scenery or subject described'.[2] And another critic (1798) who accepted the representational theory of language—'when, therefore, we use words, we revive in the minds of those that understand our language, the pictures of the objects of which we speak'—indicated that, for him, the function of literary language was to appeal to the passions, and that this language was 'the summit of his [the poet's] art'.[3]

Both of these statements exemplified the accommodation of criticism to increased knowledge. The critic sought to accommodate what he knew to what was known. The efforts to convert the picture theory into defensible criticism required some cognizance of the contemporary objections. And the dissolution of literal reality as a criterion was achieved when it no longer permitted accommodations. There had been developed in the previous half-century attacks on the concept of sight and imagination, on literal details as a single concept, on the picture theory of language, on vividness as a reality concept; there had been developed a body of descriptive poems by poets who looked at the object but wrote dull 'poetry'. The issue was dissolved because there had finally developed a comprehensive series of objections to the assumption of a visual truth. The procedure, therefore, was to redefine 'truth', to re-examine terms, and to reformulate principles. In the redefining of 'truth', Dyer's definition was one of several—'there is a poetical as well as metaphysical truth'; in the re-examination of the critical vocabulary, 'description' grew to include a genre in Aikin, and though still an embellishment in Blair it was the 'great test of a Poet's imagination'. 'Description' developed 'chiefly owing to a strong imagination, which first received a lively impression of the object; and then by employing a proper selection of circumstances in describing it, transmits that impression in full force to the

[1] George Dyer, *Poetics* (London, 1812), II, 116.

[2] Dyer, II, 118.

[3] 'On the Characteristics of Poetry', *Monthly Magazine* (1797), pp. 538–545.

imagination of others'. The eye of the poet became a synonym for 'mind'. And as to the reformulation of description, an obvious example was the use of Cunningham's painting metaphor to explain that Thomson painted by means of the imagination: Thomson, Cunningham wrote in 1841, 'was a close observer of Nature: she sat for every picture he draws'. And he reserved his highest praise for the poet's method of drawing: 'He saw all by the charmed light of his imagination.'

John Hughes (1713) had pointed out that the poet, in his descriptions, formed ideas drawn from sight, and this process was 'sometimes too called imaging, and [the ideas] are thus, in a manner like pictures, made objects of the sight'. The poet created pictures based on his direct observation; his poetry created images or pictures which became objects of sight. 'Sight' was the process of seeing, and the poet was capable of reflecting the images to the reader by what Hughes called the 'Visionary Power' of the imagination. Richardson (1715) referred to the beauty of shape and form as the 'Pleasures of the Eye' though the 'eye' was an organ to be trained how to see. Hazlitt (1818), however, and Sir Harris Nicolas (1831) referred to the 'eye' of the mind.

Hughes posited a passive power of seeing—a mind's eye—in the imagination in order to explain how words called up pictures, for the 'Visionary Power' of the imagination referred to persons, places, and things, not to ideas, sentiments, or reflections. But the 'eye' of Hazlitt was recreative, not passive. Who, said Sir Harris, does not *feel* Thomson's descriptions rush upon the mind—'feel', not 'see'.

(2) *Robert Andrews: From Image to Imagination*

> I become a transparent eyeball; I am nothing; I see all; the currents of the Universal Being circulate through me.
>
> EMERSON

The difference between direct sight and visionary imagination, while indicating the active functions of the eye and passive functions of the imagination, nevertheless tied the two together. The operation of sight and the operation of the imagination were intertwined in the practice of the poet and the response of the reader. When Thomson in his *Spring* addressed the reader seated under a spreading ash, 'catch thyself the landscape, gliding swift / Athwart imagination's vivid eye', he used 'eye' to see the imagined and recreated vividness of landscape. Because of the importance of 'sight' in landscape poetry, the blind poet Thomas Blacklock constituted a test of things seen in contrast to their expression. In Joseph Spence's essay on Blacklock (1754) published with Blacklock's poems in 1756, the critic explained that this poet's use of visible objects 'must have been acquir'd only from the Characters he has learnt of them from Books and Conversation; and some suppos'd Analogies between those Characters, and any of the Ideas in the Stock he has laid in, either from his other Senses, or his own Reflections upon them'.[1] Spence implied that observation was not essential for descriptive poetry. The ideas of nature could be derived from reading or conversation. It was not surprising, therefore, to find that Blacklock 'seems to use the words, eye, view, and sight indifferently, either for the mind, or for ideas in the mind'.

In the same year (1756), Burke supported Spence's view, but objected to the claim that Blacklock's descriptive errors were due to faulty recollection. Burke argued that it was not necessary for Blacklock to see in order to be affected by descriptions. Poets who 'saw' could write worse descriptions than those who didn't, and thus the sounds of words rather than their representation was essential to poetry. This was an extravagant theory of language, but it offered an alternative to the theory of visual imagination.

> Mr. Spence, in an elegant preface which he has written to the works of this poet, reasons very ingeniously, and I imagine for the most part very rightly upon the cause of this extraordinary phenomenon; but I cannot altogether agree with him, that some improprieties in language and thought which occur in these poems have arisen from the blind poet's imperfect conception of visual objects, since such improprieties, and much greater, may be found in writers even of an higher class than Mr. Blacklock, and who, notwithstanding, possessed the faculty of seeing in its full perfection. Here is a poet doubtless as much affected by his own descriptions as any that reads them can be; and yet he is affected with

[1] Joseph Spence, ed., *An Account of the Life, Character, and Poems of Mr. Blacklock* (London, 1754), p. 37. For discussions of sight and blindness in eighteenth-century poetry, see Kenneth MacLean, *John Locke and English Literature of the Eighteenth Century* (New Haven, 1936), pp. 106–8, and Majorie Nicolson, *Newton Demands the Muse* (Princeton, 1946), pp. 81–85. See also Austin Wright, *Joseph Spence: A Critical Biography* (Chicago, 1950), pp. 153–4.

> this strong enthusiasm by things of which he neither has, nor can possibly have any idea further than that of a bare sound; and why may not those who read his works be affected in the same manner that he was, with as little of any real ideas of the things described?[1]

Mrs. Barbauld, arguing that other senses as well as sight were the sources of our response to poetic language declared (1806) that Akenside correctly included 'every source, by which, through any of our senses or perceptions, we receive notices of the world around us' not merely through the sense of sight. For 'who would deny that the elegant mind of Blacklock was capable of receiving, and even of imparting them in no small degree?'[2] The use of imagination's eye, fancy's eye, mental eye, mind's eye to describe the internal process of vision or image in the mind was, in 1757, reduced by Robert Andrews to a single term, 'imagery', that is, visual images, which formed the essence of poetry. If, to Warton, visual imagery was characteristic of descriptive poetry, for Andrews it became the essence of all poetry.

In his 1757 preface to *Eidyllia*, Robert Andrews defined all poetry as visual imagery. Thus the pathetic narrator and the natural description all became part of a single entity called 'imagery'. Andrews began by enumerating three types of description: description (description of fact), imaginary description (objects or people which never existed but which are like those which do), and creative description (objects which exist only in the poet's imagination). All these Andrews reduced to the inclusive term 'imagery':

> I begin to be out of humour with the distinction of the imaginary and creative kinds, and am willing to retain only the former of these terms, including in it the idea of both; and if you will also include in it the historical, we shall take the word *imagery* in its common acceptation; which I call one constituent of Poetry, but very improperly; for it is rather its essence, its soul and body: so that the more or less any composition has of it, it has the more or less of Poetry.[3]

[1] Burke, pp. 168–9. For an attack on Burke, see Stewart, *Elements*, I, 495–6.

[2] Mrs. A. Barbauld, 'A Critical Essay on the Poem', *The Pleasures of Imagination* (London, 1794), p. 10.

[3] Robert Andrews, 'A Hint to British Poets', *Eidyllia* (Edinburgh, 1757), p. 4. For a discussion of eighteenth-century psychological critics on images

Andrews, like Warton and Trapp, sought the 'essence', the 'soul and body' of poetry. But although 'imagery' served him as a unifying term in dealing with all poetry, his explanation revealed that composition had 'more or less' of it. He was committed, therefore, to the same dilemma as Warton in so far as the poetic quality was to be distinguished from the non-poetic quality in the poem. This became the position of Coleridge, who explained that no long poem could be all poetry, of Shelley who referred to passages containing poetry in prose, and Poe who found that the *Iliad* and the *Odyssey* were not all poetry, merely series of different poems. These critics were not concerned, therefore, with the actual composition of a poem—for example, whether *The Seasons* was composed in parts, and how these parts exhibited poetic qualities—but with poetic quality, defined in different ways, as a basis for unified feeling. Thus Andrews found visual imagery to be the poetic quality; Coleridge the reconciliation of opposites; Shelley the transcendent image, and Poe certain 'essential' feelings and references.

According to Andrews, then, poetry presented visual images to the mind, images of natural description, of actions and events. For Andrews's version of 'description' was based on the term 'imagery' in its 'common acceptation', and Johnson's dictionary gave the following definitions of 'imagery': '1. Sensible representations; pictures, statutes. 2. Show; appearance. 3. Forms of the fancy; fake ideas; imaginary phantoms. 4. Representations in writing; such descriptions as force the image of the Thing described upon the mind.' The common acceptations of the term referred to visible representations outside or inside the mind.

Andrews sought to distinguish between the visual elements of poetry and the non-visual which were not identified as poetry, while bringing factual and non-factual imaginative events under the same denomination. He was not, however, concerned with the procedure by which this imaginative process took place, that is, the reader's perception of the visual image or the author's development of it, and how it was communicated. He was concerned with the harmony that showed it off to best advantage.[1]

Andrews's absorption of all types of descriptive detail into a poetic

[1] Andrews, p. 5 ff.

and imagination, see Gordon McKenzie, *Critical Responsiveness* (Berkeley and Los Angeles, 1948), *Univ. of California Publications in English*, No. 20, pp. 180–206. 229–66.

quality called 'imagery' revealed that although the problem of 'details' was thus resolved, another issue became dominant. For absorption seemingly converted the problem of ornamental details into a problem of the nature of poetry, as soon as the details were defined in terms of poetry as a form. For critics like Andrews and Coleridge and Shelley, the selection of details was not a descriptive problem; the definition of poetic quality was. Trapp's reference to the 'true' and the 'genuine' quality, Warton's to the indestructible 'true poetical spirit', Andrews's to the 'soul and body' of poetry, all implied that they were referring to qualities that formed the crucial, the essential differentia of poetry. But an analysis of these essentializing qualities reveals not only that critics do not agree on the qualities, but that these were no more essential to understanding poetry than inquiries about the creativity of the poet in his work, the consonance of poet and critic, the relation of unity to diction and character.

The chief objection to 'essentializing' is its reduction of the poem to selected passages or qualities and a disregard for the given. The basis for undermining these views was to illustrate their inadequate conception of the traits selected as 'essential'—whether of form or language—and to insist on the inclusiveness of the poem.

The reference to poetic qualities in poetry was not an inquiry into every aspect of poetry, for in Trapp and Warton, such references were undertaken simultaneously with discussions of imitative vividness and imitation of nature. That 'quality' to which Warton referred was a quality in words and in feelings. It created vividness, and seemed, in Warton's phrase, to be identified with a forceful imagination. He assumed that certain expressions and thoughts possessed an imaginative force irrespective of their function, and this theory was, therefore, examinable in terms of the indestructible force of imaginative expressions. It was a theory which, given the test of transposition, other critics found untenable.

The transition from 'image' to 'imagery' presupposed that the imaginative process, the affective process was more important than literal observation. When Johnson wrote that Thomson always looked out upon nature with the 'eye' of a poet, he was not writing of literal observation but of viewing that was done through individual perception. When Mrs. Piozzi provided a conversational synonym for 'eye', she used 'sight' because the organ of sight (eye) and the process of seeing (sight) were 'in somewhat like a figurative sense, nearly synonymous.'[1] The landscape of the 'eye' could be used as the landscape of the mind. H. M. McLuhan's view that the landscape of the mind was a late nineteenth-century development based on the physical or literal landscape is a rewarding insight, yet only as the landscape ceased to be literal did it begin to be internalized. And when Robert Heron (1793), in discussing Thomson's *Seasons*, wrote that sentiment and imagery 'constitute the composition Poetry, whatever its style or form', he interpreted 'imagery' and 'sentiment' as the 'only means by which the feelings of the human heart can be agitated'.[2] It was this imagery which Hazlitt referred to as one of the essentials of *all* poetry, not merely descriptive poetry.

In 1815 Wordsworth declared that between *Paradise Lost* and *The Seasons* there was no poetry to show 'that the eye of the Poet had been steadily fixed upon his object', but he did not consider this close observation the basis for literal reality. The eye on the object was not to treat of 'things' 'as they *are* but as they appear'.[3] In tracing the history of descriptive poetry, Wordsworth declared that the poetry of the period 'intervening between the publication of the *Paradise Lost* and *The Seasons* does not contain a single new image of external nature; and scarcely presents a familiar one from which it can be inferred that the eye of the Poet had been steadily fixed upon his object, much less that his feelings had urged him to work upon it in the spirit of genuine imagination.'[4]

The function of the poet was to observe the object and to let his feelings and imagination recreate it. The function of things was to be observed by the senses and refined by feelings and imagination. Wordsworth was wrong about nature imagery, as any reference to Thomson's previous critics would have made clear: John More (1777) referred to Jeremy Taylor's descriptions of morning, Scott (1785) had a series of essays on descriptive poetry beginning with *Cooper's Hill*; Blair (1783) and Barron (1806) discussed Parnell as a descriptive poet. Indeed, John Wilson (1831) did attack Wordsworth for his inaccuracy.

[1] Hester L. Piozzi, *British Synonymy* (London, 1794), I, 208.

[2] Robert Heron, 'A Critical Essay on The Seasons', *The Seasons* (Perth, 1793), pp. 4, 2.

[3] William Wordsworth, 'Essay Supplementary to Preface' (1815), *Wordsworth's Literary Criticism*, ed. Nowell C. Smith (London, 1905), pp. 185, 169. See pp. 407 ff. below for additional discussion of this passage.

[4] Wordsworth, p. 185.

But no critic denied that Thomson kept his eye on the object. After the comments of Aikin and Seward (1798), critics ceased to measure Thomson by the criterion of literal reality. 'Thomson was a man of piety and benevolence,' wrote James Beattie (1776), 'and a warm admirer of the beauties of nature; and every description in his delightful poem on the Seasons tends to raise the same laudable affections in his reader. The parts of nature that attract his notice are those which an impious or hard-hearted man would neither attend to nor be affected with, at least in the same manner.'[1] And John Wilson (1831) writing on description in *The Seasons* declared, 'There are a thousand ways of dealing in description with Nature so as to make her poetical; but sentiment there always must be, else it is stark nought.' Thomson's close observations were combined in his imagination. Each of the critics in the first half of the nineteenth century undertook to explain the nature of Thomson's imaginative creativity, but none sought the test of literal accuracy.

But in the second half of the nineteenth century, the eye on the object came to be identified not with what Wordsworth meant, but with what he did. Matthew Arnold defined this procedure as a lyrical language and a profound insight, and he distinguished between 'genuine poetry and the poetry of Dryden, Pope and all their school'.

> The poetic language of our eighteenth century in general is the language of man composing *without their eyes on the object*, as Wordsworth excellently said of Dryden; language merely recalling the object, as the common language of prose does, and then dressing it out with a certain smartness and brilliancy for the fancy and understanding. This is called 'splendid diction'. . . . The language of genuine poetry, on the other hand, is the language of one composing with his eye on the object; its evolution is that of a thing which has been plunged in the poet's soul until it comes forth naturally and necessarily.[2]

To Walter Pater, Wordsworth's phrase meant 'a sense of life in natural objects', a sensuousness which perceived a soul in inanimate things due to 'an exceptional susceptibility to the impressions of the eye and ear'.

And in 1897, D. C. Tovey's 'Memoir of Thomson' applied these interpretations to *The Seasons*, reducing the natural description

[1] Beattie, p. 54; Wilson, *Recreations*, II, 263.

[2] Matthew Arnold, 'Thomas Gray', *Essays in Criticism*, Second Series (London, 1886), pp. 95–96.

merely to 'choice of theme', not to any genuine difference between Thomson's poetry and Pope's.

> Wordsworth himself tells us that we find in the 'Seasons' that evidence of 'the eye steadily fixed upon the object', which is the distinctive mark of the true poet of Nature; and Cowper, certainly with the 'Seasons' in mind, mistrusted Thomson, more or less, when in that poem, he described what he never saw. If Wordsworth's oft-quoted phrase be limited to actual observation, Cowper's misgivings cover, it may be suspected, a very large amount of ground; and if on the other hand we extend it, as Matthew Arnold has extended it, and understand Wordsworth to mean that the poet should at least write as if he beheld, and as if the impressions he records were spontaneous, the special merit of Thomson as compared with Pope may be due not so much to the generic difference between them, on which Wordsworth seems to insist, as to a more fortunate choice of theme.[1]

These critics converted a statement of actual behaviour into a social or metaphysical position. For Arnold, Thomson was a part of a period in which lyrical poetry could not be written; for Pater, Wordsworth expressed a metaphysical position; for Tovey, Thomson ought to have sought, though he never achieved a Wordsworthian imaginative wholeness: 'Even if we grant that Thomson once had a law of his mind, analogous to Wordsworth's, urging him to present man and Nature in a contact and communion, not sentimental only, but predestined and innate, we must admit that the law was so crudely conceived and imperfectly developed, that it came to be forgotten altogether for a more imperious law written in his members and in his surroundings.' Tovey denied to Thomson that imaginative wholeness he ascribed to Wordsworth because neither *Liberty* nor the dramas reflected the 'law'.

Oscar Wilde in 'The Critic as Artist' denied that 'the proper aim of Criticism is to see the object as in itself it really is', arguing that 'this is a very serious error, and takes no cognizance of Criticism's most perfect form, which is in its essence purely subjective, and seeks to

[1] Duncan C. Tovey, ed. 'Memoir of Thomson', *The Poetical Works of James Thomson* (London, 1897), I, xxxviii; for the following quotation see p. xliv. For a definition of Thomson's 'eye on the object' which refers to the spotting of characteristic traits, see James L. Robertson, *Nature in Books* (Oxford, 1914), p. 17: 'Certainly in his delineation of individual birds, he presents the characteristic features . . . he furnishes the means of a rapid and perfect identification. He writes, in a word, with his eye on the object.'

reveal its own secret and not the secret of another'.[1] He may have been aiming at paradox, but he was describing the transformation of Wordsworth's phrase in the statements of his contemporaries. The depiction of Thomson's nature had long left behind any careful study of good and bad passages, of particular usages and their discriminations, and had substituted generalizations based on a different language and a different kind of descriptive poetry.

There is an obvious wrongness in seeking Wordsworth in Thomson, but for purposes of criticism, it is important to recognize that the eye which was originally fixed on the object had, in Tovey, become dislocated in the imagination. For Tovey ascribed to Thomson the 'heavenly gift of second sight' capable of 'intense imagination'. This theory of imagination concealed the need for disengaging moments of skill from those of failure. In critic after critic imagination arose to take the place of the eighteenth-century 'genius' or '*je ne sais quoi*' and to explain values or shortcomings by 'imagination' or its absence. This is not the place to rehearse the history of the primary, secondary, passive, active, representative, pictorial, landscape, idealizing, symbolical, sexual imagination; [2] but if power of recall, vivid presentation and 'unified' work are at least essential character-

[1] Oscar Wilde, 'The Critic as Artist', *Works* (London, 1948), p. 967. See also Edward Dowden, 'The Interpretation of Literature,' *Transcripts and Studies* (London, 1888), p. 255. For a discussion of the comments of Arnold, Peter, and Wilde, see Elmer Edgar Stoll, 'Critics at Cross Purposes,' *ELH*, XIV (1947), 320–8. Stoll points out that Wordsworth referred to the poet's eye on the object; the later writers to the critic's eye on the work of literature. This shift is attributable to the investigative character of nineteenth-century criticism as expressed in 'developmental' personifications and is discussed in Chapter IV. Here it can be noted that there is a considerable lag in the application of critical personifications from analysis of poetry to analysis of criticism.

[2] For discussions of imagination, see A. S. P. Woodhouse, 'Collins and the Creative Imagination', *Studies in English by Members of University College, Toronto* (Toronto, 1931); Donald F. Bond, 'Distrust of Imagination in English Neoclassicism', *PQ*, XIV (1955), 54–69; Walter J. Bate, 'The Sympathetic Imagination in Eighteenth-Century English Criticism', *ELH*, XII (1945), 144–64; I. A. Richards, *Coleridge on Imagination* (London, 1954); Wilma Kennedy, *The English Heritage of Coleridge of Bristol*, 1798 (New Haven, 1947); Ernest Tuveson, *Imagination as a Means of Grace* (Berkeley and Los Angeles, 1960); for varieties of 'landscape' imagination, see Philip Hamerton, *Imagination in Landscape Painting* (London, 1887). For a recent discussion with bibliographical references, see Wimsatt and Brooks, *Literary History*, pp. 283–312, 384–411.

istics of all definitions, then works which possess imagination can only be indicated by different proportions of these characteristics or by different aspects of them. But in using 'imagination' as a single quality rather than a group of qualities—and a single quality derived from the poetry of Wordsworth for whom, said Tovey, 'communion with nature was a law of life'—the varieties of Thomson's descriptions, their deliberate discriminations, were overlooked.

The very conception of observation had altered from the belief that things had a clear and distinct existence apart from the viewer's feelings and imagination. Hazlitt in 1818 explained that Thomson 'describes the vivid impression which the whole makes upon his imagination; and thus transfers the same unbroken, unimpaired impression to the imagination of his readers'.[1] Sir Harris Nicolas (1831) found Thomson's description marked by a placidity of religious feeling in the contemplation of nature. Thomson's value as a descriptive writer was associative: 'who is there that has reflected on the magnificence of an extended landscape . . . and does not feel his [Thomson's] descriptions rush upon the mind?'[2] In 1841 Allan Cunningham praised Thomson's descriptions because 'no poet, save the inspired one who wrote the eighth Psalm, attempted, like Thomson, to raise the beauties of nature out of the low regions of sensual delight, and make them objects of moral grandeur and spiritual contemplation'.[3]

In explaining the decline of the criterion of literal reality, I have traced the theory of poetic creativity and conditioned perception, showing how concepts of imagination made untenable a literal reality. Thomson, however, did not hold such a theory, but offered a Shaftesburyan basis for denying this reality. In the treatment of poetic language there were at least two traditions, one of which aimed at economy and brevity and the other of which arrived at vividness and plenitude of thing and word. *The Seasons* supported the second, especially in the construction of a critical view toward details. But it is now, perhaps, pertinent to coordinate the methods of criticism with the problems of description.

Warton's attack on descriptive clichés led him to assume that Thomson's observation of nature was responsible for his original description. But even Warton realized that the inference he drew was

[1] Hazlitt, *Lectures*, p. 167.
[2] Nicolas, *Thomson*, I, lxxxii.
[3] A. Cunningham, p. xlv.

questionable since he pointed out that if other poets observed carefully they would be bound to describe the same details. A more adequate explanation of the value of details was made in the same year (1756) in Burke's treatise. Burke found the roots of the beautiful in social affection. Thus the physical qualities of small objects and the practice of domestic manners became the basis of the 'beautiful', seen as equal in importance to sublime objects and feelings. When William Gilpin proposed the 'picturesque' as a third term in the explanation of nature, there were distinguished three critical areas each of which had its own 'literal' details, each of which provided somewhat different effects upon the beholder and each of which was based on somewhat different subjects and manners of expression.

Yet these critical concepts, developed to explain types of diversity in nature, proved insufficient to categorize the diversity of descriptive poetry. Criticism, in its procedures, recognized the non-literal character of details. The attempt to specify the type of imaginative organization or the uses of language in description led critics to refined explanations of selectivity. This procedure was made possible by the publication of poems similar to *The Seasons*, but especially by William Cowper's *The Task* (1785). Descriptive poetry had been demonstrating in its own implicit way the aspects of continuity from *The Seasons*. Thus articulate criticism followed the poetry proper, recognizing in *The Task* a basis for precision in defining the description of *The Seasons*. By attention to a poem, proceeding in a manner similar to *The Seasons*, the critics became more precisely aware of its non-Virgilian qualities: it was also apparent that generalizations about the sublime, the beautiful, and the picturesque in *The Seasons* proved these categories overly exclusive.

In substituting imaginative attitudes towards details or the enumeration of details, the critics of *The Seasons* minimized the range and scope of the particular descriptions. In 1765 John Gregory wrote that Thomson's 'greatest merit consists in impressing the Mind with numberless beauties of Nature in her various and successive forms, which formerly passed unheeded'.[1] But nineteenth-century critics did not enumerate the numberless beauties or compare them with those of other poems, a practice followed by Robert Heron (1793). Just as the imaginative unity minimized the need for variety of details, a few representative ones being sufficient evidence for 'wholeness', so too

[1] John Gregory, *A Comparative View of the State and Faculties of Man* (London, 1765), p. 153.

the need for extensive comparisons diminished accordingly. Thus the procedure of focussing on a few details in the poetry of Wordsworth was applied in the criticism of *The Seasons*, and the practice of extensive comparisons disappeared from analysis.

Even intelligent critics, in developing generalizations about poetry, often use examples that have ceased to be pertinent or that show little practical knowledge of the poetry about which they are generalizing. When in 1829, John Henry Newman declared that poetry involved the imaginative transfusion of literal details—an assumption shared by most critics of his time, including those who wrote on Thomson—he objected to Warton's praise for Thomson's novelty and literalness: 'Thomson has sometimes been commended for the novelty and minuteness of his remarks upon nature. There is not the praise of a poet; whose office is rather to present known phenomenon in a new connection or medium.'[1] Newman did not distinguish between Warton's praise of novelty and his theory of imagination, but further, he did not distinguish between the comments and the emotive power of Thomson's poetry. As Geoffrey Tillotson points out, 'part of Thomson's praise as a poet—as the author, for example, of lines like

> The yellow wall-flower, stained with iron brown
> . . . auriculas, enriched
> With shining meal o'er all their velvet leaves—
> [*Spring*, ll. 533 ff.]

is precisely that he did paint facts with a meaning, beauty and harmonious order not their own, in a new connection or medium (by 'medium' Newman meant the intervening substance through which an object is seen)'.[2] Whatever the religious generalization Newman may have wished to make about poetry, in his comments upon this particular poem, it had little applicability, other than as an expression of personal preference.

[1] John Henry Newman, 'Poetry with Reference to Aristotle's Poetics' (written in 1828), *Essays Critical and Historical* (London, 1872), I, 12.

[2] Geoffrey Tillotson, 'Newman's Essay on Poetry: An Exposition and Comment', *Criticism and the Nineteenth Century* (University of London, 1951), p. 179. See also Alba H. Warren, Jr., *English Poetic Theory, 1825–1865* (Princeton, 1950), pp. 35–45.

(d) THE ROLE OF COMPARISON IN ANALYSES OF DESCRIPTION

> It is impossible to continue in the practice of contemplating any order of beauty, without being frequently obliged to form comparisons between the several species and degrees of excellence, and estimating their proportion to each other.
>
> HUME

Criticisms of Thomson's descriptions underwent two major changes: with the advent of William Cowper's *The Task* (1785), the criticism changed focus from the details of description to attitudes implied in such details; and with the advent of Wordsworth's nature poetry, Thomson's descriptions were found to express objective attitudes rather than moving religious views of nature. This extension of critical consciousness—and here again it is necessary to state that this applied to particular critics rather than to all—discriminating different aspects of description implied that all such discussions were grounded in comparison. The preceding analysis has demonstrated how explanations of description were circumscribed by practical or philosophical contexts. The range of the term depended upon its references; it is the function of this section to study the comparative procedures involved in such delimitation.

For Robert Shiels (1753), descriptions were compared with their appropriateness to each season, that is, with the assumed general characteristics of spring, summer, autumn, and winter. Such comparisons had as their end the imitation of nature: 'we tremble at his thunder in summer; we shiver at his winter's cold, and we rejoice at the renovation of nature, by the sweet influence of spring'. But *The Seasons* required special justification within the theory of imitation because its diction was marked by 'stiffness'. Shiels therefore argued that the intensity, the particularity, of the description was achieved by the 'singular' language: 'The object he paints stands full before the eye, we admire it in all its lustre'. Shiels was puzzled how this was achieved, but he assumed that there might be some relation between the awkwardness of expression and the particularity of thought which Thomson had successfully managed. Yet when he compared the descriptions of *The Seasons* with those of *The Castle of Indolence*, it appeared at once that he preferred the regular and traditional descriptions of Thomson's last poem because they involved no such perplexities: 'the descriptions rise in a beautiful succession' and the work discovered 'more genius and poetical judgment than all his other works put together'.[1]

For Shiels, the discussion of Thomson's descriptions was altered by the poet's later poems. The concept of 'appropriateness' to nature was more clearly defined by the descriptions that Thomson was capable of, and given the same criteria, the later poem accomplished without awkwardness what the earlier poem did with it. Yet Shiels passed over the question of whether the two types of description were indeed comparable, and if they were, why success which involved irregularity, 'stiffness', showed less 'genius' than 'regular' or 'successive' descriptions. Warton's analysis of the descriptions, though it, too, was governed by truth to nature, nevertheless identified this 'truth' with novel details of nature rather than traditional clichés, and the criterion of adequacy was the transmission of the image to the mind. Warton, therefore, found that—despite occasional infelicities of diction and versification—the poem communicated the precision and novelty of nature.

The comparison used in locating qualities for analysis was governed by the particular critical ends in view despite the fact that many critics subscribed to descriptive poetry as imitation of nature. Both of the above examples were instances in which the critic sought to accommodate new material to established assumptions. The recognition of the difficulty created by Thomson's diction was minimized in order to praise his precision and appropriateness. Yet both critics recognized that Thomson's descriptions were different from those of earlier poets, but his differences were determined by comparisons with them. A new basis for comparison was introduced with Cowper's *The Task* (1785).

The impact of *The Task* upon descriptive analysis can be traced in 'An Essay on the Plan and Character of Thomson's Seasons' (1778) published by John Aikin before *The Task* (1785) and his later essay, 'A Comparison Between Thomson and Cowper as Descriptive Poets'. The first essay identified *The Seasons* as a new genre, descriptive poetry, and justified the poem's unity, by arguing that its very structure rested on the laws of natural history. In the later essay, Aikin consciously set out to distinguish poetry from natural history: 'The qualities enumerated must not be so lax and general as to apply to several species of things . . . nor yet so methodically precise as the

[1] Shiels, 'Thomson', *Lives*, V, 197, 202, 205.

descriptions in natural history, which are addresses more to the intellect than to the imagination.'[1]

In distinguishing between the 'different manners of the *Task* and the *Seasons* in the description of natural objects', Aikin found that one of the key traits of Thomson's poem was a 'combination of elevated language with common matter'. Aikin noted two other characteristics of Thomson's descriptions: the process of humanizing animals in a natural scene in order to dignify a humble topic, and the use of compound epithets for compression. These characteristics could have been analysed without *The Task*, but the later poem demonstrated that low subject matter could be made moving without 'artificial' diction and thus directed attention to a procedure for which no previous examples existed: 'When his [Cowper's] subject is low, he is content to leave it so, without any effort to raise it by the ambitious ornaments of artificial diction, secure of interesting his reader by the truth and liveliness of his delineation.'[2]

The new work not only demonstrated the possibility of handling the same material differently, it helped define the manner in which it had been handled. Thus in the first essay, Aikin wrote that the introduction of 'draughts of human life and manners, will be sufficient

[1] John Aikin, 'A Comparison between Thomson and Cowper as Descriptive Poets', *Memoir of John Aikin*, by Lucy Aikin (London, 1823), II, 181. For 'images of grandeur or beauty', see Aikin, *An Essay*, p. x. For a bibliography of Cowperian studies from 1895 to 1960, see Lodwick Hartley, *William Cowper The Continuing Revaluation* (Chapel Hill, 1960). Aikin's original position was developed by comparison. St. Lambert had pointed out that nature poetry started a new genre: 'By the union of eloquence and philosophy, *physics* is become an agreeable study; its principles have become widely diffused and knowledge is grown popular . . . Poems may be written which require a very considerable knowledge of nature, and their authors may notwithstanding hope to find readers. The English and the Germans are the fathers of this kind of poetry' (p. 492). In comparing his poem, *Les Saisons*, with Thomson's *Seasons*, St. Lambert wrote: 'the designs of our poems were not the same; and the difference of the plan naturally produced a difference in the conduct: when we have painted the same objects, we have not given them the same proportions; and when our pictures have been the same in the drawing, the colouring has been different' (p. 497). See the Summary of St. Lambert's preface to *Les Saisons, Poëme*, *The Monthly Review*, XLI (1769), 496, 497. For comparison of descriptions in Milton and Thomson, see Edward Mangin, 'Letters XIV, XV', *A View of Pleasures Arising from Love of Books* (London, 1814).

[2] Aikin, 'Comparison', II, 181, 185–90.

to call to mind the admirable use which Thomson throughout his whole poem has made of them'. But in the second essay, he declared: 'It is generally admitted that the style of Thomson is little suited to the narrative of common life. Destitute of ease, and wholly unlike the language of real conversation, it proves an awkward vehicle for the dialogue and incidents of story-telling; and though an interest is excited by the pathetic of the circumstances, as in the maid struck by lightning, and the man lost in the snow, it owes nothing to the manner of narration.'[1]

It should be noted that the critic's range of reference could be redirected, without causing him to reconsider his standards. For Aikin, who defended descriptive poetry as a new genre, was not equally prepared to defend the mixture of elevated language and humble matter. His scientific bias encouraged the recognition of new evidence, but at the same time it substituted what could be done for what had been done. *The Task*, by expressing common matter in common language, provided a guide to what could be done, but Aikin assumed that Thomson's descriptions should be judged by this accomplishment, not interpreted by it. He treated the comparison as two attempts to achieve the same end, whereas what the comparison implied was that there now existed another possibility of achieving similar but not identical ends. Instead, therefore, of representing an additional possibility of the kind of poem Thomson wrote, *The Task* became a standard for evaluating Thomson's language.

Yet Aikin himself was unhappy with this procedure and sought to explain that the poems were, as wholes, incomparable, even though he had compared some of their parts.

> Between the two poems no comparison can subsist; for while the Seasons is the completion of an extensive plan, necessarily comprising a great variety of topics, most of which would occur to every poetical mind occupied in the same design, the Task owes nothing to a preconceived argument, but is the extemporaneous product of the very singular mind and genius of the author. It had no model and can have no parallel.[2]

Aikin quite easily included *The Task* in his reality theory of poetry. Data were welcomed in so far as they could be absorbed

[1] Aikin, 'An Essay', p. xxxviii; 'Comparison', II, 195.
[2] Aikin, 'Comparison', II, 197–8.

by a method which insisted upon verifiable improvement: if *The Task* did what other poems did not, it became the basis for judging the others. The readiness to accept new particulars was implicit in the concepts of revision and adaptation in which changes in the means were accepted as diverse ways of achieving the 'same' ends. This attitude had, of course, been accepted in the descriptive view that the object would be seen similarly but expressed differently. Thomson's poem, precisely because it created dilemmas about the relation of thought to expression, urged upon critics the realization that it achieved its values in some contradictory way, that is, in despite of its awkward diction through some resolution of it.

The function of particular comparison in the development of Thomson criticism was twofold: by its specific and particular references, it insisted upon the differentness of *The Seasons* and *The Task,* thus causing these poems to be seen as possessing different descriptive ends; by accumulating a body of comparisons with reference to particular devices and subjects within the poem, the comparative procedure stimulated other inquiries, and the value attributed to the poem as a whole involved weighing the importance of the different accomplishments. Thus, although Thomson's value as a descriptive writer was not questioned, it was nevertheless possible for Jeffrey (1808) to prefer *The Castle of Indolence* to *The Seasons* and for J. C. Shairp to minimize the importance of *The Seasons* because its moral attitude was 'thoughtlessly thankful'.[1]

In 1796, in a 'Critique of the Poetry of Cowper', *The Flapper*, an Irish journal, pointed out that Thomson and Cowper were 'poets of nature', but the descriptions of the first were 'highly finished paintings of the Flemish-school; those of *Cowper* are little more than sketches, but they are the sketches of a *Raphael*'. Thomson's description was more laboured and detailed than Cowper's, 'but although Cowper shuns minuteness of description, he very frequently, as has been already observed, describes minute or trivial matters'.[2] But Aikin,

[1] John C. Shairp, *On Poetic Interpretation of Nature* (Edinburgh, 1877), p. 191.

[2] Alexander Knox, No. 30 (14 May 1795), *The Flapper* (Dublin, 1796), p. 118; 34, p. 134. The comparison extended over issues 30, 34 (28 May 1796), and 38 (11 June 1796). For criticisms of Cowper at the end of the eighteenth century, see Lodwick Hartley, ' "The Stricken Deer" and his Contemporary Reputation', *SP*, XXXVI (1939), 637–50.

in his second essay, found the poets equally detailed and minute, identifying not Thomson but Cowper with the Flemish School: 'equally minute and circumstantial with Thomson in his mode of description . . . he sometimes paints in a manner resembling the Dutch or Flemish school—but always with touches of the true picturesque'.[1]

Hazlitt (1818) declared that Thomson did 'not go into the *minutiae* of a landscape, but describes the vivid impression which the whole makes upon his own imagination'.[2] And Thomas Campbell (1819) wrote: 'Cowper's image of nature is more curiously distinct and familiar: Thomson carries our association through a wider circuit of speculation and sympathy; his touches cannot be more faithful than Cowper's, but they are more soft and select, and less disturbed by the intrusion of homely objects'.[3]

The apparent disagreement with regard to the minuteness of Thomson's descriptions indicated that comparison, as a method, operated within selected contexts. If *The Flapper* considered Thomson's descriptions as 'finished', it was comparing the red-breast description in *Winter* with the 'sketch' of 'The Woodman' in *The Task* ('equally minute and circumstantial') and the reference to the Flemish School could have been to the harvest scene. Hazlitt, on the other hand, had reference to the views of prospects, like that from Hagley Hall in *Spring*, where Thomson created the effect of the whole. Campbell referred to faithful descriptions like the thunderstorm in *Summer* and its associated phenomena, or the 'descriptions' of the passion of the groves in *Spring* ('soft and select') in contrast to Cowper's familiar and homely objects.

Comparison, therefore, entailed no necessarily identical references; comparison with regard to minute and circumstantial detail developed a series of distinctions which helped define the term 'circumstantial'—the finished quality of Flemish painting, the reference to domestic subject matter, the distinction between close and distant views, and between effects of detail which were 'finished' and those which presented 'broad strokes'. The method of providing extensive examples—in Robert Heron (1793) and *The Flapper* (1796)—was not matched in the usages of Hazlitt and Campbell; despite their discussion of similar details, the critics were actually using them

[1] Aikin, 'Comparison', II, 189. [2] Hazlitt, p. 167.

[3] Thomas Campbell, 'James Thomson', *Specimens of the British Poets* (1819) (London, 1841), p. 403.

for diverse purposes. *The Flapper* critic (Alexander Knox) was interested in illustrating the different impact which associations had upon the mind of the poet, and the comparison functioned as an example of such variety.

> It is obvious that poetry owes its very existence to that natural exercise of the human mind which is usually termed the association of ideas. Of this in a greater or less degree we are all sensible. We look at an object—that brings another to our mind, and that another, and so on in succession. We see, for example, a distant city; we are led to think of its inhabitants—to form conjectures about their occupations and pursuits—their pleasures and their pains. We turn our view to the country, and our fancy immediately begins to range amongst the probabilities of rustic life. A poet chiefly differs from a common man in the superior liveliness and justness with which he exercises this faculty. The greater his ability in forming these ideal pictures—in conceiving them with strength, with nearness to nature and fact, and with discriminative selection—and in expressing what he himself feels so as to make others participate in his feelings, the more, undoubtedly, does he possess of the radical qualities of a poet.
>
> But in order to give full delight, it is not enough that the powers of his mind merely, should be employed. His heart must be engaged, else the pleasure which he feels himself, or causes others to feel, must be comparatively dull and vapid.[1]

Aikin was interested in demonstrating the range of Cowper and his superior 'correctness' in natural science; he therefore sought to show Cowper's descriptions as equal in extent and superior in accuracy. But neither of these descriptive comparisons dealt with the varied types of descriptions in the two poems; the first focussed upon the subject matter, the second stressed 'correctness'. Alexander Knox wrote that Thomson described 'what every man may see, and what indeed almost every man has seen at one time or other; but Cowper describes what every man *must* see; he takes his materials from the every-day walks of life; he seizes on those little domestic circumstances, which perhaps no poet before him ever thought of making use of; and he forms from them pictures which astonish no less than they please'.[2]

By referring to specific details in the poem, the critics found considerable dissimilarities, and one consequence was, in the case of

[1] *Flapper*, 38, p. 149.

[2] *Flapper*, 30, p. 118.

Aikin, that *The Seasons* and *The Task* as wholes were found incomparable, each being an original. But he did make comparisons of details. Hazlitt (1818), on the other hand, sought to compare not details, but the different affective qualities of the two poems. Arguing from a concept of imagination marked by spontaneity and vigor, Hazlitt said that Thomson saw nature 'growing around us, fresh and lusty as in itself'. He saw the descriptions of 'the snow drifting against the broken casement without. . . . The first scattered drops of a vernal shower' as nature unfolding. Hazlitt accepted the hypothesis of the sympathetic imagination and he assumed that to feel deeply was to transfer 'the same unbroken, unimpaired impression to the imagination of his readers'. Thomson had artificialities, false ornaments, but his original genius could not be destroyed by these.

Led by his sympathetic reading, not his elusive theoretical claims, Hazlitt identified qualities in the poem which had previously been overlooked. The meaning of the descriptions was not merely in the profound sentiments; it was in the inevitable changes of nature. Hazlitt continued the fiction of Thomson's unforced creativity, although he attributed the 'vivid impressions' of the poem to the descriptions of a dynamic nature, and he speculated upon the achievement of vividness as due to early associations of the poem transformed by the imagination: 'The whole of the description of the frozen zone is perhaps even finer and more thoroughly felt, as being done from early associations, than that of the torrid zone in his Summer.' Hazlitt's use of the comparison with Cowper was not to discriminate the diverse qualities of these poets by use of examples, but rather to serve as a summary of points already made and to suggest the kind of affective response the poem created.

These comparisons indicated the shift in the function of description that was taking place: from a study of particular examples of the same kind, the comparisons had become a series of evaluations of diverse subjects and devices such as diction (manly or weak, pompous or simple, energetic or bland); moral attitude (*constantly* benevolent or varied); description (distinct, familiar or sublime and general); subject matter (soft, domestic or sublime and in process). The 'general' value of the poem, therefore, depended upon the preferences which the critic had with regard to these qualities or with regard to other poems by Thomson. Thus Hazlitt preferred *The Seasons* to *The Task*, but Campbell did not. But Campbell also found that to ' "The Castle of Indolence", Thomson brought not only the full nature, but the perfect art of a poet'. Such perfection implied a preference for regularity and smoothness which *The Seasons* did not possess. Another aspect of subjective preference with regard to areas within the poem was apparent in relating the moral didacticism to the description.

Aikin in 1778 recognized that the moral passages were those in which Thomson could most easily be rivalled, and in 1785 John Scott wrote that the moral sentiment was the cheapest commodity of the poem. Both these critics minimized the importance of such passages in dealing with the originality of the work as a descriptive poem. But the 1816 editor objected to Thomson's moral sentiments as a serious flaw in the poem because of his own religious feelings: 'The Religion of the Seasons is of that general kind which Nature's self might teach to those who had no knowledge of the God of Revelation. It is a lofty and complacent sentiment . . . but has no reference to the quality of our belief, to the dispositions of the heart, or to the habitual tendency of the character; still less does it involve a devotional recognition of the revealed character of the Divine Being'.[1] The critic minimized the value of the poem precisely because its moral attitude was commonplace, and though he praised the description, he did so for its merely visual accuracy. The concept of value as proportionate was accepted, but the proportions were altered. Earlier Beattie (1776) and Stockdale (1806) had praised Thomson's benevolence because it made the poet see the love within nature. Their views, therefore, were rejected by the 1816 critic because he rejected the occasional deism of the poem, whereas the earlier critics approved it. But the argument had, in a sense, little pertinence for the subsequent comment of Hazlitt in which nature was seen as 'growing around us, fresh and lusty as in itself'. The poem's interpretation involved the implications of storms and of death, and although earlier comments approved Thomson's didacticism, the decision rested upon the number, frequency and pertinence of such passages, for the poem obviously contained varied views of nature.

Because *The Task* dealt with such varied sublime and trivial scenes, it became a test case in the Bowles–Byron controversy, a demonstration that the execution, not the subject made great poetry: 'the delight we experience from the perusal of . . . *The Task*, is not to be attributed to the *objects*, as they exist in nature, but is a participation of the

[1] 'Critical Observations', *The Seasons* (London, 1816), p. x.

feelings of the poet.'[1] Bowles and Roscoe did agree about the value of execution, but the point was that nature poetry was not by 'subject' superior to any other kind. Thus *The Task*, because it dealt with subjects, often trivial, and not always with outward nature, was a model of the transforming power of the poet. But neither Bowles nor any of his opponents could analyse 'execution' in terms different from those offered by the late eighteenth-century critics.

Such moral comments, however, increased with the substitution of Wordsworth for Cowper as a basis for comparison. Stopford Brooke (1862) indicated that Thomson was a predecessor of Wordsworth who lacked his moral insight into nature and J. C. Shairp (1877), continuing this comparison, declared that Thomson's natural description suggested a religion 'easily satisfied and thoughtlessly thankful!' Thomson's religion of nature was part of the culture around him, but it showed 'no perception of that deeper mystery—that the whole creation groaneth and travaileth in pain, waiting for a deliverance'.[2] Wordsworth felt the travail, but Thomson only saw it. The proportionate weight of the vivid description decreased as the insight of Wordsworth was held up as a model.

The proportionate method in determining value had been a commonplace in criticism; Longinus, for example, in comparing Demosthenes with other orators, declared, 'in those Parts wherein he excels, he is so far superior to them, that he makes full amends for those [points] wherein he is defective'.[3] The sublime was recompense for defects because it provided an insight into the magnificence of nature. Longinus recognized the ideal of a 'sovereign Perfection of good Writing', but his discussion admitted the difficulty of attaining the ideal. Neander, in Dryden's *Of Dramatick Poesie* (1668), found vividness and liveliness of action and expression the dominant criteria in drama and judged the proportions accordingly. Though the English 'are not altogether so punctual as the French, in observing the basis of Comedy, yet our errors are so few, and little, and those things wherein we excel them so considerable, that we ought

[1] William Roscoe, *A Letter to the Reverend William Lisle Bowles, A.M.* (London, 1825), p. 42. See also Walter Bagehot, 'William Cowper' (1855), *Literary Studies* (London, 1905), I, 129–32. For Cowper's significance in early nineteenth-century comparisons, see Upali Amarasinghe, *Dryden and Pope in the Early Nineteenth Century* (Cambridge, 1962), pp. 78–82.

[2] Shairp, *On Poetic Interpretation of Nature*, p. 193

[3] *On the Sublime*, tr. L. Welsted, pp. 230, 235.

of right to be preferred before them'.[1] Pope set up proportions between the inexactness of poetry and the 'joint force and full result of all', that is, the vividness and energy which the work possessed.

In terms of final explanations, one might say, with Pope, that proportionate theories derive from the belief that man is a limited creature. ''Tis certain there is no art whatsoever brought to so great a Degree of Perfection, as to be entirely without Fault.'[2] For Thomson's critics, the elements in the proportions often differed. When the Edinburgh editor of Thomson's works (1768) admitted that *The Seasons* contained 'some inaccuracies', he did so only to point out their inconsequence and to attack those critics 'insensible of the true merit of poetry, noble sentiments and lively descriptions, and dwelling on trivial transgressions of minute critical rules'.[3] Such proportioning involved a hierarchy of 'true' and 'trivial' qualities in the poem and some assumptions about their interrelations. Such assumptions possessed more than mere subjectivity even when including statements about 'correctness', 'moral digressions', 'unity', or 'accuracy'; and when critics shared comparative contexts, the evaluation tended to be fairly consistent. Thus up to the late nineteenth century no critic ever denied the accuracy and vividness of Thomson's natural descriptions. When Shairp (1877) and Palgrave (1898) denied it, they did so because they identified vivid description not with accuracy or emotive language, but with particular moral assumptions as a condition of perception. Among critics who agreed on conditions of perception, differences occurred in the kind of approval, based on the comparative contexts provided by other (earlier and later) authors.

Critics who objected to comparisons of proportions, of parts of one work with those of another did so on the ground that such comparisons lacked an ideal truth. William Gilpin attacked La Bruyère because his concept of proportioning was incapable of 'that masterly judgment' derived from the truth of nature and the solid rules of art.

[1] Dryden, *Essays*, I, 75.

[2] Charles Lamotte, *An Essay on Poetry and Painting* (London, 1742), p. 53.

[3] 'An Account of the Life and Writings of Mr. James Thomson' (dated Edin., 15 July 1768). Prefixed to *The Seasons*, *Works* (Edinburgh, 1772), I, 8.

> In one sense all judgment must be formed on comparison. But Bruyère, who is speaking of poetry, means, that the inferior critic has no scale of judging a work of art, but by comparing it with some other work of the same kind. He judges of Virgil by a comparison with Homer; and of Spenser by comparing him with Tasso. By such criticism he may indeed arrive at certain truths; but he will never form that masterly judgment, which he might do by comparing the work before him with the great archetypes of nature, and the solid rules of his art.[1]

But judgements of the 'solid rules of art' were dependent upon some practical works, even if never again achieved. The grounds for establishing 'solid rules', therefore, had to relate to what could be done, or what ought to be done, but the manner of indicating failure in particular works would, nevertheless, involve the same evidence as that used by proportioning critics. Gilpin's objection, therefore, although posed as an attack on these critics, suggested an ideal end, the practical attainment of which involved methods similar to those used by them. As one aspect of Thomson's religion grew clearer, the distance between the Victorian view of nature and Thomson's increased. For those critics to whom nature meant the direct interrelation between God and man, Thomson's conception of the forces of the natural world was inhospitable because it viewed man as one element in the operations of nature, capable of being tossed and terrified by storms and seas. In a world in which man was concerned with his self-made 'groaning' and 'travailings', Thomson's view was, perhaps correctly, consigned to the 'rising generation' rather than the risen.

There continued to exist, therefore, a valuation which required historical insight for its foundation, but which neglected to re-examine the meaning of history as presented in *The Seasons*. The valuation of Shairp was refutable if it could be shown that Thomson's view of nature was not 'thoughtlessly thankful', and such a task was

[1] William Gilpin, 'Notes' to 'On Landscape Painting', *Three Essays* (London, 1792), p. 43. Gilpin's reference to nature as ideal or archetypal is an attempt to compare characteristics in a poem or a painting with those characteristics in nature. The critic is not to be limited by past achievements in a genre, by recognizing what had been done; he judges a poem by the ideal possibilities of nature. Such criticism confuses the translation of nature into art—of sight into language or colour and form with 'untranslated' nature. To know what can be done with the medium requires a knowledge of other poems and other paintings.

begun by Léon Morel and Myra Reynolds. Comparative value, therefore, was not only amenable to analysis, it also recognized that given particular parts of the poem values could be located therein. Thus circumstantial analysis of Thomson and circumstantial analysis of Cowper were both valuable because they functioned expressively (in given instances) to exploit the subjects, versification and language of poetry. In so far as choice of parts for comparison differs, conclusions about them are neither complementary nor contradictory but coextensive—and the usefulness of such comparisons depends upon their relation to the end assigned or reached.

The purpose of comparison is to permit keener distinctions and to make interpretation more exact. But comparison depends upon careful and relevant selection of passages: such 'relevance' is not beyond argument. Comparison, moreover, must be understood as a guide to valuing a passage, not a judgement of it. In determining proper comparisons, one is always limited to parts of poems, and so-called comparisons of 'wholes' are comparisons of some selected parts or qualities.

The exactness of interpretation that results from a 'part' may lead to recognizing its importance in the whole poem, and, indeed, any interpretation of parts depends upon a determination of the kind of poem one is reading. The role of description in a descriptive poem is considerably diminished if one discovers the poem to be a didactic exercise in deism. Yet the end in view is not as relativistic as may at first appear. If one begins with the assumption that the poem is a given, not what is in the mind of the author or in some ideal mind, but in the text as established (or established to the best of our poor knowledge), diverse interpretations of the end, at least in *The Seasons*, are examples of misinterpretation or reductionism rather than defensible positions.

Comparative interpretations help define the 'end', i.e. the relatedness of parts to whole, and in becoming more precise make the unfolding of the poem more so. Critics who compare parts, nevertheless refer to the quality of the poem as a 'whole'. Such statements, however, must be understood as proportionate divisions. The 'poem' may be valued despite its 'stiff' or 'artificial' diction, or because the descriptions of nature are considered more relevant to the end than the didactic passages. Or the 'stiffness' may invalidate any responsiveness to the poem so that it is considered a 'bad' poem because unreadable. But even here, the 'unreadability' is applicable either to the whole or to parts—and if the poem has—as *The Seasons* has—several kinds of diction, 'unreadability' would then have to apply to all types of such diction or only to some, sufficient to create proportions making the poem 'bad'. It may even be possible to argue that critics agree on interpretations of parts, but disagree upon the proportionate value they attribute to each. But whatever the judgement, the critics deal with parts and their interrelation, and in the comparative analysis of Thomson's description, there exists a very substantial concord.

IV

THE SCOPE OF CRITICAL ANALOGY: *UT PICTURA POESIS*

> Is there not something very fanciful in the analogy which some people have discovered between the arts? I do not deny the *commune quoddam vinculum*, but would keep the principle within its proper bounds.
>
> WILLIAM JACKSON

THE COMPARISON OF THE ARTS seems to persist in criticism without providing any conclusive evidence for its significance. This is, perhaps, reasonable since analogy is not a form of 'proof'. The criticism of *The Seasons* offers a special instance of the tenacity of the analogy since the poem has been compared with landscape painting from its publication, and although the analogy has not been equally important to all critics, it seems, in contrast to other forms of critical language, to possess unusual durability.

I wish in this chapter to study the critical functions of this analogy with reference to *The Seasons*: what it contributed to the interpretation of the poem and what arguments were necessary to reject any particular use. In doing this, I have had to explain eighteenth-century justifications of this analogy and objections brought against it. Critics shifted the analogy from sight to sound, from painting to music; in the transition it merely relinquished aspects of the painting analogy which science refuted, not the assumptions underlying the analogy.

Comparisons of poetry or music to painting led to increased discriminations which repeatedly proved self-corrective so long as examples were given—without such examples analogy remained speculative and groping. The major change in the painting analogy occurred when it was temporarily displaced by the evolutionary or developmental analogy. The displacement led to attempts to provide 'objective' evidence for its application; but this 'new' evidence demonstrated only that poets knew painting traditions and that these were incorporated in poetry, not that the poetry derived any structural properties from this knowledge.

The critical use of analogy defended the status of poetry, increased discriminations within the media of poetry and painting, broadened the range of shared knowledge which the arts practised, reflected the dependence of analogy upon scientific and other non-literary assumptions. Assumptions always underlie the analogy, whether assumptions about the divinity of nature, about science, about correspondences between media. Some may be more readily disposed of than others, but they do not necessarily shake the comparison, just as the painting or sight analogy was converted, without distortion, to that of music or sound. The reason is that analogies can exemplify relations for which no adequate explanation is available and, by relying upon two arts, the arguments seem more persuasive than if they rely upon one. The use of analogy demands of critics at least an extension of their knowledge of the arts. One analogy, in all its implications, can be supplanted by another resulting from new scientific or religious attitudes, but the innovating analogy does not necessarily reflect or indicate either new literary insights or new literary evidence. In this respect, the study of analogy buttresses the view that the shift of critical problems belongs to the second half of the nineteenth century.

(a) DESCRIPTION: THE ANALOGICAL BASIS

> It is difficult to discourse on either of them [poetry and painting], without a mutual borrowing of Images and Terms.
>
> H. JACOB

In the early eighteenth century poetry was compared with painting to illustrate that each possessed (1) social status, (2) common sources of subject matter, (3) a shared mode of apprehension, and (4) similar stylistic characteristics like design, colour, characters, etc. This comparison sought for description a poetic status which the drama already had, so that its defence sometimes involved competition with the drama: 'Every one', wrote John Hughes (1713), 'immediately perceives the Resemblance of Nature in the Description of a Tempest, a Palace or a Garden; but the Beauty of proper Sentiments in the Speeches of a Prince, a General, or a Counsellor is more remote, and discern'd by a kind of second Thought or Reflection'.[1] This argument had serious drawbacks as a theory of language, for there was no reason why sentiment should require more or less thought than a tempest which was never experienced. And it permitted a critic in *The Plain Dealer* (1726) to turn the entire argument against poetry because painting appealed directly to the imagination and understanding, but the poet's words lacked the directness of sight: 'The *Painter* informs the Understanding, and warms the Imagination, by striking the *Sight* strongly, and giving it the Height of Pleasure; while all that can be done, of that kind, by the greatest Poet that ever liv'd is to make us merely *imagine*, that he sets Things before our *Eyes*.'[2] The critic distinguished between the direct response of the senses and the imaginative recall of such responses. It was a position disputed by Addison who, quite justly, found recall often more intense than the reality. Yet the imagination was subordinated to the theory of sense data and critics who praised it, like Henry Needler, considered it less vivid than reality: 'there is a sort of Painting to the Imagination as well as the Eye' which 'nothing but that arising from the actual Enjoyment of the thing describ'd could exceed'.[3] In the family of arts comparison always involved a dialectical tug, with victory being awarded to the art that the critic considered the most important. But the analogical 'family' of the eighteenth century was

[1] Hughes, 439 (12 Feb. 1713), *The Lay Monastery*, 227–8. 'Resemblance', 'parallel', 'comparison', 'affinity', were the terms used to discuss poetry and painting in the early eighteenth century. 'Analogy' was not, at the beginning of the century, used with reference to the arts. The phrase '*ut pictura poesis*' was conveyed in diverse ways by translators of Horace: the Earl of Roscommon rendered it, '*Poems*, like Pictures, are of different Sorts' (1684); S. Dunster rendered it, 'Poetry and Painting have so near and close a Resemblance to each other, that in effect they are both the same' (1712); Philip Francis translated it 'Like painting, poetry' (1743); S. Patrick translated it, 'Poetry very much resembles Painting' (1750, 3rd ed.); and George Colman translated it, 'Pictures and poems are adjudged alike' (1783).

[2] *The Plain Dealer* (London, 1730), II, 26–27.

[3] Henry Needler, *Works*, ed. William Duncombe (London, 1728), pp. 91–92. For a commentary on Needler's theory and a bibliography, see Marcia Allentuck, ed., *Works of Henry Needler* (a selection), (Los Angeles, 1961), Augustan Reprint 90.

based on authority, propriety, decorum; that of the nineteenth on love and personal obligation.

The language of painters and their supporters in claiming social status for their art, and the language of poets and critics analogizing poetry to painting or the drama, assumed, that—regardless of the accuracy of these claims—one art was more eminent, more culturally useful than the other. Thus poetry sometimes clung to the skirts of painting for the social values already granted to the latter, e.g. its educational function in broadening the scope and knowledge of the new classes. Richardson in the *Science of a Connoisseur* insisted on the educative function of painting, and George Turnbull wrote his *Treatise* as an attempt to reveal the arts as the proper humanistic sources of value.[1] He wished, he explained, that the grand tour should be undertaken with a knowledge of the values of the humanistic arts, and Daniel Webb in 1760 explained, 'the persons for whom I write, are our young travellers, who set out with much eagerness, and little preparation'.[2]

Painting was, in a social sense, an aristocratic art; portrait painting was the 'darling passion' of both sexes, but especially of women, and it served their self-interest. Moreover, the painter had only one original, while the poem had many copies fully as good as the original. The painter spoke to a universal polite audience, whereas the poet was confined to those in his own country.

> The great Painter speaks to all Countries as intelligibly, as to his own. Nay, more intelligibly, more gracefully, more forcibly, to those Countries which are polite; and, therefore his fame keeps equal Pace with his Merit . . .
>
> Few persons pretend to decide sovereignly in Painting, but they who are acquainted with the Rules of the Art . . . whereas the Rabble of Mankind pretending to Judge of *Poetry*, sovereignly,

[1] Jonathan Richardson, *A Discourse on the Dignity, Certainty, Pleasure and Advantage of the Science of a Connoisseur*, *Works*, ed. J. Richardson (London, 1773), pp. 247–56. George Turnbull, *A Treatise on Ancient Painting* (London, 1740), p. ix. For a modern discussion of the family of the arts and their history in the eighteenth century, see Paul A. Kristeller, 'The Modern System of the Arts: A Study in the History of Aesthetics (I)', *JHI*, XII (1951), 496–527; 'The Modern System of the Arts (II)', *JHI*, XIII (1952), 7–46. See also Hugh Boyd, 'The Indian Observer' (23 Oct. 1793), *The Miscellaneous Works* (London, 1800), II, 342.

[2] Daniel Webb, *An Inquiry into the Beauties of Painting* (London, 1760), p. vi.

and without Appeal, wretched *Poetasters* have been often *applauded*, and *excellent Poets neglected.*[1]

The limited and 'decaying' language of poetry was compared with the assumed universal and unchanging language of painting, and in so doing brought the two 'languages' closer as they reflected each other's characteristics. Pope wrote, 'And such as Chaucer is, shall Dryden be', and indicated that poetic language changed but colours never lost their original hue. But Jonathan Richardson explained that colours faded, just as language did. The revival of medieval ballads and early English poetry demonstrated that language was not so decayed as had been thought.

The two arts could form a single body and soul, and through their different means could become a moral model. 'They both agree', wrote Joseph Trapp, in his *Lectures* (1713, 1749), 'in representing to the Mind Images of Things, and ought both of them to be govern'd by Nature and Probability. So near is their Affinity, that by a very natural and common Metaphor, Poetry is said to paint Things, Painting to describe them. Both give us *Draughts* of the Body, as well as the Soul; but with this Difference, that the former is chiefly expressed by Painting, the latter by Poetry.'[2]

Painting, according to Trapp, chiefly expressed the physical, poetry the spiritual aspects of human behaviour, though each gave 'Draughts of the Body, as well as the Soul'. The two arts together formed a complete example of human experience, and complemented each other by their means of expression, but singly they lacked this completeness, because each art stressed a different aspect of human activity. Even the critic in *The Plain Dealer* (1724) contrasted the means of expression in poetry with the permanent and universal language of painting—''tis not so much the fault of our Writers, as the Language itself that they are not read with Pleasure at this Day'—and suggested that the two arts would supplement their two different means. 'Two *Sister Arts*', he wrote, 'uniting their different *Powers*,

[1] *The Plain Dealer*, II, 23–24, 25. It should be noted that the late eighteenth-century use of 'poetic' to refer to painting indicated a strategic shift in the importance of the poet as well as an attempt to subsume poetry and painting under 'imagination'.

[2] Joseph Trapp, *Lectures*, p. 17. For Trapp's view of metaphor, see Vincent Freimarck, 'Joseph Trapp's Advanced Conception of Metaphor', *PQ* (1950), 412–16. For another comparison of poet and painter, see *The Free-Thinker*, No. 63 (27 Oct. 1718) (London, 1722), II, 51–54.

the one transmitting *Souls*, the other *Bodies* (or the outward Form of Bodies), their combining Influence would be of Force to frustrate *Death Itself:* And all the Ages of the world would seem to be *Contemporaries*.'[1]

Throughout the eighteenth century, the analogy of descriptive poetry with landscape painting served the purpose of poetry far more than that of painting. Critics seized upon the authority of a century of landscape painters to explain what classical criticism had minimized. If at the beginning of the eighteenth century poetry was compared to painting, at the beginning of the nineteenth century this practice was reversed and painting was compared with description or poetry. In the twentieth century, critics have compared *The Seasons* with specific scenes and paintings to display the confusions of poetry or to prove the ingenuity of language in achieving visual effects, but such positions have substituted for metaphoric terminology an 'inductive' or 'objective' language.

(b) JAMES THOMSON: THE 'PAINTING' OF NATURE

But who can paint / Like Nature?
JAMES THOMSON

The comparison of poetry to painting with regard to the vividness and particularity of visual experience was recognized by Thomson, but using the divine analogy, he compared poetry not to the vividness of the sister art, but to the vividness of nature. Those qualities which Thomson found in nature—the hues mixed with matchless skill 'in every bud that blows'—even extended to the olfactory sensations of nature, 'those aromatic gales / That inexhaustive flow continual round'. Thomson found poetry and painting unable to

[1] *The Plain Dealer*, II, 20. For histories of comparisons of poetry with painting—not of the critical use of analogy—see William G. Howard, '*Ut Pictura Poesis*', *PMLA*, XXIV (1909), 40–123; Cicely Davies, '*Ut Pictura Poesis*,' *MLR*, XXX (1935), 159–69; Rennselaer Lee, '*Ut Pictura Poesis:* The Humanistic Theory of Painting,' *Art Bulletin*, XXII (1940), 197–269; William Carter, Jr., *Ut Pictura Poesis: A Study of the Parallel Between Painting and Poetry from Classical Times through the Seventeenth Century* (Unpublished Dissertation, Harvard, 1951); Wimsatt and Brooks, *Literary Criticism*, pp. 264–76; Daniel Jones, *Common Trends in Landscape Painting and Nature Poetry in the Eighteenth Century* (Unpublished Master's Thesis, University of Wales, Aberystwyth, 1954); Rémy G. Saisselin, 'Ut Pictura Poesis: DuBos to Diderot', *JAAC* (1961), 145–56.

create the vividness of sensations derived from nature itself. This picture view of language had already been refuted by Addison with the argument that sensations from art could, in imagination, stimulate hues even more vivid than the original. But for Thomson, imagination's painting was inferior to nature in the mixing and variety of its hues.

> Behold yon breathing prospect bids the Muse
> Throw all her beauty forth. But who can paint
> Like Nature? Can imagination boast,
> Amid its gay creation, hues like hers?
> Or can it mix them with that matchless skill,
> And lose them in each other, as appears
> In every bud that blows? If fancy then
> Unequal fails beneath the pleasing task,
> Ah, what shall language do? ah, where find words
> Tinged with so many colours and whose power,
> To life approaching, may perfume my lays
> With that fine oil, those aromatic gales
> That inexhaustive flow continual round?
> Yet, though successless, will the toil delight.
> [*Spring*, *ll.* 467–80]

The efforts of the poetic imagination to rival the vividness and gaiety of nature were doomed to failure, but the attempt to achieve the ideal made failure delightful. Words lacked the actual presence of nature, but their references evoked some of its colours and odours. Thomson characteristically moved, in comparing language to nature, from one sense to another. Words, like flowers, were tinged with colours—but where find words with so many colours, with odours, with 'aromatic gales that inexhaustive flow continual round'? The sensuous implications sought for in language were vividly present in Thomson's use of the analogy, and when James Delacour, in his poem 'To Mr. Thomson on his Seasons' (1734), used the painting metaphor, he did so to explain that *The Seasons* painted nature more vividly, not less. The 'purer blue', the 'peculiar green' of spring, these were Thomson's achievement. Thomson's art created an ideal vividness.

> Beneath thy touch description paints anew,
> And the skies brighten to a purer blue;
> Spring owes thy pencil her peculiar green,
> And drown'd in redder roses summer's seen:

While hoary winter whitens into cold,
And Autumn bends beneath her bearded gold.

. . . . .

Your sky dipt pencil adds the proper glow,
Stains each bright stone, and lets their lustre flow,
Tempers the colours shifting from each beam,
And bids them flash in one continual stream.

Patrick Murdoch in his biography of Thomson (1762) also pointed out that the poet was able to describe monuments of antiquity more vividly 'than if we saw them with our eyes'.[1]

Both Thomson and Delacour, writing as users of the poetry-painting analogy, found the common ends of these two arts in the vividness of nature. Thomson found such effects to be less vivid, Delacour more vivid than nature. Delacour, however, was discussing the selectivity and intensity of the poem, Thomson the variety and scope of nature. But the variety and scope were never *directly* imitated in art, nor were they ever intended to be. If Thomson implied that, he was urging a theory held by no critic. But if he referred to the skill and vividness in creating imagined colours, then he was opposed to the views expressed by Delacour and Murdoch. Thomson's views were ill founded and one praise of *The Seasons* was its vividness, a vividness greater than nature's. It is unnecessary to belabour the irrelevance of Thomson's theory in the production or evaluation of poetry. But it may serve to explain the insertions of extensive information in order to rival the variety of nature.

Only John More (1777) selected Thomson's 'painting' passage to illustrate the poet's descriptive powers; but no critic selected Thomson's critical statements as a basis for discussing his descriptive powers. Indeed, if they had, it would have been apparent that his display of the poetry-painting analogy was a refutation of his argument. Thomson's image (*Spring*, ll. 467–80) began by comparing the

[1] Murdoch, I, xviii. For Thomson's indebtedness to John Norris' neoplatonism, see Herbert J. Drennon, 'James Thomson and John Norris', *PMLA*, LIII (1938), 1094–1101. For his indebtedness to Shaftesbury see Drennon, 'The Source of James Thomson's "The Works and Wonders of Almighty Power" ', *MP*, XXXII (1934), 33–36; Cecil Moore, 'Shaftesbury and the Ethical Poets in England, 1700–1760', *PMLA* (1916), 281–91. There is no need to point out that Thomson's scientific and ethical ideas involve no necessary contradiction as was claimed by Drennon.

painting imagination of nature with the painting imagination of the artist, and the imaginative painting skill of nature with that of the painter; it then compared the inadequate role of language as colour with the vivid colour of nature, and concluded with a transfer from words as colours to words as odours, 'aromatic gales' like the flowers of nature which could give sweetness to the poem. The transference of the image from painting to language to odour was one example of that very variety and transforming quality which the poet attributed to nature and of which his own lines were a demonstration even while they were supposed to deny this transformation. It was to the felt qualities of language, not to its didacticism, that Delacour and Murdoch pointed when they found his description more vivid than nature itself.

The example of Thomson's own use of the divine analogy provides a basis for explaining the limitations of critical language. Contemporary critics who sympathize with or share the same culture as the poet are involved with him in certain common views expressed by critical analogies. In using them, they convey the same content as the poet, thus paralleling rather than explaining his poetry. This is especially true in the use of continuing metaphors such as those of the elements, or of imitation, reflection, inspiration, and other enduring aspects of human experience. The critical use of the poetic analogy conceals the ingenuity or skill of the poet; modern critics who turn to this criticism often discover in it examples of the very procedures it is supposed to explain.

Prior to the late seventeenth century, for example, the reflective analogy referred to a theory of mind or to human actions as reflections (imitations). Its application to description began when images of nature could be considered not only mere sense data but complicated impositions or fancied impositions of one type of sense data upon another. Such views led to a consciousness of reflections, and to contemplations upon God, the Author of such reflections. Thomson's use of the reflective analogy was typical:

> Cheered by the milder beam, the sprightly youth
> Speeds to the well-known pool, whose crystal depth
> A sandy bottom shows. Awhile he stands
> Gazing the inverted landscape, half-afraid
> To meditate the blue profound below;
> Then plunges headlong down the circling flood.
>
> [*Summer*, ll. 1244–9]

Newton explained sight as the result not of images from an object, but of the internal structure of the eye, and Locke's definition of 'reflection'—'By Reflection then . . . I would be understood to mean, that notice which the Mind takes of its own Operations, and the manner of them'—is listed by the *OED* as the earliest use of the term (1690) to mean 'the mode, operation, or faculty by which the mind has knowledge of itself and its operations, or by which it deals with the ideas received from sensation and perception'. The use of 'reflective' in this sense is dated 1678, and 'reflect' in the sense of 'ponder', or 'meditation', 1605. The seventeenth century, therefore, provided a literature in which the physical properties of the natural world in their sensuous variety, came to reflect God and create reflections in man.

The subject matter of the images—the reflection of the heavens in the still waters of the earth, a relation between the natural and the supernatural world, the picture of one in the rural streams of the other—was the reflection either of the supernatural or the natural in nature. The very image called for reflection upon the divine analogy and to this extent it was 'functional to his [the poet's] total meaning and necessary to the completeness of his art'.[1] Criticism, however, assumed that the use of reflections was in itself good; a 1726 critic declared that in *The Seasons* the poet showed 'a *new* and *masterly manner* in which he has introduced his reflections, and made them to succeed his several Descriptions', and a 1728 critic wrote, 'Descriptive Poetry seems the most happy Art, to fix and charm the Mind to a close and constant Reflection upon all the various Beauties of Art and Nature'.[2] In this context, 'reflection' was interpreted as an ordered relation between observation and contemplation; it implied a 'new' and well-structured use of 'reflection', but it kept 'reflection' limited to moral comment rather than to the extensive implications of it everywhere in the poetry. Poetry was like painting, in this sense, because it imitated nature and thus served as 'comment' upon God's power.

[1] Earl R. Wasserman, 'Nature Moralized: the Divine Analogy in the Eighteenth Century', *ELH*, XXI (1955), 70. The features of landscape most admired in the first half of the seventeenth century are discussed by H. V. S. and M. S. Ogden, *English Taste in Landscape in the Seventeenth Century* (Ann Arbor, 1955), pp. 36–40.

[2] Quoted in McKillop, *Backgrounds*, pp. 176, 1.

(c) R. BLACKMORE, J. G. COOPER, J. WARTON: THE TRANSFORMATION OF THE ANALOGY

But *descriptive* poetry operates chiefly by *substitution*; by the means of sounds, which by custom have the effect of realities. Nothing is an imitation further than as it resembles some other thing; and words undoubtedly have no sort of resemblance to the ideas for which they stand.

EDMUND BURKE

The analogy of poetry to painting was predominantly applied in *The Seasons* to the accuracy of poetic description. As the analogy demanded particularized references, some particular comparisons, like Delacour's (1734), suggested that the poem was more vivid (redder, greener, whiter) than nature. Others, like Warton, found in *The Seasons* precise and accurate descriptions of nature's variety. Warton explained that the 'scenes of Thomson are frequently as wild and romantic as those of Salvator Rosa, pleasingly varied with precipices and torrents, and "castled cliffs", and deep vallies, with piny mountains, and the gloomiest caverns. Innumerable are the little circumstances in his descriptions, totally unobserved by all his predecessors'. And in describing a scene that might be painted, he described the flocks and herds in and near the brook in *Summer*.

A groupe worthy the pencil of Giacomo da Bassano, and so minutely delineated, that he might have worked from this sketch;

> . . . On the grassy bank
> Some ruminating lie; while others stand
> Half in the flood, and often bending sip
> The circling surface . . .
>
> [*Summer*, ll. 486–9]

He adds, that the ox in the middle of them,

> . . . From his sides
> The troublous insects lashes, to his sides
> Returning still.[1]
>
> [*Summer*, ll. 491–3]

[1] Warton, I, 46. For examples of Thomson's poetry which could be depicted in landscape painting, see 'Letter XII', (27 Feb. 1738), *Letters of the Critical Club* (Edinburgh, 1738), pp. 32–85.

Warton's analogy called attention to the precision of nature, the complex multitude of particular physical objects. The comparison of scenes in poetry to possible paintings, demanded an exercise, especially when no painting existed, of imaginative recreation. In so far as the poem was to be visually apprehended, it placed a premium upon a visually imaginative response—what Hughes called the 'visionary power'—thus indicating the neglect of the auditory elements.

As here applied, the shortcomings and advantages of the analogy were recognizable: to judge a scene or a metaphor by a prospective painting meant to provide measurable poetic criteria derived from visual, and thus demonstrable, sources. The analogy created a method for evaluating the accuracy and originality of poetry that avoided the fallacy of ancient and irrelevant models or rational rather than actual criteria. Nevertheless, the criteria proposed were just as tenuous, since they were 'imagined' rather than actual paintings and since they neglected significant poetic areas.

Another shortcoming in this use of the analogy was pointed out by John G. Cooper in his *Letters on Taste* (1752), who declared that certain metaphors could not be painted, and these were often the triumph of the poet's art.

> Many Objects, it is true, such as the following Night-Pieces for Example, may be so described even by the greatest Poets, that Painters of equal Genius might produce Pictures, betwixt which and them, the Palm of Glory would hang wavering . . . Now tho', I confess, *these* beautiful Strokes of the three greatest Poets the World ever produced, may be equalled by Painting, yet I will prove that one adventitious Circumstance *might* be thrown into such a Landscape by Poetry, as the utmost glow of Colours could never emulate. This too Shakespear has done by a metaphorical Expression in one single line,
>
> How sweet the Moonlight *sleeps* upon that Bank!
> *Merch. of Ven.*
>
> That Verb [sleeps] taken from animal Life and transferred by the irresistible Magic of Poetry, to the before lifeless Objects of the Creation, animates the whole Scene, and conveys an instantaneous Idea to the Imagination what a solemn Stillness is required, when the *peerless Queen* of Night is, in the full Splendor of her Majesty, thus lulled to Repose. When I once urged this, to an enthusiastical Admirer of the *Lombard* School of Painters, in favour of the

> Pre-eminence of Poetry over his beloved Art, he ingenuously confessed it was beyond the Power of the Pencil to convey any Idea adequate to this; and the ingenious Reason he gave, why it was so, gave me no small Satisfaction.
>
> Painting, said he, passes gently thro' one of the Senses, namely that of Seeing, to the Imagination; but this adventitious Beauty of Shakespear's seizes the Imagination at once, before we can reduce the Image to a sensible Object, which every *meer* Picture in Poetry ought, for a Test of its Truth, to be reduced to.[1]

For Cooper, the visual test of poetic imagery did have exceptions because some images involved connotations of stillness (of sound) not paintable, but appealing to the imagination.

The analogy led Cooper to 'imagination's vivid eye' rather than to the body's eye. Because Cooper accepted the theory of impressions entering through the eye, he had to explain 'vividness' by a special theory—certain images were not 'sensed', they went directly to the imagination. Even those details which the painter borrowed from the poet, he used as the 'sketch' for his painting; as Warton explained, 'he might have worked from this sketch'. The language of Cooper and Warton expressed the linguistic consequences of the comparison; Cooper used 'stroke' to mean a paintable poetic image, and Warton used 'sketch' to mean a poetic scene which was paintable, and Cooper used 'outline' as a synonym for 'sketch' when he declared that an image had very strong Outlines'. The poet and painter were analogous in their use of common details which one provided for the other. Addison in his *Remarks on Italy* interpreted the landscape in the country he was visiting by reference to poetry; Spence used this procedure to explain the cultural basis of ancient art and literature.

> What I have been saying to you hitherto, of the mutual use of the remains of the ancient artists and the classic writers towards explaining one another, is meant in general; and on any subject you could name: whether relating to their religion; their history; their arts, or manners of living; in short, to every thing known or practised among them; and so would include all their authors too, indifferently, whether in prose or verse.[2]

[1] John Gilbert Cooper, *Letters on Taste* (1752) (London, 1757), pp. 42–44. For a use of the term 'hard lines' applied to *The Seasons*, see 'Review of *A Poetical Epistle to Sir Christopher Anstey, Esq.*' (Wilkie, 1773), *Critical Review*, XLVIII (1773), 147–8.

[2] Joseph Addison, *Remarks on Italy*, *Works*, ed. G. W. Greene (New

Spence's explanation of the mutual use of the two media was historical and cultural: each interpreted a period and an art that were no longer readily and immediately understandable. In this respect the study of poetry and painting for their cultural implications had pertinence to the rise of a new class of readers and viewers who were not themselves capable of grasping the classics and their implications.

Traditionally, painting and sculpture had served as the subject of poetry, and poetry had, of course, served as the subject of history painting. But Thomson's use of nature poetry in *The Seasons* offered the painter a subject matter which he could discover for himself by looking abroad on nature, and it was apparent that landscape painters were not, as Richard Blackmore had assumed, to 'be justly compared to the Writers of Pastorals, whose Province it is to exhibit to the Imagination the same Objects'.[1]

Blackmore's speculation was based on a consistent application of the principle of analogy: the new genres of landscape painting were to be analogized with the established forms of poetry. But the principle was immediately in question because pastoral poetry had an existence as a form long before landscape painting: was there an analogy when no analogous form existed? Landscape painting, therefore, fitted but poorly into the analogy of forms. When the painters after Kent began to illustrate *The Seasons*, some of them sought to idealize the subjects of the poem and create modern pastoral landscapes. For them, the human figures, not the landscape, were central to the poem. The analogy as used by the painter and the poet did not necessarily serve the same purpose in any particular application.

There was, however, another area in which the scope of the analogy was challenged: the sensuous surface of the medium. Newton in the *Opticks*, discussing the agreement and disagreement of colours in terms of harmony, tension and discord, set up the language to discuss vision in terms of sound.

> May not the harmony and discord of Colours arise from the proportions of the vibrations propagated through the Fibres of the

[1] Richard Blackmore, see *The Lay Monastery* (London, 1714), p. 184.

York, 1856), II, 138; Joseph Spence, *Polymetis* (London, 1747), p. 291. For an analysis of Lessing and his views of descriptive poetry, see C. V. Deane, *Aspects of 18th Century Nature Poetry* (Oxford, 1935), pp. 84–92. For a balanced evaluation of *Polymetis*, see Austin Wright, *Joseph Spence* (Chicago, 1937), pp. 84–112.

> Optick Nerves into the Brain, as the harmony and discord of Sounds arise from the proportions of the Vibrations of the Air? For some Colours, if they be view'd together, are agreeable to one another, as those of Gold and Indigo, and others disagree.[1]

The critics repeatedly used the metaphor of 'striking' to convey the vividness of visual impression: 'an imagination so poetical as Thomson's', wrote Robert Shiels in 1753, 'could not but furnish those awful and striking images, which fill the soul with a solemn dread of *those Vapours, and Storms, and Clouds*, he has so well painted'.[2] Warton wrote that 'in describing the pestilence that destroyed the British troops at the siege of Carthagena, he has used a circumstance inimitable lively, picturesque, and striking to the imagination'. And Murdoch, describing Thomson's originality, wrote that he 'could not bear to write what was not strictly his own, what had not more immediately struck his imagination, or touched his heart'.[3]

In each of these statements 'striking' was identified with the vividness and liveliness of painting and its effect upon the imagination; and indeed, Cooper's use of 'strike' confirmed this painting application. But also in each of these uses the metaphor of 'striking' extended beyond the painting analogy: in Shiels to an analogy with the awful power of sublime nature, in Warton with the sounds of the passage to which he referred—the dropping of dead bodies into the sea—and in Murdoch with sensibility and the physical vibrations latent in the concept of sensibility. When the analogy moved from comparison of image with nature to vividness of apprehension or imagination, it extended beyond the visual, and the image itself called up references which were felt rather than seen. Such were the sensitive feelings, vibrations, responses to the emotive elements of the poem. And for this process auditory elements in the analogy were more relevant than the visual. Thus sound and touch were used to explain the sensibility of reader to poem and the relation of sound

[1] Isaac Newton, *Opticks* (based on 4th ed., London, 1730) (New York, 1952), p. 346. For a discussion of the impact of the *Opticks* on descriptive poetry, see Marjorie H. Nicolson, *Newton Demands the Muse* (Princeton, 1946). The language of sight included terms of 'striking', of sound and motion, and was thus, from the beginning of the century, potentially available as a sound as well as sight analogy. The gradual diminution of the importance of sight to language resulted in a corresponding increase in the place of 'sound'.

[2] Shiels, *Lives*, I, 197.

[3] Murdoch, *Account*, I, xvii.

to touch was more appropriate than sight to touch [impression]. Moreover, there was a learned physical explanation of sensibility in Hartley, as there was a popular explanation of it in *Theory of Agreeable Sensations* (1750).

> From what mechanism does it proceed, that the vibrations of the fibres of the brain have a power to transmit themselves to that of another person? The ingenious M. de Mairan upon the communication of sounds, throws some light upon this mystery. Sound reaches us, because there are certain fibres in sonorous bodies, together with the parcels of air, the fibres of the ear, and lastly, those of the brain, which form a continued train of chords, which communicate their motions to each other. Since the motions of the body, the colour of the face, and the disposition of the eye, point out to others the particular state of our soul, may we not with some reason conclude, that there is a chain with chords in unison, which convey from one brain the vibrations of the fibres of another?[1]

The development of the analogy to music arose simultaneously with the critical awareness of the kinesthetic function of the metaphor used to describe visible as well as invisible phenomena. One explanation, therefore, suggested a 'sound' basis for the analogy. Another, by Murdoch (1762), compared poetry to painting, limiting 'colour' or 'clothing' to images, but stressed the force with which Thomson seized expressions and made them part of 'his own expressive language'. Imagery was identified with inventive freedom, not status or hierarchy of poetic composition. 'In his first pieces, the *Seasons*, we see him at once assume the majestic freedom of an Eastern writer; seizing the grand images as they rise, cloathing them in his own expressive language, and preserving, throughout, the grace, the variety, and the dignity which belong to a just composition.'[2] Murdoch not only seized upon a different aspect of the traditional analogy regarding language, but he also used the analogy of poetry to music to explain the process of poetic response or sympathy:

[1] Lévesque de Pouilly, *The Theory of Agreeable Sensations* (London, 1749), pp. 104–5. For an extended discussion of the analogy between music and painting, see Charles Avison, 'On the Analogies between Music and Painting,' *An Essay on Musical Expression* (London, 1753) (original ed. 1752), pp. 20–28.

[2] Murdoch, *Account*, I, iv. For the freedom attributed to the writings of the prophets and other 'eastern' writers, see John Husbands, 'The Preface', *A Miscellany of Poems* (Oxford, 1731).

'when the readers' faculties are not *tuned in a certain consonance* to those of the poet', he could not be the best judge of poetry. The auditory analogy did not arise from the musical qualities of Thomson's poetry, but sprang from the physical and 'sympathetic' analogy.

As a remarkable example of how science was deceived by its analogies, John Aikin at the beginning of the nineteenth century analysed the unscientific physical basis of the 'sympathy' analogy. But in doing so, he also made very clear how this comparison served the musical analogy in literature.

> Errors in science have almost universally been the offspring of false or imperfect analogies; it is curious to observe how a single term, used by way of illustration, has engendered an entire theory with all its appendages. Thus the *nerves* have been called, as they really are in appearance, *strings*; but strings are capable of different degrees of *tension*, and according to these *vibrate* with greater or less force. Hence the nervous system was said to be *braced* or *relaxed*; its function depended upon its *tone*; the sympathies of one nerve with another were owing to similarity of tension, as had been remarked with respect to fiddle-strings: nerves communicated their vibrations to the brain, and excited in that organ tremulous motions which were the immediate cause of sensation; and so forth. It is a pity that all this ingenious and well-connected system is overthrown by the simple fact, that the nerves always lie unstretched in a soft bed of cellular substance, to which they are attached by innumerable minute threads, so as to be utterly incapable of any motion like the vibrating of a cord.[1]

[1] John Aikin, 'Analogy', pp. 427–8. According to Alba H. Warren, *English Poetic Theory, 1825–1865*, p. 28, the 'tendency to refer to the formal qualities of poetry in terms of another art was at least partially due to the lack of a critical vocabulary—one thinks of the universal use of the Dutch painters to stand for the concept of realism in both painting and poetry—and it marks the almost total absence of any interest in the problems of the medium in the Early Victorian period.' This argument from the poverty of a critical vocabulary seems untenable in view of the recurrent analogy between poetry and painting, and at this particular time, the application of poetic terms to painting. There existed at the end of the eighteenth century a highly involved nomenclature in formal criticism; critics continued to use analogies to reveal qualities not elicited by such terms. In the writing of Condillac and his follower Lavoisier, nomenclature was considered important in relating words to things. See Lavoisier, 'Preface', *Elements of Chemistry*, tr. Robert Kerr (Edinburgh, 1790), pp. xiii–xv, and his follower in this assumption, John Landseer, *Lectures on Engraving* (London, 1806), p. 108.

Some theories of the musical analogy with poetry relied on identical scientific evidence, and George Dyer (1812) objected to such assumptions.

> A writer, therefore, who discusses 'the correspondence between poetry and music' [Daniel Webb] sets out with a very doubtful principle. 'We are then to take it for granted', says he, 'that the mind, under particular affections, excites certain vibrations on the nerves, and impresses certain movements on the animal spirits.'
>
> This circumstance, without any other consideration, is reason enough for not entering into inquiries in this place about causes, but for confining ourselves to influences and effects.[1]

In criticism the nerve-tone-tension-string analogy was used to explain a 'vividness' or 'force' different from that of precise observation. It drew attention to a response which involved the nerves, brain, and 'sympathies'. In accounting for the values of the poem, the 'tonal' and visual analogy moved from a physiological to a psychological explanation of imagination. The predominance of the auditory rather than the visual elements in the analogy was due in part to the disproof of the visual 'fibre' theory, and the greater ease with which tension, the *concordia discors*, was more readily adapted to the auditory rather than the visual analogy, but more precisely, both analogies were subsumed under the concept of 'imagination' or 'mind' in which the tensions were found to exist. Thus one psychological explanation was supplanted by another.

Even the discussion of personification reflected the change in critical language and concept from Blackmore's (1713) consistent 'striking' the mind to John More's 'figuring' as a 'stroke'.

> The Sister Arts to heighten their Images, and strike our Minds with greater Force, agree to represent human Qualities as Persons, and to endow them with their peculiar Properties. They describe Vertues in the form of *Goddesses* and Vices in that of *Furies*, and give to each emblematical Distinctions.[2]

This was, of course, what Thomson had done in his repeated personifications—'in every breeze the Power / Of Philosophic Melancholy comes' (*Autumn*, ll. 1004–5), 'Where now, ye lying vanities of life!' (*Winter*, l. 209). Blackmore found that in this visual

[1] George Dyer, 'Music', *Poetics* (London, 1812), II, 184–5.

[2] Richard Blackmore, 32 (27 Jan. 1713), *The Lay Monastery* (London, 1714), pp. 186–7.

aspect poetry had a greater affinity for painting than for music: 'Tho' the Melody of the Voice, and that of Musical Instruments, bear a great Resemblance to the Charms of Poetry, as they are express'd in harmonious Numbers, and a pleasing Cadence of words; yet the Affinity between *Poetry* and *Painting* must be allowed to be much greater.'[1] By 1777, the explanation for personification was not mere 'heightening', or 'striking' resulting from art, but part of the fullness of language in an impassioned state. 'We *pause*, *personify* and *apostrophize*', wrote John More, 'not to enrich our style, but solely to exhibit the real state of our minds; and because no common language can do justice to such an impassioned sensibility.' More was aware, however, that common language as well as poetry was impassioned, and he distinguished between them by the extent of 'energy' and 'animation'. 'His figuring the dismal *waste*, as listening to the wild notes of the *Plover*, for instance, is a stroke singularly happy and natural, and, which none but a genius highly poetical would have hit.'[2]

(d) JOHN MORE: ANALOGY AND ITS MORAL IMPLICATIONS

> This is the great archetype whence the genius of poetry borrows all her fairest and most elegant forms.
>
> JOHN MORE

John More's *Strictures, Critical and Sentimental, on Thomson's Seasons* (1777) presented a theory of moral impressionism—a delicate responsiveness to the divine in nature—that embraced the painting and music analogies and placed them within a single context. He used the landscape analogy to suggest certain descriptive qualities and the musical analogy to convey the poem's indescribable qualities. In the chapter 'On Thomson's Powers of Description', More compared the poem with landscape painting; to demonstrate the tradition

[1] Blackmore, p. 183.

[2] John More, *Strictures*, pp. 108–9. For identification of More, see Appendix II. Pertinent additional bibliographical materials by More [John Moir] include: *Discourses on Practical Subjects* (London, 1776); *Female Tuition* (London, 1784); *Gleanings, or Fugitive Pieces* (London, 1785), 2 vols. For a similar analysis of personification, see John Donaldson, *The Elements of Beauty* (Edinburgh, 1780), pp. 46–47. Personification 'enlivened' and 'animated' abstractions giving them 'force' which was not emblematic but human, that is, visual, auditory, and emotive. For a relation of More's comment to the rhetorical sublime see Wasserman, 'Personification', *PMLA*, LXV (1950), 448.

in which he was writing the chapter, he concluded with most of Warton's digression on Thomson in the *Essay*. Confining descriptive poetry to 'external nature', More wrote: 'Now that the view should be properly bounded, that everything should be distinctly specified, that all the objects should be coloured from Nature, are three particulars which, to one who knows but little of the art, appear peculiarly indispensible in landscape painting. Do but examine the *Seasons* by these principles, and you should find them preserved almost inviolate through the whole poem.'[1]

For More, the purpose of the analogy was to win approval for what Thomson was writing, rather than to defend the poem as painting. By the three divisions of landscape painting, divisions not readily accepted by authorities on painting, More was able to call upon conventional implications of the analogy, while expressing it in a language of moral impressionism and disregarding the particular poetic or painting relationships. In discussing the unity of subject, he explained the digression of Palemon and Lavinia as follows:

> But the well known story of Palemon and Lavinia, does equal honour to the warmth of his heart, and the justness of his taste. As he intends it for a panegyric on Benevolence and Humanity, the introduction of it here, is happy and striking. For it follows an exhortation which he urges with an earnestness that marks the good man, not less than it does the true poet.
>
> Be not too narrow, husbandmen! but fling
> From the full sheaf, with charitable stealth,
> The liberal handful. Think, oh grateful think!
> How good the God of harvest is to you;
> Who pours abundance o'er your flowing fields;
> While these unhappy partners of your kind
> Wide hover round you, like the fowls of heaven,
> And ask their humble dole. The various turns
> Of fortune ponder; that your sons may want
> What now, with hard reluctance, faint, ye give.[2]
> [*Autumn*, ll. 167–76]

[1] More, p. 33. For the theory of 'archetypal analogies' see M. H. Abrams, *The Mirror and the Lamp* (New York, 1953), p. 31, and see also R. S. Crane, *The Language of Criticism and The Structure of Poetry* (Toronto, 1953). My views on critical analogy appear in 'Philosophy and Criticism: the Challenge of Discipline', University of Utah, Advancement of Learning Series [Mar. 10, 1961] (Utah, 1962).

[2] More, pp. 47–48.

'Earnestness', 'good man' and 'true poet' are not the language of painting though they 'paint' to the heart. The passage itself was an example of the kind of moral declamation which painting could not convey. Expressions like 'Think, oh grateful think!' and 'The various turns / Of fortune ponder' were neither descriptive scenes nor paintable actions. But for More, the examples of unity of subject had little to do with painting unity. The examples, therefore, extended the painting analogy, while they served to minimize its relevance.

The language of More's criticism was that of associated impressions dominated by morality. 'Objects in poetry, as well as in painting', he declared, 'should exhibit their natural and respective characters; at the same time, they occupy, their natural and respective positions'. The specification of detail in painting, to which Warton referred, was discoverable for More through identification with the narrator and the 'delineations' were based on correspondence of the feelings of the reader with the action of the passage. In the spring shower, for example, More did not analyse the 'masterly minuteness' but concluded with the moral passage which was not minutely specified. And although he used terms like 'delineated', 'figured,' 'deciphered', he made no distinctions between the picture of the slumbering swain and a passage of talk (sound) and motion which was not of the same pictorial quality.

> Perhaps, the most striking and characteristic circumstance in this description, is the conscious hilarity of the human mind. For, after making you a spectator of all nature, in a state of wistful expectation for the reviving nutriment of heaven, he brings forth the Lord of this lower world, in that sort of majesty which best becomes him. The idea can never be too often repeated, and deserves the recollection and approbation of every generous and worthy mind.
>
> . . . Man superior walks
> Amid the glad creation, musing praise
> And looking lively gratitude.
>
> [*Spring*, ll. 170–3]
>
> His Summer in particular, is crouded with beautiful delineations of every rural kind. Cows milking, sheep shearing, hay making, are scenes which he describes at length, and with a striking exactness. No sight can be more natural than the herds and flocks, which he figures lolling on the bank of a stream, and panting under the noon-tide blaze. The lounging posture of their keeper, is thus beautifully specified:

. . . Amid his subjects safe
Slumbers the monarch swain, his careless arms
Thrown round his head, on downy moss sustained;
Here, laid his scrip with wholesome viands fill'd,
There list'ning every noise, his watchful dog.
[ll. 493–7]

The harvest scene is also well deciphered. Here we find the reapers begin with the dawning day, their hardy toil, we see them all in motion, in four lines we learn the subject, the manner, and happy effects of their rustic conversation.

. . . Through their cheerful band, the rural talk,
The rural scandal, and the rural jest,
Fly harmless, to deceive the tedious time,
And steal unfelt, the sultry hours away.[1]
[*Autumn*, ll. 158–61]

As for More's use of the term 'colouring' in 'colouring from nature', i.e. recognizing in nature 'that original and independent Being, who is himself the soul and beauty of every thing amiable in what he has made', More coupled the language of description, with the moral image of sound and devotion.

Here then is a key to that peculiar art of description, for which the genius of Thomson was so happily adapted. The multifarious phenomena of the year, struck him as so many different means, by which the great Father of the universe, promotes the happiness, and smiles benignant on the glad creation. With what propriety, for example, does he conclude his address to the Sun! How elegant and natural the transition from that glorious luminary to the great Origin of light and life, of comfort and joy to all beings and all worlds! We are lost in the pleasing but awful sublimity, to which we find our hearts exalted, by strains so consonant to the rational raptures of devotional minds.

How shall I then attempt to sing of Him!
Who, Light Himself, in uncreated light
Invested deep, dwells awfully retir'd
From moral eye, or angel's purer ken;
Whose single smile has, from the first of time,
Fill'd, overflowing, all those lamps of Heaven,
That beam for ever thro' the boundless sky:
But, should he hide his face, th'astonish'd sun,

[1] More, pp. 56–57.

And all th'extinguish'd stars, would loosening reel
Wide from their spheres, and Chaos come again.
And yet was every faultering tongue of Man,
Almighty Father! silent in thy praise?
Thy Works themselves would raise a general voice,
Even in the depth of solitary woods
By human foot untrod; proclaim thy power,
And to the quire celestial Thee resound,
Th'eternal cause, support, and end of all!
[*Summer*, ll.174–91]

Thus, under the influence of a conviction, at once so affecting and sublime, he seizes, wherever his fancy roams, the identical circumstance, in all its variety of combinations, which strikes the deepest and pleases the most.[1]

More described Thomson's harmony with his subject matter—nature—as a musical harmony: 'To this strange mysterious and sympathetic harmony, by which the finest sensations of mind and fairest forms and assemblages of things are so happily and sweetly united, the muse of Thomson was constantly attuned.' The musical analogy was applied to the poet's creativity, his relation to his subject matter and to the readers' apprehension of the poem. This musical analogy, developed from More's concept of morally conditioned sensibility, explained the harmony of man, nature, and refined imaginations. Not only was the musical analogy identified in a physical sense with vibrations of sound; it also accounted for his images of soaring, of ardour and fire.

The relation of 'flight', 'ardour', 'effusions', and 'enthusiasm' to the analogy with music was identified in More with the exertions necessary in striking the right key of the understanding and the heart. Sensibility of poet and reader required exertion, were the opposite of mere imitation or mechanical art: 'There is a key in every sort of composition to which we are always in tune, but as difficult to hit, as productive of the best effects when it is.'[2] There was an ardour involved in the production and apprehension of unmechanical poetry; when this was intense it became a 'flight', and More deliberately used 'flight' to include 'poignancy', and rejected the contemptuous use of 'flight' in earlier criticism; 'whatever captivates the affections, surprises the fancy, or strikes the attention, they [the critics] denominate a *flight*, which in their dictionary is always a term of contempt. . . .

[1] More, pp. 67–68. [2] More, pp. 121–2; pp. 194–5. See also p. 232.

Ask what they mean by that opprobrious term, and ten to one, they censure the best passage of the best book you can put into their hands'. John More was wrong about 'flight'; George Etherege and William Temple, for example, had used it approvingly, but the assertion of More's criticism demanded the tone of the natural man who lived with the elements.

More compared the critic who spontaneously responded to the emotional particularities of the poem with the critic who had systems but no sensations, or who had sensations but no sympathy and praised only poetry of force, dazzle, or agitation. His criticism sought to convey the poet's 'effusions' or 'spirit'. 'Effusion' was defined by Blount as 'a pouring out, prodigality' (1674) and by Johnson as '1. The art of pouring out; 2. Waste, the art of spilling or shedding; 3. The art of pouring out words; 4. Bounteous donation; 5. The thing poured out.' The image of pouring and the image of soaring were both used by More to describe what vulgar critics could not feel or recognize. For More, such spirit was a moralistic 'relish' of the poem. Nature, according to More, was characterized by a sympathetic interrelationship between animate and inanimate creation, an intimate emotional commonwealth between man and his environment.

> Now the peculiar business of all sentimental poetry is to trace minutely every fibre of the heart, through all the windings, intricacies, and variety of its motions, and to touch every occasional delicacy in its proper tone. This is the great archetype whence the genius of poetry borrows all her fairest and most elegant forms; whatever she creates or fabricates, is so far excellent only as it bears this resemblance, must still be in nature and truth, otherwise her fables were monsters without a likeness, were images without an original.[1]

[1] More, pp. 8–9. For 'flight', see More, p. 13; for 'spirit', p. 11. For a discussion of 'breathe', 'wind', and similar images in romantic poetry, see M. H. Abrams, 'The Correspondent Breeze: A Romantic Metaphor', *KR*, XIX (1957), 113–30. For references to 'breathe' in earlier criticism, see John C. Shairp, *On Poetic Interpretation of Nature* (London, 1817), p. 79, and Geoffrey Tillotson, 'Newman's Essay on Poetry: An exposition and Comment', *Criticism and the Nineteenth Century* (London, 1951), pp. 163–6. For another example of the mixture of 'sight' with 'sound' terms in criticism, see [John Young] *A Criticism on the Elegy Written in a Country Church Yard* (London, 1783), p. 16: 'The idea of making *sounds* of a certain kind give a *relief* (to speak in the language of artists) to *silence* is not new.'

Thus poetry did not require verse and 'the muse of Sterne, though perhaps he never made a couplet in his life, we often surprise warbling as it were by accident in the sweetest and tenderest strains'.

Now the concept of moral sympathy which More expressed used the mixed language of painting and music. The 'tracing' of fibres, the 'variety of motions', 'delicacy in its proper tone', were instances of what was suggested as the transformation of the painting analogy. But this transformation, it must be noted, was not from a spatial to a temporal analogy. The analogy with painting, in so far as words created 'moving' pictures in the mind, was a temporal analogy with the spatial character of language used to point up characteristics of poetry.

Hildebrand Jacob had written that painting did not convey its images in so quick and unwearied a succession as did poetry, which was characterized by this succession, this number of 'things' or impressions. The associationist explanation for trains of thought related time to sequences of ideas or pictures. In 1762 Lord Kames declared that the 'only natural measure we have, is the train of our thoughts',[1] and ideas provided a series of moving pictures. The difference, therefore, between Warton's attention to particular images, and More's use of flight or vibration analogies was the shift not from one type of poetic theory to another but between different conceptions of association of ideas. The images of flight and effusion pointed to the unity of impressions in movement, and it must not be overlooked that 'flying' and 'pouring' were actual visual images, as was, too, the imagery of vibration and tension.

The characteristic view of the 'double idea'—'by thus comparing the image of the poet with its original in nature or memory, the double idea, like counterparts of the same tune, produces quite a different and new sensation'—placed the musical analogy and the visual analogy within the theory of temporal sensations resulting from comparison of mortal with immortal time. For More, the divine analogy embraced the visual elements of painting and the tonal characteristics of music: it formed the comparative basis for sight and sound. To this extent, the moral analogy was superior to either of the others. But at the same time, it disregarded the specific characteristics necessary for critical analysis and discrimination.

More's language, the 'strings' of the fibres of the heart, the

[1] Henry Home, Lord Kames, *Elements of Criticism* (London, 1762), I, 201.

'borrowing' of forms, the 'polished expressions', the 'effusions' and 'tones' of sympathy, was a combination of images which formed part of the divine analogies of painting and poetry. More used them as persuasion, combining the widest possible range of critical terms to convey the moral quality of the poem. At the same time, this appeal to the readers advocated a certain kind of reading—a heightened emotional sympathy, and, in this respect, the critical language of More urged a form of moral impressionism upon his readers. How his criticism altered customary terms by divesting them of critical import or placing them within uses which were noncritical—in More's case religious—can be seen by examining the diversity of implication of 'exercise' (or 'practice')—More's moral term for heightened moral feeling in sympathetic reading.

In 1707, 'practice' (substantive) was defined as 'custom, use, or the actual Exercise of any Art or Science', a usage which related it to repetition as well as exertion (exercise). In Dryden's use it was distinguished from abstract knowledge given by rules irrelevant to the 'mystery' of literature: 'This is the mystery of that noble trade, which yet no master can teach to his apprentice; he may give the rules, but the scholar is never the nearer in his practice.'

Kersey's dictionary (1715) also identified 'Exercitation' with criticism, declaring it to mean 'frequent exercising: Also a kind of Critical Commentary upon Authors'. The term 'practice' was thus identified physiologically with health in terms of the bodily motions and in this sense the stirring of the animal spirits was, as Addison suggested, the physiological basis of aesthetic pleasure. As healthy movement, 'practice' was related to exercise of critical as well as physical discipline. 'The Mind of Man', wrote Joseph Trapp (1713), 'does not love to have everything too minutely laid before it; it pleases itself in having Room for Exercise, and to walk alone, as it were, without leading.' In the pejorative sense, however, 'practice' was related to deviousness in contrast to simplicity; the absence of practice was openness, behaviour unpractised and ingenuous. Thus 'practice', identified in the vocabulary of Locke and his followers with custom, usage, and, in Hartley's system, mechanism, was used in criticism by Neele (1825), for example, as a term opposed to spontaneity. Indeed, one meaning of 'exercise' in our time has come to be mechanical 'drill' which is supposed to create ease in learning. For a critic like John Pinkerton, who identified practice with knowledge, (1785), practice was what taught the critic and the poet to make careful distinctions; but for critics who used 'practice' in opposition to 'spontaneity' or who felt the need for system rather than for mere observation, 'practice' was seen as necessary but nevertheless insufficient for creating 'systems' of criticism.

There were by the middle of the eighteenth century eight different uses of 'practice' catalogued by Johnson (1755), the first of which was the neutral explanation: 'The habit of doing any thing.' But the explanation of 'practice' by 'habit' suggested the manner in which the term was beginning to be identified with a type of mechanical behaviour buttressed in philosophy by mechanism and associationism. In insisting upon the emotional elements in creativity, Wordsworth and John Wilson objected to Thomson's 'practices' and praised his uncontrolled expressions of feeling. And when in 1864 Thomson's increased 'skill' was identified with his continued 'practice', his practice referred not to greater refinement and subtlety, but to establishing an appeal to a wider audience, to habits which were widely shared.[1]

More's language was highly metaphoric, establishing a series of relations between the reader and the poem based on the four elements: nature (earth), spirit or force (fire), flight (air), and effusion (water). He exemplified in his language the 'presence' of God in nature which he claimed the poem illustrated. Thus his own use of analogy paralleled what he found to be the underlying message of the poem. This reference to the 'divine analogy' sermonized the poem, as one of More's critics noted. But the metaphoric use of criticism, while interpreting few passages, did seek to make clear the kind of 'sympathy' necessary to read Thomson.[2] The reading of poetry was not a mere matter of subduing prejudice or creating a dream state, but an emotional preparedness to understand the author.[3] In this respect, the divine analogy provided a guide for proper contemplation:

> Paradoxical as it may appear, it is a truth suggested by constant experience, that most enjoyments are never less relished than in the

[1] Preface, *The Seasons* (Edinburgh, 1864).

[2] See *Critical Review*, XLV (1778), 430, *Monthly Review*, LVIII (1778), 285. See John Wilson, *Recreations*, II, 272–3.

[3] Jeremy Collier, 'Upon General Kindness', *Essays Upon Several Moral Subjects* (London, 1705), pp. 175–6. More, p. 232; pp. 172–4. For discussions and bibliography of 'sympathy', see Kenneth MacLean, 'Imagination and Sympathy: Sterne and Adam Smith,' *JHI*, X (1949), 399–410, and Roy R. Male, Jr., 'Shelley and the Doctrine of Sympathy', *University of Texas Studies in English*, XXIX (1950), 183–302.

very instant of fruition. We exult while they are yet remote, and give all our souls to the pleasing palpitations of hope, but possess them with the most unaccountable indifference, and pathetically regret their absence the moment they are gone. Such is the natural caprice of the heart, and such the evanescent quality of every mortal delight! We never know the worth of health till in sickness, of plenty till in want, of youth till in age, of happiness till in misery. Our awakening to a sense of what we might once have been, is only when the acquisition is no longer in our power. Nor have we any thing then to compensate our loss, but the cutting reflection, that our fate, however bitter, is no more than the natural consequence of our own folly.

It is only in such a train of thinking as this, or something similar, that we can possibly enter into the spirit, or relish the Pathetic of Thomson's poetry. His various allusions to human misery particularly indicate a disposition of heart, which nothing but the deepest reflections on manners and life could thus happily mature. To this sweet sympathizing temper of mind he turns and improves the minutest circumstance.[1]

These reflections suggested too limited a view of responsiveness, for how was one to read the burlesque passages? Involvement was necessary provided it did not prevent acceptance of the different speakers the poem created. More's limited use of the divine analogy led him to assume that those passages which expressed Thomson's own feelings—his personal recollections—were bound to be the best, yet Thomson's epitaph on Elizabeth Stanley was considerably inferior to his later passages on the same subject in *The Seasons*.

But despite the objections to More's moralizing, his use of critical analogy created speculative insights that could, at his time, have had no evidence to support them. Through the elemental analogy he conveyed the sense of Thomson's unfolding nature, and he demonstrated how the visual and auditory comparisons could be subsumed under one analogy. In his strategic use of criticism, he attributed to Thomson's descriptions an individual sensibility, an originality and sense of place that none of his contemporaries recognized.[2]

[1] More, pp. 235–6.

[2] More, pp. 50, 179–80. The first stanza of Thomson's poem on Elizabeth Stanley written in 1738 read as follows:

> Here, Stanley, rest! escaped this mortal strife,
> Above the joys, beyond the woes of life,

(e) THE DECLINE OF THE PAINTING ANALOGY AND ITS SUBSTITUTES

> It must not be supposed that Thomson's writing of this kind consists wholly, or even mainly, of pure description, or of what is sometimes called 'word painting'.
>
> SIR GEORGE DOUGLAS, 1911

At the end of the eighteenth century *The Seasons* was compared to 'painting' in terms of the precision, accuracy, and vividness which had become identified with imaginative power. Thomson was, said Percival Stockdale (1793), a poetical painter and a sage. His paintings of the seasons were 'transcripts made immediately from the living volume of *Nature* . . . the whole groupe of objects in *his* descriptions is always peculiarly striking or affecting, from their natural and happy

---

Fierce pangs no more thy lively beauties stain,
And sternly try thee with a year of pain;
No more sweet patience, feigning oft relief,
Lights thy sick eye to cheat a parent's grief:
With tender art to save her anxious groan,
No more thy bosom presses down its own:
Now well earned peace is thine, and bliss sincere:
Ours be the lament, not unpleasing tear!

A revised version appeared in the 1744 *Seasons*:

And art thou, Stanley, of that sacred band?
Alas, for us how soon! Tho' raised above
The reach of human pain, above the flight
Of human joy; yet with a mingled ray
Of sadly pleased remembrance, must thou feel
A mother's love, a mother's tender love:
Who seeks thee still, in many a former scene;
Seeks thy fair form, thy lovely beaming eyes,
Thy pleasing converse, by gay lively sense
Inspir'd: where moral wisdom mildly shone,
Without the toil of art; and virtue glow'd
In all her smiles, without forbidding pride.
But, O thou best of parents! Wipe thy tears;
Or rather to *Parental Nature* pay
The tears of grateful joy, who for a while
Lent thee this younger self, this opening bloom
Of thy enlighten'd mind and gentle worth.
[*Summer*, ll. 564–80]

relation to one another'.[1] But Thomson was also a moral painter because of his amiable and benevolent morality.

The divine analogy diminished in importance because Thomson's critics identified the morality as the easiest and most commonplace part of the poem. The painting analogy was separated from the divine analogy, one creating vividness, the other a commonplace poetry, or both were made part of an imaginative power which did not explain either. In 1841 Allan Cunningham wrote that the divine analogy was involved in the aim of the poem: 'by the contemplation of the beauties of nature, to raise man's thoughts to God'. The moral commentary of the poem was valuable because of the imaginative power, 'the glow, and the upward flame-like spirit of his poetry'. The moral transitions and descriptions were held together by Thomson's imaginative fervour as a poet. The moral analogy and the painting analogy were subordinated to the more general imaginative power, although as Cunningham remarked, 'that the author had a fine taste and accurate eye for painting, may be gathered from groupings and descriptions without end'.[2]

'Groupings' and 'descriptions' were used by Cunningham to denote Thomson's selectivity, and he had himself, in outlining the poem, illustrated just this. But the analogy of 'groupings' in a poem with those in a painting did not imply any centrality to the use of analogy, and, indeed, it was possible to argue that such groupings were in no necessary way connected with painting, that they were what Thomson saw and felt. This statement was expressed by the Scottish geologist Hugh Miller in 1845 in his *First Impressions of England and Its People*. He visited Hagley Hall and, following the description in the poem, he discovered, to his surprise, that it explained the kind of selectivity made by Thomson. Miller wrote that 'it must often have struck the Scotch reader, that in dealing with very extended prospects, he rather enumerates than describes. His pictures are often mere catalogues in which single words stand for classes of objects, and in which the entire poetry seems to consist in an overmastering sense of vast extent, occupied by amazing multiplicity.' The non-analogical language of Miller—'extended', 'enumerates', 'catalogues', 'classes', 'extent'—drawn from science, put to

[1] Percival Stockdale, ed., 'Notes to The Seasons', *The Seasons* (London, 1793), unnumbered. For the John Sharpe quotation, see McKillop, *Backgrounds*, p. 6.

[2] Cunningham, pp. xlvi, lxi, lii.

a test the selective description without in any way implying a painting analogy. Miller quoted the introductory description to the 'Panegyric on Great Britain'.

> Heavens! what a goodly prospect spreads around
> Of hills, and dales, and woods, and lawns, and spires,
> And glittering towns, and gilded streams till all
> The stretching landscape into smoke decays!
> [*Summer*, ll. 1438–41]

> Now, the prospect from the hill at Hagley furnished me with the true explanation of this enumerative style. Measured along the horizon, it must, on the lowest estimate, be at least fifty miles in longitudinal extent; measured literally, from the spectator forwards, at least twenty. . . . Here the surface is dimpled by unreckoned hollows; there fretted by uncounted mounds; all is amazing overpowering multiplicity—a multiplicity which neither the pen nor the pencil can adequately express; and so description, in even the hands of a master, sinks into mere enumeration. The picture becomes a catalogue; and all that genius can accomplish in the circumstances is just to do with its catalogue what Homer did with his—dip it in poetry. I found, however, that the innumerable details of the prospect, and its want of strong leading features, served to dissipate and distract the mind, and to associate with the vast whole an idea of littleness.[1]

[1] Hugh Miller, *First Impressions of England and Its People* (1845) (New York, 1882), pp. 135–6. This passage was also quoted by J. R. Boyd in 1852 and by Henry Beers in 1898. According to H. F. Clark, *The English Landscape Garden* (London, 1948), p. 15, these lines describe 'the scene at Esher with visual imagery as carefully composed as any of Claude's landscapes'. But 'careful' composition, while contrasting with 'careless', ought not to be confused with 'careful' in the same respects as painting, especially since Thomson's details developed a quite different view of man from Claude's presence of the past. See also Horace E. Hamilton, 'James Thomson Recollects Hagley Park', *MLN*, LXII (1947), 194–7, who points out that Thomson's letter to Miss Young, dated 23 August 1743, contained many of the descriptions which the poet included in his Hagley Park passage in the revised 1744 edition (Zippel, 'Spring', Text C, ll. 901–37). For a description of Hagley Park, see Thomas Maurice, *Hagley, A Descriptive Poem* (Oxford, 1776), and Joseph Heely, *A Description of Hagley Park* (London, 1777). For a modern repetition of Thomson's so-called 'Recollective Imagination'—elaborately phrased enumeration of details—see William Allan Neilson, *Essentials of Poetry* (Boston, 1912), pp. 140–1.

The actual sight provided an explanation for Thomson's 'enumerative style'; the multiplicity of the scene was responsible for lines like 'hills, and dales, and woods, and lawns, and spires, / And glittering towns'. The geologist recognized the catalogue as an attempt to convey the quality of multiplicity to the scene, but he found that 'description, even in the hands of a master, sinks into mere enumeration'. Now Miller was a good example of the scientist who destroyed the fiction of the painting analogy of Hagley Park, yet the evaluation of the poetry showed an insensitivity to the subtlety of the enumeration as well as to its function as a literary device. He did not perceive the 'goodly prospect' and 'stretching landscape' enclosing the catalogue so that, in observing from Hagley Hall, he found only innumerable details which served 'to dissipate and abstract the mind'. However, demonstrating that the analogy was irrelevant, he proved the need to turn to poetic analysis, to 'dip' reality into poetry.

Yet as A. Hamilton Thompson (1913) observed of another of Thomson's enumerations from Hagley Hall: 'Thomson's description of the stock elements of conventional scenery, of

> . . . hill and dale, and wood and lawn
> And verdant field, and darkening heath between,
> And villages embosom'd soft in trees,
> And spiry towns by surging columns mark'd
> Of household smoak,
>
> [ll. 952–6]

was governed by an accuracy of observation and depth of enjoyment which, while perpetrating the Miltonic tradition in poetry, distinguished Thomson from poets who, without observation and feeling for nature, had passively accepted the superficial qualities of that tradition.'[1]

The enumeration was a poetic device used by Milton and by the Augustans, and what Thomson achieved was a sense of the heights and depths, of town and stream (man and nature), of the 'goodly prospect' which distantly 'glitters' and is reflective of nature and finally overcome by the smoke of man, 'into smoke decays'.

This inductive test of the analogy was characteristic of distinctions

[1] A. Hamilton Thompson, 'Thomson and the Poetry of Natural Description', *Cambridge History of English Literature* (London, 1913), X, 109–10.

made between the history of painting and the history of poetry. Thomas Twining in 1789 had declared that the Greeks 'had no Thomsons because they had no Claudes', but critics showed that Scottish landscape or nature poetry existed long before Claude, and that Thomson was part of a tradition, independent of landscape painters. This view was first proposed in 1862 by Stopford Brooke:

> The first poem devoted to natural description appeared, while Pope was yet alive, in the very midst of the town poetry. It was the *Seasons* 1726–30; and it is curious, remembering what I have said about the peculiar turn of the Scotch for natural description, that it was the work of James Thomson a Scotchman. . . . He wrote with his eye upon their scenery, and even when he wrote of it in his room, it was with 'a recollected love'. The descriptions were too much like catalogues, the very fault of the previous Scotch poets, and his style was always heavy and often cold, but he was the first poet who led the English people into that new world of nature.[1]

By removing *The Seasons* from the Claudian 'glow', Brooke compared the poem with those of Shelley and Keats. The 'heaviness' of style was a reference to the poem's diction, and 'cold' a reference to absence of expressions of personal feeling. But 'cold' and 'heavy' were also terms which, in the last half of the nineteenth century, became part of the personifications of literary movement and style. In a later work, Brooke wrote (1902): 'This is the story of a hundred years; the pregnancy, carrying, birth and manhood of Naturalism in English poetry. Its strong and beautiful manhood, worn with its passion for revolution, for fullness of life, died with Shelley, Keats, and Byron. There was then a period after their deaths of silence or inefficiency. But, it had left a child behind it; one of its own blood, of its own methods, of its own imagination.'[2]

The adjectives 'heavy' and 'cold' are physical properties as well as human ones, and they form part of the analogy of style in contrast to the personification of process or unfolding: 'he was the first poet . . .' The purpose of the critical personification or the organic analogy was to create a sense of the cyclical pattern of poetic development. But the organic analogy concealed the diverse qualities of

[1] Stopford Brooke, *History of English Literature* (London, 1862), p. 162.
[2] Stopford Brooke, *Naturalism in English Poetry* (London, 1902), pp. 11–12.

poetry so that the analogy implied a consistency of literary development which Brooke himself could not accept. In *Naturalism in English Poetry* (1902), he found Thomson naturalistic and neo-classic in *The Seasons* with a 'touch' of romanticism in *The Castle of Indolence*. The theory of organic development found in the common natural analogy—'English poetry is one tree, with an organic unity, and all its developments, however strange, share in the life of the whole and are linked to the being of one another'—implied germ, growth and decay; but in the application of this to Thomson's poetry, Brooke showed that the analogy buttressed particular statements about *The Seasons* which were made to conform to the unfolding analogy, disregarding the practice of Thomson. He found Thomson's unity a patchwork, though he could not explain why scenes were shifted from one season to another. He noted important aspects of Thomson's subject matter—his cosmopolitanism and his humanity—but when he came to natural descriptions, he wrote: 'He not only restored natural description to poetry . . . but he made a new kind of it—direct description of the doings and appearance of Nature; without any reference to man—for his own sake.'[1] But Thomson's descriptions implied a relation between man and nature which John Veitch, John Shairp, and Léon Morel all noted previously. For Brooke, the progressive unfolding of naturalism limited the understanding of the poem itself.

Brooke's view of the Scottish tradition assumed a continuity, whereas Veitch pointed out that Thomson seemed unfamiliar with Scottish poetry, and the Scottish poems that do resemble *The Seasons* —those of Riccaltoun, Armstrong, Mallet—were not those mentioned by Brooke. Moreover, Brooke's organicism here was based on an unfounded racial theory which he persistently used to account for Scottish nationalism: 'I have always said and still maintain that it descended to the Lowland poets from the strong admixture of Celtic blood which prevailed over the whole of the south-west of Scotland above the border . . . The Celtic spirit had its way, and added to the English blood in Scotland its own natural love of wild nature.'[2]

The nationalistic study of literature ascribed by Brooke to Scotland, to England and then to the union of both was earlier sounded

[1] Brooke, *Naturalism*, p. 47. See also pp. 54–55. For 'cosmopolitanism', see Joseph Texte, *Jean-Jacques Rousseau and the Cosmopolitan Spirit in Literature* (London, 1899).

[2] Brooke, *Naturalism*, p. 49.

by Charles Kingsley in his lecture on English literature (1848). The teaching of literature was 'to comprehend the English spirit, thoroughly to see that the English mind has its peculiar calling upon God's earth, which alone and no other, it can fulfil'. The personification of the English mind with its calling was used to establish the continuity of vocation and the continuity of English literature as a religious vocation. The shift from the poetry-painting image to the history of man or nature analogy meant a shift from the study of particulars within a work to common or uncommon qualities in the history of literature. And even when the Pre-Raphaelites continued the poetry-painting analogy, the 'poetic' was identified with qualities in paintings of the past, and these were developmental or 'creative' qualities rather than those of the finished work. Oswald Doughty has pointed out that for Rossetti, the personal, the pictorial, and the poetic were identified 'with a romantic mood or dream-state which was obviously a profoundly important element in his own aesthetic development'.[1]

In criticism of *The Seasons*, the painting analogy did not completely disappear, but the details to which it referred became minimal, when compared to the personifications of literary movements and their causes. But in order to explain such developments, it was necessary to select qualities in the poetry which could be shown changing, and thus Brooke selected catalogues which became unified, John Dennis selected precision which became 'more accurate', Clarence E. Stedman types of suggestiveness.[2] Such selectivity, however, revealed a considerable departure from the analysis of parts undertaken by earlier critics. Moreover, the selectivity was almost entirely conditioned by the characteristics of the ideal to which the progression led. To the extent that the analogy correlated attitudes toward the society —cosmopolitanism and religion—it offered new areas of investigation, but when it correlated diction, or types of unity, or 'accuracy' of detail, it merely contrasted these divisions with the achievements of later writers to the denigration of the earlier poets.

What caused the developmental analogy to secure the prominence in critical language formerly held by the arts analogy? The answer

[1] Oswald Doughty, 'Rossetti's Conception of the "Poetic" in Poetry and Painting', *Essays by Divers Hands*, N.S. XXVI (London, 1953), p. 96. For Kingsley, see 'On English Literature', *Literary and General Lectures and Essays, The Works of Charles Kingsley* (London, 1880), XX, 262.

[2] Clarence E. Stedman, *Victorian Poets* (Boston, 1876), pp. 188, 368–9.

to this lay first in theories of language. The poetry-painting-music analogy had rested on a picture theory of language, and on an associative theory of imaginative suggestiveness. Without completely supplanting poetic 'suggestiveness', the developmental analogy opposed the 'suggestiveness' of associationism on the grounds of false perception of language. 'Suggestiveness' or 'day-dreaming' was an incorrect perception of poetic language which was best studied by its context or by the metaphoric (or metaphysical) implications of language. (By the mid-nineteenth century poetic-painting had become 'word painting'.)[1] The developmental analogy attacked the loose methodological assumptions of associationism which gave no satisfactory explanation of historical continuity and which denied or, at best, minimized cause-effect relationships.

By comparing earlier with later nineteenth-century critical terms, it can be noted that a thoroughgoing transformation of emphasis was taking place within the continuing issues: 'sympathy' became 'influence', 'parallels' became 'sources', 'habit' became 'history'. Sympathy and influence', for example, originally shared astrological and 'scientific' meanings, but the difference now was that 'influence' was a chronological and developmental term, whereas 'sympathy' was a specific and momentary exchange. Moreover, 'sympathy' implied a moral and aesthetic exchange whereas 'influence' implied causes and effects. 'Sympathy' dealt with a multitude of qualities, 'influence' with isolatable, examinable parts. 'Sympathy' was discernible by individual sensibility; 'influence' was a statistical matter, and when it branched out to literary ancestry, it still remained a matter of fact. Those critics, like E. S. Dallas, who ridiculed facts in the analysis of literature,[2] offered a completely mental defence of literary value, a completely impressionistic alternative to associationism. It was, indeed, only in the second half of the nineteenth century and by comparison with the mysticism of Wordsworth, that Thomson's description was defined as 'objective'.

At first, the painting analogy was limited to references to 'colours' of language or to 'touches' of description, and in such terms as implied shifting relations between the painting analogy and the body analogy. In 1876, for example, John Dennis in an essay on 'English Rural Poetry' wrote:

[1] Edward Dowden, *Considerations on the Criticism of Literature* (Dublin, 1864), pp. 22–23.

[2] E. S. Dallas, *Poetics: An Essay on Poetry* (London, 1852), pp. 283–4.

> It is possible, as we have seen, to discover many gems of rural verse hidden amidst the works of our earlier poets; but just as landscape painting in England may be said to have commenced with Gainsborough and Wilson, although English landscape painters existed before their day, so, speaking broadly, may Thomson and Cowper be accounted the genuine fathers of English rural poetry. Their descriptions of nature are fuller, and, if we except the incidental touches of our greatest poets, more truthful than those produced at an earlier period, and they led to the more reverent, and accurate, study of nature exhibited by Wordsworth, Shelley, Scott and Tennyson.[1]

Dennis used the poetry-painting analogy to parallel the development of landscape painting with poetry, though neither Richard Wilson nor Thomas Gainsborough were Thomson's contemporaries. In Dennis there was a continuation of the critical personification of stylistic traits so that he described the qualities of early nineteenth-century poetry as 'a splendour of imagination, a passionate force which imparted new life to language, an ardent love of nature that produced as profound an influence in poetry as Turner exercised in plastic art'. In this critical language of love, the period was seen as a lover and all literature part of the human family. The critic sought to define the 'attitude' of a period, and the artificial style of the early eighteenth century, in Stopford Brooke's words, 'succeeded to and extinguished the natural'.

Brooke saw the development of literature as a progress resulting

[1] John Dennis, 'English Rural Poetry', *Studies in English Literature* (London, 1876), pp. 372–3. The term 'landscape' with reference to eighteenth-century nature poets was first used by Thomas B. Shaw (1849). By the end of the nineteenth century the 'landscape poets' or the poets of 'natural description' were compared with the 'nature' poets of the early nineteenth century who included, but went beyond, mere landscape. According to Pevsner, 'The Genesis of the Picturesque', *Architectural Review*, XCVI (1944), 142, the word 'landscape' first appeared in the sixteenth or early seventeenth century to designate painted scenery and 'already in Milton's *Allegro* (1632) was used for real scenery of an appeal similar to that of a picture. The term Picturesque, so important during the second half of the eighteenth century is heralded in this use.' For early definitions of 'landscape' and for a study of painting treatises, see Henry V. S. Ogden and Margaret S. Ogden, *English Taste in Landscape in the Seventeenth Century* (Ann Arbor, 1955), Chapters I and II. For an early use of 'picturesque' referring to the creation of pictures in poetry, see George Sewell, *A New Collection of Original Poems* (London, 1720), p. 71.

from sibling rivalry. John C. Shairp (1877) saw the progress of nature poetry in terms of increased religious awareness. He used the poetry-painting analogy as a genre comparison suggesting that Thomson was like Claude in that he led to a better poet as Claude led to Turner, and that his digressions were, like the figures and temples of Claude, trivial and irrelevant.

> Thomson has been called the Claude of poets. And his way of handling Nature stands to that of Wordsworth or Tennyson much as Claude's landscapes do to those of Turner or some of the modern painters. It may be added that Thomson's somewhat vapid digressions about Amelia and Lavinia have not more meaning than the conventional lay figures which Claude introduces into the foreground of his landscapes.[1]

The purpose of the analogy was to minimize the significance of Thomson in the history of poetry; by comparing Claude with Turner whose eminence Ruskin publicized, Shairp was able to use the analogy as a form of strategic disesteem. This negative use of analogy appeared in Henry A. Beers' comment:

> Thomson has been likened, as a colorist, to Rubens; and possibly the glow, the breadth, and the vital energy of his best passages, as one of Rubens' canvases, leave our finer perceptions untouched, and we ask for something more esoteric, more intense.[2]

This analogy suggested Thomson as Wordsworth's forerunner in religious handling of nature, but Wordsworth at times reflected the kind of optimism Shairp found in Thomson's nature. Thomson's handling of particularity and vastness was not, moreover, the forerunner of Wordsworth's mysticism—indeed, it is a strange argument, for these critics, to derive mysticism from deism. The analogy itself

[1] Shairp, *Poetic Interpretation*, pp. 189–90.

[2] Henry Beers, *History of Romanticism in the Eighteenth Century* (London, 1898), p. 107. For the evolutionary or developmental analogy as related to a theory of criticism, see René Wellek, 'The Concept of Evolution in Literary History'. *For Roman Jakobson* (Hague, 1956), pp. 653–61. For an early essay listing some definitions for organic critical terms, see J. Isaacs, 'Coleridge's Critical Terminology', *Essays and Studies 1935* (London, 1936), 97–104. See also Harry H. Clark, "The Influence of Science on American Literary Criticism, 1860–1910', *Transactions of the Wisconsin Academy of Science, Arts and Letters*, XLIV (1955), 109–64; additional bibliographical references are included in Donald Pizer, 'Evolution and Criticism: Thomas Sergeant Perry', *Texas Studies in Literature and Language*, III (1961), 348–59.

was strangely put because Turner and Constable drew the inspiration for some of their paintings from *The Seasons* and they were, therefore, involved with the inspiration from *The Seasons*, the very poem which was a 'prelude' to Wordsworth.

Analogies are not refuted; they are ignored. The resort to painting-poetry analogy by William Bayne in 1900 was a return to the praiseworthy uses of it at the beginning of the century, but his essay on Thomson was completely defensive, though it was surely defensible: 'The harvest scene in "Autumn" or that of the haymakers in "Summer", forms a finely-conceived, finished, and effective drawing.'[1] Bayne analysed the characteristics of Thomson's natural description, pointing out that his landscapes were not inanimate. He joined his analogy to Thomson's nationalism and a defence of his religion. The defence of Thomson's 'painting' could no longer be made in the terms of 'highly wrought' pictures because Léon Morel (1895) and Myra Reynolds (1898) had made convincingly clear the movement of Thomson's language. In 1911, Sir George Douglas denied the analogy with painting if it meant 'still-life'.

> As a matter of fact there is very little 'still life' in Thomson's work; and what there is, is always in the proper place. No; Thomson's art is far more than that of the mere scene-painter—an art which does not rank high in literature: Thomson's art is rather that of the playwright himself, for he gives us the *life* and action of every scene, and raises his own function to that of the dramatist of the forces of Nature. And this it is which gives the quality of greatness to his work; which informs his vast landscape with a moving interest, and transforms his pages to the living theatre of a grandiose spectacle, or pageant.[2]

Douglas's examples indicated that he was referring to the motion in Thomson's scenes, and the frequency of quotation clarified his analogy of the poem as drama which Aikin in 1778 had used to imply an ordered unity. Douglas's analogy coincided with what was known of Thomson's language; Aikin's did not unless we remove—as he was prepared to do—the inconsistencies in the poem.

In this respect the organic personifications which analogized *The Seasons* as part of literary history possessed a curious critical ambivalence. While attacking *The Seasons* for artificial diction, the criticism expressed itself in 'natural' language which was 'unnatural'

[1] William Bayne, ed., *Poems by James Thomson* (London, 1900), p. xxvi.
[2] George Douglas, *Scottish Poetry* (Glasgow, 1911), p. 60.

as descriptions of literary movements. William Lyon Phelps, for example, in 1893 defined literature, after Arnold, as the crystallization of tendencies of thought and found that 'the Queen Anne school of English Literature expressed the popular dominating ideas about the problems of life'.[1] It is hard to take seriously a view of the eighteenth century which finds that Swift was destitute 'of positive religious belief', but what needs to be considered is the view of the analogy of man in explaining literary changes. Thomson chose blank verse instead of couplets for *The Seasons*, Phelps explained, because 'he was doubtless weary of its monotony. Possibly one of his reasons for forsaking the couplet was the fact that Pope had brought it to its utmost refinement and polish, and that it was not capable of any further development.'[2]

Continuity and change were analogized in imagery of man, the family, trees, and rivers. Samuel Croxall, Lady Winchelsea, Thomas Parnell were 'currents flowing in a direction opposite to the general stream'. To be accurate, this generalization required more qualifications than Phelps made, yet the explanation of the genesis of movements was expressed for him and for Edmund Gosse and Thomas S. Perry in analogies that implied motion and growth. But the major cause for dissatisfaction with this developmental view was its indiscriminate selection of aspects which changed. The analogy implied a whole group of reasons for change in such words as 'weary', 'exhausted', or 'love of nature'. The analogy thus avoided the specific details necessary to define what the characteristics of Thomson's blank verse were, when Johnson, for example, had noted that it was an independent growth. In assuming that some elements were constant the analogy created a poetry divided in itself, and the human analogy or the 'current' analogy provided a fictional 'wholeness'.

The chief critical term for the evolutionary theory was 'influence', a conscious or unconscious current from writer to writer within a given genre; 'influence', with its implication of flow, could embrace the human analogy, and, in nature poetry, suggested the departure from and 'return to' nature. In seeking to understand the shift in analogical, critical terms, it is necessary to realize that the earlier poetry-painting analogies used the body as a basis for the union of the two arts or as an example of the force of visual perception upon the mind of writer and reader. The comparative basis for such

[1] William Lyon Phelps, *The Beginnings of the English Romantic Movement* (London, 1893), p. 7.
[2] Phelps, pp. 37–38.

analogies was the vigour or force of the impression from each of the arts. The developmental analogy kept as its basis the concept of force and energy to explain the rise or decline of a type. Blank verse was 'exhausted', the poet found new energy through 'love' of nature. In 1756 Joseph Warton wrote that Thomson 'was accustomed to wander away into the country for days and weeks, attentive to "each rural sight, each rural sound"', but in 1898 Henry A. Beers expressed the same information in terms of love: Thomson 'was something of a naturalist, who wrote lovingly and with "his eye upon the object"', and in the same year Myra Reynolds wrote of Thomson's 'strong love of nature'.[1]

The 'force', 'freedom', 'new spirit' which Thomson introduced was the 'energy' and 'vividness' that belonged to earlier analogies, still maintained as a value, though now derived from the innovating force rather than the precision of description. The developmental analogies and personifications placed *The Seasons* within the tradition of nature poetry, though it was not clear whether Thomson belonged here since he lacked knowledge of Scottish poetry. As early as 1777, John More had pointed to Scottish scenes in *The Seasons* and the recollections of Scottish storms. The development of nature poetry meant that 'force' was to be identified with increasing intensity or

[1] Beers, p. 107; Myra Reynolds, *Treatment of Nature* (London, 1898), p. 94. See also terms like 'literary ancestry', 'adore', and the personification of stylistic traits. Discussions of Thomson's 'influence' often recognize that the concept is slippery, and terms like 'verbal echoes', 'borrowings', 'parallels', and 'similarities' do not permit very reliable inferences. Discriminations of 'influence' which deal with style or families of style (traditions) are still meagre, and the tracing of words, phrases, and fragments provide only the most mechanical critical data. Studies of Thomson's 'influence' are found in the following: Gjerset, *Der Einfluss von James Thomson's Jahreszeiten auf die deutsche Literatur des 18. Jahrhunderts* (Heidelberg, 1898); John A. Walz, 'Schiller's *Spaziergang* and Thomson's *Seasons*', *MLN*, IV (1906), 117–20; Otto Zippel, *Entstehungs- und Entwicklungeschichte von Thomson's 'Winter'*, Franklin Bliss Snyder, 'Notes on Burns and Thomson', *JEGP*, XIX (1920), 305–17; C. H. Ibershoff, 'Bodmer and Thomson's *Seasons*', *MLN*, XLI (1926), 29–32; Margaret M. Cameron, *L'Influence des Saisons de Thomson sur la poésie descriptive en France (1759–1810)* (Paris, 1927); Walter G. Johnson, *James Thomson's Influence on Swedish Literature in the 18th Century* (Illinois, 1936). One of the major attacks on 'influence' and evolutionary terms and personifications in criticism was made by Arthur Quiller-Couch, 'On the Terms "Classical" and "Romantic"', *Studies in Literature* (Cambridge, 1918), pp. 76–95.

some form of religious mysticism as its highest stage so that the development of a type was governed by qualities considered to be the culmination of a form, and the form itself was disengaged from comparison with non-literary arts.

The developmental analogy, therefore, found that Thomson's precision of description was not as 'vivid' as Wordsworth's nor as personal as Shelley's. Because it evaluated *The Seasons* by what was assumed to be the ideal of the form, it minimized even the description. Its value was historical—it led men back to nature. But the developmental analogy could not answer some of the questions it raised. Even the selection of traits which were influences upon Thomson were not clear. Milton and John Philips were named, but the respects in which they 'influenced' *The Seasons* was not specified. Nor could the analogy seriously maintain that Thomson was 'tired' of couplets, considering how few he had written. In deciding the traits of romanticism, it was discovered that Thomson was not the best choice for a forerunner, since Arnold had named Gray. But the most obvious and most serious dilemma of the evolutionists was their indictment of a whole culture in a theory of development; it was the 'spirit of the age', Phelps wrote, that spoke out in Lady Mary Wortley Montagu when she replied to Pope in a 'coarse, doggerel burlesque'. In 1880, Arnold had written that Thomas Gray never spoke out because he, 'a born poet, fell upon an age of prose'. Gray was isolated in his century, and in 1911, Sir George Douglas wrote in the critical analogues of love and nationalism:

> Blame the age in which he lived, if so you are minded. It was an age of reason, of mild enlightenment . . . it was an age of prose rather than of poetry. So by all means blame the age, if such be your pleasure, for Thomson's stiffness, his artificiality. . . . But I for my part cannot help believing that Thomson would have stood a better chance of giving himself up, whole-hearted, to the goddess he adored—to Nature who alone is good—if, instead of joining Pope upon the banks of the Thames, he had stayed here at home, in Scotland, with Allan Ramsay![1]

The language of progress and organicism did not eliminate the difficulties which critics had with 'imagination', with 'unity', with the unresolved particulars of the poem. The placing of the poem within

[1] Douglas, pp. 71–72. For a view which attacked Arnold's essay and (by implication) Douglas's acceptance of it, see Arthur F. Bell, Ed., 'Introduction', *Gray Poems Published in 1768* (Oxford, 1915) pp. xxxviii–xlii.

a tradition was obviously dependent upon this kind of knowledge; without it, there were only speculative assumptions about tradition and about the relation of the unity to the poem. The new analogy, in other words, began by superimposing upon the poem assumptions about language and religious views that were untenable. It was only when the analogy was applied directly to literature that its applicability had any value as criticism; that is, when counting and enumeration revealed that Thomson was not involved in conflict with Pope's language or Pope's ideas, but shared aspects of common beliefs in different ways. The individualism, the traditionalism, could become apparent in literature only as the critic studied innovation as well as convention.

The most complete attack upon the painting analogy and the 'age' appeared in 1910: it was Irving Babbitt's *The New Laocoon, An Essay on the Confusion of the Arts*. Within the language of the developmental analogy—of arrival and departure, of family relationships—Babbitt identified the eighteenth-century poetry-painting analogy with the 'following' of Aristotle and Horace, while losing the right direction of the Aristotelian norm. The 'influence' theory formed the basis for the age and Babbitt explained that although 'the immense influence of Horace was in the main beneficial', Aristotle's *Poetics* tended, in the Renaissance, 'under the influence of the literary casuists, towards a pure formalism; and when we examine more closely we discover that the means used for thus exalting questions of form and neglecting what we should call nowadays the subjective side of art, was a certain idea of imitation'.[1]

The idea of imitating not action but models was developed by the 'pseudo-classic' theorists—as Babbitt called them—and one of the chief consequences was the belief in correspondence between pictorial art and poetry. Granting disagreements on such correspondences, Babbitt declared that the theorists 'did, however, finally reach a fair agreement as to what constitutes the element of poetical colouring'.

> The poet, then, is an imitator, and a painter who in drawing his design, that is, in choosing a subject and mode of treatment, is to be unspontaneous and traditional. He is also to be unspontaneous and traditional in laying on his poetical colors; and by poetical colors the neo-classicist understands words, elegant phrases, figures

[1] Irving Babbitt, *The New Laocoon* (Boston, 1910).

of speech and the like. Horace already speaks of words as poetical colors in much this sense, and the expression is found even in Wordsworth. Both words and imagery are regarded by the neo-classicist as being laid on like pigments from the outside. They are not, in Wordsworth's phrase, the spontaneous overflow of powerful feelings; they lack the vital thrill that would save them from artificiality. The result might not have been so bad if the poet had painted with his eye on the object. But at this point the other theory of imitation intervened, and in supplying his palette with poetical colors (that is, words, happy phrases, figures of speech, etc.) he must not look to nature but to models.[1]

Babbitt attacked this view as a 'confusion' which led to a 'romantic confusion' in the next century based on spontaneity, but Babbitt's criticism is a representative example of how his own developmental analogy removed him from the inquiries necessary to provide confirming data for his statements. His own use of analogy was strategic: it was to defend a humanistic position against the extremes of post-Renaissance doctrine: 'I trust that I have at least justified in this book the statement I made at the beginning, that an inquiry into the nature of the *genres* and the boundaries of the arts is far-reaching and involves one's attitude not merely toward literature but toward life.'[2]

The objection to the diction-colour analogy involved no reference to eighteenth-century diction and it was completely consistent with his theory that he did not seek to discover in the nature poetry what 'laying on words from the outside' might mean to a writer like Thomson, who affirmed of his epithets that 'I must chuse, what appears to me the most significant Epithet or I cannot, with any Heart, proceed'. Babbitt wrote of Thomson's poem as an 'influence': 'Whatever it may be in itself, considered as an influence, Thomson's "Seasons" is a pseudo-classical document. It led to a school of descriptive and pictorial poetry, but pictorial in a pseudo-classic sense—that is conceiving of words and phrases as pigments to be laid on from without; and this school was not slow to justify itself by an appeal to the maxim *ut pictura poesis*.'[3] But granted that Thomson's followers wrote poor nature poetry, that nature poets shared common images, the writing of bad poetry must be distinguished from the shared cultural language, whether this be 'poetic diction' or the romantic imagery of birds and breath. Babbitt's

[1] Babbitt, pp. 18, 22–24. [2] Babbitt, p. 252. [3] Babbitt, p. 31.

discussion neglected the distinction between good and bad uses of poetry—although he conceded that Thomson may have used language well—and thus he did not distinguish between the doctrines of critics and the actual language of poets. Babbitt could not explain the difference between right and wrong linguistic preferences any more than he could explain originality within a theory of models. But both were significant to poets and essential in understanding what 'colours' meant, since nature did appear in colours, and these were not 'laid on'.

Babbitt's misunderstanding of the eighteenth-century analogy arose from the naïve view of development, from an imposed Greek ideal and from a neglect of the poems he was describing. He interpreted literary changes in terms of psychological or scientific analogues which involved opposites or action-reaction, and his own view of inner check was itself formulated by this untenable view of opposites. For the development of eighteenth-century views of poetry and poetic techniques themselves was not a single entity, but contained elements which had more or less continuity and Thomson, who, as Warton and Wordsworth recognized, did have his eye on objects, composed moving poetry without 'discrediting' poetic diction. Indeed, the followers of Thomson repeatedly kept their eye on the object, though their poetry proved, too often, dull. For Babbitt, the poetical diction became the key to the analogy, although not one single example of poetic diction appeared in his book, and the poetry-painting analogy was, in the eighteenth century, based on theories of picture language, of perception, of appropriateness of language to subject.

Although his own language reflected some elements of the developmental analogy, Babbitt objected to this analogy when it denied the independence of genres. He objected to applying the biological analogy to literature:

> Because the genera and species evolve and run together in this way on the physical plane, it is easy to take the next step and assume that the literary *genres* evolve and run together in the same way. This is what is known as the biological analogy. But any one who would make of this comparison between the natural genus and the literary *genre* anything beside a more or less useful metaphor, at once falls into pseudo-science. Brunetière, for example, is pseudo-scientific in his literary Darwinism or *évolution des genres*. The reason is obvious: the *genres* are related not merely to the natural law, but in a vastly higher degree to the 'law for man'.[1]

[1] Babbitt, p. 215.

Babbitt believed that each genre had a unity, measure, purpose of its own and that this development had to be charted by critics; but he made an arbitrary assumption that descriptive poetry was not a genre, just as there was an arbitrary decision preferring natural language to artificial diction when in each case the poet had his eye on the object. Such 'laws for man' ignored the serious literary issues of determining what the ends of a genre were. The accurate descriptions were bound to be considered occasional exceptions despite the obvious fact that they were not, because then the concept of 'age' would have had to be reconsidered.

The theory of development or evolution, coming as it did from science, led to considerable research into the facts of English literary history. Such facts together with the historical tracing of 'influence', 'followers', and 'imitators' supplanted careful study of particular works. Criticisms of *The Seasons* did not, however, reflect any change in substance, only a reproportioning of accepted information. But when the poem began to be discussed as part of 'attitudes' or 'philosophies' in John C. Shairp's *Poetic Interpretation of Nature* (1877), aspects of the poem began again to be seen in terms of particular elements—such as natural description, diction, philosophic ideas, Scottish background. The analysis of its nature elements was continued in John Veitch's *The Feeling for Nature in Scottish Poetry* (1887); and in Léon Morel's *James Thomson: sa vie et ses œuvres* (1895) the attempt to trace stylistic traits by examination of particular words and phrases began. 'Influence' became identified with quantitative studies of literary characteristics, and the poem again became the subject of intensive study.

Veitch's work and that of Myra Reynolds (1898) separated the discussion of landscape painters from that of 'landscape' poets—Henry A. Beers referred to Thomson and his followers as 'landscape poets' (1898)—and Reynolds referred to the sunset after the rain in *Spring* as 'one of the best examples of Thomson's power to paint word pictures'. Sir George Douglas (1911) also referred to Thomson's word-painting and A. Hamilton Thompson (1913) wrote that

> the village haymaking and sheepwashing in *Summer* are mild attempts at *genre* pictures; the 'rural smell' of the harvest, the 'dusky wave' of mown hay on the meadow, the 'russet hay-cock' of the one, the 'pebbled shore' and 'flashing wave' of the washing-pool in the other, meant more to Thomson than the perfunctory rustics who form part of the scene. His one elaborate picture of

the pursuits of his fellow-men is the description of a feast after a day's hunting.[1]

The use of word-painting implied the power of suggestion of words to create pictures, and formed no extended analogy with painting other than the perception of a picture, and the use of the term 'picture' by A. H. Thompson did not imply any serious analogy with painting. It is necessary, therefore, to insist that the 'return to nature' theorists demonstrated a literary development for Thomson rather than a pictorial one—a tradition of poetry rather than a tradition of painting. And it should be added that by insisting on Thomson's close observation of nature they tended to deny that his sight or his value as poet was conditioned by painting; on the contrary, the point was that the analogy with painting was of negative value whereas his direct response to nature was the basis for his poetic force. The return to nature denoted, in great part, a departure from painting.

The documentation of this return to nature meant for Myra Reynolds an enumeration of those words and phrases which depicted the sounds, sights, smells, and actions of nature and those which reflected the continuation of the classical 'influences'. Thomson 'looked on Nature with the eye of an artist, but not of an artist in black and white. It was not form but colour that attracted him.' Yet his awareness of colour involved 'broad masses of strong, clear colour'—'blue as seen in the sky or reflected in water'—and with 'such words as indicate colour in general without specification as to kind'—'the boundless blush of spring', 'the innumerous-coloured scene of things'. The examples of Thomson as colourist showed little relation to artistic use of colour and the 'eye of the artist' merely implied that he attended to the idea of colour, but not to distinctions of hue, saturation, and brilliance.

Reynolds recognized in *The Seasons* a pervasive 'dislike of boundaries'. It was the sense of exuberance and abundance, and she identified this with the wide views: 'He loved to seek out some proud eminence and there let his eye wander "far excursive" and dwell on "boundless prospects".' Such a view had been described in

[1] Thompson, pp. 112–13. For quotations from Myra Reynolds, see pp. 85–86, 93, 339. For 'colour' in *The Seasons*, see William H. Browne, 'Colour-Chords in Thomson's Seasons,' *MLN*, XII (1897), 282–3. For a statistical discussion of colour terms and adjectives based on Morel's and Reynolds's compilation, see Cornelius E. De Haas, *Nature and the Country in English Poetry* (Amsterdam, 1928), pp. 103–5.

1845 by Hugh Miller, and it did not necessarily involve a landscape way of seeing but merely a view from a height. But the developmental view put a premium upon originality or innovation and Miss Reynolds declared that looking at particular elements in nature often produced 'exceptional vividness of statement. What took rank in the poet's mind as his own discovery brought out a natural freshness of phrase . . . These specific references are of real importance in showing new powers of perception.' Direct experience of nature did not, however, as Thomson's followers proved, lead to 'freshness of phrase' and the 'new powers of perception' seemed an untenable conception.

The kind of query which this implied—why was there no Thomson in 1700?—could not be answered by the developmentalists with any adequacy any more than it can be answered today. But the development of an interest in nature can only be concealed by the attribution of 'new powers' to explain what the old powers cannot. The same kind of claim, with the same kind of validity, is made by modern critics in explaining a misunderstanding of eighteenth-century personification. Although personification of allegorical traits and characters was common in eighteenth-century poetry, there is a need to distinguish between adequate and inadequate personification; and the basis for this is a knowledge of the poetry, not an 'allegorical imagination' or a 'visual imagination'.

The 'influence' of landscape painting upon poetry was developed in a now-famous study by Elizabeth W. Manwaring, *Italian Landscape in Eighteenth Century England*. She pointed out that eighteenth-century writers developed a technical language which distinguished between 'landscape' and 'prospect': 'with them *landscape* means about what Shenstone meant by it, a more unified, less vast, paintable scene, though often still extensive, and *prospect* a view from a height, too vast for the canvas'. Thomson was '*par excellence*, the poet of pictorial landscape'. Although his *Winter* (1726) had few landscapes, *Summer* (1727) contained 'Claudian sunrises and sunsets, extended views, pastoral scenes', and in *Autumn* (1730) 'the landscapes are well constructed, but less Italian'.[1]

[1] Elizabeth W. Manwaring, *Italian Landscape in Eighteenth Century England* (New York, 1925), pp. 96, 104. For Claude's paintings as related to artificial rather than natural landscape, see Rev. Stopford Brooke, ed., 'Critical Notice of "Bridge with boate" ', *Liber Studiorum of J. M. W. Turner, R.A.* (London, 1882): 'Claude did not work from nature, nor did

The case for Claude and Rosa as part of the cultural background of eighteenth-century literature was convincingly made, but there was reason to doubt that *The Seasons* was, in any but the most general way, 'influenced' by these painters, and, granting this influence, the importance of its contribution to the poem. For Elizabeth Manwaring did not expound the 'influence' of the Dutch realists upon the poem, although this was one of the bases for comparison in Warton and others. And of the examples she gave, the view from Hagley Park which Thomson included in *Spring* in 1744 was described as 'the most elaborately composed of all his landscapes, with real Claudian distances'. It was this very view which the geologist Hugh Miller (1854) found to be a careful replica of the scene—instead of an artificial composition—and there is reason to believe that many of Thomson's landscapes are described as he saw them. Another example, the personification of day in *Summer* (ll. 81–90), has been found by Jean Hagstrum to resemble Guido's 'Aurora' rather than a Claudian sunrise.

> In one of Thomson's most celebrated and beautiful passages he describes the rising of the sun as a royal progress.
>
> But yonder comes the powerful king of day
> Rejoicing in the east. The lessening cloud,
> The kindling azure, and the mountain's brow
> Illumed with fluid gold, his near approach
> Betoken glad. Lo! now, apparent all,
> Aslant the dew-bright earth and coloured air,
> He looks in boundless majesty abroad,
> And sheds the shining day, that burnished plays
> On rocks, and hills, and towers, and wandering streams
> High-gleaming from afar
>
> [*Summer*, ll. 81–90].
>
> This has been considered a Claudian sunrise. But because its most striking feature is the personification of day as a powerful king, coming in golden pomp to the earth, it is closer to Guido's 'Aurora'. Thomson's imagination seems to have kindled at this fresco, in which the sky streams not only with vague unembodied

---

he see or care for natural truth, but he composed his properties into beautifully disposed masses, and with a view to awaken through noble composition an ideal pleasure. It was always a conventional idealism, having no secure basis of truth, and resembles the landscape of Pope, and when it is best, of Collins or Gray.'

> glories but with glories attached to large and lovely human figures in general progress and also in graceful motion within that forward progress.[1]

Now although Miller's view included more than the selected elements of the poem, he was able to test what Thomson could have seen. It might have been possible to argue that some of Claude's distances resembled those from Hagley Hall, but such a contention would in no way indicate that Thomson was imitating Claude. What it did indicate was that enumeration as a poetic device could be understood either by familiarity with the subject or by familiarity with the techniques of poetry and their possible implications. Miss Manwaring sought to explain what the 'influence' of the three landscape painters was in England, 'what were the early traces of its appearance; by what means their influence spread; the conceptions of landscape beauty which it established for a hundred years in literature, in gardening, in general taste'.

In order to prove that landscape conceptions in literature were established by the painters, she demonstrated the prevalence of landscape views in eighteenth-century poetry and then sought to derive them from the knowledge of the landscape painters.

> Throughout the century a literary landscape was formed, generally, on these models: extended prospect, variety of objects, amphitheatre form, sunset and sunrise lights; or cliffs, cascades, hanging woods, torrents, 'delightful horrors'. Not until late was the beauty of quiet and gentle scenery generally recognized, or indeed, in literature recognized at all.[2]

This implied a shared vocabulary of landscape description, but it did not distinguish between painting terms and paintable scenes. In the example of the 'young day' given by the author there was, as Robert Heron (1793) realized, no very paintable description.

> Young day pours in apace,
> And opens all the lawny prospect wide.
> The dripping rock, the mountain's misty top
> Swell on the sight and brighten with the dawn.
>
> [*Summer*, ll. 52–55]

[1] Jean Hagstrum, *The Sister Arts* (Chicago, 1958), pp. 262–3. For an attack upon Hagstrum's use of the analogy, see William Wimsatt, Jr., 'Review of *The Sister Arts*', *PQ*, XXXVIII (1959), 288–9. For support of Hagstrum's views, see Alan D. McKillop, 'Review of *The Sister Arts*', *MLQ*, XX (1959), 198–9.

[2] Manwaring, p. 95.

The day 'pouring' in was a mixed personification, and the 'swelling'—the gradually revealed sight—was a progressive, not static action. 'None of these [images] . . .' wrote Heron, 'are pictured with any very expressive or very delicate strokes of the pencil. But they delight the imagination with a very agreeable group of objects, and a sweetly placid scene.' The 'king of day' passage, however, was a very 'expressive' painting passage:

> Painting could not more expressively represent the rising sun's appearance, than the poet, when he marks it by
>
> . . . The lessening cloud
> The kindling azure, and the mountain's brow
> Illum'd with fluid gold . . .

The conversion of landscape to language may have been responsible for the development of landscape clichés, but Miss Manwaring was aware that in landscape a poet like Gilbert West 'shows the influence of Thomson', so that the relation of landscape to poetry could be the result of poet 'influencing' poet without any reference to landscape painting. The assumption that landscape poetry was predominantly visual resulted in an unfounded assumption that visual language did not create intellectually felt views of the world, and C. V. Deane (1935) was quite correct in writing that 'if Miss Manwaring's conclusions are accepted, then Lessing's case against eighteenth-century descriptive poetry would appear to be substantiated beyond question'.[1]

In arguing against the influence of landscape artists upon Thomson, Deane quoted the 'king of day' and the 'Hagley Park' passages and argued with regard to the first that it contained nothing 'to suggest imitation of or rivalry with a Claudian view' and 'that in thus depicting a sunrise in general terms that poet may have been unconsciously influenced by an aggregate of memories drawn from the artist's early work'. The second description was 'not a formal composition at all. It is what Thomson names it, a "prospect" ', probably written from an exact impression.

The value of Miss Manwaring's book for criticism was that it created a need for modern critics of eighteenth-century poetry to know another art even if they disagreed with the application of it in

[1] C. V. Deane, *Aspects of 18th Century Nature Poetry* (Oxford, 1935), p. 67. For Robert Heron, see 'A Critical Essay on *The Seasons*', *The Seasons* (Perth, 1793).

Italian Landscape in Eighteenth Century England. In drawing attention to certain stereotypes of landscape, the book caused critics to distinguish varied characteristics of poetic landscape which permitted original poetic expressions to be discriminated from those of 'descriptive versifiers'. In attempting to render the analogy from painting more defensible, Deane tried to place the *ut pictura poesis* maxim 'on a new footing, so far as concerns eighteenth-century nature poems of detailed description—to show that the "precise suggestion of a visible whole" which characterizes the best of them is contrived by methods of composition and grouping analogous to, and often identical in aim with those of landscape painting, but purely poetic in substance and execution'.[1]

The passage in *Autumn* selected for analysis was:

> Now, by the cool declining year condensed,
> Descend the copious exhalations, checked
> As up the middle sky unseen they stole,
> And roll the doubling fogs around the hill.
> No more the mountain, horrid, vast, sublime,
> Who pours a sweep of rivers from his sides,
> And high between contending kingdoms rears
> The rocky long division, fills the view
> With great variety; but, in a night
> Of gathering vapour, from the baffled sense
> Sinks dark and dreary. Thence expanding far,
> The huge dusk, gradual swallows up the plain:
> Vanish the woods; the dim-seen river seems,
> Sullen and slow, to roll the misty wave.
> Even in the height of noon oppressed, the sun
> Sheds, weak and blunt, his wide refracted ray;
> Whence, glaring oft, with many a broadened orb,
> He frights the nations. Indistinct on earth,
> Seen through the turbid air, beyond the life,
> Objects appear; and, wildered, o'er the waste
> The shepherd stalks gigantic...
>
> [ll. 707–27]

[1] Deane, pp. 99–100. See also W. L. Renwick, 'Notes on Some Lesser Poets of the Eighteenth Century', *Essays on the Eighteenth Century* (Oxford, 1945), pp. 130–46: 'The point is, that the eighteenth-century poets assumed the value of a pictorial sense. Their landscapes are composed. In Wordsworth there is no scenery' (p. 137).

This passage describes the transformation of man and nature caused by fogs and reveals the blunting, dull qualities of nature as they overpower and distort normal views. The passage was assumed to be analogous to a painting because it selected the essentials of the scene with a feeling for the 'structural succession of images'.

> A few characteristic yet widely varied features have been chosen in the Carter Fell passage so as to exhibit the essentials of the scene; a mountainous mass separated from rolling sullen moorlands by a wooded river valley. The order in which the objects are described follows the course that would naturally be taken in casting the eye over the view. Arrested first by the dominating height, our vision follows its slope down to the valley and thence up to the wastes which stretch into the distance. . . . The course followed is rhythmical in line, and . . . the impression of depth is secured by leaving the remoter images to the end of the description.[1]

Since Deane's use of the analogy was to help his readers understand eighteenth-century descriptive poetry, it must be asked to what extent his explanation did help. The rise and descent of the 'copious exhalations' which now roll 'doubling fogs' around set the tone for the passage. This 'check' to height referred to the mountain which sank under the 'gathering vapour', and 'sinks' was an irony of nature. The sense of sullen, greedy nature was not an example of landscape but a suggestive use of personification which played with submerged imagery of the sublime: dusk 'swallows up' the plain, the river seems 'to roll the misty wave', the sun 'glaring oft'. There are instances of personification which are emblematic and which are modelled on pictures and of such Jean Hagstrum has given examples. But these can be considered as uses of paintings, not as incorporating painting techniques in poetry.

In 1936, taking off from the poetry-painting analogy of Elizabeth Manwaring and C. V. Deane, Bernard Fehr declared that since 1845 when 'the geologist Hugh Miller drew special attention to that description [Hagley Park] by Thomson, the accuracy of which he confirmed by supplying details of his own, undue importance has ever since been attached to this passage, which is devoid of Thomson's Baroque characteristics, his grandeur, sweeping movement, and pompous rhetoric'. But this identification of Thomson's 'characteristic'

[1] Deane, p. 99.

features was not shared by earlier 'characteristic' discoverers: (1) particular description by Joseph Warton, (2) this plus knowledge of natural science and the development of description as a genre by Aikin, (3) the sense of process in nature by Hazlitt and Sir George Douglas, (4) the influence of landscape painting—Manwaring.

Fehr began by assuming that whatever did not conform to the canons of his version of Baroque was not characteristic. But this analysis is much too easy, and one must consult the theoretical grounds for his assumptions. These were that Thomson was most characteristic in his metrical opposition to Pope, and that the return to blank verse was a return to Miltonic Baroque expression. But putting aside the determination of Baroque characteristics, there was no satisfactory procedure for distinguishing Thomson's Baroque characteristics if one did not examine his blank verse in the drama; in an example of representative verse characteristics, Fehr found the 'lavish decorative display of Rococo'.

> Rent is the fleecy mantle of the sky;
> The clouds fly different. And the *sudden* sun
> By fits *effulgent* gilds the *illumined* field.
> And *black* by fits the shadows sweep along.
> A *gaily* checker'd heart expanding view,
> Far as the *circling* eye can shoot around,
> *Unbounded* tossing in a flood of corn.
> [*Autumn*, ll. 36–42]

> This famous autumn piece expresses movement and the visual delights caused by it, in convolutions followed by undulations. Thomson's motional effects are, moreover, heightened by the choice of verbal imagery: fly, fits, sweep, shoot, tossing, flood. The images, however, are weighted by decorative epithets, all of them logically redundant. 'Sudden', naturally if the sun is having 'fits'. 'Illumined', certainly if an 'effulgent' fit is 'gilding' the field, 'black', exactly if these are 'shadows', 'gaily' of course if the view is 'checkered'. 'Circling', what else if it is an eye shooting 'around', 'Unbounded', indeed if it is a 'flood'. This is the lavish decorative display of Rococo and recalls Thomson's age when interior decoration in the big houses began to run riot . . .[1]

[1] Bernard Fehr, 'The Antagonism of Forms in the Eighteenth Century', *English Studies XVIII* (1936), 201, 202. Fehr acknowledges that his comparison was first suggested by F. W. Bateson, *English Poetry and the English Language* (Oxford, 1934), pp. 76–77. For a discussion of Fehr and his presentation of the issue, see René Wellek, 'The Parallelism Between

Fehr's analysis of the 'Rococo' characteristics assumed that the epithets were 'decorative' and 'logically redundant'. Now the quoted passage was contrasted with the preceding lines 12–35 (not noted by Fehr) which described the 'pleasing calm' (ll. 36–42) of departing summer. Thomson's use of language, therefore, was not redundant but comparative, so that the 'fierce effulgence' of departing summer—the prolonged, intense heat of summer—differed in extent and intensity from the 'fits effulgent' of autumn. The 'sudden' sun of autumn was contrasted with the 'attemper'd suns' of its summer and the 'fits' were not redundant because the sun arose 'sudden' but was 'effulgent' and 'black' in turn.

If one compares the original passage with its revision Thomson's procedure becomes clearer. He had written in 1730 (ll. 30–31):

> while broad, and brown, below,
> Unbounded harvests hang the heavy head.

and ll. 40–42 (1730):

> A gayly checker'd, wide-extended view,
> Far as the circling eye can shoot around,
> Convolv'd, and tossing in a flood of corn.

These he revised in 1744 as follows:

ll. 30–31 while broad and brown, below,
Extensive harvests hang the heavy head.

ll. 40–42 A gayly chequered, heart-expanding view,
Far as the circling eye can shoot around,
Unbounded tossing in a flood of corn.

The key terms in the revisions were 'unbounded', 'extended', 'extensive', 'convolv'd', and 'expanding'. By contrasting repetitions Thomson built distinctions in word usage as well as in the meanings of storms, love, death, and the other continuing themes. In a poem which dealt with repetitions of natural phenomena this procedure was not surprising, but it was used to contrast with other methods of

---

Literature and the Arts', *English Institute Annual*, 1941 (New York, 1942), pp. 40–42. For another example of a vague and unrewarding parallel, in which Richard Wilson's 'freshness of conception and technique' is paralleled with Thomson's 'more natural freedom of blank verse', see Herbert Read, 'Parallels in English Painting and Poetry', *In Defence of Shelley and Other Essays* (London, 1936), pp. 242–3.

deriving meaning—like the prospect views, declamations, and lyric personal references. In this passage the original contrasted the heavy, motionless harvest with the wind-blown (convolv'd), sea-tossing harvest resulting from autumn breezes. The revised passage established a more direct point of view from a narrator who, observing the 'heart-expanding' view, found himself part of the autumnal nature rather than that of declining summer.

In distinguishing the alleged 'Rococo' qualities, Fehr misconstrued Thomson's usage. In implying a parallel between poetry and Baroque architecture and gardens, he examined sentence syntax and suggested the examination of versification. But in implying that different arts all formed part of a whole, he studied the verses in order to establish similarities rather than differences. The failure to trace Thomson's usage, therefore, was not inherent in the comparison but in his use of it—namely, that it would reveal common ends. For the very assumption of 'evolution' implied the kind of response he anticipated. 'Now let us, instead of going on with the story of literature, consult the Fine Arts. What kind of evolution of forms do they reveal in the 17th and 18th centuries?'

Fehr's attempt to identify columns in architecture with sentence structure in poetry, is one of several attempts to identify stylistic effects in literature and the other arts. The major difficulty is the failure as yet to establish adequate tools for stylistic discrimination. To assume that columns and lines are analogical is one matter; to speculate about them, another. This sort of speculation is based on the assumption that common bonds of some type exist among the arts. This may be so, but little progress can be made so long as speculation relies on the weakest tools and false comparisons, and considers the issue settled before it is begun.

Just as C. V. Deane pointed out that direct imitations of painting views were infrequent and offered other explanations for the same phenomena, Majorie H. Nicolson has demonstrated that the use of colour by Thomson was not dependent upon painting but upon current interest in Newton's theory of optics. In a recent summary of Thomson's achievement in 'visual description', Jean Hagstrum has named four characteristics:

> (1) he has responded to the *light* (and the lights) of the natural world, giving us what may be the best poetic light-imagery of natural light ever written. (2) He has rendered the *color* of the natural world with greater eloquence and fidelity than any other

> writer on so large a scale. (3) He has achieved on his verbal canvas the grace of *natural motion* that was greatly admired in seventeenth- and eighteenth-century aesthetic thought. (4) He has attempted to solve the problem of landscape form in verbal description by humanizing and mythologizing the world in the manner of baroque and Renaissance landscape.[1]

There seems no reason to assume that the first three characteristics require, in any way, the attempt to compose paintings in poetry, and Hagstrum recognizes this by explaining that 'the technique most peculiarly amenable to verbal art is natural personification, and by means of it Thomson achieves his characteristic form'.[2]

Personification is a characteristic device of Thomson's, and Hagstrum distinguished between implicit, unvisualized figures and fully developed 'pictorial action', and he further distinguished between moral personifications which tend to be 'lifeless' in contrast to natural personifications which 'are usually bright, individual and moving. It is here that his characteristic excellence resides'. This excellence is identified as 'motion', as excited outbursts on contemplating the personifications, as supplications which convey personal intimacy and reverential responsiveness.

The examples of personifications which function like 'personae' or allegorical figures in painting are not those which function best as poetry. Not only was the invocation to *Spring*, 'Come, gentle Spring, ethereal mildness, come,' considered ineffective by some eighteenth-century critics because of its vagueness, but *Winter*, which was also vague—'sullen and sad'—had a suggested revision by Lyttelton making it more specific and in closer agreement with Kent's illustration; but Thomson rejected the revision. There are other examples in *Autumn* to suggest that Thomson was not consistent in increasing visuality: thus while in *Winter* (1726) 'angel forms are seen' (l. 77) became more visual in 'Where angel forms athwart the solemn dusk, / Tremendous sweep, or seem to sweep along' (*Autumn*, 1730, ll. 1033–4), the personification of the western sun in *Winter* (1726, ll. 80–84)

> Now, when the Western Sun withdraws the Day,
> And humid Evening, gliding o'er the Sky,
> In her chill Progress, checks the straggling Beams,
> And robs them of their gathered vapoury Prey,

[1] Hagstrum, p. 252. [2] Hagstrum, p. 259; see also pp. 263–4.

became more generalized (*Autumn*, ll. 1082–5)

> The western sun withdraws the shortened day;
> And humid evening, gliding o'er the sky,
> In her chill progress, to the ground condensed
> The vapours throws.

The personifications to which Hagstrum pointed were often formal invocations; the assumption that invocations create a sense of personal intimacy seems difficult to defend in the examples given:

> Welcome, ye shades! ye bowery thickets, hail!
> Ye lofty pines! ye venerable oaks!
> Ye ashes wild, resounding o'er the steep!
> Delicious is your shelter to the soul . . .
> [*Summer*, ll. 469–72]

'Bowery thickets', 'lofty pines', and 'venerable oaks' were conventional objects, formally addressed. The qualities in Thomson's personification which convey aesthetic value are the relation between personifying and natural qualities, the conception of a universe in which man and nature share characteristics so that the moon is a 'disk' and a 'visage', shifting between them. That motion to which Hagstrum correctly calls attention is, however, graceful motion in the sense that it conveys transformations in conventional postures. The process imagery of Thomson is characterized by a series of postures, forms, gestures, and sounds reflecting the universe which includes man and nature. And its artistic power often derives from the conversion of such norms to new power.

These poetic qualities are not the result of paintings; the painting characteristics in personifications seem to be formal set pieces. The assumption that such pieces require to be '*seen* if we are ever again to recover the pleasures of reading Thomson' disregards the fact that many critics felt that the best part of poetry was not able to be seen, and many of Thomson's critics recognized that the creation of the sublime and the pathetic rather than the allegorical passages were the best parts of the poem. To construct a theory which defends personification is one thing; to assume that all personification is good is another. The eighteenth-century critics distinguished between these procedures, and there is no need to create a theory of visual poetry when we admit that much of the poem is not subject to it.

In summarizing the critical function of analogy, one can begin with the strategic use of critical language. Analogy of poetry with painting served to defend the status of description, to excuse the 'unplanned' design, to urge the philosophical unity of mind and body. It acted to persuade, and in this persuasion it helped change attitudes towards the arts. Analogy also functioned to create more careful discriminations within the arts. Since comparisons were always of elements or devices, it demonstrated that some critical generalizations were unsound and that care was needed to discriminate the use of metaphors in poetry from those in painting. In this respect the analogy could be self-corrective, testing the theory of picture language, and creating the need for more accurate distinctions.

The study of analogy illustrates that the shift from a painting to a musical analogy was not a shifting of philosophical assumptions, but a change of reference within them. Precisely because the musical analogy was consistent with the language of sight, it fitted nicely into these assumptions, and supplanted the painting analogy that was seriously damaged by scientific discoveries. But these two analogies could rest on an assumption of a divinity reflected in nature, discoverable by looking abroad upon it. So long as language was considered 'pictured' in the eye of the imagination, the critic quite correctly compared particulars of poetry with those of painting and created discriminations which coincided with this view. Historically, therefore, the analogy explained why eighteenth-century poets assumed they were 'painting' images. But some critics found evidence to deny such assumptions and others, who accepted them, nevertheless distinguished between successful and unsuccessful 'paintings'. All who accepted pictured language postulated discriminations based on shared perception of the arts. The refutation of the analogy began with a denial of such sharing.

The muting of the poetry-painting analogy came from an investigative method based on a theory of progress which carefully traced developments within a single genre. Without any new information, therefore, this evolutionary or developmental analogy substituted 'love' for 'sight' (internal for external nature) and literary ancestry for the family of the arts. This analogy, because it was developmental, at first neglected the eighteenth century as an independent entity, but even in its error it practised investigation, counting colours and prospects in *The Seasons*. The painting analogy began to recur, therefore, in an attempt to 'prove' the 'influence' of painting on poetry. Thus analogy, buttressed by investigative procedure rather than mere assertive comparisons, led to a clear study of painting assumptions and traditions available to poets. But critics have been too hasty to make applications of this knowledge to particular poetic devices, ignoring the alertness of eighteenth-century critics to the discrimination between adequate and inadequate examples.

Eighteenth-century poetry used many subjects found in landscape painting, and even if we concede that Thomson had particular paintings in mind for passages in *The Seasons*, it is a misunderstanding to argue that a passage (a part) is organized like a painting (a whole), or that verbal and visual organization are interchangeable. If there are 'translations' from poetry to painting and painting to poetry, then the language of this translation must be sufficiently specific to be examined. The examples which have thus far been offered are welcome but not very rewarding speculations.

V

LITERARY CRITICISM AND ILLUSTRATIONS OF *THE SEASONS*

> Poetry being in some respects an art of designing as well as painting or sculpture, they may serve as comments upon each other.
>
> J. ADDISON

THAT POETRY or painting or sculpture could serve as interpretation or explanation of each other was widely recognized in the eighteenth century; Addison declared that 'poetry being in some respects an art of designing as well as painting or sculpture, they may serve as comments upon each other'.[1] Lord Roscommon had earlier noted that looking at painting and looking at drama involved common visual terms. Charles Lamotte wrote that art gives subjects to poetry as poetry gives subjects to art.[2] Joseph Spence in *Polymetis* used

[1] Joseph Addison, *Dialogues upon the Usefulness of Ancient Medals*, in *Works*, ed. by Thomas Tickell (London, 1804), V, 20–21; Robert Wolseley, 'Preface to Rochester's *Valentinian* (1685),' *Critical Essays of the Seventeenth Century*, ed. by J. E. Spingarn (Bloomington, 1957), III, 16–17; John Dryden, *Essays*, ed. by W. P. Ker (Oxford, 1900), II, 130–1; Richard Blackmore, *The Lay Monastery*, 31 (25 Jan. 1713), quoted in Nathan Drake, *The Gleaner* (London, 1811), I, 33–35. For a modern interpretation of visual symbols by an art historian, see R. Wittkower, 'Interpretation of Visual Symbols in the Arts', *Studies in Communication* (London, 1955), pp. 109–24. For a general discussion of non-verbal criticism, see James S. Smith, 'Visual Criticism: A New Medium for Critical Comment', *Criticism*, IV (1962), 241–55.

[2] Charles Lamotte, *An Essay upon Poetry and Painting* (Dublin, 1742), pp. 41–49; see also Lord Roscommon, 'Notes to Horace of the Art of Poetry', *Poems* (London, 1717), p. 278. For a discussion of the interpreta-

poetry to explain the iconography of ancient sculpture;[1] the development of the very word 'illustration' is an example of this interpretative function.

The original meaning of 'illustration' was 'explanation', or 'spiritual enlightenment'. Bullokar in 1676 defined 'to illustrate' as 'to make famous, or noble, to unfold or explain'. 'Illustration', 'illustrious', 'lustre' continued to be applied in 1713 by Henry Felton to spiritual illumination in literature or life.[2] By the end of the eighteenth century, however, the term had come to be identified with engravings and the meaning was extended to 'embellishment' as well as 'explanation'. The reason for this was that illustrations had become, as a result of increased production and lowering of artistic standards, merely decoration. Solomon Gessner wrote that the 'warmth of imagination, without which there can be no invention, is either

[1] Joseph Spence, *Polymetis* (London, 1755), 2nd ed., p. 291. See also, John Scott, *Critical Essays* (London, 1785), p. 205 n., who proposed an interpretative illustration for ll. 49–52 of Gray's 'Elegy'. For study of interrelation of the arts in emblem literature see Henri Stegemeier, 'Problems of Emblem Literature', *JEGP*, XLV (1946), 26–37; for bibliography see Robert J. Clements, 'Iconography on the Nature and Inspiration of Poetry in Renaissance Emblem Literature', *PMLA*, LXX (1955), 781–804.

[2] Henry Felton, *A Dissertation on Reading the Classics* (London, 1713), pp. 7, 225, 'lustre'; p. 7, 'illustrious'; pp. 95, 120, 'illustrations'. See also (John Bullokar) *An English Expositour* (Cambridge, 1676). For a study of the term 'ornament', see Ruth Wallerstein, *Studies in Seventeenth-Century Poetry* (Wisconsin, 1950), pp. 13–15, and Bray, *A History of English Critical Terms* (Boston, 1898), pp. 212–14.

tive significance of stage setting, paintings, and book illustration upon Shakespeare criticism, see W. Moelwyn Merchant, *Shakespeare and the Artist* (London, Oxford, 1959). For a discussion of a Milton illustrator, see Helen Gardner, 'Milton's First Illustrator', *Essays and Studies 1956* (London, 1956), pp. 27–32; Miss Gardner shows a keen awareness of the relations between text and illustration: 'the interest in the illustrations to the student of Milton lies, I think, in two things. First . . . Medina was making a serious attempt to illustrate and interpret and not merely to decorate the poem, and . . . we must be struck by the variety of treatment he found necessary . . .

'The second point that is of great interest is the difficulty Medina found in representing Satan, and the means by which he tried to solve the problem' (pp. 35–36). For eighteenth-century novel illustrations, see Thomas D. C. Eaves, *Graphic Illustrations of the Principal English Novels of the Eighteenth Century* (Unpublished Dissertation, Harvard, 1951). For book illustrations as 'marginal notes', see Roger Fry, 'Book Illustration and a Modern Example', *Transformations* (London, 1926), p. 158.

enfeebled or totally lost',[1] by constantly engraving works of others. The explanatory basis of illustration, therefore, tended to be minimized and its decorative function exploited; the defenders of book illustration at the beginning of the nineteenth century sought to win status for illustration as an independent art and brought in 'explanation' only as a subsidiary function. In 1824, for example, Richard Plowman defined 'illustration' as 'nothing more than the exemplification of works of literature by works of art',[2] but urged that it could also be an incentive to topographical and biographical (portrait) study as well as to interpretation by causing the reader to reflect on the words and the seen (scene).

The Seasons was for more than one hundred and fifty years the most illustrated poem in the English language. By examining the verbal criticism in the light of interpretative illustrations, the range of literary inquiry can be gauged. For there were subjects, tones, insights which this inquiry could have investigated, but neglected or resisted. Literary criticism, for example, neglected the emotive unity of each season which Kent illustrated in 1730, and did not develop explanations for it until 1753. Moreover, the critics neglected—until the nineteenth century—the mythological and natural interrelations so that the processes of nature were not seen as recurrent forces which man had in all seasons to accept. Even Thomson's concern for diverse social and economic classes was neglected by critics until John Wilson stressed it in 1831.

The literary critics, however, recognized the independence of Thomson's nature descriptions, and Warton (1756) even singled out a number of scenes for painting, but landscape illustrations in which the figures were insignificant began at the very end of the eighteenth century and only became characteristic in the mid-nineteenth

[1] Solomon Gessner, 'Letter on Landscape Painting', *New Idylles*, trans. by W. Hooper (London, 1776), p. 99; *Eighteenth Century Book Illustration*, ed. by Philip Hofer (Los Angeles, 1956), p. iii. For early eighteenth-century book illustration, see Iolo A. Williams, 'English Book Illustration, 1700–1775', *The Library*, XVII (1936), 1–21.

[2] Richard Plowman, *An Essay on the Illustration of Books* (London, 1824), p. 9; William Gilpin, *An Essay on Prints* (1768; London, 1802), 5th ed., pp. 1–30; Carl P. Moritz, *Travels of Carl Philipp Moritz in England in 1782* (reprint of English trans. of 1795), intro. by P. E. Matheson (London, 1924), p. 9; 'Address', *The Poetical Works of James Thomson* (London, C. Cooke, 1800), pp. v–vi. See also George M. Woodward, *Eccentric Excursions* (London, 1807), p. ii.

century. Literary critics obviously dealt with a great many subjects, such as diction, imagery, comparisons between different works which illustration could not depict, but even within the range of illustration there was a frequent disregard for moving descriptive passages such as the walk in *Spring* or the falling of the snow in *Winter*.

Literary critics often took offence at Thomson's burlesque passages—Lord Lyttelton removed the fox-hunt from the 1751 edition of Thomson's works; illustrations, however, presented caricature as an element of the poem. Wordsworth's comment—that in 'any well-used copy of the Seasons the book generally opens of itself with the rhapsody on love, or with one of the stories (perhaps Damon and Musidora)'[1] —reflected the prudish critical fears, whereas the tradition of the nude led artists to illustrate the passage, some even recognizing the ironic tone of the description.

Illustration can function as non-verbal criticism, it can also function as an independent work of art, but it cannot function as both simultaneously. Thomas Pennant praised Thomson as a naturalist and sprigs of flowers often served as end pieces or side pieces—see C. F. Sargent's illustrations (1857)—with no identifiable relevance to the poem. This function of illustration began as early as 1730 in B. Picart's engravings of the statues of the seasons at Versailles which had no relevance to Thomson's mythology. Illustrations sometimes show no actual knowledge of the poem, as Raymond Picart has remarked of Racine's eighteenth-century illustrators: 'engravers who think out for themselves the problem of illustrating, by re-reading the text they have to illustrate are very few'.[2] But most of Thomson's eighteenth-century illustrators did read the text, and William Kent, for example, revised his depiction of Musidora in the *Summer* illustration (1744) to accord with Thomson's revision of the Musidora passage (Figs. 1 and 2).

Thomson's *Seasons* provided the text as well as even the incentive for many of Turner's and Constable's paintings. 'How I pity the unfeeling landscape painter, whom the sublime pictures of Thomson cannot inspire', wrote Solomon Gessner. But the inspiration of one art by another must not be confused with the interpretation of one art by another. This confusion of function has steered discussions of the two arts, especially in *The Seasons*, into blind alleys. Thomas

[1] William Wordsworth, *Works* (London, 1909), p. 871.

[2] 'Racine and Chauveau', *Journal of the Warburg and Courtauld Institutes*, XIV (1951), 260; Gessner, p. 102.

Twining remarked in 1789 that Greek Poetry 'had no Thomsons, because they had no Claudes'; Sir Harris Nicolas wrote in 1830 that Thomson's 'pictures of scenery and of rural life are the productions of a master, and render him the Claude of Poets', and the 1855 editor of Thomson remarked that 'no other poet combined to an equal extent the glow of Claude and the gloom of Salvator'.[1] Such remarks are statements about the causes of poetry or the similarity (or identity) of subject matter or effects in two arts. Neither Elizabeth Manwaring nor any other critic has provided information demonstrating that Thomson was familiar with Claude or Rosa in 1730, the publication date of the first edition of the poem. Ralph Williams has argued that *Summer* (1727) included many more 'prospect' scenes than *Winter* (1726) because Thomson was close to the poet-painter John Dyer during this period.[2] But *Spring* (1728) published the following year indicates no continuity of this approach and underlines the unlikeliness of Williams' explanation. Although nature could serve poet and painter as subject, the examination of effects requires at least specific works which can be examined. Passages have been compared with paintings which Thomson may or may not have seen, and 'effects' derived from similarities in subject matter rather than from an analysis of artistic qualities. Such approaches overlook the fact that the poets themselves were aware of classical and renaissance traditions governing 'poetical pictures'. John Hughes, for example, traced descriptions of morning in poets from Homer to Otway indicating the consistency of pictorial imagery: 'In some of these Poetical Pictures which I have here set before the Reader, the Heavens only are shewn, and the first Springing of Light there. In others the Earth is taken into the Prospect, with her Flowers wet with Dew, and her rising Vapours. And sometimes the Occupations of living Creatures, proper to the Season, are represented and afford a yet greater Diversity of amusing Images.'[3]

[1] Thomas Twining, *Aristotle's Treatise on Poetry* (London, 1789), p. 35: *The Poetical Works of James Thomson*, ed. by Sir Harris Nicolas, p. lxxxi; *The Poetical Works of Thomson, Goldsmith, and Gray* (London, 1855), p. xxvi.

[2] Ralph Williams, 'Thomson and Dyer: Poet and Painter', *The Age of Johnson* (New Haven, 1949), pp. 209–16. For discussions of poetry and painting in *The Seasons*, see Elizabeth Manwaring, *Italian Landscape in Eighteenth Century England* (New York, 1925), pp. 100–8; Jean Hagstrum, *The Sister Arts* (Chicago, 1958), pp. 243–67; Alan D. McKillop, *The Background of Thomson's Seasons* (Minnesota, 1942), p. 71.

[3] John Hughes, *Poems on Several Occasions* (London, 1735), II, 334.

To avoid the vagueness of such discussions, this chapter locates specific interrelations of the arts; these occur in the illustrations to specific passages in the poem and in the interpretation of these passages. The illustrations need to be 'read' with the text, and in this respect they partake of Hogarth's concept of narrative paintings. Early eighteenth-century definitions of 'read' meant not only 'to read a book' (peruse) but (Bailey) 'to guess, divine, or foretell' and Johnson included 'to discover by character or marks; to learn by observation'. To consider illustrations as needing to be read is not inconsistent with these definitions, and the illustrations from 1730 to 1900 are governed by diverse 'reading premises'. It need only be added that references to the 'language' of art are common and confirm this assumption.[1]

From 1730 to the 1790's the dominant illustrations—William Kent's 1730 plates—contained a plate for each season in which were depicted numerous scenes from the poem. Kent's plates presented the unity of each season, and the extent of this unity could only be understood if one read the widely dispersed pertinent passages. These indicated the range as well as the limits of the unity. The next major illustrations appeared in the editions from 1790–1810. These presented single scenes or an occasional example of more than one action—but no attempt at Kent's multiple actions. These scenes were clustered around the principles of the sublime and the pathetic. They could not be read as illustrative of the poem's unity, but rather as examples of its chief emotive qualities. Amidst the variety, there developed consistent iconography of illustration whether of the man fishing or the shepherd perishing in the snow, and it attempted to convey the 'poetry' of 'painting'. These illustrations sought to capture the qualities of poetry by relying upon theories of association and picture language. The third major period of illustration, 1840–60, attempted an artistic and narrative fusion of poem with engraving. Illustrations were placed around the margins and dispersed through the text, contrary to the earlier practice severely limiting the number of illustrations so that the most extensively illustrated text (1797) before 1841, contained only seventeen. The fusion was based on the theory that illustration was to create a coherent imaginative entity of the poem so that Thomson's personifications and images blossomed on the page together with the naturalistic world he described, all becoming part of a single view.

[1] George Turnbull, *A Treatise on Ancient Painting* (London, 1749), p. ix.

The development of new theories of illustration did not completely eliminate reproduction of former engravings; for example, Richard Westall's 'poetic' illustrations were reprinted in 1876, long after this approach had ceased to govern illustrators. But the significance of illustrations for the theory of criticism is irrefutable: they supported, supplemented or contradicted verbal criticisms, but above all they tested theories of assumed relations between descriptive poetry and painting. This test concept was clearly and forcefully expressed in 1807:

> I have often thought that there is no better way to prove the defects or excellences of a poet, in respect to his descriptive powers or knowledge of nature, than by making a composition for a picture from the images which he raises, and from his own description of his characters and their actions. You by these means put him on trial; you will detect every deviation from nature; and when his performance is brought to this strict examination, it will sometimes happen, that what in words might seem like a true representation of nature to the poet, to the painter may appear much like a false witness in the court of justice, and he will soon be convinced that the admired work is no more than an ingenious falsehood.[1]

One critical theory that was 'put on trial' by the illustrations was that 'words . . . are but Pictures of the Thought'. The illustrations constituted a refutation of this doctrine by making explicit that pictures always involved more than the words, or a selection of the words; that the same words created different pictures; that some words led not to specific pictures but to imaginative associations expressed in pictures. John Landseer (1807), even though he admitted that the arts could not always achieve similar effects, explained that an image such as 'the breezy call of incense-breathing morn' could be engraved—was indeed in the Aurora of Count Goudt—but that those 'who have not enjoyed this early freshness, in a romantic country, cannot forcibly enjoy this print, because it operates, like all the higher efforts in art, by stimulating the imagination to more than is exhibited'.[2]

[1] *The Artist*, IX (9 May 1807), 3–4. Abraham Cowley, 'To the Royal Society' (1667), l. 69.

[2] *Lectures on the Art of Engraving* (London, 1807), p. 174. 'The Life of James Thomson', in *The Lives of the Poets*, ed. by T. Cibber (London, 1753), V, 202.

At the beginning of the nineteenth century, this theory that knowledge of the original was necessary to create imaginative associations with the representation, identified imagination with recollected associations. But this very same type of auditory, tactile, and olfactory image—'the breezy call of incense-breathing morn'—led other theorists to the separation of literary from artistic imagination, identifying imagination as expression through a medium: 'notwithstanding that many flights of imagination arising in the mind of the poet, and particularly fitted to *his* art, may have given vast delight . . . we shall yet, on the trial, be convinced that they are not adapted to that of the painter'.[1] For this critic illustration demonstrated that perception of painting and perception of language involved different kinds of imagination, each of which was expressed in the manipulation of a medium, not in associations with the end-product.

Illustrations also tested the critic's application of painting vocabulary to poetry. Robert Shiels wrote of Thomson that 'the object he paints stands full before the eye, we admire it in all its lustre'. But the English illustrations to *The Seasons* up to 1753 did not display close views of objects so that the kind of 'painting' Shiels described was independent of the available examples to the poem and prescriptive of other types. And in 1852, James R. Boyd pointed out that eighteenth-century literary critics tended to use 'picturesque' in contexts quite different from artists.

> Black from the stroke etc. ['Summer,' ll. 1050–6]: Dugald Stewart selects this passage as an example of the *picturesque* in writing, by which he means that graphical power by which poetry and eloquence produce effects on the mind analogous to those of a picture. He does not limit that epithet to objects of sight, but extends it to all those details, of whatever kind, by a happy selection of which the imagination may be forcibly impressed. The epithet *picturesque* is also applied by Dr. Warton to a passage in 'Winter' (732–8), where every circumstance mentioned recalls some impression on the ear alone.[2]

Another kind of criticism directly tested by illustrations was the naming of passages that were excellent 'paintings'. Joseph Warton, for example, referred to a summer scene (ll. 485–9) as 'worthy the pencil of Giacomo da Bassano, and so minutely delineated, that he

[1] *The Artist*, p. 4.

[2] *The Seasons*, ed. by James R. Boyd (New York, 1852), p. 156. *An Essay on the Genius and Writings of Pope* (1756; London, 1782), I, 46.

might have worked from this sketch'. The 'various groups' of herds and flocks had been included in Kent's design for summer (Fig. 1) and were a small part of the plenitude of the summer landscape, not a minutely delineated painting. It was not until 1793 that Thomas Stothard drew the 'group' as a single illustration (Fig. 3) revealing that the illustrative concept had changed from a picture of the unity of the season to a fragmented detail of the emotive coherence of man and animal, as seen in the shape of the shepherd and the sheep. The two designs presented quite different interpretations despite the fact that they used the same scene as subject. The appropriateness of illustration, moreover, depended upon the interpreter—the designer—and it further indicated that the qualities of poetic excellence and those of 'painting' were not identical, for the minute excellence in the poem was not the basis for excellence either in Kent or Stothard. The necessary consequences of this view were that (1) excellence in poetry led to no predictable excellence in illustration; (2) the language of poetry had more extensive implications than Warton assumed; (3) any passage could lead to interpretations unsuspected by critics—some pictures of 'Musidora' were in this category.

The illustrations supplemented literary criticism by presenting each season as a unity. The very first illustration (1730) implied that poetic as well as artistic vision was selective and emotive, but although the art critic Jonathan Richardson recognized this, literary critics developed a theory of imagined use of reality only in the second half of the century. Kent's emotive or associative view of unity, shared by Robert Shiels (1753), eventually came to be taken for granted, although not, perhaps, as a result of his illustrations. By the last decade of the century, some literary criticism stressed the need for heightened selectivity or perspectives, and the contemporary illustrations, abounding in the presentation of a variety of specific scenes, supported this view. Some literary criticism still insisted on the literal accuracy of the descriptions, but each illustration served to refute the literalness of the poem.

In treating the pathetic of *The Seasons*, the illustrators of the 1790's supplemented criticism by interpreting benevolence and 'goodness' in terms of the human family; with regard to the sublime of *The Seasons*—what Robert Shiels had called Thomson's finest quality—they presented sufficiently varied instances to question the concept for criticism. The illustrations seized upon certain poetic characteristics of *The Seasons* and these were reshuffled in importance, depending upon the interpretation. The choice among the total possibilities within the four seasons tended to be restricted, but even within these limits certain scenes—such as fishing (*Spring*, ll. 379–442), Musidora (*Summer*, ll. 1269–1370), Celadon and Amelia (*Summer*, ll. 1171–1222), the man dying in the snow (*Winter*, ll. 275–321), boys skating (*Winter*, ll. 760–71)—were frequently redone, whereas the lonely mariner (*Summer*, ll. 939–50), Stothard's bare winter scene, or the drowning sailor (*Summer*, ll. 992–1000) were only undertaken once in the eighteenth century. Such repetition not only served to clarify individual interpretations, but provided examples of the robustness, vigour and broad social range of *The Seasons* (in 'Haying' [*Summer*, ll. 352–60] and 'Sheep-shearing' [*Summer*, ll. 394–411]) deliberately rejected by literary critics for moral or social reasons.[1]

The illustrations, moreover, provided an iconography which suggested the interchangeability of certain images and actions in the poem, such as the lonely wayfaring stranger (*Winter*, ll. 179–80) and the shepherd who himself becomes a lonely stranger in the storm (*Winter*, ll. 277–83). And especially in illustrations which were reworked and reinterpreted, such as the education of the young or the meeting of Palemon and Lavinia, it was possible to recognize the legitimate range of interpretation, that is, the provision of foreground, background and expressive behaviour which the poet omitted and the illustrator required. The differences, therefore, between William Hamilton's parents teaching the young at the table (1797) and Henry Singleton's parents observing the children at their prayers, the books still lying open, specified an increased morality and sentimentality of interpretation.

The interpretative shifts from the Kent illustrations to those of the last two decades of the eighteenth century revealed, where diverse actions were included in a single scene, a considerable reduction in detail and number of actions; unity became more representative and less inclusive or encyclopædic. The variety of detail applied to one activity rather than a multiplicity of activities—ploughing and planting, for example, became representative of spring. The narrowed selection supported the verbal arguments of critics like Patrick Murdoch and James Beattie, who sought to identify in the poem what the former called Thomson's 'distinguishing qualities of *mind* and

[1] See John Scott, *Critical Essays* (London, 1785), pp. 322–5.

heart'. These later illustrations sought to capture the characteristic elements of the seasons with reference to their expressiveness, whereas Kent's sought the characteristic elements with reference to conventions of a genre.

Simultaneous with continued interpretations of unity were single scenes of representative moments. These scenes fragmented the poem far more than Kent's illustrations but, by their selection, they insisted that some passages were more typical than others. Single scenes rather than multiple scenes predominated, but within these there existed a diversity of interpretative comments far more related to current literary criticism than to the earlier comments of Thomson or his contemporaries.

There was an obvious increase in the number of scenes depicted so that the concept of 'typical' was called into question by the varied attempt to picture typicality. But despite the increase, the areas of the typical were limited to the sublime, the pathetic, and the picturesque. The high frequency of domestic scenes supported verbal statements by critics like John Aikin, Percival Stockdale, and James Beattie, who found Thomson's benevolence and piety throughout the poem. 'The rural character,' wrote Aikin, 'as delineated in his feelings, contains all the softness, purity, and simplicity that are feigned of the golden age.'[1]

At the beginning of the twentieth century, illustration was disengaged from the poem; only one single set of engravings has been published in the last sixty years (1900–60). The scientific and formalistic grounds of criticism have excluded non-verbal commentary from the domain of criticism. The insistence upon the independence of the arts has neglected the value of their interrelation, and in Henry James's words, the function of illustration was not to interpret but 'to stand off and on its own feet . . . as a separate and independent subject of publication, carrying its text in its spirit'.[2] The consequence of this limitation has been to reduce the range of criticism, to misunderstand past criticism and to neglect or misconstrue interrelations between the arts because the tests for such premises have been abandoned.

[1] 'An Essay on the Plan and Character of Thomson's Seasons' (1778), reprinted in *The Seasons* (London, 1802), p. lxii. Patrick Murdoch, 'An Account of the Life and Writings of Mr. James Thomson', in *The Works of James Thomson* (London, 1762), I, xix.

[2] Henry James, 'Preface', *The Golden Bowl* (1905) (London, 1923), I, xii.

AND ILLUSTRATIONS OF 'THE SEASONS'

(a) WILLIAM KENT'S SEASONS

Read the history in connection with the picture, to see if everything is appropriate to the subject.

N. POUSSIN

In 1730 two sets of engravings were published for *The Seasons*, one for the octavo edition and another for the quarto. The octavo edition, issued twice in 1730, contained engravings for each season (B. Picart, designer; J. Clark, engraver) based on 'marble statues in the Garden of Versailles 7 foot high (Fig. 4).' There were also tail pieces which had no relation to the poem (*Summer* and *Autumn* both showed a knight on horseback slaying a dragon), but the head piece to *Summer* showed one man assisting another in sowing, and *Autumn* displayed a man in an attitude of contemplation with a book in his hand, sitting near a tree, a scene that at the end of the century became a clue to the lonely poet.

In the quarto edition of 1730 were published the Kent–Tardieu engravings containing a frontispiece for each season. The Picart–Clark illustrations were reprinted only once again in 1735, but the Kent designs were re-engraved for smaller editions twice by Pierre Fourdrinier during Thomson's lifetime and by Neist, Ridge, Donaldson, and others after his death. There exist no comments by Thomson on these engravings, but it appears likely that the continuation of this set and the discontinuance of Picart's was in itself an expression of preference, perhaps also a judgement. Moreover, Thomson's respect for Kent as a landscaper was written into *The Seasons* in his praise of Esher Park (*Summer*, ll. 1431–2): 'Enchanting vale! beyond whate'er the Muse / Has of Achaia or Hesperia sung!'

Jean Hagstrum has suggested that the Kent illustrations suffered from badly drawn allegorical figures (Figs. 5, 6, 7), and Edgar Breitenbach has objected to the allegorical figures because they are 'hollow, wornout metaphorical imagery'.[1] But it should be stated that there exist different criteria for the illustration as interpretation and the illustration as independent work of art; a 'bad' engraving may still be a valuable commentary upon artistic tradition. The artistic quality depends upon a wholeness in the illustration independent of any narrative.

The engravings to *The Seasons* were marked, from the very

[1] Edgar Breitenbach, 'The Bibliography of Illustrated Books', *The Library Association Record* (May 1935), II, 179. Hagstrum, p. 263.

beginning, by conflicting allegorical and naturalistic tendencies. Just as the poem addressed 'gentle Spring' and personified it (*Spring*, l. 1), so, too, the illustrations in 1730 sought to convey this allegorical and naturalistic view of spring. In his designs Kent attempted to create a representative picture of the unity of each season, governed by the great chain of being leading in a series of inclined planes from natural to allegorical figures, and including earth, water, clouds, animals, man, and heavenly figures. The analogical unity which the engravings suggested was not that of the subject matter of each season, but of the relation between the distant past and the immediate present.

Margaret Jourdain has written that Kent's designs for *The Seasons* show Italian influences, and Bertrand Bronson has called the lower halves of the engravings 'faintly Claudian',[1] but a comparison between Claude's *An Autumnal Evening* and Kent's *Autumn* reveals that only the trees as a framing device and the faint mountains in the background suggests a similarity; the management of movement and the handling of planes are considerably different. Kent's designs were representations of types of unity in *The Seasons*, composed from a close knowledge of the poem, and they differed from the single-scene designs he created for other poems, *The Faerie Queene* and Gay's *Fables*. The artistic landscape tradition was absorbed and altered by the literary text.

These early illustrations for *The Seasons* show a concentration on the unity rather than the particularity of each season that Warton was to recommend in 1756. At least for the designer in 1730, the unity of the poem did not represent an issue, just as the letter to the *London Journal* in 1726 praised Thomson for the manner in which he connected reflections with descriptions. Swift objected to the lack of unity of action in *The Seasons*, declaring (1732) that the seasons 'are all description, and nothing is doing; whereas Milton engages me in actions of the highest importance',[2] but Kent's illustrations implied a unity of feeling and moral value.

The unity which Kent created involved a spatial view of the

[1] Margaret Jourdain, *The Work of William Kent* (London, 1948), p. 73; Bronson, *Printing as an Index of Taste in Eighteenth Century England* (New York, The New York Public Library, 1958), p. 35; *London Journal* (1726), as quoted in McKillop, p. 175.

[2] Jonathan Swift, Letter to Charles Wogan (2 Aug. 1732), in *The Correspondence of Jonathan Swift*, ed. by F. Elrington Ball (London, 1913), IV, 330.

supernatural and natural worlds. The upper half of each season represented the personified allegorical introduction to the season, and the bottom half several naturalistic scenes from the poem. Each of the four plates was seen from a direct and central point of view from which the countryside ascended either to the right or the left. In the central background each plate had a mountain, faintly drawn. The engraving moved to the background in a series of inclined planes, each of which grew fainter as one looked out on the mountain. Clouds separated these planes from the allegorical figures which presided over the entire scene.

Since each season included men, women, animals, and supernatural beings, Kent was able to convey a relation between the orders of nature, beast, man, and the heavens that Thomson himself accepted. In *Spring* (ll. 860–6) Thomson wrote:

> The informing Author in his works appears:
> Chief, lovely Spring, in thee and thy soft scenes
> The smiling God is seen—while water, earth,
> And air attest his bounty, which exalts
> The brute-creation to this finer thought,
> And annual melts their undesigning hearts
> Profusely thus in tenderness and joy.

This attempt to convey in design the relation between heaven and earth which Thomson's *Spring* included, involved, for Kent, a careful selection of scenes. The whole top half of the design was devoted to the first allegorical lines of the poem, and to those dealing with surly winter and the 'bright bull' of the zodiac, although these passages occupied a very small part of the season.

> Come, gentle Spring, ethereal mildness, come;
> And from the bosom of yon dropping cloud,
> While music wakes around, veiled in a shower
> Of shadowing roses, on our plains descend.
> [ll. 1–4]

In addition to the area occupied, it was connected to the earth by the rainbow, a description indicated in the poem (ll. 203–12). As for the naturalistic scenes, the engraving included the poet as a swain playing to the Countess of Hertford (ll. 5–10), the shepherd pointing to the rainbow (ll. 212–17), the ducks and swans in the pond (ll. 776–82), the cooing dove in amorous chase (ll. 786–8), the shepherd on the mountain brow with his sportive lambs (ll. 832–8), a hall (the home of one of the lovers?), a lover and his beloved (ll. 962–79). Kent omitted all scenes involving violence or sorrow—the robbing of the nightingale's nest, the violent love excitement of the bulls (ll. 792–808), the lover's dream of death (ll. 1052–73); what he included were specific scenes representing the benevolent variety of the universe.

The interpretation was not based, therefore, upon mere subject matter because the order and manner of treatment were different. It conveyed the activity of the allegorical figures who were in motion, and while the heavens were moving and acting, the natural universe received their benefits. In visual terms Kent interpreted Thomson's argument to *Spring*: 'This Season is described as it affects the various parts of Nature, ascending from the lower to the higher; and mixed with digressions arising from the Subject.'[1] Spring and her train were sportively in motion, matched only by the earthly gambolling lambs. Thus the significance of the introduction to spring was not a mere personification, but the expression of those forces attributed to God:

> Chief, lovely Spring, in thee and thy soft scenes
> The smiling God is seen—
>
> [*Spring*, ll. 861–2]

The function of the rainbow, too, was central to this interpretation of *Spring* as a smiling season because the beauty of the heavens was reflected in the pond, and like a smile, it was engaging and ephemeral. Thomson had the 'swain' chasing the rainbow in the field, and it was an example of Kent's presentation of heavenly effects to create heaven's reflection in the pond. Not only did Kent find a painter's analogy for the relation between heaven and man, but he also created a structural relation between the earth and the heavens. When, in 1744, Thomson added a poetic prospect from Hagley Hall, it was a possibility that the poetic passage was placed next to the lovers not only because of the ideal love of Lyttelton and his wife but also because of the 'hall' that already existed in the illustration (despite the fact that it was not a prospect view). For Thomson's description summarized the dusky landscape and the mountains 'like far clouds':

> your eye excursive roams—
> Wide-stretching from the Hall, in whose kind haunt
> The hospitable Genius lingers still,

[1] Thomson, 'Argument to Spring' (1728).

To where the broken landscape, by degrees
Ascending, roughens into rigid hills
O'er which the Cambrian mountains, like far clouds
That skirt the blue horizon, dusky rise.
[*Spring*, ll. 956–62]

The mountains, compared to 'far clouds', were marked by the arc-like quality of the clouds supporting and surrounding spring. Thus the rising hills were the earthly counterparts of the beclouded heaven; by establishing a relation between foreground and background (mountains) which was analogous to that between earth and heaven (top and bottom of the design) Kent created a visual unity between the hill and dales, reflective of that benevolence to be found in the allegorical heavens.

The use of inclined planes conveyed a series of incidents in the poem. But despite the fact that Shaftesbury and later Lessing argued that a painting revealed instantaneous time, it was not possible to see all the incidents simultaneously. Moreover, the diverse scenes implied a succession of some type, whether circular or random, all appropriate to spring, and in that sense implied a period—a season —of time rather than simultaneous occurrences. Kent's illustration could be properly understood only if read within the context of specific passages. Perception was not a matter of mere instantaneous response; Dryden earlier had noted this despite the assumption that the action, passions and manners in a picture were theoretically to be discerned 'in the twinkling of an eye'. For, as he remarked in the discussion of Poussin's painting of '*The Institution of the Blessed Sacrament*', there was 'but one indivisible point of time observed; but one action performed by so many persons, in one room, and at the same table; yet the eye cannot comprehend at once the whole object, nor the mind follow it so fast; 'tis considered at leisure and seen by intervals'.[1] Kent's presentation, therefore, was characteristic of an artistic conception of literary unity and George S. Layard has pointed to a similar procedure in the 1720 illustrations to the third part of Robinson Crusoe.[2]

The failure to see Kent's illustration 'by intervals' and with the text has caused some misinterpretation. Thus Jean Hagstrum's comments on *Spring*, while displaying knowledge of heroic, pastoral,

[1] Dryden, *Essays*, II, 132.

[2] George S. Layard, 'Robinson Crusoe and his Illustrators', *Bibliographica*, II (1896), 185.

and ideal conventions inherited by Kent, miss the point that the engraving presents a fusion of some scenes only, while omitting other, more violent ones. The unity, moreover, while involving conventions, was not itself conventional because it included scenes from the text not common to seventeenth-century landscape.

The variety of incident in the poem, involving shifts in place and time, was incorporated in the engraving through artistic concepts of place and time. By the use of heavy and light shading, the mountain in the distance appeared faint and the immediate foreground very dark. But the relation between them was such that the different actions—the swain playing to the lady and the faint shepherd on the brow of the mountain—which had been seen precisely and closely in the poem were seen at receding distances in the engraving. And the simultaneous and similar actions such as the swain and the sportive lambs in the foreground and on the mountain which could be both vivid and faint gave to the illustration a meaning independent of distance.

The poem and the illustration expressed common views of nature and man, Kent's interpretation being the smiling reflection on earth of the heavenly benevolence in *Spring*, of the astonishing power and ferocity of nature in *Winter*. This was, of course, a highly selective view of Thomson's *Spring*, but it was one view that Thomson developed. There were, too, other methods by which Kent interpreted the poem: Kent developed a series of correspondences between physical shapes on earth and heaven, just as Thomson compared the Cambrian mountains to 'far clouds' and the mountains of snow to 'an atmosphere of clouds':

> And icy mountains high on mountains piled
> Seem to the shivering sailor from afar,
> Shapeless and white, an atmosphere of clouds.
>
> [*Winter*, ll. 906–8]

Kent used particular scenes from the poem in his design, but the significance of these incidents was not identical with that in the poem. Neither the order nor the emphasis were the same. He illustrated the introduction to *Spring*, the rainbow, the passion of the groves and others, but the subjects and their role in the poem became materials—what Henry James has called 'compositional resources'[1]—to be converted into a different kind of entity in the

[1] Henry James, 'Preface', *The Golden Bowl*, I, vii.

engraving. The incidents served to establish an identification for the illustration, but the basis for the comparison was in the attitude which the artist had toward his materials, the manner in which he joined the incidents together. Thus, the introduction to *Spring*, which functioned in the poem as a formal device to create aesthetic distance, became in the illustration the central allegorical force presiding over all the events and, because of its role in the design, formed a basis for correspondence between the heavens and earth. The framing or formal device was accomplished by the marginal trees within which the whole scene was viewed.

Kent's illustration supported the proposition voiced by Addison and others that in the arts the same effects could be achieved by different means. But the second interpretative implication was that 'unity' involved selective elements and that 'wholeness' in the poem was not the same as wholeness of interpretation. The illustration depended upon a variety of detail both of incident and nature so that the lambs in the foreground and on the mountain's brow, the shepherd piping to his lady and the man making love to the woman, the classical structure and the cluster of farm houses served to convey the contrasting views of simplicity and refinement. But the illustration lacked the sensuousness, the awareness of natural processes characteristic of Thomson's description, for example, of spring flowers:

> And in yon mingled wilderness of flowers,
> Fair-handed Spring unbosoms every grace—
> Throws out the snow-drop and the crocus first,
> The daisy, primrose, violet darkly blue,
> And polyanthus of unnumbered dyes;
>
> [*Spring*, ll. 528–32]

(b) VARIATIONS OF SOCIALIZATION AND EXPRESSION

> How I pity the unfeeling landscape painter, whom the sublime pictures of Thomson cannot inspire!
>
> S. GESSNER

For approximately fifty years (1730–80) the illustrations which dominated *The Seasons* were those by William Kent. These illustrations or re-engravings of them appeared in English editions of 1736, 1738, 1744, 1746, 1750, 1752, 1756, 1757, 1758, 1761, 1762, 1763, 1764, 1766, 1767, 1768, 1773, 1774, 1778, 1782. In the 1770's, however, there appeared three sets of illustrations—those by George Wright–E. Malpas (1770?), those of 1773 unsigned, and those by David Allan, William Hamilton–[James?] Caldwell, 1778—which, while continuing some aspects of Kent's work, moved in different directions. It was not, however, until 1793, when reworkings of the Kent plates were reprinted for the last time—Dodd–Cook—that Kent's direct influence disappeared from illustrations of *The Seasons*. In 1770[?] George Wright, while still presenting several scenes from the poem in a single plate (Fig. 8), was nevertheless intent upon a purely naturalistic unity; the 1773 illustrations were formal seasonal illustrations unrelated to the poem (Fig. 9), and the 1778 illustrations separated the allegorical sculptures for each season from plates presenting single, naturalistic scenes from the poem. The 1770[?] and 1778 illustrations, were at one in moralizing the poem by eliminating or isolating the personified seasons. The poem was studded with classical references and reworkings of the *Georgics*, and Kent's illustration had conveyed the relation between classical and Christian concepts by means of artistic conventions. But subsequent illustrations began to disengage the classical from the Christian view.

Wright's designs, inept as they were, had significance because they were the first which completely naturalized the poem, separating country from city and allegory from actuality, unsupported by Thomson's own version. To the illustrated edition George Wright appended notes for the new audience; he was beginning his task of moral anthologist. In 1782, his anthology *Dear Variety, Suited to All Ages and Conditions of Life* contained the following advertisement: 'The ensuing compilation may be justly stiled *Variety*, as it consists of a *Variety* of extracts from *various* authors, upon *various* subjects; a *Variety* of sentiments from *various* publications, collected at *various* times, and will doubtless be perused by *various* readers.' And in *Gentleman's Miscellany* (1797) he quoted in the preface a Monthly Reviewer of 1788 on a previous collection, *Pleasing Reflections on Life and Manners:* 'Miscellaneous collections of this kind are become very numerous; but as they generally consist of *moral* pieces, they are, to say the least of them, innocent as well as entertaining. The multiplication, therefore, of such compliments, is of no disservice to society.'[1]

Wright's illustrations, therefore, were directed at the same class

[1] George Wright, *Gentlemen's Miscellany*, 1797. George Wright, *Dear Variety*, 1782.

which purchased the anthologies, and his badly designed frontispiece was based on the poet who retreated into the 'mid-wood shade'.

> Hence let me haste into the mid-wood shade,
> Where scarce a sunbeam wanders through the gloom,
> And on the dark-green grass, beside the brink
> Of haunted stream, that by the roots of oak
> Rolls o'er the rocky channel, lie at large
> And sing the glories of the circling year.
>
> [*Summer*, ll. 9–14]

The subject which he chose to illustrate was one which, after 1790, became a commonplace in Thomson illustration: the isolated poet. Poets at this period, in the process of creating their own work, were aware of the division within criticism and of their increasing isolation. But the literary critics of *The Seasons* did not consider the wandering narrator as a significant figure in the work, except as he framed the point of view: in this respect the illustrations of Stothard, Cranmer, and Roberts were at odds with the general run of critical thought.

The key passage was that of the lonely lover (*Spring*, ll. 1004–73), distraught and driven by the agonies of love. The Stothard illustration with the young man leaning against a tree in the moonlight with his arms folded conveyed neither the 'soften'd soul' (l. 1039) of the description nor the shared woes of the 'bird of eve'. Stothard's elegant young man had a firm grip on his woes (Fig. 10). A considerably more literal design was published by Corbould (A. Strahan, 1802) and re-engraved by the American engraver Roberts (1816) (for another example, see Fig. 11). There the young man was lying on the bank amid the drooping lilies and behind him an ancient tree: 'or on the bank / Thrown, amid drooping lilies, swells the breeze / With sighs unceasing and the brook with tears' (ll. 1030–2).

In the background through the hanging boughs the moon 'peeps through'. And the more literal the illustration, the more obvious was the expressive interpretation of the scene. Corbould's illuminated young man gleamed in bright contrast to the bank and trees, whereas the poem drew a comparison between the painful restlessness, the irrepressibility of love and the gentleness of nature. The point is that even misinterpretations such as this draw attention to specific passages of man's agonized involvement with nature which literary critics ignored.

In criticism, the disengagement of Virgilian personification from moralized nature was argued by John Aikin (1778), who identified the unity of the poem with the seasonal laws of natural science and who rejected the urban passages. Aikin sought not only to limit the poem to natural subjects, with religious digressions, but he was the first to declare that the poem was the beginning of a new genre—description.

The David Allan–William Hamilton and J. Caldwell illustrations to the very edition for which Aikin wrote his 'Essay on the Plan and Character of Thomson's *Seasons*' still contained pseudo-classical allegorical figures (Fig. 12) representing each of the seasons. Thus the illustrations presented two views of the poem, one of which insisted upon the applicability of the classical heritage as represented in sculpture. Not only did these illustrations (reprinted 1779, 1792, 1796) continue a double focus on the poem, but when the allegorical figures were removed to the title page as vignettes or ornaments they represented a reduction in their importance from the central place given them by Kent. In 1792 Charles Ansell designed and A. Birrell engraved a title page which contained a globe surrounded in a circle by the signs of the zodiac, but their illustrations to the text were naturalistic. In 1794 Thomas Stothard engraved a title page to *The Seasons* in which four allegorized female figures in a ring illustrated the lines from the 'Hymn' (Fig. 13):

> Mysterious round! What skill, what force divine,
> Deep-felt, in these appear! a simple train,
> Yet so delightful mixed with such kind art,
> Such beauty and beneficence combined.
>
> [*Hymn*, ll. 21–24]

The allegorized seasons had become four maidens, and the personifications in *The Seasons* who were masculine and feminine were supplanted by a naturalistic and prettified view. Even William Hamilton's attempt to recombine the allegorical and the naturalistic in 1797 failed. His head piece to *Spring* was a combination of a single allegorical balloon-like figure of Spring floating on clouds with a garland of roses in the background on which appeared the signs of the zodiac; in the foreground there were two farming scenes: ploughing and planting. The naturalistic scenes were separate frames quite unrelated to allegorical spring (Fig. 14). In the 1805 edition edited by the Rev. Mr. J. Evans, the allegorized female figures of the seasons were relegated to the ends of each season and placed as tailpieces, in emblematic poses, although *Summer* and *Autumn* were the same figures. And in the title-piece to the 1818 edition from the Chiswick Press, engraved by Thompson, the four seasons were naturalistic figures, walking with representative burdens, spring being, as Thomson created her, the only woman among the seasons. But in addition to the reduction of importance of the allegorical figures, usually females, and their incorporation into the females of the naturalistic scenes, a similar process was apparent in the transfer of emblematic attributes from cherubs—as indicative of the seasons—to children. In the Ansell–Birrell (1792) illustrations, a cherub introduced each season, but the cherub was not clearly distinguishable from an infant, and in Hamilton's *Winter* the cherub had become a child skating (Figs. 15, 16).

The literary critics at the end of the eighteenth century and the beginning of the nineteenth did not attend to the allegorical figures in the poem, and to that extent neglected the historical quality. Illustrations such as those of the 1801 French edition (Le Barbier) pictured Thomson's personifications of the powerful king of day or winter on his throne, and Hamilton's headpiece to *Spring* (1797) represented the allegorized season. The illustrators clung to the dual characteristics of the poem, the classical and Christian qualities, the allegorical and natural views. In this respect their historical understanding of the poem persisted in contrast to that of the critics who insisted exclusively on the naturalistic interpretations until the twentieth century.

According to Edgar Breitenbach, Kent's personifications of *Spring* and her train belong to a tradition of the late Middle Ages: 'The scheme of composition is astonishingly similar to the ones of the 'planet children' representations in the fifteenth century, which likewise show, under the reign of the astral rules of providence, a survey of human occupations.'[1] Another possible tradition for the zodiac and multiple occupations is to be found in Books of Hours of which Alfred W. Pollard remarks that both 'in manuscript and in printed *Horae* it [the 'Kalendar'] is usually found illustrated with the signs of the Zodiac and pictures of the occupations or pastimes appropriate to the month'.[2] But whether 'planet children' or 'putti', Kent's

[1] Breitenbach, 197.

[2] Alfred W. Pollard, 'The Illustrations in French Books of Hours', *Bibliographica*, III (1897), 430–73. Multiple activities in seasonal land-

figures were moved from an allegorical tradition to a more literal personification (by Hamilton) and to naturalistic poses by Stothard and others. Of the roles of children, there existed three types: the child as representative of the season as a whole (Ansell-Birrell's *Winter*), the child within the family related to the past through adults, home, books,—involving idealized relationships within the group (Hamilton's *Paternal Instruction*), and one example (Ansell–Birrell) of children as malicious—nest-snatching (previously illustrated by Eisen).

The domestication of *The Seasons*, a process apparent in the illustrations of the last decade of the eighteenth century, involved simultaneously its praise as a poem expressing sentiments and feelings. Regardless of the obvious attempt to sell editions by sentiment, the absence of nature as an entity, that is, without people, was especially notable. The engravings, by disengaging themselves from a single point of view, also left behind a significant artistic tradition: the allegorical imagery.

The Kent illustrations contained no children, not even the swain chasing the rainbow. But beginning in 1792, the illustrations for an entire decade celebrated and sentimentalized the role of the child. The passage from the poem on paternal instruction—*Spring*, ll. 1152–6—was illustrated by Stothard (1794) as were the passages on sheep-shearing, skating, and story-telling (*Winter*, ll. 617–20) (Fig. 17). Thomson had in *Autumn* referred among many values of rural life to the love of kindred: 'the little strong embrace / Of prattling children, twined around his neck' (ll. 1341–2). But in the Cruikshank–Laurie illustrations, scenes from the poem which did not contain children suddenly accumulated them; thus the fisherman urged 'to thy sport repair' (*Spring*, ll. 396–442) brought his family, and instead of the lover gathering nuts for his beloved (*Autumn*, ll. 610–19), a child shook the tree and another held the basket (Stothard, 1793). Children swam and children skated, and in the 1797

scapes were not uncommon. According to Henry V. S. and Margaret S. Ogden, such paintings in the early seventeenth century 'are differentiated from the ordinary prospect . . . by the emphasis on the scenery and the outdoor activities of a certain time of year, as well as by various conventional characteristics. Owing to the natural activities of peasants in winter, the winter picture usually showed more buildings and less scenery than those of other seasons.' *English Taste in Landscape in the Seventeenth Century* (Ann Arbor, 1955), p. 48.

illustrations by Hamilton, five out of seventeen illustrations to the four seasons included children, a far greater proportion than the space devoted to them even in the last draft of the poem. The justification for this interpretation of the poem was clearly put by John Landseer (1807): 'Every artist that is worthy of his appellation, desires and endeavours by his works, that the average or general feeling of the society to which these works address themselves, shall sympathize or accord with his own.'[1]

The domestication of *The Seasons* had its complementary development in literary criticism with John More's argument (1777) of the moral value of the poem, and the attention to narratives and moralizing in Aikin's essay. Such comments were, however, beginning to be seriously questioned by the end of the century, though still repeated. John Aikin himself pointed out that in this respect Thomson was most easily imitated: 'excellent as the moral and sentimental part of his work must appear to every congenial mind, it is, perhaps, that in which he may most easily be rivalled'. 'Moral sentiment', wrote John Scott (1785), quoting an 'ingenious Critic', 'is the cheapest product of the human mind.'[2] But another aspect of the importance of childhood in Thomsonian criticism was the Earl of Buchan's assumption—obviously dependent upon Rousseau—that Thomson's infancy and early years were spent in the 'pastoral country of Teviotdale in Scotland, which is full of the elements of natural beauty, wood, water, eminence and rock, with intermixture of rich and beautiful meadow', and there a child will receive impressions most conducive to genius 'more readily than in towns or villages'.[3]

The increase in Thomson's child population was the effort of illustrators, and the frequent editions during this period—there were thirty-two publications of the poem, exclusive of American and foreign, from 1790 to 1799—indicated the widened appeal of the poem and its illustrations.

The social illustrations presented idealized views of the family, but in so far as these views were single scenes, they served as fragmentary insights which could be representative or particular but

[1] Landseer, p. 219.

[2] Scott, p. 143. John More, *Strictures Critical and Sentimental on Thomson's Seasons* (London, 1777), p. 166; Aikin, pp. lxii–lxiii.

[3] Earl of Buchan (David Stuart), *Essays on the Life and Writings of Fletcher of Saltoun and the Poet Thomson* (London, 1792), p. 183.

could not be indicative of the poem's diversity. Nevertheless, this fragmentation, by moving social behaviour—or its opposite—to the foreground, concentrated on expressiveness, acuteness of detail, and the contrast between the sharpness of human form and the encompassing vagueness of nature.

Scenes of death in *Winter* were sometimes included with scenes of domestic bliss even in the same season. The illustrations conveyed the poem's unevenness of attitude though Stockdale and Beattie insisted upon its benevolence or purity as central. A good example of this procedure was the 1793 Perth edition which contained the fishing scene populated with children uncreated by Thomson and an illustration of the terrified sailor. In the illustration, the very mouth of the fish can be seen caught on the hook (Fig. 18), and in Catton's design of the terrified sailor (Fig. 19), the scene is pictured as though the spectator were directly in front of the open-eyed, open-mouthed mariner and his sinking ship. Thus a sense of immediacy was created by closeness, and the expressiveness of the scene made possible direct sympathy from the viewer.

This view of expression provided an interpretation similar to that developed by Robert Heron in an essay on *The Seasons* in the same volume. Heron defined poetry as the operation of sentiments and images (in this order) on the imagination and feelings and then proceeded to compare the imagery of *The Seasons* with that of other works. Thomson's passage was as follows:

> A faint deceitful calm,
> A fluttering gale, the demon sends before,
> To tempt the spreading sail. Then down at once
> Precipitant descends a mingled mass
> Of roaring winds and flame and rushing floods.
> In wild amazement fixed the sailor stands.
> Art is too slow. By rapid fate oppressed,
> His broad-winged vessel drinks the whelming tide,
> Hid in the bosom of the black abyss.
> [*Summer*, ll. 992–1000]

The passage described the contrast between the 'deceitful calm' and the precipitant onslaught of the waves, the manner in which the forces of nature suddenly surrounded and 'hid' the sinking ship. The insignificance of the sailor and his fright before the powers of nature was noted by the single line 'In wild amazement fixed the sailor stands'. But the illustrator, Catton, made the expression of the sailor central, and he interpreted the passage as the terror of man in the face of the violent forces of nature. The sailor, standing with eyes popping, mouth open, jacket unbuttoned, legs set apart—in the position of terrified amazement, of immovable uncontrol—was surrounded by a cave of waves, a 'black abyss'. The open-mouthed man was about to be swallowed by the huge mouth of waves, one sailor having already been sucked from the vessel, others clutching supports of the sinking ship. Thus man and nature were seen as two forces, the expressiveness of man helplessly overcome by the dark surrounding power, the circular tide and hollow wave indicating continuous time as well as continuous action. The interpretation of the illustration, therefore, conveyed the poem's development of clashing forces, despite the fact that it did so by altering the action of conflict. The critic, however, who examined Thomson's imagery would have discovered that the vessel was personified—'drinks the whelming tide, / Hid in the bosom of the black abyss'—and that the ship was seen in a suicidal image of comfort or love ('hid in the bosom of the black abyss').

The artistic interpretation was expressed through associations, and indeed, the centrality of the mariner was the result of a painting tradition, for he was not equally central in the poetic passage. For this reason, the 'reading' of these illustrations demanded a language of gesture that was often associative rather than directly responsive to the poem. The 'reading' or 'interpretation' required for single scenes, containing frequently the pertinent passage at the foot of the illustration, was different from that applied to Kent's designs. The mariner involved a considerable alteration of emphasis as well as fact, for Thomson had made reference to 'the sailor', not to a crew, though a crew was legitimately implied. Such changes of detail occurred in most illustrations: G. Wright annotated 'steers' as 'oxen' (*Spring*, ll. 35–36) and then drew horses or donkeys as plough animals. But the difference between factual changes and interpretative changes was considerable. Expressive illustrations of the seventeen-nineties attempted to interpret not facts or literal statements, but associative or emotive qualities by direct proximity. The confinement of each illustration to a single action, therefore, was an attempt to create immediacy rather than an artistic procedure which presupposed instantaneous response. And the amorphous shape of the background—as in William Hamilton's illustration of Celadon and Amelia (Fig. 20)—became the deliberately undefined nature in which man lived and died. (For a different interpretation, see Richard Wilson's painting, Fig. 20*a*.)

Thomson's use of nature as background can be studied in these illustrations with respect to a concept such as the 'sublime'. Illustrations of 'sublime' passages in *The Seasons* revealed that Thomson's 'sublime' language and his situations were used in diverse contexts. The poetic terms used by Thomson for the sublime included 'astonish', 'astound', 'admire', 'daunt', 'dreadful' ('dreadful motion'), 'howling' ('howling waste'), 'stiffened' ('stiffened corpse'), 'froze', 'polished', 'marbled'. The terms were related to death, to the final absence of mobility, to dread of death, to awe, moral and physical, though they could be used to suggest the pleasurable sublime in such a phrase as 'pleasing dread'.

Critics have pointed to Thomson's use of one element of the sublime—the 'statuesque'—and have seen it as a contrast with motion or as a continuation of the Greek tradition of beauty. McKillop has written that Thomson had an 'interest in what we may call the statuesque . . . There is no classic austerity about Thomson's statues, however; they are both realistic and sentimental; they often represent natural catastrophes that are bizarre rather than sublime and are used as decorations that surprise and shock by an odd life-likeness. They are, in fact, poetical waxworks.'[1] McKillop quite rightly points to the function of statuesque references as contrasts to movement, but the 'statuesque' functions not only as an image of fixity but as an image of silence. Such images as those of Celadon, of Musidora, of the stiffened corpse in *Winter* create the poetry of silence; they describe moments of speechlessness, shock, contemplation, irony (in Musidora), which poetry can only suggest. The reference to sculpture in these contexts was to underline the inadequacy of poetic expression by comparison with non-verbal art ('So, faint resemblance', 'In Fancy's Eye') which permitted the scene to be prolonged, stressing the silence and sight of death which, if it could not be matched by art, could be made more enduring. This

[1] Allan D. McKillop, *Background of Thomson's Seasons*, pp. 70–71. For the importance of silence and its relation to sincerity, see *The Wanderer*, XXIII, 4 July (London, 1718):

> 'Tho' there generally is so little Communication between the Heart and the Tongue that it is difficult to guess at a Man's Meaning by his Words, they ever differ most in Things of greatest Consequence.'
>
> 'Hence wise Men study the Art of Silence to prevent their Sincerity being call'd in Question.'

contextual view of these images and their appropriateness can be defended by pointing to the descriptions of sculpture in *Autumn* which insisted on the imaginative life (not speech) of sculpture, not its lifelessness (immortality).

> the statue seemed to breathe
> And soften into flesh beneath the touch
> Of forming art, imagination-flushed.
> [*Autumn*, ll. 138–40]

Because sculpture was identified with silence, it pointed to the verbal limits of poetry and to the need to attend to its silences. Thus Thomson's use of 'silence' differed from Wordsworth's contemplative awareness of it.

> Wordsworth, from the peculiar delicacy of his perceptions and perhaps from his contemplative Nature, was deeply sensitive to the silences in the world about him. There is some though but little indication of a similar pleasure in preceding poetry. One of the best passages is Thomson's description of the boding silence before a storm.[1]

Thomson's silence is a recognition of the inscrutableness of nature, and sculpture and 'fixity' represent the buried yet insoluble life of man. The appeals to man to be benevolent and to trust in God must be understood as resulting from a recognition that innocence and beauty die—and for no recognizable reason. Silence constitutes one mode of response to unanswerable dilemmas.

The Seasons contained varied uses of the sublime: the cattle killed by lightning—'and, stretched below, / A lifeless group the blasted cattle lie' (*Summer*, ll. 1151–2)—the sailor in 'wild amazement fixed' (*Summer*, l. 997), the amazed swain who 'runs/To catch the falling glory' (*Spring*, ll. 214–15), the Eastern tyrants who know not love but only 'bosom-slaves, meanly possessed/Of a mere lifeless, violated form' (*Spring*, ll. 1133–4), Celadon staring at the dead Amelia:

> But who can paint the lover, as he stood
> Pierced by severe amazement, hating life,
> Speechless, and fixed in all the death of woe?
> So, faint resemblance! on the marble tomb

[1] Myra Reynolds, *The Treatment of Nature in English Poetry* (London, 1898), p. 338.

The well-dissembled mourner stooping stands,
For ever silent and for ever sad.
[*Summer*, ll. 1217–22]

and the nude Musidora returning from her swim, discovering the note from Damon,

With wild surprise,
As if to marble struck, devoid of sense,
A stupid moment motionless she stood:
[*Summer*, ll. 1344–6]

The illustrations of the sailor, the swain, Celadon, and Musidora involved not only situations and places, but applied to good or bad situations, to serious, ironic, or sentimental ones. Johnson's definition of 'amazement'—'astonishment or perplexity, caused by an unexpected object, whether good or bad—in the former case it is mixed with admiration, in the latter with fear'—summarized only some of the uses of the term in *The Seasons*. The critical value of illustrations of passages identified as 'sublime' was that they interpreted a variety of specific instances. Both these illustrations and John Scott's and Robert Heron's examination of specific passages were the consequence of a view insisting on the critical descent to particulars. But the illustrations also drew attention to concepts assumed to be clear in one art, but not equally clear or traditional in another. Thus the illustrations supported the diversity of meaning of 'sublime' by indicating the variety of contextual characteristics.

An example of how artistic variations could extend literary concepts can be observed in the illustrations of the man perishing in the snow.

and down he sinks
Beneath the shelter of the shapeless drift,
Thinking o'er all the bitterness of death,
Mixed with the tender anguish nature shoots
Through the wrung bosom of the dying man—
His wife, his children, and his friends unseen.

. . . .

Alas!
Nor wife nor children more shall he behold,
Nor friends, nor sacred home. On every nerve
The deadly Winter seizes, shuts up sense,

Fig. 1. Wm. Kent–N. Tardieu, *Summer* (1730).

Fig. 2. Wm. Kent–P. Fourdrinier, Revised *Summer* (1744).

Fig. 3. T. Stothard–P. Audinet, *Shepherding* (1794).

Fig. 4. B. Picart, *Winter* (1730).

Fig. 5. Wm. Kent–N. Tardieu, *Spring* (1730).

Fig. 6. Wm. Kent–N. Tardieu (1703), Reduced by P. Fourdrinier, 1744, *Autumn* (1744).

Fig. 7. Wm. Kent–N. Tardieu (1730), Reduced by P. Fourdrinier, 1744, *Winter* (1744).

Fig. 8. G. Wright–E. Malpas, *Spring* (1770?).

Fig. 9. Unsigned, *Autumn* (1773).

Fig. 10. T. Stothard–P. Audinet, *Contemplation* (1794).

Fig. 11. T. Kirk–J. P. de Moulinville, *The Young Lover* (1798).

Fig. 12. D. Allan–J. Caldwell, *Winter* (1778).

Fig. 13. T. Stothard, *The Four Seasons* (1794).

Fig. 14. Wm. Hamilton–P. Tomkins, Headpiece to *Spring* (1797).

Fig. 15. C. Ansell–A. Birrell, *Spring* and *Winter* (1792).

Fig. 16. Wm. Hamilton–P. Tomkins, *Skating* (1797).

Fig. 17. T. Uwins–C. Warren, *The Touch of Kindred* (1816).

Fig. 19. C. Catton–F. Chesham, *The Drowning Sailor* (1793).

Fig. 20. Wm. Hamilton–F. Bartolozzi, *Celadon and Amelia* (1797).

Fig. 20*a*. R. Wilson–Wm. Woollett, *Celadon and Amelia* (1766).

Fig. 21. H. Fuseli–Wm. Bromley, *The Dying Shepherd* (1802).

Fig. 22. R. Westall–Wm. Finden, *The Dying Shepherd* (1819).

Fig. 24. Wm. Hamilton–J. Caldwell, *Palemon and Lavinia* (1778).

Fig. 25. Wm. Hamilton-F. Bartolozzi, *Palemon and Lavinia* (1797).

Fig. 26. Wm. Hamilton–R. Rhodes, *Palemon and Lavinia* (1802).

Fig. 27. Alexander Anderson, *Hunter and Hare* (1797).

Fig. 28. G. L. Crusius, *Spring* (1758).

Fig. 29. C. Eisen–C. Baquoy, *Musidora* (1759).

Fig. 30. C. Eisen–C. Baquoy, *Palemon and Lavinia* (1759).

Fig. 31. R. Westall–C. Heath, *Musidora's Answer* (1819).

ig. 32. J. C. Horsley–
. Thompson, *Musidora* (1842).

Fig. 33 Thurston, T. Bewick, *The Fleeing Lover* (1805)

Fig. 34. Kirk–Ridley, *Musidora* (1802).

Fig. 35. Thurston–T. Bewick, *Doctor, of Tremendous Paunch* (1805).

Fig. 36. R. Westall–C. Heath, *Lavinia's Mother* (1819).

Fig. 37. J. Bell, *Spring* (1842).

Fig. 38. G. Hay–S. Paterson, *The Dying Shepherd* (1864).

Fig. 39. J. Wolf–Dalziel, *The Timid Hare* (1859).

Fig. 40. B. Foster–Dalziel, *Shepherd and Flock* (1859).

Fig. 41. Kronheim Plate, *Summer*—Shepherd and Flock (1868).

Fig. 42. J. McWhirter–J. Corner, *Autumn*—the Falling Leaves (1864).

Fig. 43. John Powell, *The Whole Air Whitens* (1802).

Fig. 44. T. Seccombe, *Spring* (1873).

And, o'er his inmost vitals creeping cold,
Lays him along the snows a stiffened corse,
Stretched out, and bleaching in the northern blast.
[*Winter*, ll. 305–21]

Hamilton in 1778 first drew the man perishing in the snow, sitting against a snowbank, 'Thinking o'er all the bitterness of death'. It was an attempt to picture the pathetic in Thomson's passage. The shepherd was separated from the snowdrift by a careful attention to details: his hat beside him, his staff lying across his lap, the detailed clasp on his shoes. The howling storm of the poem—'And every tempest howling o'er his head/Renders the savage wilderness more wild' ll. 295–6—was tamed by the shepherd's ease in death and his sympathetic appeal to heaven. In 1802, Henry Fuseli undertook to illustrate the line '. . . down he sinks' by showing the cowering insignificance of insecure man in the storms of nature (Fig. 21). The shepherd was seen crouching on the dark ground near a body of water, his knees drawn up to his chest, his body covered with his cloak and his dog also seeking shelter under his cloak. A storm was raining down upon them, the dark clouds hiding flashes of light—and the illustration was consistent in its dark-grey colours. The white snow of Thomson was absent, and the crouching frightened man, analogous in shape to the clouds, was part of the shapelessness of nature described by Thomson. By establishing an artistic shapeliness between the human objects and natural objects, so that the cloak covering the man formed another drift or hill against which he was huddled, Fuseli created a reciprocal relation in terms of function: as the clouds were used so was the man used. The open-mouthed amazement of the sailor, his terrified uncontrol was one view of the sublime; another was Fuseli's closed, confined, circular view of the smallness of man, the triviality of his effort at safety. This ironic attitude was supported by the protruding tail and rear of the dog, side by side with the face of the shepherd, whose safety consisted of hiding under a cloak.

But the next major set of engravings—those based on the designs of Richard Westall and first published in 1816—showed the man perishing in the snow with his hands clasped and 'thinking o'er all the bitterness of death' (Fig. 22). It stressed the pitiful situation of the man, leaning against a 'shapeless drift', and, by isolating the individual without carefully framing the background, 'sketched to the imagination'. But this illustration, with its interpretation of the sublime as pity, clashed with interpretations of the detailed and awesome power of nature, and thus reduced the vigour and significance of the passage. Westall's illustration suggested (1816) a concept of imagination stressing predominance of internal or mental action, a view governed by 'association' or 'suggestion'. In 1824, T. Wright declared, 'Mr. Gilpin just remarks, 'all the real artist wishes, is to give *such characteristic touches* to his pictures, as may be able to rouse the imagination of the beholder. The picture is not so much the *ultimate* end as it is the *medium* through which the ravishing scenes of nature are excited in the imagination; for the true *enjoyment* of the *picture* depends chiefly on the *imagination* of the spectator.'[1]

Thomson's literary critics, however, applied another concept of the imagination dealing with the craft by which the poet vivified nature and made possible the new or renewed recognition of nature. This view, which insisted on richness of particularity and detail, resulted in different emphases given to space, action, and expressiveness. The sense of nature's profusion appeared in the Kent illustrations as the unity of the great chain; but a theory of particular imagination which stressed feeling for detail seemed to apply also to illustrations which made single scenes dense and encompassing such as that of Charles Catton or in the remarkable 'nutting' engraving of Richard Corbould and Francis Chesham (Fig. 23). There was substituted for Kent's details, the lushness of particular objects, or the contrast between highly expressive particulars and amorphous nature.

Otte Benesche has recognized that some early eighteenth-century characteristics of book illustration persisted at the beginning of the next century. This period, he wrote, 'kept alive achievements and features of the Baroque, although on the surface of style and fashion Neo-classicism was completely dominant and gave to this era its name in the history of style'.[2] But it 'kept alive' only certain themes, types of gesture, conceptions of interpretation. The reconstitution of these—like Hamilton's reworking of personification or Catton's sublime—was made within altered theories of space, time, nature, and imagination.

[1] W. Gilpin on *Picturesque Beauty* as quoted in T. Wright, *Some Account of the Life of Richard Wilson Esq. R.A.* (London, 1824) p. 47.

[2] Otto Benesche, *Artistic and Intellectual Trends from Rubens to Daumier* (Cambridge, Mass., 1943), p. 61.

The criticisms implicit in the illustrations, governed by artistic traditions, were not as extensive as literary criticisms, even when both were interpretative. For it was self-evident that artistic interpretation, keyed to specific passages, dealt with the range of the poet, his attitude toward his material, his organization or unity, and his attitude to the audience. The Kent illustrations, for example, dealt with unity in a formalized rural or landscape view. But Stothard's illustrations (1793) domesticating the poem were directed at an audience with sentimental attitudes toward the family and nature. That *The Seasons* contained both these elements could be certified by an analysis of specific passages. The illustrations of Stothard and other designers who did individual scenes seemed to encourage interpreting *The Seasons* as a series of poems—what Robert Shiels in 1753 had called an 'assemblage of poetical ideas'. But the random quality of the illustrations seemed sufficient warranty against such procedure. Interpretation, in other words, had to be analysed with respect to specific concepts such as unity, the sublime, or the pathetic.

There were many critical areas to which illustrations were not relevant. Even within analysis, they could not portray versification, and they could handle imagery only if language was assumed to be pictured. The tests of poetic value could be applied only if they were based on vividness, visual or imaged, and illustration could only eliminate such inadequate theories, not provide better ones. But the study of illustrations reveals that they implied solutions to such literary problems as emotive unity, often before such unity was articulated and that they pointed to a range of meaning which criticism for social or literary reasons often ignored. Such illustrations also demonstrated, in the last decade of the eighteenth century, that valuable interpretative practices often resulted from pressures external to the poem. In the 1790's twelve new sets of illustrations were published, exclusive of the reprints of earlier illustrations. (This flurry of interpretation continued for two more decades—seven from 1800 to 1810, five from 1810 to 1820). Such variety of interpretation did not always do justice either to the art or the poem. But in themes of the isolated poet, or the lover's dream, the illustrations called attention to subjects completely ignored in the literary comments on the poem.

The illustrations in the eighteenth century conveyed the interpretative transitions from the hierarchical views of landscape to the expressed interrelation between man and nature. From the fusion of convention and diversity seen as inclined planes in a great chain, it moved to man as an object of nature surrounded and often engulfed by it. From illustrations of 'unified' views, it moved to single fragments, representative either of 'wholes' or of significant actions. In moving from the significance of background as hierarchical to the foreground as detailed and particularized, it moved from a view of eternity governed by status to eternity as connected with past and future (of nature or family). And it moved finally from an interrelation of personified nature and naturalistic activity to man's representative role, both of forces which surrounded him and those which shaped him. Only Charles Catton and Henry Fuseli among the illustrators at the turn of the century saw the forces of nature, as Thomson did, in process, but among the critics such insight had to wait for William Hazlitt.

(c) SIR WILLIAM HAMILTON AND ALEXANDER ANDERSON: TWO TYPES OF ARTISTIC REVISION

Hence let me haste into the mid-wood shade,
Where scarce a sunbeam wanders through the gloom.

J. THOMSON [*Summer*, ll. 9–10]

(1) *The Enclosures of Nature*

Paradise is the Passion for 'a walled enclosure', and it may well be that the peculiar value set on gardens in the later middle ages is a legacy of the Crusades.

K. CLARK

Palemon and Lavinia (*Autumn*, ll. 177–310) was one of the three formal narratives in *The Seasons*: the others were Musidora, and Celadon and Amelia. All these stories dealt with love, and all were characterized by 'innocence and undissembling truth' and by retirement amidst the shades of nature: 'Alone amid the shades, / Still in harmonious intercourse they lived / The rural day' (*Summer*, ll. 1185–7). The Musidora episode began 'Close in the covert of an hazel copse' (*Summer*, l. 1269) and Lavinia 'with her widowed mother, feeble, old, / And poor, lived in a cottage far retired / Among the windings of a woody vale; / By solitude and deep surrounding shades, / But more by bashful modesty, concealed' (*Autumn*, ll. 181–5). The concept of idyllic retirement, associated with the Horatian retreat to nature and the innocence of pastoral life, was in *The Seasons* seen as pierced and interrupted. Just as Lavinia had to leave her retreat, so in her retreat Amelia is killed by lightning and Musidora is spied upon by her lover. The concept was, therefore, treated as tragic, ironic or unendurable—'compelled / By strong necessity's supreme command, / With smiling patience in her looks she went / To glean Palemon's fields.' (*Autumn*, ll. 214–17).

Thomson's use of enclosure imagery applied to more than the narratives: the vessel which 'drinks the whelming tide / Hid in the bosom of the black abyss' (*Summer*, ll. 999–1000) or the caravan 'buried deep' beneath descending hills or the embracing and menacing fog: 'in deeper circles still / Successive closing, sits the general fog / Unbounded o'er the world, and, mingling thick, / A formless grey confusion covers all.' (*Autumn*, ll. 728–31). Thomson's imagery suggested the manner in which, in tender situations, the enclosure was entered by forces beyond the control of the inhabitant. The individual was taken from the breast or bosom of nature, and as in Gray, he desired to return to it.

> As in the hollow breast of Appenine,
> Beneath the shelter of encircling hills,
> A myrtle rises, far from human eye,
> And breathes its balmy fragrance o'er the wild—
> So flourished blooming, and unseen by all,
> The sweet Lavinia . . .
>
> [*Autumn*, ll. 209–14]

The enclosure gave to the individual an innocent freedom—'And breathes its balmy fragrance o'er the wild'—exactly as the flower born to blush unseen retained its immense potentialities for ever. However, another aspect of the enclosure, in the sublime and tragic instances, permitted no escape; the individual found himself 'fixed' and 'amazed'. The study of illustrations to Palemon and Lavinia by William Hamilton, who three times—1778, 1797, 1802—drew designs (Figs. 24, 25, 26) of Palemon meeting Lavinia while she was gleaning in his fields, reveals the shifting interpretation of enclosure imagery in the hands of a single painter and how, by reproportioning elements within the same scene, he minimized or exaggerated its sentimentality.

The illustrators repeatedly made Thomson's narratives their

subjects but the literary critics, even Thomson's most sympathetic admirers, felt that they were not the best parts of the poem. In 1778 Aikin declared 'writers much inferior in respect to the powers of description and imagery, have equalled our poet in elegant and benevolent sentiment, and perhaps excelled him in interesting narration'.[1] Aikin found the narratives commonplace and objected to them because they approached common life, unlike the descriptions which were original views. But neither Thomson's literary defenders —Sir Harris Nicolas wrote that 'every one who has read them will admit that the History of Celadon and Amelia, and of Lavinia, for example, have afforded as much pleasure as any other part'[2]— nor his detractors attended to the function of these narratives apparent in the illustrations. The narratives—Celadon and Amelia, and Musidora in *Summer*, Lavinia and the burlesque fox-hunt in *Autumn*—formed contrasting views of experience, the naturalistic and burlesque as opposed to the idealistic and angelic. The latter, describing innocence and love, depicted them as innocently victorious or defeated, victors or victims. The critics, by attending to Thomson's didactic comments about the 'varied God', neglected the inferences from his examples. The artists, however, related Palemon and Lavinia to the recurrent cycle of nature or to the religious idealizing of woman—the story had echoes of Ruth and Boaz. Hamilton's revised illustrations reduced the implications of the turns of fortune and the mystery of nature's cycle to a success story, but he never lost touch with the text, though he interpreted less and less of it. But the literary critics, excepting John More (1777), neglected the interpretations of these tales.

Hamilton's illustrations consistently focussed upon the sentimental aspects of the narrative, gradually omitting the ambiguous and accidental relationship—one might call it the open relationship—between man and nature, and substituting for it the idyllic aspect of the enclosure and the innocence and idyllic quality of Lavinia. Thomson wrote of the external shade as a reflection of internal modesty—'By solitude and deep surrounding shades, / But more by bashful modesty, concealed'. But one of the chief characteristics by which Hamilton developed the sentimentality of interpretation was gradually to close off the horizon of the field in which Lavinia was

[1] Aikin, *Essay*, p. xxxix.

[2] Sir Harris Nicolas, ed., *The Poems of James Thomson* (London, 1830), I, lxxxiii.

gleaning to stress expressive gestures and to ignore the cyclical range of nature.

Thomson told the story of Lavinia and Palemon from the view of the omniscient narrator and then from that of Palemon. In it, the idealized virtue and purity of Lavinia were contrasted with the elegant but generous rural wealth of Palemon. Both aspects represented Thomson's attempt to idealize rural England. The harvest myth, therefore, was interwoven with the story, the glee of those who harvest and the sadness of those who glean. The reversals of fortune were implicit in the scene, but the selection for interpretation dealt with love and the reward of virtue, not of friendship—for there was nothing in the illustration to convey Palemon's benevolence as well as love to Acasto's daughter.

In the 1778 engraving, Palemon is addressing Lavinia in the left foreground, a tree occupies the left background and is contrasted with the bright view of the field on the right in which two figures are bent, gleaning. The right hand of Palemon is upon his breast, his left is extended and he is gesturally speaking the language of the heart. Below the illustration appear the following lines:

> Then throw that shameful pittance from thy hand,
> But ill applied to such a rugged task;
> The fields, the master, all, my fair, are thine.
> [*Autumn*, ll. 288–90]

The first interpretation of Hamilton, badly drawn as it was, contrasted the simple smock of Lavinia with the elegance of Palemon. Another contrast placed the figures in balance against the field, the other gleaners and the open horizon, the pittance and the plenty. The illustration represented not only the immensity of Palemon's wealth but the obligation of elegance to virtue and the freedom offered to it.

By neglecting to centre the character, Hamilton sought to suggest Palemon's chancing 'beside his reaper-train/To walk'. (*Autumn*, ll. 2256). In 1797, this literal quality was replaced by an attempt to capture Palemon's Arcadian splendour. The illustration was structurally divided into two frames with the tree as border. In the background were bushes and a partial view of a house. Hamilton sought to relate Lavinia to the simple tasks of the poor, to the natural scenes of which she, holding some grains, was a human image. The light rays of the sun and the light of her dress created the idealized relation between woman and nature which Thomson had expressed:

> Her form was fresher than the morning-rose
> When the dew wets its leaves; unstained and pure
> As is the lily or the mountain-snow.
>
> [*Autumn*, ll. 192–4]

Establishing Palemon as the centre of the point of view through whose eyes Lavinia was seen, Hamilton in 1797 made him the elegant swain, giving him a faithful dog at his feet and an impressive hall as his home. This illustration lost the relationship between simplicity and freedom, between Lavinia and the other gleaners. The original illustration suggested the accidental turn of fortune, but there was nothing accidental in the 1797 engraving. Thomson's poem suggested the irony of Palemon's status awareness, but in 1797 he had become a wealthy swain proposing to a beauty so that the meaning of harvest, poverty and misfortune disappeared.

In the 1802 edition, the backgrounds were considerably reduced and Lavinia became the central figure with a white smock and a halo of bushes behind her. The point of view was shifted to a sentimental glorification of the woman, and although the left background showed some gleaners and the right the house, Lavinia represented the idealized model of purity and Palemon, dressed as a young squire, was paying homage to her. The shift in point of view idealized Lavinia, but it sacrificed the sense of the past which the background accomplished and it lost the relation between nature and man characteristic of Thomson's description.

The three illustrations of Hamilton were marked by an increasing diminution of the view. The 1778 illustration contained a long view of the horizon moving on an inclined plane from the figures in the left foreground. The gradual disappearance of the horizon was the consequence of a changing conception of space and time in interpreting descriptive poetry. Kent's spatial continuum was a series of objects and events in space, part of a hierarchical structure. By the end of the century, although the stylized gestures of the characters remained fairly constant, the horizontal plane (or planes) gave importance and priority to the foreground, placing the characters in a dominant role. It also conveyed a distinction between the known and the unknown. Each of the illustrations presented a single scene, but they all showed an increasing attempt to picture the sentimental discovery of love and the immortalizing of Lavinia. The first example contrasted the particular material scene with the perennial vista of nature, Palemon and Lavinia with the enduring cycle of nature. The diminution of the horizon in the 1802 edition, attempted to create a symbolic use of the woman: she had a white halo around her head, and the natural scene became the basis for eternal time.

In the 1797 illustration the horizon was confined to the left background and in the 1802 engraving the horizon almost completely disappeared behind the branches of a tree that occupied the centre background. The illustrations moved from an extended descriptive view of the sky to portraits with several objects as background. The dominance of character minimized the enclosure concept of Thomson as it did the sense of the harvest and the rewards of nature and man. Thomson did not describe the sunrise or the prospect; he merely wrote that Palemon 'chanc'd beside his reaper-train / To walk'. The composition of Hamilton moved from the open field and the chance meeting to the central role of the meeting and the disregard of the naturalistic environment. The increased domestication of the illustration was marked by two features, neither of which had any factual relation to the incident in the poem. The 1778 illustration was located in the field, but in 1797 Hamilton placed a portion of the house in the right background indicative of Palemon's rural wealth whereas the background of Lavinia was a view of the horizon. Moreover, in each of the engravings a dog was introduced. In 1778 the dog was an ornamental animal. But in the subsequent engravings, the dog was placed between the figures, representing the friend to man and creating a scene of rural devotion.

The narrative of Palemon and Lavinia grew, in the hands of Hamilton, less and less related to the turns of fortune, the contrast between retreat and exposure, simplicity versus elegance. The critic in *The Artist* (1807) objected to the florid quality of Thomson's language, but Hamilton's illustrations had become more rather than less florid, and revealed an increasing attempt to capture the scene's literal point of view rather than to supplement the scene with descriptive views. Thomson had written of Lavinia:

> for loveliness
> Needs not the foreign aid of ornament,
> But is when unadorned, adorned the most.
> Thoughtless of beauty, she was beauty's self...
> [*Autumn*, ll. 204–7]

But of Hamilton's Lavinia in the 1790's it was hard to believe that she was indeed 'thoughtless of beauty'. And it was equally difficult to discover the loneliness of the poor gleaner among the supposed riches of the harvest.

(2) *Alexander Anderson: The Loneliness of Nature*

> Lone on the midnight steep, and all aghast,
> The dark wayfaring stranger breathless toils,
> And, often falling, climbs against the blast.
> J. THOMSON [*Winter*, ll. 178–80]

The development shown by Sir William Hamilton was considerably different from that of the American engraver, Alexander Anderson, who engraved *The Seasons* more times than any other artist and who in the closing of the horizon achieved a sense of the loneliness and desperation of man's condition. According to Sinclair Hamilton, 'the decade of the nineties . . . derives its chief importance from the fact that in it Alexander Anderson, the most famous of our early wood engravers, began to work'.[1]

Anderson began in 1797 with a series of four engravings, apparently from original designs. In 1802 he engraved four headpieces, one for each season. In 1803 he prepared, for a miniature edition, four plates and four tailpieces. In 1805 he redesigned and engraved the 1797 plates. In 1807 he engraved for a Portland company the Cranmer illustrations to the Evans 1802 edition. And in 1812, he designed and engraved one plate for each season. In a period of fifteen years, Anderson prepared six sets of engravings for *The Seasons*.

The 1797 edition contained four plates (a fisherman, Celadon and Amelia, the hunter and the hare (Fig. 27), the ship 'entangled in the gathering ice' (*Winter*, l. 921)). The illustrations contained little scenery; in fact they tended to minimize the nature descriptions of

[1] Sinclair Hamilton, *Early American Book Illustrators and Wood Engravers 1670–1870* (Princeton, 1958), p. xxxi. For information about Anderson, see the biographical notice by B. J. Lossing, *Art Journal*, XX (London, 1858), 271–2; see also Evert A. Duyckinck, *A Brief Catalogue of Books Illustrated with Engravings by Dr. Alexander Anderson* (New York, 1885); Frederic M. Burr, *Life and Works of Alexander Anderson* (New York, 1893); and Helen M. Knubel, 'Alexander Anderson and Early American Book Illustration', *Princeton University Library Chronicle* (1940), pp. 8–18.

the text. They had a childish simplicity of gesture, like the boy with his hunting horn and dog, and a scampering rabbit. The second set (1802) showed Anderson's concern with horizon light as a clue to the season, *Spring* and *Autumn* being about the same grey hue and *Summer* and *Winter* being light and dark. The Anderson illustrations of a farmer ploughing and another who 'his lusty steers / Drives from their stalls' (*Spring*, ll. 35–6) created an inconspicuousness in the activities, completely at odds with Thomson's joyous invocation. Even the sheep-shearing scene in *Summer*, described by Thomson as a pastoral kingdom, appeared as a solemn rather than a gay occasion:

> The housewife waits to roll her fleecy stores,
> With all her gay-drest maids attending round.
> One, chief, in gracious dignity enthroned,
> Shines o'er the rest, the pastoral queen, and rays
> Her smiles sweet-beaming, on her shepherd-king;
> While the glad circle round them yield their souls
> To festive mirth, and wit that knows no gall.
> [ll. 398–404]

The boy dragging the sheep from the river, the small group involved in the shearing, all tended to create a sense of recalcitrant beast and effortful work. In these illustrations Anderson avoided any precise expressiveness so that the man dying 'in the northern blast' (*Winter*, l. 321) had his face averted, only the barrenness of death being clear, with snow drifts accumulating in the background.

The 1803 miniature edition—four plates and a tailpiece for each season—pictured in *Spring* the ploughman and his steers returning from the field and *Summer* showed the shepherd returning with his flock. Each of these with the theme of 'return' and the lonely identity of man and animal created a sense of barrenness and isolation—as though the home represented a lonely outpost of civilization. The horizon, with the exception of *Summer*, was grey or black. Even the male reapers in *Autumn*, sitting and drinking before the huge wheat field, seemed dwarfed by the immensity of the task before them, and the sky seemed a reflection of the shape of the field. Anderson's view of the poem, in these illustrations, reflected its rural quality, reflected it to the exclusion of all else, and the small tailpieces (a hare, a bird, a stag, and a boy on the mountain cliff) with the absence of people and the neglect of sentimentality created a sense of the fragmentary quality of the action. For Anderson it became central to the meaning of *The Seasons*.

Anderson's interpretation of *The Seasons* was based on an American locale and an American austerity. In contrast to the domestication of the poem in England and its socialized qualities during this period, this American view saw the poem as an expression of the vigour and loneliness of rural life. There were many passages in *The Seasons* which substantiated this view. The English illustrations often created densely populated scenes, but Anderson, aiming at the isolation of the rural environment, reduced the number of figures. These American illustrations served to show not only Anderson's increasing skill, but at least one kind of appeal that Thomson's poem had for an American audience. The values of *The Seasons* transcended local cultures, and the illustrations displayed some of its wide-ranging relevance.

In 1759, when C. Eisen and C. Baquoy illustrated the first French translation of *The Seasons*, they provided scenes quite independent of the Kent plates picturing allegorical cherubs for each season as well as single characteristic scenes. Their procedure contrasted with that of the German G. L. Crusius who, in 1758, designed *Spring* (Fig. 28) relating, as Kent did, the natural to the allegorical figures. Eisen's four designs described four social acts—nest-snatching, Damon spying on Musidora (Fig. 29), Palemon's appeal to Lavinia (Fig. 30), and winter dancing—two of which involved disorder between man and nature and two demonstrating plenitude and union. The hair styles and clothing were French, and there was a notable absence of the violence and sublime of the poem. The naughtiness and sociability of the single scenes established a far narrower range than Kent's multiple scenes, but with the frontispieces they conveyed a sense of playfulness and diverse social behaviour which the poem captured, but which English critics did not observe. So, too, when Anderson almost forty years later began illustrating *The Seasons*, he did so by ignoring the English traditions which he had available and proceeded to interpret the work irrespective of its environment. Yet such interpretations were valid in so far as they described qualities in the poem which did exist, and they are significant for criticism because they supplement the remarks of critics.

But in the 1805 revisions of the illustrations to Stafford's edition, Anderson either imitated those scenes of English illustrators which created a maze of nature—so that he used George Wright's illustration to *Spring* as the basis for the fishing scene—or by his own revisions, created a nature threatening, dark and profuse. The hunter was now deep in the forest (*Autumn*) and in *Winter* the huge icy walls seemed to block the ship, with the added setting sun the colour of icebergs. By 1812, the darkness had descended upon the illustrations: the man fishing and Palemon addressing Lavinia were surrounded by the darkness of nature, and the lonely sailor (*Summer*) 'who from the first of joys,/Society, cut off' (*Summer*, ll. 939–40) was pictured sitting, sad, on the jutting eminence, viewing the raging waves below. Anderson created a pervasive sense of isolation, of the elements pressing and burdensome even in man's pleasant activities, like fishing or wooing, whereas Thomson found desolation only in certain moments in each season. The sense of gaiety, of sentimentality, of the glorification of woman and child, had no place in Anderson's illustrations.

In 1802, the Richard Corbould–Parker illustrations were reprinted in America, and in 1804 Hamilton's 1802 plates (with Kirk's *Musidora*) were reprinted (Philadelphia, Budd and Bartram); the Cranmer designs were reprinted in 1807 and 1819. It must, therefore, be assumed that Anderson had available other interpretations from which to choose. Yet when he illustrated the story of Palemon and Lavinia, keyed to the passage

> 'And art thou then Acasto's dear remains?
> She whom my restless gratitude has sought
> So long in vain?'
>
> [*Autumn*, ll. 265–7]

he substituted benevolence for ardour. In his interpretation, the scene was one of utmost seriousness, and the tree with overhanging branches created an enclosure which represented not the idealization of woman or the secret of love, but an act of benevolence and charity done in private. As each character seemed to look away from the other, the sense of disengagement was fortified, and Thomson's idealized love was interpreted as Christian obligation.

A number of essays have been written, beginning with Walter L. Nathan's 'Thomas Cole and Romantic Landscape',[1] dealing with the

[1] Walter L. Nathan, 'Thomas Cole and Romantic Landscape', *Romanticism in America*, ed. George Boas (Baltimore, 1940), p. 33. Other essays which deal with the relation between American 'romantic' landscape and literature include Donald Ringe, 'Kindred Spirits: Bryant and Cole', *AQ*, VI (1954), 235 ff.; 'Painting as Poem', *AQ*, XII (1960), 71–83; Paul Shepard, Jr., 'Paintings of the New England Landscape', *College Art Journal*, XVII (1957), 30–52; Charles L. Sanford, 'The Concept of the

concepts of the 'picturesque' and the sublime in early American paintings, especially Thomas Cole's, but an analysis of Anderson's engravings reveals an absence both of the picturesque and of an 'unending variety of hills and dales, woods and streams'. The meagreness of detail and the reduction of expressiveness pictured a sublime in which nature was awesome and threatening. But the tradition was not that of Catton and Fuseli, it was a view of the poem in terms of an American environment divorced in the 1797 edition from the illustrated English editions. Anderson's innovation was to insist on the austerity of nature in the poem, not its sentimentality. The illustrations involved a disregard for historical context—or rather a neglect of such context—in order to suggest the emotional tone of isolation, which captured a relation between the bleakness of Scotland and that of the frontier. In fact, one of Thomson's English critics in 1777 had pointed to Thomson's reliance upon his knowledge of Scottish winter in his poem. 'The story of the man perishing in the snow ("Winter") is, to say the least, finely and feelingly told. This accident, is the more natural and affecting, that it happens so frequently among those wild romantic hills and deserts in the South of Scotland, where our poet was born. There we have but few beaten tracks, and only mere foot-paths, through the fields from one house to another; which, by the way, are often single, and situated at a most uncomfortable and inconvenient distance.'[1]

There were many 'sublimes'—the loneliness and barrenness of Anderson was one; the gigantic and awesome nature of Cole another. America was present in Anderson's *Seasons* but it was not the result of nationalistic art. It resulted from the penetration of a point of view which gave significance to the poem. But the total 'poem' was no more completely available to this point of view than it was to any in literary criticism.

Arthur Barker, in his discussion of views of Milton's 'sublimity' and Satan throughout the eighteenth century, points out that by the close of the eighteenth century 'Milton's sublimity was being transformed from a theory of religious elevation to a delightful sensationalism'.[2] But neither 'delightful sensationalism' nor 'pity and

[1] More, p. 48.

[2] Arthur Barker, 'And on his Crest Sat Honor', *UTQ*, XI (1942), 430.

Sublime in the Works of Thomas Cole and William Cullen Bryant', *AL*, XXVIII (1957), 434–48. See also Asher B. Durand, 'Letters on Landscape Painting', *The Crayon*, I (1855).

admiration' can sufficiently account for changes in the interpretations of the dying shepherd in *Winter*—from Hamilton's 1778, Fuseli's 1802, and Westall's 1816 illustrations. Only by gauging the way in which these were reproportioned can the characteristics of change and continuity in criticism be assessed. If there was Hugh Blair, there was Samuel Johnson. If there was William Jones, there was John Scott. If there was in Fuseli an increase in sensationalism, there was also an awareness of irony; if in Westall an increase in sentimentalism, there was also a disengagement from 'sensationalism' in order to express the typical simplicity of man and nature.

(d) THE CONFLICT OF TRADITIONS: THE NUDE AND THE PRUDE

> His description of the rural bath, and the incident it suggests, are natural and interesting.
>
> J. MORE

> It is in his 'Damon and Musidora', that Thomson displays the cloven hoof. It is appalling to think that with him and his generation of Englishmen, this sort of thing could have passed for delicacy of sentiment.
>
> D. C. TOVEY

In so far as illustrators engraved passages in the poem which critics considered inferior or undesirable, there must be considered to have existed a conflict on the issues. Such conflicts existed among critics and among engravers as well as between the two groups. Regarding these disagreements, there were two persistent areas in which they occurred; the illustrations of the narratives, especially Musidora, and the illustration of the burlesque passages.

George Wright, who published his illustrated and annotated edition in 1770[?], wrote: 'The story of Damon and Musidora here related, tho' it may be much admired for its natural simplicity and artless dress, is rendered extremely disgustful to the modest reader, by the too particular description of Musidora undressing herself, which might better have been left out, for any beneficial instruction

Barker points out that the illustrations were responsible for critical misrepresentation: 'All three critics [Patrick Hume, William Smith, and Jonathan Richardson] are intent on seeing what Milton has described; and because of the misrepresentation of the illustrators, all three emphasize the human qualities through which Milton makes Satan possible' (p. 434).

it can convey, unless raising indelicate or indecent ideas in the breast, may be stil'd useful.'[1] The passage to which Wright referred read as follows:

> . . . as from the snowy leg
> And slender foot the inverted silk she drew;
> As the soft touch dissolved the virgin zone;
> And, through the parting robe, the alternate breast,
> With youth wild-throbbing, on thy [Damon's] lawless gaze
> In full luxuriance rose. But, desperate youth,
> How durst thou risk the soul-distracting view
> As from her naked limbs of glowing white,
> Harmonious swelled by nature's finest hand,
> In folds loose-floating fell the fainter lawn,
> And fair exposed she stood, shrunk from herself,
> With fancy blushing, at the doubtful breeze
> Alarmed, and starting like the fearful fawn?
> Then to the flood she rushed: the parted flood
> Its lovely guest with closing waves received;
> And every beauty softening, every grace
> Flushing anew, a mellow lustre shed—
> As shines the lily through the crystal mild,
> Or as the rose amid the morning dew,
> Fresh from Aurora's hand, more sweetly glows.
> [*Summer*, ll. 1308–28]

Musidora had been part of Kent's *Summer*, but in the French 1759 edition she had a plate to herself which set the model for later English editions. In 1778 she was treated individually for the first time in an English edition (Hamilton–Caldwell) and again in an incompleted painting by Gainsborough (1782?), (National Gallery); other treatments appeared in 1793 (Henry Singleton–Thornthwaite), 1794 (Thomas Stothard–William Bromley), 1797 (Hamilton–Bartolozzi?), 1802 (Kirk–Ridley), 1805 (Thurston–Bewick), 1816 (Westall–Heath), 1842 (J. C. Horsley–J. Thompson) (Figs. 31, 32). In some illustrations she was more clothed than others, depending upon whether she had just arrived to bathe, was on the verge of entering the water, or had dressed and was answering Damon's note. The objection to the passage was almost exclusively moral. The 1792 critic explained that 'the tales introduced by Thomson in the different Seasons are the most exceptional parts of the poem.'[2] Wordsworth in 1815 declared, 'In any well-used copy of the *Seasons* the book generally opens of

[1] G. Wright, *Seasons*, p. 205. [2] 'Preface', *Seasons*, 1792.

itself with the rhapsody on love, or with one of the stories (perhaps Damon and Musidora).' [1] Musidora represented the vulgarity of popular taste. In 1816 the editor of the Sharpe edition wrote: 'We know we shall offend common prejudice in pronouncing the Tale of Musidora, which has furnished so many artists with a subject, and the publishers of so many editions of Thomson with a captivating embellishment, to be as vulgarly conceived, and to be as coarse in sentiment, though not in expression, as a Dutch painting. But Thomson is chastity and purity itself in comparison with his contemporaries.'[2]

Thomson was not fortunate in the literary defenders of Musidora. John More (1777) found the scene 'modest' and 'chaste': 'The fortunate discovery of Damon on that occasion, the proof he gives in her modesty and diffidence, of a chaste and respectful attachment, and the generous acknowledgement of his bashful mistress, are touched with inimitable delicacy and tenderness.'[3] 'To point out the particular beauties of Celadon and Amelia; of his [Thomson's] Damon and Musidora, would be, to affront the good sense, and good sentiments of my readers.' A somewhat more adequate defence was made in 1830 by Sir Harris Nicolas. He explained that 'a poem descriptive of scenery and of changes in the weather requires the introduction of human beings to give it life'.[4] Sir Harris did not mention Musidora, but the same argument applied. The issue, however, was not so simply resolved, it being obvious that not digressions, but these particular ones, were what had to be defended. The best that his critics could do, apparently was done in Robert Chambers's *Cyclopaedia of English Literature*: 'Every alteration was an improvement in delicacy of thought and language, of which we may mention one instance. In the scene betwixt Damon and Musidora—"the solemnly-ridiculous bathing" as Campbell [1819] has justly termed it —the poet had originally introduced three damsels!'[5] The best that

[1] Wordsworth, *Literary Criticism*, pp. 186–7.

[2] 'Critical Observations', 1816, p. xi. [3] More, p. 48.

[4] Nicolas, I, cxxix–cxxx.

[5] *Cyclopaedia of English Literature* (Edinburgh, 1844), II, 13. According to Robert Bell, ed., *Poetical Works of James Thomson* (London, 1855), I, 156, n., Lord Byron referred to Thomson's 'sexual imagination': 'Byron, speaking of Thomson's portraits of beauty, observes, that they "prove the peculiar turn of thought, and, if the term may be allowed, the sexual imagination of the descriptive poet".' Alfred Noyes recognized the humour of the Musidora episode, but assumed that this was an example of 'unconscious humor'. Thomson lacked 'that deeper vision'; his 'chief merits

was said about the passage was that it was an improvement over the original.

There were two critical functions which these illustrations served: they counterbalanced the sexual prejudices of the literary critics and they demonstrated the application of an artistic tradition within a literary tradition. For Thomson not only described Musidora originally in terms of the 'Venus of Medici', but by creating peeping Damon he ironically satirized prudish attitudes to sex: 'Ye prudes in virtue, say / Say, ye severest, what would you have done?' (ll. 1298–1299). The literary critics who objected to the passage did not see it as playful irony:—many of the engravers did, and in so doing created a basis, not taken in criticism, for re-evaluating the passage. But even among engravers there were those who removed peeping Damon, as did an American publisher—A. Sherman, Philadelphia—censoring Kirk's Musidora.

It is perhaps necessary to defend the interpretation of Musidora as playful irony, and this can be done by recognizing the place of this passage in *Summer*. It follows a praise of swimming which concludes with the lines, 'Even from the body's purity the mind / Receives a secret sympathetic aid' (ll. 1267–8). But the 'pure' action of the episode is that Musidora, returning from swimming, confesses her love for peeping Damon who has fled, declaring ,'the time may come you need not fly' (l. 1370). This sensuous invitation comes after a previous description of Musidora's coyness, shyness and 'maiden pride' (l. 1278).

The design of the episode is to illustrate how Musidora's concealed feelings become exposed when her body is exposed. The attitude to Damon, who observes Musidora undressing, is mock heroic.

> Thrice happy swain!
> A lucky chance, that oft decides the fate
> Of mighty monarchs, then decided thine!
> For, lo! conducted by the laughing Loves,
> This cool retreat his Musidora sought.
> [*Summer*, ll. 1285–9]

The 'dubious flutterings' of Damon's soul are stilled after no serious conflict and he resigns himself to watching his beloved disrobe. The

---

are those of keen observation, his alertness to sights and sounds and fragrance, to atmospheric effects, and especially to colours.' 'The Nature Poet of the Eighteenth Century', *Some Aspects of Modern Poetry* (London, 1924), pp. 239, 241.

description of Musidora proceeds with extravagant sexual imagery and Damon is compared to Paris:

> when aside
> The rival goddesses the veil divine
> Cast unconfined, and gave him all their charms.
> [*Summer*, ll. 1305–7]

The comparison of peeping Damon with heroic Paris, and the rather dissimilar situations involved, plays with the tradition of immortal sexuality; and Damon is seen as near madness from this 'soul-distracting view'. Thomson creates an analogy between Damon's sensuousness and that of nature:

> Then to the flood she rushed: the parted flood
> Its lovely guest with closing waves received.
> [*Summer*, ll. 1321–2]

The departure of Damon, 'Checked, at last, / By love's respectful modesty' is described in burlesque terms of the distraught lover, for 'struggling from the shade / With headlong hurry fled: but first these lines, / Traced by his ready pencil' (ll. 1337–9). The return of Musidora to the shore continues the mock-heroic comparison only to conclude with an invitation to love. The next line of the poem begins a description of the sun: 'The Sun has lost his rage . . .' (l. 1371). The revisions of the original passage, which was a maturation sequence rather than a mock-heroic sexual one, suggested the irony. Thus there was added the 'dubious flutterings', and the lines, while gazing on naked Musidora, 'But, desperate youth,/How durst thou risk the soul-distracting view.' The exchange of notes together with its sensual, teasing implications was also added.

The irony of the scene was captured by Thurston (Fig. 33) in his description of the lover fleeing as Musidora moves to the shore, and the peeping lover of Kirk was observing with obvious pleasure the disrobing of his beloved here removed from the Venus posture (Fig. 34). (For an attempt to prettify the scene, see Fig. 32, 1842.)

There is no doubt, too, that in illustrating this passage, designers were able to defend themselves by the tradition of the nude in painting. They thus drew attention to the prejudices of the literary critics, though by the middle of the nineteenth century there were relatively few illustrations of the nude Musidora, the designers themselves having been defeated by the social pressures. The critical argument that the passage was incompetent poetry, however, could not be answered by illustrations. These could suggest that the passage was ironic or serious, that it was richly or thinly sensuous, these could demand a re-reading of the passage for proper interpretation, but the value of the poetry could only be determined by an analysis of the passage.

Equally important in defining the critical range, and related to caricature rather than the playfulness applied to Musidora, was the attitude toward the comic or burlesque passages in the poem. Thomson had written of the need for wit and 'folly-painting humour' when the 'serious thought' failed.

> But, when with these the serious thought is foiled,
> We, shifting for relief, would play the shapes
> Of frolic fancy; and incessant form
> Those rapid pictures, that assembled train
> Of fleet ideas, never joined before,
> Whence lively wit excites to gay surprise,
> Or folly-painting humour, grave himself,
> Calls laughter forth, deep-shaking, every nerve.
> [*Winter*, ll. 609–16]

The critics did not discuss Thomson's humour or his conception of the comic, and when Lyttelton edited Thomson's works in 1750, he removed 'A ludicrous account of foxhunting' from *Autumn* and published it as a separate poem on the grounds that it was inappropriate and he was aiding Thomson's immortality. And when Thomson in *Summer* described the 'jovial mead' and 'the ruddy maid, / Half-naked, swelling on the sight, and all / Her kindled graces burning o'er her cheek' (ll. 355–7), John Scott (1785) declared it was 'indelicate'. Yet the illustration by Kirk–Neagle (1798, 1800) of the maid interpreted the sensuousness and the Thurston–Bewick (1805) illustration of the 'doctor of tremendous paunch' caricatured the vulgarity of some types of rural behaviour (Fig. 35).

The neglect of the comic by the critics occurred not merely because of its 'indelicacy', but because they found the moral sentiments and the comic a mixed form. Thus, despite the insistence upon rural activities of a critic like Aikin (1778), he denied to the rural burlesque and comic sections the 'congruence' he sought. But, further, the Miltonic assumptions made about Thomson's blank verse kept the critics from understanding the exaggeration involved in the spider and the fly or the Musidora episodes.

It should further be noted that the engravings involved a bid for an audience which was less learned and of a somewhat different class from the original. Coleridge's remark upon finding *The Seasons* in a farmer's hut—'This indeed is fame'—and John Wilson's insistence that Scottish farmers read it, indicated that for the early nineteenth century the illustrations kept alive a class element which the critics did not discuss. The illustrations of the reapers who make 'The rural scandal, and the rural jest / Fly harmless, to deceive the tedious time / And steal unfelt the sultry hours away' (*Autumn*, ll. 159–61) implied an awareness of the lower classes and a respect for their tasks which the critics ignored. The critics treated Thomson's benevolence and his sentiment, his awareness of domestic bliss or anxiety, but one needed only to look at the illustrations to determine the social status of the characters. The illustrations, therefore, kept in balance the different classes to which the poem referred as well as their diverse activities. Most of the illustrations, whether in Kent's edition or Corney's (1842), dealt with more than one class, and to this extent the illustrations performed a necessary contribution in controlling the interpretation of the poem for the reader, regardless of whether it functioned similarly for the critic. Wolfgang Stechow has declared that 'while in the fifteenth and sixteenth centuries it was the life, labors and pastimes of the lower and middle classes that were primarily represented in paintings, the eighteenth century concentrated almost wholly on the pastimes of the upper strata of society'.[1] The illustrations to *The Seasons*, however, are a refutation of this statement whether one examines the illustrations of Kent, Hamilton or subsequent designers. Moreover, by ironical use of convention (a peeper looking at Venus di Medici), illustration interpreted a quality of the poem completely neglected by literary critics—ironic sensuousness.

(e) RICHARD WESTALL: THE POETRY OF PAINTING

> . . . from the study of mere outer pictures of Nature and human action, we, necessarily, enter within the realm of ideal thought . . .
>
> *The Crayon*, 1855

In 1816 John Sharpe issued an edition of *The Seasons* designed by

[1] Wolfgang Stechow, 'The Winter Landscape in the History of Art', *Criticism*, II (Spring, 1960), 185.

Richard Westall and engraved by Heath. For the next twenty-five years, these illustrations were the most frequently reprinted in England and the United States. Sharpe reprinted them in 1817, 1824 (twice), while in the United States they were reprinted in 1817, 1819, 1830, 1832, 1842. Their last printing occurred in 1889, in Glasgow and New York. The illustrations included a frontispiece from the hymn, a plate for each season and another for the hymn.

Each illustration—a sort of circular vignette—was keyed to a passage in the poem: *Spring*: to 'together let us tread / The morning dews and gather in their prime / Fresh-blooming flowers to grace thy braided hair /', omitting even in the quotation the following 'indelicate' line: 'And thy loved bosom, that improves their sweets' (ll. 490–492); *Summer* to Musidora carving a note to Damon; *Autumn* to Lavinia's need to glean Palemon's fields; and *Winter* to the man dying in the snow. Each of these passages was related to the tender passions and in each illustration the human beings occupied the centre, surrounded by nature so that in *Spring* even the clouds resembled the heads of trees. Westall selected for illustration those passages most susceptible of sentimentality regardless of surrounding nature so that Amanda and her lover did not see 'where the winding vale its lavish stores, / Irriguous, spreads' (*Spring*, ll. 494–5). Each of the three women had been praised by Thomson for her loveliness—Amanda 'Formed by the Graces' (*Spring*, l. 484), Musidora compared with the 'Venus of Medici', Lavinia, 'Thoughtless of beauty, she was beauty's self, / Recluse amid the close-embowering woods'. (*Autumn*, ll. 207–8).

Westall stressed the idealization of woman, seeking by placing her within the sole confines of nature to suggest her modesty and virtue, all the greater because of its concealment. 'Far retired / Among the windings of a woody vale; / By solitude and deep surrounding shades, / But more by bashful modesty, concealed' (*Autumn*, ll. 182–5). Even the man perishing in the snow seemed to lean against the 'shapeless drift' and to clasp his hands in prayerful resignation (Fig. 22), just as Lavinia's mother sat with clasped hands looking at her daughter about to leave the shelter of the retired cottage to glean Palemon's field (Fig. 36).

Westall's vignettes excluded details of nature; his figures in contrast to those in Hamilton's foregrounds were seen from a distance. Thus the miniatures created a softness (compare Westall's *Musidora* with those of Cranmer and Thurston) derived from the vagueness and indefiniteness of the surroundings. Westall selected for illustration passages dealing with inner human qualities—'with smiling patience in her looks' (*Autumn*, l. 216) or 'thinking o'er all the bitterness of death' (*Winter*, l. 307) so that his illustrations were indefinite because 'suggestive' or associative or 'poetic' and because, as an American critic remarked, 'by the process of reasoning ourselves into the Beautiful, from the study of mere outer pictures of Nature and human action, we, necessarily, enter within the realm of ideal thought, which is ever at work, to give variety, complexity and infinity to the range of the human mind'. It was not, perhaps, surprising that there were more reprintings of this set of illustrations in the United States than there were in England.

The interpretation of *The Seasons* which Westall pursued was that of tenderness and pity as the dominant qualities of the poem. The result was a reduction in the range of the poem, and a deliberate excision of passages, such as the one in *Spring* (ll. 489–93) from which the sexual reference was deliberately omitted, and a neglect of nature in process, violent, ironic, or unknown. So, too, in his illustration of the shepherd perishing in the snow, the darkness of nature and the shapeless drift of snow possessed a softness in marked contrast to the possibilities of the power of nature in the same passage: 'On every nerve / The deadly Winter seizes, shuts up sense, / And, o'er his inmost vitals creeping cold, / Lays him along the snows a stiffened corse [*sic*] / Stretched out, and bleaching in the northern blast' (ll. 317–21).

One characteristic of these plates was to give *The Seasons* a single tone. This tone, however, was not based on Thomson's descriptions of nature, neither his 'circumstantial' nor prospect views, and though he seemed to illustrate the 'pathetic', the preface to the 1816 edition found that the chief quality of Thomson's style and diction was a 'gait of natural pomp which it is mimicry to adopt' and called Thomson 'the Johnson of poetry'.[1] And the critic, in opposition to Westall, declared that 'throughout the *Seasons*, it is to the senses, however, rather than to the heart, that the appeal is made'.

The appeal to which this critic referred was quite obviously different from the appeal to the heart which Westall painted. For Westall, this appeal was found in a reduction of external expressiveness in order to suggest internal feeling, an absence of planes in order

[1] 'Critical Observations', 1816, p. vi.

to suggest the oneness of nature and man, and the use of pathetic gestures. Thomson's poem was occasionally sentimental, as in the reference to the dying shepherd's family, but such sentimentality was submerged by nature's authority over man. What the critic meant was that the religion of 'the Seasons is of that general kind which Nature's self might teach to those who had no knowledge of the God of Revelation. It is a lofty and complacent sentiment, which plays upon the feelings like the ineffable power of solemn harmony, but has no reference to the quality of our belief, to the dispositions of the heart, or to the habitual tendency of the character.'

This view was an appropriate attack on the illustrations in its own edition, but it did not adequately describe Thomson's uneven views or the illustrations of Fuseli, Catton, or Corbould who recognized the need for man's acceptance of a world dominated by nature's powers and processes.

(f) THE COLLABORATIONISTS

> Now it is one thing for an illustrator to come into direct collision with his author. This, I take it, is absolutely contrary to all the ethics of collaboration. It is quite another thing for the artist to import into his work particulars that have been ignored in, but are not inconsistent with the author's production. Indeed, when we consider the matter closely, it is inevitable throughout that this should be the case.
>
> G. S. LAYARD

By the mid-nineteenth century there were available three major traditions of Thomson illustrations. The first marked a return to the conception of 'innumerable nature'—a view of the poem dominated by its variety. In contrast to Kent, this variety was not governed by the attempt to view scenes within a single plate, but rather to prepare a continuous narrative of illustrations. The first such set was published in 1841, designed and engraved by Samuel Williams. The second, under the editorship of Bolton Corney, with designs by members of the Etching Club, was published in 1842 (reprinted 1847, 1860). The third, in 1859, contained illustrations by Birket Foster, F. Pickersgill, J. Wolf, G. Thomas, and Noel Humphreys. This procedure involved an attempt to remove the fragmentation which characterized individual and representative scenes of the poem. By creating a series of pictorial narratives, these illustrations insisted on the action in the poem, on movement, thus subscribing to the contemporary belief which sought motion in decoration as opposed to stability or idleness. But still another factor was the attempt to create an entity of illustration and poem.

The second tradition was that developed by Westall: the foreground and background equally indefinite, the minimizing of human figures and the humanity of nature. It could contain wide landscape views as well as vignettes and was not necessarily keyed to the poem. Some, as in the Kronheim colour plates (1868), contained landscape illustrations stressing particular qualities in the landscape and associated with, rather than illustrative of, the poem. Such associations led to naturalistic illustrations of birds and animals named in *The Seasons* (1859, 1892, Estes and Lauriat, Boston).

The third tradition was that of single scenes containing interpretations of passages such as 'the ruddy maid' (*Summer*) and the shepherd perishing in the snow.

Samuel Williams (1841) restricted his miniature drawings, placed within lines of the text, to naturalistic events and rural scenes. The 1842 Bolton Corney edition had a series of illustrations around the margins of the page in imitation of illuminated manuscripts, marking the return to the 'putti' (Fig. 37). Moreover, by placing a series of illustrations around the margins of the page, a deliberate attempt was made to fuse illustration and poem in a physical as well as interpretative sense. The ground for the union was a theory of the visual imagination, suggesting that the poem not only described scenes and actions but also the imagined life of man. Thus in *Spring* the freeing of souls in death was illustrated: 'Together down they sink in social sleep; / Together freed, their gentle spirits fly / To scenes where love and bliss immortal reign' (ll. 1174–6); in *Summer*, the pestilence (ll. 1083–4) and the 'fairy people' (l. 1673).

The eighteenth-century illustrations of the classical and Christian elements of *The Seasons* had involved conventionalized personifications of the seasons or sculptured representations of them. By 1830, these conventionalized seasonal figures had become so stereotyped as to be the objects of ridicule.[1] Attacks on engravings which could be shifted indiscriminately from one nature poem to another derided stereotyped figures, postures and allegorical details. Serious engravers,

[1] John Wilson, 'Winter Rhapsody', *Blackwood's Magazine*, XXVIII (1830), 870–1.

therefore, sought to interpret the poem more precisely or to engrave in a highly personal style. The division had undergone alterations in terms of the proportion devoted to allegorical figures and to naturalistic ones, but the new fusion of non-natural with natural figures was premised on the existence of an imaginary and naturalistic world. Thus Thomson's images of the souls in sleep were visualized, whereas the only eighteenth-century illustration of *The Seasons* devoted to the poet's imagination was Thomas Stothard's *The Lover's Dream*. There were, of course, illustrations to *Macbeth*, which represented witches, but these belonged to a different genre from descriptive poetry.

The literary theorists of the mid-eighteenth century, like Arthur Murphy, who urged that metaphors were to be tested by the pictures they made, considered such pictures creations of the mind. But these pictures were confined to images of action or to traditionally visual allegorical or emblematical figures. There was, therefore, a considerable difference between the images which served as references for these eighteenth-century critics and the nineteenth-century imaginary images in the world of the artist. There were two quite different views involved, and the type of vision which the eighteenth century personified in ambition or pride—personifications for which emblems and artistic conventions existed—was not the other-worldly mythological imagination which was worked out for the poem in the 1842 edition. The distinction between the vision of action and the vision of dreams and fantasy was a distinction in two theories of imagination.

Such undertakings in the mid-nineteenth century were made possible by theories of mental action which saw poetry and illustration as forms of imagination. The illustrations to the Corney edition, therefore, required to be read differently from those of the Kent or Hamilton or Westall illustrations. Where they contained several scenes they not only required to be read from top to bottom, like the text, but they had to be read in series with reference to the order of ideas. Thus though the man dying in the snow preceded references to his family—in the illustration the family was at the top of the page and at the bottom the dying shepherd—the illustrations sought to create a unity of narrative which the poem did not possess, but its advantage lay in seeking to create variety by sequence of actions rather than single representative instances.

The critical value of these illustrations in defining the eighteenth-century concepts of visual imagery (by exhibiting what the nineteenth century interpreted visual imagery to be) is extremely important. They revealed that eighteenth-century poetry was visual in the sense of allegory, emblem and action, but that the 'fairy' world to which Addison referred, the world of dreams and phantasy, was not part of this. The illustration of these had to wait for a view of imagination from which neither actual nor imagined sights were excluded.

In the second half of the nineteenth century some illustrations interpreted the poem as unsentimental, based upon the Pre-Raphaelite doctrine of realism. The Pre-Raphaelites followed Raphael, wrote Ruskin in 1851, 'by painting the truths around them as they appeared to each man's mind, not as he had been taught to see them, except by the God who made both him and them'.[1] In *The Seasons* this meant—in the shepherd dying in the snow, for example—the treatment of man as an object of nature (Fig. 38).

The conception of man as an object of nature was expressed in several ways. The 1859 volume included descriptive scenes without humans, and sought to approximate the balance which the poem had. In the illustrations of man, Celadon and Amelia for example, Celadon was gripping the hand of the dead Amelia and it was not the sculptured image of the poem nor the view of man hidden in the bosom of nature, but man exposed at the height of desperation—the two human beings occupying almost the entire illustration. This detailed realism of expression was matched by the realistic details of the animal illustrations; for example, in the illustration 'Poor is the triumph o'er the timid hare' (*Autumn*, l. 401) (Fig. 39) the frightened face of the hare hidden in the rushy fen, surrounded but not shielded by the plenitude of nature, conveyed Thomson's sense of the frightening reality of nature without the didacticism.

In the Bolton Corney (1842) and the 1859 volumes, the varied illustrators presented no single interpretation of the poem. But the range of interpretation differed from that at the turn of the century. In addition to the effort to construct a continuous imaginative whole, there were realistic illustrations which expressed the isolation of man and animal and moments of subdued despair, the view of man as a trivial object in overarching nature. These two interpretations were complementary because both saw man overwhelmed by nature either within the 'whole' or as an objective but insignificant part of a huge universe. These illustrations defined the element of distortion in such

[1] John Ruskin, *Pre-Raphaelitism* (London, 1851), p. 59.

mid-nineteenth century interpretations. That the illustrators treated man as a fragment or object can be seen by comparing the dominant role of the shepherd in Stothard's 1794 (Fig. 3) illustration, and the vague, imprecise and uncentred role in the illustrations of Birket Foster (1859) (Fig. 40) and the Kronheim plate to *Summer* [1868?] (Fig. 41). In Foster, the shepherd in the left middle ground is less definite and less precise than the animals in the foreground. Thomson had called the shepherd a 'monarch-swain' and had begun and concluded this section with him as the guardian of 'his subjects'. But these illustrations picture man as an insignificant though organic part of the natural environment. In both nature is seen as unconfined, extending into the horizon, but in Foster nature's variety is pictured through the varied shapes and positions of the animals, whereas in the Kronheim plate nature appears cyclical and circular in the rolling hills, and the density and variety of vegetation. (That such rolling hills do exist in England and Scotland is quite irrelevant to the interpretative issue.)

These illustrators, by attending to contemporary values, interpreted the poem to their audience; this interpretation involved the fragmentation of the individual as a trivial, even isolated part of nature, an awareness of the individual's shared isolation with other elements in nature, and a sense of man's symbolic smallness. The trends of literary naturalism and symbolism are far more apparent from the illustrations than from the studies of contemporary literary critics.

In the 1859 Birket Foster–Dalziel illustration—'Hence, let me haste into the mid-wood shade, / Where scarce a sunbeam wanders through the gloom', (*Summer*, ll. 9–10) in the autumn sketch—'Oft let me wander o'er the russet mead', (*Autumn*, l. 971) in 'While Nature lies around deep-lulled in noon,' (*Summer*, l. 630, Schmoltze, 1857), in J. McWhirter's–Corner's illustration of the latter scene in 1864, there was apparent the immensity of the trees, the extravagant detail of nature in leaf, branch, grass, and stubble and the meagreness of human outline, the isolation and weakness of the individual, the endurance of nature. Within these views there were of course differences so that Birket Foster drew the variety—water, trees, sky—of natural details and McWhirter the disproportion between nature and man (Fig. 42).

The loss of the portrait identity of man in nature was characteristic of the 'reading' demanded by these illustrations. By the accumulation of details of nature, especially in the types of variety proposed, and by reducing the role and description of man, these illustrations asserted the non-verbal, non-literal qualities of art so that the disproportion between the stated text and the illustration was considerable. In this respect, such illustrations indicated the limitations of Thomson's descriptions, even in what he described so well. But such discrepancy does not sufficiently account for the vagueness of the human elements. This vagueness reveals the perplexing dilemma of human identity, and this dilemma was seen by Thomson in his refusal to explain the death of innocent Amelia or the death of the shepherd in winter—it was seen in his storms, his sinking ships, his plague.

In the illustrations by Foster and others in the 1850's and 1860's, the vagueness of man was seen as resulting from the size of the actual landscape, but in a painter like Turner, nature itself was seen as vague and unfinished. Both Constable and Turner had careful knowledge of *The Seasons*, and one critic has declared that 'Turner's close familiarity with the detailed clauses of Thomson's descriptive passages is as clear as his sympathy with Thomson's intense and accurate vision of nature'.[1] Yet Turner did not illustrate *The Seasons* though he appended passages of the poem to several of his paintings. For Turner's conception of nature as a process, as an immense vague power, was similar to Thomson's only in the threatening, transforming quality. Thomson saw this transformation in shifts from nature to personification and back, whereas man formed no central image for Turner.

It does not appear unduly speculative to inquire why, in the first quarter of the nineteenth century, Turner and Constable found Thomson congenial, for it was at this time that the illustrators caught up with the literary critics in considering the poem as a descriptive work. Beginning with Warton in 1756, the literary critics had seen the poem as predominantly a descriptive work; the first illustration which was pure landscape without human figures was a 1794 tailpiece of *Winter* by Thomas Stothard, who also placed on the title page a vignette of a waterfall (*Summer*, ll. 590–606). There was a series of water-colours executed by John Powell and included in one 1802 edition (Fig. 43), but these were not reprinted. These water-colours were unusual illustrations to the poem. Although they

[1] Ann Livermore, 'J. M. W. Turner's Unknown Verse Book', *The Connoisseur Year Book 1957*, ed. L. G. G. Ramsey (London, 1957), p. 78. For additional references to Thomson and Turner, see C. B. Tinker, *Painter and Poet* (Cambridge, Mass., 1938), *passim*.

included scenes frequently handled, such as Palemon and Lavinia, Musidora, Celadon and Amelia, the shepherd perishing in the snow, the sower—they also contained three landscape scenes which sought to interpret the mood of nature. These included the setting of the sun in *Spring* (ll. 1009–10) which reflected the lover's feelings, the waters glistening against the mountain in *Autumn*, and the 'roused-up' river in *Winter*. The autumn scene captured nature in motion so that the dark clouds, the sea, the river, the birds, even the jagged mountains were painted in motion. Thomson's passage read:

> Nor stops the restless fluid, mounting still,
> Though oft amidst the irriguous vale it springs;
> But, to the mountain courted by the sand,
> That leads it darkling on in faithful maze,
> Far from the parent main, it boils again
> Fresh into day, and all the glittering hill
> Is bright with spouting rills. But hence this vain
> Amusive dream!
>
> [*Autumn*, ll. 750–7]

It is important to note that although in this 1744 version Thomson calls his 1730 theory a 'vain / Amusive dream' and even offers an alternative, he retains the earlier imagery and its implications. Thomson described the river and sand in an image of courtship and pursuit which shifted between personification and naturalism. For 'courted' to the mountain 'darkling', it burst forth 'fresh into day', casting its freshness upon the surroundings. Nature was both led and leader, in darkness and bright day. Powell achieved these contrasts by light and by stroke, but the magnitude of nature 'wide and wild' was also the result of a merging of the sea and clouds, ocean, and mountains.

This conception of nature significant in itself became dominant only at mid-century, and it serves to confirm the theory that a major shift in critical ideas took place at that time rather than at the end of the previous century. A series of major efforts were then undertaken to create an imaginative unity between poem and illustration, to treat the poem as a visual narrative, to interpret the allegorical images as part of a coherent view of man and nature, to re-create balance between man and nature by giving balanced emphasis to each, to restore a relation between the violent and mystical and the benevolent and practical.

(g) THE DECLINE OF ILLUSTRATION

> The question then arises whether a work of the imagination should ever be illustrated . . .
>
> H. S. ASHBEE

The illustrations of the mid-century pointed to an iconography in which each person reflected the relation between man and nature; they thus conveyed the seasonal recurrence of the poem differently from the 'pathetic' of children and family at the beginning of the century.

The major differences after the sixties included a change from pastoral to rural nature, the prominence of birds and beasts and natural landscape, an abandonment of caricature for serious illustration, the interpretation of the sublime without accompanying figures, the disappearance of invented children and the neglect of classical personifications. The frequently illustrated scene of fishing or of sheepshearing disappeared from the text after the 1860's, and the pastoral paradise was supplanted by walkers in the forest or by rural landscape without figures. (See T. Seccombe's illustrations (1873) to *Spring*, 'The rapid radiance instantaneous strikes / The illumined mountain' (ll. 192–3) (Fig. 44), and *Summer*, 'And falling fast from gradual slope to slope', (l. 603) the illustration to *Winter* in 1881, 'Drooping, the labourer-ox / Stands covered o'er with snow', (ll. 240–1) and the numerous naturalistic illustrations in the 1892 Estes and Lauriat editions.) Even the shepherd scenes reduced the role of the shepherd because the pastoral activities had lost pertinence for society. In this respect the illustrations supported the view of at least one literary critic. John Dennis in 1876 distinguished 'pastoral'—'a slavish mimicry of classical remains'—from 'rural':

> There was a time when the term Rural Poetry was regarded as synonymous, or nearly as, with Pastoral Poetry. The most artificial verse ever written, and which, in its legitimate form, was 'a slavish mimicry of classical remains', was confounded, at the beginning of the last century, with the poetry that describes the simple sights, sounds, and occupations of country life, the changes of the seasons, the colour of wayside flowers, the song of birds, the beauty of woods and meadows, and the manifold charms of rivers winding through rich pasture—lands, of sunny nooks, shady lanes, and forest glades lying close to the haunts of rustics.[1]

[1] John Dennis, 'English Rural Poetry', *Studies in English Poetry*, p. 356.

In this period of declining illustration earlier illustrations were reprinted—the Williams 1841 illustrations together with the Gilbert–Greatbach designs (1869) in 1876 and the Westall designs in 1889, selections from Metz (1802) in 1874 and 1888—and scenes such as reaping or the jovial mead or the lover's finding of 'the clustering nuts' become disembodied from the text (see the 1881 edition) so that the 'secret shade'—'the clustering nuts for you / The lover finds amid the secret shade' (*Autumn*, ll. 615–16)—is in Seccombe's illustration full of light—neither secret nor a shade.

The recurrent pattern formed, however, no basis for literary comments at this time. The critics sought to place *The Seasons* within the Augustan tradition and it was seen as an antithesis to Pope. 'Thomson', wrote a critic in 1864, 'was the first poet of eminence who rebelled against the artificial importations from the continent, and strove, we believe in part unconsciously, to bring literature back to a purer style, and to imbue it with a spirit closer to nature.'[1]

This historical conception of the poem formed one of the reasons for the gradual separation of illustration from poetry. The historical function placed the poem among other poems or among the social forces of the time, but it removed the poem from particular analysis—originally, the chief contribution of illustration. Illustration demanded interpretation of particular passages or of the unity of the whole, but in the interpretation of the poem as a formal stylistic entity, illustration could only serve as embellishment. As the poem, therefore, became identified with a literary tradition, it lost significance as artistic expression. Moreover, the theory of the picture language of poetry was by the last quarter of the nineteenth century widely discredited; illustration was therefore an appendage to the poem. It had become so, in part, through the cheapening and conventionalizing of engravings which disregarded the particular poem. Artists themselves insisted on the independence of illustration as an art. Holman Hunt explained in an illustration of *David Copperfield*, 'My object was not to illustrate any special incident in the book, but to take the suggestion of the lover seeking the fallen girl coming upon the object of his search.'[2] And in 1895 Laurence Housman declared

[1] 'Preface', *The Seasons* (Edinburgh, 1864).

[2] Quoted in D. Welland, *The Pre-Raphaelites in Literature and Art* (London, 1953), p. 25. The theory of independent inspiration for illustrators and poets is also stated by Robert Bell, ed., 'Introduction', *Art and Song* (London, 1867), p. viii.

that the 'illustrations of the pre-Raphaelites were personal and intellectual readings of the poems to which they belonged, not mere echoes in line of words in the text. Often they were an effort to sum up the drift of an entire poem within the space of a single picture, as in Rossetti's first illustration (1857) to *The Palace of Art*'.[1]

The major changes in the relation between illustration and the poem after the 1860's were the disengagement of the two arts and the frequency of reprinting of older illustrations or engraving imitations of them. A literary criticism or a theory of book illustration which left no room for non-verbal interpretation or only for 'imaginative' or fanciful interpretations lost touch with the kind of linguistic theories from which the poem derived as it also neglected the analysis or interpretation of particulars. This major change in the concept of illustration resulted, finally, in the abandonment of illustration as an interpretative technique so that in the twentieth century there has been but one illustrated edition (1927).

But for purposes of criticism the change corresponded with the critical attack upon the poem in the last quarter of the nineteenth century. The literary critics found, within an evolutionary view, that Thomson's concept of nature was incorporated in that of other poets, so that John C. Shairp remarked that Thomson's view corresponded to Wordsworth's childish pleasure, the first of three increasingly metaphysical phases. Or the critics found Thomson the initiator of a nature movement which led up to Wordsworth, or they found him a member of Pope's coterie, dominated by artificiality. But each of these critical views was tied to general considerations hostile to illustration. For illustration by its contemporaneity could not reduce the poem to its evolutionary inadequacy, especially since illustrators insisted on the independence of illustrations as works of art. Furthermore, the insistence upon Thomson's realistic descriptions was for the critics an inadequate religious view, but the illustrators created landscapes which conveyed quite different views of Thomson's lines, such as the McWhirter–Hay interpretations, Thomas Seccombe's two nature views (1873, 1880), and the imitations of mid-century narrative illustration in 1892.

But these interpretations, dependent upon earlier insights into passages and the whole, were substituted for an immediacy of response to the poem. Especially for theories which seize upon

[1] Laurence Housman, 'A Forgotten Book Illustrator', *Bibliographica*, I (1895), 276–7.

immediacy as a characteristic of illustrations, such responses were failures of the contemporaneity of interpretation. In this repetitive development, the varieties of illustration, like the varieties of literary interpretation in the first half of the century, stabilized alternatives while neglecting the very function of such alternatives—that non-verbal interpretation should derive from a careful and current response to parts or versions of the whole.

The return to Westall's sentimental view or Gilbert's imitations of Hamilton or Metz's benevolent squires or McWhirter's or Hay's naturalizing of man or even the imitation of narrative unity in the 1892 edition depicted varieties which applied to other periods and revealed for criticism the dilemma of the choice of ends. For the adequacy of means to ends in an interpretation is not sufficient ground for approval of the criticism. Only as the ends themselves are defensible are the examinations of means critically rewarding. These illustrations were the equivalent of circumventing the attack on *The Seasons* by relying upon authority, upon earlier approval. But the literary critics objected to the simplicity, the benevolence of the poem, though they continued to praise Thomson as an initiator. There existed interpretations of Thomson as a sublime poet of nature's power, of human tragedy, of the loneliness of man amidst the hugeness of nature, but the illustrations sought to avoid these interpretations by reducing the poem to a series of pretty sketches. It was thus used to avoid the mainstream of literature and to support views of the world which avoided the dreadful questionings of Victorian man. The gap, therefore, between the literary and non-verbal critics was immense because by separating the arts their ends had become disparate. The literary critics analysed the religious implications of the poem for contemporary thinkers, but the illustrators sought to placate the fears of a middle-class audience and to teach them—even at this late hour—how to find peace in nature.

The prowess of *The Seasons* as a nature poem depended upon the poems with which it was compared. By the latter half of the nineteenth century it was considered an optimistic and naïve poem compared to Wordsworth's poetry. The illustrators, therefore, were presenting a view of nature that, in painting, was taken for granted as a moving and profound view, but in criticism had come to be considered inferior to the interaction of man with nature. In this respect the Kronheim plates captured the moving prospects of the poem more accurately than Shairp's attack upon it.

But other critics and illustrators were at one in moving from the poem to an imagined exercise rather than an interpretation of specific passages. The literary critics sought to place the poem within the early eighteenth century, providing a place for it in the history of literature, but the illustrators, seeking to stress the contemporaneity of the poem, placed the characters in nineteenth-century costume.

Because of the divergence between illustration and criticism, artistic objections were raised to the entire process of illustration, based on the premise that illustration was valuable only as an independent art form. In 1895 H. S. Ashbee wrote:

> The question then arises whether a work of the imagination should ever be illustrated—whether it were not better to leave the reader entirely in the author's hands without the intervention of a second party. To have thoroughly satisfactory illustrations there would seem to be but two alternatives: either the author must illustrate his own work; or he must have at his elbow an artist of equal and similar genius to his own. Both combinations are alike difficult.[1]

This argument against illustrations made them either independent works of art or continuations of the spirit of the author. It led, therefore, to the view which Forrest Reid attacked: 'illustration has come to be regarded as a dubious mixture of art and something that is not art. Probably the lectures and writings of Whistler did more than anything else to create this prejudice.'[2] Although illustrations could be both—those of Turner or of Blake were examples of each—such a view did not realize the function of illustrations as interpretation or criticism. The grounds for this view were derived from an organic theory of the work of art in which illustration and poem formed one unified art object. Such a unity was attempted in the multiple illustrations for *The Seasons* in the 1841, 1842, 1857, and 1859 editions. But neither the action nor the episodes could be rendered in the succession or unity of poetry.

The division between the illustrators and the literary critics became increasingly more marked in the growing attacks upon the poem and resulted in a consistent reduction in illustrations. In the 1860's there were seven illustrated editions in England and the United States (1860, 1861, 1863, 1864, 1868, 1869, 1869), in the next decade six (1870, 1874, 1874, 1876, 1876, 1876), in the 1880's two (1881, 1889),

[1] H. S. Ashbee, *An Iconography of Don Quixote* (London, 1895), p. x.
[2] Forrest Reid, *Illustrators of the Sixties* (London, 1928), p. 2.

and in the last decade two (1892, 1892). In the twentieth century there have been five editions of *The Seasons*, but only one illustrated edition—1927.

Yet although the illustrations made it possible for poetry to continue to exploit the usual particularities of nature so that a literary theory of realism (later naturalism) came to defend the use of particulars in every kind of literature, the illustrations of this poem, *The Seasons*, came to a virtual end by the end of the nineteenth century. Illustration and literary theory were in unison on the artistic independence of illustration, and this unity denied the importance of illustration for the poem. This view was, in fact, what Henry James sought when he preferred photographs to drawings for illustrations to his New York edition because 'the proposed photographic studies were to seek the way, which they have happily found, I think, not to keep, or to pretend to keep, anything like dramatic step with their suggestive matter'.[1] One consequence was the separation of poetry and illustration; another was the attempt of poetry and fiction to incorporate artistic techniques. The antagonism of the arts derives from the failure of a merger, and these two tendencies are dependent upon the successful acceptance of a common ground, whether it be a picture theory of language or a common theory of imitation. The failure of such theories to account for new poetry leads to renewed antagonism. But out of each effort at reciprocal merging there always has come, as John L. Lowes remarked, 'a certain widening of the scope of each of the arts involved'.[2]

Joseph Frank has pointed to the spatial attempt in the modern novel to describe the instantaneous flow of ideas. This was but one of the ways in which the independence of the arts sought to incorporate qualities derived from the two arts in conjunction. Symbolist fragmentation and imagist vision were more than mere analogues. By creating a kind of fragmentary poetry, fragments of sentences, of associations, of objects, with the suggestion of a huge and unlimited nature, the technique of the sketched or unformed background has been carried into poetry. Such approaches did, of

[1] Henry James, 'Preface', *The Golden Bowl*, I, xii. For a discussion of 'scene' and 'picture' as critical terms, see R. W. Short, 'Some Critical Terms of Henry James', *PMLA*, LXV (1950), 673–80. For art devices in the work of Henry James, see Viola Hopkins, 'Visual Art Devices and Parallels in the Fiction of Henry James', *PMLA*, LXXVI (1961), 561–74.

[2] John L. Lowes, *Convention and Revolt in Poetry* (Boston, 1919), p. 293.

course, come from other sources than illustrations, but the point is that they created a comparative basis in techniques. But the very need for such independence of the arts is indicative of the desire to substitute individual growth for co-operation. The neglect of illustration as interpretation at the end of the nineteenth century denied the implied subordination involved, and in this respect each of the arts became 'nationalistic', imperialistic, and authoritative. By current critical insistence on the verbal, explanatory discipline of criticism as the only criticism, interpretative illustrations have been systematically ignored, and criticism has been narrowed.

The illustrations at the beginning of the nineteenth century were profuse, but there were few new essays on *The Seasons*. Murdoch, Aikin, and Johnson were frequently reprinted and Hazlitt and Campbell added their comments before the new study in 1831 of Sir Harris Nicolas. The number of illustrated editions far exceeded the comments upon Thomson, and they served to keep alive the possibilities of interpretation. At the beginning of the twentieth century this situation was reversed. In 1927 there appeared the only twentieth-century illustrated edition. But critical notices of Thomson appeared not only in the editions of William Bayne (1900), Henry D. Roberts (1906), Otto Zippel (1908), James Logie Robertson (1908), and John Beresford (1927), but in the critical studies of Stopford Brooke (1902), G. C. Macaulay (1908), Myra Reynolds (1909), John Dennis (1896), Elizabeth Manwaring (1926), the histories of Scottish and English literature, and the articles of Herbert Drennon, C. A. Moore, etc. The diversity of criticism thus seems to perform the role which illustration did in the last century, but such a conclusion would be untenable. For the kind of interpretation which illustration performs stems from a different tradition from that of literary criticism.

Of the five illustrations by Jacquier to the 1927 edition—they are called 'pictures', one for each season and the 'Hymn'—each seeks a different quality in the poem, characterized by contrast. Thus the picture to *Spring* depicts the lonely lover 'sad amid the social band' (l. 1017), while over his head his 'wafted spirit flies'. The picture to *Summer* depicts a male *Summer* from whom a coquettish but vulgar *Spring* 'Averts her blushful face' (l. 7). In this illustration Thomson's description of the personified seasons is interpreted in sexual terms so that the allegory is burdened with a burlesque interpretation, appropriate to the Musidora episode, but not to the invocation if one examines the four invocations. Each of the four illustrations is pertinent to the interpretation of the poem as a series of love cycles: the pining lover, the ardent summer, the husband separated from wife and children, and Thomson himself in *Winter*, 'Pleased have I wandered through your rough domain; / Trod the pure virgin-snows, myself as pure.' (ll. 10–11). This conception of the poem as a series of contrasting love episodes, interpreting love as a natural, social, familiar, and sexual phenomenon provides another recurrent pattern, and it serves to return the nature concept to the social role it possessed at the beginning of the eighteenth century. It is not an adequate characterization of the poem, but it belies the disrespect for illustration as interpretation in our time.

Among the themes which persist in illustration from 1730 to 1927 are personifications of a season, a scene of suffering and death, and a scene of isolation contrasted with gaiety. These scenes do not always refer to the same passages so that Kent's wayfaring stranger in *Winter* and Stothard's shepherd wandering in the snow and Jacquier's rider and horse perishing 'amid the miry gulph' (*Autumn*, l. 1156) are all examples of suffering and death, but it is the conception of the illustrations that these themes, like the seasons, become part of a cyclical pattern. These three themes form the continuing elements of the poem for the illustrators: the supernatural forces, the natural forces of gaiety, isolation, and death. Within these there occur major changes from 1730, beginning with the 1770's and again in the 1840's, so that there are periods of considerable overlap in the handling of these and other themes. The need for discrimination is in the tools for defining the shifts in concept, the extension or abandonment of types of illustration, and the development of others. This study reveals that literary interpretation narrowed the range of analysis and that the discontinuance of illustrations in the past thirty years has coincided with increased formalization of criticism, a neglect of the major cyclical pattern of the poem, and a failure to concentrate on the present values which every illustration must make meaningful.

VI

DICTION, STYLE AND LANGUAGE: THE DILEMMA OF CRITICAL AGREEMENT

> Mr. Thomson's poetical diction in *The Seasons* is very peculiar to him: His manner of writing is entirely his own.
>
> R. SHIELS, 1753

> Thomson was a conscientious watcher and lover of Nature; his matter, which was his own, was hindered by his manner, which was somebody else's.
>
> A. AINGER, 1898

JUDGEMENTS OF THOMSON'S LANGUAGE in *The Seasons* have tended, for more than two hundred years, to concede it force and vividness while attributing to it artificiality and inflation. Such judgements diversely define 'force', 'vividness', 'artificiality', and 'inflation' as characteristics of poetry either essential or subsidiary, and they identify either the value or faults of the poem with this essential quality, or they excuse, defend, attack, or overlook the language because other qualities are proportionately more significant in determining judgement.

In the history of Thomson criticism, the terms 'diction', 'style', and 'language' are used separately, together, or interchangeably to explain 'force' in poetry; 'forcefulness' or 'vigour' remains a constant in criticism despite the different examples of it. Each of these terms calls forth some method of verification—language innovation or imitation or Miltonic diction or obscurity of reference or relation of philosophy to particular description—and such verification can be examined with reference to the range of its applicability. Such range indicates the adequacy of a particular explanation for all possible uses regardless of the agreement which all may have about Thomson's images or 'epithets'. Indeed, one of the most perplexing problems of this criticism is to discover which aspects of language are included and which excluded from statements about 'diction', 'style', and 'language'. Even with regard to the number of images and epithets, exclusive of the number of nouns and verbs in any line or sentence, the critics of the late eighteenth century give only so-called representative samples of clarity or obscurity, appropriateness or inappropriateness, correctness or incorrectness of a particular usage. Those nineteenth-century critics who divide the diction of the poem into artificial or simple clusters as representative passages evaluate a passage by some theory of spontaneity or simplicity in contrast to labouring or artificiality of expression. At the end of the nineteenth century and during the twentieth, efforts have been made to count types of terms or figures and even to identify the kinds of passages which seem aesthetically more active than others. Yet there does not exist a concordance for *The Seasons* by which it might be possible to discover the frequency of word usages in the original publication of each season and in the revisions.

Critics reveal similar responses to artistic unevenness of the language, yet the explanations for this unevenness vary considerably in their adequacy and reasoning. The examination of particular passages by John More, John Scott, John Aikin, and Robert Heron illustrated both the taste with which passages were selected and the 'scientific' bias of particular explanatory methods. There was, however, no necessary connection between such methodological procedures applied to language and 'scientific' gathering of biographical data in the works of Sir Harris Nicolas (1831), Allan Cunningham (1841), Bolton Corney (1842), and others. Neither the essay by John Scott (1785) nor, with one exception in America, the essay of Robert Heron (1793) was reprinted in the nineteenth century. For this eighteenth-century methodological approach to language there were, in the succeeding century, substituted (1) the 'imaginative' uses of language in terms of its impact upon the spectator or its source in the poet, (2) the speculative assumption made by Robert Bell that Thomson used certain recurrent patterns which needed to be exposed, (3) the attitude to language as mere data (in the school uses of *The Seasons* that made information a criterion of value). In the last half of the nineteenth century, despite the absence of new information regarding language, the artificiality of the language was indicative of Thomson's age as a whole, and, therefore, indicative of his inability to rise beyond it. A second view was that the subject matter of the poem expressed deistical optimism incompatible with the nature of evil, thus reducing the significance of the poem as a whole, regardless of its natural description.

The return to measurement in analysis, the quantitative approach to Thomson's language, took place in isolated instances in England, France and Germany in the response to positivistic gathering of data. Later, Thomson's language was studied by James Logie Robertson, by Léon Morel, by Myra Reynolds. Part of their statistical approach resulted from renewed efforts to collate all the texts and achieve a variorum edition; part resulted from identifying Thomson with his own time, because, in doing so, it became necessary to trace similarities and differences. Thus not the mere factual approach, but the factual approach become cultural, led back to a re-examination of the language and ideas of the poem.

The accumulation of language data, however, has not yet led to sufficiently reliable generalizations. Thomson's *The Seasons* does use Miltonic language, but in ways different from Milton. The discrimination of adequate from inadequate uses is what needs to be determined, and such determination is bound up with the diverse qualities of poetic language. The recourse to versification statements is an indication of such diverse qualities. The counting of Miltonic usages is not a sufficient guide to the function of language, just as there is insufficient evidence to assume that the aesthetic value of nature passages derives from certain philosophical assumptions unless one is prepared to argue that sound rhythm, and choice of words, images, and sentence structure are all the reflections of philosophic ideas.

(a) ROBERT SHIELS, JOHN MORE, JOHN SCOTT: CLARITY, CORRECTNESS, AND OBSCURITY OF DICTION

> Obscurity is often inseparable from elaborate writing. In struggling hard for a full description, it is sometimes impossible to avoid perplexity.
>
> J. MORE

In his life of Thomson in 1753, Robert Shiels sought to explain Thomson's diction by reference to his originality, his 'air peculiarly his own'. The 'diction' or 'style' or 'manner'—terms used interchangeably by Shiels—were characterized by certain traits of writing:

> Mr. Thomson's poetical diction in the Seasons is very peculiar to him: His manner of writing is entirely his own: He has introduced a number of compound words; converted substantives into verbs, and in short has created a new language for himself.[1]

Shiels admitted that Thomson's style was justly 'blamed for its singularity and stiffness', but claimed that it was admirably fitted for description. The criterion for description was, in the critic's usage, vividness and accuracy, and Thomson's language was like a 'microscope capable of discovering all the minute beauties'. Shiels did not indicate specific examples of Thomson's 'stiffness', but the reader's response was apparently unhindered by it. Thus vividness of effect, of which precision of detail was one characteristic, formed the basis for approving the language despite its departure from customary poetic usage.

Joseph Warton's digression on *The Seasons* (1756) identified the best examples of its diction with vividness and distinctness, the characteristics of truth; he did not deny that 'the diction of the *Seasons* is sometimes harsh and unharmonious, and sometimes turgid and obscure'; even 'though in many instances, the numbers are not sufficiently diversified by different pauses, yet is this poem on the whole, from the numberless strokes of nature with which it abounds, one of the most captivating and amusing in our language'.[2] Warton considered the criterion for poetry the perfect idea it created in the mind; thus the vividness of detail and the visual quality outweighed for him all the other negative characteristics of turgidity, obscurity, and inharmoniousness. Warton identified Thomson's descriptive diction with reference to particularity of detail:

> What poet hath ever taken notice of the leaf, that towards the end of autumn

[1] Robert Shiels, 'Thomson', *Lives of the Poets*, ed. T. Cibber (London, 1753), V, 202. Shiels's use of 'poetic diction' possessed no disrespectful implication. The use of 'diction' to mean 'poetic diction' first came into use at the end of the seventeenth century. See Thomas Quayle, *Poetic Diction* (London, 1924), p. 7. 'Style' had extensive definitions in this period. 'Manner' was sometimes distinguished from 'style' by referring to the characteristics of a writer, 'style' to the characteristics of a genre.

[2] Joseph Warton, *Essay on the Life and Writings of Pope* (London, 1782), I, 43.

> Incessant rustles from the mournful grove,
> Oft startling such as, studious, walk below,
> And slowly circles through the waving air?
> [*Autumn*, ll. 990–2]

Or, who, in speaking of a summer evening, hath ever mentioned

> The quail that clamours for his running mate?[1]

['. . . the quail clamours for his running mate', *Summer*, l. 1657]

This particularity of detail was indicative of Thomson's originality, and it provided, in contrast to Shiels's argument joining originality with genius, a critical and exact basis for contrasting Thomson's diction with the clichés of other descriptive poets. While sharing Shiels's view of vividness, that is, of the evocation of the description, Warton made an important distinction—the vividness was created by establishing an identity of reader with the narrator-spectator. Such identification defined vividness ideally, and, although it depended upon a theory of picture language, distinguished any reader's response from the proper one of the present spectator.

There are a number of important characteristics to be noted in this criticism, not the least of which is that although *The Seasons* was excellent of its kind, neither Warton nor his immediate followers thought this poetry to be the highest kind: 'I will not presume to say it is equal, either in dignity or utility, to those compositions that lay open the internal constitution of man, and that IMITATE characters, manners and sentiments.'[2] The specific images, quoted by Warton, contain none of Thomson's compounds, nor does his discussion go beyond 'minuteness'. Yet all the examples are instances of sound, action, and motion—'The living surface of the ground'.

The examples of Warton function as verification for the reader, and the critic often appeals to the reader to confirm his statements.

[1] Warton, *Essay*, I, 44. According to Chambers's *Cyclopaedia* (1741), 'turgid' or 'tumid' or 'swollen' was defined as that style 'enriched and heightened with figures and flowers of rhetoric . . . Longinus uses the terms *florid* and *affected* style, indifferently and lays them down as quite contrary to the true sublime'. The 'tumid' style is 'that immediately stuffed with big words and sentences'.

[2] Ibid., I, 50–51. 'Obscurity', according to Chambers (1741), 'is a fault that may either be in the perception, or the diction.' '*Obscurity in the diction*, may arise, first, from the ambiguity of the sense of words; secondly, from the figures or ornaments of rhetoric; thirdly, from the novelty or obsoleteness of the words.'

But when the examples of John More (1777) are examined, examples of poetic simplicity—descriptions of 'natural' affections in readily understandable language—they differ in content and expressiveness from those of Warton despite the fact that More shared Warton's criteria of vividness and truth.

> I submit it to better judges, whether the following passages, which are among the first that accrued [occurred?] to me, do not breathe as much simplicity, as a proper conciseness of language, and the necessary closeness of ideas could well permit? The first, refers to the various and amiable sensations which fill the contemplative mind, as she looks wistfully around her on the fall of the year.
>
> Ten thousand thousand fleet ideas, such
> As never mingled with the vulgar dream,
> Croud fast into the mind's creative eye.
> As fast the correspondent passions rise,
> As varied, and as high: Devotion rais'd
> To rapture, and divine astonishment;
> The love of nature unconfin'd, and, chief,
> Of human race; the large ambitious wish,
> To make them blest; the sigh for suffering worth
> Lost in obscurity; the noble scorn
> Of tyrant-pride; the fearless great resolve;
> The wonder which the dying patriot draws,
> Inspiring glory thro' remotest time;
> Th'awakened throb for virtue, and for fame;
> The sympathies of love, and friendship dear;
> With all the social Offspring of the heart.[1]
>
> [*Autumn*, ll. 1014–29]

This passage, which celebrated the power of philosophic melancholy in autumn to exalt 'the swelling thought' was an amplification of a passage taken from the 1726 version of *Winter AC* (ll. 64–73). The sublime thoughts were 'simple' in the sense that they expressed humanitarian—'amiable'—sentiments, in non-metaphoric language, for the language of 'simplicity' was, to More, natural diction. But although More's theory of diction was part of his view of poetry as

[1] John More, *Strictures Critical and Sentimental on Thomson's Seasons* (London, 1777), pp. 84–85. For a study of 'simplicity' in the eighteenth century, see Raymond D. Havens, 'Simplicity, a Changing Concept', *JHI*, XIV (1953), 3–32.

expressive of truths of nature, his example, nevertheless, revealed the bias of his taste for moral declamation. The examples of Warton were artistically defensible, but the passage quoted by More revealed that his view of simplicity did not prevent him from providing inept instances of morality as 'simple' poetry.

The passage quoted achieved the 'swelling thought' by asserting rather than evoking the sublime; 'ten thousand thousand', 'Devotion', 'divine astonishment', etc. The use of 'as' in the second line was part of the comparative 'such as', but 'as' in lines four and five referred to the 'fleet ideas' which 'croud fast'. Thus 'As fast the correspondent passions rise, / As varied, and as high' were both puzzling and awkward—puzzling because of their parallelism and awkward because of their failure to indicate the speed they were supposed to exhibit. The series of exclamatory ideas followed no increasing sequence of emotion, and the emotion of love referred to in 'the love of nature unconfin'd, and, chief, / Of human race' was found at the end in a tamer form—'the sympathies of love, and friendship dear'.[1]

It is perfectly possible in criticism to agree upon the ends of diction —e.g. the expression of precise sight or feeling—and to disagree upon the means. It is possible, also, as eighteenth-century critics only too well observed, to use the same terms but to mean different things by them. But the issue here was agreement upon ends and the 'simplicity' to arrive at them, without capacity to distinguish good from bad examples—appropriate from inappropriate examples—of simplicity. For within the same theory, the examples furnished instances of language working more complexly than the theory accounted for. Thus such examples were not only instances, as in More, of simple and 'amiable' sentiments, but of the diverse characteristics used in poetry to express them. And unless the theory was to distinguish good sentiments from good poetry, as some critics did, the example reflected the inadequacy of the critic's judgement.

Considerable examples of this occurred in the criticism of John Scott (1785), who wrote an essay devoted solely to the diction of *The Seasons*. Scott's essay was far less fragmentary than Warton's digression or More's comments on diction; it pointed out that John Aikin had explained the plan and character of *The Seasons*, 'and to Dr. Johnson's opinion of them, there is no great reason to object.

[1] *Winter A*, ll. 64–73.

Particular criticism cannot be expected to pursue her task regularly, through a Poem of such length; but the examination of some detached passages, will perhaps sufficiently point out the nature of its beauties and defects'.[1] The beauties and defects of Thomson's diction were tied, for John Scott, to a general theory of the descriptive poem: 'A descriptive poem ought to be easily intelligible. *Cooper's Hill* is so obscure, that repeated perusals are necessary to discover its meaning, which when discovered is often found to be absurd'.[2] The descriptive poem was to be readily intelligible, that is simple and clear, and vivid or forceful.

> Thomson observed closely and described forcibly. He seldom distracts the reader's attention by the introduction of heterogeneous ideas; he has few similes and few allusions; but he errs, by endeavouring to impress his subject on the mind, with a pomp and reduplication of expression. He often, in attempting energy and dignity, produces bombast and obscurity; and in avoiding meanness, becomes guilty of affectation. His language is indeed a kind of anamoly [anomaly], for which he had no example, and which it would not be easy to imitate.[3]

'Precision', 'clarity', 'simplicity', 'intelligibility', 'force', 'dignity', 'correctness', were the beauties of diction, whereas 'pomp', 'reduplication', 'meanness', 'obscurity', 'incorrectness', and 'affectation' were faults. It was, however, possible for a passage to be 'precise', but 'incorrect', or to be 'forceful' and 'pompous'. The criterion in the descriptive poem was a forceful simplicity of diction, but the theory of 'beauties' and 'faults' mixed these in the same passages, disregarding the kind of poetry which the poem or passage presented. Scott used 'classical' simplicity as the criterion of the ideal poem and in a letter to James Beattie wrote, 'My criterion of merit is classical simplicity; that is to say, the manner of Homer, the Greek tragic poets, Virgil, Milton, Pope, in contradistinction to every species of false ornament'.[4] His comments on particular characteristics of diction, therefore, while offering specific examples, made no effort to assess the private rather than the 'classic' poetic usage. Thus his

[1] John Scott, *Critical Essays* (London, 1785), p. 295. For a biographical and critical account of Scott, see Lawrence D. Stewart, *John Scott of Amwell* (Berkeley and Los Angeles, 1956). See also John Scott, *A Letter to the Critical Reviewers* (London, 1782).

[2] Scott, *Essays*, p. 13.

[3] Scott, *Essays*, p. 296.

[4] Stewart, p. 165.

use of examples did not explain Thomson's general manner, but compared it to his criterion:

> Our poet's picture of the approach and descent of a '*vernal shower*' is one of his capital pieces. It is a fair specimen of his general manner; its beauties and defects are so intermixed, that it is no easy matter to separate them.
>
> Gradual sinks the breeze
> Into a perfect calm; that not a breath
> Is heard to quiver through the *closing* woods,
> Or rustling turn the *many-twinkling* leaves
> Of aspen tall. The uncurling floods, diffused
> In glossy breadth, *seem through delusive lapse*
> *Forgetful of their course*. 'Tis silence all,
> And pleasing expectation. Herds and flocks
> Drop the dry sprig, *and mute-imploring eye*
> The *falling verdure*. Hushed in short suspense,
> *The plumy people streak their wings with oil*
> To throw the *lucid moisture* trickling off,
> And wait the approaching sign to strike at once
> Into the general choir. Even mountains, vales,
> And forests *seem*, *impatient*, to demand
> The *promised sweetness*. Man superior walks
> Amid the glad creation, musing praise
> And looking lively gratitude. At last
> The clouds consign their treasures to the fields,
> And, softly shaking on the dimpled pool
> Prelusive drops, let all their moisture flow
> *In large effusion o'er the freshened world.*
>
> [*Spring*, ll. 155–76]

There are here two kinds of circumstances, one actually existent in nature, and one the product of the Poet's imagination. The calm is of the first sort, and is forcibly expressed by the quietness of the aspen, and the glassiness of the water. The '*floods seeming forgetful of their course*' is of the second, and might be an allowable hyperbole; but in the present case it wants propriety. A poetical mind too seldom thinks with precision; imagination is apt to act without judgment, and confound one object with another. The floods could not seem '*forgetful of their course*,' for their *course* was not stopped. On the cessation of the wind, the curl or undulation on the surface would cease, but the motion of the current would not be destroyed. When the gale sank, a pool would become smooth; but a river which ran before, would run still, and with the same velocity. To say that the floods seem forgetful of their course, 'through delusive lapse' is to talk nonsense . . . The '*prelusive drops on the dimpled pool,*' is a beautiful stroke; but it was unnecessary to say, first, that '*The clouds consign their treasures to the fields,*' and next, that they '*let all their moisture flow in large effusion o'er the freshen'd world.*'[1]

This passage was characteristic of Scott's close analysis and indicates his awareness of good passages, and the limitations of his critical method. For Scott, imagination and reality were distinguished, and he treated the reality-sense of the description, and the imagery or 'product of the Poet's imagination'. Thomson forcefully expressed the natural environment, but inappropriately used his imagery. Lack of 'propriety' here characterized an untrue image, one contrary to fact. But the image, 'the uncurling floods, diffused / In glassy breadth, seem through delusive lapse / Forgetful of their course', was not contrary to fact. Thomson wrote 'seem' and the river, become smooth and glassy and broad, seems not to move, that is, forgetful of its course. But the circling waves which become uncurled and smooth as glass seem, by becoming something other than themselves, also to forget themselves. The narrator is explaining that the sinking of the breeze preparatory to the storm creates a bewitching calm of the trees, leaves, and rivers, and an expectation in the animals and man. The argument from reality misread the image, though the implied personification was, no doubt, here as elsewhere in the poem, a further reason for objection. For the flood, 'diffused / In glassy breadth'—terms appropriate to a river, but not to a human being—also seems 'forgetful', an attribute of a human being. But just this kind of metaphorical transfer characterized Thomson's illustrations of man and nature as common objects of the universe.

Scott was quite right in declaring that 'Even mountains, vales / And forests seem, impatient, to demand / The promised sweetness' was misplaced, since the order appeared that of nature, animals, and man. But even if one considered 'Man superior' as a factual rather than a value assertion, and thus justified the order of Thomson, the lines were inept poetry because they asserted the emotion they should have evoked.

But the statement made by Scott's contemporary, John Pinkerton, in the same year, 1785, in which Scott's essay was published drew

[1] Scott, *Essays*, pp. 298–9.

attention to one of the implications of the essay on diction. Pinkerton wrote:

> Of any works which have obtained considerable applause, Thomson's poem of The Seasons is the most incorrect. Any reader who understands grammar and classic composition, is disgusted in every page of that poem by faults, which, tho in themselves minute, yet to a refined eye hide and obscure every beauty however great, as a very small intervening object will intercept the view of the sun. This reason makes me very much suspect the fame of the Seasons will not be of long existence; for I know of no work that has inherited long reputation which is deficient in style, as the Seasons undoubtedly are to a most remarkable degree.[1]

Pinkerton did not disagree with Scott on the mixture of beauties and faults in *The Seasons*, although his evaluation of it was also governed by 'grammar and classic composition'—the basis for a proper 'style'. Now Shiels had identified Thomson's style in this poem with 'an air peculiarly his own'—'style' was here the manner of expression which characterized a work or a writer, a summary of his peculiar characteristics. And this individuality was supported by Patrick Murdoch, by John More, and by Samuel Johnson: 'As a writer he is entitled to one praise of the highest kind: his mode of thinking, and of expressing his thoughts, is original . . . His numbers, his pauses, his diction, are of his own growth, without transcription, without imitation.'[2]

In distinguishing between theories which identified 'style' with particular traits of a writer, and those which identified it with a particular kind of writing, it is significant to inquire what it would mean 'to be deficient in style'. For Shiels, such a question is meaningless when 'style' is used in his accustomed sense, the poet's manner of expression. The 'style' may not be suitable for certain genres, but it cannot be 'deficient'. For Pinkerton and Scott such a question is answered by the departures from a 'classic style'. It seems reasonable to assert that the criterion of a 'classic style' is appropriate only if, indeed, it is the kind of style a writer is using. Whatever inadequacies one may find in the enumeration of specific traits composing a poetic 'manner', these are relevant to the discovery of 'style' but

[1] John Pinkerton (R. Heron, pseud.), *Letters on Literature* (London, 1785), pp. 64–65.

[2] Samuel Johnson, *Lives of the English Poets*, ed. George Birkbeck Hill (Oxford, 1905), III, 298.

not to its denial. Pinkerton was declaring what *The Seasons* ought to do, not what it did or sought to do in diction.

Scott had written that Thomson's 'language is indeed a kind of anamoly [anomaly], for which he had no example, and which it would not be easy to imitate'.[1] But in his detailed method of example, commentary, and evaluation, Scott made several points which were not, in his terms, crucial, and which indicated that the method called forth explanations that were important, but incidental to his general conception. Scott referred to the use of 'favourite words'—words which a writer used time and again—and he tried to distinguish between contexts which used compound words and those which did not.

The 'favourite word' which an author used Scott called a defect because it meant succumbing to a natural inclination which led to artistic dependence.

> It is a circumstance that cannot have escaped notice, that most authors have their favourite words, which they are apt to introduce too often. There seems a natural inclination to commit this fault, and I have perhaps committed it myself, though it has disgusted me in the work of others. I have already remarked, that Goldsmith, in his Deserted Village, has used the substantive '*Sports*,' and the adjective '*sweet*' to an excess. Thomson seemed to have a predilection for this word 'snatch'd'; his fishing line is 'snatch'd from the hoary steed.' Spring, line 384 [*Spring*, l. 386] has been noticed; and in line 516 [*Spring*, l. 518], he talks of 'snatching a hurried eye through a verdant maze.' He once uses it properly: The kiss 'snatch'd hasty from the sidelong maid.' *Winter*, l. 625.[2]

Scott's own poetry made him aware of factors that his theory explained away, but it cannot be denied that the frequency of terms like 'bounded', 'snatched', and others drew attention to traits of Thomson's language. But the 'detached' method of Scott's criticism, the absence of adequate statistical data and the readiness to assimilate all instances of linguistic usage into 'propriety' and 'correctness' despite his admission that specific words and passages were nevertheless effective—the attempt to consider the poem in ideal terms—limited the effectiveness of his commentary. Scott recognized that 'diction' revealed diverse attributes of a word, but 'force', 'clarity', 'simplicity', 'propriety', did not, in Scott's theory, alter its given

[1] Scott, *Essays*, p. 296. [2] Ibid., pp. 320–1.

meaning. Thus the line 'Snatched through the verdant maze, the hurried eye / Distracted wanders' (*Spring*, ll. 518–19) implied the vigour with which the view seized the eye, and the synecdoche dealt with the forceful pull of the verdant maze. The 'snatched' in the *Winter* line, 'The kiss, snatched hasty from the sidelong maid / On purpose guardless, or pretending sleep' (ll.625–6) implied a seizure unresisted, even welcomed, so that that 'snatched' implied playfulness without opposition or force.

Scott was cognizant of Thomson's compounds and new-coined words, as well as his 'metaphorical expressions'. He saw them as efforts to elevate or vary the diction, and found them unsuccessful because exceptional, yet there seemed in his theory of language no room for the exception.

> Where a subject occupies any considerable number of lines, it is commonly necessary to mention it repeatedly, either in the same terms or in others. The permitting one word to recur frequently, has been justly termed a slovenly practice; and writers, to avoid it, often have recourse to a kind of metonymical, or rather catachrestical expressions which are mostly either improper or inelegant. Thomson has a great number of these quaint phrases of his own construction . . . The single circumstance of rain, is described by no less than seven different appellations [above passage]; it is called 'falling verdure,' 'lucid moisture,' 'promised sweetness,' 'treasures of the clouds,' 'heaven descending in universal bounty,' 'fruits and flowers,' and lastly, 'milky nutriment.'[1]

The reason given by Scott for the use of these images—the avoidance of repetition of 'rain' or 'shower'—seems in the light of eighteenth-century descriptive poetry as well as of *The Seasons* to be inadequate. These terms were considered 'improper', 'inelegant', and 'catachrestical' because, for the most part, they were extravagant comparisons. But 'falling verdure', 'promised sweetness', 'treasures of the clouds', 'heaven descending in universal bounty', 'fruits and flowers', and 'milky nutriment' are instances of the consequences of the shower. In this language of Thomson, the future appears *in potentia* in the present, and the shower is described by the products it will bring forth. 'Lucid moisture' is not an image but a factual description, and in the language of growing nature there was a distinction between 'falling verdure', 'treasures of the clouds', and 'milky nutriment'. The first was an example of the falling shower seen in

[1] Scott, *Essays*, pp. 303–4.

terms of its natural product—the second was part of a formal contrasting with an informal image and 'milky nutriment' was scientific terminology. Each of these functioned in a special way to achieve poetic meaning, and it was an unfortunate reduction to attribute one function to all these images.

Scott recognized their function as poetic diction and variation, but he did not see their relevance to a continually transforming nature. Some of his particular examples, like 'promised sweetness', were improper, but since all were judged by a general theory of language propriety which admitted that passages frequently incorrect were moving and poetically forceful, the general theory was not very helpful. It was for this reason that critics like John Pinkerton, who shared the assumption of 'correctness' with Scott, advocated abandonment of general theory for the collection of specific observations, though even observations would have to be undertaken with some linguistic assumptions—no doubt those of the discarded theory. But the point is that observations would make data available and make release from inadequate generalizations more likely.

But this was not the direction which the study of diction in *The Seasons* took. The method of comparative analysis used incidentally by Scott and extensively by Robert Heron (1793) became one of several approaches to diction. Instead of attending to particular details, comparing the general characteristics of Thomson in *The Seasons* with those of other poets, many critics made diction an expression—spontaneous or otherwise—of the imagination, usually the associative imagination, analysable on the basis of whatever assumptions the critic had about imagination.

The decline of particular dictional analysis followed from another consequence—the variety of terms for diction had become so diverse and controversial that distinctions were reduced rather than increased during the nineteenth century. 'Obscurity' of diction could be a necessary consequence of obscure subject matter, or the result of a failure in poetic communication. 'I only observe in one Word', wrote Joseph Trapp in 1713, 'that a clear Style is never faulty, an obscure and uncouth one always so; but that the easy or the strong, the short or prolix, the loose or close, the brisk or slow, the sweet or soft, or the rough and harsh, are all of them sometimes proper, sometimes improper, according to the Subject Matter of the Poem they appear in.'[1] Clarity, for Trapp, was the use of language appropriate to the

[1] Joseph Trapp, *Lectures on Poetry* (1713) (London, 1742), pp. 92–93.

subject, and obscurity a neglect of such use. But this view of 'obscurity' was tied to simplicity of thought expressed in simple words, in Locke's definition of 'perspicuity'—'the using of proper terms for thoughts, which a man would have passed from his own mind to that of another's'.[1] It did not, however, take account of the obscurity of the scriptures, and, in the words of Patrick Murdoch (1762), the *Hymn to the Seasons* was in this scriptural tradition: 'In imitation of the Hebrew Bard, all nature is called forth to do homage to the Creator, and the reader is left enraptured in silent adoration and praise.'[2]

The argument of obscurity in scripture was sometimes separated from that in secular books, the latter being judged by common knowledge. But even Bishop Butler saw analogies between the scriptural argument and satire. He went into considerable detail in analysing the problem of obscurity in scripture and he pointed out that the 'mythological [fable], and the satirical, where the satire is, to a certain degree, concealed', were analogical to scripture in appearing obscure. He declared that a critic 'might be fully assured, that such Persons and Events were intended in a Satyrical Writing, merely from its being applicable to them . . . For, his Satisfaction, that he understood the Meaning, the intended Meaning, of these Writings, would be greater or less in Proportion as he saw the general Turn of them to be capable of such Application: and in Proportion to the Number of particular things capable of it.'[3]

Bishop Butler did not prepare very clear criteria for adequacy of interpretation, for he implied that the critic's satisfaction (that he understood the meaning) was the proper criterion. He also pointed out an argument which, again, was directed at a distinction between literature and scripture, but which was clearly applicable to literature when the assumptions about man's rationality altered. For Butler assumed that 'the meaning of a book is nothing but the meaning of the author'.[4] Butler assumed too readily that the 'meaning of the author' was uncomplicated, but even he realized that in editing memoirs the editor often did not know the full meaning of the work and that the reader sometimes saw what the editor did not.

With regard to scripture, the authors of the books were obviously

[1] Samuel Johnson, *Dictionary of the English Language* (London, 1755).
[2] Patrick Murdoch, *The Works of James Thomson* (London, 1762), I, ix.
[3] Joseph Butler, *Analogy of Religion* (London, 1736), p. 252.
[4] Ibid., p. 253.

inspired, and thus they did not know the full intent of what they were writing. Butler, of course, accepted the assumption that truth was attainable, if God chose to reveal it, and in his analogy to literature he implied that there always was a 'whole' meaning, though he tended to avoid the question whether variant interpretations were wrong or merely part of the whole: 'though I think it clear, that the Prophets did not understand the full Meaning of their Predictions; it is another Question how far they thought they did, and in what Sense they understood them'.[1]

Another argument defending obscurity in scripture was developed by John Husbands in the preface to *A Miscellany* (1731).[2] He argued that scriptural language was the primitive language of man and that as a result of man's refinement he had ceased to understand the beauty of this language. The language was obscure because its beauty was hidden from corrupted man; it was a language composed in the East by a strange people and time and custom had made it obscure. Its obscurity could be overcome only by immersing oneself in belief.

But the fullest defence of obscurity in didactic poetry came from Bishop Lowth in his discussion of Hebrew parables and proverbs. Proverbs, wrote Bishop Lowth (1753), 'instantaneously stimulate or affect the mind; they penetrate deeply, and are firmly retained'.[3]

The argument in justification of some types of obscurity was based on subject matter and the effect upon the reader: some subjects 'of their own nature can't admit that clearness and perspicuity which must be in other occasions, wherein Aristotle has reason to place perspicuity as the first and most necessary point of writing well. Yet *metaphysical* notions, excess of passion as rage or despair, perplexities of mind, speculative and contemplative reflections, and the like can hardly ever be totally free from something of obscurity and confusion.' But not only were there subjects which did not permit clarity because they dealt with speculative or hidden matters, but 'in

[1] Butler, p. 254.

[2] John Husbands, *A Miscellany of Poems by Several Hands* (Oxford, 1731), Preface. Selections from the essay appear in *Eighteenth Century Critical Essays*, ed. Scott Elledge (Ithaca, 1961), II, 416–31. For a discussion of John Husbands see R. C. Crane, 'An Early Eighteenth Century Enthusiast for Primitive Poetry: John Husbands', *MLN*, XXXVII (1922), 27–36.

[3] Robert Lowth, *Lectures on the Sacred Poetry of the Hebrews* (London, 1787), II, 168, originally published in Latin, 1753.

writing room must be left for the reader's wit and sharpness in seeing beyond the surface of words'.[1]

> For as I have read somewhere, we are then doubly pleased with an Author, who while thus we see his wit, makes us reflect upon his own; and gives us occasion to flatter ourselves, that we penetrate farther than every vulgar reader, who, as we imagine, will never take the hint and carry it to the thoughts we have upon it.[2]

Obscurity which made it possible for the reader to exercise his feeling and intelligence, discriminated between vulgar and sensitive readers. Defence of obscurity, therefore, could imply a differentiation of audience. John More (1777), like those critics who defined poetry as the communication of feeling, insisted on ready response of any 'common' reader as a guide to clarity. 'I should imagine most of the obscurity we meet with in *The Seasons* to arise from violent inversions of style, over-wrought descriptions, and a culpable use of technical phrases.'[3] In giving examples of this obscurity More named two instances 'in which the leading idea is almost buried among a multitude of accessory ones, and where for me, at least, he is much too profound to be plain'. The second instance was the description of frost which, 'masterly and expressive, has no other fault indeed, but that it requires rather too much attention, either to comprehend its meaning, or relish its beauties'.[4]

But this very same passage was defended, from different views, by two other critics. John Aikin (1778) declared that 'to reject those grand and beautiful ideas which a philosophical view of nature offers to the mind, merely because they are above the comprehension of vulgar readers, is surely an unnecessary degradation of this noble art'.[5] The ground for Aikin's position was the truth value of these ideas, and the failure to grasp this truth did not deny its poetic significance. Scott's view, however, that the passage was 'graphical even to the very greatest minuteness, and . . . not justly charged with . . . verbosity', was based on knowledge of the scientific theory

[1] Lowth, *Lectures*, II, 168–9.

[2] John Constable, *Reflections upon Accuracy of Style* (London, 1734), p. 122.

[3] John More, *Strictures Critical and Sentimental on Thomson's Seasons* (London, 1777), p. 91.

[4] More, *Strictures*, p. 95.

[5] John Aikin, 'An Essay on the Plan and Character of the Poem', *The Seasons* (London, 1778), p. xvii.

of frost and the almost-scientific precision of the description, 'minuteness' here referring to detailed accuracy.

By the end of the eighteenth century, 'obscurity' as applied to the diction of *The Seasons* was used infrequently, and 'pompous', 'turgid', 'affected', remained throughout the nineteenth century the terms of disapprobation. But the discussions of diction did not continue close (minute) comparison between similar passages or images. In the discussions of 'obscurity' and other terms, the diversity led not to analysis and evaluation of diversity but to a justification for it. In so far as nature poets began to develop the tradition made famous by Thomson, the procedure was to explain the diction by reference to some type of associationism. Another reason for this methodological change was the accepted hostility to an eighteenth-century 'poetic diction'—in Wordsworth's terms—for it was he who said that Thomson wrote a vicious 'style'.

Wordsworth had set down his interpretation of eighteenth-century poetic diction in his 1800 preface and the 1802 'Appendix'. In 1800 Wordsworth wrote:

> The Reader will find that personifications of abstract ideas rarely occur in these volumes; and are utterly rejected, as an ordinary device to elevate the style, and raise it above prose. My purpose was to imitate, and, as far as possible, to adopt the very language of men; and assuredly such personifications do not make any natural or regular part of that language. They are, indeed, a figure of speech occasionally prompted by passion, and I have made use of them as such; but have endeavoured utterly to reject them as a mechanical device of style, or as a family language which Writers in metre seem to lay claim to by prescription . . . There will also be found in these volumes little of what is usually called poetic diction.[1]

[1] W. J. B. Owen, ed., *Wordsworth's Preface to Lyrical Ballads* (Copenhagen, 1957), pp. 117–18. See also Marjorie L. Barstow, *Wordsworth's Theory of Poetic Diction* (New Haven, 1917). For a contemporary attack on Wordsworth's poetic language theory, and an attempt to reject it by reference to the Pope–Bowles controversy (the romantic-classic controversy), see Martin McDermot, 'Preliminary View of Literature of the Age', *The Beauties of Modern Literature* (London, 1824), pp. xxvi–xxxvi. As an example of the perverted taste of natural and simple language, McDermot quoted from epitaphs on tombstones (pp. xxx–xxxiii). The argument that these epitaphs were undistinguished and tasteless poetry was directed against the assumption that language which led to religious musings or reflections had inherent poetic suggestiveness. For a typical example of epitaph poetry, see George Wright, *Pleasing Melancholy or a Walk among*

Wordsworth attacked personification, pompous language, inherited images, because these were impermanent in their appeal. As W. J. B. Owen has pointed out, the comment on diction 'means no more than that his [Wordsworth's] language avoids conventional poeticisms'.[1] In 1802, when Wordsworth added the 'Appendix' on poetic diction, he provided a primitivistic theory derived from John Brown and others, to explain what theories of classical simplicity or 'Eastern' freedom had attacked or defended.

There was the authority of the past for noting the force and turgidity of Thomson's language and no new theory of language led to a classification of his 'diction'. Thus critical assertions accumulated, and the characteristics which in Scott and Heron made it possible, by specific examination, to judge the reliability of these assertions ceased to appear. The major concern was with the explanation for force and vigour as qualities of imagination or spontaneous skill.

In 1806 there appeared in the *Edinburgh Review* an analysis of J. Poulin's translation of *The Seasons*, and the critic declared that 'upon the whole, without being unfaithful, it is perhaps an improvement on the original. Many of these brilliant and masterly expressions have indeed been overlooked, which are scattered here and there, like gems, in the poetry of Thomson; but the general heaviness and encumbrance of his style has been relieved, without any material deviation from his leading thoughts and expressions.'[2] There were three major faults in *The Seasons*: (1) blank verse which was really

[1] Owen, p. 27. For the primitivistic assumptions of Wordsworth's 'Appendix', see Owen, pp. 192–4. See also Roy Harvey Pearce, 'The Eighteenth Century Scottish Primitivists: Some Reconsiderations', *ELH*, XII (1945), 203–20.

[2] 'Les Saisons de J. Thomson. Traduits en Vers Français par J. Poulin', *Edinburgh Review*, VII (Edinburgh, 1806), 329. For a bibliography and discussion of German translations of *The Seasons*, see Morton Collins Stewart, 'Barthold Heinrich Broches' Rendering of Thomson's *Seasons* and the Later German Translations', *JEGP*, X (1911), 20–41, 197–213, 378–414. See also C. H. Ibershoff, 'A German Translation of Passages in Thomson's *Seasons*,' *MLN*, XXVI (1911), 107–9.

the Tombs in a Country Church Yard, in the Stile and Manner of Hervey's Meditations; To Which Are Added Epitaphs, Elegies and Inscriptions, In Prose and Verse (London, 1793). For Wordsworth's view on epitaphs and their language that McDermot was attacking, see 'Upon Epitaphs' (1810), *Wordsworth's Literary Criticism*, ed. Nowell C. Smith (London, 1905), pp. 79–143. For the Bowles–Byron controversy, see J. J. Van Rennes, *Bowles, Byron and the Pope-Controversy* (Amsterdam, 1927).

couplets with the rhyme erased; (2) incoherent unity; (3) 'the laboured, pedantic, and injudicious phraseology, which frequently destroys the effect of ideas the most happily conceived and skilfully detailed'. The basis for (1) was the frequency of Thomson's end-stopped lines which created the expectancy of rhyme. Although the critic wisely selected as example the farmer's check of the plague (*Spring*, ll. 127–36), a passage which was full of end-stops, his example from Lavinia and Palemon was not convincing: 'Some expressions in his description of Lavinia have great beauty; but the whole bears the appearance of having been written with rhymes, and afterwards *done into blank verse*; and here the French poetry has some advantage, we think, over the original.'[1]

But despite the fact that this critical selectivity was exceedingly strange, since the nature passages would seem the most appropriate in which to test the verse, the translation of the famous passage did not support the critic:

A native grace
Sat fair-proportioned on her polished limbs,
Veiled in a simple robe, their best attire,
Beyond the pomp of dress; for loveliness
Needs not the foreign aid of ornament,
But is when unadorned adorned the most.
Thoughtless of beauty, she was beauty's self,
Recluse amid the close-embowering woods.
[*Autumn*, ll. 201–8]

Car, pour plaire et toucher, l'amabilité pure
Dédaigne le secours d'une vaine parure,
Et brille d'autant plus qu'elle a moins d'ornemens.
Sans connoitre de prix de ses attraits charmans,
Sans connoitre le beau, c'étoit la beauté même.
Derobant aux regards la puissance suprême.

But the critic's view of Thomson's injudicious phraseology led him to praise the elimination of one of Thomson's most interesting images on the grounds of a more correct language:

And o'er the high piled hills of fractur'd earth
Wide-dash'd the waves in undulation vast;
Till from the center to the streaming clouds
A shoreless ocean *tumbled round* the globe.
[*Spring*, ll. 313–6]

[1] *Edinburgh Review*, VII, 329.

> Aussitôt a sa voix les ondes elancées
> Engloutirent les monts sous leur masse pressées;
> Et jusque dans son centre, avec force entr'ouvert,
> D'un océan sans bords le globe fut couvert.[1]

And in an associative analysis of some of Thomson's diction in 1809, Edward Mangin demonstrated that 'imaginative' associative principles were governed by appropriate selection of associated details—and in the specific example 'gallant Vernon' quoted by Warton and Heron, Mangin resorted to the same explanation merely couching it in terms of proper associationist language.

> In Thomson's description of a scene of this kind on the coast of Carthagena, that engaging poet has omitted every loathsome circumstance, and touched the terrible with but a gentle hand, while he holds up to view the particulars which are calculated to awaken our tenderest compassion.
>
> You, gallant Vernon, saw
> The miserable scene; you pitying saw
> To infant weakness sunk the warrior's arm;
> Saw the deep-racking pang . . .
> [*Summer*, ll. 1041–4]
>
> In those distressful scenes which we form in our imagination, or which are presented to us by the novelist or dramatic poet, the whole story is brought at once before us, and all the pathetic circumstances, which are unknown or overlooked in real life, may be exhibited in their full force.[2]

(b) WILLIAM HAZLITT, ALLAN CUNNINGHAM, ROBERT BELL, ETC.: THE STABILITY OF JUDGEMENT

> His faults were those of his style—of the author and the man.
>
> W. HAZLITT

The judgement regarding Thomson's diction was continued by Wordsworth who, in 1815, declared that 'notwithstanding his high powers, he writes a vicious style; and his false ornaments are exactly

[1] *Edinburgh Review*, VII, 331.

[2] Edward Mangin, *Essays on the Sources of Pleasure Received from Literary Compositions* (London, 1809), p. 26; also pp. 76–77. See also J. B., 'Comparison of Virgil and Thomson', *The Northern Star*, I (1817), 344.

of that kind which would be most likely to strike the undiscerning. He likewise abounds with sentimental commonplaces.'[1] Now Wordsworth continued Warton's tradition of praising Thomson for his precision, but his 'false ornaments' were the result of a body of readers who welcomed bad taste. Thomson's originality went, according to Wordsworth, unappreciated by the many. This view was attacked by John Wilson (1831) on the grounds that some statements were wrong, others exaggerated. Although Thomson sometimes wrote a vicious style and commonplace sentiments, such sins are not very frequent in the 'Seasons', and were all committed in the glow of that fine enthusiasm, which to his imagination arrayed all things, and all words, in a light that seemed to him at the time to be poetry—though sometimes it was but 'false glitter'.[2] Wilson recognized that Thomson sometimes wrote with inaccurate knowledge and a false sense of the emotions he worked to evoke. The example suggests that his control over his material was sometimes ambiguous —and this had to be considered in the 'wholeness' of Thomson.

> The godlike face of man avails him naught.
> Even Beauty, force divine! at whose bright glance
> The generous lion stands in softened gaze,
> Here bleeds, a hapless undistinguished prey.
> But if, apprised of the severe attack,
> The country be shut up, lured by the scent,
> On churchyards drear (inhuman to relate!)
> The disappointed prowlers fall, and dig
> The shrouded body from the grave; o'er which,
> Mixed with foul shades and frighted ghosts, they howl.
> [*Winter*, ll. 404–13]

Wilson ridiculed the softened gaze of the lion and declared that Thomson 'so far from making poetry of it in this passage has vulgarized and blurred by it the natural and inevitable emotion of terror and pity. Famished wolves *waking* up the dead is a dreadful image—but "*human to relate*" is not an expression heavily laden with meaning'. In comparing Wilson's comments on the rain passage

[1] William Wordsworth, 'Essay Supplementary to Preface', *Wordsworth's Literary Criticism*, ed. Nowell Smith (London, 1905), p. 186. For a discussion of the term 'style' in art criticism applicable to literary theory, see Meyer Schapiro, 'Style', *Aesthetics Today*, ed. Morris Philipson (New York, 1961), pp. 81–113.

[2] John Wilson (Christopher North), 'Winter Rhapsody', *Blackwood's Magazine*, XXIX (1831), 296.

in *Spring* with Scott's, it is apparent that despite the similar judgements, Wilson's understanding of Thomson's language was more adequate than that of Wordsworth or Scott.

> Equally great are the words—
>
> Herds and flocks
> Drop the dry sprig, and, mute-imploring, eye
> The falling verdure.
>
> [*Spring*, ll. 162–4]
>
> The verdure is seen in the shower—to be the very shower—by the poet at least—perhaps by the cattle, in their thirsty hunger forgetful of the brown ground, and swallowing the dropping herbage.[1]

Wilson recognized that Thomson used language to refer to transforming nature—he explained it associatively—and he was cognizant of him here in the roles of 'humane' and 'religious' poet.

In 1843 the reviewer of Wilson's *Recreations of Christopher North* pointed out that the particular criticism of Wilson, 'its minute dissection of particular passages, both as to thought and diction, carries us back to the thought and diction of Addison and Johnson, rather than to our own time'.[2] The reviewer saw the history of criticism as a series of periodic evolutions due to the exhaustion of a particular kind of criticism. The development of general criticism at the beginning of the nineteenth century was 'the natural reaction which followed against an effete and worn-out system'.

> By degrees it was found to be much easier to deal with these generalities and abstractions than to descend to particulars;—to frame a theory, or write a philosophical essay having the slenderest application to the case in hand, than to direct the criticism to the real appreciation of the work to be reviewed. At best, our criticism became in great measure limited to some sketch of the general design of the work, and its relation to the particular theory patronised for the time by the critic.[3]

To these strictures there were occasional exceptions, and John Wilson was one: 'to this system of praise and blame, unaccompanied by a due application of critical particulars, the practice of the writer of these Recreations stands opposed'.

[1] John Wilson, *Recreations*, II, 260–1.

[2] *Edinburgh Review*, LXXVII (Edinburgh, 1846), 86. Note that this statement about history is expressed in customary cyclical personifications.

[3] *Edinburgh Review*, LXXVII, 87.

In Wilson's criticism the references to the 'poet' and to the 'imagination' supplied no proper guide to the critic's values, but his examples did. Robert Heron, Wordsworth, Nicolas, A. Cunningham, and others referred to the imagination in explaining the language of the poet, whereas Warton referred to the force and vigour of his description. But the difference in explanation of 'imagination' among the critics themselves was not the result of any shared theory, merely a shared expression. Wordsworth's theory was based on the response of the audience, Heron's on a theory of imagery, Wilson's on a sense of enthusiasm, Hazlitt's on character and personality, Nicolas's on conscious and non-conscious intent, and Cunningham's on the response of the common reader. But the significant difference between these critics and Scott (but not Warton, Murdoch, and Stockdale) was the fact that they sought to characterize the writer as a whole. They were not interested in the beauties and faults, but in the characteristic qualities.

There existed for them no new information about Thomson's language; they sought to apply generalizations from associationism and from Thomson's life to his language. But these generalizations did not explain the language; they constituted excuses for, rather than analyses of, the uneven diction. Yet the stability of judgement offers two conclusions about the development of criticism: (1) the irrelevancy of certain kinds of generalization, (2) the importance of retrospective validity.

The use of generalizations to explain data is relevant only if the data are or can be derived from the generalization that forms the basis for them. The imposition of theories of imagination upon diction did not explain the diction, and in the examples of Wilson, the insights into Thomson's usage were the result of a particular analysis of the passage in terms of its implications rather than in terms of any prescribed 'classical simplicity'. The characteristic quality became an implied quantitative criterion, not one based on analysis of usage. The recommendation of varied types of 'imagination', therefore, became exploratory or speculative generalizations, but in Hazlitt and Wilson, the contribution to Thomson's diction rested on statements about the poetry or on the comparisons of *The Seasons* with *The Task*. In these comparisons the generalizations became of little relevance. Where the generalizations were most prominent, there led to unreliable and inaccurate statements about Thomson, and they created a history of irrelevance.

Hazlitt (1818) had written that the defects of Thomson's writing were the defects of his character. Thomson was indolent, 'frequently pedantic and ostentatious in his style, because he had no consciousness of these vices in himself . . . He takes advantage of all the most trite and mechanical common-places of imagery and diction as a kindly relief to his Muse, and as if he thought them quite as good, and likely to be quite as acceptable to the reader, as his own poetry.'[1] Nevertheless, Thomson's original genius could not be submerged by affectation or false ornaments.

Although in *The Castle of Indolence* there was John Armstrong's stanza which traditionally referred to Thomson as one who on 'nature's pleasing themes, / Pour'd forth his unpremeditated strain', there was no reason to assume that Thomson was indolent about writing—he certainly was not about rewriting. Craik in 1861 declared that Thomson 'pours forth his unpremeditated song apparently without the thought ever occurring to him that he could improve it by any study or elaboration',[2] but the 1864 edition of *The Seasons* pointed out that the numerous corrections 'manifest how gradually, and with how much premeditation, the poet's style actually was formed'.[3]

Hazlitt identified Thomson's transformational language: 'nature in his descriptions is seen growing around us, fresh and lusty as in itself'. This sense of the growth and unfolding of nature resulted from Hazlitt's insight into the poem, and an analysis of Thomson's language and imagery does, indeed, confirm this view. Thus there

[1] William Hazlitt, *Lectures on the English Poets* (London, 1841), p. 165. See David Nichol Smith, *Some Observations on Eighteenth Century Poetry* (Oxford, 1937).

[2] George L. Craik, *A Compendious History of English Literature* (London, 1861), II, 268. Thomas Arnold, however, disagreed with him about Thomson's 'inspiration' or 'imagination', confusing 'imagination' with dreamy mysticism and finding only 'correctness' in Thomson's descriptions. Thomas Arnold, *A Manual of English Literature* (London, 1862), pp. 312–13: 'Even in describing nature, Thomson betrays a signal want of imagination; he saw correctly what was before him—the outward shows of things—but never had a glimpse of

> The light that never was on sea or land,
> The inspiration, and the poet's dream.'

For the attribution of an 'objective' view of nature to Thomson's *Seasons*, see Chapter IV.

[3] Preface, *The Seasons* (Edinburgh, 1864).

is here an example of what might properly be called *retrospective validity*. As a result of our knowledge now of what Thomson was doing, it becomes possible to point out that such criticism was not dependent upon the generalization of imagination, but upon Hazlitt's differentiation of Thomson from Cowper. Within the theories of imagination, the comments of some critics are more adequate than those of others, but their adequacy is the result of their insight into characteristics of the poem which the theory itself does not account for. Hazlitt wished to evoke the spirit of the poet for his listeners, but, so too, did John More, the first 'appreciator' of *The Seasons*. Yet More did not find in the poem the same qualities as Hazlitt, though he, too, found the poem an imaginative expression of Thomson. Hazlitt evoked the enthusiasm of Thomson's descriptions, but he and subsequent critics distinguished between the episodes or narratives and the natural description. More, for example, discussed these episodes as 'descriptions'—Celadon and Amelia, Damon and Musidora, Palemon and Lavinia. In referring to the Damon episode, he wrote 'there is in the whole Episode . . . a beautiful assemblage of the most luxuriant images, yet couched in a language so peculiarly inoffensive and expressive'. But Hazlitt wrote that the 'selections which have been made from his [Thomson's] works in Enfield's Speaker, and other books of extracts, do not convey the most formidable idea of his genius and taste; such as Palemon and Lavinia, Damon and Musidora, Celadon and Amelia'.[1] The diction of these episodes was not discussed and the shift in evaluation was based in Musidora on the implied immorality noticed by Wordsworth and other sophisticated readers. But the other two episodes lost their authority, in Hazlitt's view, because they were examples of artificial—'framed and glazed'—poetry.

In 1830 Sir Harris Nicolas reiterated that 'it has been said that the style of that work is pompous, and that it contains many faults. The remark is partially true. His style is, in some places, monotonous, from its unvaried elevation; but to him Nature was a subject of the profoundest reverence, and he, doubtless, considered that she ought to be spoken of with solemnity; though it is evident from one of his verses, which is often cited, that he was aware simplicity is the most becoming garb of majesty and beauty.'[2]

[1] Hazlitt, *Lectures*, pp. 173–4.

[2] Sir Harris Nicolas, *The Poetical Works of James Thomson* (London, 1830), I, lxxxii.

These remarks were less a statement about Thomson's diction than an apology for his faults in terms of intent. Since nature was the subject of profound reverence, Thomson sought to write constantly in a tone of 'unvaried elevation'. But here it must be noticed that Sir Harris Nicolas, who printed a number of letters, gathered information unknown till then, and printed a number of specimen alterations of the revised *Winter* (1726), conveyed misinformation in his comments on the diction and lacked the knowledge that Scott and Heron had provided. For the diction of the poem was not 'unvaried elevation'; it contained variant styles of the pathetic, the sublime, the comic, and the burlesque. The comments upon diction remained untouched by the careful historical method employed in marshalling facts about Thomson's life.

Simultaneous with this view there developed other excuses for Thomson's diction, excuses derived from the historical study of literature, concealed by an appeal to Thomson's originality. In Warton and again in Aikin (1777,1778), Thomson's originality was seen to consist in certain precise uses of language. Aikin identified such uses with a new era in poetry. But George Moir in 1839 used Thomson's independence of Pope as an example of his originality, and this originality was sufficient to excuse his pompous and redundant use of language, since these were instances in which he was unable to break away from the language of his period. This view appeared in the *Encyclopaedia Britannica*, and in another reference work, Robert Chambers's *Biographical Dictionary of Eminent Scotsmen* (1835); Johnson was quoted on Thomson's original diction, but the passage on the inflation of language was omitted.

Allan Cunningham, however, did not omit this passage, but explained the language on two grounds, both of which were previously mentioned by Sir Harris Nicolas. Thomson's 'pomp' was the result of a theory of poetic language which sought 'to elevate verse which sung of the humble toils of the shepherd, the husbandman and the mechanic', and, despite the pomp, the language had a power that overcomes its defects.

> His language has been called, by high authorities, swelling and redundant; but Thomson, with other great poets, held that a certain pomp and measured march of words was necessary to elevate verse which sung of the humble toils of the shepherd, the husbandman and the mechanic; and though Campbell prefers the idiomatic simplicity of Cowper, and Coleridge his chastity of

> diction, to the unvaried pomp of Thomson, yet both confess their preference of the latter, as a lofty and born poet. I believe this conclusion will be that of all who can feel the power, the glow, and the upward flame-like spirit of his poetry.[1]

Addison had pointed out that phrases used in ordinary conversation 'become too familiar to the ear, and contract a kind of meanness by passing through the mouths of the vulgar'[2] and should be avoided; and Gray and Blair, among others, had given similar reasons for the elevation of poetic language. Neither Nicolas nor Cunningham provided a new analysis of language, and the critics who did gloss Thomson's language for students—A. T. Thomson (1847), Gilbert Maxwell Gibson (2nd ed., 1855), James R. Boyd (1852), etc., glossed the language for its derivations, its grammar, and only occasionally, unsystematically, and at random, commented upon its appropriateness.

James R. Boyd, for example, referred to Thomson's use of personification as a fine awareness of poetic imagery, and gave one example of what was meant by Thomson's cumbersome style: 'innumerous-coloured'. Robert Bell (1860), although he made some effort to distinguish the types of poetry containing 'ornament' from those which were redundant, was aware of the need for some further analysis of language.

> Thomson's descriptions betray hardly any marks of effort or artifice. The grace, beauty and sweetness with which they are invested seem to be inherent in them. They are never loaded with expletives, or decorated by 'the foreign aid of ornament'; and notwithstanding the richness and luxury of phrase in which he indulges on some occasions, he always employs homely and familiar terms to express homely and familiar things.[3]

Bell objected, on moral grounds, to the Musidora episode, and found that 'even the chaste pastoral of Lavinia is slightly stained by the same taste'.

Bell's comments upon Thomson's 'style' and 'diction'—his characteristic 'peculiarity' and his choice of words—revealed that no new information had been gathered on these subjects so that only a

[1] Allan Cunningham, 'Life of James Thomson', *The Seasons* (London, 1841), p. xlii.

[2] Joseph Addison, *Works*, ed. G. W. Greene (New York, 1856), VI, 50.

[3] Robert Bell, *Poetical Works of James Thomson* (London, 1855), II, 10.

different theory was engrafted upon Scott's observations. Bell wrote:

> Poetry, like handwriting, has its secret and unconscious signs, which, in conjunction with more decisive evidence, may sometimes enable a vigilant critic to identify the style. The most noticeable peculiarity of Thomson is his habit of repeating himself. He frequently recurs to the same, or similar, turns of expression. He seems to have been haunted by particular words, which, being generally inelegant and unusual, or employed in strange combinations, are soon perceived by the reader. The structure of his sentences, also, exhibits some singularities by which a strict grammarian could not fail to detect the authorship.[1]

Yet when Bell came to 'snatch'd', the key word selected by Scott, he did not footnote it, nor did he footnote any of the 'unconscious signs' to which he had referred. His footnotes, a combination of those of John Mitford in the *Gentleman's Magazine* (1841) and those of Anthony Todd Thomson, were instances of sources and analogues —or influences. But he did come up with a judgement about Thomsons's language and versification which took account of Thomson's 'remarkable labours of revision', and minimized, therefore, the fault of luxuriance on the grounds of its suitability to the kind of poetry Thomson was writing. Such an approach was the result of John Mitford's publication of some of the revisions found in his 1738 edition, and the effort at revising, therefore, was equated by Bell with the success of revision.

> The versification of *The Seasons* is not founded either upon an imitation of any previous writer, or upon any settled system. It fluctuates with the demands of the occasion, and presents a perpetual variety. The breaks and rests wait upon the sense, which is never strained to accommodate the numbers, or produce rhythmical effects. Thomson rarely resorts to inversions, or any of the artifices or surprises incidental to the blank verse of his predecessors. He generally completes his meaning with clearness and precision; but incoherent passages sometimes occur, which involve his intention in obscurity or leave it unfinished. His diction, which he cultivated with infinite pains, is copious and luxuriant; occasionally but very seldom exuberant; and almost always elevated and appropriate. He evidently considered the choice of language a matter of paramount importance; and to this object he almost

[1] Bell, II, 11.

exclusively devoted the remarkable labours of revision he bestowed upon the poems.[1]

This argument was to be used by the 1864 edition to deny spontaneity, but it was coupled with an admission of Thomson's 'pomp'.

(c) TAINE, PHELPS, ROBERTSON, MOREL, TOVEY, REYNOLDS, BEERS, MACAULAY, ETC.: THE BREAKDOWN OF DICTION AND ITS RECOVERY

> Independently of Thomson's more generally recognized merits, he made some valuable contributions to the diction of English poetry.
>
> G. MACAULAY, 1908

By 1863, when Taine's *Histoire de la Littèrature anglaise* was published, Thomson had been placed within the Augustan period, in accordance with the various theories of contrasting currents in the early eighteenth century. But his diction remained secure, even Taine noting both the artificialities and the genuine delight in nature which resulted in precision. Once Thomson was placed within a literary tradition, his style was found to derive from Milton and Virgil; and John C. Shairp declared (1877): 'It is heavy, cumbrous, oratorical, overloaded with epithets, full of artificial invocations, "personified abstractions", and insipid classicalities. It is a composite style of language formed from the recollection partly of Milton, partly of Virgil's *Georgics*.'[2]

Shairp quoted several passages conveying an accurate picture of nature—'How true to nature this picture! how happily rendered.' And he admitted that in spite of all the 'obstructions which repel pure taste and natural feeling, no one can read the four books of the "Seasons" through, without seeing that Thomson, for all his false style, wrote with his eye upon Nature, and laid his finger on many a fact and image never before touched in poetry'. But his 'tawdry diction' was now seen as characteristic of a whole society and what, in early critics, had been a view dominated by the force and vigour of

[1] Bell, II, 11. Bell attempted to use his theory of 'handwriting', i.e. the characteristic traits of a writer, to identify the 'Ode to Congreve' as Thomson's. His difficulty lay in the insufficiency of his distinctions, not in his assumptions.

[2] John C. Shairp, *On Poetic Interpretation of Nature* (Edinburgh, 1877), pp. 186–7.

language, despite its cumbersomeness, had now become a diction which was part of a century, cold and artificial. In comparing him with Cowper, Shairp found that nature was seen 'separate and apart from human passion, or relieved only by some vapid episodes of a false Arcadianism. Hence, great as is Thomson's merit for having, first of his age, gone back to Nature, the interest he awakes in it is feeble, because with him Nature is so divorced from individuality and from man'.[1]

There was no doubt that for Shairp, as for the other critics discussed, vigour of expression and feeling was a criterion of value, but such expression was seen as reflective of emotion and therefore there was 'an essential kinship between the waves of excited feeling within the breast . . . and a corresponding rhythmical cadence in the words which utter it'. The artificiality of Thomson's diction obscured the feeling, though it would seem that there could be no poetic way to reveal that the feeling was genuine. And, indeed, to an American critic, John Bascom (1874) Thomson was cold, was artificial, and his only value lay in directing others to nature. Such a value, it must be added, was not that of poetry but that of social sensitivity. A comparison of the examples of Shairp with those of John Bascom reveal a disagreement about particulars though agreement on generals. Bascom declared of the famous shower passage in *Spring:*

> So cold an enthusiasm and fearful a search for precedents might well be followed by a feeble dressing up of homely things in poetic verbiage, like the following:
>
> Hushed in short suspense,
> The plumy people streak their wings with oil,
> To throw the lucid moisture trickling off.
> [*Spring*, ll. 164–6]
>
> Or this:
>
> Urged to the giddy break, much is the toil,
> The clamour much, of men and boys and dogs,
> Ere the soft fearful people to the flood
> Commit their woolly sides.
> [*Summer*, ll. 376–9]
>
> When we can wash sheep in a way no more straightforward than this, our muse is too dainty for husbandry.[2]

[1] Shairp, p. 204.

[2] John Bascom, *Philosophy of English Literature* (New York, 1874),

Referring to the conclusion of the shower passage, Shairp wrote that it was an example of Thomson's 'close observation and peculiar manner' which showed his 'minute faithfulness'. This disagreement depended upon the selection of a context—the shower and the sheep-shearing selections were insufficient in Bascom to convey a sense of Thomson's usage—but granted the insufficiency, simplicity of diction was the criterion of vividness for Bascom, and the strange language of Thomson was not 'simple', whereas for Shairp, such vividness was able to penetrate the artificiality of language because of its precision. There might be reservations at particular uses such as 'plumy people' or 'soft fearful people', but they were objectionable on artistic grounds whereas the 'streaking the wings with oil' was part of the scientific language, not bad taste. In the examples, therefore, distinctions had to be implied which the criticism itself had taken no notice of since Scott and Heron.

The reasons for Thomson's uneven diction had been discussed in the criticism of the mid-century, but no systematic technique had been developed for dealing with the diction. The disagreement of Shairp and Bascom was but one of several that arose without additional information. Nevertheless the attempt to explain the writer in his own time in terms of contrasting forces led to an analysis not only of the period but of the uses of language and the 'influences' of the period. In the G. M. Gibson and A. T. Thomson school texts there had been annotations of the Latin roots of some of Thomson's terms and the scientific explanations of the thrush (*Spring*, l. 598), the woodlark (*Spring*, l. 599), the stockdove (*Summer*, l. 616), etc. And John Mitford (1841), Robert Bell (1861) and others had suggested a series of sources for different passages in the poem. One of the conceptions relevant to diction, therefore, was an attempt to note the sources of the poem. The purpose of these sources was to establish the reference range of Thomson, to suggest the comparative nature of literary study and its continuity, to locate the originality of the poem as well as its indebtedness. But this study served as an example of the discrimination necessary to handle 'diction'. For what took

---

p. 214. For an opposing view of the 'straightforwardness' of Thomson's description which accepts poetic diction as capable of naturalness, see Edmund Gosse, *A History of Eighteenth Century Literature* (London, 1889), p. 223: 'Yet, even in *Summer*, and, specially in the beautiful picture of the washing and shearing of sheep, we find Thomson, as ever when he deals with what he has himself known and seen, glowing and felicitous.'

place in the 1880's and 1890's—keeping in mind that the unevenness of Thomson's diction was reasserted as before—was a division of 'diction' into selection of words—Anglo-Saxon or Latin in their roots, types of compounds, neologisms, Miltonic and Spenserian usages, kinds of sentence structure, line structure, and versification.

This study required, above all, particular facts about linguistic usage in the poem, and the accumulation of such data came about simultaneously from France, Germany, and England. In France, Alexandre Beljame had begun the study of English literature by seeking to explore the relation of the early eighteenth-century writer to his culture. In 1895 Léon Morel published the most important critical work on Thomson that had been produced. In Germany, renewed work had begun on establishing the text of *The Seasons*, and in 1891 J. Logie Robertson published a thoroughly annotated edition of the poem, and this edition was followed in 1895 by D. C. Tovey's edition. This intense critical activity, an attempt to place literary history under an evolutionary theory and thus to redefine 'romanticism' and its relation to the preceding period, did not develop a special theory of poetic language, but it did begin to gather new data on linguistic use in *The Seasons*, and to specify the needs of scholarship: 'a variorum edition of the *Seasons*, a task often promised but never fulfilled, would be a boon to students of English literature'.[1]

Morel in *James Thomson: sa vie et ses œuvres* set himself to analyse the vocabulary, grammar, imagery, and versification of the poem as part of an overall study of its language and style: 'Nous relèverons ce qui appartient en propre à Thomson et ce qui lui est inspiré par les influences alors régnantes, en analysant la langue du poète dans son vocabulaire, dans sa grammaire, dans les figures de sa langue poétique, dans le rythme général et dans les particularités prosodiques de son vers.'[2]

With regard to Thomson's innovations, Morel pointed to noun combinations, 'insect-tribes', 'forest-walks', 'reaper-train', then combinations of nouns and adjectives functioning as epithets—'blood-happy', 'sage-instructed eye', 'love-enlivened cheeks', 'romp-loving miss', etc., and combinations in which the first term was an adjective —'bitter-breathing frost', 'deep-loaded bough'. Adjectives were sometimes given the function of adverbs—Morel called this usage

[1] Edmund Gosse, *Eighteenth Century Literature* (London, 1880), p. 222.

[2] Léon Morel, *James Thomson: sa vie et ses œuvres* (Paris, 1895), p. 412.

one of the familiar traits of the style of *The Seasons*: 'Nous en avons, au courant de la plume, relevé dans l' "Automne" vingt-six exemples, et trente-quatre dans le "Printemps".' Morel pointed to a series of epithets which were used as past participles by adding 'ed', for example, 'rocky-channelled maze', 'rosy-footed May', 'innumerous-coloured scene', 'young-eyed health', 'rosy-bosomed Spring', 'various-blossomed Spring', etc. There were combinations which combined two qualities such as 'white-empurpled shower' and 'wide-dejected waste' and expressions like 'world-rejoicing state' which were difficult to justify logically.

The critic recognized many valuable and vivid innovations in the use of these compounds to convey many precise and graphic descriptive qualities. But many combinations of Latin terms easily became stiff and clumsy. In 'frequent-pausing', 'secret-winding', etc., there was an awkwardness of form, and the frequency of repetitions of such forms merited the rebuke of pomp and monotony.

> Le nombre seul de ces formes suffirait à donner au style du poète un caractère artificiel; et ce défaut est aggravé par la répétition complaisante des mêmes combinaisons. Nous citions tout à l'heure 'mazy-running brook', de l' 'Été'; le 'Printemps' nous fournit 'the mazy-runnig [sic] clefts' et l' 'Automne' [']mazy-running clefts.[']—[']The many-twinkling leaves' est charmant; mais dans le même chant vient 'many-bleating flocks,['] et dans l' 'Automne'[']many-coloured woods'. Dans le seul 'Printemps' nous avons: 'the well-used plough, well-showered, the well-dissembled fly.' Dans l' 'Automne', à moins de cent vers d'intervalle,[']wide-projected heaps, et wide-refracted ray.[']—[']All-surrounding heaven,['] du 'Printemps', est rappelé par ces deux expressions de l' 'Automne': [']Nature's all-refining hand, et all-enlivening trade.[']—[']Seagirt reign['] est, dans l' 'Automne', bientôt suivi de [']sea-encircled globe.[']—'Never-cloyed desire,['] et [']ever changing views', du 'Printemps', sont rappelés comme par un écho dans 'ever-dripping fogs'.[1]

Morel found that Thomson repeated expressions such as 'think', 'convolved', 'invest', 'detruded', and that such repetition seemed indiscriminate. Moreover, Thomson tended to form words directly from Latin in order to give his language an elegance and elevation, and in this respect he used words more appropriate to the language

[2] Morel, p. 418.

of reason, logic, and science. Morel referred to a number of Scottish uses that had been catalogued by J. Logie Robertson.

In the grammar of the poem, the critic noted very few formal errors and found the characteristic Thomsonian inversion to be placing the qualifier after the word qualified:

> Contrairement au génie de la langue, Thomson place volontiers le déterminatif après le terme déterminé, l'épithète après le substantif, le complément avant le verbe ou l'adjectif, l'adverbe après le verbe: 'on churchyards drear', 'the quire celestial', etc.[1]

Morel also turned to Thomson's ellipses and archaisms. And he found that the grammar showed a desire for independence; Thomson pushed to excess the search for forceful and elevated language.

Soon after Morel published his study, D. C. Tovey (1897) published his edition of *The Seasons*, urging only cautions against the imitation of Thomson's language and poetry. And in 1898, in an essay on Cowper, Alfred Ainger found that the 'form and diction of those once famous poems repel us'. Thomson had sensibly followed a model, Milton, and although 'Thomson was a conscientious watcher and lover of Nature; his matter, which was his own, was hindered by his manner, which was somebody else's'. For Ainger, Thomson's poetry 'had gone through some process of adaptation to the supposed claims of poetic convention'. But it was now possible to point to the divergencies from convention and the independence of Thomson's diction, though there was, of course, no ground for denying the autobiographical assertion: 'We of this day, I must admit, can hardly read Thomson with patience.' And he was supported in this view by Tovey and Stephen Gwynn (1904):

> There is no particular reason why anyone nowadays should read *The Seasons* . . . we can all own Wordsworth, Scott, Shelley and the rest, who have done so much better what Thomson was the first to do—that is, to express in verse the charm and suggestions of landscape.[2]

It was inevitable that the argument of Thomson's originality in turning to nature should be discarded as a critical argument for reading him because it provided no such justification; it substituted historical innovation for literary quality. Moreover, Stopford Brooke

[1] Morel, pp. 430–1.

[2] Stephen Gwynn, *Masters of English Literature* (London, 1904), p. 202.

as early as 1865 had pointed to a Scottish tradition of nature poetry and placed Thomson within it. Thus there were even reservations about the originality of the return to nature. The defence of the value of *The Seasons*, even by one of its firmest supporters, William Bayne, was made in 1898 and 1900, in terms of 'expansiveness', 'precision' and 'freshness' of description, but in the 'artistic part' of the work, Bayne conceded that Thomson was 'bombastic, cumbrous and vapid'. And the same rebuke was given to his versification; here Milton served as a basis for comparison.

> The chief fault of Thomson's poetry in general is its infelicity of style, linguistic and poetical. It was, of course, impossible that Thomson could altogether avoid the peculiar diction of his age, though it may be wished that he had occasionally less emphasized its verbosity; but he erred deliberately when he attempted to copy the rhythmical harmonies of Milton. No doubt, his success, after all, is surprising. The freshness and beauty of his conceptions invest language as well as rhythm with a transforming charm.[1]

Tovey sought to put the poetry of Thomson in the tradition of his period and not only pointed to his turgidity and occasional vulgarity (Damon and Musidora) but found that Thomson had considerably less vitality than Keats. He quoted the lines at the conclusion of the Celadon and Amelia episode and compared them with similar lines in the 'Urn':

> Yet when we encounter the same essential thought in Thomson and in Keats, we feel that in Keats it appears under new conditions and with a new animating principle. This, for instance, of emotion fixed in sculptures:
>
> . . . On the marble tomb
> The well-dissembled mourner stooping stands,
> For ever silent, and for ever sad.
> [*Summer*, ll. 1220–2]
>
> So writes Thomson; very beautifully, yet with sobriety, with measure; he is quite conscious of the illusion, and lets you know it—in fact it is but a simile. To turn from this to the 'Ode on a Grecian Urn' is to pass from Praxiteles, if not to Prometheus, at least to Pygmalion; there is not 'well-dissembled' sorrow here, but real and perennial joy in the 'pipes and timbrels' and 'wild ecstasy';

[1] William Bayne, *Poems by James Thomson* (London, 1900), p. xxviii.

he is alive—that 'bold lover'—and can hear a kindred spirit say:

> . . . never shalt thou kiss
> Though winning near the goal; yet do not grieve;
> She cannot fade, though thou hast not thy bliss,
> For ever wilt thou love and she be fair.

We see here all the difference between an easy receptivity, and the passionate *desiderium* for a fairer world. Again, we have seen Thomson's theory of 'life rising still on life'—the comfortable optimism of his belief in progress, development, perfection; let us note in Keats the change that has come over the spirit of the dream; the new thought of renunciation, self-denial, due ultimately to collision with hard and cruel fact.[1]

The limitation of Thomson's language was not based, here, on the turgid or vulgar or monotonous; the language lacked animation because it presupposed an optimistic view of life. Thomson's passage did not, however, present this view, since it compared the actuality of suffering with the 'well-dissembled', the artificiality of art. It conveyed the view, expressed elsewhere in Thomson, that no one could paint like nature. And 'well-dissembled' referred to the marble mourner whose expression of mourning was grievous and finally artistic but dissembled nevertheless in contrast to the lover who had just lost his beloved.

> But who can paint the lover, as he stood,
> Pierced by severe amazement, hating life,
> Speechless, and fixed in all the death of woe?
> So, faint resemblance! on the marble tomb

[1] D. C. Tovey, *The Poetical Works of Thomson* (London, 1897), I, xciv–xcv. Tovey's preference for Keats's knowledge of 'hard and cruel fact' was not identical with a preference for particularity. This assumption was developed by critics in the following decades often using the same quotation. One critic pointed out that this passage 'released' Keats's imagination; others quoted the 'auriculas' passage:

> 'auriculas, enriched
> With shining meal o'er all their velvet leaves'.
> *Spring*, ll. 536–7.

But particularity was one kind of description used in *The Seasons*; critics who sought to see it as the model of what could have been but was not done, had little idea of how Thomson was using language or to what end.

> The well-dissembled mourner stooping stands,
> For ever silent and for ever sad.
>
> [*Summer*, ll. 1217–22]

Keats was comparing mortality with immortality, the pains of the flesh with the pleasures of art, and the pains of denial with the pleasures of renunciation. It is questionable which view is more 'optimistic', although the term 'optimistic' seems inappropriate to either selections. But granting the term, it seems reasonable to assume that 'optimism' is in itself not a criterion for aesthetic value since the comic, for example, would thus be excluded from a theory of art.

But the view of Thomson's language in so far as it was explained by the period was further narrowed by Sir George Douglas (1911), who granted to Thomson's art the dramatizing of nature's forces—their movements:

> Take the opening of his *Spring* for an example: Spring's imperceptible assertion of benignant influence; the massing of the clouds before the south-wind; Nature's assumption of green robes; the joyous pairing of the birds, the breaking forth of trees into leaf and blossom; the timely industry of careful man, with plough, seed-sheet, and harrow. All this is largely, grandly, set before us![1]

Yet the invocations, the directly didactic portions of the poem—the passage on industry in *Autumn*—had lost their interest and vitality as had what Douglas called the academic pieces—the lover in *Spring* and the *Winter* storm (ll. 153–74).

The grounds for objecting to this passage were that it lacked 'inspiration'—the quality of a Byron, Shelley, or Swinburne. 'And it is not only that Thomson's genius was meditative rather than passionate; his very method of work—his polish, his artifice, the conventionality of his vocabulary: all these were inimical to spontaneity. He was tethered to the formalism of the age he lived in.' But this storm passage, when compared to those in the other seasons, is marked by a chaotic violence different from the gloomy swelling of the autumn rivers. Douglas's criticism confused the composition of poetry with its effects, and although he imposed a historical criticism upon the poem, the particular examples, unlike those given by Morel, did not have validity:

> Blame the age in which he lived, if so you are minded. It was an age of reason, of mild enlightenment; comfortable, prosperous,

[1] George Douglas, *Scottish Poetry* (Glasgow, 1911), p. 60.

> picturesque; the golden mediocrity of Anne and of the first two Georges: but it was an age of prose rather than of poetry. So by all means blame the age, if such be your pleasure, for Thomson's stiffness, his artificiality.[1]

After Léon Morel, the most extensive study of the language of *The Seasons* was undertaken by George Macaulay (1908) who, while recognizing Thomson's originality, sought to trace his literary debt to Milton, the Bible, Virgil, Lucretius, and others. Indeed, in the same year Otto Zippel published a list of 'Models' and Sources' for the poem. The critical idea behind the search for parallels, sources, and influences was to identify Thomson's individuality—to study what he did with these and, at the same time, to provide a more careful statement of the tradition embodied in his diction. One of the important points which Macaulay was thus able to make was that Thomson seemed to be closer often to John Philips's diction than to Milton's: 'In Philips there was always a vein of ironical humour, not sufficient to turn his work into burlesque, but redeeming its heroic style from absurdity; while Thomson, whose genius was more enthusiastically poetical sometimes fell into the fault of unredeemed grandiloquence.'[2] Macaulay, moreover, discussed Thomson's diction in terms of his general conception of nature. And it was this which led him to recognize that the poet's originality was due not to his turning to nature, but to his particular expressions of it:

> The literary obligations of various kinds which have been traced affect only a very small portion of Thomson's work, and ought not to be allowed to detract from his credit for essential originality. At the same time, it must be noted that Thomson was not so much the independent founder of a school of poetry, as the most eminent member of a group of young poets, who were all working in the same direction, and who exercised mutual influence upon one another.[3]

With respect to diction, versification, and style, Macaulay was, to a large extent, dependent upon the findings of Morel. 'Style' used as the all-inclusive term for poetic expression included Thomson's 'undue amplification' and want of simplicity, but it also included a number of original words and compounds. Just as Morel did,

[1] Douglas, p. 71.
[2] George Macaulay, *James Thomson* (London, 1908), p. 148.
[3] Macaulay, p. 153.

Macaulay relied upon his sensitivity in distinguishing good compounds from bad ones.

> Many of his newly-formed compounds are expressive and beautiful. He invented the adjective 'many-twinkling', which is used by him of leaves in the sunlight. 'The dewy-skirted clouds,' 'the dew-bright earth,' 'the dimply pool,' 'the dusty-mantled lawn,' 'bitter-breathing' as applied to frost, 'faint gleaming' to the dawn, 'rocky-channelled' and 'mossy-tinctured' to the brook, and 'forest-crowned' to the mountain;—these are examples of new combinations for which we may reasonably be grateful, and in some of which Thomson was the precursor of Keats.[1]

Macaulay, like Morel, dealt with Thomson's favourite words—'convolved', 'diffused', 'unessential'—with his Latinisms—'affective', 'amusive', 'excursive', 'prelusive', 'repercussive', 'innumerous', 'irriguous', 'umbrageous', 'clamant', 'emergent', etc.—his syntactical transpositions, compound-words and periphrases. This latter was partly the result of Miltonic imitation but

> more in consequence of the general debasement of taste in poetry, a system of periphrasis had been adopted in the poetical diction of the early eighteenth century, by which it was thought that dignity was given to the mention of the common things of everyday life. John Philips, in his *Blenheim*, speaks of 'the brazen instruments of war' when he means cannons, Gay calls fish 'the finny brood,' and even Pope, who is usually more direct, gives us 'the scaly breed' in *Windsor Forest*, and 'the fleecy winter,' as a periphrasis for snow, in the *Iliad*. Thomson, in *The Seasons*, carries this mannerism rather to an excess. He speaks of 'the flowery race,' 'the household feathery people,' 'the bleating kind,' 'the fearful flying race,' 'the plumy nations,' 'the glittering finny swarms,' when he wishes to indicate flowers, domestic fowls, sheep, birds or fish.[2]

This procedure he attributed to a want of simplicity.

The statistical analysis of Morel and Macaulay played a very important role in criticism of *The Seasons*, in understanding eighteenth-century criticism as a whole, and in understanding eighteenth-century poetry, for by providing an analysis of 'artificiality', that is, imitation of skilful but not spontaneous invention, a complexity rather than simplicity of invention, this type of criticism made possible distinctions within uses of diction, distinguishing

[1] Macaulay, p. 171. [2] Macaulay, pp. 162–3.

poetic terms previously used from those invented. Moreover, on the basis of individual taste, Morel and Macaulay argued for the preference of some terms to others. Thus not only did they provide a basis for refuting artificiality of diction as a concept, but by distinguishing some types of diction they also made possible further distinctions. The importance of their accomplishment can best be understood by realizing that they undertook to deal in detail with what had become the chief basis for Thomsonian attack—the artificiality of diction. Within the overall opposition to this diction, they sought to discriminate among categories of diction.

It is now clear that in setting up these categories and distinguishing between good and bad uses of diction, they were dependent upon a received theory of artificial language and 'simple' poetry. The frequency of compounds or periphrasis was attributed to the 'age', but the 'age' was considered an age of prose; the age went wrong. The need to understand the values for which the age prized this diction extended no further than their consistency with the general artificiality. The distinction between usages of the same terms either by the same poet or by several poets of the period did not lead to a re-examination of this explanation.

In trusting to individual phrases and words rather than to passages, they were unable to develop generalizations about style as a whole, but they encouraged further inquiry into diction, into sources and analogues, into history of ideas. The important elements in discrimination became available as antecedents closer than Milton and Virgil to Thomson began to be discovered, and Milton and Virgil themselves began to be canvassed for the poetical basis of parallels, derivations, and 'influences'. In Raymond D. Havens's study, *The Influence of Milton on English Poetry* (1922), and in several studies of Virgil's influence on English poetry, statistical counts of word usage and parallel passages began to accumulate, and the originality of Thomson as well as his indebtedness began to be documented.

In the work of Havens the immense documentation led him to reassert Thomson's value as poet and as eighteenth-century 'influence', while denying his originality as nature poet, 'for though he is a figure of the first importance in this field, he did not create the taste by which he was appreciated . . . he was by no means the first writer of his time to feel, or the first to give effective expression to the feeling, that 'night and day, sun, moon and stars, likewise a wind on the heath, are all sweet things'. The tabulation of poems in blank verse throughout the eighteenth century led the critic to sense their inferiority without being able to account for it in poetic terms. He therefore found that 'the principal significance of *The Seasons* lies in its popularity'.[1]

The documentation of this statement was a listing of editions of *The Seasons* and of poems which sought to imitate *The Seasons*, but when Havens analysed the Miltonic influence he found that the poem tended to reflect the faults of diction described by Morel and Macaulay. The dilemma of this documentation was clearly presented in Havens: he selected a series of traits in *Paradise Lost* which differentiated the poem from other poetry and prose. These characteristics pertained to language and versification, but their selection was based on what the critic considered the proper differentiae.

1. Dignity, reserve and stateliness
2. The organ tone
3. Inversion of the natural order of words and phrases
4. Omission of words not necessary to the sense
5. Parenthesis and apposition
6. The use of one part of speech for another
7. Departure from ordinary vocabulary
8. Introduction into a short passage of a considerable number of proper names
9. Unusual compound epithets

Other characteristics not distinctively Miltonic but used by him frequently included intentional repetition of a word or phrase, an uninterrupted series of words in the same construction, and the forming of adjectives in -ean or -ian from proper nouns.

Since eighteenth-century poets did not consciously follow these Miltonic traits, their use of them had to be explained in terms of bad imitation. Thomson created poetry out of other poetry, and he adopted Milton's manner 'without realizing that what was fitting, necessary even, in picturing the wars of archangels and the creation of the solar system'; and it became ridiculous when applied to Musidora's bathing or to the shearing of sheep.[2]

In explaining why Thomson was able to do what his contemporaries were not, Havens reiterated the theory of the Scottish past developed

[1] Raymond Dexter Havens, *The Influence of Milton on English Poetry* (Cambridge, Mass., 1922), p. 124.

[2] Havens, p. 139.

by Stopford Brooke: *The Seasons* 'was written by a Scot, it was suggested by Scottish verses, it pictures Scottish scenes'. But Mallet, who was also a Scot, did not write poetry of the same quality as Thomson, and Hinchliffe, who was not, did. Moreover, in his 1726 preface Thomson pointed out that the poem was suggested by Virgil and the Scriptures, and Collins said that Thomson got the idea of *The Seasons* from Pope's pastorals. The poem, moreover, pictured, along with Scottish scenes, others that Thomson never saw, and expressed moral and didactic sentiments in no way dependent upon Scottish scenery or traditions.

The diction of *The Seasons* was catalogued in the tradition of Morel and Macaulay, and Havens remarked that 'the feature of Thomson's diction that is likely to attract most attention is his use of uncommon words derived from the Latin. He has, for example, "vernant", "clamant", "prelusive", "amusive", "inprisive", "diffusive", "effulgent", etc'. He declared that if there was a "pompous, contorted way of saying a thing, Thomson is likely to hit upon it; that of two words he prefers the one of Latin origin and of two Latin words that which is less common. Calling things by their right names and speaking simply, directly, and naturally, as in conversation, seems to have been his abhorrence.' And again, 'Thomson has a penchant for words which are today particularly disliked, such as "swain", "glebe", "gelid", "lucid", "verdant", "umbrage", "mead", "verdure", "the fair", "the muse". He also delighted in unnatural and inflated circumlocutions, like "the household feathery people" (hens), "the copious fry" or "the finny race" or "the glittering finny swarms" (fish) . . . For birds he had more than fifteen periphrases, speaking of them in one place as "the plumy burden" that "winnow the waving element".' Havens concluded that 'this is all bad, very bad. Indeed, the turgid diction and the distorted, pompous style of *The Seasons* are largely responsible for the current underestimate of the poem. These qualities are the more objectionable because they are used in picturing simple country life; for, according to our twentieth-century feeling, nature poetry ought above all kinds to be natural.'[1]

[1] Havens, p. 138. See also Raymond D. Havens, 'The Poetic Diction of the English Classicists', *Kittridge Anniversary Papers* (Boston, 1913), pp. 435–44. Havens's view of 'poetic diction' in his 1913 article was that it avoided prosaic, harsh, vulgar words (p. 438), though in his Milton volume he recognized that many of Thomson's words were 'prosaic' and 'harsh'. Havens declared (1913) that 'eighteenth-century periphrases are

The explanations for Thomson's use of this diction were that (1) he wished to banish the drab uniformity of neo-classic verse; (2) his defects sprang from lack of fineness of taste and want of skill in handling a strange medium; (3) his effort was part of the general eighteenth-century view of the separation of poetic language from prose. The quandary of Havens's view was that other poets of the period apparently accepted Thomson's use of blank verse and the conception of the development of poetry was the result of such 'influence'. But influence did away with the kind of discrimination that Havens began by establishing. While giving a particularity to Miltonic words and phrases in Thomson, he was unable, except in personal terms, to explain why some critics approved the diction and others did not. Thomson's diction in the early eighteenth century did not meet with complete approval, but why critics approved some passages and not others, why Shiels and Warton and Aikin and indeed all subsequent critics had divided responses, the theory of 'influence' could not answer because it presupposed that the value of poetic diction had to be accounted for in terms of Milton's usage and not that of the eighteenth century. Thomson might indeed have been guilty of bad taste, but not merely by using poetic diction; the issue was that the period offered a proper as well as an improper use of this diction, and Thomson was praised for some uses and attacked for others. The theory of 'influence' distorted the problem of poetic value by setting up a criterion of usage irrespective of the writer 'influenced', because it traced similarities rather than dissimilarities and differences, and because it confined 'influence' to words, phrases, and disparate elements rather than analysing these in terms of crucial or important and unimportant uses of extensive poetic passages.

As late as 1924, Thomas Quayle in *Poetic Diction*, while trying to be sympathetic to the poetic language of the eighteenth century, nevertheless judged it by 'suggestiveness', by 'spontaneity', by the language of romantic poetry. Referring to Thomson's 'latinisms' he wrote: 'not only do they possess none of that mysterious power of suggestion which comes to words in virtue of their employment through generations of prose and song, but also not infrequently

---

vague, unnatural, and mechanical . . . They add nothing, but are simply attempts to be elegant and poetical in an artificial way' (p. 442). For a view of eighteenth-century misuse of Milton—'how literary reminiscence sometimes strangles poetry' (p. 255)—see Walter Raleigh, *Milton* (London, 1900), pp. 252–5.

their meaning is far from clear. They are never the spontaneous reflection of the poet's thought, but, on the contrary, they appear only too often to have been dragged in merely for effect.'[1] As Bertrand H. Bronson pointed out some twenty years later, Quayle's comments on eighteenth-century abstractions were similar to Wordsworth's.[2]

The attack on the view that eighteenth-century poetry lacked imagination, 'spontaneity', and adhered to outworn conventions because of a theory of imitation focussed above all on assumptions about poetic diction although other objections were also voiced. Scholarship had become computation and had lost touch with value distinctions; the study of literature while cognizant of the landscape arts blinded critics to important uses of language; literary history could not be properly formulated by ignoring the 'expectations' or 'ends' of each particular time. With regard to poetic language, the attack began in 1934 with F. W. Bateson's *English Poetry and the English Language*: 'the danger into which modern English scholarship is running is of not knowing when to stop. If to be relentlessly thorough and impeccably accurate is to be scholarly, what is there to prevent the aspiring scholar from tabulating the rhymes, let us say, in the *Theophila* of Edward Benlowes ("propitious still to blockheads")? What could be more thorough—or more futile'?[3] The

[1] Thomas Quayle, *Poetic Diction* (London, 1924), p. 68.

[2] Bertrand H. Bronson, 'Personification Reconsidered', *ELH*, XIV (1947), 170. For other works on this subject, see John Arthos, *The Language of Natural Description* (Ann Arbor, 1949); Robert A. Aubin, *Topographical Poetry in Eighteenth Century England* (New York, 1936), Earl R. Wasserman, 'The Inherent Values of Eighteenth Century Personification', *PMLA*, LXV (1950), 435–63; Edward A. Bloom, 'The Allegorical Principle', *ELH*, XVIII (1951), 163–90; Rachel Trickett, 'The Augustan Pantheon; Mythology and Personification in Eighteenth Century Poetry', *Essays and Studies 1953* (London, 1953), pp. 71–86; Donald Davie, *The Purity of Diction in English Verse* (London, 1952) pp. 38–61; Chester F. Chapin, *Personification in Eighteenth Century English Poetry* (New York, 1955). For a recent view attacking personification, see Norman Maclean, 'Personification but not Poetry', *ELH*, XXIII (1956), 163–70.

[3] F. W. Bateson, *English Poetry and the English Language* (Oxford, 1934), pp. v–vi. For another explanation of the attack on earlier theories of the developmental analogy, see David N. Smith, *Some Observations on Eighteenth Century Poetry* (London, 1937), p. 56: 'I ask you to distrust the familiar labels—"classical", "neo-classical", "pseudo-classical", "pre-romantic", and all the others. I sometimes doubt if we shall ever understand the poetry of this century till we get rid of the terms "classical" and "romantic" in one and all forms.' The first use of 'neo-classical' that I have

alternative was to study the language of poetry and the 'real' history of poetry was 'the history of the changes in the kind of language in which successive poems have been written'.

Bateson distinguished two theories of poetic diction—one which proposed that some words were not suitable for poetry, and the other, that there were some words only (or especially) suitable for poetry. This was the theory of the nature poets. Bateson declared:

> the vocabulary of poetic diction can be paralleled in the numerous technical terms of science, philosophy and politics that were coined in the eighteenth century. The motives that led chemists to create a word like 'phlogiston' (first used in 1733) were ultimately identical with those that induced Thomson and the rest to call fishes a 'finny tribe' . . . By restricting a general notion to a particular field they represented a gain in precision.[1]

The important change introduced by Bateson's view was due to his question, what function was the poetic diction intended to perform? He lacked the evidence to do more than suggest that such language was deliberate, and he fell back upon a comparison of this diction with Baroque architecture that created a 'confused dignity which can be called sublime'. Bateson made important distinctions, but he neglected many more adequate answers to the functions of poetic diction than he gave. In the following years, C. V. Deane's *Aspects of Eighteenth-Century Nature Poetry* (1935), Geoffrey Tillotson's two essays on poetic diction (1935, 1939), and David Nichol Smith's discussion of eighteenth-century poetry attempted to construct a rationale for such diction. This development stemmed from many sources: the recognition of a series of trends within the period differing on the use of poetic diction, the data accumulated by

[1] Bateson, p. 69.

been able to trace occurred in 1863 in William Rushton's lecture, 'The Classic and Romantic Schools of English Literature', *The Afternoon Lectures on English Literature* (London, 1863), p. 44: 'When we speak of the classical school in English literature, we refer to those writers who have formed their style upon ancient models, and, for the sake of distinction, we might call it the Revived Classical or Neo-Classical school.' This appellation, at the end of the century, came often to be used synonymously with 'pseudo-classical'. For 'neo-classic' and 'pseudo-classic', see William Allan Neilson, *Essentials of Poetry* (Boston, 1912), pp. 118–19. For the use of 'Augustan' as a general term for the early eighteenth century and the multiplicity of its meanings, see James W. Johnson, 'The Meaning of "Augustan",' *JHI*, XIX (1958), 507–22.

'influence' studies stressing diversity of usage and the fact that poets using the same diction did not use it equally well. The concept of 'discrimination', therefore, demanded some explanation distinguishing 'good' from 'bad' uses. Referring to phrases like 'fleecy care', Tillotson declared, 'In the work of good poets they are not there simply as a means of avoiding the mention of low material. . . . The good poets discriminate their use.'[1] Thomson and Pope used 'fish' and 'birds' in uncompromisingly straightforward terms, 'when Thomson calls birds "the glossy kind" it is because he is going on to show that glossiness counts in the mating season . . . When Thomson speaks of young birds as "the feathered youth" he means that the birds though young are not too young to have feathers. He is compressing into two words a long meaning, compressing it in a way common at the time for other materials than those of nature.'[2] The analysis of the terms also presupposed a reading of eighteenth-century poets in which the procedure was to explain language rather than trace it. To this view support was originally derived from the attack on the eighteenth-century view of Arnold that the age itself was wrong; no age, T. S. Eliot remarked, could go wrong, and it was indeed necessary to explain what was right in terms of the age in order to know how its 'norm' went wrong. Deane and Tillotson, therefore, were constructing the 'norm' of eighteenth-century poetic language.

In a brilliant essay (1939), Geoffrey Tillotson sought to explain the grounds for the use of poetic diction, while conceding that in discussing poetic diction 'we are comparing the best poetry of the nineteenth century with the less-than-best poetry of the eighteenth'. The eighteenth-century nature poets who were the chief users of

[1] Geoffrey Tillotson, *Essays in Criticism and Research* (Cambridge, 1942), pp. 60–61.

[2] Tillotson, p. 61. See also D. Nichol Smith, pp. 64–65: 'On a style naturally rhetorical and Latinized, Thomson superimposed a Miltonic element. He found in Milton a language after his heart. "Chimerae huge", "in endless mazes, intricate, perplexed"—such words and phrases as these made their way into *The Seasons*, much more easily than we are apt to suppose. *The Seasons* is sometimes spoken of as if it were a long exercise in aureate diction; but it is too vital a poem for its language to be a continuous artifice. The style came easily to Thomson; it was natural to him.' 'Natural' is here used as an antithetical term to 'artifice', but Thomson did not use the same diction throughout *The Seasons*, nor did he use it in the plays. The relation between 'vitality' and 'naturalness' is not a necessary one.

poetic diction have Virgil's *Georgics* at the base of their metre and diction. Many of the single syllable nouns were derived from the *Georgics*—'race', 'tribe', 'train', 'gale', 'vale', 'swain', 'tide', etc. 'As the reverence for Virgil faded [in the nineteenth century], the capacity to supply the connotation faded with it. In the eighteenth century the meanings of the favourite Virgilian words are not defined in the dictionaries. They are beyond definition in the same way that Keats's words are, though often for other reasons'.[1] Virgil celebrated the control of man over land and animal, and this view was shared by the poets. As for the avoidance of 'low' words, a periphrasis was often a means for skirting the company of parodists who ridiculed the Saxon elements in language. The remedy, remarks Tillotson, was 'sometimes worse than the disease. But the disease was a real one.'

In illustrating how good poets used poetic diction, he quoted the passage from *Winter*, ll. 256 ff.

> . . . The foodless wilds
> Pour forth their brown inhabitants. The hare,
> Though timorous of heart, and hard beset
> By death in various forms, dark snares, and dogs,
> And more unpitying men, the garden seeks
> Urg'd on by fearless want. The bleating kind
> Eye the bleak heaven, and next the glistening earth,
> With looks of dumb despair; then, sad-dispersed,
> Dig for the withered herb through heaps of snow.

> Here the diction is parcel of the meaning. 'Brown inhabitants' is a neat way of grouping creatures which inhabit the scene described and whose brownness is the most evident thing about them in the snow. 'Bleating kind' is anything but an unthinking substitute for 'sheep'. Thomson is saying: we think of sheep as creatures who bleat, but they are silent enough in the snow; it is the dumb eye and not the voice that tells us of their despair.[2]

And, finally, poetic diction helped express 'some part of the contemporary interest in the theological and scientific significance of

[1] Tillotson, p. 61.

[2] Tillotson, p. 81. For some recent discussions which disregard this research into the techniques and values of Augustan nature poetry, see Dorothy M. Stuart, 'Landscape in Augustan Verse', *Essays and Studies*, XXVI (1940), 73–87, and W. Lamplough Doughty, 'The Place of James Thomson in the Poetry of Nature', *The London Quarterly* (1949), pp. 154–8, 249–54.

natural phenomena'. Poetic diction was a means of differentiating God's creatures in diverse ways, whether 'scaly breed' for the 'clothing' of fish or 'watery breed' for their environment.

This latter view of Tillotson was fully documented by John Arthos in 1949, when he demonstrated that many terms of the 'stock vocabulary of natural description' had both a long poetic history and contemporary scientific use. Thus words considered by Havens as words unpalatable to modern tastes or unbearable periphrases, such as 'verdant', 'lucid', 'fry', 'race', 'nation', 'tribe', were parts of a traditional rather than an eighteenth-century vocabulary.

And in the following year (1950) John Butt wrote:

> But we should take care not to regard Thomson as Milton's sedulous ape. Thomson's latinisms came naturally to a lowland Scot writing Southern English, and his periphrases were used not to escape vulgarity, but precisely and evocatively. It was not the meanness of the word 'egg' that he wished to avoid when describing the young birds in *Spring* breaking 'their brittle bondage'. The periphrasis enabled him to draw attention to a single attribute of the egg required by the context. Nor did he aim at the grandeur of generality in referring to birds as 'the fearful race', for 'fearful' is the most apt generic term to describe both the 'white winged plover' when she
>
> wheels
> Her sounding flight, and then directly on
> In long excursion skims the level lawn
> [*Spring*, ll. 695–7]
>
> to tempt 'the unfeeling schoolboy' from her nest, and the heath-hen fluttering 'o'er the trackless waste . . . to lead The hot pursuing spaniel far astray'. Thomson needed these periphrases and must have found them even if Milton had never written . . .[1]

The analysis of 'poetic diction' and periphrasis was followed by analysis of eighteenth-century personification and its implications. 'It is with personification as with diction', wrote Alan D. McKillop (1956), 'discussion has shifted from the question of the absolute value of a figure or word . . . to the effectiveness of a figure or word in its full context, in its relation to the intentions and expectations of poet, critic, reader.'[2] The unevenness of Thomson's language,

[1] John Butt, *The Augustan Age* (London, 1950), pp. 93–94.
[2] Alan D. McKillop, 'Review of Personification in Eighteenth Century English Poetry', *PQ*, XXXV (1956), 254.

therefore, could no longer be ascribed to periphrases, latinizing and compounds. Since this was so, Thomson's unevenness was moved to his variant uses of the same terms, and his dull passages therefore were attributed to almost direct transcription from secondary sources or to a neglect of his original intent in his first *Winter* (1726) as revised in his last version (1746).

But these conclusions revealed, once again, the overwhelming agreement established regarding the unevenness of the language, this time resulting from an implied comparison of Thomson's language with that of his contemporaries. But the generalizations used to explain why some kinds of diction functioned better than others were not very satisfactory. If we compare the evaluations of passages by eighteenth-century critics with those by modern critics, it will, perhaps, clarify the issue. Robert Heron (1793) had written of the image, 'a shoreless ocean tumbled round the globe', that it did not 'present a very happy image', meaning that 'tumble' for the ocean was an inappropriate comparison, and he may have had reference to its colloquial quality—'to towze or rumple'—although it also meant to cast or throw violently. But in our time Bonamy Dobrée quoting the passage preceding the image, has declared:

> so far the effect is a little laboured; but then we get a transition which brings us to a last line which is miraculous, even though it may be derived from Milton:
>
> Till, from the centre to the streaming clouds
> A shoreless ocean tumbled round the globe.
> [*Spring*, ll. 315–16]
>
> And here it was not science that captivated Thomson . . . Thomson himself referred to 'fabling Burnet'. What spurred him was the sudden vision, and here, perhaps, is the clearest example of Thomson exploring his imagination, and so releasing that of the reader.[1]

What Dobrée may have discovered in Thomson's use of language was the imaginative sublimity of the 'shoreless ocean'—J. L. Robertson annotated 'tumbled' in 1914 (*Nature in Books*, p. 16) with the comment, 'often with a single word or phrase which has caught the significant characteristic of his subject he flashes upon our imagination a whole vast and varied scene'—the immense tumbling waters

[1] Bonamy Dobrée, *English Literature in the Early Eighteenth Century* (London, 1959), pp. 492–3.

which made the world a 'globe' and implied that in the floods unleashed by God the boundaries were submerged, the clouds and waters tumbling and streaming side by side. Heron's objection was due to a limited view of poetic language—and one of the values of Thomson's diction, therefore, was that sometimes it was far more subtle than the theories which his own contemporaries brought to bear and became valued only as poetic theory became more comprehensive. But there were passages in Thomson which were honoured by his contemporaries and by all subsequent critics, and although the reasons for admiration changed, the location of such passages serves as part of a definition of critical sensitivity. Such sensitivity also includes defence of passages not consistent with the critic's principles but resulting from a speculative grasp of poetic aims. In Thomson, because of his frequent revisions, such aims are visible though not always decipherable. It was possible, of course, merely to repeat some of Warton's examples, but in that case, the knowledge of other passages—the range of the critic—needed to be examined. As an example of the sensitivity of a critic in opposition to his linguistic assumptions one may take John Scott's analysis of the word 'kind oppression' in the *Summer* hay-making passage [Scott's italics]:

> Now swarms the village o'er the jovial mead:
> The rustic youth brown with meridian soil,
> Healthful and strong; *full* as the summer rose
> Blown by prevailing suns, the ruddy maid,
> Half-naked, swelling on the sight, and all
> *Her kindled graces burning o'er her cheek.*
> Ev'n stooping age is here; and infant hands
> Trail the long rake, or with the fragrant load
> O'er charg'd amid the *kind oppression* roll.
> [ll. 352–60]

Scott pointed out that 'fragrant load' was one of Thomson's 'new-coined discriminations and "kind oppression" is a phrase of that sort, which one scarcely knows whether to blame, or praise: it consists of two words, directly opposite in their signification; and yet, perhaps, no phrase whatever could have better conveyed the idea of easy uninjurious weight'. Scott suggested, however, that if it wasn't an unfortunate periphrasis, it was redundant, referring apparently to 'o'ercharg'd' and 'oppression'. Nevertheless, this use of oxymoron, a form of paradox, to which modern critics have developed a special awareness, was at least recognized and recognized with approval. Scott limited himself, as always, to the reality of 'oppression' rather than to the playful fact that the children become a part of the load they carry when they become 'overcharged'.

It is possible to test judgements about diction by the alternatives they propose, and in the *Summer* storm passage (ll. 1128–43), Scott attempted a revision of what Thomson had written (1746) in order 'only to explain my meaning, when I talk of classical and correct composition'. Granting the accuracy of Thomson's observation, Scott declared:

> No author, ancient or modern, (so far as I know) has described the grand electrical phenomena of the atmosphere, with such dignity and precision. The diction as usual, is rather too diffuse.
>
> 'Tis listening fear and dumb amazement all:
> When to the startled eye the sudden glance
> Appears far south, eruptive through the cloud,
> And following slower *in explosion vast*,
> The thunder raises his tremendous voice.
> At first heard solemn o'er the verge of heaven,
> The tempest *growls*; but as it nearer comes,
> And rolls its awful burden on the wind,
> The lightnings flash a larger curve, and more
> The noise astounds; till overhead a sheet
> Of livid flame discloses wide, then shuts
> And opens wider, shuts and opens still
> Expansive, wrapping ether in a blaze,
> Follows the loosen'd aggravated roar
> Enlarging, deep'ning, mingling; peal on peal
> Crush'd horrible, convulsing heaven and earth.

Scott declared that the first eight lines 'might possibly be compressed to advantage' in the following way:

> 'Tis list'ning fear and dumb amazement all:
> When to the startled eye the sudden glance,
> Appears far south eruptive through the cloud;
> And following slow the solemn thunder rolls.
> Long, dark and threatening o'er the verge of heav'n
> The tempest swells, but as it nearer comes,
> And spreads its awful burden on the wind,
> The lightnings flash, etc.

The explanation of the revision was as follows: 'Storms arise from all quarters of the horizon, but perhaps oftenest from the south; the mention of that point is therefore equally natural and picturesque; specification of position always gives a kind of reality to a supposed scene. The "sudden glance of distant lightning", should have been followed by the thunder heard remote, not by the "*tremendous voice*", and vast explosion; these are introduced too early in the description. The tempest rolling its awful burden on the wind, is a just and noble idea.'[1] What governed Scott's view of 'diffuse', therefore, was the introduction of personified thunder which disrupted the consistency of natural description. He removed, too, 'the tempest growls', again substituting natural description for personification and again in 'spreads' for 'rolls its awful burden'.

What the revision did was to reduce the Thomsonian characteristic of mingling natural with personified description in order to create a continuity between the universe of man and nature. Not only did Scott abuse the music of 'And following slower in explosion vast, / The thunder raises his tremendous voice', but he missed the sequential unfolding of the storm in terms of lightning, then thunder, then the tempest as a whole. The picturesqueness of Thomson is lost in the commonplace simplicity urged by Scott of making the tempest 'long, dark and threatening', and because he makes the thunder 'roll', he is compelled to make the tempest 'spread its awful burden' rather than amass the cumulative power which the passage requires and which is found in 'rolls'.

Adequate criticism of any passage depends upon an inference about what the passage seeks to do; thus the commentary poses an end and analyses how it has or has not been achieved, indicating or implying what might have been done. It is possible to recognize what Thomson sought to develop in this passage by referring to its similarity to an earlier version. Scott's criticism did not accept Thomson's use of personification, just as it was not sensitive to the order of the passage. The criticism did not recognize Thomson's characteristic use of personification and attributed it to a lack of control of language or to diffuseness. But Thomson in his original version had sought the personification and indicated the religious-scientific basis for it:

> 'Tis dumb Amaze, and listening Terror all;
> When, to the quicker Eye, the livid Glance
> Appears, far South, emissive thro' the Cloud;
> And, by the powerful Breath of God inflate,

[1] Scott, *Critical Essays*, pp. 322–4 (for other passages, see pp. 371–3).

> The Thunder raises his tremendous Voice,
> At first low-muttering; but, at each Approach,
> The lightnings flash a larger Curve . . .
> [*Summer*, 'A', ll. 757–63]

Critical sensitivity to language, therefore, can lead to reliable statements about aims, but the determination of aims, linguistic and otherwise, based on the naked poem clearly presents a problem. John More (1777) was a more sensitive critic of Thomson than Scott and in the famous moon passage from *Autumn* he undertook the same type of revision as did Scott; and in doing so, he created a very close approximation to Thomson's original version. More made clear that he preferred the non-scientific passages to the technical ones, and he was, though he did not know it, preferring one kind of Thomsonian poetry to another. He was limited in the kind of poetry he could appreciate, but what he could appreciate was in the tradition of Thomson's own verse. In 1746 Thomson had written:

> Meanwhile the moon,
> Full-orbed and breaking through the scattered clouds,
> Shows her broad visage in the crimsoned east.
> Turned to the sun direct, her spotted disk
> (Where mountains rise, umbrageous dales descend,
> And caverns deep, as optic tube descries)
> A smaller earth, gives all his blaze again,
> Void of its flame, and sheds a softer day.
> Now through the passing cloud she seems to stoop,
> Now up the pure cerulean rides sublime.
> Wide the pale deluge floats, and streaming mild
> O'er the skied mountain to the shadowy vale,
> While rocks and floods reflect the quivering gleam,
> The whole air whitens with a boundless tide
> Of silver radiance trembling round the world.
> [*Autumn*, ll. 1088–1102]

Of this More declared:

> His description of the moon, may perhaps be thought a little too severely wrought. For grandeur suffers essentially from the least want of simplicity. The truth is, Thomson generally explains at the same time that he describes. This unavoidably wears an air of obscurity, to such readers at least, as are not previously acquainted with the subject. Fortunately, the exceptionable lines may here be omitted, without injuring the rest, which apart from these, cannot

but leave some pleasing impressions of sublimity on every susceptible heart:

> Meanwhile the moon
> Full orb'd and *breaking* thro' the *scatter'd* cloulds [clouds],
> Shews her *broad visage* in the *crimson'd east.*
> Now thro' the *passing cloud* she seems to *stoop,*
> Now up the pure cerulean *rides sublime*!
> Wide the pale deluge floods [floats] and streaming mild
> O'er the sky'd mountain to the shadowy vale,
> While rocks and flood reflect the *quivering* gleam,
> The whole air whitens with a boundless tide
> Of silver radiance, *trembling* round the world.[1]

More found obscurity and explanation to be technical and artificial, 'too severely wrought' because he assumed that an indiscriminate audience was the basis for judging the value of poetry. When More's statement is compared with that of a modern critic who analyses Thomson's original version of this passage, it is recognizable at once that the information of the modern critic explains what some of the eighteenth-century critics took for granted, but that the grounds for value are not distant from Warton's. The original passage and the critical comment follow:

> The vivid Stars shine out, in radiant Files;
> And boundless Ether glows, till the fair Moon
> Shows her broad Visage, in the crimson'd East;
> Now, stooping, seems to kiss the passing Cloud:
> Now, o'er the pure Cerulean, rides sublime.
> Wide the pale Deluge floats, with silver Waves,
> O'er the sky'd Mountain, to the low-laid Vale;
> From the white Rocks, with dim Reflexion, gleams,
> And faintly glitters thro' the waving Shades.
> [*Winter*, 'A', ll. 88–96]

No noun lacks its preceding adjective, and adjectives and adverbs do most of the work of the description. Yet this is effective poetry. It conveys a sense of vision and scope; the movement of the lines itself suggests the slow majesty of the moon's progress; specific details ('the pale Deluge,' 'the sky'd Mountain') show the poet's eye; and a certain restraint lends emphasis. Close observation is suggested here, and interest in the aesthetic observation of nature; the generalized vocabulary emphasizes by implication the moon's

[1] More, *Strictures*, pp. 256–7.

impartiality, lack of particularity, and thus adds to the sense of universality which the passage successfully evokes.[1]

The universality of the passage is identified by Patricia Spacks (1960) as 'partly the product of the poet's special vision of the cosmos as a beautifully structured interconnected whole'. More, whose reconstruction was very close to the original, valued the passage for his underlined words such as 'moon', 'breaking', 'scattered clouds', 'broad visage', 'crimson'd east', 'passing cloud', 'stoop', 'rides sublime', 'quivering', 'trembling', which belonged to the diction of 'pleasing impressions of sublimity'. The modern critic found that close observation and generalized vocabulary contributed to the sense of an ordered universe based on the moon's progress.

A pertinent language context was, for More, any passage that he could hold up to the criterion of simplicity or audience approval, but for the modern critic to do the same is to neglect the ways in which poetic passages accumulate meanings. Words are shaped not merely by their past but by their uses within a poem, and it is necessary to define or demonstrate what makes a context sufficient; for example, what the 'vivid Stars' are related to, or the sailing of the moon. The entire passage which begins, in the original *Winter*, with line 80 and concludes with line 104 is a description of the sunset, night, and sunrise. In the total passage there are many nouns without adjectives, and significant verbs. The passage which represents the cycle of the sunset and sunrise, develops its fullness from the images of interchange, the gliding, riding, rising forces of nature.

This passage was also analysed by John Veitch (1887):

> This passage shows Thomson in his weakness and in his strength. The description is of the most literal kind—a noting simply of what the eye may observe, but the eye of a poet. Then it is made up from many scenes, not extracted, as it were, as an essence from one striking vision, and thus rendered typical of many; it is rather a generalized and adapted picture. It is marred, moreover, by explanations of how certain of the features arise, are seen, and may be seen. But the last seven lines contain as true, characteristic, and noble a delineation as can be found in the English, or, I believe, in any language. The moon seeming to stoop through the passing clouds, then riding clear and sublime; the light streaming over 'the skied mountain'; the gleam of rock and flood; and, finally,

[1] Patricia Meyer Spacks, *The Varied God* (Berkeley and Los Angeles, 1959), p. 61.

the 'boundless tide of silver radiance trembling round the world',—are elements of a picture complete in the beauty of its impressiveness and unity.[1]

According to Veitch, the faults of the passage are the over-enumeration of scenes without a single 'essence' or 'wholeness', especially in the first part, and a too general reference to marshes, rivers, fogs. It contains, moreover, an explanation of sight from the 'optic tube' rather than an imagined presentation. The last six lines, however, dealing with the moon and concentrated into a single view or essence, relate all details to the beauty of moonlight. The objections of Veitch were the same as those of More but governed by a theory of imaginative wholeness instead of obscurity. Yet the concept of 'wholeness' is no more adequate than 'obscurity' to explain the passage because the passage is not about the moon, but of the relation of three types of nature's progress, resulting from the cyclical pattern of the sun casting down vapour which becomes fogs (darkness and dreariness) and shining upon the moon which becomes radiant. The cyclical rise and fall exists not only from heaven to earth but even from one object in heaven to another—setting and rising, sun and earth, mountains and dales. The passage, therefore, is a complexly woven whole, and the weakness of the first part is not an enumeration but a somewhat dulled comparison—in a musical sense—of the gliding sun, the rolling fogs and the riding moon. The shortened day is not sufficiently abrupt, nor the fogs—though three subordinate clauses developing the 'clustering' do set up preparation for the coming radiance. The shimmering radiance is dependent for its effect upon the reflection and cumulative cycle and contrast, and the whole is an example of the varied and conflicting natural qualities. The concept of 'essence' or whole, therefore, is of a type which the critics do not see because they expect the transforming universe of Thomson to be conceived in terms of a single image rather than a series of reflective images forming a 'whole'. And for Veitch, the perception of this view is impeded by the false scientific contrast of explanation as opposed to poetic description.

Now in order for critical interpretation to take cognizance of a different kind of 'whole', it had to permit looseness to exist as a value, or to assume that the concepts of wholes were tentative or to

[1] John Veitch, *The Feeling for Nature in Scottish Poetry* (Edinburgh, 1887), II, 58–59.

see wholes in terms not only of Wordsworth but of Pope and of Dryden, or it had to reject scientific induction for personal sympathy. Without such alternatives, criticism was committed to negative judgements determined by its assumptions, and a consequence of this commitment can be observed in Patricia Spacks's volume. She argues that the 'good' passages in *The Seasons* are the result of Thomson's sense of the objectivity of nature, and she sees the above moon passage unfortunately revised to show man's scientific accomplishments. In supporting her statement, linking artistic value with a world view, she seriously delimits her understanding of the language and structure of the passage.

> In the final section of this transferred passage, Thomson increases the descriptive emphasis on the moon. In doing so, he is unable to avoid referring parenthetically to the scientific achievements of man: the spotted disk of the moon shows
>
> (Where mountains rise, umbrageous vales descend,
> And oceans roll, as optic tube descries)
> [*Autumn* 'A', ll. 988–9]
>
> Moreover the moon is, after all, only 'a lesser earth' (l. 990)—the domain of man is temporarily of supreme importance in the universe. That the poet's purely descriptive skill has not deserted him, however, is indicated by the last two lines added to this passage:
>
> The whole air whitens with a boundless tide
> Of silver radiance, trembling round the world.[1]
> [ll. 1101–2]

Such criticism, predicated on the badness of revisions, must resort not to an awareness of poetic structure but to some personal explanation—Thomson's 'purely descriptive skill has not deserted him'—to explain what is good, as though poetic skill exists exclusive of poems and their structure. The inattention, in other words, to the inner relations of language, to 'rise' and 'descend', to 'whitens' and

[1] Spacks, pp. 115–16. For an examination of another *Autumn* revision, ll. 743–56, see Gertrude Greene Cronk, 'Lucretius and Thomson's Autumnal Fogs', *AJP*, LI (1930), 233–42. The author declares that in the revision, the 'at first unapparent economy is perhaps the most remarkable quality which he has here achieved. It is an economy resulting not from scant material or idea, but from extreme compression, from fusing almost inseparably, the harvest of the eye and of the mind.'

'boundless' merely increased the fragmenting of the poem by the fragmentation of the explanation.

There exist an abundant number of passages from the 1746 revision which almost all critics agree in praising: in *Spring*, the fishing scene and the shower, the descriptions of the birds; in *Summer*, the purling brook, sheep shearing and haying, the storm, the Nile, the sand storm; in *Autumn*, the moon scene; in *Winter*, the storm, the dying shepherd, the robin redbreast, the frozen river, the conclusion.

Passages of the poem have won continuing approval (since Warton) for a diversity of reasons detailed in this chapter, and perhaps the criterion of poetic value is precisely the capacity of a passage to have reference not only to developed and consistent values within the poem, but clear references to nature as well, depending upon the place of the poem in the culture examining it. The force of language in the poem depends upon more, and more complex, criteria than have yet been discovered. And, indeed, those that have been discovered have often served to verify unproved earlier hypotheses. The 'style' of Thomson has not been made clear although more elements of its originality are now available than at any time previous. But the humour of Thomson in his obvious burlesque passages as well as in those of Musidora, haymaking, etc., have not been disclosed. There are numerous 'tones' in *The Seasons*, but some of these have still to be discriminated by criticism. The versification of Thomson is now seen to be more diverse than was assumed, but his invocations to his patrons, to industry, and his catalogues of history seem irretrievable.

A NOTE TO CHAPTER VI: A DISAGREEMENT ON PERSONIFICATION

There have been a number of disagreements on the first four lines of *Spring*, and since these pertain to poetic language, especially personification, it might prove valuable to study the grounds of such disagreements and the possible methods for handling them.

In 1753 Robert Shiels wrote:

> The author next published the Spring, the introduction to which is very poetical and beautiful.

> Come gentle Spring, ethereal mildness come,
> And from the bosom of yon dropping cloud,
> While music wakes around, veil'd in a show'r
> Of shadowing roses, on our plains descend.
> [*Spring*, ll. 1–4]

'Poetical' and 'beautiful' were but two of the common critical terms which expressed his critical judgements. *Winter* was a 'picturesque' poem and he wished to 'take an opportunity of pointing out some of its most striking beauties'. Just as the 'induction' to *Winter* was celebrated 'for its sublimity, so the conclusion has likewise a claim to praise, for the tenderness of the sentiments, and the pathetic force of the expression'. *Autumn* was not 'without its beauties, of which many have considered the story of Lavinia, naturally and artfully introduced, as the most affecting. The story is in itself moving and tender'. The 'induction' to *Spring* 'is very poetical and beautiful', and *Summer* 'has many manly and striking beauties, of which the Hymn to the Sun is one of the sublimest and most masterly efforts of genius we have ever seen'.

'Striking beauties', 'sublimity', 'picturesque', 'tenderness of the sentiments', 'pathetic force of the expression', 'naturally and artfully introduced', 'most affecting', 'moving', 'poetical', 'beautiful'—these terms formed the inheritance of Shiels's critical vocabulary, but they served as impressionistic comments rather than critical explanations. 'Poetical' and 'beautiful' were followed by a particular example, but the example merely restated the poem and was not analysed by selecting the 'poetical' or the 'beautiful'—though the first might, perhaps, be defined as the use of personification—a 'poetical' figure—and the second as indicative of the attributes of spring—'music' and 'shadowing roses'. Subsequent critical comments on the same passage need to be quoted before the analytical issues can be understood.

In 1777 John More commented that Thomson 'speaks in the first period of his *Spring*, of *Music veil'd in a shower of shadowing roses*. These delicate and tender flowers are not certainly quite so early in our island. Had he wrote in a warmer climate, where vegetation is much more forward than here, fact, perhaps, might have countenanced this beautiful exordium'. Anna Seward in 1798 in terms similar to this wrote:

> There is a striking inaccuracy in the very front and head of these charming poems—in the exordium of Spring. We are astonished that so nice an observer of nature should have permitted such an

anachronism to remain, through all the editions he so carefully revised, viz. putting roses into the garland of an English Spring, when she first appears, and in their ripe luxuriance too!

Veil'd in a shower
Of shadowing roses on our plains descend!

A proper invocation for Summer, not for Spring. Milton more accurately distinguishes:

Nor sight of vernal bloom, nor Summer's rose.

Certainly the rose is summer's boast, nor ever ripens naturally in our climate till he has attained his strength.

John Aikin supported Anna Seward and added, 'The epithet "ethereal mildness" which he gives to Spring presents no visual image'. Robert Heron (1793) explained that:

In the *Invocation* to Spring, Thomson, personifying the season which he is about to celebrate, presents a lovely, but, I think, rather too faint a picture.

. . . *gentle Spring, ethereal mildness* . . .

give no image to the imagination, nothing but a personification almost without attributes. The circumstances, however, in which the heavenly form is invited to appear, are such as may aid the fancy to distinguish its features and figure:

. . . *from the bosom of yon dropping cloud,*
While music wakes around, veil'd in a shower
Of shadowing roses, on our plains descend.

The poet seems to stand in rapt attention, to gaze eagerly on the *dropping cloud*, to listen, with fond awe, to the aerial *music*, *waking around*; and, amid these emotions, to fancy, that he sees a Being, august and charming as Venus,—like Flora, invested in the fairest ornaments of vegetation,—but, in timid delicacy, in modest dignity, surpassing both,—descend, with majestic motion, beside him.

William Hazlitt (1818) attacked the passage:

[Thomson] overloads an exquisitely natural sentiment or image with a cloud of painted, pompous, cumbrous phrases, like the shower of roses, in which he represents the Spring, his own lovely, fresh, and innocent Spring, as descending to the earth . . . a flimsy, round-about unmeaning commencement.

In 1830 John Wilson declared:

> That picture is indistinctly and obscurely beautiful to the imagination, and there is not a syllable about sex—though 'ethereal mildness', which is an Impersonation, and hardly an Impersonation, must be, it is felt, a Virgin Goddess, whom all the divinities that dwell between heaven and earth must love. Never, to our taste—but our taste is inferior to our feeling and our genius— . . . had poem a more beautiful beginning. It is not simple—nor ought it to be—it is rich, and even gorgeous—for the Bard came to his subject full of inspiration, and as it was the inspiration, here, not of profound thought, but of passionate emotion, it was right that music at the very first moment should overflow the page, and that it should be literally strewed with roses. An imperfect Impersonation is often proof positive of the highest state of poetical enthusiasm. The forms of nature undergo a half-humanizing process under the intensity of our love, yet still retain the character of the insensate creation, thus affecting us with a sweet, strange, almost bewildering, blended emotion that scarcely belongs to either separately, but to both together clings as to a phenomenon that only the eye of genius sees, because only the soul of genius can give it a presence—though afterwards all eyes dimly recognise it, on its being shewn to them, as something more vivid than their own faint experience, yet either kindred to it, or virtually one and the same.

In examination of a single passage by diverse critics one may look hopefully for some sort of continuity in critical endeavour. Such continuity made discrimination possible, for the passage was carefully analysed, disclosing critical assumptions and explanations. Such analyses were neither directly progressive nor even directly continuous—they did not reveal an advance in method or in the study of language or imagery, but they did make clear that some explanations were based on more careful evidence and individual perception than others.

The 'beautiful' and 'poetical' of Shiels, followed by an example, indicated that he used the poem as a substitute for critical explanation. The difficulty with such uses was not merely that Shiels presupposed a unity in his audience's interpretation of 'beautiful' which did not exist, but that he failed to provide a context of usage sufficiently defined so that within the induction to the poem the 'beautiful' elements would be apparent. The term 'beautiful' was used by Shiels seven different times in the essay; it was applied to the whole poem, to its parts, to the subject of the poem and to its construction—

'beautiful transition'. The several uses of a critical term in one essay are not necessarily confusing, provided they are not contradictory. But the value of their use depends upon the contexts of discrimination in which they are placed.

The attack of Anna Seward upon the passage was based on the assumption that the 'shower' of 'roses' was factually inaccurate, 'an anachronism'. Though one must realize that her comment was made lightly, her argument insisted the poem was to be judged by its truth to fact. In this she was supported by John Aikin, who added that, expressively, the metaphor 'ethereal mildness' was a failure because it failed to paint a picture. And, indeed, Priestley and others explained that the test of a metaphor was 'its being examined as a painting'.

Hazlitt did not assert that 'shower of shadowing roses' was a phrase unable to paint a picture, but he objected to it because it was 'painted' or artificial, arguing that a 'natural'—a spontaneous—sentiment should be expressed in spontaneous language. The disagreement about 'shower of shadowing roses'—whether it was factually inaccurate, a description of the 'fairest ornaments' or merely a cumbrous phrase—indicated that critics could agree on the area, the basis of disagreement.

Heron and Hazlitt disagreed on the inference from the shower metaphor. Both agreed that it was an 'ornamental' metaphor, though Heron found the vegetation ornaments vivid, whereas Hazlitt found such description merely 'cumbrous' and artificial. The critical dilemma, if the appeal is made merely to the critical presuppositions, is that both arguments involve tautologies. Vividness is an aesthetic value; the passage has vividness; therefore it has value. Artificiality is an aesthetic fault; the passage has artificiality; therefore it is faulty.

If critical dilemmas were, however, merely tautologies, then no resolution could follow. But such dilemmas are resolvable by reference to other inquiries or to other agreements—the basis for determining vividness, or the agreement on how meaning is identified or the agreement on similar uses or contexts within the same poem, or reference to the manner of perceiving the passage. By reference, for example, to the use of 'shadowing' or 'bosom of yon dropping cloud' some basis can be established by which to compare adequate with inadequate uses. By reference to such agreements, tautological arguments become empirical distinctions, the validity for which rests on what Hume called 'matters of fact' and the refutations of which depend upon more adequate 'facts' or a refutation of the presented evidence. In this particular passage, for example, the 'shower of shadowing roses' was functioning to introduce the sexual implications of spring—the rosy innocence of spring (a fountain personified as well as a season) was descending veiled in a spray or shower 'of shadowing roses', a rain foreshadowing the coming fruition or reflecting the coming rebirth of nature. The use of a metaphor in which future qualities—'shadowing roses'—are attributed to present actions was a frequent device in Thomson's *Spring* as when 'Heaven descends / In universal bounty, shedding herbs / And fruits and flowers on Nature's ample lap' (ll. 180–2). Thus it is possible to argue that what appeared 'cumbrous' is a characteristic of Thomson's writing and as 'spontaneous' as the other passages referred to. The argument for 'cumbrous' can thus not be made in the terms presented, and must now be conducted in terms of function, which is also reducible to matters of fact.

These criticisms, by confining the analysis to the particular passage only, were involved in the method of 'beauties' and 'blemishes'—a method in which the atomic portions of the work were evaluated with reference to general principles rather than other parts of the same work and without realization that contexts of language were necessary to determine (*a*) whether passages were or were not 'artificial', that is, whether artificiality as a mode of composition was apparent in 'ethereal mildness' and in a 'shower of shadowing roses', and (*b*) whether identification of particular implications—vegetative ornaments—was consistent with the inferences drawn. The resolution of the dilemma here is dependent upon the kind of inference to be drawn from any one particular passage without providing for inferences from the components.

It could be argued that such resolutions merely pose another theory of inference with contextual assumptions. But this would be wrong. For explanation depends upon data; insufficient, inadequate as well as inaccurate data or inferences can be and need to be refuted or corrected.

If the critical issue were raised, inquiring what refutation would be sufficient to demonstrate that factual errors—such as English roses in summer—in the induction to *Spring* are not aesthetic errors, is it not sufficient to argue that truth to fact as an *aesthetic* principle is irrelevant, for it makes all personification unpoetic—a procedure surely contradictory to the position of Anna Seward.

One of the dilemmas of these particular critical comments was that they all shared a neglect of the poem as a whole. Granted that the different seasons were governed by different emotional 'tones', these comments did not undertake to relate the 'tone' of the part to that of the season. Compared to Shiels's comments, the assumptions of explanatory criticism are apparent in the analyses which critics offered. Reasons were given and particular references made. These practices encouraged discussions of the particularities of the poem, while revealing at the same time their critical limitations. And it was precisely because they provided such explanations that it is possible to examine them and to discover the basis of critical discrimination and the types of data, psychological or scientific or literary, on which their discriminations rested.

When, therefore, Wilson pointed out that 'ethereal mildness' was an indistinct image, he was describing what the other critics also recognized. His approval of this faintness was that it was not associated with sex and that it was associated, in the critic's mind, with a 'Virgin Goddess'. His inferences—that the poet came to the passage full of inspiration—a position opposite to Hazlitt's which denied Thomson's inspiration here, is obviously an inference incapable of demonstration and valuable only if the point were pursued by analysis of the passage. He claimed that the reference to 'roses', while vague, was in keeping with the poet's 'passionate emotion', and an 'imperfect Impersonation is often proof positive of the highest state of poetical enthusiasm'. But 'proof positive' in any *particular* case requires more than references to some other situations.

If one analyses the function of the personification it seems that it belongs with the succeeding apostrophe to Hartford:

> O Hartford, fitted or to shine in courts
> With unaffected grace, or walk the plain
> With innocence and meditation joined
> In soft assemblage, listen to my song,
> Which thy own season paints—when nature all
> Is blooming and benevolent, like thee.
> [*Spring*, ll. 5–10]

The *Spring* personification addresses the season and the apostrophe addresses the human embodiment of the season. Thus, in Thomson's customary way, there is a relation between man and the heavens which includes both as subject to or characterized by the same forces.

But in this comparison, the language describing Spring ('ethereal mildness') and its activities (music 'waking' and a 'shower' which is 'veiled' descending), creates a plethora of reference and activity in contrast to the simplicity and innocence of Hartford. Thus the 'gentle' and 'unaffected' seem to contrast with the secretiveness of Spring, and instead of reflecting each other, Spring and Hartford have contrasting powers. Thus the poet must 'explain' their similarity by stating that 'nature all / Is blooming and benevolent, like thee'—a summary which indicates that the comparison has somewhat failed to be clearly developed—and indeed it has. It is a failure all the more noticeable by comparison with the induction to *Winter* in which the poet's formal voice is, as in *Spring*, followed by his innocent one, yet, by having one recall the other the transition succeeds, whereas in *Spring* it fails.

VII

THE APPEALS TO THE PAST: CRITICS AND AUDIENCES

> A general love of literature was not so diffused in Thomson's time as it is in ours.
>
> A. CUNNINGHAM

THERE WAS A TIME when *The Seasons* was the most popular poem in the English language; and 'popularity' meaning unanimity of response was a common eighteenth-century theory of evaluation. The problem of 'popularity' belongs to this study of criticism because, as a popular poem, *The Seasons* was the model for other poems, because critics sometimes explained its value as a result of its popular subject, and because critics were diverted from certain theories of analysis by the very power of this popularity. To study the rise and fall of this popularity is to study the development of indiscriminate but extensive analyses of words, lines, and passages, and the decline of aesthetic discrimination.

The problem of popularity can be seen in the diffusion of criticism; the critics who were the defenders of the poet and the poem in the mid-eighteenth century and who saw criticism as a defence of artistic integrity, were supplemented at the end of the century by critics who looked upon themselves as teachers of youth. They assumed that an unconscious 'tuition' was learned from nature or from works about nature, and such hypotheses were in conflict with particular literary analyses of the poem. These teacher-critics set out to make the poem understandable to an audience composed of young men and women, suppressing the classical backgrounds and exalting the moral teachings and rural references. The 'tuitionists' took for granted the literary value of the poem, but their precise grounds became more and more obscure.

Their 'grants' did not survive the shift from a rural to an industrial society, and except for a small, classically educated audience, there were no critics equipped to expound the poetic value of *The Seasons*. So long as the society supported the poem and so long as its values could be tested by looking abroad on nature, its critical abuses as an educative instrument could be borne. But the use of the poem as a textbook, its institutionalization, systematically undermined the poetic values by substituting for them social, scientific, or grammatical guides.

The poem was used to teach natural science, philology, grammar, and history; its critical fate, in the schools, was in the hands of teachers. From 1840 to 1870 there were numerous school editions—some more reliable than others—but the dreary conclusion must be that literary discrimination was corrupted by these texts. At the beginning of the nineteenth century, despite the moralizing of the 'tuitionists', readers could recognize the precision of nature description by looking abroad on nature. But with increasing industrialization, the balance maintained by the society, a balance which stabilized the poem's literary value even though the critics did not concentrate upon it, was upset. The poem which had been used for teaching information rather than poetic craft was attacked for its thinness of cultural values, especially since the annotations provided only an arbitrary historical background. The collapse of its popularity coincided with the decline of respect for eighteenth-century society as a whole so that generalizations about the society were only rarely opposed when critics applied them to *The Seasons*.

Critics who defended the poem as a cultural document had first to correct the indiscriminate attack upon the eighteenth century. But in countering the developmental theory, such critics continued to disregard the aesthetic values of the poem, often arguing that these were irrelevant. Their view of literary history as an adjunct of history proper overlooked the fact that expressive devices of language and structure had their own histories, often altering the meaning of overt poetical statements.

The attempt to establish the poem as an eighteenth-century document, however, demanded an adherence to quantitative measurements, to studies of words, of images, of ideas. By adhering to quantitative historical studies, critics were sometimes led to the individuality of poets and their distinctive uses of shared content and vocabulary. Thus in opposition to the poem as document critics began to re-examine the expression of ideas and the meaning of literary as distinct from other kinds of history. This has led back to reconsiderations of 'process', to the search for philosophic assumptions in the so-called language of objective description and to distinctions between successful and unsuccessful uses of subject matter. These investigations are, as yet, tentative and speculative, but they reflect the shift in criticism in which the burden of discrimination must now be borne by the scholar. In a commanding position for the preservation of the past he can no longer afford to neglect discriminations since the values he discloses are the only ones likely to be transmitted, there no longer being a society and a popular audience to preserve what he ignores.

(a) R. SHIELS, J. WARTON, P. MURDOCH, J. AIKIN AND THOMSON'S OWN AUDIENCES

But in a short time, the applause became unanimous.

P. MURDOCH

The possibility of composing a popular poem was already present to Thomson while working on *Summer*; at that time (21–27 Aug. 1726) he wrote to David Mallet of his verses: 'They contain a Panegyric on Brittain, which may perhaps contribute to make my Poem popular. The English People are not a little vain of Themselves, and their Country. Brittannia too includes our native Country, Scotland.'[1] 'Popularity' was to be achieved by an appeal to national feeling, and as Horace E. Hamilton remarked (1942), if Thomson 'could see his way clear to insert in *Summer* the Panegyric on Britain' on the expectation that it would contribute, as he says, 'to make my poem popular', is there any reason to suppose that he would not also have admitted other materials which in his estimation of public taste would have the same effect?'[2]

[1] Alan Dugald McKillop, *Letters and Documents* (Lawrence, 1958), p. 48.

[2] Horace E. Hamilton, *Travel and Science in Thomson's Seasons* (Unpublished Dissertation, Yale University, 1942), p. 115. See also Horace E. Hamilton, 'James Thomson's *Seasons*: Shifts in the Treatment of Popular Subject Matter', *ELH* (1948), 112. It should be noted that some of the most inept passages are the result of Thomson's eulogies and his bid for 'popularity' a matter of temptation, not discrimination.

Thomson may have made a bid for popular approval by incorporating appeals to different groups, but his poem shared elements with Mallet's *Excursion* and Savage's *The Wanderer*. All may have wished their poems to be 'popular', but they differed in the handling of 'popular' material. Without such discrimination, criticism cannot distinguish common subject material from individual treatment of it. Thomson's friends constituted one group of critics who recognized such differences although they did not always approve of Thomson's particular versions.

There were other readers of Thomson's work about whom we know little except that they, like Thomson's own friends, did not all approve. The critics who wrote after Thomson's death tried to explain this audience with reference to its clannish quality and its disregard for merit. In 1753 Robert Shiels wrote: 'a work that has only its intrinsic merit to depend on, may be long dormant in a Bookseller's shop, 'till some person eminent for taste, points out its worth to the many, declares the bullion sterling, stamps its value with his name, and makes it pass current with the world'. '*Winter*', he explained, was unsold until Mr. Whatley urged its value. He brought it to the attention of readers, who, now judging it for themselves, 'found it so completely beautiful, that they could not but think themselves happy in doing justice to a man of so much merit'.[1]

For Shiels (1753), the approval of literary value was not an issue; the distribution of a new work was. Himself a Grub-Street writer, he saw literary recognition as the chief issue, along with the neglect of social status that writing entailed. That his view of the poem's distribution was, in fact, inaccurate, does not deny its importance. Neither William Somerville nor Joseph Mitchell gave the poem wholehearted approval; moreover, it had no distribution difficulty, the poem in 1726 going into four editions. And who was Whatley that all should lend him their ears? In 1897 D. C. Tovey remarked that, considering *Winter* was published in March, 'Mr. Whatley must have been quick, if he anticipated Aaron Hill, who had commended the poem, to which Mallet called his attention, before April 5th and received from Thomson that day a letter of thanks of incredible fulsomeness'.[2]

In 1756 Joseph Warton suggested that the proper candidate for Thomson's 'patron' was Joseph Spence; for Spence 'made honourable

[1] Shiels, 'Thomson', *Lives*, V, 196 n., 197.

[2] Tovey, 'Memoir', *Thomson's Poetical Works*, I, xxii.

mention of it [*The Seasons*] in his *Essay on the Odyssey*, which becoming a popular book, made the poem universally known'.[1] Since Spence's book was published after at least two editions of *Winter* had been printed, Spence could not have been responsible for its success, even though he may have stimulated it. But even such stimulation was highly questionable, considering that the comment which Spence had made appeared in a footnote that referred to Thomson's use of obsolete words: 'beside several other Beauties, [he] is by no means unhappy in his Management of this sort of Words'.[2]

The reviewer of Warton's book in 1756 pointed out that his praise of Spence was overdone: 'He imputes more to Mr. Spence's recommendation of Thomson's Winter than probably it produced. For tho' the character which Mr. Spence gave of that poem may have increased its popularity, it is certain, that other gentlemen gave earlier testimonies of their applause.'[3] The conception of readers who disregarded the poet until he was sponsored by a powerful patron expressed the sense of injustice which Shiels and Warton felt for the disregard of talent.

The first critic who made an effort to explain the impact of the poem upon its readers was Patrick Murdoch (1762), who insisted that prejudice alone prevented the readers from responding to Thomson's original subject. The development of a theory of sympathy was, for him, a necessary weapon to combat wrong expectations and to direct proper evaluation.

> The Poem of *Winter*, published in *March* 1726, was no sooner read than universally admired: those only excepted who had not been used to feel, or to look for any thing in poetry, beyond a *point* of satirical or epigrammatic wit, a smart *antithesis* richly trimmed with rhime, or the softness of an *elegiac* complaint. To such his manly classical spirit could not readily recommend itself; till after a more attentive perusal, they had got the better of their

[1] J. Warton, ed., *The Works of Alexander Pope* (London, 1797), I, 236 n.

[2] Joseph Spence, *An Essay on Pope's Odyssey* (London, 1726), Part II, p. 15. For a discussion of Spence and Thomson, see Austin Wright, *Joseph Spence: A Critical Biography* (Chicago, 1950), pp. 37–39.

[3] 'Review of *An Essay on the Genius and Writings of Pope*', *Monthly Review*, XIV (1756), 547. Edmund Gosse nominated Aaron Hill as the man who 'sounded the praises of the new descriptive poem through London': *A History of Eighteenth Century Literature* (London, 1889), p. 222. His grounds for this choice were no more adequate than those of earlier critics.

> prejudices, and either acquired or affected a truer taste. A few others stood aloof, merely because they had long before fixed the articles of their poetical creed, and resigned themselves to an absolute despair of ever seeing anything new and original. These were somewhat mortified to find their notions disturbed by the appearance of a poet, who seemed to owe nothing but to nature and his own genius. But, in a short time, the applause became unanimous; every one wondering how so many pictures, and pictures so familiar, should have moved them but faintly to what they felt in his descriptions.[1]

Murdoch's analysis of Thomson's audience had a threefold purpose: to create for his own audience an acceptance of the concept of sympathy in reading Thomson, to suggest that the historical failure to do so was the result of trivial poetic principles, and to encourage the continued 'universal' acceptance of *The Seasons*. The use of 'universal' and 'unanimous' is not quite sufficient to remove the disagreements which persisted. Warton's peculiar use of the word 'universal'—Spence made the poem 'universally known'—and Murdoch's use of 'universally admired' and 'unanimous'—the applause became unanimous—may imply absoluteness, but they obviously apply to limited contexts of responsive readers. Such uses of 'universal' and 'unanimous' applied to a 'company of one mind' or a 'union of sentiments', but such company was self-contained; admiration was not always for the same qualities, nor was there always admiration.

The need to which Murdoch pointed for creating an audience hospitable to newness and originality was repeated by other critics who, in the latter part of the eighteenth century, attacked earlier readers for demanding conformity and enforcing it, even against the talent of the author. That such an argument was as damaging to the author as to the audience was not without implications for the critics' contemporaries. In 1785 Thomas Warton wrote the following comment on the readers of Milton's minor poems.

> The poems which compose the present volume were published almost thirty years before the appearance of *Paradise Lost*. During that interval they were so totally disregarded, at least by the general reader, as scarcely to have conferred on their author the reputation of a writer of verses; much less the distinction and character of a true poet. After the publication of the *Paradise Lost*,

[1] Murdoch, *Account*, I, vii.

whose acknowledged merit and increasing celebrity might have naturally contributed to call other pieces of the same author, and of a kindred excellence, into a more conspicuous point of view, they long continued to remain in their original state of neglect and obscurity. At the infancy of their circulation, and for some years afterwards, they were overwhelmed in the commotions of faction, the conflict of religious disputation, and the professional ignorance of fanaticism. In succeeding years, when tumults and usurpations were at an end, and leisure and literature returned, the times were still unpropitious, and the public taste was unprepared for their reception. Wit and rhyme, sentiment and satire, polished numbers, sparkling couplets and pointed periods, having so long kept undisturbed possession in our poetry, would not easily give way to fiction and fancy, to picturesque description, and romantic imagery.[1]

Warton found Milton's poems neglected because the readers were overwhelmed by social and religious tumults, and when the 'commotions' subsided, 'the public taste was unprepared for their reception'. He implied the need to prepare the public for new poetry at the same time that general readers preferred poetic conventions conflicting with those of the poet. The readers were dominated by interests often quite irrelevant to poetry or directly antagonistic to the particular efforts of a Milton or a Thomson. Now George Sherburn has shown that Thomas Warton was factually inaccurate in assuming that Milton's minor poems were disregarded. If, therefore, the wrong assumptions of disregard by Shiels, Joseph Warton, Murdoch, and Thomas Warton be placed against the information available to them but not pursued, there seems to be either an investigative failure in gathering information, or a dominating hypothesis that 'public taste' could not be divorced from prejudice or uninterest without some patronizing efforts. These statements tried to account for obvious differences of response and assumed that when prejudice was eliminated, the poems became 'popular'. But the question of the readers for whom the poets wrote was concealed in these assumptions—the author wrote as a form of self-knowledge, but his knowledge was communicable to all who would read 'sympathetically'. But if, for these, the 'self' of the poet was accessible, by the end of the eighteenth century critics recognized that, for others, it was not; when a poet

[1] Thomas Warton, ed., *Poems upon Several Occasions*, by John Milton (London, 1785), p. iii.

won immediate popularity, therefore, 'sympathetic' critics suspected a toadying to fashion.

In 1786, in his *Memoir* of William Whitehead, William Mason quoted portions of Warton's passage to explain how fashion controlled the early poetry of Whitehead and limited his imagination.

> This, however, I think, would not have been the case, had he taken the versification of Spenser, Fairfax, Milton and poets similar to them for his model, rather than the close and condensed couplets of Pope; for, in that way of writing, his fancy would have developed itself earlier, and, perhaps have obtained greater strength and powers of exertion. But, though he had read Spenser in childhood with avidity, and was fully capable, as I shall shew presently, of catching his manner, yet the fashion of the time led him to exercise himself in that mode of versification which was then (almost exclusively of all others) esteemed the best; for those writers which may be called of the Italian School, were in no request.[1]

Mason explained that for Whitehead to adapt himself to fashionable taste 'was perfectly prudent, in order to procure a more favourable reception of his production'. It may have been more prudent for success but it was also more damaging to talent. These views of the 'general reader'—in contrast to the special reader—urged upon the poet an independent exercise of his originality and upon the reader a sympathetic response or a more appropriate response to the poetry based on the knowledge of its form and content. In criticisms of *The Seasons* this movement took two directions: defence of the poet's originality in form and subject matter, and attempts to educate the general reader in order to appreciate the poem more fully. Both these directions set off from the assumption that the poem was moving and vivid.

Thomson's originality in form and subject matter was first treated in detail by John Aikin in an *Essay on the Application of Natural History to Poetry* (1777). Aikin quoted Warton (1756), who had derived Thomson's vividness from literal knowledge of nature, and he also knew of Thomas Pennant's (1768) claim that the 'great beauty of that celebrated poet consists in his elegant and just descriptions of the œconomy of animals; and the happy use he hath made of natural knowledge in descriptive poetry, shines through almost every

[1] William Mason, 'Memoir of his [Whitehead's] Life and Writings', *Poems of William Whitehead* (York, 1786), III, 11, 14.

page of his *Seasons*'. Aikin addressed himself to contemporary poets and urged them to abandon feeble imagery and seek out fruitful novelty based on scientific truths.

Since Aikin sought to explain both the unity of the poem and its vividness of natural description, he obviously began by assuming that the poem did, in fact, possess unity and vividness. He attributed this vividness to scientific accuracy, and he gave reasons for claiming that *The Seasons* marked a new era in poetry. When *Winter* was first published, it was thought that descriptions 'could not legitimately constitute the whole, or even the principal part, of a capital piece. Something of a more solid nature was required as the ground-work of a poetical fabric.'[1] Aikin explained that Thomson had such a ground-work—the laws of natural science; he assumed, therefore, that Thomson's poem had become a model for descriptive poets because it was based on scientific truth, and that readers who enjoyed it did so for its precise observations, its science or both.

> Every grand and beautiful appearance in nature, that distinguishes one portion of the annual circuit from another, is a proper source of materials for the Poet of the Seasons. Of these, some are obvious to the common observer, and require only justness and elegance of taste for the selection: others discover themselves only to the mind opened and enlarged by science and philosophy.[2]

Aikin was quite right in assuming that some of Thomson's materials required scientific knowledge if they were to be fully understood, but he confused scientific materials with their poetic function. Even the common observer could not always perceive the beauties of the descriptions without a knowledge of other poetry, and the learned reader did not necessarily appreciate the poetry merely because he knew science.

The equation of scientific accuracy with poetic vividness seemed to explain the continuing authority of *The Seasons* so that almost

[1] John Aikin, 'An Essay on the Plan and Character of Thomson's Seasons' (1778), p. ix. For Pennant's reference, see Thomas Pennant, *British Zoology* (London, 1768), II, 260–1. See also 'Preface', I, ix, for Pennant's assumption that scientific knowledge corrected taste. Benjamin Martin, 'Dialogue IX', *The Young Gentleman and Lady's Philosophy* (London, 1759), I, 220–54, used *The Seasons* and other poems to illustrate the natural history of the four seasons. His book began with a poem, 'On the Usefulness of Natural Philosophy: A Poem'.

[2] Aikin, 'Essay', reprinted in *The Seasons* (London, 1792), p. xvi.

fifty years after its original publication (1730) it retained its force as a descriptive poem. The poets and the 'common' and 'learned' observers could all receive pleasure from the poem because, like science, it survived the test of truth. The examples Aikin gave were often 'vivid', though not for the reasons given. In 1777, Aikin quoted from *Summer* (ll. 224–36) and declared that Thomson

> has drawn a scene so surprisingly natural that our perception of it is no less lively than if it really existed before our eyes. It is perfect still life; the representation of a hot summer's noon
>
> The daw,
> The rook and magpie, to the grey-grown oaks
> That the calm village in their verdant arms,
> Sheltering, embrace, direct their lazy flight;
> Where on the mingling boughs they sit embower'd
> All the hot noon, till cooler hours arise.
> Faint, underneath, the household fowls convene;
> And in a corner of the buzzing shade,
> The house-dog with the vacant grey-hound, lies
> Out-stretch'd and sleepy. In his slumbers one
> Attacks the nightly thief, and one exults
> O'er hill and dale; till, wakened by the wasp,
> They, starting, snap.
>
> A striking instance of the extraordinary effect of a well-chosen epithet in adding life and force to a description, is shown in the expression '*buzzing* shade'. A single word here conveys to the mind all the imagery of a passage in the same author which Mr. Warton justly commends as equally new and picturesque.
>
> Resounds the living surface of the ground:
> Nor undelightful is the ceaseless hum
> To him that muses through the woods at noon;
> Or drowsy shepherd, as he lies reclin'd
> With half-shut eyes.
>
> [*Summer*, ll. 281–5]
>
> It is by such bold comprehensive touches as these, that Poetry is frequently enabled to produce more lively representations than Painting, even of sensible objects.[1]

To assume that the use of 'buzzing' or 'the living surface of the

[1] John Aikin, *An Essay on the Application of Natural History to Poetry* (Warrington, 1777), pp. 71–73.

ground' was dependent upon actual personal experience implied a theory of art which made all observers potential poets. But many observers who wrote poetry did not make it vivid, and, in many moving passages, Thomson wrote of what he never saw. The theory of scientific accuracy in the early work of Aikin could not disengage expression from impression, and led him to make distinctions between 'vulgar' and 'learned' readers that he later regretted. He found it necessary to assume that the accurate images would operate upon the reader only if he recognized their accuracy.

> Although it be true, that poetical composition, being rather calculated for amusement than instruction, and addressing itself to the many who feel, rather than to the few who reason, is improperly occupied about the abstruse and argumentative parts of a science; yet to reject those grand and beautiful ideas which a philosophical view of nature offers to the mind, merely because they are above the comprehension of vulgar readers, is surely an unnecessary degradation of this noble art.[1]

Reliance upon knowledge divided the readers in one way; reliance upon feelings divided them in another. As one reader of Aikin remarked, 'I insist that genuine Poetry, that consists of the Sublime and Pathetic, addresses itself to the *Few* who feel rather than to the *Many* that reason. There are a thousand Men of Sense to one Man of Taste.'[2] Aikin's belief that scientifically correct subject matter was more vivid than fiction did not create the demand for a learned audience since notes could keep the audience informed and even the 'vulgar' could understand. But Aikin's position was unsound, and his friend Thomas Percival in his essay, 'Miscellaneous Observations on the Alliance of Natural History, and Philosophy with Poetry' (1789), began to modify it by acknowledging that some deviation from truth was acceptable if congruous, although

> in delineations of nature, they [fictions] have no legitimate place; and the judgment rejects, with disgust, whatever falsifies the truth of description, by its obvious incongruity . . . The poet is not, upon all occasions, to be confined within the precise boundaries of truth. What writer, of lively fancy, in describing a morning walk on the banks of the Keswick, would not embellish the beauty of the scene by the *Melody of Birds*; and thus add the charms of

[1] Aikin, 'An Essay on Thomson's Seasons', p. xvii.
[2] MS. notes in Aikin (London, 1792), p. xvii (B.M.).

> music to all the enchantments of vision? Yet, I believe, there is not a feathered songster to be found in those delightful vales.[1]

But if 'congruity 'of the imagination could operate on one occasion there was no reason to believe that it could not operate on all. The need to provide a theory of congruity which would account for the imaginative 'charms' of poetic expression led Aikin to suggest the concept of 'temporary illusion' (1794), but it merely converted reality into recalled reality, and thus did not satisfactorily explain poetic passages of which the poet had no original impressions. Aikin could not completely relinquish his assumption that scientific truth, where available, formed the basis for poetic value, and more than twenty years after the *Application* in comparing *Winter* (ll. 746–9) with a similar passage in Cowper's *The Task*, he found the latter 'more accurate'.

> That Thomson was in general an exact, as well as a minute observer of nature is evinced in almost every page of the Seasons; yet there are some instances in which Cowper, in touching upon the same circumstances, has displayed superior correctness. Thus, where Thomson, with a truly picturesque selection of incidents, represents the effects of a hard frost, he augments the real wonders of the scene by painting a cascade as if it were congealed into ice at the instant of falling:
>
> [Then appears
> The various labour of the silent night; 'tis
> Prone from the dripping eave,] and dumb cascade,
> Whose idle torrents only seem to roar.
> [*Winter*, ll. 746–9]

[1] Thomas Percival, *Moral and Literary Dissertations* (Warrington, 1789), p. 252. 'Congruity' was a term for harmony or mathematical figures though it had earlier been applied commonly to religious 'grace'. To the scientist-critics it implied consistency with a particular end in the poem and was distinguished from 'harmony' as an ideally imposed form. The term 'congruity' was used with 'combination', 'association', 'accommodation', as identifying transitions loosely related to ends. In one philosophic sense it belonged to the 'theory which places virtue in the nature, reason and fitness of things'—and this usage contrasted with innate or unconscious qualities in art. For an extensive discussion of 'congruity' and its relation to 'propriety', see 'Congruity', *Encyclopaedia Britannica* (Edinburgh, 1771), II, 265–8. For a continuing distinction between natural sciences and poetry, see J. S. Mill, 'Poetry and Its Varieties', *Monthly Repository* (1833), reprinted in *Dissertations and Discussions* (London, 1859), I, 69–70. See also George H. Lewes, 'The Inner Life of Art', *The Principles of Success in Literature* (1865), ed. T. Sharper Knowlson (London, 1898), pp. 183–9.

But this is an impossibility, and is regarded as such by Cowper, who has formed a beautiful frost picture from the opposite appearances. Speaking of a stream stealing away beneath its frozen surface, he says,—

> Not so, where scornful of a check, it leaps
> The mill-dam, dashes on the restless wheel,
> And washes in the pebbly gulf below,
> No frost can bind it there: its utmost force
> Can but arrest the light and smoky mist
> That in its fall the liquid sheet throws wide.

In this passage, too, Cowper is more accurate in the silent stealthy flow of the frost-bound stream, than Thomson, who, probably for the sake of poetical effect, represents it as indignantly murmuring at its chains:

> The whole imprison'd river *growls* below.[1]
> [*Winter*, l. 731]

To refer to 'dumb cascade / Whose idle torrents only seem to roar' as an impossibility was to fail to understand that Thomson was comparing the postures of nature, its normal noise and motion, with the congealing of its power—the control of one part of nature over another—although such control could not hide the beauty of motion and form. That water flows under the cascade is quite irrelevant to the evaluation of the passage, And this kind of irrelevance was inherent in Aikin's reality principle—although it should be noted, too, that even factually Aikin was wrong, for cascades can freeze.

Although he sought to distinguish between two kinds of readers, he recognized that, for him, there were the many who felt. And as far as their feelings resulted from knowledge of people and nature, the poem conveyed its message. Critics like Hume, Johnson, Scott, and Heron insisted on perception as conditioned by knowledge of poetic structure—proper responses to poetry were based on particular knowledge of poems. But the reality principle confused knowledge of fact with knowledge of poetry that expressed these facts.

[1] Aikin, 'A Comparison between Thomson and Cowper as Descriptive Poets', *Memoir of John Aikin, M.D.*, ed. Lucy Aikin (London, 1823), II, 191–2. See John Wilson, 'Winter Rhapsody', *Blackwood's Magazine*, XXIX [1831], 295: 'The whole imprison'd river growls below.' 'Here again, how pleasant to see the peculiar genius of Cowper contrasted with that of Thomson. The gentle Cowper delighting—for the most part—in tranquil images—for his life was passed amidst tranquil nature; the enthusiastic Thomson, more pleased with images of power.' For Aikin's comparative method, see pp. 175–81 above.

The critics and readers who responded to nature and morality could do so on the ground that moral declamation and pictures of rural and family life were most moving because commonly experienced. Popularity was confused with value because it eliminated the intermediary knowledge of other poems. The general nature of Johnson was based on assumptions of norms of behaviour expressed in poetry, but the reality principle was based on familiarity, on particular knowledge itself. The popularity of *The Seasons*, therefore, at the beginning of the nineteenth century was reflected in the varied illustrations of family and social behaviour, in the appeals to morality and benevolence, in the love scenes of different classes. 'Reality' was not defended as scientific but as psychological, and at the beginning of the nineteenth century as the poem lost for its readers its relation to Virgil and the classical tradition, it achieved a contemporaneity beyond any it had previously had; and in this decline of critical discrimination, Aikin represented a test case. From 1777 to 1820 he wrote of *The Seasons* six times, and his views represent a gradual succumbing to the decline of literary standards.

Aikin treated *The Seasons* in 1777, 1778, *Letters to a Young Woman* (1804), 'A Comparison between Thomson and Cowper as Descriptive Poets,' *General Biography* (1814), and *Select Work on the British Poets* (1820) based on the life in *General Biography*. His repeated returns to the poem demonstrated his need to revise both his strategy and his theory of poetry. His statement of its 'plan' or 'end' was revised by his changing awareness of its 'means' or operation as a poem: (1) by comparison with Cowper, Aikin discriminated Thomson's descriptive characteristics more sharply; (2) by considering the audience as innocent young women rather than as learned men or poets, Aikin insisted on the availability of the poem to all readers. In 1778 he had declared that 'to reject those grand and beautiful ideas which a philosophical view of nature offers to the mind, merely because they are above the comprehension of vulgar readers, is surely an unnecessary degradation of this noble art', but in 1804 he wrote that Thomson had 'judiciously avoided any parade of abstruse speculation which might prove repulsive to the generality of his readers'.[1] By applying criteria of correctness and novelty he found Thomson growing less novel as he compared him with later poets. Cowper saw nature 'at an advanced period of life, when the novelty

[1] Aikin, *Letters to a Young Woman* (London, 1804), p. 168.

of common subjects being exhausted, the rural solitary is reduced to pry more closely into surrounding scenes, in order to excite a new interest in them. Hence his observations are commonly of a more curious and recondite kind than those of Thomson, who usually takes what lies obvious upon the surface of things.'[1]

In summing up his views of *The Seasons* in 1814 and 1820, Aikin still presented novelty as a criterion, but it was no longer based on natural science; the unity of the poem was somewhat altered from its clear plan in 1778; 'to its general plan, of a history of the year through its changes, as affected by the vicissitudes of the seasons, it adheres sufficiently to preserve a continuity of subject, allowing for the moral and philosophical digressions by which it is varied'. And he added the praise for its morality which he originally had felt was easiest to imitate: 'No poet has deserved more praise for the moral tenor of his work. Unbounded philanthropy, enlarged ideas of the dignity of man, and of his rights, love of virtue public and private, and a devotional spirit narrowed by no views of sect or party, give soul to his verse when not merely descriptive' (1814, 1820).

Aikin's later views of poetic value were tied to his assumption of an audience without specialized education, and he saw poetry, therefore, as a guide to moral tuition. The criteria of value depended upon a need for moral vigour in the contemporary audience. The durable value of Thomson had originally been seen in terms of specific scientific ends. But the ends of the poem were no longer tenable in these terms because they reduced the value of the moral passages. Thus the novelty was identified with personal rather than with scientific observation.

It is possible to understand Aikin's shift toward social and away from literary standards because of his editing for a popular audience. The conditions of his artistic observation, moreover, grew less rigid as Aikin grew more permissive. The analysis of literary value was confused with social needs rather than artistic demands. Wordsworth's attack associated popular taste with artistic badness, but if there was here no necessary connection, it was equally meretricious to couple popular taste with artistic goodness. The argument for unanimity on the part of Thomson's mid-eighteenth-century critics implied a small and select group of readers; when Aikin argued for popularity as a criterion he was not describing the same audience assumed by Murdoch.

[1] Aikin, 'Comparison', II, 193.

The concept of 'popularity' created a serious issue in the domain of literary history. For if contemporary critics found the audience 'unanimously' supporting the poem, there was every reason to assume that this was an example of durable value. But there existed contemporary poems, such as those of Wordsworth, which had only a limited audience, and there were poems like *The Seasons* which had originally met with an uneven reception. In the theories of sympathy there was an obvious assumption that only readers who 'sympathized' with the poem could give it a proper reading, and to this extent sympathy meant literate readers of 'taste'. But there existed other critics who argued not for the 'universal' approval of the learned but for approval of all readers. For these critics, response to the poem was not conditional upon its artistry as the basis for truth to human nature, but upon any emotional appeal it made to the reader.

(b) G. WRIGHT, P. STOCKDALE, J. EVANS: THE IMPLICATIONS OF POPULARITY

> The object of most of the notes is to keep alive the attention of the young reader.
>
> J. EVANS

The appeal to a wider audience at the end of the eighteenth century implied that the poem did not need to be fully understood to be appreciated; and that some readers appreciated more of the poem than others. A critic like George Wright (1770?), for example, could leave the artistic response to his readers and annotate only the moral and technical passages. There were many reasons for this confidence in the artistic value of descriptive poetry. In 1777 the *Evangelical Magazine* pointed out that proper descriptive poetry was bound to reflect heavenly wisdom:

> When we view a sketch of nature, drawn by a judicious poet, of lively fancy and correct taste, and there trace the numberless and inimitable strokes of heavenly wisdom . . . our minds are enriched with sacred knowledge, and our hearts burn with seraphic love.[1]

[1] *Detached Essays* (Newcastle-upon-Tyne, 1777), pp. 18–19. For the continuing associative reflections upon nature and the different seasons, see Nathan Drake, 'On the Influence of Autumnal Scenery over the Mind and Heart', *Evenings in Autumn* (London, 1822), I, 5–6. Drake quotes *Autumn*, ll. 1312–26, on the contemplative man and declares that he

Walter Whiter, Robert Burrowes, and later Sir Harris Nicolas assumed that some kind of unconscious power operated in the production of poetry, and that responses to it were vivid and immediate. The Rousseauistic theory of the innocence of childhood impressions had been applied to Thomson's composition by Lord Buchan (1792), implying that the impression of literature upon the young shaped their character, and nature poetry shaped it into Christian benevolence and love of man and God. Because Thomson's poem had won overwhelming approval as a literary work by the end of the eighteenth century, editors and critics supplemented the published analyses of Murdoch, Aikin, and Johnson by addressing their remarks to unlearned readers and directing them to historical facts and moral guides.

Although the poem was interpreted as moving, poetic analysis permitted critics to separate the message from its expression. Since some of them considered the diction 'cumbrous', they preferred to attend to the message. Between 1790 and 1810 there were more than eighty English editions published; critics used this interest to teach matters other than poetry, the conventional acceptance of such instruction being deduced from the didactic theory of poetry. Although no critic doubted that poetry moved, instruction was never far from the surface of feeling. As Daniel Sandford explained (1841),

---

'watches with discriminating admiration the phenomena of the revolving year, and who from all he sees and feels derives a source of the present and most permanent enjoyment' (p. 6). As an example of Drake's associative sentimentalizing and misinterpretation of Thomson, see his comments on *Autumn*, ll. 989–97 (p. 8). See also Drake, 'The Sheltered Solitude of a Summer's Noon, Favourable to the Indulgence of Fancy and Meditation', *Noontide Leisure* (London, 1824), I, 1–17; 'On the Moral and Literary Associations Connected with the Spring of the Year', *Mornings in Spring* (London, 1828), I, 1–12. There are a number of discussions of the change in the audience of the eighteenth century, but they reflect insufficient care in their data and their conclusions. See A. S. Collins, 'The Growth of the Reading Public during the Eighteenth Century', *RES*, II (1926), 284–94, 428–38. See also, Leo Lowenthal (with Marjorie Fiske), 'The Debate over Art and Popular Culture: English Eighteenth Century as a Case Study', *Literature, Popular Culture, and Society* (Englewood Cliffs, New Jersey, 1961), pp. 52–108. Lowenthal's study is unreliable in its use of quoted material and in its conclusions. For valuable studies see Alexandre Beljame, *Men of Letters and the English Public in the Eighteenth Century* (1881), tr. E. O. Lorimer (London, 1948), and Richard D. Altick, *The English Common Reader* (Chicago, 1957).

the aims and tendencies of science and literature were essentially distinct: even when both were incorporated in poetry: 'Science seeks to convince the understanding; literature to captivate the heart. Even when the two are so conjoined, by a happy effort of genius, that scientific truths assume the attraction of literary dress, it is still easy to recognize the separate elements, and assign to each its native province.'[1]

In 1773 it was still possible for a Dublin editor to see the poem as an introduction to polite literature and to consider that it taught the beauties of trope and figure which 'refine the taste, enlarge the Conception, and so improve the Mind, as to fit it for the most rational of all Amusements, that of studying a good Author, entering thoroughly into his Meaning, and as it were imbibing his Spirit'.[2] Thomson's passage from *Spring* (ll. 1152–6) was quoted in support of this theory:

> to rear the tender thought,
> To teach the young idea how to shoot,
> To pour the fresh instruction o'er the mind,
> To breathe the enlivening spirit, and to fix,
> The generous purpose in the glowing breast.

Refining the conception and enlarging the mind were accomplished through the moving expressiveness of the poem, but the view was considerably narrowed and obscured by the identification of 'instruction' with moral faculties and the assumption that tropes and figures—images—were irrelevant to the 'spirit' of the poem. There was thus concealed in this regard for the audience a view of poetic language not shared by the eighteenth-century critics, nor by Wordsworth or Hazlitt. It was a theory that ignored the necessary conditions for response and permitted and encouraged private meditation rather than literary analysis.

The new editions of *The Seasons* were being addressed to an unlearned audience, and George Wright in his 1770? preface appended a considerable number of notes to his edition, the first annotated edition of the poem. He deliberately omitted '*learned* criticisms' and classical quotations because he 'rather wished to draw some moral and entertaining reflections from the whole (where it could be done with propriety) to assist the reader's more private meditations, than

[1] Daniel K. Sandford, 'On the Rise and Progress of Literature', *The Popular Encyclopedia* (Glasgow, 1841), IV, iv.

[2] 'To the Reader', *The Seasons* (Dublin, 1773), p. 2.

to shew his own learning'.[1] The notes consisted predominantly of moral declamation: they assumed an interest in the artistry, but they annotated only the obvious moral reflections. Such notes for the 'modern' reader separated poetic values from the values considered important for the 'unlearned'. To Aikin, the scientific facts were, at least in 1778, considered essential for mastery of literary value, but in the 'Notes' of Wright such information played no part.

In 1779 in a review of Aikin's edition of *The Seasons* in the *Monthly Review*, the critic summarized in detail the reasons for the poem's value to youth. It captivated imagination and thus infused a love of nature into the readers, and its precepts could not fail to have a great influence on the heart. The precepts were palatable because 'set off with all the allurements of poetry'. It was an argument that seemed tenable if it could be related to a particular kind of reading and controlled perception with regard to nature, but the 'influence' on the heart seemed suspect even then.

> As a school book, there is, perhaps, no poem that can stand in competition with Thomson's Seasons. While the richness and luxuriance of his imagery captivate the imagination, the warmth and fidelity with which he copies from truth and nature, imperceptibly infuse a love of nature and truth into his readers: The variety of learning that he displays, at the same time that it informs, awakens curiosity: And the precepts, both moral and religious, with which his poem supereminently abounds, and which are set off with all the allurements of poetry, cannot fail to have great influence on the heart. On every account, therefore, his poem is excellently calculated for the study of youth.[2]

[1] George Wright, ed., *The Seasons* (London, 1770?), p. 190. George Wright was an extensive popularizer and anthologist of rural moral-reflective poetry and prose. In addition to his edition of *The Seasons* (1770?), he edited Blair's *The Grave* (1776) and Young's *Night Thoughts* (1777). He was the author of *The Rural Christian* (1776), *Thoughts in Younger Life* (1778)—this volume contains a short and not very informative memoir—*Dear Variety* (1782), *The Young Moralist* (1782) a compilation, *Retired Pleasures* (1787)—'chiefly extracted from approved writers', *Pleasing Reflections on Life and Manners* (1788), *Pleasing Melancholy or a Walk Among the Tombs in a Country Church Yard* (1793), *The Lady's Miscellany* (1793)—an anthology, *The Gentleman's Miscellany* (First Amer. Edition, Exeter, 1797)—an anthology. On the need for commentators on contemporary works, see Matthew Concanen, 'Of Commentators' [3 Sept. 1726], *The Speculatist* (London, 1730), pp. 185–8.

[2] 'Review of John Aikin, ed., *The Seasons*, by James Thomson', *Monthly*

The attempt to distinguish literary notes from summarizing or exhortation which performed a religious and social function was made in the 1792 Strahan edition. The references to rural life, the scientific terms of the early eighteenth century were becoming obscure and reading was thus impeded; the notes sought only to remove such encumbrances. The editor did not seek to appeal to the unlearned; he took for granted that 'every person possessed of a real taste' would not require artistic assistance in the notes.

> The use of Notes is either to explain the sense of passages that are obscure, or to ascertain the meaning of words, which, from being used in a new or peculiar sense, are not generally understood. To do more is superfluous. In the Seasons few such passages will be found; but from the nature of the Poem which treats principally of rural affairs, and from the Author's education in the country, which must early have familiarized to his mind the technical terms used in agricultural occupations, many words and phrases occur unintelligible to the inhabitants of cities. Such we shall try to explain; or, when a subject slightly mentioned in the Poem requires illustration, we shall endeavour to throw every light upon it in our power. But we shall not attempt to point out the beauties, or criticise the defects of particular passages: the perusal of *The Seasons* cannot fail to gratify every person possessed of a real taste, or a relish for elegant description of the beauties of Nature.[1]

While pointing to the consequences of social change for literary criticism, the critic refused to substitute morality for taste. Evaluation was the province of the reader of taste, and it was separated from the 'facts', which required annotation. Persons 'possessed of a real taste' relished the natural descriptions antecedent to any knowledge about rural occupations. Such knowledge, therefore, supplemented but did not create artistic responses; it provided information

[1] Introduction to Notes, *The Seasons* (London, 1792), unnumbered. For opposition to notes pointing out beauties and faults, see William Roscoe, 'Preface, *The Works of Alexander Pope* (1824), as quoted in Upali Amarasinghe, *Dryden and Pope in the Early Nineteenth Century* (Cambridge, 1962), p. 58 n. See also Anthony Todd Thomson, ed., *The Seasons by James Thomson* (London, 1847), p. viii: 'With regard to the poems themselves, their merits are so universally acknowledged, that little is required from me, the editor, upon that head.'

Review, LXI (1779), 119. See also 'The Life of James Thomson', *British Biography* (London, 1780), X, 331–2.

and removed encumbrances in the reading. These procedures continued to be popular guides to facts and dates, assuming in the reader an immediate relish for description or other elegant beauties. Arguments for popularity of the poem must, therefore, be seen as assuming an interest in or perception of unannotated beauties, directing readers to familiar morality, nature, science, and rural classes and activities.

There was as much diversity in the application of these notes as in the annotation of Shakespeare, Milton, and the classics. 'Notes' were, at the beginning of the eighteenth century, regarded as 'brief Remarks upon an Author for the better understanding him.' But a more general definition was that of Kersey (1715): 'A Remark or Explication set in the Margin of a Book; a short Writing containing an Account of Business, Repute, Esteem, Credit.'[1] Notes written by a poet upon his own work—as those of Pope on *The Rape of the Lock* or Thomson's on *The Seasons*—could be interpreted either as serious or ironic comments. The defence of the objectivity of notes or annotations—'annotation' was in the above dictionaries commonly defined as 'notes, remarks, observations'—accepted a separation of 'taste' from 'facts', though Stockdale (1793) refused to accept such divorce because of his rejection of the poem as a historical entity, and he felt that the need for 'frequent' annotation showed the failure of poetry to appeal to the common sentiments of mankind.

> Notes, indeed, to the works of true poets are principally useful [he wrote] when they illustrate facts, which, by a long degree of time may not be generally known: to *such* facts there is hardly one allusion in the Seasons; their author judiciously, never refers you, but to celebrated persons or events. His sentiments, and descriptions are (what poetry should ever be) always perspicuous. The mind is rather distracted than delighted by the poet whose thoughts and pictures must be illustrated by frequent annotations:—Such a poet is but a Tyro in the divine act; indeed, he deserves not the honourable and distinguishing name.[2]

For this reason Stockdale found Thomson's *Autumn* somewhat inferior to the other seasons: 'As soon as a poet becomes scientifick, he rather forgets and leaves his province; because he ceases to

[1] John Kersey, *A General English Dictionary* (London, 1715).

[2] Percival Stockdale, ed., 'Notes to the Seasons, "Spring" ', *The Seasons* (London, 1793), unnumbered.

address the common knowledge, and the common sentiments of mankind.'[1]

Stockdale's view of the common knowledge and the common sentiments of mankind disagreed with Aikin's initial interpretation (1778). For the kind of scientifically accurate information that Aikin took for granted, Stockdale assumed to be beyond mankind's common knowledge. That neither critic had a proper guide to such common sentiments is self-evident, but this is far less significant than their appeal to an audience of taste and judgement. For Aikin realized that full appreciation of the scientific truths of the poem demanded more than merely common readers.[2]

Some of the scientific knowledge to which Aikin referred was, in a short time, reduced to scientific error and, in 1792, the editor explained that Thomson's interpretation of thunder in a summer storm was incorrect (l. 1110): 'Thomson here details the philosophy of the day.' When Thomson wrote of 'nitre' in the winter air—'for sight too fine, the ethereal nitre flies' (*Winter*, l. 694), the critic urged wariness upon the poet in giving 'place in a permanent work to the transient opinions of the day. It is now well known that there is no more *nitre* in the air in winter than in summer.'[3] Inaccuracies of fact, however, served to confirm the distinction between poetic and factual truth and provided a reason for reliance upon taste rather than knowledge, a justification to prevent prejudice among the learned. At the same time, other critics argued for the extension of the audience, unprejudiced because unlearned, and appealed to the uses of the poem as education and morality, defending those poets whom the learned disdained. In 1805 the Rev. John Evans wrote:

> There are very few parts of the poem that want explanation, and therefore the object of most of the notes is to keep alive the attention of the young reader—by drawing his notice to the beauties both of language and sentiment scattered throughout this delightful work. Happy shall be deem himself, provided the trouble now taken, may conduce to promote the virtue and piety of the Rising Generation.[4]

[1] Stockdale, 'Notes to the Seasons, "Autumn" ', unnumbered.

[2] Aikin, 'An Essay on Thomson's Seasons', p. x.

[3] 'Notes', *The Seasons* (London, 1792).

[4] Rev. John Evans, 'Advertisement to the Second Edition', *The Seasons* (London, 1805). Rev. John Evans was a Baptist minister and master of a seminary in Islington (1799). His educational programme is found in *An Essay on the Education of Youth* (London, 1799). Some anecdotes of

This appeal to the 'modern' young reader continued, in the notes, to refer to particular passages, but the literary quality of the passages was no longer a warranty for its annotation. Wright, for example, quoted (*Autumn*, ll. 169–70): '. . . Think, Oh! grateful, think / How good the God of harvest is to you,' and commented, 'The poet's humane, benevolent and charitable disposition, here discovers itself in striking colours.'[1] This exclamation, however, was neither 'striking' nor 'colourful', and indicated the decline in taste that was accompanying some of the moral instruction for the audience. Such moral instruction did not seem able to distinguish morality as good poetry from morality as bad poetry. According to a critic in 1816, the editors did not even seem able to distinguish proper from improper moral sentiments, for the 'greatest defect in *The Seasons* respects the cast of its moral sentiments; but in this respect it is not the less adapted to the more numerous class of the readers of poetry'.[2] In 1815 Wordsworth had declared: 'Away, then, with the senseless iteration of the word *popular*, applied to new works in poetry, as if there were no test of excellence in this first of the fine arts, but that all men should run after its productions, as if urged by an appetite, or constrained by a spell.'[3]

To the critics who sought to appeal to the unlearned, the poem was considered an emotive stimulus which led, in a very direct way, to moral acts. *The Seasons*, therefore, while attracting the readers to the pleasures of sense, was used to elevate the mind.[4] Critically, this implied the direct action of the statements in the poem upon its readers, whereas the theories of imagination had been at pains to recommend the separation of art from the reality it represented.

The introduction of 'tuitionists', who were often clergymen, into the interpretation or analysis of *The Seasons* created a body of moral commentators who passed as literary critics. Yet their criticism did not attempt to create critical readers, but rather literary 'intuitionists'.

[1] Wright, p. 210.

[2] 'Critical Observations', p. x.

[3] 'Essay Supplementary to Preface (1815)', *Wordsworth's Literary Criticism*, ed. Nowell Smith (London, 1805), p. 199.

[4] William Godwin, 'Of the Happiness of Youth', *The Enquirer* (Dublin, 1797), p. 69. See also John Leyden, *Scenes of Infancy: Descriptive of Teviotdale* (Edinburgh, 1803), pp. 96–100.

Thomson appear in another volume by Evans, *Richmond and Its Vicinity* (Richmond, 1825), 2nd ed., pp. 131–48. See also 'Preface', *The Parnassian Garland*, ed. John Evans (Albion Press, 1807).

Although conditions for literary response were taken for granted, these critics tended to identify knowledge in the poem with knowledge of the poem. In contrast to the 'spirit' of the author that John More attempted to capture in 1777, these critics found in Thomson the common moral declamation available in sermons and in most other reflective-descriptive poetry. For them, *The Seasons* lost that artistic individuality which earlier critics sought to define, and they took for granted the qualities which others sought to distinguish. Thus the popularity of the poem tended to reduce the number of discussions of its artistry and supported generalizations about 'spirit' and 'imagination' which took the place of analysis. In this sense Wordsworth's comment that Thomson 'was fortunate in the very title of his poem, which seemed to bring it home to the prepared sympathies of every one', applied more to the early nineteenth than to the early eighteenth century. For nature as an archetype—that nature described, for example, in Charles Bucke's *Philosophy of Nature* (1813)—presupposed a universality of early interest in the subject unsupported by the facts. But Wordsworth, and Thomson's 1816 critic who followed his lead, resisted the implication of 'popularity' as a value in itself or as concealing defensible literary values. And the controversy between Wordsworth and John Wilson can clearly represent the opposing views.

(c) WILLIAM WORDSWORTH AND JOHN WILSON: THE TWO AUDIENCES

> The poet must reconcile himself for a season to few and scattered hearers.
>
> W. WORDSWORTH

In his 'Essay Supplementary to the Preface, 1815' Wordsworth explained the grounds for the reading of poetry, having stated that the 'appropriate business of Poetry (which nevertheless, if genuine, is as permanent as pure science), her appropriate employment, her privilege and her *duty*, is to treat of things not as they *are*, but as they *appear*: not as they exist in themselves, but as they *seem* to exist to the *senses*, and to the *passions*'.[1] This world of the imagination was

[1] Wordsworth, p. 169. For the early relation between Wordsworth and Wilson, see Alan Long Strout, 'William Wordsworth and John Wilson: A Review of their Relationship between 1802 and 1817', *PMLA* (1934), 143–81.

properly penetrable only under highly exclusive conditions so that Wordsworth's readers were indeed few.

> Whither then shall we turn for that union of qualifications which must necessarily exist before the decisions of a critic can be of absolute value? For a mind at once poetical and philosophical; for a critic whose affections are as free and kindly as the spirit of society, and whose understanding is as severe as that of dispassionate government? Where are we to look for that initiatory composure of mind which no selfishness can disturb? For a natural sensibility that has been tutored into correctness without losing anything of its quickness; and for active faculties capable of answering the demands which an Author of original imagination shall make upon them, associated with a judgment that cannot be duped into admiration by aught that is unworthy of it?—among those and those only, who, never having suffered their youthful love of poetry to remit much of its force, have applied to the consideration of the laws of this art the best power of their understandings.[1]

This disinterested, philosophical, educated sensibility characterized the worthy critic or reader, but there were other types whom Wordsworth felt to be misreaders. The proper readers were, therefore, compared with the improper readers, and only the former were capable of decisions of 'absolute value'. But these same readers could also be guilty of the worst possible decisions. They could be, as Wordsworth remarked, the best as well as the most erroneous and perverse critics. And this view demonstrated the speculative futility of interpreting an aesthetic transaction by omitting controls governing responses or references.

The question which Wordsworth raised was a very significant one: to what extent was it possible for an attentive perusal of a poem to make a good reader out of a poorly trained one? This issue arose in Wordsworth's opposition to Murdoch's view that 'the poem of *Winter*, published in March 1726, was no sooner read than universally admired'. Wordsworth denied that the poem was universally admired because no good poem was ever 'universally admired'. He distinguished between 'wonder' and 'genuine admiration' and he pointed out that genuine admiration of the poem could take place only if the reader had already possessed the 'art of seeing'—and very few did.

[1] Wordsworth, pp. 173–4.

> Wonder is the natural product of Ignorance; and as the soil was *in such good condition* at the time of the publication of the *Seasons*, the crop was doubtless abundant. Neither individuals nor nations become corrupt all at once, nor are they enlightened in a moment. Thomson was an inspired poet, but he could not work miracles; in cases where the art of seeing had in some degree been learned, the teacher would further the proficiency of his pupils, but he could do little *more*.[1]

Wordsworth was justified in objecting to Murdoch's language, but he did not realize that Murdoch was presenting a quite different issue. Murdoch was comparing the initial apathy to the poem with the enthusiasm for it once the apathy was overcome. Wordsworth was concerned with the quality of enthusiastic responses, comparing proper with improper types of evaluation. The major problem which he undertook to answer in the essay was the relation between critic or reader and poem, and the extent to which such relationship created a new insight in the reader. This poetic sensibility—'The profound and the exquisite in feeling, the lofty and universal in thought and imagination; or in ordinary language, the pathetic and the sublime'—demanded a response from the reader not only immediate but complex and difficult, especially since the language of such poetry demanded submission to the poet's usages and meanings.

> But in everything which is to send the soul into herself, to be admonished of her weakness, or to be made conscious of her power; —wherever life and nature are described as operated upon by the creative or abstracting virtue of the imagination; wherever the instinctive wisdom of antiquity and her heroic passions uniting, in the heart of the poet, with the meditative wisdom of later ages, have produced that accord of sublimated humanity, which is at once a history of the remote past and a prophetic enunciation of the remotest future, *there*, the Poet must reconcile himself for a season to few and scattered hearers.[2]

Wordsworth assumed the irrelevance of a historical approach to the imagination: the values of a good work continued to be recognized and maintained throughout time. In the examples which Wordsworth gave, in the 1815 edition, of the operation of the imagination, he extended the meanings of words by their function in the poems. But his analysis of the history of literary criticism was not based on the accumulation of particular examples. Aside from the

[1] Wordsworth, p. 186.

[2] Wordsworth, p. 200.

reference to Warton's comments and to Thomson as an 'inspired poet', he provided no positive statements about the poem's values, although he listed the 'title', the 'vicious style', false ornaments, and the sentimental commonplaces as reasons for wrong admiration.

His famous remark about literary history provided a further clue to his absolute values; for his judgement of poetry conceived of 'genuine' imagination in terms of imagery of nature rather than social imagery:

> The poetry of the period intervening between the publication of *Paradise Lost* and the *Seasons* does not contain a single new image of external nature; and scarcely presents a familiar one from which it can be inferred that the eye of the Poet had been steadily fixed upon his object, much less that his feelings had urged him to work upon it in the spirit of genuine imagination.[1]

Now it was perfectly possible for readers to appreciate those parts of the poem which described familiar events, especially descriptions such as sheep-shearing, fishing, the visit of the robin. In such descriptions, the poem was subtilizing the responses of popular readers, and creating through literary skill a heightened awareness of actual, known situations. There were readers who responded merely to the moral declamation or to the idealized story of Lavinia, but there was no reason to assume that the poem's popularity was due only to them.

Popularity has tended to be confused with wrong values because critics have assumed that the lowest common denominator was shared by all readers. But Johnson's general nature, for example, did not assume that the norms of society were the lowest common denominators of approval. The identification of popular appreciation with false values can be attributed, in part, to the reality principle itself. In so far as good poetry was identified as knowledge—scientific or otherwise—only the learned could understand it or, if the general reader understood it, the knowledge was confined to elementary expressions of known principles. But if it is assumed that such reality is not, in itself, a sound critical principle, then the popularity of a poem like *The Seasons* can be attributed to the moving manner in which known experiences are described. As Johnson put it, 'the reader of the *Seasons* wonders that he never saw before what Thomson shows him, and that he never yet has felt what Thomson impresses'.

[1] Wordsworth, p. 185. For a history of this passage, see pp. 167–71 above.

When in December, 1830, John Wilson criticized Wordsworth's judgements of Thomson, he refused to accept Wordsworth's limits either of imagination or of the aesthetic transaction (difficult and exclusive). It is necessary to disengage the verbal controversy over meanings of 'admiration', 'wonder', 'title', 'prepared sympathies' from the serious issue of conflicting views of imagination and its operation. It is necessary also to disengage from this controversy the strategies of polemics: Wordsworth would not have written this if he had known how popular his own poetry was to become. For Wordsworth pointed to a serious difference between popularity and genuine admiration, and no polemical answer removed the issue.

Wilson found that the 'art of seeing' had not been lost even though little descriptive poetry was written from Milton to Thomson: 'Though descriptive poetry may not have flourished during the period between Paradise Lost and the Seasons, did not mankind enjoy the use of their seven senses? Could they not see and hear without the aid of those oculists and aurists the Poets? Were all the shepherds and agriculturists of England and Scotland blind and deaf to all the sights and sounds of nature?' His major objection to Wordsworth's theory of imagination, therefore, was that it was hierarchical in theory and monistic in practice: 'And, doubtless, in the works of every true poet will be found passages of that species of excellence, which is proved by effects immediate and universal.' Such statements would have made mandatory the view that many passages in *The Seasons* were immediately recognized and 'universally' appreciated. These were, indeed, the passages to which Wilson pointed because the passages of Scottish winter and Scottish experience were those felt and appreciated by the Scottish peasantry.

> 'The art of seeing' has flourished for many centuries in Scotland. Men, women, and children, all look up to her loveful blue or wrathful black skies, with a weather-wisdom that keeps growing from the cradle to the grave . . . The Scottish Peasantry—Highland and Lowland—look much and often on nature thus; and of nature they live in the heart of the knowledge and the religion. Therefore do they love Thomson as an inspired Bard—only a little lower than the Prophets. In like manner have the people of Scotland—from time immemorial—enjoyed the use of their ears. Even persons somewhat hard of hearing are not deaf to her waterfalls. In the sublime invocation to Winter, which we have quoted—we hear Thomson recording his own worship of nature in his

> boyish days, when he roamed among the hills of his father's parish, far away from the manse. In those strange and stormy delights did not thousands of thousands of the Scottish boyhood familiarly live among the mists and snows? Of all that number he alone had the genius to 'here eternize on earth' his joy—but many millions have had souls to join religiously in the hymns he chanted! [1]

The major dilemma of Wilson as well as of Wordsworth was the assumption that the identical qualities were responded to in 1730, in 1815, in 1830, for there were readers who were not Scotsmen, and for whom the art of seeing was not identical with that of Wilson's countrymen. Wilson overlooked the importance of Wordsworth's theory of depth imagination, but when he asked whether no progress had been made in seeing for a hundred years, he was obviously attacking the exclusionist basis of Wordsworth's theory. The poem did not remain the same entity for one hundred years, nor were the critics still searching for the same values.

Wordsworth's exclusionist theory of value used history as a demonstration of initial principles, and the evaluation of *The Seasons* as a whole was not the result, as it had been for Aikin and John Scott (1785) and Robert Heron (1793), of a study of specific passages and their quality. Interpretation and evaluation of specific passages was irrelevant to the general theory of poetic imagination. Wordsworth had shown in his 1815 preface that he was aware of specific interpretation, but he rejected it for evaluation in terms of the premises of imagination and exclusion. The neglect of specific interpretation for evaluation of the whole was the result of the absolute values attributed to the imagination.[2]

A further conflict on the extension of the audience was introduced by the associationist theories of audiences. In 1821, comparing *The*

[1] John Wilson, 'Winter Rhapsody', *Blackwood's Magazine*, XXVIII (1830), 877.

[2] See 'Upon Epitaphs (2)' (1810), *Wordsworth's Literary Criticism*, ed. Nowell C. Smith (London, 1905), p. 120, for a statement of Wordsworth's dislike but acceptance of minute criticism: 'Minute criticism is in its nature irksome, and as commonly practised in books and conversation, is both irksome and injurious. Yet every mind must occasionally be exercised in this discipline, else it cannot learn the art of bringing words rigorously to the test of thoughts; and these again to a comparison with things, their archetypes, contemplated first in themselves, and secondly in relation to each other; in all which processes the mind must be skilful, otherwise it will be imposed upon.'

Seasons with *Night Thoughts*, a critic pointed out that inborn associations dictated the poet's audience which was limited to those whose tastes sympathized with the poet's. Homer alone was an exception because he 'was so transcendently superior to ordinary lucubrators, as to stimulate the feelings indiscriminately of all who were capable of understanding him'.[1]

But granting the absolute relativity of taste, the critic nevertheless had to define the kind of taste *The Seasons* represented. 'The 'Seasons' of Thomson . . . exhibit in their prevailing feature all the gaiety and cheerfulness of that Spring which he so admirably delineates, and may be said, as a whole, to display, notwithstanding their serious pictures of grave and reflexive tendency, all the airy and sportive features of this blest season of universal smiles.'[2] The critic was aware that Thomson's poetry was often serious and moral but 'this does not prevent his speculations from wearing, on the whole, an amiable and exhilarating aspect,—from exhibiting that contentment whose countenance is illumined by a perpetual smile, and whose language habitually breathes serenity of mind'.[3]

The objections to this view were that it represented a moral not a poetic response, and that the habitual optimism overlooked the complex responses in each season. But important to the kind of analysis that prevailed was the view attributed to the whole, rather than to an analysis of parts. And a further point is that such comments made criticism into a series of personal responses inaccessible to argument. For if readers found that the poem did not display gaiety 'on the whole', then their associations were not in sympathy with this poem, but some other poem identified as *The Seasons*. Yet despite different associations with different poems, some were superior to others because of their moral teaching.

This view demanded an absoluteness of response which even the contemporaries of the critics did not feel. The 1816 critic deplored Thomson's optimism but the 1821 critic praised Thomson 'for leading the minds of readers to an habitual reminiscence, and a grateful acknowledgement of the Great Author of their own and of all being, who, it is more probable, would have cautiously shunned the more

[1] E. P., 'Literary Retrospections: with remarks on the Divers Tastes that Characterize the Intellectual Order of Society, and a View of the Poetry of Thomson and Young', *Gentleman's Magazine*, XCI (Part II, 1821), 223.

[2] *Gentleman's Magazine*, 223. [3] *Gentleman's Magazine*, 223–4.

direct calls of piety, and declined all such exhortations, if administered in a less pleasing shape'.[1]

The difference between these two critics depended upon a speculative issue quite irrelevant to the value of the poem. One critic assumed that revealed religion provided a standard for poetic value; the other that the rational religion did. Such theories involved a different order of 'facts' from Aikin's natural science, but they were involved in the same dilemma, attributing poetic value to historical facts or moral preferences.

A somewhat different associative theory was applied to the literature by John Mitford in order to answer Wordsworth's exclusionist assumptions. Writers who wrote out of narrow habits of association were bound to have narrow and limited audiences, because their view of nature was narrow.

> The compositions of all good writers have, of necessity, that difference which arises from the habits of association formed by them: and in the degree in which those habits unite with or differ from those of the world in general, arises the popularity or neglect of the poet. He who had formed his associations upon a narrow system, and from a confined and partial acquaintance with general nature, must expect his admirers will naturally be few.[2]

[1] *Gentleman's Magazine* (1821), 339. In 1827 the poet James Montgomery in opposition to the 1816 critic and with more precision than the *Gentleman's Magazine* writer, pointed out that sections of *The Seasons* did possess revelatory qualities, and, therefore, he considered the poem 'religious' in these sections. See James Montgomery, 'Introductory Essay', *The Christian Poet* (Glasgow, 1827), pp. vi–vii:

> 'There are only *four* long poems in the English language, that are often reprinted, and consequently better known and more read than any other similar compositions of equal bulk. Three of these are decidedly religious in their whole or their prevailing character—*Paradise Lost*, *The Night Thoughts* and *The Task*: and of the fourth, *The Seasons*, it may be said, that one of its greatest charms is the pure and elevated spirit of devotion which occasionally breathes out amidst the reveries of fancy and the descriptions of nature, as though the poet had sudden and transporting glimpses of the Creator himself through the perspective of his works; while the crowning Hymn of the whole is one of the most magnificent specimens of verse in any language, and only inferior to the inspired original in the Book of Psalms, of which it is for the most part a paraphrase.'

[2] John Mitford, ed., *The Works of Thomas Gray* (London, 1835), II, xliv–xlv.

Mitford's view was based on an inadequate awareness of the resources of language, but it did not, as Wordsworth's theory did, make a virtue of exclusion. Nevertheless associationism served, in these two instances, to create relative views of poetic composition and its readers which were not, however, subject to change or the conditions of society.

The associationist critics accepted two sources for popularity: the extensive associations of a poem (defined quantitatively) and the transmission of such associations. Other critics argued that the popularity of the poem lay in its capacity to lead men to knowledge and action. Poets and readers looked anew on nature, and its popularity rested on what it made men think and do. Thus the difference between a popular poem and an exclusive or private poem was the kind of social action to which it led. At the beginning of the eighteenth century the opposite of 'popular' was 'obscure', but a century later the opposite of 'popular' was 'over-refined' or anti-democratic or 'restricted to the few'.

The Seasons was till late in the nineteenth century a poem which functioned on both these levels. Its development as a popular poem rested on an extension of the predominantly urban audience of Thomson's own time to those rural readers to whom John More referred in 1777. And it is possible that its extension among urban readers was connected with a nostalgia for nature. In the beginning of the nineteenth century Thomas Campbell wrote that Thomson was the 'author who has first or chiefly reflected back to our minds a heightened and refined sensation of the delight which rural scenery affords us'.[1] *The Seasons* caused poets to see nature differently, and consequently to write of it differently.

The reasons critics gave for its popularity had often little to do with literature: Wordsworth named the salacious passages, others passages of moral purity. (In 1862 the Society for Promoting Christian Knowledge published an edition of the poem.) The obvious moral didacticism held an attraction for its audience readily noted by scornful critics. But the poem also provided an alternative to lower forms of literature because it was poetry at the same time that it contained stories. Its nature views involved a return to English and Scottish nationalism and a rejection of Greek mythology. In this

[1] Campbell, *English Poets*, p. 42. On the significance of *The Seasons* as model and stimulus for other poets, see Nathan Drake, 'On the Farmer's Boy of Bloomfield', *Literary Hours* (Sudbury, 1800), II, 441–3.

respect, rejection of 'artificial' Greek mythology was supported by the eulogy of local, regional, and national traits exemplified in descriptive poetry.[1] Social and humane qualities began in the home and were tied to local places and people. Their sentimentalism and nationalism could march side by side in descriptive poetry. 'The *Love of Home*,' wrote Nathan Drake (1820), 'or the attachment to local objects which have been intimately associated with the pleasures and affections of opening life, is a feeling, or rather, indeed, a passion which has been found to exist, in a greater or less degree, in every age and nation, and may therefore be deemed natural to, and, for the most part, adherent in man.' [2]

The poem, because it dealt with varied classes, served as an education in class behaviour, and in this respect the point made by Robert Thomson about the development of the novel applied to *The Seasons*.

> Every thing interesting in the character or condition of all the different classes in society was thus brought out into the broadest light, and a general taste was excited for each delineation, when given in the unpretending form of novels, which indicated to poets that they might occupy this new field with an assurance of success.[3]

The Seasons possessed a wide range of subjects and its political no less than its social range was appreciated, and by its scientific and geographic details it taught people about nature and the world. It was a poem ideally suited for instruction. It still continued to attract readers and to make them respond authentically to nature and to

[1] Robert Thomson, *Treatise on the Progress of Literature* (Edinburgh, 1834), p. 172.

[2] Nathan Drake, 'On the Love of Country and of Home', *Winter Nights* (London, 1820), I, 219–20. The entire essay (pp. 219–41) is a sentimental exposition of the values of local affection. See also Drake, 'On the Feelings of Regret Which Accompany a Long Absence from our Country and our Home', *Winter Nights*, II, 1–25; 'On Returning to Home After Long Absence', *Winter Nights*, II, 245–66. See also Richard Polwhele, *The Influence of Local Attachment with Respect to Home* (London, 1796). For a discussion of 'love of country' as an instinct, and love of local place or habitation as the result of habit and association, see Charles Parr Burney, *The Love of Our Country*, a Prize Essay recited in the Theatre at Oxford, Wednesday, 14 June 1809 (Oxford, 1809). For Scottish nationalism of the late eighteenth century which regretted that Thomson did not compose in his 'mother-tongue', see John Ramsay, *Scotland and Scotsmen in the Eighteenth Century*, ed. Alexander Allardyce (Edinburgh, 1888), I, 25–26.

[3] Robert Thomson, *Treatise*, p. 186.

serve as an example for the theory (repeated in 1842) that there was 'a perfect identity between the instinctive tendencies of earliest youth, and the most characteristic elements of poetry; and by this alone might be explained the powerful influence which poetry exerts in the culture of the youthful mind'.[1] It was a theory bound to be overcome by the acknowledgement of the complexity of poetry, but at the middle of the nineteenth century it served to support the ease with which *The Seasons* could convey varied subjects.

The Seasons was ideal for instruction: teachers could use it to illustrate the separation of subject matter from its expression, and to argue that the ideal poem was superior to any particular model—that Thomson's responses were often far more moving than his expression of them. Such theories found it unnecessary to examine the particular uses of Thomson's language and structure since this was taken for granted. As critics pointed out, Thomson's position as a fine nature poet was stabilized, and this permitted him to be used for other purposes. 'Thomson's place in English literature has been long ago fixed, and criticism of his poems', wrote a critic in 1864, 'must in great degree be mere repetition of what others have written.'[2] No one arose to question his position because neither the psychological nor the linguistic theories offered alternatives. Thus it was that in 1847 *The Seasons* was inducted into academic institutions which provided it with a controlled youthful audience, a basis for continuing popularity. The poem began to be institutionalized.

When *The Seasons* was taken into the schools, it was a 'popular' poem. Its popularity—so far as this is evident from statements and illustrations—was attributable to a complex of reasons which did not necessarily clash with those of the established critics. In fact, the critics—Murdoch and Aikin and Johnson—were repeatedly reprinted in the first half of the nineteenth century and their statements served to keep the popular and the critical claims close together. It is, of course, difficult to explore all the reasons for popularity, but Johnson's claim was shared by many who lacked his knowledge. The 'tuitionists' who supported Thomson's morality were opposed in editions such as the frequently reprinted 1816 one which was itself a 'popular' edition attacking the false popularity of the poem. What can be said about 'popularity' is that the reasons for reading the

[1] Rev. W. M. Hetherington, 'On the Moral Influence of Modern Poetical Literature', *A Course of Lectures to Young Men* (Glasgow, 1842), p. 324.

[2] *The Seasons* (Edinburgh, 1864), Preface.

poem were more extensive in the early nineteenth century than they had ever been. And that particular analysis had become so tied to factual annotation that the grounds for value, while taken for granted became more and more concealed from view.

(d) ANTHONY T. THOMSON, JAMES R. BOYD, GILBERT M. GIBSON: THE INSTITUTIONALIZING OF THE 'SEASONS'

> May I be allowed to add here, what I have long suspected; that the method of education, which is followed now, and has been followed for many ages in our schools, is chiefly founded on a mistake?
>
> JOSEPH SPENCE, *Polymetis*

In 1847 Anthony T. Thomson published an edition of *The Seasons* fully annotated with scientific and naturalistic lore. In 1852 James R. Boyd published a school edition of the poem in America; in 1855 Gilbert Maxwell Gibson published an edition for English schools; numerous other editions appeared in the 1860's.

A. T. Thomson's scientific annotations, which were more extensive than the text of *The Seasons*, reflected the interest in the poem as a mine of scientific information and misinformation. It exemplified a characteristic critical procedure in the school editions: the overdetermination of the text. The literary value of the poem was assumed, but the pages were littered with commentary which threw little light on the poetic quality, or even on the poem as knowledge. The poem formed the starting-point for the display of information, and the poetry assumed the role of the honey to make the medicine palatable.

Boyd, in his American edition, defended the study of English poets in the schools. 'I cannot doubt,' he wrote, 'that at no distant day, a thorough and critical study of such works as these will be deemed essential, and will be demanded in all seminaries above the grade of the primary school.'[1] He conceded that even in primary schools the

[1] James R. Boyd, ed., *The Seasons* (New York, 1852), p. 4. Anthony Todd Thomson, ed., *The Seasons by James Thomson* (London, 1847), p. vi: 'It is true, that the volume of Nature is open to every one, although every age which looks upon it is not fitted to profit by the perusal of its pages . . . all [aspects of nature] afford objects of interest to the mind enlarged by education, which, blending with the pleasures of imagination, not only exalt the character, but heighten the moral feeling. It is to afford this assistance to the readers of The Seasons, that I have ventured to lay the

poems were studied extensively 'but, in almost all instances, it is for no higher purpose than grammatical parsing. This, indeed, has its benefits, but there are much higher purposes to be attained in the proper study of these authors, which, it is to be hoped, may be secured by the diligent study of them in connection with the commentaries now before the public.' The 'proper' study of *The Seasons* was based on the vast amount of information it contained:

> *While it is not devoid of sentiment, general and refined, its more striking characteristic is the large extent and compass of knowledge it displays.* I have looked upon it as preeminently valuable, from *the fulness and beauty of its teachings in all the prominent departments of Natural History*, and have thought, that, by a somewhat ample explanation of these subjects in the notes, a taste may be formed or matured, in this interesting branch of study, and a foundation laid for prosecuting it with happy success. The desire is strongly felt, moreover, to encourage and *aid the formation of the habit*, so seldom formed, and yet so valuable, *of connecting with the study of Nature the study of its great Author* . . . there would be furnished an unfailing source of profitable entertainment and delight that would strongly *tend to raise the mind above the danger of vicious associations and the pursuit of vicious practices.*[1]

The study of the subject matter of the poem—its 'proper' study as a school poem—treated poetry as information and neglected the distinctions between poetry and science as subject matter because it took such differences for granted. The pursuit of biographical and scientific information which characterized Thomson's biography, so that in 1842, for example, Bolton Corney reprinted Murdoch's 1762 life of Thomson, with proof or disproof of each fact, was applied to facts in the poem itself.[2] For students, *The Seasons* served quite different needs from those of the literate and classical readers. Not only did the poem as textbook not exploit literary value, but in Boyd's use, critical notes served even to blur poetic values. 'The notes will be

[1] Boyd, p. 6.

[2] Bolton Corney, ed., *The Seasons* (London, 1742).

annotations appended to this edition before the public.' For an earlier misuse of poetry to teach correct natural science, see Robert Patterson, *The Natural History of the Insects Mentioned in Shakespeare's Plays* (London, 1842). For a discussion of natural science and poetry at mid-century, see Hans Christian Oersted, 'The Relation between Natural Science and Poetry', *The Soul in Nature*, tr. L. and J. B. Horner (London, 1852), pp. 143–63.

found', he wrote, 'to embrace a tolerably extensive Cyclopedia of erudite and tasteful criticism',[1] but Aikin and Johnson, who were quoted, could not possibly agree on the position that the importance of the poem was its information. It is not surprising, therefore, that the schools became the corrupters of poetic values by their teaching of poetry; the consequences of the school editions was a disregard for the stylistic traits of Thomson, a gradual decline in the initial interest in the poem, a fragmentation of the poem more damaging than the 'elegant extracts'.[2]

The use of notes for school editions had special purposes, and Gilbert Maxwell Gibson (1855) pointed out that only if one did not understand this function of notes did they present 'the appearance of a crude, inert, and indigent mass, without shape, without soul, and without aim; whereas, viewed in this—their true light, they assume form and consistency of parts, life and definedness of object'.[3]

This purpose of his notes, far removed from literary interpretation or assessment of value, was based on a distinction between *lingua*, the common colloquial language, and *eloquentia*, the learned and refined language: 'This eloquentia, as it is an effect of civilization, so it is the test, by which a nation's refinement is to be proved—the standard, whereby it is to be measured.'[4] The notes in Gibson's 1855 edition sought to display the Latin derivation of many of Thomson's literary terms and to demonstrate that the 'most elegant of our modern classics have obviously drawn their inspiration, formed their taste, and most diligently modelled their style of diction and sentiment, from the choice spirits and exquisite patterns of antiquity'. Gibson pointed to Latin and English sources of Thomson's expressions, but such notes lacked critical applicability. Thomson did possess a Latinate vocabulary, but Gibson did not systematically annotate Latin derivations. His use of such notes was to show the family of terms depended upon Latin derivations; as such, he occasionally

[1] Boyd, p. 5.

[2] Wordsworth, p. 187. See Edmund Blunden, 'Elegant Extracts', *Essays on the Eighteenth Century* (Oxford, 1945), pp. 225–37, and Richard D. Altick, *The English Common Reader* (Chicago, 1957), pp. 176–8.

[3] Gilbert M. Gibson, ed., *The Seasons* (Edinburgh, 1855), p. viii.

[4] Gibson, p. 12. For the following quotation, see p. 16. For discussions of classical education, see *Essays on a Liberal Education*, ed. Rev. F. W. Farrar (London, 1867), and [William Minto], *The Claims of Classical Studies* (Aberdeen, 1869). For secondary and adult education, see Altick, pp. 173–212.

referred to similar usages of a word—e.g. 'concoctive' (*Autumn*, l. 408) is referred to *Autumn*, ll. 7, 'concocted', and both were keyed to Virgil's line, 'Coquat maturis solibus aestas'—but his findings were neither systematic nor based on the extension of traditional meanings. Of the examples of Thomson's uncommon words derived from the Latin, Raymond D. Havens was later to list the following:

> 'Vernant', 'clamant', 'prelusive', 'amusive', 'infusive', 'diffusive', 'effulgent', 'effulged', 'effulgence', 'detruded', 'sublimed', 'convolved', 'convolution', 'exanimate', 'efflux', 'distent', 'emergent', 'relucent', 'turgent', 'luculent', 'conjunctive', 'incomposed', 'effused', 'infracted', 'auriferous', 'sequacious', 'ovarious', 'innoxious', 'flexile', 'illapse', 'magnific', 'concoctive', 'impurpled', 'agglomerating', 'incult', 'relumed', 'constringent'.[1]

Of these selected terms Gibson annotated 'concoctive', 'auriferous', and 'ovarious', and his philological approach is properly represented by the following comment: 'ovarious is an adj. of abundance, from lat. *ovum*, an *egg*, Lit. full of eggs; oval, i.e. in the shape of an *egg*; with *pario*, to bring forth, *oviparious*, that is, breeding by *eggs*, opposed to *viviparious*, from *vivus*, *living*, i.e. *bringing living young*. N.B. *Viviparous*, contr. form *viperous*, whence viper.' [2]

The Seasons was included in the *British India Classics* in 1869, and in justification of this its editor, E. E. Morris, wrote:

> The 'Seasons' of Thomson is a book which has attained a very wide popularity. One can appeal to the most convincing testimony —the number of editions and the sale of copies. It has been translated into the French, German, and Dutch languages, besides the Latin translation to which allusion has been made. Professor Wilson speaks of the condition in which copies may be found in every cottage and ale-house in South Scotland, battered, thumb-marked, even stinking from long and familiar use. A recent traveller in Australia speaks of the general popularity of the book at the Antipodes, though there the seasons are turned upside down. Such popularity is an answer to the question why this book is selected for study and examination in India. It contains descriptions of English scenery, in a manner which has made the book popular with learned and unlearned alike.[3]

[1] Havens, *Milton*, p. 135.
[2] Gibson, p. 214 n. 873.
[3] E. E. Morris, ed. *Thomson's Seasons* (London, 1869), p. xxxiv.

The minute description of English scenery had in the early nineteenth century been identified with specific national characteristics. 'Among the chief characteristics of our English poetry', wrote Edward Bulwer in 1835, 'are great minuteness and fidelity in rural description—a deep melancholy in moral reflection, coupled with a strong and racy aptitude to enjoy the sweets of life as well as to repine at the bitters—a glowing richness, a daring courage of expression, and a curious love of abrupt change in thought and diction.'[1] Quoting the passage on autumn fogs, Bulwer declared: 'This is *description*!—and this is national—this is English! albeit it was the Tweed, 'Whose pastoral banks first heard *that* Doric reed.'[2] And in 1849, Thomas B. Shaw in his *Outlines of English Literature* declared that the 'finest art and the most idiomatic literature of England bears testimony to the intensity of feeling for the external loveliness of nature which seems to form a distinctive feature of the national character . . . In that great and peculiar style, invented and principally cultivated in England—descriptive or landscape poetry—Thomson is by far our greatest artist.'[3]

As long as this nationalistic assumption operated, the poem was considered representative of the country, and by comparison with it, poems between the Restoration and Thomson introduced a foreign 'spirit' in English literature. The schools tended to foster this nationalism although critics sought to distinguish it from noisy 'patriotism'. The fact that natural description could be considered a peculiarly English trait permitted even the 'nature' of the poem to be turned to nationalistic purposes. *The Seasons* did describe Scottish and English landscape, but the quality and implication of the descriptions differed from the praise of industry in *Autumn* and from other nationalistic passages. To disregard such distinctions was to blot out the differences within the poem.

The school editions not only used the popularity of the poem to teach science and other subjects, but, in doing so, implied that conscious overt statements were characteristic of poetry. Granting that good instruction might avoid such obvious misunderstandings, the very selection of words and lines to be analysed showed no intelligent literary discrimination. Words were arbitrarily selected for analysis,

[1] Edward Bulwer (Bulwer Lytton), *The Student* (London, 1835), II, 291.
[2] Bulwer, II, 295.
[3] Thomas B. Shaw, *Outlines of English Literature* (London, 1849), pp. 357–8.

and in a single line different texts annotated different words, with no awareness of the appropriateness of or need for such notes. For example, in line 4, in *Winter*, 'Weak, wan and broad, he [the sun] skirts the southern sky', not only was the 'southern sky' explained, but obvious words such as 'wan' and 'broad' and 'skirts' were also explicated.

Line 49.—*The southern sky*. Capricornus and Aquarius are two of the six southern signs of the zodiac. During our winter months, the sun appears in the three last signs named in the notes to *line* 42.[1]

49. Skirts. *Skirt* signifies, primarily, the edge of anything: hence to skirt is to border, or run along the edge.[2]

49. *Wan*. Faint and pale, from Goth 'vans' wanting; so old English word, 'wanhope', despair, where it is a negative particle; so wanting colour, or pale.

Broad. Enlarged by the low-lying mists.[3]

The over-determination of the text—what the eighteenth-century called over-refinement—buried the values of the poem by neglecting to discriminate them from failures. The institutionalizing of the poem created a body of school readers who shared a body of poetry, who were taught to examine it with care and philological scrupulosity, but who did not seem to know the difference between a good passage and a bad one. An example of this can be gleaned from J. Franck Bright's introductory remarks (1874) about how to teach *Winter*, ll. 5–14.

Welcome, kindred glooms!
Congenial [cogenial] horrors, hail! with frequent foot,
Pleased have I, in my cheerful morn of life,
When nursed by careless solitude I lived,
And sung of Nature with unceasing joy,
Pleased have I wandered through your rough domain;
Trod the pure virgin-snows, myself as pure;
Heard the winds roar, and the big torrent burst;
Or seen the deep fermenting tempest brewed
In the grim evening-sky.

'Welcome—evening sky' (5–14). What is the meaning of this? I bid you hail, for there is something in your feelings which is akin

[1] Walter M'Leod, ed., *Thomson's Winter* (London, 1864), p. 48 n.
[2] Morris, II, 126 n.
[3] J. Franck Bright, *Thomson's Seasons Winter* (London, 1874), p. 29 n.

to my gloominess. Even in the time of my youth, the season of cheerfulness, and when I was without the cares of life, I have found pleasure in the roughness of winter, have found a sympathy with my own innocence in the virgin purity of the snow, and have observed with delight the sounds and sights of the winter storm.

In the above lines an opportunity would occur of explaining one or two derivations.

'Kindred glooms'. The connection of kind and kin and kindred might be pointed out, and its close similarity with the word 'congenial' in the other classical branch of the language.

The meaning of *con* in composition might be illustrated by numerous examples.

'With frequent foot'. This poetical way of expressing 'frequent' might be pointed out, and illustrated perhaps by the use of 'hot fote' for 'rapidly' in Chaucer.

'Cheerful', 'careless'. To what class of epithets do these belong? If important, in what does their importance consist?

In both instances the whole effect of the contrast depends upon them. They are in fact compressed sentences. In the morn of life, though I was cheerful and free from care, I still loved the gloom of winter.

'Brewed'. Is the word well used here? It keeps up the metaphor of the adjective 'fermenting'.[1]

This instruction was detailed and rhetorically attractive, but it did not understand the poetical implications of the very words it defined. Thomson's 'relation' to winter is that of a child to its family, for 'kindred glooms' or 'horrors' did not frighten him when young. The narrator recalls his careless and innocent childhood, in which the roughness and grimness of nature appeared as forms of pleasure because the solitude which 'nursed' him was 'careless'. But it is a reference to a time long past. The sentence structure is based upon recall—'Pleased have I' in which the inversion is a reversion to an earlier time. (C. P. Mason's edition peremptorily declared: 'Strike out the second *pleased have I*.')[2] The hailing of winter glooms in the name of childhood is part of the childish ebullience, though the conventionality of the roaring winds and the bursting torrents, activities observed rather than participated in, suggest a much more distant kinship than the virgin snows.

This instruction, with its demand for paraphrase, analysis of

[1] Bright, pp. xii–xiii.

[2] C. P. Mason, ed., *Thomson's Seasons Winter* (London, 1864), p. 35.

epithets, derivations, tended to provide a pseudo-scientific attitude to poetic language while neglecting to explain why the poem was worth reading in the first place. In this passage, characteristic of man's joy of recollected youth, there still remains the difficulty of establishing a rapport with a period long-lost. *Winter* was, for the wayfaring stranger, and the dying shepherd, a time of horror. But in the school texts, poetry became, not its own valued discipline, but a form of training for everything else.

With the disappearance of the society and associations which the poem evoked, the 'instinctive' popularity dwindled. What had begun as notes to support information became the basis for the very 'interest' it had assumed. The natural description continued to be approved, but its implications had been considerably reduced. Some school books were clearly better than others, that is, based on more reliable texts, or supplied with more appropriate notes. But even so good an edition as E. E. Morris's for the *British India Classics* had to treat the poem as an instruction book for foreigners. And in justifying the kind of edition that was issued, W. J. Jeaffreson wrote, in 1869, that even the textbooks had to appeal to different types of students.[1]

The reaction to the corruption of poetic value led critics to insist on the 'higher value' of poetry as opposed to its grammatical analysis. Of the teaching of poetry J. C. Shairp declared:

> If criticism be needed this generation has done that work to satiety. It has edited and re-edited every great poet; found out all that can be known about each and a good deal that cannot be known; has counted and scheduled the percentage of light endings and of weak endings, of end-stopt and run-on verses in every place, has compared, corrected, annotated with most precise, worthy and sometimes with wearisome exactness. It is surely time that this work should cease.[2]

[1] Morris, 'General Introduction', I, xi. For essays on the teaching of English, see J. W. Hales, 'The Teaching of English', *Essays on a Liberal Education*, ed. Rev. F. W. Farrar (London, 1867), pp. 293–312; J. R. Seeley, 'English in Schools', *Lectures and Essays* (London, 1870), pp. 217–44.

[2] Shairp as quoted in W. H. Stanley, *Poetry: A Popular Analysis* (Eastbourne, 1895), epigraph. For an attack on the misuse of *The Seasons* in the schools, see George Saintsbury, *The Peace of the Augustans* (London, 1916), pp. 79–80: 'Perhaps no one, with the possible exception of Milton, has been worse served than Thomson by the modern habit of using for

The objections to the teaching of poetry included its disregard of poetic value and its pedantic concern with grammar and rhetoric. In 1895, W. H. Stanley remarked that poetry 'is still to be learned by rote; intellect and taste are not scientifically appealed to: aid in analysis or in securing cultured appreciation is not provided, or even thought of it would seem'. And he offered a handbook that would point out 'Firstly, what poetry is; and Secondly, in what its most striking beauties consist'.[1] Since the *Seasons* was one of the poems frequently misused, Stanley used a sample from it to illustrate how nature's spirit was expressed in art. He took the example of the Russian exile in *Winter* (ll. 799–809):

> There, through the prison of unbounded wilds,
> Barred by the hand of nature from escape,
> Wide roams the Russian exile. Naught around
> Strikes his sad eye but deserts lost in snow,
> And heavy-loaded groves, and solid floods
> That stretch athwart the solitary vast
> Their icy horrors to the frozen main,
> And cheerless towns far distant—never blessed,
> Save when its annual course the caravan
> Bends to the golden coast of rich Cathay,
> With news of human-kind.

With his view of poetry as 'thought tinged with emotion', Stanley found the imagery and sentence structure of poetry as constitutive of this 'feeling'. He related the study of poetry to presentation of emotion, and sought to associate 'feeling' with expression of the sublime and pathetic. Stanley sought to bring back 'appreciation' to the study of poetry, but he founded value on the commonplaces of

[1] Stanley, p. 3. For discussion of this passage see pp. 24–27 above. See also George Sampson, 'Literature in the Class-room', *Essays and Studies*, XX [Oxford, 1935], 123–34.

---

quite, or at any rate moderately young children English classics instead of ancient as instruments of linguistic and literary "drill".' Earlier Duncan C. Tovey, 'The Teaching of English Literature', *Reviews and Essays in English Literature* (London, 1897), pp. 1–21, had attacked the over-annotation and the wrong annotation of English literature: 'a boy who in order to understand the "Excursion" really needs an explanation of such words as "downs" and "landscape" ought to be studying not the "Excursion", but the horn-book' (p. 13). Tovey listed as good annotated texts, Payne's selections from Burke and Pattison's editions of Pope's 'Essay on Man' (1871) and 'Satires' (1872).

poetic language and sentence structure. To Stanley the passage was moving because 'more desolate surroundings 'twould be difficult to imagine', not because it contrasted an unbounded 'prison', a roaming exile amid endless vastness of ice with the bounded caravan that annually, in its marked course, 'bended' 'to the golden coast of rich Cathay'. It was a picture of man roaming unbounded but solitary, and the caravan, bounded and fixed, but blessed, giving some blessing even to the borders seen by the exile. Stanley's effort, therefore, provided a 'scientific' alternative that tended to retrieve a value that no longer seemed fully relevant to his own generation.

(e) THE SHRINKING OF THE AUDIENCE: THOMSON AS PHILOSOPHER, SCIENTIST, SCHOLAR

> From 1750 to 1850 Thomson was in England the poet, *par excellence*, not of the eclectic and literary few, but of the large and increasing middle class.
>
> THOMAS SECCOMBE

In 1841, Allan Cunningham explained the modern audience for Thomson in terms of a 'general love of literature' as compared to the limited and prejudiced coteries of 1726.

> . . . A general love of literature was not so diffused in Thomson's time as it is in ours: nor had it appealed from individual patronage to that of the public: each great author had his own coterie of patrons and admirers, who had staked their taste on his merits, and were interested in vindicating their own judgment . . . The approbation of his friends required the confirmation of the public, before he could be ranked with safety among the great authors; and though many of the finest wits and judges had, ere this, classed him with the loftiest, it must not be concealed that some who stood high with the learned and discerning, hesitated to admit him among the sons of light.[1]

But by the end of the nineteenth century, critic after critic asserted that the general audience for *The Seasons* had diminished. In 1880 George Saintsbury wrote that 'making allowance for the time over which his influence has extended, no poet has given the special pleasure which poetry is capable of giving to so large a number of persons in so large

[1] Cunningham, *The Seasons*, pp. xxvi–vii.

a measure as Thomson'.[1] And John Dennis sixteen years later (1896) declared:

> The *Seasons* was at one time, and for many years the most popular volume of poetry in the country. It was to be found in every cottage, and passages from the poem were familiar to every schoolboy. The appreciation of the work was more affectionate than critical, and Thomson's faults were sometimes mistaken for beauties: but the popularity of the *Seasons* was a healthy sign, and the poem a forerunner of Cowper's *Task*, brought into vigorous life, feeling and sympathies that had been long dormant.[2]

The critics agreed that the audience of the poem had considerably diminished, and although they provided no statistics, the drop in editions in the last decade of the nineteenth century and the decline in illustrations tended to support the view that the number of readers had dropped off. But during the last decade of the century there began to be more essays on Thomson and more references to him in histories of literature than at any previous time. As the poem ceased to be read for values that were current, it was grafted on the organic unfolding of literature to give it simulated interest or to treat it as a curiosity whose history was to be explored.

In explaining the reasons for its loss of popularity John Churton Collins (1907) asked, 'How is it then that the Nature-poetry of the eighteenth century ceases to appeal to us?' If one asks who the 'us' is that Collins writes about, it would seem to refer to his critical contemporaries, to the students, the middle-class readers—to all who read poetry. The question was not raised in such a way as to imply the divorce of critics from popular readers, but rather the inclusion of both groups. In giving reasons for Thomson's loss of popularity, Collins attacked the age and its poetic failure; the implication was that those who had found value in the poem either as natural description, or as morality, or as music, or as imagery, had no proper understanding of the relation of the poem to the period since the poem was intertwined in some organic way with the age. The decline in popularity had to be interpreted as an attack upon all earlier supporters of the poem because it was based on the inadequacy of *The Seasons* as art.

Such a position was critically untenable because it disregarded all

[1] George Saintsbury, 'James Thomson', *The English Poets* (ed. Thomas H. Ward, London, 1880), III, 169.

[2] John Dennis, *The Age of Pope* (London, 1896), pp. 91–92.

distinctions made previously; and even supporters of the attack on an 'age' as though it was a single entity began to make excuses for or even claims for exceptions. Even Collins himself found Thomson 'inspired'. Collins listed the following reasons for the decline of popularity: (1) the poets were encumbered with traditions inappropriate for the treatment of nature; (2) they lived in an age of conventionality and prose; (3) their style was stilted, cumbrous and pompous; (4) their realism was undiscriminating, and (5) their Christianity was mere convention.[1]

[1] John Churton Collins, 'The Descriptive Poetry of the Eighteenth Century', *Poet's Country*, Andrew Lang, ed. (London, 1907), pp. 147–8. See also the explanation given by Francis T. Palgrave, *Landscape in Poetry* (London, 1897), p. 166: 'We now reach that well-known period, covering about seventy years after the Restoration, when a style of poetry, admirably clear, yet in regard to Nature and often to Man, superficial or restricted, supplanted earlier truth and simplicity, and the true landscape wellnigh vanished from English verse. Upon the several causes of this change or decline it will be here enough to touch slightly. They will be partly found in the English politics of the day, which brought French writers, in their exactness of style, lucidity and common sense forward—partly in the degeneracy to which the Elizabethan style had fallen. The French Renaissance, in fact, had now its moment with us; for the time the Italian impulse was exhausted. It was a critical age; and, as such, essentially antagonistic to an imaginative—an age, broadly speaking, of light without warmth. Poetry now mainly addressed the wealthy, the well-born, and cultivated classes.' See also Henry Beers, 'The Modern Feeling for Nature', *Points at Issue* (New York, 1904), pp. 121–59.

For a patronizing view of the eighteenth century, dismissing 'inspiration' and feeling, and treating Thomson as a curiosity, see John Oldcastle, 'Preface', *The Seasons by James Thomson* (London, 1888), *Illustrated Gleanings from the Classics*, Number 3, pp. 8–9:

> 'What we like in Thomson is his *last centuryness*. We like to hear him speak of young birds as "the feathered youth"; of his lady readers as "the British Fair"; of Sir Thomas More as having withstood "the brutal tyrant's useful rage". The man who could write these phrases speaks to us from another world than ours, a world into which what we feel as poetry, emotion, pregnancy and truth, had not been born—that curious world, in short, of the Eighteenth century, in which there was so much culture, and a complete suspension of one gift of the gods—inspiration. The Eighteenth century is extremely amusing to us; its artificial yet simple moods make us laugh. There is nothing that reposes us so much from Elizabethan and modern intensity as to step into the shallow regions, the cool and elegant twilight, which unaccountably prevailed for a long hundred years in England, beginning when the cycles of Redemption changed their date, and when Thomson was born, in 1700.'

These 'reasons' began, by assuming with Arnold and Leslie Stephen, that the eighteenth century was 'an age of commonplaces' unfortunate for nature poetry. Hindered by this untenable theory of progress, it was necessary to argue that *The Seasons* was 'popular', had 'appeal' for the wrong reasons or that its previous readers failed to recognize its serious defects.

> The Seasons [Collins wrote], it must be admitted, does not hold the same place in modern estimation as it did in that of our forefathers. It is a poem heavily clogged with diffuse commonplace, and still more intolerable didactic platitudes. Its versification is frequently harsh and cumbrous, its diction vicious, it is a poem with very little imagination and with no architecture. But Thomson was an inspired poet: he had true enthusiasm.[1]

Considering the defects of the poem, Collins' statement that Thomson was an 'inspired' poet—although he had little imagination—was a bid to explain qualities which the critic could not understand. Indeed, because of the misunderstanding of Thomson's popularity, critics like Collins continued to select isolated passages, or lines, or statements about philosophy without a recognition of the experimental quality of Thomson's verse or its individuality.

The popular audience may have attended to associations and sentimentalities, but these were not all that were attended to. Thomson's natural descriptions formed the basis for associations but they also inspired feelings about nature. Neither Collins nor many of his contemporaries recognized that learned critics were responding to passages which had originally won popular approval because their value, as Johnson and Wilson noted, was immediately testable by rural experience. When such tests disappeared, and more complicated grounds for approval were required, that is, grounds based on the structure of language and sentences, the critics resorted to fragmentation of the poem by 'memory tests' of single lines, by continuing annotations of words and passages as though these formed cultural interests in and for themselves. And these 'cultural' interests equated didactic passages in the poem with eighteenth-century ideas in science, philosophy, and religion.

Even a critic like William J. Courthope, sympathetic to the eighteenth century, comparing a passage from *Winter* with one at the end of the century from *The Botanic Garden*, used these not to study

[1] Collins, pp. 165–6.

differences between types of nature poetry, but to prove that the social ease of the late eighteenth century killed off its creative impulse. Referring to the later poem, Courthope declared (1885): 'Poetry of this kind is as sure a symptom as the lethargy of the Church or the prevalence of petty faction in politics that the vigorous and constructive Conservatism of the eighteenth century . . . has become crystallized in lifeless forms and conventions.'[1] Courthope's view of literary history as sharing the general exhaustion and revitalization of English culture made it unnecessary to analyse the differences within a single poem, but it insisted that in a poet like Thomson, such vitalizing principles did exist, and those existed in an enduring way.

The annotations of the poem in the first half of the nineteenth century were connected with a view of the poem as social action, as a cause for the reader's behaviour. The notes exhorted or informed him, but did not assume some past wholly separated from his own time. The theory expressed by Leslie Stephen (1881), however, that the 'whole character of contemporary literature, in short, is moulded by the social conditions of the class for which and by which it was written, still more distinctly than by the ideas current in contemporary speculation',[2] made Thomson somewhat exceptional 'by reason of his original descriptions of natural scenery . . . and by his powerful representation of sensuous nature'. But his conception of nature was 'substantially that of his age'. Stephen was wrong in ascribing to Thomson a view of nature as a 'comparatively lifeless series of phenomena'. Locating the poet in the period, he was unable to explain

[1] William J. Courthope, *The Liberal Movement in English Literature* (London, 1885), p. 78. For an early statement of Courthope's views, see his essay, *The Genius of Spenser* (London, 1868).

[2] Leslie Stephen, *History of English Thought in the Eighteenth Century* (New York, 1881), II, 349. For an important review of this book, see Mark Pattison, 'The Age of Reason', *The Fortnightly Review*, New Series, XXI (1877), 343–61. Pattison described the historian of 'thought' or 'ideas' as follows: 'He investigates the varied phenomena of expression in order to elicit from them the common thoughts which underlie all the phenomena . . . The business of the historian of thought is to find this central idea . . . to evaporate the facts until they leave behind only their metaphysical essence, to pass through the fleeting phenomena to their ideal causes, this process, though it may demand peculiar powers of philosophical analysis, does not seem one of impossible magnitude or overwhelming labour' (p. 345). For an attempt at a social and economic explanation for the beginning of modern nature poetry, see Vernon Lee, 'The Outdoor Poetry', *Euphorion* (London, 1884), I, 111–66.

the meaning of poetic 'power' which, despite its didacticism or bombast, created moving passages, since such 'power' depended not on the period but on the poetic transformation of philosophical or social materials.

Seeking the 'social class', 'social conditions', and 'ideas current in contemporary speculation', the critics were no longer engaged in defending the present value of Thomson's poetry, for there was considerable ambiguity about the audience for whom they themselves were writing. The study of the eighteenth century as a period of 'transition' implied that critics were engaged in criticism as a form of scientific inquiry. In 1898 Myra Reynolds explained this as follows:

> The detailed study of a barren field in its most barren aspects would be inexcusably dull and dreary from any but the historical point of view. The moment that point of view is adopted interest begins. The study of literature as a growth, and evolution, gives a new significance to periods of transition. The pleasure of the biologist in the lower forms of life is paralleled by the delight of the student of literature in tracing out the first vague, ineffective attempts to express ideas that are afterwards regnant.[1]

This clinical view of eighteenth-century scholarship—it was not, of course, applied to the nineteenth century—concealed prejudices that were religious, philosophic, or literary. Without continuing analyses of the literary value of *The Seasons*—these were assumed—its value was attributed to its effort to be romantic poetry. Such a claim could be made only if there had ceased to be qualitative distinctions between the two kinds of poetry. For such distinctions to be made again, it was necessary to reassemble data about the relation of subject to expression.

The view of scholarship as a historical enterprise pursued for itself and, therefore, studying rather than valuing the poetry was resisted by those critics who still sought to make a defence of *The Seasons*. This defence was made by Léon Morel, William Bayne, Edmund

[1] Myra Reynolds, *Treatment of Nature in English Poetry 1898* (Chicago, 1909), p. 364. See Collins, p. 145: 'The descriptive poetry of the first half of the eighteenth century has scarcely any intrinsic value, with the exception of that produced by Thomson, Dyer and Collins. The interest of that produced during the second half is chiefly historical: it lies in its anticipation, faint it must be owned and feeble, of what the poets of the fuller day of the revolutionary period developed and matured.'

Gosse, James Logie Robertson, and George C. Macaulay who valued its presentation of nature (with reservations). The statement of Bayne in 1900 which defended its philosophy appealed to readers to recognize its serious religious premises:

> It is not usual to lay stress on the religious view of Thomson's poetry of Nature; with himself in truth, it was kept in the background, and in comparison with such a poet as Wordsworth, his philosophical tendency is far from emphatically asserted. Yet there is obvious reason to believe that Thomson, too, despite his formal acknowledgement of the strictly-defined metaphysic of his day, thought and systematised for himself on the all-engaging problems of Nature and of man. In various passages of *The Seasons* especially, and in the rapt emotion of the 'Hymn' he withdrew his fealty from the cold speculation of his time, and adopted a purely intuitional faith in agreement with the idea of the supernatural in revelation.[1]

The claim that the *Hymn* represented intuitional faith was defensible though not by Bayne's argument that Thomson 'experienced no less than Wordsworth and Coleridge that spiritual travail of man's life and destiny'. Thomson, however, expressed it objectively rather than abstractly and philosophically. Bayne's appeal sought to maintain Thomson's modernity without any careful discrimination, but this approach accepted a bipartite poem—its natural description and its stated or overt philosophy. So long as the poem was considered artistic all its characteristics were subsumed under poetic qualities, but when it became an evolutionary forerunner of later poetry, when it became a 'transitional' poem, not valuable in itself, attempts were made to outline which of its parts led to the full and whole Wordsworthian philosophy of nature. In 1905 W. J. Courthope wrote: 'His "mode of thinking" in *The Seasons* is partly inspired by Virgil, partly by the Deistical tendencies of the day; in the "expression of his thoughts" he directly imitates both Milton and the author of *Cider*'.[2] Courthope's separation of thought from expression, although

[1] William Bayne, ed., *Poems by James Thomson* (London, 1900), pp. xxxiv, xxxvi. For earlier comments on Thomson's occasional 'Spirit of Devotion', see James Montgomery, 'Introductory Essay', *The Christian Poet* (Glasgow, 1827), pp. vi-vii. See also George Macdonald, *England's Antiphon* (London, 1868), p. 295.

[2] William J. Courthope, *A History of English Poetry* (London, 1905), V, 304. For an earlier statement about Thomson and philosophy, see Anthony Todd Thomson, ed., *The Seasons by James Thomson* (London, 1847),

supposedly in support of Johnson's statement that Thomson's 'mode of thinking and expressing his thoughts, is original', divided the philosophy from the natural description. Courthope now noted a 'conspicuous absence' of Christian theology; the passage he quoted was that of the 'smiling God' in *Spring* (ll. 849–63):

> What is this mighty breath, ye curious, say,
> That in a powerful language, felt, not heard,
> Instructs the fowls of heaven, and through their breast
> These arts of love diffuses? What, but God?
> Inspiring God! who, boundless spirit all
> And unremitting energy, pervades,
> Adjusts, sustains, and agitates the whole.
> He ceaseless works alone, and yet alone
> Seems not to work; with such perfection framed
> Is this complex, stupendous scheme of things.
> But, though concealed, to every purer eye
> The informing Author in his work appears:
> Chief, lovely Spring, in thee and thy soft scenes
> The smiling God is seen—while water, earth,
> And air attest his bounty . . .

This was to become one of the key passages in exploration of Thomson's 'deism', but as Alan McKillop pointed out, the first version contained 'lines that describe the God of the Old Testament'.[1] This passage followed a description of love among the fowl, 'the rougher world of brutes', 'the broad monsters of the foaming deep', and the 'sportive lambs'. Spring was the time of love, the time of the 'smiling' in contrast to the violent God. The passage, attributing to God the varied 'acts of love', found in love a boundless spirit and energy. God was a wild and powerful as well as gentle force, and only the 'purer eye' could see him 'informing' his works. The misunderstanding of the passage came from neglecting to reconcile the ideas of the period with the language of the poet, and George Macaulay (1908) quite rightly demurred in the appellation of

[1] McKillop, *Background*, p. 40.

Preface, p. vii: 'Our poet was only moderately acquainted with philosophy, but he was deeply read in natural history, voyages and travels; he had also successfully cultivated a taste for the fine arts and architecture; and although he did not perform on any instrument, he was passionately fond of music. With his attention directed to such a variety of subjects, it is not surprising that he should have implicitly adopted several erroneous theories of natural phenomena.'

'philosophic poet' to Thomson: 'a strange aberration of criticism which has been reserved for our own time'.[1] Thomson's religious ideas had been recognized from the beginning, but they were not studied as characteristic of eighteenth-century deism or the reflection of eighteenth-century conflicts.

Thomson's religion in *The Seasons* included inspirational and deistical elements, and it was possible to find both in the 1746 version because both were there. The attention to God's works, benevolence and beauty were noted by Courthope, but his view of history in poetry did not take account of the implied rather than stated concepts. He neglected the dreadfulness of the drowning lover in *Spring*, of the drowning sailors, the buried caravan, the primitive savagery in *Summer*, of the husbandman made homeless by the storm and the innocent Amelia killed by lightning in *Autumn*, of the shepherd killed by the snows in *Winter*. Yet such passages as these could not be explained as deistical manifestations—they were mysteries which man did not understand and which elicited from him a faith in God.

Historically, the cultural critics of Thomson's religious beliefs did not examine the reliability of his claim that *Job* was one of his two models, nor did they seek to understand why eighteenth-century critics found the 'sublime' to be one of the poem's most impressive qualities. In fact, the attempt to discover the ideas in the poem—the religious, social, moral attitudes—revealed how limited was their view of poetic ideas. Thomson's beliefs were equated with statements in the poem, but the role of such statements in the structure of the poem—how they fitted into its organization—was completely overlooked. Thus the critics' selectivity tended to support their prejudices. The cultural assumption that the eighteenth century was a shallow religious age marked by deistical views was derived from the religious controversies and imposed, by a theory of organic unity, upon the poetry; and it distorted the interpretation of *The Seasons*. This distortion did not, however, prevent the methodological search for 'facts' in literature. The search provided a very wide body of knowledge about Thomson's stated beliefs, his nationalism, his reading, his sources, his education, but it has only now begun to correct itself.

The early development of the 'historical' view was expressed by Cecil Moore.

[1] Macaulay, p. 96.

> One of Thomson's recent biographers [G. Macaulay], however, is disturbed by what he considers a modern tendency to associate the poet with the philosophers . . . The truth is, it would be a strange oversight in criticism not to do so. If in a period when most of the literature was didactic there is any poet more frankly committed to philosophy than Mark Akenside, it is James Thomson.[1]

Moore (1916) began by rejecting the descriptive passages as 'conscientious realism' and rejecting them as irrelevant to Thomson's 'historic importance'. But surely lines like

> The bittern knows his time with bill engulfed
> To shake the sounding marsh; or from the shore
> The plovers when to scatter o'er the heath,
> And ring their wild notes to the listening waste.
> [*Spring*, ll. 22–25]

or

> When from the pallid sky the Sun descends,
> With many a spot, that o'er his glaring orb
> Uncertain wanders, stained; red fiery streaks
> Begin to flush around. The reeling clouds
> Stagger with dizzy poise, as doubting yet
> Which master to obey; while, rising slow,
> Blank in the leaden-coloured east, the moon
> Wears a wan circle round her blunted horns.
> [*Winter*, ll. 118–25]

[1] Cecil A. Moore, 'Shaftesbury and the Ethical Poets in England, 1700–1760', *PMLA* (1916), pp. 282–3, reprinted in *Backgrounds of English Literature* (Minnesota, 1953), pp. 98–99. R. S. Crane, 'Review of Cecil A. Moore, *Backgrounds of English Literature, 1700–1760*', *PQ*, XXXIII (1954), 253, stated that when Moore wrote his essays 'the dominant problem was still one, in the main, of rescuing the history and appreciation of this [eighteenth-century] literature from the patterns imposed by Phelps and Beers . . . What he did, in essence, was to shift the focus of attention from the old quarrel over "classical" and "romantic" literary tastes, and their distribution between the parts of the century, to the still largely unexplored province of early eighteenth-century moral and theological ideas as these bore on contemporary changes in the context and tone of popular literature.' What Moore did was to redefine concepts of total culture or spirit as developed by Arnold and Pattison to refer to parts of such culture, i.e. to moral and philosophical ideas. He thus refined and discriminated among types of 'thought'. For an attack on critics who neglected Thomson's deliberate and significant innovations as a nature poet, see G. Gregory Smith, *Scottish Literature* (London, 1919), pp. 164, 168–9.

are not mere realism, but forms of selective personification implying relations between man and nature. Moore brought Thomson's 'worship of nature' into social passages that seemed unrelated, and he did resist seeing Thomson as a mere 'forerunner' or pre-romantic. These were important corrections to the 'transitional' view, but he shared the mistake of critics who did not distinguish qualitative differences, thus attributing equal weight and importance to quite unequal passages.

The developmental generalization which defined an age as a cultural whole, a stage in man's progress, extended to all areas of literature, expressing itself in many variations. But critics like Stephen and Collins made excuses for Thomson by attributing to him certain 'powers' or 'inspiration' which other eighteenth-century poets did not possess. But such attribution could not explain why he was no longer popular. Such terms implied poetic powers which did not require learning. The failure of Thomson to remain 'popular' was not a failure of the poetry; it was the result of a change from the kind of society which Thomson described and from the kind of language Thomson used. The attempt to explain this within the developmental context led to repeated exceptions. For Thomson was joined by Gray, by Parnell, by Collins and, later, by Smart and by Johnson.

Attempts to disregard particular exceptions meant ignoring particular passages, and it was possible, for example, for A. Clutton-Brock to argue in 1911 that the 'chief error of eighteenth-century taste and practice in poetry' was 'to judge of descriptive passages, not by their relation to the main theme of the poem, but by their dignity and freedom from mean associations'.[1] But this application of the organic principle implied that the only proper relation of descriptive passages was their closeness to the main theme, a premise untenable in the face of the descriptive poetry.

Yet the loosening of the generalization was inevitable if the poetry was carefully read, and in 1921 A. H. Cruickshank wrote, 'It does not help much to say it was an artificial age. This is only to state what may be a fact without assigning a cause.'[2] The critic had to discover good reasons for its artificiality, not to question whether there could

[1] A. Clutton-Brock, 'Description in Poetry', *Essays and Studies*, II (Oxford, 1911), 95.

[2] A. H. Cruickshank, 'Thomas Parnell; or, What Was Wrong with the Eighteenth Century', *Essays and Studies*, VII (Oxford, 1921), 77; see also pp. 80–81.

The decision remained, ultimately, that
enth-century poets were 'acute, correct,
they had genuine power and passion . . .
ley had not penetrated her mystery; they
ad little hold on its higher aspirations and
While assigning reasons for 'artificiality',
urnell be given a hearing. It was not yet
the 1930's, that the basis for understand-
dy of poetic language and ideas through
cept of a 'learned' as opposed to an 'un-
omson, the separation of 'critical' from
nction. Yet the kind of value that critics
em back to a reinterpretation of 'popular'.
Some assumed that 'popularity' was to be equated with the common ideas of the period, and set about discovering the 'ideas' of Thomson.

The elements of culture included Thomson's deism, nationalism, and, in 1932, his primitivism. Raymond D. Havens found that Thomson's views on primitivism were an unresolved antagonism; Thomson expressed an 'enthusiasm for progress and likewise for pastoral simplicity . . . The dichotomy was not superficial but profound; it sprang from a cleavage in his life and led to one in his work, in his taste and in his sense of value.'[1]

Although Havens granted that the most vital force in Thomson's poetry was his love of nature and simple country life, he attributed his love of primitivism to his indolence and carefree dreams, and his progress-views to the influence of his associates after Thomson came to London. Putting aside the unwise speculation involved in this hypothesis—as more was learned of Thomson's reading there were good reasons to doubt at least his literary indolence—the conception of Thomson as a divided (not merely inconsistent) poet reflected the shortcomings of neglecting the progressive unfolding of the poem. For example, Havens quoted parts from *Summer*, ll. 860–90.

> But what avails this wondrous waste of wealth,
> This gay profusion of luxurious blue,
> This pomp of Nature? . . .
> Progressive truth, the patient force of thought,
> Investigation calm whose silent powers
> Command the world, the light that leads to Heaven,

[1] Raymond Dexter Havens, 'Primitivism and the Idea of Progress', *SP* (1932), 41.

Kind equal rule, the government of laws,
And all-protecting freedom which alone
Sustains the name and dignity of man—
These are not theirs. The parent sun himself
Seems o'er the world of slaves to tyrannise,
And, with oppressive ray the roseate bloom
Of beauty blasting, gives the gloomy hue
And features gross—or, worse, to ruthless deeds,
Mad jealousy, blind rage, and fell revenge,
Their fervid spirit fires. Love dwells not there.

He then declared that 'passages in this tenor' are likely to follow almost immediately pictures of the idealized savage. For example, only four lines separate the extract just quoted from a reference to

many a happy isle,
The seat of blameless Pan, yet undisturbed
By Christian crimes and Europe's cruel sons.[1]
[*Summer*, ll. 853–5]

Now Thomson was not always consistent in different passages added at different times, but in the passage quoted Thomson was describing the equatorial rivers as indicative of the violence, gentleness, and variety of nature. Just as the rivers raged and swept through the land, they also gave bounty to the land ('they fair-diffusive flow/ And many a nation feed' ll. 851–2), a happy isle uncorrupted by evil society and Christian crimes. But all this bounty, this pomp of nature was of no avail to those savages who themselves were savage, not needing corrupt Christianity to teach them 'selfish fierce desire'. Thus Thomson's view of primitivism here was that primitive man could be idyllic or savage, just as the Christian could know love or crime, just as nature could give beauty or destruction.

The critics who placed *The Seasons* within the 'culture' of its own

[1] Havens, 'Primitivism', *SP*, 50. In 1932, Dougald Macmillan, 'Recent Publications: Studies in the Seventeenth and Eighteenth Centuries', *SP*, XXIX (1932), 506, wrote: 'Though "the twilight of the Augustans" is a picturesque phrase with some meaning in it, the age of Johnson has qualities of its own; and, as has been pointed out, James Thomson did not intend to make himself a precursor.' But this warning was not uniformly heeded. See Mona Wilson, 'The Twilight of the Augustans', *Essays and Studies*, XX (Oxford, 1935), pp. 75–85, who wrote that Thomson, 'the most contented member of the [Augustan] garrison', 'loosened the first stone' and that painting helped weakened Augustan conventions to lead, apparently, to the romantic sunrise.

time greatly added to our knowledge of Thomson's education and reading by a remarkable display of ingenuity and effort, considering the limited documents with which they worked. Herbert Drennon demonstrated and Douglas Grant added to our knowledge of Thomson's education in science. Alan D. McKillop and Horace E. Hamilton provided information about sources and readings. This accumulation disposed of a number of earlier interpretations of Thomson's period: the 1816 critic had denied to Thomson any love affair, but Douglas Grant convincingly demonstrated that Thomson was in love with Amanda Young; Allan Cunningham had written, 'Of the studies of Thomson, in Edinburgh, the little that is known is chiefly found in his correspondence with his friend Cranstoun, minister of Ancrum',[1] but Herbert Drennon provided data on the kind of studies Thomson probably had at Edinburgh. The sources listed by Zippel in 1908 were corrected by subsequent findings of Dwight Durling, Alan McKillop, and others.

The progress which these critics made destroyed many of the earlier assumptions about Thomson: he was not literarily indolent—he read extensively. His diction was not the arbitrary language of a poet, but part of the common scientific vocabulary of the period. He wrote his work with considerable support from his extensive reading and he frequently revised his work—whatever was meant by 'spontaneous', it could not be defined as drawn from the immediate and unthought responses of his imagination.

But in providing this information, the critics could not explain either why the poem was popular in its own time or why it should be read in theirs. The search for contemporary ideas did not carry with it a response to the literary values of the poem. The interest seemed that specified by Myra Reynolds, an interest in the facts themselves rather than in the poet's use of them. For even the view of what a literary fact was, seemed puzzling. The denial that Thomson's natural description revealed no philosophic assumptions seemed to disregard what Hazlitt had pointed to as the special quality of Thomson's nature. And those who didn't disregard it, misconceived it.

The critics continued to grant the poem's value as natural description, but the grant had been considerably diminished so that it was difficult to understand what they valued in it. Terms like 'skill' and 'poetic sensibility' serve as substitution for careful analysis, but more

[1] A. Cunningham, ed., *The Seasons* (London, 1841), p. xv.

remarkable than the omissions were the inclusions. For these critics omitted the most moving nature passages and failed to recognize in those they quoted differences in tone, in kind of speaker, in the importance of the words spoken. Referring to Damon in *Summer*, Fairchild (1939) declared that, like Damon, 'the true poet possesses

> A pure ingenuous elegance of soul
> A delicate refinement, known to few.'[1]

But the tone of the entire passage is playfully ironic, for it reads—

> In sweet confusion lost,
> And dubious flutterings, he a while remained.
> A pure ingenuous elegance of soul,
> A delicate refinement, known to few,
> Perplexed his breast, and urged him to retire:
> But love forbade. Ye prudes in virtue, say,
> Say, ye severest, what would you have done?
> [*Summer*, ll. 1293–9]

Again, referring to the social content of the poem, Fairchild wrote: 'God himself is so social and smiling that one is tempted to compare Him to the last glimpse of the Cheshire Cat in *Alice in Wonderland*. All of Him has faded away except the cosmic grin. In the "soft scenes" of spring "the smiling God is seen".'[2] But Thomson's point here was that in the 'soft scenes' there was God's benevolence, but in the violence of love, in the storms and tempests of the other seasons, God was not 'smiling'.

So, too, in passages by other historians of ideas, the poem was fragmented and distorted by the selection of a particular idea being pursued, without the accompanying sense of artistic control. As a substitute for this, the critics speculated about Thomson's mind and Thomson's beliefs, though even if they discovered them these would have to be considered together with their poetical implications. Lionel Trilling and R. S. Crane have both criticized this artistic neglect by exponents of the historians of ideas, but in the social critics of *The Seasons* there seems a historical failure as well. For concealed in these analyses of *The Seasons* is a view of the period which is, if not

[1] Hoxie N. Fairchild, *Religious Trends in English Poetry* (New York, 1939), I, 519. For a discussion of the ideal of "the happy man" in *The Seasons*, see Maren-Sofie Røstvig, *The Happy Man* (Oslo University Press, 1958), II, 247–93.

[2] Fairchild, 521.

'transitional', at least dualistic. At the beginning of the second half of the nineteenth century this dualism opposed naturalism to artificiality; Courthope saw this as part of a perpetual conflict between liberalism and conservatism; later critics have seen it as contradictory factors in the period or in Thomson himself. But *The Seasons*, reflecting the variety of nature and man, does not set up such dualism; it does, however, imply the need for constant discrimination between the explainable and controllable social order, and the puzzling and unanswerable 'givens' of nature and of man's origin (primitivism). Praises of science, therefore, and praises of the social order are not contradictory to views of primitive man as vicious or angelic because they deal with different orders of society. The historians of Thomson are inevitably dependent upon the poem as culture, but the expressive techniques of poetry are themselves the embodiment of culture—and if the poem is to have value, however limited, as poetry, it must be because this 'culture' retains a value for present readers.

Towards this goal critics have begun, though only begun, to re-examine the language and subject matter of *The Seasons*. In the works of Geoffrey Tillotson, John Arthos, Chester Chapin, Marjorie Nicolson, there is present a more comprehensive conception of 'culture', a reconsideration of the kind of 'history' in which poetic ideas are embodied.

VIII

CONCLUSION: CRITICISM AND DISCRIMINATION

> The temple of science requires for its elevation the united labours of myriads of different artists; and the construction of it will be perpetually incident to delays, by the indolence, unskilfulness, and mistakes of those who are employed on the undertaking.
>
> THOMAS PERCIVAL

DISCRIMINATION is among the most difficult critical tasks, depending upon the subtlety, the insight, as well as the knowledge of the critic. There is no retreat from the personal element, just as there can be no substitute for actual knowledge of literature and society. I have tried to show how the limits of knowledge can be and have been extended, how concepts like 'genius', 'unity', and 'obscurity' have become clarified as methods were provided for dealing with them. Aspects of Thomson's unity, natural description, variety of subject, use of language came to be understood, even though such understanding did not, unfortunately, always endure.

'Discrimination' has been used by critics to refer to different tasks and its derivation reflects this practice. But after examining all these uses, it appears that 'discrimination' is no single task but a characteristic of all, a feature of thinking about literature. Discrimination combines subtle insight with knowledge in the making of distinctions, and all criticism demands distinctions. The decisions of the critic are supported, rejected, or neglected by various methods and arguments. It has been the aim of this book to illustrate discriminations, and to explain how and why they were made, ignored, discarded, or transmitted.

CRITICISM AND DISCRIMINATION

(a) THE TYPES OF CRITICISM

Critical approaches of the most diverse sorts can coexist without implying either contradiction or inconsistency.

R. S. CRANE

(1) *'Process'*

In defining criticisms of *The Seasons* as the explanation, interpretation, or evaluation of poetry, I have distinguished three types: Criticism as decision-making in the writing of the poem, as interpretation of the poem, as principles or philosophical views of literature tested by particulars. Some critics have identified philosophic views with frameworks governing criticism. To these critics, the choice of a criticism appears purely strategic, though they acknowledge that some criticisms are more carefully constructed and ask more, and more pertinent, questions than others. Such a view of criticism seems unnecessarily limiting, not only because it does not account for what critics have called 'criticism' and the practices they have identified as such but because it assumes that the limitations as well as the advantages of a criticism depend upon preferential choices in frameworks. Ought not the question in criticism to be its receptivity to new data by admitting the kinds of refutation its premises make possible?

Poets learn from poems and critical interpretations can be made from pictures. In composing, a poet makes some decisions that are consciously dictated by the ends he seeks. Such ends are sometimes put into words by the poet or his friends, but if they are not, they do not necessarily deprive the poet of his critical activity. To insist that as a discipline criticism must be addressed only to an audience of non-poets, and to address them only in language, is to establish a dichotomy between name and practice, or to insist that different names can be given to the same practice. Criticism has indeed suffered from irrelevant discriminations so that it has been divided into biographical, psychological, sociological, historical, linguistic criticisms, though all of these are interpretative and imply far more diversity than they possess.

To consider 'process' as an activity of criticism means to conceive of data as not confined to the questions of any specified framework and to admit that some data are necessary for understanding the poem but not available. Philosophers have suggested that a framework creates the kind of questions for which its structure provides answers, but criticism, if understood as 'process', must specify the kinds of data that might have been available but are not; must, in other words, know what it does not know. To deny the relevance of information because it appears unavailable is to create a framework in which the unknown becomes unnecessary.

A poet learns and borrows from other poets and their poems, but his 'learning' is found in the poem. Thomson borrowed from Virgil and Milton, but his translation from the *Georgics* in his preface to *Winter* (1726, 2nd ed.) differed from his incorporation of the same passage in *Autumn* (1730, ll. 1248–69). Yet so little is known either about stylistic tradition or 'process' that statements about Thomson's contribution to the styles of other poets or even about the identification of his own style or styles lack the precision necessary for informed distinctions.

Nevertheless, criticism needs to try to define a poet's 'process' in order to understand the tradition of which he is a part. Thomson's transformation imagery and Shelley's transformation imagery both suggest a world in which nature is constantly undergoing changes—in Thomson such changes, characterized by personification, show that man and nature are moved by God's power, whereas for Shelley such changes indicate the external variety of the internal absolute. Yet the characteristic of Thomson's transformations is a playfulness and experimentalism, a constant trying-out of poetic skill and discovery of nature—and it is this exploratory quality which gives his poem its range as well as its unevenness.

In Thomson's own lifetime his 'process' underwent change, and no student of his poetry has yet studied with sufficient care the idiom that was his in *The Seasons*. The attempt of explanatory criticism to deal with this process during Thomson's lifetime must be distinguished from criticism which sought to explain the finished product without reference to the poet. For Thomson's friends—Mallet and Aaron Hill and later Lyttelton—did criticize portions of *The Seasons*, and the poem was often revised in accordance with their suggestions. Criticism has suffered a serious loss here, since valuable information is no longer available, and indeed, if John Mitford had not in 1814 discovered a revised 1738 edition with many of Lyttelton's emendations, we would not even know that Thomson resisted certain revisions while accepting others. Understanding of 'process' criticism, then, operates within severe informational limitations. But such restrictions ought not to be a warrant for ignoring them; what Thomson wrote of poetry may be applied to this criticism: 'Is there no end of that clamorous argument against the use of things from the abuse of them?'

Whatever private poetic needs the poet had, they were shaped by his knowledge of other poetry and by his audience of friends who made recommendations. Thus the stated definition of poetry in Thomson's preface (1726) has to be checked against and compared with the actual practice of composition. It is, however, self-contradictory to attempt to interpret *The Seasons* merely in terms of its own period. Putting aside the obvious difficulties of defining what its period was or how a modern critic can place his responses within it, the contemporary interpretative criticism of the poem saw its unity and morality as traditional.

Thomson's contemporaries had only their past and their present to consider. Even a critic like John Hughes, who defended description as a new form, was dependent upon theories of vision which are untenable as explanations for a modern reading of the poem. On the other hand, the modern critics who have found 'rules' characteristic of the early eighteenth century have not been able to establish the individuality of the poet which a study of 'process' would have revealed.

There is still no clear analysis of Thomson's transpositions, but process would make untenable a theoretical view based on organic or dramatic unity. To know what was excluded—for example the dead figures in *Summer* ('A', ll. 780–7, 'B', ll.718–49)—is to know that interpretative statements about Thomson's sculptures ought to distinguish what 'fitted' the poem from what did not, just as Thomson's rejection of a more specific 'picture' in the initial *Spring* image belies the adequacy of a criticism which finds the poem merely adding painting passages. To interpret *The Seasons* without attending to revisions as guides for interpretation is to overlook the possibility of interpreting Thomson's linguistic uses and to manifest over-confidence in the adequacy of one's 'objective' information.

(2) *Explanatory Criticism*

In order to provide a criterion to gauge the limits of verbal commentary, I have sought to reconstruct a theory of non-verbal criticism based on illustrations keyed to specific passages in the poem. Illustrators defined the 'sublime' more precisely than the verbal critics, and they recognized the playfulness of the Musidora passage and the presence of buxom maids which the critics ignored for moral reasons. As interpretation, the illustrations tested the theories of picture language and they refuted assumptions about the visual basis of metaphor. Such refutations were made in words, too, but the illustrations offered proof that vividness was in no necessary way identified with sight. The illustrations extended the range of interpretation, dealing with themes that the critics, operating merely within a limited literary tradition, tended to overlook.

In the unfolding of the types of criticism of *The Seasons*, 'process' criticism ceased with the poet's disengagement from the poem; interpretations and poetic theories continued, though interpretations and theories differed. Each type can be best understood in terms of whom it serves and how it serves. For the poet, 'process' is the most important kind of criticism and comments of others are tested by their usefulness to him in the poem. For a time in the eighteenth century the shared quality of criticism was such that editors revised and adapted the works of others. There were moral and social as well as literary reasons for this shared authorship, and critics who assume that Lyttelton's changes were governed by literary theories of appropriateness do not realize that his views of appropriateness were obviously not those of Thomson in a great many passages of the poem.

The formal comments upon *The Seasons* appeared in lives of the poet or in essays on poetry up to the middle of the nineteenth century, but in the second half of the century, and up to our time, the bulk of commentary has appeared in histories of literature. Yet in the first half of the nineteenth century the most varied and prevalent criticism was that in the illustrations to *The Seasons*. It may have appealed to those readers Wordsworth despised and John Wilson admired, but if criticism has different audiences, different audiences do not necessarily demand different criticisms.

The phenomenon, which critics note at the end of the nineteenth century, of a narrowed audience for poetry seems to develop simultaneously with a restricted criticism. The cessation (with one exception) of illustrations reflected the reduction of variety within interpretative criticism, and there arose a criticism which sought to eliminate any attempt to reconstruct 'process' or to take account of it in interpretation while most of those who did take account of it removed it from interpretation or evaluation.

Explanatory criticism includes articulate statements and illustrations interpreting particular passages. Articulate statements can describe a particular passage, interpret it, or assert a value based on interpretation. (1) *The Seasons* 'are a miscellany, and really consist of passages of poetry laced together by passages of verse; (2) 'The time was ripe for a long, meditative poem on the beauties of nature'; (3) 'Thomson is an original poet of the first order'. These statements contrast with the series of words collected by Morel and Reynolds and Havens in which they categorize parts of speech or provide word-lists of Thomson's vocabulary. Yet even in making statements about such 'facts', they must relate them to assumptions about poetry.

Explanations which distinguish poetry from non-poetry, as Oliver Elton's statement (1), are common in criticism because they serve to identify the 'crucial' ('poetic') passages and to explain or illustrate what the critic means by poetry. Such distinctions, therefore, are not in themselves important because without some specific examples they can be statements about characteristics like unity or diction rather than a whole called 'poetry'. Such statements as traced in Joseph Trapp and Joseph Warton reveal quite different 'poetic' characteristics. Without confirming examples, they remain ambiguous despite their insistence on the 'real' poetry.

Critics have assumed that such 'essentializing' procedures necessarily lead to statements different from those of categorizing critics, but I have explained in dealing with Thomson's 'eye on the object' the omnipresence of 'precision' as a characteristic of his description, despite the varied theories which present these views. To refute such a statement, that is, to argue the poem is all 'poetry' requires some specific knowledge of Elton's distinctions. The inadequacy of such a statement, therefore, results from its ambiguity, i.e. lack of information, or, if it means that many passages are 'poor' poetry ('verse'), from a disagreement over standards. But such statements are amenable to examination despite their generalizations exactly as (2) is analysable despite its use of an organic metaphor to describe a literary situation. The 'ripeness' of time, as John Butt explained, was defined by certain popularly held views expressed by Addison and supported by the rationalizations of Sir Isaac Newton. The time was 'ripe' meant that there was a commonly held view of natural philosophy as the subject for poetry and Thomson shared this view. This use of analogy must be distinguished from statements about the age as one of prose and reason. These latter statements defined the age by imposing characteristics upon it. To refute such statements meant to invoke a different theory of history or to demonstrate that characteristics assumed to belong to another age did actually find a place in this one. The difference between the two generalizations was a difference between an imposed framework and a statement pertaining only to selected data.

The third kind of statement (3) is an evaluative generalization based upon the critic's own grounds. To say that Thomson is an 'original poet' of the first order, does not deny that he might be a craftsman of the second order, or a philosophical poet of the third. The meaning of such statements is limited by the critic's definitions; it is not, however, necessarily redundant. The meaning of 'originality' for Cunningham, as for Warton and Johnson, referred to the use of new images in poetry. 'First order', therefore, was defined by these uses of Thomson. And these could be checked against the usages of other poets; critics might prefer not to call this procedure 'first order', but there would then be a dispute over naming the order, not to what the order referred.

Critics use terms like 'imagination', 'context', 'ends', 'elements', which permit statements about particulars to be made without themselves referring to very clear concepts. 'Imagination' characterized ways of seeing—though each different way was identified as a different imagination. Critical language is strategic as well as referential, and many of its terms create the basis for an inquiry into facts. In the same way the language of gesture in non-verbal criticism creates diversity of interpretation—as in the Lavinia illustrations—and the explanation of a particular passage is defined by the relation of foreground, background, posture, and place to the textual passage.

In each explanatory criticism I have tried to point out the importance of refutation. Explanation in criticism, if it is to be understood, requires that the grounds for alteration be clear. If Warton argues that the summer scene leaves a clear idea in the mind, it is necessary to know what would make such a description unclear. If the language of Thomson is called 'artificial', it is necessary to know what would make this language 'natural'. Illustrations, in this respect, constitute no special case; misinterpretations do occur, as the illustration of the fishing scene which makes it a social occasion instead of an isolated sport involving man and nature. Illustrations must be read, and if it is granted that they can be read, there is no reason to assume that readings cannot be validated by comparison with particular passages.

(3) *Philosophic Criticism*

As the epigraph to 'choice of subject', I quoted a passage from Suzanne Langer expressing the view that the way a philosophic question is put limits the ways in which any answer to it can be given. But this statement, when applied to criticism, needs considerable 'hedging', especially upon 'can'. For within common statements of a problem there are answers available which 'can' be, but are not, given. This was apparent in the study of revisions which could have, but did not for fifty years, lead to a study of 'progress' in 'text' or art. So, too, the difficulties with establishing the author of revisions could have led, but did not for many years lead, to a comparison of Lord Lyttelton's edition with Thomson's. The possible answers, in other words, may be available, but critics do not often find them, and in this philosophers are probably little different from critics. Because of this, one is never quite sure of the 'limits' imposed by a question, just as John Mitford's find of an annotated edition raised unanticipated questions.

The difference in answers depends upon the insight of the critic, like More's or Hazlitt's sense of the kind of poem Thomson was writing. Particular critics discover such answers for many reasons, some probably far removed from literature, but others are the result of discriminations already made and known. The application of aesthetic or other philosophic generalizations are valuable so long as specific elements within the poem are brought as tests for them. But generalizations like those of imagination or organicism, imposed upon the poem, merely serve to conceal difficulties. Such difficulties are avoided when philosophers derive generalizations from practices sufficiently particular and similar to be informative—like the generalization about descriptive details based upon the varieties urged by critics.

When a generalization, like Aristotle's about the author speaking in his own person, is tested, it can only be examined by specific instances, thus making the instance coincide with the generalization or extending the generalization to take account of the exception. In criticism the neglect of the exception—assuming that it 'proves' the rule—is governed by some theory of evidence. Such theories, however, are amenable to examination like other statements about literature; the rejection of such examination is a rejection of criticism, because it provides no possible refutation.

Some philosophers imply that differences in interpretation are due to differences in basic assumptions, and leave criticism at that, but I have tried to explain that types of differences should be discriminated. Differences about Thomson's 'obscurity' can be referred to language use or language mistakes, but there are limits to our knowledge of language. Critics who disagree about specific uses of language may be stalemated; yet it is not their assumptions but human ignorance which sometimes accounts for this.

Philosophic generalizations also keep alive the relatedness of the arts. More than theoretically, they encourage illustrations and other efforts of union. Some of these, as I have shown, serve to explain the poem and to mark more clearly the types of criticism that exist. Philosophic generalizations like that of the 'history of ideas' do relate criticism to other kinds of knowledge. Generalizations which deal with the arts do so by discriminating common areas and suggesting relations among them. What criticism must constantly do is to find instances which test these or provide the basis for more adequate generalizations.

(b) NEGLECT AND ATTENTION

> Where the exertion of Attention has been habitually neglected, the senses lose their vigour and the perceptions become languid and confused; but where, on the contrary, the perceptions have been exercised by attention, they acquire new strength, and are brought to a degree of perfection, which in some instances, appears quite extraordinary.
>
> E. HAMILTON, 1802

In considering the poles of 'attention' and 'neglect' within which critics operate, one observes that critics always treat some aspect of the work and that the organized commentary or interpretation makes decisions about inclusion and exclusion. These may be matters of preference or occasion or system so that it is necessary to distinguish fragmentary from comprehensive criticisms. But what is neglected and what is minded cannot be critical 'givens'. Much is given to the critic, but what he chooses cannot be free from attack.

That critics should neglect problems for which no knowledge exists is understandable, but ought they to neglect material and problems pertinent to their inquiry? The critics from Lyttelton to Johnson knew of Thomson's revisions and discussed when and to what extent to refine. But they did not analyse Thomson's revisions, nor even tabulate them with any care.

Prejudice in favour of the poet might explain why critics ignored what they considered early efforts, but the very same respect for the poet led Anna Seward to analyse revisions and illustrate Thomson's progressive taste. Some critics were guilty of ignorance: John More and John Scott both revised passages as critical comparison, not aware, apparently, that Thomson himself had revised them. Others argued that Thomson didn't revise or didn't revise carefully. Such statements were wrong—and there is no need to pursue them. But neglect was sometimes not a literary but a social decision—as Lyttelton's was—a desire to appease the 'best' critics after the death of Thomson.

In the late eighteenth century neglect of revisions could have been due to methodological difficulties. Although critics knew of the revisions, they had not been tabulated, and the task was too cumbersome for them to undertake. But in the succeeding half-century, studies of Thomson's diction also came to be neglected; that is, no attempt was made to inquire into what was received. The revisions, even though some were publicly available, led to no statistical study. Attention was turned to the emotive unity of the poem, and terms like 'imagination' and 'spirit' concealed the fact that no new data had been provided, merely new generalizations. During this period attention focussed upon establishing a reliable text—finally achieved by Bolton Corney in 1842—and verifying biographical details about Thomson.

It was during this period that a revised 1738 edition was turned up and Thomson's 'progress' in taste was questioned. The critics, however, discussed the revisions without any satisfactory basis for distinguishing their number, quality or 'maker'. Here it is important to note that neglect of diction resulted not from lack of information but from agreement upon conclusions inherited from the eighteenth century. Although all criticism has strategic aims in directing particular attention upon issues, the critic cannot be absolved from responsibility for repeating conclusions which are not reliable. Warton, Scott, and Heron analysed particular uses of Thomson's language;

nineteenth-century critics who repeated their generalizations with their own vocabulary lost the precision which the earlier statements had. Neglect can be the result of ease, of the refusal to make discriminations, as well as of ignorance, because 'poetry' is substituted for a 'poem', and 'imagination' for comparative analysis of passages.

'Attention' as a critical concept in the late eighteenth century implied careful observation of particulars and required specified perceptual conditions for it to be practised. In the nineteenth century, terms for the imagination—the 'spirit', the 'energy', the 'motive' of the whole—implied that this 'attention' was governed by some inner, undefined sensibility which went beyond the mere letter of the work. Later, when the expression and the subject were seen as inextricable, attention focussed again upon specific details and testable interpretations. The early nineteenth-centuries neglect of the specific text of *The Seasons*, therefore, could be justified on the theoretical grounds that the text did not reveal the true poem, but then the true poem was discoverable by some kind of sensibility.

The neglect of revisions as interpretation constituted a special case in criticism of *The Seasons* since Mitford's claim that Pope substantially revised the poem for the 1744 edition made such discussions extremely complicated. This neglect, therefore was the result of ambiguous information. On the other hand, neglect of the sexual passages and of the burlesque passages by literary critics of the eighteenth and early nineteenth century was based on agreed moral assumptions, sometimes disguised as genre consistency, although *The Seasons* was, in the late eighteenth century, generally accepted as a loosely structured poem capable of considerable variations. The Musidora episode continued to be illustrated at the time, and it was occasionally discussed to defend the poet from the charge of immorality or bad taste.

In the twentieth century attention has been directed at the moral, religious and philosophical portions of the poem with deliberate disregard of the narratives, except to consider them as instances of *The Seasons* as 'miscellany'. This disregard is due to the principle of organic unity expected in the poem and to the attempt to recreate expectations which contemporary readers had for the poem. But these are 'neglects' which had nothing to do with principle, only with the impact of the inherited commentaries of the past fifty years, i.e. with prejudice about the kind of nature the poet is describing and the kinds of language and personae the poem presents. Here, too, the reference to the poet's lack of 'discrimination' is another example of language concealing the absence of any new knowledge about the poem's organization, including even a disregard for the recurrences within it. It would be comforting to assume that 'attention' in our time has studied all the details and interrelations, but although we know more about Thomson's language than ever before, we know little more about the organization of the poem; although we know more about its stated religion, morals, philosophy, we have still to draw inferences from narratives and action.

But neglect has sometimes been overcome, and concealed issues have been made apparent by a shift in critical assumptions, or by methodological changes which have only a tangential relation to the critical problem. Thus the language began to be attended to because the school annotations provided an over-determination of the text. In E. E. Morris's edition (1869) there appeared systematic lists of alliterative uses, types of adjectives, etc.—analyses which made it possible for criticism to compute uses and then to distinguish them. It is possible to argue that the method used to accumulate biographic and textual detail was applied to the language of the poem because of new developmental assumptions. But it is equally reasonable to argue that critical generalizations collapse before the analytical demands of the classroom and that they lose the validity infused into them by readers when the environment to which they refer disappears.

(c) PRINCIPLES, PERCEPTIONS AND PREDICTIONS

> In each case we form a hypothesis as to the motive of the composition, and endeavour to colligate the facts under that hypothesis. Should our hypothesis fail to colligate the facts, we reject it and try another and yet another.
>
> E. DOWDEN, 1888

In attending or not attending to problems, passages, words, the critics are governed by assumptions or principles, formulated or not, systematic or not. In the face of new poems, principles can turn into prejudices or predictions. The looseness or tightness with which principles or assumptions are held is often a cultural matter, depending upon how principles are attained and the welcome given to their opposition. Yet even at the beginning of the eighteenth century, when many critics identified literary principles with permanent truths, there was always room within principle for originality and for circumventing principle by snatching graces beyond the reach of art. Such snatching involved risks, and Pope warned writers not to undertake them, but he did not himself wholly avoid them.

Thomson's poem demanded a reconsideration of the importance of description and the re-examination of unity. For a critic like Johnson, governed by empirical premises, it was possible to trust to his perceptions when they clashed with his principles. For critics like John Scott or Wordsworth or recent critics like Fairchild or Drennon, principles seem unshaken by perceptions. For this reason it is important to know what kind of evidence, what kind of perceptions would be necessary to shake principles. For some critics, only time can be considered proper evidence, that is, only the accumulation of knowledge not presently available. But in such cases there exists some guide to the proper evidence that time brings. For Scott it was a comparative method arguing what the poem 'ought' to be and only when it became clear that his 'ought' was different from Thomson's did his criticism become irrelevant. So, too, Fairchild's analysis of the poem as 'smiling optimism' shows a disregard for those passages which state the reverse position and for the quality of the passages which imply rather than state philosophic positions.

The tenacity with which principles are held is often incommensurate with the evidence brought to support them. Because critics see their task as defenders of public morality or purveyors of knowledge or guardians of certain kinds of Christian religion, they apply to poetry hypotheses which are deeply felt but only tangentially pertinent to poetry. The critic who has a wide toleration of poetic differences operates by discovering or attending to particulars, unnoticed by others, or by demonstrating a sensibility for the working of the poem that is in the nature of a prediction. Johnson's toleration of Thomson's unity, awareness of his poetic language and consciousness of revisions required a speculative willingness to trust perceptions. And, in the face of present information, he was correct on unity and language, and, in selected instances, even on revisions.

The readiness to descend to particulars was practised by Hazlitt, the most astute of Thomson's critics in the first half of the nineteenth century. Hazlitt recognized that Thomson's descriptions showed nature in growth and transformation, and although he repeated the conclusions about cumbrous language, he understood the kind of action the language described and the vividness of the description.

Breaking through generalizations about imagination, he conveyed a direct impression of Thomson's nature.

Johnson was able to challenge the established principle of poetic unity because in *Cooper's Hill*, in *Windsor Forest*, in other subsequent descriptive poems there existed sufficient examples for the new generalization, and Johnson trusted his knowledge and taste. The generalization applied to a type of poem, and although it remained a prediction about how unity served, it came to be accepted for the next half-century because as a critical proposition, it was sufficiently loose to include associative and imaginative interpretations. The difference between Johnson's statement and Shiels's statement which was not dissimilar lay in the language of Johnson, in the accumulated authority of Johnson, in the fact that, being a statement about Thomson—a supporter of liberty—it had behind it the impartiality of the maker.

Shiels's view of unity, while similar to Johnson's, tended to reduce the poem to an assemblage of poetical ideas rather than a whole work, and although some modern critics have returned to this position, they have not referred to Shiels. The reason is that Shiels saw the poem as failing to possess customary dramatic or narrative order—an order that Thomson neither wanted nor achieved. The modern version of this claim against Thomson has rested on two counts: a lack of organic unity and a lack of knowing when to stop (indiscrimination). But the principle of organic unity is itself irrelevant when applied to *The Seasons*, and lack of discrimination (as used by modern critics) implies that the poem ought to have been other than it is rather than better of its own kind—principles not relevant to the poem as it exists.

The questioning of particular principles presents a somewhat different aspect when the period accepts the individuality of each poem. For Hazlitt, the inquiry into Thomson's expressiveness was not an attack on firmly held principles, and it required, therefore, a more considerable reliance upon individual taste since a basis for comparison was given in *The Task*. The conception of Thomson's description as growth and transformation resulted from an examination of particular passages. Hazlitt did not deny the cumbrousness of the language, nor did he have much to say about the unity, but in conveying the impressions of Thomson's nature, he achieved an understanding which critics like Morel and D. Nichol Smith have been able to substantiate.

In the second half of the nineteenth century, Johnson's theory of unity remained unquestioned but was not considered relevant, and Hazlitt's view was challenged.

Thomson's nature—its growth, its reflection of God's omnipresent power—was treated as an 'objective', 'landscape', mere 'visual', 'word-painting' view of nature. The substitution of this so-called 'objective' view for Thomson's actual conception was the result of finding in Wordsworth the ideal inner expressiveness of nature. If one asks at what point prejudice interferes with principles adopted or assumed, the answers must lie in the application of non-literary views to literature without careful provision for their transfer, in the use of a specific comparison as a criterion rather than an inquiry, in the strategic attempt to convey differences without regard to similarities.

The adoption of extreme statements as new principles—that Thomson was interesting only because he was artificial—represented just this combination of critical taunting with a disregard for particulars. In the study of Thomson as philosopher in *The Seasons* the bridge between ideas and expression was not crossed and the apparent newness of this view showed a continuing disregard of literary 'ideas' other than those overtly stated. At the end of the nineteenth century and during the twentieth century, the investigative methods of inquiry have tied the development of principles to what has been investigated rather than to what can, should, and ought to be investigated. Thus there have been accumulations of details about Thomson's texts without any careful exploration of their interpretative significance, and the same applies to his sources. Efforts at predicting Thomson's 'style' by comparison with the other arts have acted as pertinent correctives to this mere statistical study, but at the worst, as in Fehr's studies, they have divorced predictions from any verifiable stylistic comparisons, and, at best, they have established common sources of subject matter or shared interests. But they still lack the 'translation' techniques necessary to explicate one art in terms of another.

(d) THE SELF-DEVELOPMENT OF CRITICISM

> The first step in developing a genuine poetics is to recognize and get rid of meaningless criticism.
>
> N. FRYE

Neglect, attention, and the trust in perception show criticism as related to external forces, but it also possesses some self-determination; it passes on some of its data and insights so that for periods of time accumulations do occur. To the extent that methods, facts, and assumptions are accumulated and testable, criticism does have a self-developing quality. This is apparent in problems which continue, recur, or disappear. The attempt of verbal interpretations and theory, for example, to absorb 'process' and non-verbal criticism, reduces the types of criticism while ignoring the difficulties which such reduction creates. Thomson in *The Seasons* incorporated material and subjects from the *Georgics* and from contemporary poetry. Critics like Dwight L. Durling and Raymond D. Havens, who have sought to reconstruct aspects of 'tradition', have tended to overlook the complexity involved in a 'source' and its poetic re-working. The limits of such re-working which would indicate the 'end' of a tradition have not been sought; although every poem makes independent use of its materials there is no easy answer to the originality of eighteenth-century poets in their 'tradition' and the traditionalism of nineteenth-century poets in their originality.

In considering self-development with regard to 'process', it is clear that revisions of the same poem do not always provide artistically superior passages. *The Seasons* is especially illuminating as a study of this kind. But only as one considers the variety of revisions—words, phrases, images, stanzas, scenes, transpositions—can one discriminate differences among them which permit a study of successes and failures. The development of Thomson is puzzling because, although his *Seasons* was most successful in description, he avoided it in the dramas and in most of *Liberty*. Thus without some interpretation of this omission it is difficult to see the kind of 'end' he sought as a descriptive poet.

In addition to a poet's 'process', there is the phenomenon of critics who seek to reconstruct it—the phenomenon of recurrent problems. For example, in the criticism of *The Seasons* the problem of Thomson's diction was treated in extensive detail by Scott and Heron and Aikin and, after a period of neglect, it was again considered by Morel, by Reynolds, by Havens, and by other modern critics. 'Recurrence', however, does not necessarily mean that the problem was abandoned and later resumed; after Aikin's essay in the early nineteenth century the statements about diction were overwhelmingly repetitious and general, continuing but minimizing the findings of earlier critics. These studied diction in terms of appropriateness, simplicity, and clarity. Their discussions of it were connected with a methodological procedure of suggesting alternatives either by rewriting Thomson or by giving 'similar' examples from other poets. Modern analyses, however, resulted from historical and scientific studies of poetic language.

Throughout the nineteenth century Thomson's diction was treated as a 'whole', as a single entity, until the recurrence of a statistical method in Morel, Reynolds, and Havens. 'Continuity' and 'recurrence' in criticism can, therefore, be distinguished by discriminating judgement from methods of judgement. Judgements continued to be made about diction, but since they neglected to pursue the method of particularity, they became generalizations insufficiently grounded.

Critics who considered Thomson's diction as a single imagined entity identified it by its lowest common denominator; that is, discussed it in terms of ease or difficulty of creation rather than in its implications as linguistic behaviour. In assuming an accumulated body of knowledge regarding diction, the critics assumed a 'natural' end for the poem and found the diction 'artificial'. The difficulty was that critics took for granted 'self-development' and the statements of earlier critics. Thus the values of the poem were seen to exist despite, rather than because of, its diction.

In interpretations of *The Seasons* certain types of information pertinent to unity, diction, versification, philosophy became available, and although there were always critics who seemed not to know what others had achieved, there did exist an accumulation of information. It would, for example, be an anachronism now to maintain that Thomson's unity is analogous to the life of man, or that his vocabulary is 'artificial', i.e. deliberately literary, or that the philosophy is to be found only in overt statements.

Critics take particular passages to interpret, explore, defend, or attack. They thus discover the possible interpretations and make available the grounds for agreement, disagreement, or speculation. Pertinent to this is the method of locating a key criticism like Johnson's and using it as a basis for agreement or dissent. Thus it becomes possible to detect differences in criticism and to infer the grounds for such differences. The care with which differences are discriminated and positions shared is essential to the self-development of criticism. Without proper theoretical distinctions, differences become confused, and ignorance is substituted for knowledge. The 'new' theories of John Aikin and Robert Heron both derived, according to their own statements, from Warton (while Warton himself admitted his indebtedness to Addison), but they did not understand that the theories of language they proposed could not both be derived from Warton. 'Development', therefore, depends upon knowledge, not upon assertions of knowledge.

Criticism develops also by implied agreement. The agreement upon a point of view such as imaginative vigour in natural description, or awkwardness and artificiality of diction, leads to a series of statements which take for granted the information necessary to demonstrate the point. In thus departing from the critical, particular method which formed the basis of such judgements, this procedure leads to a neglect of examination, loses the precision to which it had been tied, and creates fictions about 'wholes', 'imagination', 'force'.

Criticism is self-developing in the sense of confronting what earlier criticism had deliberately neglected. That is, self-development in critical behaviour implies the recognition of diverse possibilities within a single point of view. This was apparent in the study of revisions and again in the quantitative approach to 'influence'. The analysis of revisions began with objections to tampering with the text, but since these objections were based on the author's independence and the critic's ignorance, they could, contradictorily, support the view of the author's development in his rewritings. Such recognition was not without assistance from other sources, for there were political implications in this defence of the author, but criticism did develop its own explanations. This procedure was even more characteristic in the response of criticism to the particular poem. So long as the particular poem could not be considered an exception to the critical generalization, responses to it were completely determined by prior assumptions. But when criticism took a sceptical view of generalizations not based on particular data, the particular poem could be the cause for changes in generalizations. Criticism expressed the experimental view of data accumulation, and it thus established a readiness to respond to differences in the poem.

But criticism constantly reflects its own limitations. The unity of *The Seasons* was recognized as new and its newness could be subsumed under new philosophic concepts and therefore accepted; its language, however, had no such support, and did not lead to new investigations or to readiness to abandon received principles. Wordsworth continued John Scott's theory of simplicity, and critics did not understand Thomson's use of personification. Readiness, therefore, existed only as a readiness to examine certain received principles, not all. *Cooper's Hill* and *Windsor Forest* had served as a basis for accepting the new unity of *The Seasons*, but no study had been made differentiating the kinds of diction in Milton and Virgil. The diction of Thomson, therefore, had only limited guides to distinguish its kind so that it was difficult for critics to explain proper and improper uses. Thus, unless there existed a basis for close discrimination, there seemed no reason to alter the received view. Such a basis depended upon the most discriminating comparison, and although every critic accepted comparison as a necessary critical procedure, only precise comparisons were needed if criticism was to become more accurate.

The critics who have written on *The Seasons* have all accepted comparison as a critical technique, but they have compared passages as 'beauties' or they have compared them for scientific accuracy, for imagery, for philosophy, science, taste, and skill. As a method, 'comparison' has been applied to every problem discussed. Yet the discovery of the appropriate comparison remains definable only by the 'insight' and diligence of the critic. Comparison forms not only a basis for critical inferences; it is also a basis for critical discovery. It presupposes certain critical ends which must be defensible in themselves before one even raises the question of the appropriateness of the choices. To compare Thomson with Lucretius when he is working with Richard Bradley is an example of an obviously wrong comparison. In comparing Thomson with himself, for example, Bonamy Dobrée found certain impressive lines missing, but this omission is no necessary loss of taste since the omission was undertaken for other purposes equally significant to the poetry. Comparison, in other words, makes demands upon the critic's judgement in determining the passages to be compared and in discovering what particular elements in one passage are relevant to those in another. Thus, comparing Thomson with himself can reveal a use of 'posture' terms, just as comparison with Cowper can yield differences in personification and imagery. But critics do not compare the 'whole' poem with other poems, although their language implies at times that they do. Even within the hierarchy of genres the bases for discrimination are subject matter, range, ends, or other parts or characteristics such as sentence structure or intensity of language.

CRITICISM AND DISCRIMINATION

(e) THE PERIODS OF CRITICISM

> A history, however, is more than a succession of discrete events; if it is to be fully intelligible, as a history, the events must be exhibited in a context of collective causes sufficient to account both for the common elements that persist through the criticism of the period and for the variant combinations of these that appear in different writers at different times.
>
> R. S. CRANE

In defining the periods of criticism in any other than a chronological fashion, it is necessary to attend to methods, problems, assumptions of different critics. A period is obviously a range of time and ideas, and it is as necessary to note which problems are included as well as which are omitted. Beginning, therefore, in purely chronological fashion, one notes that the criticisms of Patrick Murdoch, John Aikin, and Samuel Johnson continued to be published together with Thomson's poems, until the mid-nineteenth century. Whatever major change Wordsworth is claimed to have introduced in his prefaces of 1800–15, in the criticism of Thomson his comments fell within the customary range of critical questions and answers given to *The Seasons*.

The critics of *The Seasons* from the mid-eighteenth to the mid-nineteenth century form a group of critics who were moral, empirical, or ideal impressionists. And they were supplanted by a group that might be called metaphysical, empirical, or ideal organicists. The 'impressionists' based their response to the poem upon particular impressions of it, whether fragmentary (empirical) or moral (in terms of a divine analogy operating in it) or ideal (in comparing it to some ideal values or ideal poem of the same type).

The impressionists, therefore, speculated about theories of poetic perception in order to discuss the problems they selected. The various theories of the sympathetic imagination of the reader were summoned to justify acceptance of irregularities. In More, the irregularities of diction, in Stockdale and Murdoch, the irregularities of unity were to be 'understood' and accepted by means of a reading which found the values of the poem in other parts. In Aikin, the theory of sympathy or temporary illusion was used as a corrective for the theory of scientific reality because it made irrelevant the truth quality of the drama. Critics like John Scott and Robert Heron compared passages in the poem with passages supposed to reveal the 'true' assumptions about nature poetry or about all poetry. But these theories were about the nature of poetry or the distinction between one genre of poetry and another, although the comparison of particular passages implied an associative theory of perception.

The assumptions of these critics were different, but their actual comments upon the poem placed analysis of parts above analysis of it as a 'whole'. In this criticism, therefore, unity was seen as a value only if the work possessed 'vividness' to begin with, or if unity of character or tone was sought, such unity was explained in speculative terms in order to make more acceptable the statements about obscurity or inaccuracies or artificiality. The quotations used implied a 'group' orientation: John More quoted Warton as did John Aikin, Hugh Blair, Robert Heron, and the editor of Cooke's edition (1794). John Scott quoted John Aikin and Samuel Johnson.

I have suggested that the concept of proportionate comparison is inherent in evaluation, and it seems to me that a similar procedure is desirable in discussing periods in criticism. Such periods include a wide diversity of problems, subjects, language, ends, and audiences so that no one approach defines a period. In any period, moreover, there are obvious carry-overs from earlier criticisms. The issue in defining a period would seem to be based on discriminating the importance or unimportance of certain problems, the neglect or innovation of others.

The 'importance' of a problem in criticism is its actual relation to explanation, interpretation, or evaluation of poetry. In terms of 'process' such criticism forms models for poetry, and when it ceases to function in this way it is no longer significant as criticism for poets. When illustrations leave the text behind, they cease to be interpretations, and when critical discourse discusses 'poetry' without reference to poems, it creates difficulties in explaining, interpreting or evaluating particular poems. 'Importance', therefore, is definable by inquiries into poems, and to distinguish it from 'unimportance' or 'lack of importance' is a matter defended or refuted by argument. To discuss a period merely by reference to philosophic generalizations without descending to specific poems, leads critics into serious anachronistic errors. Theories of imagination and of sympathy in the early nineteenth century are based on views of association developed in the eighteenth. The frequency of the term 'imagination' does not imply its newness.

One must distinguish, however, the strategic use of problems, speculation, and language from their referential use. Theories of a poet's progress are often announced in the eighteenth century to permit critics to point out numerous failures to progress, just as theories of communication are invoked in order to permit attacks on certain types of obscurity. The problems of the years 1750–1960 include: what is a poem, how is it to be read, what is to be explained or interpreted in it, how are these to be verified, how is the poem to be placed with other poems, and who is to evaluate it, and what are the grounds for evaluation? These represent the persistent inquiries in criticism, and the critics of *The Seasons* provide variations to these which make them part of two major groups: from the mid-eighteenth to the mid-nineteenth century, and from the mid-nineteenth century to the present.

The first group of critics, for all their variations, reduce the question of poetry to some type of associative relation conveying force and vigour, whether in poetry or some other art (painting). For them, *The Seasons* has some type of associative, tonal, or imaginative unity, but its unity is not the basis for its value. Rather its imaginative force or vigour is. The meaning of imaginative force or vigour becomes part of the inquiry of how it is to be read or perceived. The theories of visual imagination, moral imagination, sympathetic imagination all form part of the inquiry about the conditions for perceiving; this inquiry is obviously more important than that of the nature of poetry because it makes possible the formal analysis of poetry as fiction rather than reality. It permits absorption of theories of imitation while resting upon theories of empirical impressions. At the same time such theories permit comparison of parts based upon 'force' or 'vigour', and even genres are governed by such hierarchies. 'Force' and 'vigour' are defined in formal and psychological terms and they are considered the result of certain diction, images, subjects which are norms to which the critic responds if he perceives in the proper way. Evaluation was a matter of comparing appropriate possibilities, that is, other 'similar' passages, made or found by the critic, in poetry or nature.

The second group of critics see all poetry as a huge continuum or tradition and they seek to place *The Seasons* within this stream by finding characteristics it shares with earlier poems or characteristics it shares with other streams than poetry (painting). The critics, therefore, seek to explain the history of influences or ideas within poetry or society or the other arts. They take for granted certain conceptual theories about verse, or force, or form, and explain language or form by reference to sources and models, and they develop theories of verification of data. These critics analyse the poem as a cultural object, overlooking or minimizing the relation between subject matter and its value. Modern critics, however, have insisted on 'culture' in the poem as part of its poetic wholeness and have insisted on a rejection of influences in order to study the organic unity of the poem. Yet these critics, too, have tended to neglect the bases for evaluation of such wholes or the applicability of them to *The Seasons*.

There were, of course, variations within each period not only in the treatment of problems but in the critical language in which these were stated. The theory of Thomson's artificial language, for example, took for granted that his language ought to be 'spontaneous' or 'natural', but eighteenth-century critics found this language 'obscure' and 'turgid'. The terms were not identical, but they involved no new distinctions. The concept of the imagination, too, from Robert Andrews to Allan Cunningham, permitted critics to find unity in tone or in the moral analogy or in the unconscious creation of the poet; but the purpose of such generalizations was still to defend the immediate vividness and intensity of the poem and explain or excuse its failings.

Certain generalizations merely attempt to explain away known facts; they reflect divergencies of preference, the use of current theories imposed upon known facts. Sir Harris Nicolas defended the digressions as forms of unconscious activity and Hazlitt attacked them as conscious and artificial. But neither attempted to study the revisions or the writing habits of the poet in order to bring new information to bear upon the poem. Such generalizations in criticism are speculative in the worst sense because they apply non-literary theories to criticism without establishing the kinds of interrelations necessary to demonstrate their validity. Proper attempts at interrelations form the basis for new 'periods' only because they test the theories and alter the assumptions of criticism. Floating ideas, however, cannot be said to change literary theory. Hazlitt's analysis of the transformational language of the poem was a far more significant contribution to a theory of Thomson's language than his theory either of artificiality or of sympathy. But no critic attempted to provide a quantitative study of Thomson's images until the end of the century, and then it was part of a different kind of theory.

In this respect Coleridge's organicism, the analytical method of which has become so significant for modern critics, did not exert upon Thomson's critics nor upon English criticism that power which it now possesses. The problems with which Coleridge dealt, especially those pertinent to contrasting forces in creating a whole, were not fully understood by his contemporaries, but in our time he has come to represent a theory of analytical organicism. He forms part of two 'periods' exactly as the method of Anna Seward formed part of the method of 'organicism' in the writing of James L. Robertson and George Macaulay, but for them the analysis of revision to indicate 'taste' and 'skill' formed part of a larger inquiry into the poet's 'unity'.

Within the earlier period a number of inquiries were discontinued, that is, a number of problems which were continued from previous critical doctrines were abandoned. Shiels's inquiry into 'beauties' and 'faults' as characteristic of an 'assemblage of poetical ideas', for example, was replaced by some type of unity of tone or character that served as basis for evaluation. There was discontinued, too, the tampering with the manuscript carried on by Lyttelton. The comments by Thomson's friends were forgotten or ignored in the criticism, and a historical factual approach to the text and to data about the poet took its place. In this respect the accidental discovery of Lyttelton's emendations of the 1738 edition, thought for a long time to be Pope's, led to misconceptions about Thomson's 'skill' and 'progress', and to a cessation of analysis of his revisions, though critics, being people, continued to express convictions about Thomson's revisions without seeing them all or even knowing whose they were.

Changes in the periods of criticism, moreover, are supported by non-verbal criticism. In the illustrations, the continuity of Kent's interpretation of the moral unity was interrupted in the 1770's with sentimental and idealized versions of *The Seasons*, and these continued in various interpretations, each emphasizing some social or accurate natural aspect of the poem until the gradual reduction of illustrations at the end of the nineteenth century. The illustration in 1927 dealt with the poem as a mythological-natural love poem, not unrelated to the organic view of nature and man in contemporary criticism.

(f) THE DILEMMAS OF DISCRIMINATION

> But where are such [true] critics to be found? By what marks are they known? How distinguish them from pretenders? These questions are embarrassing.
>
> D. HUME

Discriminations are involved in critical process, interpretation, judgement, and prediction, in making, transmitting, and supporting critical acts. To understand the dilemmas of discrimination is to understand the limits of objective responses, the ineradicable personal element in criticism. It is self-evident that the critic is himself a datum, but assuming that the critic is prepared to attend to all the relevant knowledge available, with a readiness to respond to novelty and to the individuality—the particularity—of each work, there is, nevertheless, an inevitable reliance upon one's own taste. For the poet-critic, this expresses itself in the act of selection, the risks of novelty, the decisions to stop, to continue, to refine. For the interpreter, there are decisions about the adequacy of information—the evaluation of what has already been done—and the trust placed in responses which differ from those of other critics.

Discrimination in criticism of poetry operates by responses to parts which are then related to wholes, but such responses while accurate in emotional tone, may be completely wrong in the kind of explanation given. Thus John Aikin recognized that Thomson's nature implied philosophic attitudes, and he argued that the natural description was impressive because it was true. Although he did not distinguish between the different expressions of nature, he recognized that it was no mere objective picture. Yet his explanation was refuted by the discovery that many of the facts in *The Seasons* were scientifically false; the poetry remained impressive; his explanation did not.

A similar dilemma arose when, at the end of the nineteenth century, some critics denied the transforming quality of Thomson's nature. Such a denial, without severe accompanying distinctions, was as untenable as the claim that scientific accuracy was the basis for artistic quality.

The reverse of this practice is equally relevant to the dilemma of discrimination. Thomson's earliest critics found his greatest powers in the sublime, though they recognized that in the same poem he wrote of the pathetic and tried his hand at burlesque. It was the practice of Lyttelton to eliminate the burlesque, and of later critics to find the 'tender' or the gentle or the optimistic qualities as those 'characteristic' of *The Seasons*. Yet the problem of proper discrimination is to recognize the diverse qualities within the poem and not to begin by depriving it of the variations it contains. Critics who prefer one or another of Thomson's qualities reveal this dilemma of criticism—the identification of preferences with representative instances. Thomson is optimistic in parts of *Spring*—but without determining the relation of part to whole, of optimism to its opposite, 'optimism' not only ceases to be correct, it becomes a false discrimination.

There is, however, no reason to assume that any analysis of every word or passage will provide any more adequate discrimination than reductionism. This over-determination of the text—so conspicuous in school editions—did not imply a qualitative awareness of different passages and usages within the poem. Even the quotations from different poets were often misleading about the implications of words and passages. And the argument that such analyses served to teach novices in literature was as fallacious as the use of moral passages to teach benevolent Christianity.

There are discriminations that are accepted so long as their dangers are concealed by forces which prevent their being tested; but when such forces disappear, the discriminations disappear along with them. Thus bad discriminations seem to have a puzzling durability whereas they are not exposed only because of the complicated character of artistic responses.

In this respect, the discriminations made by the bulk of Thomson's readers in the early nineteenth century are just not known. Discussions about the common readers by reference to the statements of highly literate and educated critics do not provide the kind of information from which to draw reliable inferences. Yet the critics themselves respond to the poem in terms of new views of nature, and this aspect of *The Seasons* seems capable of being shared by all observers of or participants in rural life.

Each criticism tends to distinguish a correct from an incorrect discrimination. For defenders of Thomson's variety, over-refinement and exclusive subtleties formed wrong distinctions. For the exclusionists led by Wordsworth, false discrimination was the bad taste attributed to common readers. For the imaginative idealists, false discrimination was over-emphasis on faults. For the religious defenders of Wordsworth, it was praise for description which lacked mystical and emblematic qualities. For cultural critics (of the late nineteenth century) it was a failure to see that all early eighteenth-century poets were part of an age of prose and reason. For modern critics of organic form, wrong discrimination is to deny that Thomson failed to compose an organically unified poem or that he could not recognize his good from his poor lines.

But despite the widespread meanings attributed to correct or incorrect discrimination, the test of discriminations rested in the examples given or the explanations provided—and among these there was far more room for agreement than appears. Critics who prefer Thomson's 'auriculas' passage to his description of a winter storm, state a preference rather than a contradiction, and critics who accept variety do not necessarily oppose all hostile criticism of the poem. Wordsworth's exclusionist assumptions, speculative as they are, can be tested by an examination of the 1726 *Winter*, a poem which did not lack the qualities of good poetry. It is, in other words, in the quality of the explanation, in the reliability of the evidence brought to support one's interpretation or judgement that disagreements exist.

Every interpretation of *The Seasons* relies upon some previous responses either to this poem or other poems. And inherent in the actual process—as in all learning processes—this is a reliance upon prior information. So long as such knowledge is held with an understanding of how it was attained, and the kinds of instances to which it refers, it can be manipulated to explain new examples. But when a gap occurs between the generalization and the instances to which it refers, empty phrases substitute for critical insight.

Discrimination proceeds by particular problems and the study of *The Seasons*, for example, from Warton to Heron and Aikin is a continuing analysis of literary images which are taken for granted until the latter part of the nineteenth century when attempts were made to compute the kind of metaphors, their usages and derivations. The 'return' resulted from a view of artificial diction that was to be compared to the non-artificial language. It was a recurrence to a study of language based on a developmental and organic theory of literature, and it took more than thirty years before an understanding of Thomson's language made any advances pertinent to a reinterpretation of the poem. Discriminations which earlier had taken for granted the artistic quality of the poem had come to be undermined by the end of the century, and only as the researches led back to inquiry into the good and bad uses of language did they affect the interpretation of the poem. But even in our time, the term 'discrimination' can be used to conceal the need for critical analysis. Accusations against Thomson's literary indolence have ceased, but failures of artistry are still unfortunately identified with 'discrimination'—as though Thomson might have been Milton if he had worked harder. There are faults in *The Seasons* which are the result of Thomson's limits as a poet, but these can only be explained by distinctions and comparisons. 'Discrimination' ought not to be used to conceal the need for careful explanation; it then becomes itself a parody of the procedure it is to exemplify.

(g) THE ACT OF EVALUATION

> Judgment eventually submits itself to analysis, and the subjective elements in criticism can be objectified by being related to their objects and viewed in a larger perspective.
>
> H. LEVIN

In the continuity of articulate statements about the poem, the most remarkable fact has been the agreement upon the value of its natural description and the recognition of ineffectiveness in its eulogies, digressions, and some of its language. In every statement about the value of *The Seasons*, a proportion was created in which these factors were juggled, and the judgement ultimately given was approving, the only exception being the Victorian period in which some critics reduced the value of natural description because they measured it against a particular metaphysical position.

What this continuity implied, therefore, was that the evaluation of the 'poem' was an evaluation of parts, and that approval of the 'whole' meant that the natural description rather than any of the other less successful parts was considered the adequate guide for the 'end' of the poem. This critical agreement for two centuries assumed that response to the poem among literate critics was not decided by theories of poetic perception but by a knowledge of other poetry and the external world. It was in explanations of the 'goodness' of this natural description that critics differed, as they did in placing natural description in the hierarchy of genres from epic to epigram.

Even the theories of poetic perception, that is, theories of how to read poetry, whether dominated by disinterest and the absence of prejudice, or by interest in and sympathy with the narrator's attitudes, or by imaginative tone or organic unity, did not prevent this agreement as long as they led to a readiness, a willingness to accept the unfamiliar. Only critics like D. C. Tovey and Oscar Wilde, who urged that the poem should not be read, made it impossible to agree on what was valuable in it. The agreement on the value of natural description was based on a diversity of reasons: newness of detail and precision of description (Warton), vividness and accuracy (Aikin), imaginative force and moral insight (More, Nicolas, Cunningham), individuality of sight and expression (Shiels, Johnson), vividness of imagery and sentiment (Heron), the unfolding processes of nature (Hazlitt, Morel, Reynolds), the organic relation between nature and ideas (Morel, Macaulay, Spacks). Each of these critics, regardless of the literary theory to which he committed himself, named the same or similar passages as examples—the shower or Hagley Park in *Spring*, the sunrise and storms in *Summer*, the sunrise and lyric references in *Autumn*, the redbreast and storms in *Winter*. In each of these passages they valued what they, in their own time, could defend. Warton's attack on the thought and language of hereditary descriptions, and Myra Reynolds's defence of a changing nature full of colour, movement, sound implied two different views of literature. The function of those views was persuasive, to convince a particular audience at a particular time; the reference to qualities in the poem, however, was directly verifiable in a reading of it. Explanations for the audience, therefore, could lose their validity without denying the impressiveness of the particular examples.

In this regard, certain arguments became irrelevant for criticism, even if true. Thus the argument for Thomson's newness was, in the light of nineteenth-century poetry, irrelevant to a reader familiar with Wordsworth, Keats, Tennyson, and the numerous other nature poets. The novelty of *The Seasons* exists in the present or else 'novelty' refers to a quality which has ceased to be new. When G. Gregory Smith (1919) put forward the argument of novelty, he did so to place Thomson in historical perspective and distinguished his value for poetry from his value as a poet.

But some explanations, like 'precision of detail', persist. This persistence seems due to a language which implies a fusion of thought and expression so that it is possible to examine a passage with reference to the facts and to the expression of external nature. 'Precision' thus can mean 'scientific accuracy', a particular in contrast to a general description, a description using specific language, vividness, an exact impression conveyed to the reader, a selection of appropriate details, and so forth. Those explanations which permit the widest latitude of verification seem to represent the continuing critical agreements.

In explaining natural description as a value in *The Seasons*, critics found in the same passages characteristics previously unnoticed or insufficiently explored. The technique of cumulative response, of returning to passages like the introduction to *Spring*, or the *Summer* sandstorm, formed the basis for more acute discrimination. In the eighteenth century there was a considerable continuity of criticism: Warton was quoted by John More, by John Aikin, by Robert Heron so that these critics built upon his remarks and examples. And this has been the case with the remarks of Johnson in the nineteenth and twentieth centuries. This accumulation refines or resists earlier distinctions. Natural description was extended by critics to include not merely the actual sights and sounds of nature, but these as part of an attitude to nature, a rhythmic pattern, a skill in imagery. The complex of values attributed to description explained the worth of these passages and the neglect of others.

'Precision' and 'vividness' were redefined in terms of the current theories (of literature, psychology, science, etc.), but such definitions did not necessarily exclude each other or earlier comments. Some element of 'accuracy' entered into every definition of 'precision'. The reformulations, however, were the result of theories outside the poem, and what was 'precise' for George Macaulay depended upon an evolutionary theory of literature in which 'precision' was seen as a hierarchy extending to the Wordsworthian 'eye fixed on the object'.

The theory of interpreting a work on its own terms became a commonplace in late nineteenth-century criticism, but it conceals the meaning of 'terms'. For although *The Seasons* was indeed a verbal construct, critics differed about relations of words to things, about the elements which composed unity and about the contexts which provided the basis for interpretation. These were words, lines, stanzas, seasons, passages within seasons. The underlying 'terms' could be moral, religious, philosophic, scientific, imaginative, expressive. But the determination of what made the natural description 'good' involved the selection of an 'end' toward which it was directed. Such an end was discovered in the poem, but not from the poem.

Some explanations of ends were clearly more comprehensive, more accurate, more verifiable than others. None included all the aspects of a poem, but no criticism can, and if consistency of criticism is observed, there is still need to examine the kind of consistency offered. For Warton, the end involved a comparison with the descriptions of earlier poets; for Heron, it involved a comparison with images and sentiments of earlier and later poets; for Shairp, it involved a comparison with what was ideal Wordsworthian description; for Spacks, it involved a comparison with what was assumed to be the most adequate of Thomson's own descriptions. But in every case there was an overt or implied comparison necessary to discover what Thomson was doing by noting either what he could have done, what he had done, or what others had done. So long as these are recognized as comparisons, their critical relevance as well as their implied importance in the poem are examinable.

There was another sense in which the comparisons implied that the poem was not, and could not be, interpreted without knowledge beyond the poem. Thomson described both what he saw and did not see so that critics came to grant the irrelevance of literal accuracy. This was, however, supplanted by assumptions of imaginative force and vigour. Yet the response to particular passages, as John Wilson pointed out, demanded some knowledge of language and human experience. Hidden in the agreement on natural description was an understanding about human experience, whether of nature itself or of human nature implied in the personifications.

The extensive illustrations to the poem and the wide audience during the eighteenth and most of the nineteenth century, which the critics and publication statistics corroborate, indicate that there were originally levels of response to nature which later critics did not feel. But their recognition of value implied that the poem referred to phenomena which still demanded from them an exercise of their feelings and memory. Thus the critics found in the poem some exercise of their emotional life, whether a return to the wild joy of childhood or the confused violence which found man and nature part of 'one wild dazzling waste'.

When critics approved the natural description, they meant that it made them see nature differently or see an inimitable quality in the poem. Every exploration of this has referred to subject matter or individuality of thought and expression. Critical analysis has depended upon the critics' selection of particulars and these have been the basis for what the poem did well. There has been taken for granted, in other words, that the process of evaluation was implicit in interpretation. The description of the spring shower was good not because it embodied the great chain but because, in doing so, it did it well. The 'well-doing' results from the intrinsic forces of the passage—from the expectation of the storm and its fulfilment, the versification and its variety, the suspension of natural forces and their release, its comparisons with the preceding insect passage and the subsequent idealized golden age. This passage, moreover, is artistically more prominent than the surrounding ones and makes greater demands upon knowledge, feeling, and interpretation than other passages and provokes insights which extend beyond the normal usages of the poem. The imagination which 'beholds the kindling country colour round', beholds a fiery stirring, heat and light, colour and sound, fire 'springing' from water and the animation of life in nature. Such a line or passage cannot properly be interpreted without indicating its exceptional quality, and the fact that its range of implication extends beyond the neighbouring passages and thus stands out from them.

This is what critics mean when they refer to 'memorable' passages or those they 'remember', and it marks the difference between critics who attend to specific examples and those who impose generalizations upon the work of art. To suggest that the work of art imposes a pressure upon critics to attend to perceptions rather than principles is not to suggest that all critics succumb to such a pressure.

At the head of the introduction to this book stands an epigraph by John Bruce in which he explains that the 'art' of criticism must have its 'science'. Using 'art' to mean 'the power of doing something not taught by nature', 'artfulness' or 'skill', and 'science' to mean 'knowledge' or 'art attained by precepts, or built on principles', Bruce found them related in terms of ends and means. Art was achieved by science; criticism was developed by demonstrable principles, though there was always an element in art which defied 'skill'. This study has attempted to discriminate the characteristics of 'criticism', by using as a model the continuity and discontinuity of problems found in interpretations of *The Seasons*. Much remains to be learned about the 'art' and 'science' of criticism, but now, one hopes, a little less than previously.

APPENDIX I

A CHECK LIST OF EDITIONS OF *THE SEASONS*[1]

Note: The following editions were collected in the course of my research, when I had no intention of publishing a bibliography. Since the number of editions has increased beyond all anticipation, I have decided to publish the list with the hope that some scholar, interested in compiling a proper bibliography, may find it useful. I have tried to locate places for all editions and to indicate sources where I have not found editions. I recognize that there are inconsistencies in my notations and that there are probably other editions, but the time necessary to track down all the material has not been available to me. I welcome corrections and additions. Symbols used to designate American Libraries are taken from *Symbols Used in the Union Catalog of the Library of Congress*. Those used to designate other libraries are taken from Donald Wing, *Short-Title Catalogue*.

CLU-C	William Andrews Clark Library, Los Angeles, Calif.
CSmH	Henry E. Huntington Library, San Marino, Calif.
CSt	Stanford University, Stanford, Calif.
CtY	Yale University, New Haven, Conn.
DLC	Library of Congress
EN	National Library of Scotland (Advocates)
IU	University of Illinois, Urbana, Ill.
L	British Museum, London
MB	Boston Public Library
MBAt	Boston Athenaeum
MdBP	Peabody Institute, Baltimore, Md.
MH	Harvard University, Cambridge, Mass.
NN	New York Public Library
NNC	Columbia University, New York, N.Y.
NNPM	Pierpont Morgan Library, New York, N.Y.
O	Bodleian Library, Oxford
Paris	Bibliothèque Nationale
PPL	Library Co. of Philadelphia
RC	(personal copy)
TxV	University of Texas, Austin, Tex.
ViL	Jones Memorial Library, Lynchburg, Va.
VtU	University of Vermont, Burlington, Vt.
VtMiM	Middlebury College, Middlebury, Vt.

[1] This bibliography was compiled with the assistance of N. D. Baker's manuscript of illustrated editions of *The Seasons* now in possession of the Rare Book Collection, Library of Congress, and listed here as 'Baker'.

A CHECK LIST OF EDITIONS OF 'THE SEASONS'

Sources

ALLIBONE: Samuel Austin Allibone, *Critical Dictionary of English Literature and British and American Authors, Living and Deceased, from the Earliest Accounts to the Latter Half of the Ninteenth Century*. Phila., Lippincott, 1858–91. 5 v.

AMERICAN CATALOGUE: James Kelly, *American Catalogue of Books Published in the United States from Jan. 1861 to Jan. 1871*. N.Y., Wiley, 1866–71. 2 v.

American Catalogue of Books, 1876–1910. N.Y., pub. weekly, 1876–1910. 9 v. in 13.

ANNUAIRE: *Annuaire des Ventes de Livres*. Paris, Delteil, 1918–31. 13 v.

BIBLIOTHECA LINDESIANA: J. L. L. Crawford, *Bibliotheca Lindesiana*. Aberdeen, Univ. Pr., 1918–23.

'CAXTON HEAD': Thomson's Seasons, a remarkable collection of editions of Thomson's Seasons from 1728 to 1908, comprising examples of the work of the most famous eighteenth- and nineteenth-century book illustrators, from the library of the late Judge Willis. [London, Tregaskis, 1911?]

DNB: *Dictionary of National Biography*. London, Oxford University Press, 1921–22. 22 v.

EBERT: Friedrich Adolf Ebert, *Allgemeines Bibliographisches Lexikon*. Leipzig, Brockhaus, 1830. 2 v.

ENGLISH CATALOGUE: *English Catalogue of Books . . . issued in Great Britain and Ireland . . . 1801–*. London, S. Low, 1864–1901.

EVANS: Charles Evans, *American Bibliography*. Chic., 1903–34. 12 v.

GJERSET: Knut Gjerset, *Der Einfluss von James Thomson's 'Jahreszeiten' auf die Deutsche Literatur des Achtzehnten Jahrhunderts*. Heidelberg, 1898.

GRAESSE: J. G. T. Graesse, *Trésor de livres rares et précieux*. Dresden, Kuntze, 1859–69. 7 v.

HEINSIUS: Wilhelm Heinsius, *Allgemeines Bücher-Lexikon, 1700–1892*. Leipzig, Brockhaus, 1812–94. 19 v.

HOE: *A Catalogue of Books printed in Foreign Languages after the year 1600 forming a part of the Library of Robert Hoe*. 4 v.

KAYSER: Christian Gottlob Kayser, *Vollständiges Bücher-Lexikon, 1750–1910*. Leipzig, Tauchnitz, 1834–1911. 36 v.

QUÉRARD: Joseph Marie Quérard, *La France littéraire*. Paris, Didot, 1827–64. 12 v. *La Littérature française contemporaine, 1827–49*. Paris, Daguin, 1842–57. 6 v.

RYLANDS: *Catalogue of the Printed Books and Manuscripts in the John Rylands Library*. Manchester, J. E. Cornish, 1899. 3 v.

TOBIN: James Tobin, *Eighteenth Century English Literature and its Cultural Background*. New York, Fordham University Press, 1939.

1726

Winter, A Poem. London, J. Millan, 1726. 16 pp. fol. L

Winter, A Poem. 2nd ed. London, N. Blandford for J. Millan, 1726. 8°. O

APPENDIX I

Winter, A Poem. 3rd ed. London, 1726. 8°. L

Winter, A Poem. 4th ed. London, N. Blandford for J. Millan, 1726. 56 pp. 20½ cm. L

Winter, A Poem. Dublin, T. Hume for W. Smith, 1726. 27 pp. 19½ cm. DLC

1727

Summer, A Poem. London, J. Millan, 1727. 88 pp. 20½ cm. 8°. L

Summer, A Poem. Dublin, R. Norris, 1727. 59 pp. 8°. L

1728

Spring, A Poem. London, A. Millar [etc.], 1728. 57 pp. 20½ cm. 8°. L

Winter, A Poem. 5th ed. London, J. Millan, 1728. 38 pp. 8°. O

Spring, A Poem. Dublin, S. Powell for George Risk, George Ewing, William Smith, 1728. 53 pp. 8°. O

Summer, A Poem. 2nd ed. London, J. Millan. 1728. 88 pp. 8°. CtY

1729

Spring, A Poem. 2nd ed. London, A. Millar, 1729. 57 pp. 8°. O

1730

The Seasons [plus Hymns, Poem on Newton.] illus. William Kent-N. Tardieu. London, J. Millan and A. Millan, 1730. 4°. MH
[Some copies add Britannia, 2nd ed.] NNC
[and others add also 4 leaves of misc. poems.] NNC

The Seasons, A Hymn, A Poem . . . and Britannia, illus. B. Picart-J. Clark. London, J. Millan and A. Millar, 1730. 8°. L
[Collective title page for the separately published seasons.]
[Some copies add 4 leaves of misc. poems.] L

Poems, viz. Spring, Summer, Autumn, Winter. A Hymn . . . To the Memory . . . And Britannia. Dublin, S. Powell for George Risk, George Ewing, William Smith. 1730. 8°. [Collective title page for separate parts.] O

Winter, A Poem, a hymn on the seasons, a poem to the memory . . . and Britannia. London, J. Millan, 1730. 69 pp., 19. 8°. O

Winter, A Poem, a hymn on the seasons, a poem to the memory . . . and Britannia. Dublin, S. Powell for George Risk, George Ewing, William Smith, 1730. 70 pp. 8°. O

The Seasons, A Poem. London, J. Millar and A. Millar, 1730. 311 pp., 16. 20 pp. 8°. NNC

Summer, A Poem. 3rd ed. London, J. Millan, 1730. 71 pp. 8°. L

Summer, A Poem. With large additions. Dublin, S. Powell for George Risk, George Ewing, William Smith, 1730. 60 pp. 8°. O

Autumn, A Poem. 2nd ed. London, N. Blandford for J. Millan, 1730. 72 pp. 8°. L

Autumn, A Poem. Dublin, S. Powell for George Risk, George Ewing, William Smith, 1730. 60 pp. 8°. O

[*Autumn.* Edinburgh, by R. Fleming, 1730.] 62 pp. 8°. MH

A CHECK LIST OF EDITIONS OF 'THE SEASONS'

1731

Spring, A Poem. 2nd ed. London, A. Millar, 1731, 77 pp. 8°. L
[and a reprint of identical description, produced in October 1734, 250 copies]

1734

Winter, A Poem (and a hymn, etc.). London, J. Millar, 1734. 79 pp. 8°. L

1735

The Four Seasons, and other Poems, illus. B. Picart-J. Clark. London, J. Millan and A. Millar, 1735. 8°. (Contains *Spring*, 2nd ed., 1731, 77 pp., *Summer*, 3rd ed., 1730, 71 pp., *Autumn*, 2nd ed., 1730, 72 pp., *Winter, A Poem*, etc., 1734, 79 pp.) EN

Summer, A Poem. 4th ed. London, J. Millan, 1735. 64 pp. 8°. L

1736

The Works of Mr. James Thomson, illus. William Kent-P. Fourdrinier. London, A. Millar, 1730–6. 2 v. 4°. L

1738

The Works of Mr. James Thomson, illus. William Kent-P. Fourdrinier. London, A. Millar, 1738. 2 v. 8°. L

1740

Spring, A Poem. Dublin, S. Powell [for Risk, etc., as above], 1740, 54 pp. 8°. O

Summer, A Poem. Dublin, S. Powell [for Risk, etc., as above], 1740. 8°. O

1744

The Works of Mr. James Thomson, illus. William Kent-P. Fourdrinier. London, A. Millar, 1744. 2 v. 8°. [Vol. II in B.M. dated 1738.] L

The Seasons. London, A. Millar, 1744. 243 pp. 8°. L

The Seasons. London, A. Millar, 1744. 242 pp. 8°. L

1745

Jahres-Zeiten des Herrn Thomson, Eng. and Ger. ed., tr. B. H. Brockes, illus. C. Fritsch. Hamburg, 1745. 543 pp. 8°. NNC

1746

The Seasons, illus. William Kent-P. Fourdrinier. London, A. Millar, 1746. 230 pp. 17 cm. 12°. L

1749

The Works of Mr. James Thomson, illus. London, A Millar, 1738–49 [Vol. I, 1744]. 3 v. 21 cm. NNC

1750

The Works of James Thomson, ed. George, Baron Lyttelton, illus. William Kent-P. Fourdrinier. London, A. Millar, 1750. 4 v. 4°. [2nd title-page of vol. I dated 1752 in B.M. copy.] L

1751

The Poetical Works of James Thomson, illus. [Kent]-I. Ridge. Dublin, J. Exshaw, 1751. 360 pp. EN

1752

The Works of James Thomson. London, A. Millar, 1752. 4 v. CSmH
The Seasons, illus. William Kent-P. Fourdrinier. London, A. Millar, 1752. 222 pp. 16½ cm. NNC
The Seasons, London, A. Millar, 1752. 220 pp. 12°. L

1754

The Works of James Thomson. 1754. 4 v. 12°. Graesse

1756

The Works of James Thomson, illus. [Kent], Donaldson and Goodnight. London, A. Millar, 1756. 4 v. Baker

1757

The Works of James Thomson, illus. William Kent-P. Fourdrinier. London, A. Millar, 1757. 4 v. 12°. L
The Seasons, illus. William Kent-P. Fourdrinier. London, A. Millar, 1757. 216 pp. 17 cm. NNC
Jacob Thomson's Gedichte, tr. J. Tobler, Zürich, 1757. Gjerset.

1758

The Seasons, illus. William Kent-P. Fourdrinier. London, A. Millar, 1758. 209 pp. 17½ cm. L
The Seasons. illus. William Kent-P. Fourdrinier. London, A. Millar, 1758. 209 pp. 16 cm. NNC
The Seasons, Dublin, 1758. 180 pp. 16°. L
Jacob Thomson's Jahreszeiten, Ger. ed., tr. Johann Franz von Palthen, illus. Crusius. Rostock, Verlag der Koppischen Buchhandlung, 1758. 142 pp. 22 cm. NNC

1759

Les Saisons, French ed., tr. Marie Jeanne de Chatillon Bontemps, illus. Eisen-C. Baquoy. Paris, Chaubert, 1759. viii, 332 pp. 8°. L

A CHECK LIST OF EDITIONS OF 'THE SEASONS'

1760

Les Saisons, French ed., tr. Marie Jeanne de Chatillon Bontemps, illus. Berlin, Amsterdam, A. Bedin, 1760. 2 v. in 1. 17 cm. NNC

1761

The Seasons, illus. William Kent-P. Fourdrinier. Edinburgh, A. Donaldson and J. Reid, 1761. 209 pp. 8°. L

The Seasons. [Place and publisher not given], 1761. 200 pp. 8°. L

Les Saisons, French ed., tr. Marie Jeanne de Chatillon Bontemps. Berlin and Amsterdam, 1761. 8°. Paris

1762

The Works of James Thomson, ed. Patrick Murdoch, illus. William Kent-N. Tardieu. London, A. Millar, 1762. 2 v. 29 × 23½ cm. 4°. L

The Works of James Thomson, illus. [Kent]-Neist. London, A. Millar, 1762. 4 v. 12°. L

The Seasons, illus. [Kent]-Neist. London, A. Millar, 1762. xxxii, 209 pp. 17½ cm. EN

1763

The Works of James Thomson. London, 1763. 2 v. 12°. L

Les Saisons, French ed. Frankfurt, Esslinger, 1763. 8°. Heinsius

Les Saisons, French ed., tr. Marie Jeanne Chatillon Bontemps, Berlin and Amsterdam, 1763. 8°. Paris

1764

The Seasons. [Place and publisher not given], [1764]. xxiv, 204 pp. 12°. EN

The Seasons, illus. London, 1764. 209 pp. EN

1765

Jacob Thomson's Gedichte, Ger. ed., tr. J. Tobler. Zürich, 1765. 5 v. 17 cm. NNC

1766

The Works of James Thomson, illus. [Kent]-Neist. London, A. Millar, 1766. 4 v. NN

The Seasons, illus. [Kent]-Donaldson and Goodnight. London, A.Millar, 1766. 209 pp. 12°. L

Jacob Thomsons Jahreszeiten, Ger. ed., tr. Johann Franz von Palthen. Rostock, Koppisch, 1766. 142 pp. 22 cm. L

1767

The Seasons, illus. [Kent]-Neist. London, A. Millar [etc.], 1767. xxx, 206 pp. 18 cm. NN

The Seasons, illus. [Kent]-I. Ridge. Dublin, R. Bell, 1767. xxxiv, 230 pp. 17½ cm. 12°. L

1768

The Works of James Thomson. London, A. Millar, 1768. xxiv, 394 pp. 8°. L
The Works of James Thomson, illus. [Kent]-Donaldson. Edinburgh, J. Robertson for A. Kincaid, 1768. 4 v. NNC
The Works of James Thomson, illus. Edinburgh. A. Donaldson, 1768. 4 v. 17 cm. NNC
The Seasons, illus. [Kent]-Neist. London, A. Millar [etc.], 1768. xxx, 209 pp. 18 cm. L
The Seasons, illus. [Kent]-Donaldson. Edinburgh, A. Kincaid and J. Bell and J. Robertson, 1768. xxxviii, 208 pp. 18 cm. L
The Seasons, illus. Edinburgh, Printed by A. Donaldson, 1768. 209 pp. 18 cm. NNC
Die Jahreszeiten, Eng. and Ger. ed. Basel, Schweighauser, 1768. Gjerset

1769

The Seasons. Glasgow, R. and A. Foulis, 1769. xxxi, 203 pp. 12°. L
The Seasons, Eng. and Ger. ed. Basel, Schweighauser, 1769. 180 pp. 18 cm. Kayser
The Seasons. London, printed for the proprietors, 1769. 209 pp. 12°. L
Les Saisons, Poëme, French ed. Dordrecht, A. Blussé et Fils, 1769. 332 pp. 8°. EN
Les Saisons, French ed., illus. Eisen-C. Baquoy. Paris, Chaubert and Herissant, 1769. 8°. Hoe
Jacob Thomson's Gedichte, Ger. ed.. tr. J. Tobler. Zürich, 1769. Gjerset

1770

The Seasons, illus. Wright-Malpas. London, [1770?]. 8°. L
The Seasons. illus. [Kent]-I. Ridge. Dublin, by John Exshaw, 1770. 12°. L

1771

The Seasons, illus. [Kent] I. Ridge. Dublin, by John Exshaw, 1771. 12°. L

1772

The Works of James Thomson. Edinburgh, for R. Clark, 1772. 4 v. 8°. L
The Seasons. Edinburgh, Wilham Auld, 1772. xxxiv, 219 pp. 20°. L

1773

The Works of James Thomson, [illus. Kent]. London, W. Bowyer, 1773. 4 v. 12°. L
The Works of James Thomson. Edinburgh, A. Kincaid and W. Creech, 1773. 8°. In *The British Poets*. Edinburgh, A. Kincaid and W. Creech, 1773–6. vv. 38–9. L

The Seasons, [illus. Kent]. London, W. Strahan, etc. xxxviii, 209 pp. 1773. L

The Seasons . . . with *Britannia*, etc., illus. with new plates, unsigned. Dublin, Printed by W. Smith, 1773. 12°. L

1774

The Works of James Thomson. Edinburgh, A. Donaldson, 1774. 4 v. 12°. NN

The Seasons, illus. [Kent]-P. Fourdrinier. London, W. Strahan, 1774. xxxviii, 209 pp. 14 cm. L

The Seasons, illus. Edinburgh, A. Donaldson, 1774. xxviii, 209 pp. 18 cm. L

The Seasons, illus. Edinburgh, J. Robertson, 1774. CtY

Thomsons Vier Jahreszeiten, Ger. ed., illus. Zürich, Orell and Gessner, 1774. 208, 170 pp. 15 cm. NNC

1775

The Works of James Thomson. London, A. Millar, 1775. 4 v. 18 cm. NNC

The Works of James Thomson. London, John Donaldson, 1775. 4 v. 18 cm. NNC

The Seasons. Glasgow, R. Chapman and A. Duncan, 1775. xxxvi, 256 pp. 22 cm. L

The Seasons. Edinburgh, W. Darling, 1775. xxxviii, 208 pp. 12°. EN

Les Saisons, French ed., tr. Marie Jeanne de Chatillon Bontemps, illus. Moreau-Choffard, etc. Amsterdam, 1775. 8°. DNB

1776

The Seasons. London, Oxlade, 1776. 144 pp. 12°. L

The Seasons. Glasgow, R. and A. Foulis, 1776. xxxi, 203 pp. 12°. EN

1777

The Works of James Thomson. 1777. 2 v. 12°. In *The Poets of Great Britain Complete from Chaucer to Churchill*, ed. John Bell. London, John Bell, 1782. vv. 57–8. 12°. L

The Seasons, ed. George Wright, illus. Wright-Malpas. London, J. French, [1777]. xxiv, 228 pp. L

The Seasons. Philadephia, Robert Bell, 1777. 251 pp. 19½ cm. 8°. L

Les Saisons. French ed., illus. Tr. Marie Jeanne de Chatillon Bontemps, Paris [1777], 280 pp. 12°. L

1778

The Works of James Thomson, illus. London, J. Rivington, T. Payne, etc. 1778. 2 v. 18 cm. NNC

The Works of James Thomson, illus. London, J. Rivington & Sons. 3 v. 22 cm. NNC
The Works of James Thomson, illus. [Kent]-Donaldson. Edinburgh, J. Robertson for W. Anderson, 1778, (Vol. III dated 1768). 4 v. 17 cm. EN
The Seasons. [Kent designs unsigned.] London, W. Strahan [etc.], 1778. xxviii, 209 pp. 15½ cm. NNC
The Seasons, illus. Hamilton-Caldwell. London, J. Murray, 1778. xlv, 256 pp. 8°. NN
The Seasons illus. Edinburgh, Printed by J. Robertson for W. Anderson, 1778. xl, 208 pp. 18 cm. NNC

1779

The Works of James Thomson. 1779. 2 v. 8°. In *The Works of the English Poets*, ed. Samuel Johnson. London, 1779–81. vv. 48–9. 8°. L
The Works of James Thomson. Aberdeen, J. Boyle, 1779. 4 v. 16 cm. NNC
The Seasons, illus. Allan, Hamilton and Caldwell. London, J. Murray, 1779. xlv, 256 pp. 19 cm. 8°. EN
The Seasons, illus. Allan, Hamilton and Caldwell, with extra illustrations by Bartolozzi. London, J. Murray, 1779. xlv, 256 pp. 19 cm. 8°. NNPM
Les Saisons, French ed., tr. Marie Jeanne de Chatillon Bontemps, illus. Londres, 1779. 270 pp. 12 cm. L
Les Saisons, French ed., tr. Marie Jeanne de Chatillon Bontemps, illus. Paris, Pissot [etc.], 1779. 19 cm. NNC

1780

The Poetical Works of James Thomson. Edinburgh, Apollo Press, 1780. 2 v. 13 cm. [*Bell's Edition. The Poets of Great Britain, complete from Chaucer to Churchill.*] NNC
The Seasons, illus. [London, 1780?]. xii, 162 pp. 15 cm. NNC
The Seasons. Edinburgh, G. Alston, 1780. xxxviii, 206 pp. 12°. EN
The Seasons. Paris, 1780. 12°. L
Les Saisons, French ed., tr. Marie Jeanne de Chatillon Bontemps. London, 1780. xvi, 268 pp. 14 cm. NNC

1781

The Seasons. Leipzig, E. B. Schwickert, 1781. xxix, 208 pp. 19 cm. NNC
Jacob Thomson's Gedichte, Ger. ed., tr. J. Tobler. Zürich, Orell, 1781. 8°. Gjerset

1782

The Seasons, illus. [Kent]-Donaldson and Goodnight. London, A. Millar, 1782. xxxiv, 208 pp. 18 cm. NNC

Les Saisons, French ed., tr. Marie Jeanne de Chatillon Bontemps. London, Cazin, 1782. 18°. Annuaire

Les Saisons, Poëme, French ed. Paris, Pissot, 1782. xxxii, 182 pp. 14 cm. NNC

1783

The Beauties of Milton, Thomson, etc. [selections]. London, 1783. 12°. L

Les Saisons, French ed., tr. Marie Jeanne de Chatillon Bontemps, illus. Marillier. Londres, 1783. 213 pp. 11 cm. NNC

1784

The Poetical Works of James Thomson. Glasgow, Andrew Foulis, 1784. 2 v. fol. L

The Seasons. London, W. Osborne and T. Griffin, 1784. The Seventeenth Edition. xxxii, 190 pp. 16 cm. [I have not found the alleged sixteen prior editions.] EN

1785

The Works of James Thomson, illus. London, J. Rivington, 1785. 3 v. Baker.

The Seasons. Paris, Theophilus Barrois, 1785. 12°. Quérard.

1786

The Seasons, Ital. ed., illus. Milano, G. Galleazzi, 1786. NNC

1787

The Poetical Works of James Thomson. Bell's Edition. The Poets of Great Britain complete from Chaucer to Churchill. London, Printed by Fry and Couchman, 1787. 2 v. 13 cm. DLC

The Seasons, illus. William Kent. London, J. Rivington, etc., 1787. xxiii, 180 pp. 18 cm. L

De Jaargetijden, Dutch ed., tr. G. Lublink den Jongen, illus. Amsterdam, de Erven P. Meyer and G. Warnars, 1787. xxxvi, 318 pp. 8°. Graesse

1788

The Works of James Thomson, illus. Dodd-Cook. London, J. Rivington & Sons, 1788. 3 v. 8°. L

The Works of James Thomson, illus. [Kent]. London, J. Rivington & Sons [etc.], 1788. 2 v. 12°. L

The Seasons, illus. Dodd-Cook. London, A. Strahan for J. Rivington & Sons [etc.], 1788. xxxi, 191 pp. 17 cm. L

The Seasons, [Kent]. London, J. Lackington, 1788. 209 pp. 12°. EN

The Seasons. Philadelphia, Prichard and Hall, 1788. xviii, 20–196 pp. 12°. NN

Les Saisons, French ed., tr. Marie Jeanne de Chatillon Bontemps, illus. after Eisen. [London, 1788 ?]. 12°. Quérard

1789

The Seasons and The Castle of Indolence. Edinburgh, P. Hill, 1789. 12°. L

Jakob Thomson's Jahreszeiten, Ger. ed., tr. Ludwig Schubart. Berlin, C. F. Himburg, 1789. xl, 336 pp. 18 cm. NNC

Jacob Thomson's Jahreszeiten, Ger. ed., tr. Johann Franz von Palthen. Berlin, 1789. Gjerset.

179–

The Seasons, illus. [179–?]. lix, 318 pp. 16 cm. NNC

The Seasons, illus. London, for J. Badcock, [179–?]. xxxi, 222 pp. 16 cm. NNC

1790

The Poems of James Thomson. 1790. In *The Works of the English Poets*, ed. Samuel Johnson. London, M. Brown for J. Buckland, J. Rivington & Sons [etc.], 1790. 275 pp. vv. 54–5. 6½″. 8°. L

The Seasons, illus. Allan-Caldwell. London, 1790. Baker

The Seasons. Glasgow, J. Duncan, 1790. CtY

The Seasons. Newburyport, John Mycall for proprietor of the Boston book-store, [1790 ?]. xxxviii, 42–238 pp. 17½ cm. 12°. NN

The Seasons. London, John Taylor, 1790. xxxii, 33–231 pp. 4°. L

The Seasons, etc. London, J. Wenman, 1790. 176 pp. 12°. L

The Seasons. Philadelphia, H. Taylor for R. Campbell, 1790. 190 pp. 17 cm. 16°. NN

Autumn, Eng. and Latin ed., tr. R. C. Brownell. [London, 1790]. 8°. Rylands

1791

The Seasons, illus. London, William Lane, 1791. xxiv, 200 pp. 12°. L

The Seasons. Philadelphia, W. Woodhouse, 1791. Evans

The Seasons, ed. J. J. C. Timaeus. Hamburg, 1791. 179 pp. 8°. L

1792

The Seasons, illus. London, J. Murray, 1792. xlv, 256 pp. 20 cm. 8°. L

The Seasons, illus. London, J. Strahan [etc.], 1792. xxii, 229 pp. 24½ cm. L

The Seasons, illus. London, Printed for and sold by the booksellers, 1792. 240 pp. 18 cm. NNC

The Seasons. Hartford, Elisha Babcock, 1792. Evans

1793

The Seasons, illus. Dodd-Cook. London, J. Rivington & Sons [etc.], 1793. xxiii, 180 pp. 18 cm. L

The Seasons, ed. Percival Stockdale, illus. Stothard, etc. London, A. Hamilton, 1793. xxiv, 227 pp. and 'Notes to the Seasons.' 25 cm. 8°. L

The Seasons. London, L. Wayland, 1793. xxiii, 156 pp. 24°. EN

The Seasons, illus. Allan-Caldwell. London, J. Murray, 1793. xlv, 256 pp. 8°. EN

The Seasons, illus. Corbould-Parker. London, T. Longman [etc.], 1793. xxxi, 272 pp. 6¼″. 8°. EN

The Seasons, illus. London, T. Longman, B. Law & Sons, [etc.], 1793. xxxi, 272 pp. 17 cm. NNC

The Seasons, illus. Catton-Corbould. Perth, R. Morison for R. Morison & Son, 1793. lii, 250, 39 pp. 24 × 19 cm. 4°. L

The Seasons, ed. McKenzie. Dublin, 1793. 8°. L

The Seasons. Newburyport, 1793. Evans

1794

The Poetical Works of James Thomson, illus. In *Cooke's Pocket Edition of the Original and Complete Works of Select British Poets*. London, C. Cooke, [1794?]. xxiv, 314 pp. [See 1800 ed.]. L

The Poetical Works of James Thomson, illus. Cooke's edition. London, C. Cooke, [1794?]. xii, 318 pp. 14 cm. NNC

The Poetical Works of James Thomson. Edinburgh, Mundell & Son, 1794. In *Select British Poets, and Translations*, ed. Robert Anderson. London, [1794]. v. 9. 24 cm. In *A Complete Edition of the Poets of Great Britain*, ed. Robert Anderson. London, J. and A. Arch; Edinburgh, Bell and Bradfute, 1793, 1792–4. 8°. L

The Seasons. London, W. Osborne and T. Griffin, 1794. xxiii, 176 pp. 17 cm. NNC

The Seasons, illus. Metz-Neagle. London, J. Murray, 1794. xlv, 256 pp. 8°. L

The Seasons, illus. Cruikshank-Laurie. London, J. Creswick and Co., 1794. xix, 196 pp. 14½ cm. L

The Seasons, illus. T. Stothard. London, J. Stockdale, 1794. 269 pp. 16°. L

The Seasons, illus. T. Stothard. London, J. Stockdale, 1794. xix, 256 pp. 16½ cm. 12°. EN

The Seasons, illus. Perth, R. Morison, Jr., for R. Morison & Son [etc.], 1794. 2 v. in 1. 14½ cm. L

The Seasons. Parma, J. B. Bodoni, 1794. 248 pp. 32½ × 24½ cm. 4°. L

The Seasons. Revised and corrected by J. J. C. Timaeus. Leipzig, John Sommer, 1794. xlvii, 179 pp. 8°. L

The Seasons, illus. London, J. Creswick, 1794. xix, 196 pp. 15 cm. NNC

1795

The Poetical Works of James Thomson. In *A Complete Edition of the Poets of Great Britain*, ed. Robert Anderson. London. J. and A. Arch; Edinburgh, Bell and Bradfute, 1793, 1792–5. v. 9. 8°. L

The Seasons, illus. Stothard. London, J. Chapman, 1795. xiv, 233 pp. 23 cm. L

The Seasons, illus. Edinburgh, Robert Ross, 1795. xxviii, 223 pp. 12°. L

The Seasons. Philadephia, Jacob Johnson & Co., 1795. xix, 194 pp. 17 cm. 12°. NN

The Seasons. Edinburgh, James Gillies, 1795. 172 pp. 24°. EN

Tempora Thomsoni, Latin ed., tr. R. C. Brownell. Eng. and Lat. 61, 91, 57, 79 pp. London, Mr. Yates, [1795?]. 288 pp. 22 cm. L

Les Saisons, French ed., tr. Marie Jeanne Chatillon de Bontemps, illus. Binet-Blanchard. [Paris], Imp. de Patris, 1795. 284 pp. 13 cm. NNC

Les Saisons, French ed., illus. Le Barbier. Paris, Imp. de Didot Jeune, 1795. 8°. Annuaire

1796

The Seasons, illus. Allan-Caldwell. Alnwick, J. Catnach, 1796. xii, 162 pp. 15½ cm. DLC

Les Saisons, French ed., tr. Marie Jeanne de Chatillon Bontemps, illus. Le Barbier, Baquoy-Dunbroun-Dupreel-Patas. Paris, Didot, 1796. 272 pp. 8°. EN

Thomson's Jahreszeiten, Ger. ed., tr. Harries, illus. Altona, Hammerich, 1796. lxxii. 350 pp. 8°. L

Jakob Thomson's Jahreszeiten, Ger. ed., tr. Ludwig Schubart. Zweite Ausgabe. Berlin, 1796. 304 pp. 8°. L

1797

The Seasons. London, A. Millar, W. Law, R. Cater, etc., 1797. 162 pp. 15 cm. 12°. EN

The Seasons, illus. Hamilton-Bartolozzi-Tomkins. London, P. W. Tomkins, 1797. 244 pp. 48 × 39 cm. fol. L

The Seasons, illus. London, P. W. Tomkins, 1793–7. (Issued in parts.) CLU-C

The Seasons, illus. Cruikshank-Laurie. London, T. Heptinstall, 1797. xxi, 192 pp. 15 cm. NNC

The Seasons, illus. Philadephia, W. W. Woodward, 1797. [Stafford's Edition.] xxiv, 200 pp. 17½ cm. 12°. NN

The Seasons, tr. F. G. Canzler. Gottingen, 1797. 8°. Heinsius

1798

The Poetical Works of James Thomson, illus. Kirk-Neagle-De Moulinville. London, C. Cooke, 1798. 12°. 'Caxton Head'

Les Saisons, French ed., illus. Binet-Blanchard. 1798. Baker

James Thomson's Jahreszeiten, Ger. ed., tr. G. F. Herrmann. Leipzig, Weissenfels, 1798. 8°. L

1799

The Seasons, illus. Corbould-Parker. London, A. Strahan for G. G. and J. Robinson [etc.], 1799. lxiii, 238 pp. 16 cm. 12°. L

The Seasons, illus. Springsguth. London, T. Wills, 1799. Baker

Episodes des Saisons de Thomson. Paris, Langlois, Malherbe, 1799. 8°. Quérard

18—

The Seasons. London, [18—?]. xix, 196 pp. 14½ cm. [Same as J. Creswick, 1794?] NNC

1800

The Poetical Works of James Thomson, illus. Kirk-De Moulinville-Neagle-Warren-Corbould-Thurston-Warren-Reimbach. Cooke's edition. London, for C. Cooke, [1800]. xxiv, 314 pp. 14 cm. illus. NNC

The Seasons, illus. Edinburgh, Ross and Blackwood, 1800. xxix, 223 pp. 17 cm. EN

The Seasons. Wrentham, Massachusetts, Nathaniel Heaton, Jr., and David Heaton; Providence, Oliver Farnsworth; Newport, Henry Cushing; Salem, Ephraim Goodale, Mendon [etc.], 1800. xv, 168 pp. 17½ cm. 12°. L

The Seasons. Paris, Egron, 1800. 8°. DNB

The Seasons. Hamburg, Herold; Leipzig, Sommer, 1800. 8°. Heinsius

Les Saisons, French ed., tr. Marie Jeanne Chatillon Bontemps. Paris, F. Louis, 1800. 248 pp. 12°. Paris

Thomson's Jahreszeiten, Eng. with Ger. notes, ed. Halle, illus. 1800–. v. I [*Spring*, *Summer*] 20 cm. NNC

1801

The Works of James Thomson. London, R. Baldwin, 1801. 3 v. 8°. Eng. Cat.

The Poetical Works of James Thomson. In *Bell's Edition. The Poets of Great Britain complete from Chaucer to Churchill*, vv. 91–92. London, G. Cawthorn, 1801. NN

The Seasons, illus. London, G. Cawthorn, 1801. xxxii, 235 pp. NNC

The Seasons. Albany, New York, Whiting and Leavenworth for Thomas, Andrews and Penniman, 1801. xiv, 163 pp. NN

The Seasons, illus. Philadelphia, John Bioren for Benjamin and Jacob Johnson, 1801. xix, 192 pp. 17 cm. NN

The Seasons. Leipzig, Breitkopf, 1801. 8°. Heinsius

Les Saisons de Thompson, French ed., tr. J. P. F. Deleuze, illus. Eisen-Baquoy and Gravelot-DeLauney. Paris, Imp. de Guilleminet, 1801. 420 pp. 8½ cm. 8°. NNC

Las Estaciones del Año, illus. J. Ribelles. Madrid, 1801. 2 v. 13 cm. NNC

1802

The Works of Mr. James Thomson, illus. Metz-Neagle, Anker Smith, Medland. London, R. Baldwin [etc.], 1802. 3 v. 22 cm. 8°. EN

The Works of James Thomson. London, Hamilton, 1802. 3 v. 8°. Ebert

The Seasons, illus. Hamilton, Fuseli, etc. London, F. J. DuRoveray, 1802. xxiv, 262 pp. 23 cm. 8°. [19 cm. NNC] L

The Seasons, illus. Hamilton, Fuseli, etc. London, F. J. DuRoveray, 1802. xxiv, 262 pp. 8°. One of three copies printed on calendared paper, with coloured drawing of the frontispiece and proof impressions of plate. EN

The Seasons, illus. Wooley, Kirk, Brown-Northwell. London, C. Whittingham for G. and J. Robinson [etc.], 1802. lxviii, 242 pp. 22 cm. 8°. L

The Seasons, illus. Wooley, Kirk, Taylor and J. B. Longacre. London, C. Whittingham for G. and J. Robinson [etc.], 1802. lxviii, 242 pp. 24½ cm. 8°. L

The Seasons, illus. Corbould-Parker. London, A. Strahan for R. Baldwin [etc.], 1802. xviii, 166 pp. 13½ cm. 12°. EN

The Seasons, ed. Rev. J. Evans, illus. Cranmer, Thurston, Corbould, etc. London, J. Cundee for T. Hunt, 1802. xxxii, 213 pp. 15 cm. L

The Seasons. Dundee, Chalmers, Ray and Co., 1802. xv, 208 pp. 22 cm. NNC

The Seasons, illus. Corbould-Parker, Anderson and Roberts. New York, George F. Hopkins, 1802. xlvi, 217 pp. 16 cm. NN

The Seasons. Vienna, R. Sammer, 1802. xx, 268 pp. 12°. L

The Seasons, Eng. and French ed., tr. J. Poulin, illus. Eisen-Baquoy. Paris, Durand, 1802. 2 tom. 8°. xiv, 239 pp. 20 cm. L

1803

The Works of James Thomson, illus. Metz-Neagle. London, R. Baldwin, 1802. vol. I, 1803, vol. II, III, 1802. 3 v. 8°. L

The Poetical Works of James Thomson. London, L. J. Higham, 1803. xxiv, 394 pp. 18 cm. NNC

The Seasons, illus. Edinburgh, John Buchanan, 1803. 215 pp. 13 cm. NN

The Seasons, illus. Corbould-Parker and Cromek. London, A. Strahan for R. Baldwin [etc.], 1803. lxiii, 238 pp. 17 cm. L

The Seasons, illus. London, W. Suttaby, 1803. 168 pp. 4½ cm. 24°. Bibliotheca Lindesiana

The Seasons. London, T. Wills, 1803. xviii, 168 pp. 14 cm. NNC

The Seasons, illus. Dundee, Chalmers, Ray and Co., 1803. xv, 209 pp. 21 cm. 8°. EN

The Seasons, illus. Anderson. New York, L. Nichols for T. Simpson, 1803. xxii, 179 pp. 18½ cm. NN
The Seasons, illus. New York, T. B. Jansen and Co., 1803. (With life by Robert Heron.) 255 pp. 10 × 6½ cm. NN
The Seasons. Paris, for Theophilus Barrois, Jr., 1803. 2 v. 12°. L
Die Jahreszeiten, Ger. ed., tr. W. Soltau. Braunschweig, 1803. DNB

1804

The Poetical Works of James Thomson. Philadelphia, Robert Carr for Benjamin Johnson etc., 1804. 2 v. in 1. 14 cm. NN
The Seasons, illus. Burnett-Scott. London, for J. Brambles, A. Megitt and J. Waters, 1804. 20, 221 pp. 14 cm. NNC
The Seasons. Birmingham, Knott and Lloyd, 1804. xxv, 174 pp. 12°. L
The Seasons with The Castle of Indolence, illus. Hamilton and Lawson. Philadelphia, Budd and Bartram for Thomas Dobson, 1804. lix, 319 pp. 16°. NN

1805

The Poetical Works of James Thomson, illus. Westall and Stothard. 1805. In *The Works of the British Poets*, ed. Thomas Park. London, Stanhope Press by Charles Whittingham for John Sharpe, 1805–9. v. 20. 16°. L
The Seasons, ed. Rev. J. Evans, illus. [London], J. Cundee, 1805. 2nd ed. xxxii, 216 pp. 17 cm. L
The Seasons, illus. Bewick-Thurston. London, for James Wallis, 1805. xxii, 285 pp. 8°. L
The Seasons, illus. Bewick-Thurston. London, for James Wallis, 1805. xvi, 286 pp. 8°. L
The Seasons, illus. Bewick-Thurston. London, for James Wallis, 1805. xx, 286 pp. 8° (Fine Paper). L
The Seasons. London, W. Suttaby [etc.], 1805. xiv, 168 pp. 12 cm. L
The Seasons, illus. Anderson. New York, for Thomas B. Jansen, 1805. xxii, 179 pp. 18 cm. DLC
The Seasons. Philadelphia, Kelly and Austin, 1805. 239 pp. PPL
The Seasons. Coln, Rommerskirchen, 1805. 8°. In *The British Parnassus*, or, *Collection of Classical English Poets*, v. 1. Heinsius
Les Saisons, French ed., tr. J. P. F. Deleuze, illus. Roger. Paris, Levrault, Schoell et Co., 1805. 400 pp. 12°. Quérard
Die Jahreszeiten, Ger. ed., tr. J. F. Horn. Halle, Hendel, 1804–5. Heinsius
Jakob Thomsons Jahreszeiten, illus. Ger. ed., tr. Ludwig Schubart, Genilly-Stothard. Berlin, Himburg, 1805. 304 pp. 21 cm. NNC
Le Stagioni di Giacomo Thomson, Ital. ed., tr. Carlo di Ligni. Firenze, 1805. 293 pp. 8°. EN

1806

The Seasons, illus. London, Vernor, 1806. xxxiii, 182 pp. 12°. L
The Seasons, illus. Dublin, William Porter, 1806. IU

The Seasons. Coln, (Bauer in Leipzig), 1806. 12°. Heinsius
Les Saisons de Thomson, French ed., tr. J. P. F. Deleuze, illus. Roger-Brunet. Paris, 1806. 400 pp. 15 cm. NNC
Les Saisons, French ed., tr. Nic. Fremin de Beaumont. Paris, Le Normant, 1806. vii, 303 pp. 8°. EN

1807

The Seasons, illus. Hamilton-Bartolozzi, Tomkins. London, T. Bensley for Longman, Hurst, Rees and Orme, 1807. 236 pp. 33 × 26 cm. 4°. L
The Seasons, illus. Westall-Heath, Hamilton. London, Stanhope Press by C. Whittingham for W. Suttaby, 1807. 174 pp. 13½ cm. Baker
The Seasons. Brookfield, E. Merriam and Co. for I. Thomas, Jr., 1807. xv, 160 pp. 14½ cm. NN
The Seasons, illus. Evans-Anderson. Portland [Maine], Printed by Thomas B. Wait and Co., 1807. 215 pp. 18 cm. NN
Le Stagioni di Giacomo Thomson, Ital. ed., tr. Carlo di Ligni. Napoli, Simone, 1807. 255 pp. 20 cm. NNC
Foraaret, Danish ed., tr. P. Foersom. Kiobenhavn, 1807. 12°. L

1808

The Poetical Works of James Thomson. 1808. 115 pp. 8°. In *Select British Poets*, ed. Samuel Johnson. London, The Proprietors, 1810, [1808–10]. 8°. L
The Seasons, illus. Uwins-Rhodes. London, J. Walker, 1808. xii, 156 pp. 13 cm. NNC
The Seasons, [etc.], illus. C. Watson. 1808. 12°. In *The Cabinet of Poetry*, ed. Samuel Jackson Pratt. London, 1808. v. 4. 12°. L
The Seasons. Edinburgh, W. Creech, Manners, [etc.], 1808. 246 pp. 16½ cm. L
The Seasons. London, W. Suttaby, 1808. 168 pp. 12°. L
The Seasons. Boston, Manning and Loring, 1808. xliv, 135 pp. 15 cm. NNC
The Seasons. Philadelphia, Jacob Johnson, 1808. l, 166 pp. 12°. L
The Seasons, [etc.]. Bordeaux, P. Beaume, 1808. 335 pp. 12°. L

1809

The Seasons. London, Vernor, 1809. 8°. Eng. Cat.
The Seasons, Eng. and French ed. London, C. Nourse, 1809. 2 v. 24°. NN
The Seasons, Hymns, Ode and Songs of James Thomson, illus. [Bewick's woodcuts]. London, A. Wilson for Taylor and Hessey, 1809. 323 pp. 12°. EN
The Seasons, illus. T. Bewick. Edinburgh, J. Ballantyne and Co. for R. Scholey, J. Walker, etc., 1809. xxii, 262 pp. 18 cm. EN
The Seasons, illus. T. Bewick. Edinburgh, 1809. 8°. L
The Seasons, illus. Anderson. Philadelphia, Jacob Johnson, 1809. MH

The Seasons, ed. Parsons and Galignani. In *Parsons and Galignani's British Library*. Paris, 1809. 250 pp. 8°. Paris

1810

The Poems of James Thomson. In *The Works of the English Poets*, ed. Alexander Chalmers. v. 12. London, 1810. 507 pp. 24 cm. L

The Seasons, illus. Bartolozzi-Tomkins. London, Longman, 1810. Eng. Cat.

The Seasons, illus. Corbould-Heath. London, Scott and Webster, [1810]. 192 pp. 14 cm. NNC

The Seasons. London, Vernor, 1810. 8°. Eng. Cat.

The Seasons. Manchester, Hopper and Son, [1810?]. 184 pp. 12°. L

The Seasons, illus. Boston, Oliver C. Greenleaf, 1810. xviii, 196 pp. L

The Seasons. Frederick-Town [Maryland], John P. Thomson, 1810. xxxi, 226 pp. 16°. NN

The Seasons. London, Scott and Webster, [1810?]. 192 pp. 14 cm. NNC

The Seasons, Eng. and French ed. Bordeaux, P. Beaume; Paris, Brunot-Labbe, 1810. 2 v. 18°. Quérard

The Seasons. Bordeaux, P. Beaume; Paris, Brunot-Labbe, 1810. 18°. Quérard

1811

The Seasons, illus. Uwins-Rhodes. London, J. Walker [etc.], 1811. xii, 156 pp. 13 cm. 24°. L

The Seasons, illus. Uwins-Cordon. London, Wilkie and Robinson [etc.], 1811. lii, 236 pp. 21 cm. 12°. L

The Seasons, illus. London, Vernor, Hood, and Sharpe, 1811. xii, 216 pp. 15 cm. NNC

[*The Seasons*. New York, Richard Scott, 1811.] Baker

The Seasons, illus. Philadelphia, T. and G. Palmer, 1811. 188 pp. 13½ cm. Baker

1812

The Seasons, illus. London, W. Suttaby, 1812. 168 pp. 12°. L

The Seasons. Aberdeen, D. Chalmers and Co., 1812. xxiv, 203 pp. L

The Seasons, illus. New York, T. and J. Swords, 1812. 232 pp. 10½ cm. NN

The Seasons. New York, C. S. Van Winkle, 1812. 168 pp. 24°. NN

Vinteren, Danish ed., tr. P. Foersom. Kiobenhavn, 1812. 12°. L

1813

The Seasons, Hymns, Ode and Songs of James Thomson, illus. Hilton-Edwards-Rhodes. London, J. W. H. Payne, 1813. 323 pp. 18½ cm. 12°. L

The Seasons, Hymns, Ode and Songs of James Thomson, illus. Hilton-Edwards-Rhodes. London, J. W. H. Payne, 1813. 323 pp. 20½ cm. NNC

Les Saisons, French ed., tr. Marie Jeanne de Chatillon Bontemps, illus. Paris, 1813. xii, 250 pp. 14 cm. 18°. NNC

1814

The Seasons, Hymns, Ode and Songs, illus. Hilton-Edwards-Rhodes. London, J. W. H. Payne, 1814. 323 pp. 12°. EN

The Seasons, illus. Newburyport, W. B. Allen and Co., 1814. 176 pp. NN

The Seasons, illus. [Hamilton]-Maverick. Georgetown, Richards and Mallory; Philadelphia, P. H. Nicklin, 1814. 213 pp. 18°. MdBP

The Seasons, illus. Bartolozzi-Tomkins. London, Whittingham and Rowland, 1814. 4°. L

1815

The Seasons. Ludlow, H. Procter, [1815?]. xiv, 196 pp. 18 cm. NNC

The Seasons. Middlebury [Vermont], William Slade, Jr., 1815. 262 pp. 12½ cm. NNC

The Seasons. Leipzig, Sommer, 1815. 8°. L

Les Saisons, French ed., tr. Marie Jeanne de Chatillon Bontemps. Clermont, Landriot, 1815. 18°. Quérard

Jacob Thomson's Jahreszeiten, Ger. ed., tr. J. C. W. Neuendorff. Berlin, Reimer, 1815. 8°. Gjerset

1816

The Seasons and Castle of Indolence, illus. Uwins-Warren. London, Walker and Edwards, etc., 1816. xii, 204 pp. 14 cm. 12°. L

The Seasons, illus. London, John Sharpe, 1816. xii, 215 pp. 8°. EN

The Seasons, illus. New York, Richard Scott, Forbes and Co., 1816. xxvi, 234 pp. 24°. NN

The Seasons. Hanover, Hahn, 1816. 166 pp. 16°. NN

Les Saisons, French ed., tr. Marie Jeanne de Chatillon Bontemps. Tulle, Imp. de Chirac, 1816. 12°. Quérard

Les Saisons, French ed., tr. Marie Jeanne de Chatillon Bontemps. Avignon, J. A. Joly, 1816. 12°. Quérard

Jahreszeiten, Ger. ed., tr. J. C. W. Neuendorff. Berlin, 1816. 8°. Graesse

1817

The Seasons with The Castle of Indolence, illus. Westall-Heath, Finden-Pye. New York, W. B. Gilley, 1817. 287 pp. 14 cm. L

The Seasons, illus. Westall-Heath, Finden-Pye. London, J. Sharpe, 1817. 215 pp. 17 cm. 12°. EN

The Seasons, illus. Taylor. London, Suttaby, Evans and Fox, 1817. 168 pp. 15 cm. NNC

The Seasons. Boston, T. Bedlington, 1817. 264 pp. 13 cm. NN

The Seasons. London, H. Berthoud, 1817. xv, 220 pp. 8°. L

La Estate di G. Thomson, Ital. ed. Modena, 1817. 8°. L

A Portion of Summer, Romaic ed. In [P. Petriody eidopoiesis kai protasis pros tous neous tous 'Ionas dia na anorthososi ten palais' Ellados], ed. Plato Petrides. Kerkura, aoez [1817]. 8°. L

1818

The Seasons and The Castle of Indolence. Edinburgh, Fairbairn and Anderson, 1818. 279 pp. 24°. EN

The Seasons, illus. Hamilton, Singleton-I. Taylor. London, Suttaby, Evans and Fox, 1818. xiv, 168 pp. 24°. EN

The Seasons, illus. Rolls-Heath. London, John Sharpe, 1818. xii, 215 pp. 17 cm. NNC

The Seasons, illus. London, Chiswick Press by C. Whittingham, 1818. 158 pp. 13 cm. 5¼″. 12°. EN

The Seasons, illus. Anderson-Westall. New York, W. B. Gilley, 1818. 287 pp. 13½ cm. NN

Les Saisons, French ed., tr. Marie Jeanne de Chatillon Bontemps, illus. Paris, A. Delalain, 1818. 18°. Quérard

Les Saisons, French ed., Orleans, Imp. de Jacob Aine, 1818. 8°. Querard

Le Stagioni di Giacomo Thomson, Ital. ed., tr. M. Leoni. Verona, 1818. xxix, 208 pp. 22 cm. NNC

Le Stagioni di Giacomo Thomson, Ital. ed., tr. F. Schizzati. Parma, 1818. 261 pp. 8°. L

Die Freiheit, Ger. ed., tr. O. C. G. D. Hansemann. Hanover, 1818. Gjerset

1819

Poems. 1819. In *Specimens of the British Poets*, ed. Thomas Campbell. London, 1819. v. 5. 8°. L

The Poetical Works of James Thomson. Philadelphia, 1819. vi, 416 pp. In *The Works of the British Poets*, ed. E. Sanford. Philadelphia, 1819–23. v. 22. 15 cm. 12°. L

The Poetical Works of James Thomson, Philadelphia, Benjamin Johnson, 1819, 8 v, 196 pp. NN

The Seasons, etc., illus. Brown, Kirk, Woolley-Rothwell, Brown-Taylor. London, Thomas Kelley, 1819. lxxii, 310 pp. 8°. L

The Seasons, illus. New York, R. and W. A. Bartow; Richmond [Virginia], J. Gray and Co., 1819. 220 pp. 16 cm. DLC

The Seasons, illus. Westall-Scoles and Anderson. New York, W. B. Gilley, 1819. 287 pp. 14 cm. 12°. NN

The Seasons. London, John Sharpe, 1819 (with second title page dated 1818). xii, 214 pp. 8°. EN

Jahreszeiten, Ger. ed. St. Petersburg, Briefe, 1819. 4°. Kayser

APPENDIX I

1820

The Seasons, illus. Uwins-Warren. London, F. C. and J. Rivington, 1820. xii, 204 pp. 24°. L

The Seasons, illus. Uwins-Bell. Belfast, Simms and M'Intyre, 1820. xiii, 168 pp. 13 cm. DLC

The Seasons, illus. Chiswick, C. Whittingham, sold by R. Jennings, T. Tegg, A. K. Newman, 1820. 211 pp. 18 cm. L

The Seasons. New York, R. and W. A. Bartow, 1820. 220 pp. 14 cm. NN

Jahreszeiten, Ger. ed. St. Petersburg, [Halle, Hemmerde and Schw.], 1820. 4°. L

La Primavera di G. Thomson, Ital. ed., tr. Antonio Bovio Silvestri. Bologna, 1820. 4°. L

1821

The Seasons, illus. Westall-Heath, Finden, Pye. London, John Sharpe, 1821. xii, 215 pp. 17 cm. L

1822

The Poetical Works of James Thomson, illus. London, William Cole, [1822]. 260 pp. 11 cm. NNC

The Poems of James Thomson. In *The British Poets*, vols. 43 and 44. Chiswick, Press of C. Whittingham, 1822. 2 v. 16½ cm. NN

The Seasons, Odes, Songs and Hymns. London, John Bumpus, 1822. xxiii, 192 pp. 18 cm. 12°. L

The Seasons, illus. In *Whittingham's Cabinet Library*. Chiswick, C. Whittingham, 1822, 158 pp. 12°. EN

The Seasons, with a Poem to the Memory of Sir Isaac Newton. Kilmarnock, R. Mathie, 1822. 203 pp. (EN copy incomplete). 14 cm. EN, NNC

The Seasons, illus. Anderson. Boston, T. Bedlington, [etc.], 1822. xviii, 196 pp. nar. 24°. NN

Die Jahreszeiten, Ger. ed., tr. W. Soltau. Braunschweig, 1822. Heinsius

Jakob Thomson's 'Jahreszeiten', Ger. ed., tr. Friedrich Schmitthenner. Zwickau, [Schumann], 1822. 2 v. 10 cm. NNC

1823

The Seasons. London, Jones and Co., 1823. (University Edition). viii, 136 pp. 29°. EN

The Seasons, illus. Westall-G. B. Ellis. Philadelphia, Edwin T. Scott, 1823. CSt

Die Jahreszeiten, Ger. ed., tr. W. Soltau. Braunschweig, 1823. viii, 216 pp. 8°. L

1824

The Seasons, illus. R. Westall. London, J. Sharpe, 1824. xii, 215 pp. 16 cm. 12°. L

The Seasons. Edinburgh, Oliver and Boyd, 1824. 168 pp. 12°. EN
The Seasons and Castle of Indolence. London, T. and J. Allman; Edinburgh, John J. Anderson, 1824. vii, 204 pp. 15 cm. NNC
The Seasons, ed. John Williams. London, G. and W. B. Whittaker, 1824. l, 276 pp. 8°. EN
The Seasons. London, Jones and Co., 1824. viii, 136 pp. 9½ cm. [Imperfect copy.] NN
The Seasons, illus. Anderson. New York, Abraham Paul, 1824. 256 pp. 24°. NN
The Seasons, illus. Hamilton, Westall, Kirk, Woodruff. Philadelphia, A. Sherman, 1824. 204 pp. 18 cm. NNC
Die Jahreszeiten, Ger. ed., tr. W. Soltau. Braunschweig, 1824. Kayser
J. Thomson's Jahreszeiten, Ger. ed., tr. F. W. Brockbräu. 1824. DNB
Hymnus zum Schlusse der Jahreszeiten, Ger. ed., tr. K[nebel]. Jena, Cröker, 1824. Kayser

1825

The Poetical Works of James Thomson. London, Cole, [ca. 1825]. 24°. Annuaire
The Seasons and Castle of Indolence. London, Baynes, etc., 1825. 216 pp. 13 cm. NNC
The Seasons, illus. London, John Sharpe, 1825. iv, 203 pp. 14 cm. NNC
The Seasons, illus. Westall-Rolls, Romney. London, John Sharpe, 1825, xii, 215 pp. NN
The Seasons, illus. William Thomson. London, T. Tegg, 1825. 170 pp. 18 cm. NN
The Seasons, illus. Boston, T. Bedlington, 1825. 154 pp. 15 cm. NNC
The Seasons. In *Jone's* [Jones's] *Cabinet Edition of Select British Poets*, v. I. London, Jones, 1825. iv, 36 pp. 8°. Paris
Thomson's Jahreszeiten, Ger. ed., tr. K. F. von Rosenzweig. Hamburg, Perthes, 1825. Gjerset
Thomson's Jahreszeiten, Eng. and Ger. ed. St. Petersburg, N. Gretsch; Leipzig, 1825. 521 pp. 22 cm. 4°. [*Spring* only]. NNC

1826

The Seasons, illus. T. Uwins-C. Warren. London, T. Davidson for C. and J. Rivington, 1826. xii, 204 pp. 12°. L
The Seasons, illus. Anderson. Boston, T. H. Carter and Co., 1826. Baker
The Seasons, illus. Boston, T. Bedlington, 1826. 154 pp. 14 cm. NN
The Seasons. Philadelphia, E. T. Scott, 1826. 180 pp. 14½ cm. CSt
The Seasons, illus. Maverick, Durand. Philadelphia, J. H. Cunningham, 1826. 214 pp. 15½ cm. DLC
The Seasons and Castle of Indolence. Frankfurt, O.M., H. L. Broennet, 1826. xx, 234 pp. 16°. NN
Le Stagioni di Giacomo Thomson, Ital. ed., tr. P. Muschi. Firenze, G. Molini, 1826. 412 pp. 21 cm. L

1827

The Seasons. London, T. Kay for the Booksellers, 1827. xii, 204 pp. 18 cm. NNC

The Seasons, illus. Chiswick, C. and C. Whittingham by T. Tegg, 1827. 158 pp. 14½ cm. DLC

Jacob Thomson's Jahreszeiten, Ger. ed., tr. H. Harries. Wien, 1827. 212 pp. Gjerset

J. Thomson's 'Jahreszeiten', Ger. ed., tr. Friedrich W. Bruckbräu. Munich, Lindauer, 1827. 4 parts in 1 v. 14 cm. NNC

1828

The Seasons, illus. Philadelphia, E. T. Scott, 1828. MH

The Seasons. Concord, Manahan, Hoag and Co., 1828. 204 pp. 15 cm. NNC

1829

The Seasons, illus. H. Corbould-J. Mitchell. Edinburgh, Oliver and Boyd, 1829. 168 pp. 12°. EN

The Seasons, illus. Hartford, S. Andrus, 1829. 192 pp. 16°. NN

The Seasons. Paris, Baudry, 1829. xxxii, 215 pp. Paris

The Seasons. Nurnberg, F. Campe, 1829. 152 pp. 32°. Kayser

183–

The Seasons, [illus.?]. Philadelphia, James Kay, Jr., and Bros., 183–. ViL

1830

The Poetical Works of James Thomson, [edited with a memoir by Sir Harris Nicolas]. London, W. Pickering, 1830. 2 v. 8°. 17½ cm. In *The Aldine Edition of the British Poets*. L

The Seasons and The Castle of Indolence. London, W. Pickering, 1830. cxxviii, 292 pp. 12°. L

The Seasons, illus. New York, S. and D. A. Forbes, 1830. 192 pp. 18 cm. NN

The Seasons. London, Thomas, Allman, [1830?]. xii, 180 pp. 32°. L

Jahreszeiten, Ger. ed., tr. Friedrich W. Bruckbrau. Munich, Lindauer, 1830. 4 v. 12°. Heinsius

1831

The Poetical Works of James Thomson in *The Works of Cowper and Thomson*. Philadelphia, J. Grigg, 1831. [Part II]. xxxvi, 133 pp. 22½ cm. 8°. NN

The Seasons, illus. Romney-Rolls. London, John Sharpe, 1831. iv, 203 pp. 14 cm. NNC

The Seasons, illus. Philadelphia, J. Locken, 1831. 192 pp. 16°. NN

Le Stagioni, Ital. ed., tr. Michele Leoni. Palermo, 1831. 252 pp. 16°. L

1832

The Poetical Works of James Thomson. Hildburghansen at New York, Bibliographick Institution, 1832. 2 v. 16½ cm. NNC

The Seasons. Pearl Edition. London, John D. Evans, 1832. 144 pp. 9 cm. NNC

The Seasons, illus. Hartford, S. Andrus. 192 pp. 16 cm. DLC

The Seasons, Newport, N. H., French and Brown, 1832. [French and Brown's edition. For the use of schools and academies.] 201 pp. 16½ cm. NN

The Works of Cowper and Thomson. Philadelphia, J. Grigg, 1832. [Part II]. xxxvi, 133 pp. 8°. NN

1833

The Beauties of Thomson, ed. Alfred Howard [selections]. London, T. Tegg, [1833 ?]. 212 pp. 14½ cm. NN

The Seasons. Boston, 1833. 12°. L

1835

The Seasons and *Castle of Indolence*. London, Orr and Smith, 1835. 223 pp. 8°. L

1836

The Seasons. London, C. Tilt, 1836. CtY

The Seasons, illus. New York, 1836. 200 pp. 32°. NN

The Seasons. Exeter, J. and B. Williams, 1836. Baker

The Seasons. Hartford, Judd, Loomis and Co., 1836. 192 pp. 16 cm. ViL

Jahreszeiten, Ger. ed., tr. Friedrich W. Bruckbrau. Munich, Lindauer,1836. 12°. Kayser

1837

The Works of Cowper and Thomson. Philadelphia, J. Grigg, 1837. [Part II]. xxxvi, 133 pp. 8°. NNC

The Seasons. Hartford, Andrus, Judd and Franklin, 1837. 192 pp. 16°. NN

The Seasons and Castle of Indolence, illus. H. Corbould-C. Heath. London, Scott, Webster and Geary, 1837. xiv, 192 pp. 12°. EN

1838

The Seasons, illus. London, C. Daly, 1838. MB

The Seasons and Castle of Indolence. London, W. Smith, 1838. 220 pp. 17 cm. L

APPENDIX I

1839

The Poetical Works of Thomson, Milton and Young, ed. Rev. H. J. Cary. London, W. Smith, 1839. 8°. Eng. Cat.

The Poetical Works of James Thomson in *The Works of Cowper and Thomson*. Philadelphia J. Grigg and Co., 1839. 8°. [Part II]. xxxvi, 133 pp. NN

The Seasons. London, 1839. xv, 174 pp. 32°. L

The Seasons. New York, Robinson and Franklin, 1839. CtY

The Seasons, illus. Boston, Weeks, Jones and Co., 1839. CtY

The Seasons. Halifax, William Milner, 1839. xv, 174 pp. 12 cm. NNC

184–

The Seasons. New York, T. Y. Crowell, undated (184–?). 479 pp. 19 cm. NNC

The Seasons. London, Tilt and Bogue, [184–?]. In *Tilt's Miniature Classical Library*. 236 pp. 10½ cm. NNC

The Seasons. New York, D. Appleton and Co.; Philadelphia, G. S. Appleton, [184–?]. xvi, 207 pp. 10½ cm. NN

1840

Poems and Plays. London, W. Smith, 1840. In *Smith's Standard Library*. 8°. Allibone

The Seasons. Philadelphia, James B. Smith and Co., [1840?]. TxV

The Seasons, illus. Westall. London, Rivington, 1840. Eng. Cat.

The Seasons. Zelle, Schulze, 1840. 12°. Kayser

1841

The Poetical Works of John Milton, James Thomson and Edward Young, ed. H. F. Cary. London, W. Smith, 1841. viii, 203 pp. 8°. L

The Seasons and The Castle of Indolence, with a biographical and critical introduction by Allan Cunningham, illus. Samuel Williams. London, Tilt and Bogue, 1841. lxx, 271 pp. 21 cm. 8°. L

The Seasons and Castle of Indolence. Zelle, Schulze, 1841. Kayser

The Seasons, ed. Anthony Todd Thomson. London, 1841. 8°. Graesse

The Seasons, with a life of the author by George Kent and notes by Moses A. Cortland, illus. New York, Charles Wells, 1841. 4th ed. vi, 168 pp. 15 cm. NN

The Seasons. Halifax, William Milner, 1841. xv, 174 pp. 16°. L

1842

The Seasons, ed. Bolton Corney, illus. John Bell, C. W. Cope, Thomas Creswick, etc. London, Longman, Brown, Green and Longmans. 1842. xlviii, 320 pp. 22 cm. 8°. L

The Seasons. London, John D. Evans, 1842. Baker

The Seasons and Castle of Indolence, illus. Gainsborough-Archer. London, Scott, Webster and Geary, 1842. xiv, 231 pp. 16°. NN

The Seasons and Castle of Indolence. London, W. Smith, 1842. 220 pp. 8°. EN

The Seasons, ed. Bolton Corney, illus. E. Bookhout, John Bell, C. W. Cope, Thomas Creswick. New York, Harper and Brothers, [1842?]. xlviii, 320 pp. 22 cm. EN

The Seasons, illus. Westall-Ellis. Philadelphia, John Locken, 1842. VtU

James Thomson's Frühling, Ger. ed. Magdeburg, (Fabricius), 1842. Kayser

Thomsonowy Počasy, tr. F. Daucha. V Praže, Tiskem J. Spurneho. 1842 LC

The Seasons, Latin, Ital., Span. and Hebrew ed. Berlin, 1842. DNB

1844

The Seasons. Boston, Lewis and Sampson, 1844. 159 pp. 16°. NN

1845

The Seasons and Castle of Indolence. London, Clarke, 1845. 24°. Allibone

The Seasons and The Castle of Indolence. London, William Pickering, 1845. 12°. Eng. Cat.

The Seasons and Castle of Indolence. Edinburgh, R. Martin; London, J. Duncan and Whittaker, 1845. 279 pp. NNC

1846

A Phonetic Version of The Seasons. Dublin, 1846. (MS.). NN

1847

The Poetical Works of James Thomson, in *The Aldine Edition of the British Poets*. London, William Pickering, 1847. 2 v. 16½ cm. EN

The Seasons, ed. Anthony Todd Thomson. London, Longman, Brown, Green and Longmans, 1847. xii, 438 pp. 8°. L

The Seasons, illus. Bell, Cope, Creswick, Horsley, Knight, Redgrave, Stone, Stonehouse, Tayler, Townsend, Webster. London, Longman, Brown, Green and Longmans, 1847. xlviii, 320 pp. 8°. NN

The Seasons, ed. Anthony Todd Thomson. London, Longman, 1847. xii, 438 pp. 17 cm. NNC

The Seasons. Paris, Baudry, 1847. In *Baudry's European Library*. xxiv, 199 pp. Paris

1848

The Seasons and The Castle of Indolence. London, Chapman and Hall, 1848. 12°. Allibone

The Seasons and Castle of Indolence. London, Groombridge, 1848. 12°. Eng. Cat.

APPENDIX I

1849

The Poetical Works of James Thomson, ed. J. Nichols, illus. Gilbert-Greatback. London, W. Tegg and Co., 1849. lxxii, 676 pp. 12°. L

The Poetical Works of James Thomson in *The Works of Cowper and Thomson*, illus. Holmes-Heath. Philadelphia, Grigg, Elliot and Co., 1849. [Part II]. xxxvi, 133 pp. 9¾″. L

The Seasons and The Castle of Indolence, illus. Gilbert-Greatback. London, W. Tegg and Co., 1849. lxxvi, 296 pp. 8°. LC

1850

The Poetical Works of James Thomson, ed. J. Nichols, illus. Gilbert-Greatback. London, W. Tegg and Co., 1850. lxxii, 681 pp. 16½ cm. NN

The Poetical Works of James Thomson, illus. J. McWhirter and G. Hay. Edinburgh, Nimmo, [1850?]. xliii, 498 pp. 18½ cm. NNC

The Seasons and The Castle of Indolence, illus. Gilbert-Greatback. London, W. Tegg and Co., 1850. 2nd ed. lxxvi, 296 pp. 8°. EN

Les Saisons, French ed., tr. P. Moulas, Lille, L. Daniel, 1850. 257 pp. 8°. Paris

1851

The Works of Cowper and Thomson, illus. Philadelphia, Lippincott, Grambo and Co., 1851. [Part II]. xxxvi, 133 pp. 8°. NN

The Seasons, ed. Anthony Todd Thomson. London, 1851. 8°. Graesse

The Seasons. 1851. In *The Cabinet of Poetry*. London, H. G. Bohn, 1851. 4 v. 8°. L

The Seasons. London, Piper, 1851. 32 mo. Allibone

1852

The Seasons and The Castle of Indolence, illus. W. Harvey. London, H. G. Bohn, 1852. 255 pp. 12°. L

The Seasons, illus. John Bell, C. W. Cope, A.R.A., Thomas Creswick. London, Longman, Brown, Green, and Longmans, 1852. xlviii, 320 pp. 21 cm. NNC

The Seasons. New York, A. S. Barnes and Co.; Cincinnati, H. W. Derby and Co., 1852. 335 pp. 20½ cm. DLC

Thomsonowy Počasy, . . . Newé Wydání, tr. F. Daucha. V Praže, 1852. xl, 198 pp. 8°. L

1853

The Poetical Works of James Thomson, James Beattie, Gilbert West, and John Bampfylde, illus. Birket Foster. In *Routledge's British Poets*. London, G. Routledge and Co., 1853. 16½ cm. L

Thomson's Poetical Works in *Library Edition of The British Poets*. Edinburgh, James Nichol, 1853. xviii, 372 pp. 8°. L

The Poetical Works of James Thomson. 1853. In *Collection of British Authors*, ed. Bernard Tauchnitz. Leipzig, Tauchnitz, 1853. v. 279. vi, 402 pp. 16°. L

Thomson and Pollok: containing *The Seasons* by James Thomson and *The Course of Time* by Robert Pollok. Boston, Phillips, Sampson and Co., 1853. 438 pp. 12°. NN

The Seasons, ed. J. R. Boyd. New York, A. S. Barnes and Co., 1853. 8°. NN

1854

The Complete Poetical Works of James Thomson, ed. Rev. George Gilfillan. New York, D. Appleton and Co., 1854. xx, 372 pp. 8°. NN

The Poetical Works of James Thomson, ed. Rev. George Gilfillan. New York, D. Appleton and Co., 1854. xviii, 372 pp. 8°. NN

The Poetical Works of James Thomson. Boston, Little, Brown and Co., 1854. 2 v. 8°. L

The Poetical Works of James Thomson, ed. F. J. Child. Boston, 1854. 2 v. 12°. MBAt

The Seasons and The Castle of Indolence. London, A. Scott, 1854. Eng. Cat.

1855

Poetical Works of James Thomson, London, John W. Parker and Son, 1855. In *The Annotated Edition of the English Poets*, ed. Robert Bell. 2 v. L

The Poetical Works of Thomson, Goldsmith and Gray, illus. London, T. Nelson and Sons, 1855. 526 pp. 8°. L

The Seasons. London, Thomas Nelson and Sons, 1855. 136 pp. 32°. L

The Seasons, ed. Gilbert Maxwell Gibson. Edinburgh, Oliver and Boyd, Seton, 1855. 12, 288 pp. NNC

The Seasons, ed. James R. Boyd. New York, A. S. Barnes and Co.; Cincinnati, H. W. Derby and Co., 1855. 355 pp. 20½ cm. DLC

1856

The Poetical Works of James Thomson, ed. J. Nichols, illus. Gilbert-Greatback, London, W. Tegg and Co., 1856. lxxii, 681 pp. 12°. RC

The Seasons, ed. James R. Boyd. New York, A. S. Barnes and Co.; Cincinnati, H. W. Derby and Co., 1856. 335 pp. 12°. NNC

The Seasons. New York, Leavitt and Allan, 1856. 192 pp. 12 cm. NNC

1857

The Poetical Works of James Thomson. Boston, Little, Brown and Co.; Cincinnati, Truman and Spofford, 1857. 2 v. 16½ cm. DLC

The Poetical Works of Thomson, Goldsmith and Gray. London, T. Nelson, 1857. 12°. Eng. Cat.

Thomson and Pollok: containing *The Seasons* by James Thomson and *The Course of Time* by Robert Pollok. Boston, Phillips, Sampson and Co., 1857. 438 pp. 20 cm. NNC

The Seasons and Castle of Indolence, illus. G. F. Sargent-M. A. Williams. London, James Blackwood, 1857. 262 pp. 9½ cm. 4°. EN

The Seasons and The Castle of Indolence, illus. Gilbert-Greatback. London, W. Tegg and Co., 1857. lxxvi, 296 pp. 8°. EN

The Seasons. London, Groombridge and Sons, 1857. 220 pp. 18 cm. NNC

The Seasons, illus. Schmolze. Philadelphia, E. H. Butler and Co., 1857. xl, 332 pp. 22 cm. 4°. NNC

1858

The Poetical Works of James Thomson. London and Glasgow, Griffin, 1858. 8°. Allibone

Thomson and Pollok: containing *The Seasons* by James Thomson and *The Course of Time* by Robert Pollok. Boston, Phillips, Sampson and Co., 1858. 438 pp. 20 cm. NNC

The Seasons, illus. Pickersgill, Foster, Wolf, Thomas, Humphreys. London, Nisbet, 1858. 230 pp. 8°. Allibone, Eng. Cat.

The Seasons. New York, Clark, Austin and Co., 1858. 168 pp. 16°. NN

1859

The Poetical Works of Thomson, illus. London, T. Nelson and Sons, 1859. 8°. 'Caxton Head'

The Poetical and Dramatic Works of James Thomson, and Edward Young, D.D. London and Glasgow, Richard Griffin and Co. iv, 236 pp. 10″ × 6¼″. 8°. RC

The Poetical Works of Thomson and Gray. London, T. Nelson, 1859. 22 + 425 pp. NNC

The Seasons and The Castle of Indolence. London, H. G. Bohn, 1859. Eng. Cat.

The Seasons, illus. Birket Foster, F. R. Pickersgill, J. Wolf, G. Thomas and N. Humphreys. London, J. Nisbet and Co., 1859. 228 pp. 21 cm. 8°. L

The Seasons, ed. Allan Cunningham, illus. S. Williams. London, W. Kent and Co., 1859. 4°. 'Caxton Head'

The Seasons, illus. Birket Foster. New York, Robert Cortan Bros., 1859. Baker

1860

The Poetical Works of James Thomson, ed. Sir H. Nicolas, Rev. P. Cunningham. In *The Aldine Edition of the British Poets*. London, Bell and Daldy. 1860. 2 v. EN

The Poetical Works of James Thomson, ed. J. Nichols. London, W. Tegg and Co., 1860. 8°. Eng. Cat., Allibone

Thomson and Pollok: containing *The Seasons* by James Thomson and *The Course of Time* by Robert Pollok. Boston, Phillips, Sampson and Co., 1860. CtY

The Seasons, illus. Bell, Cope, Creswick. London, Longman, Green, Longman and Roberts, 1860. xlviii, 320 pp. 21 cm. LC

The Seasons, ed. James R. Boyd. New York, A. S. Barnes and Co., 1860. 335 pp. NNC

1861

The Poetical Works of James Thomson, ed. Robert Bell. London, Griffin, 1861. 2 v. 12°. Eng. Cat.

The Seasons, ed. Robert Bell, illus. London, C. Griffin, Bohn and Co., [1861]. 206 pp. 16°. NN

1862

The Poetical Works of James Thomson, ed. Sir H. Nicolas, Rev. P. Cunningham. In *The Aldine Edition of the British Poets*. London, Bell and Daldy, 1857. 2 v. 8°. L

The Seasons and Castle of Indolence. London, Bell and Daldy, 1862. 2 v. 12°. Eng. Cat.

The Seasons and Castle of Indolence. London and Glasgow, Griffin, 1862. 2 v. 12°. Allibone

Thomson and Pollok: containing *The Seasons* by James Thomson and *The Course of Time* by Robert Pollok, A.M. Boston, Crosby and Nichols, 1862. 438 pp. 19 cm. LC

The Seasons. Boston, Crosby and Nichols, 1862. 154 pp. 15½ cm. DLC

Thomson's Seasons, pt. 1, 4. London, Christian Knowledge Society, [1862]. (*Spring*, 36 pp., *Winter*, 39 pp.) 8°. L

The First Part of Thomson's Seasons, '*Spring*', ed. C. P. Mason. London, Walton and Maberley, 1862. 55 pp. L

1863

The Poetical Works of James Thomson, James Beattie, Gilbert West and John Bampfylde. New Edition, London, Routledge, etc., 1863. L

The Seasons. Boston, Houghton, Mifflin and Co., 1863. Baker

The Seasons, ed. Bolton Corney. London, Longman, Brown, Green and Longmans, 1863. xlviii, 320 pp. 21 cm. NNC

The Seasons and Castle of Indolence. Zelle, Schulze, 1863. xxiii, 285 pp. 12°. Kayser

Thomson's Spring, ed. Walter M'Leod. London, Longman, Green, Longman, Roberts and Green, 1863. v, 120 pp. In *Oxford Local Examinations*. L

1864

The Poetical Works of James Thomson. London, W. Tegg and Co., 1864. Eng. Cat.

The Poetical Works of James Thomson. London, Simpkin, 1864. 12 mo. Eng. Cat.

The Poetical Works of James Thomson, illus. J. M'Whirter, Hay. Edinburgh, W. P. Nimmo, [1864]. xliii, 498 pp. L

The Seasons and The Castle of Indolence, ed. R. Ball. London, Griffin, 1864. 12°. Eng. Cat.

The Seasons, illus. Schmolze. Philadelphia, E. H. Butler and Co., 1864. xl, 332 pp. 22 cm. NNC

The Fourth Part of Thomson's Seasons, 'Winter', ed. C. P. Mason. London, Walton and Maberly, 1864. viii, 56 pp. 8°. L

Thomson's Winter, ed. Walter M'Leod. London, Longman, Green, Longman, Roberts and Green, 1864. 2nd ed. vii, 142 pp. In *Oxford Local Examinations*. L

1865

The Poetical Works of James Thomson. Boston, Little, Brown and Co., 1865. 2 v. 17 cm. DLC

1866

The Poetical Works of James Thomson, ed. Sir Harris Nicolas, Rev. Peter Cunningham. In the *Aldine Edition of the British Poets*. London, Bell and Daldy, 1866. L

The Seasons, ed. James R. Boyd. New York, A. S. Barnes and Co., 1866. 355 pp. 19 cm. DLC

The Seasons, New York, Clark and Maynard, [1866]. Amer. Cat.

1867

The Poetical Works of James Thomson. Leipzig, Tauchnitz, 1867. 16°. Allibone

1868

The Poetical Works of James Thomson, ed. Charles Cowden Clarke, illus. Edinburgh, W. P. Nimmo, 1868. xviii, 372 pp. 22½ cm. L

The Poetical Works of James Thomson, ed. Charles Cowden Clarke, illus. New York, Sheldon and Co., [1868?]. xx, 372 pp. 22½ cm. DLC

1869

The Poetical Works of James Thomson, plates, Kronheim and Co., Edinburgh, W. P. Nimmo, 1869. xiv, 372 pp. EN

The Seasons, ed. E. E. Morris. 1869. 2 v. In *British India Classics*, ed. William Julius Jeaffreson. London, Longmans, Green and Co., 1869. 2 v. L

The Seasons, ed. Anthony Todd Thomson, illus. Gilbert-Greatback. London, W. Tegg and Co., 1869. xii, 438 pp. NNC

The Seasons. Philadelphia, Claxton, Runson and Haffelfinger, 1869. 192 pp. 16°. NN

1870

The Poetical Works of James Thomson with Memoir by R. Bell. London, Griffin, [1870?]. 2 v. 17½ cm. NNC

Thomson's Seasons, Spring, (*Winter and Hymn*). In *Chambers' English Classics for Use in Schools*. London and Edinburgh, 1870, 1871. L

1871

Spring and Winter, ed. Walter M'Leod. London, Longman, Brown, Green and Longmans, 1871. 12°. Eng. Cat.

The Poetical Works of Thomson, Falconer, and Blair. London, T. Nelson and Sons, 1871. 448 pp. RC

1872

The Poetical Works of James Thomson. In *The Aldine Edition of the British Poets*. London, Bell and Daldy, 1872. 2 v. 12°. Eng. Cat.

1873

The Poetical Works of James Thomson, ed. W. M. Rossetti, illus. T. Seccombe. London, E. Moxon, Son and Co., [1873]. xx, 508 pp. 8°. L

The Poetical Works of James Thomson, ed. C. C. Clarke. In *Cassell's Library Edition of the British Poets*. London, Cassell, [1873]. 372 pp. 8°. L

The Poetical Works of James Thomson, illus. London, James Blackwood and Co., 1873. Eng. Cat.

1874

The Works of James Thomson, illus. Metz and Hamilton. London, John Dicks, 1874. 11, 220 pp. NNC

The Poetical Works of James Thomson, illus. London, James Blackwood and Co., [1874]. 378 pp. 8°. L

Thomson's Seasons, Winter, ed. J. F. Bright. In *Rivington's English School Classics*. London, J. Rivington, 1874. xvii, 62 pp. 16°. L

1875

The Poetical Works of James Thomson, illus. London, James Blackwood and Co., [1875]. xx, 373 pp. 8°. EN

1876

The Seasons and The Castle of Indolence, illus. Gilbert-Greatback, S. Williams. London, Chatto and Windus, 1876. lxx, 271 pp. 8°. EN

1877

The Seasons, illus. Boston, James R. Osgood and Co., 1877. 4 pt. 16°. [L has *Spring*, 80 pp.] L

1878

The Poetical Works of James Thomson, ed. W. M. Rossetti. London, Ward, Lock and Co., [1878]. viii, 508 pp. 8°. L

The Poetical Works of James Thomson, illus. London and Edinburgh, W. P. Nimmo, 1878. xliii, 498 pp. NNC

The Poetical Works of James Thomson. Boston, Houghton, Osgood and Co., [1878]. 8°. Amer. Cat.

1879

The Poetical Works of James Thomson, ed. W. M. Rossetti, illus. T. Seccombe. London, E. Moxon, Son and Co., [1879]. xx, 508 pp. EN

The Seasons, illus. Schmolze. New York, James Miller, 1879. 8°. Amer. Cat.

The Spring, Ger. ed., tr. H. A. Werner. Leipzig, Teubner, 1879. viii, 53 pp. Kayser

188–

The Poetical Works of James Thomson. New York, Hurst and Co. [188–?]. 382 pp. 12°. NN

The Poetical Works of James Thomson, ed. F. J. Child. In *The Aldine Edition of the British Poets*. Boston, Houghton, Mifflin and Co. [188–?]. 2 v. 12°. L

1880

The Poetical Works of James Thomson, ed. W. M. Rossetti, illus. Thomas Seccombe. London, Ward, Lock and Co., Warwick House, [1880]. xx, 508 pp. 8!. 8″. In *Popular Poets*, ed. Edward Moxon. London, Ward, Lock and Co., [1879–83]. 8°. L

1881

The Poetical Works of James Thomson, James Beattie, Gilbert West, and John Bampfylde. 1881. 4 pt. In *Routledge's British Poets*, 1853–8. 24 v. L

The Seasons and The Castle of Indolence, ed. Robert Bell, illus. London, Griffin, Bohn and Co., [1881]. 272 pp. 17½ cm. DLC

The Seasons, illus. Boston, Houghton, Mifflin and Co.; The Riverside Press, Cambridge, 1881. 103 pp. In *Modern Classics*, v. 22. VtMiM

1883

The Poetical Works of James Thomson. Edinburgh, W. P. Nimmo and Co., 1883. xxxvii, 498 pp. 8°. L

1884

The Seasons, Student's Edition. Boston, G. D. Russell, [1884]. Amer. Cat.

1888

The Seasons, [selections], illus. London, Field and Tuer; New York, Scribner and Welford, [1888]. [1889? NNC]. In *The Leadenhall Press Six Penny Series*. 30 pp. 18 cm. NN

1889

The Seasons, illus. Glasgow, D. Bryce and Son, 1889. 215 pp. 23½ cm. 8°. L

The Seasons, illus. New York, F. A. Stokes and Bro., 1889. 215 pp. 23 cm. DLC

1891

The Seasons and The Castle of Indolence. Oxford, Clarendon Press, 1891. vi, 436 pp. 8°. EN

The Seasons and The Castle of Indolence, ed. J. L. Robertson. New York, Macmillan, 1891. 8°. Amer. Cat.

1892

The Seasons, ed. Allan Cunningham, illus. London, Chatto and Windus, 1892. 271 pp., 8°. L

Spring, illus. Boston, Estes and Lauriat, [1892]. 95 pp. 15½ cm. DLC

Summer, illus. Boston, Estes and Lauriat, [1892]. 127 pp. 15½ cm. DLC

Autumn, illus. Boston, Estes and Lauriat, [1892]. 105 pp. 15½ cm. DLC

Winter, illus. Boston, Estes and Lauriat, [1892]. 92 pp. 15½ cm. DLC

1893

Spring. (Also *Summer.—Autumn.—Winter.*) London, Gay and Bird; [Boston, Mass.], [1893]. 4 v. 12°. L

1894

The Seasons. Boston, Mass. London, Dec. 1894. 2 v. Eng. Cat.

1897

The Poetical Works of James Thomson, A New Edition with Memoir and Critical Appendices, ed. Rev. D. C. Tovey. London, George Bell and Sons, 1897. 2 v. 8°. In *The Aldine Edition of the British Poets*. L

1899

The Seasons, ed. Wilfred Meynell. London, 1899. Tobin

1900

Thomson's Winter, being a Reproduction of The First Edition. With an introduction by William Willis. London, W. H. Bartlett and Co., 1900. 45 pp. 8°. L

1901

The Poems of James Thomson, ed. William Bayne. London, W. Scott, [1900? NNC], [1901]. In *The Canterbury Poets*, ed. Joseph Skipsey, William Sharp and others. London, Walter Scott, [1884–1922]. xxxviii, 286 pp. 8°. L

1906

The Seasons, ed. Henry D. Roberts. With a bibliographical note and critical study by Edward Gosse. In *The Muses' Library*, London, G. Routledge and Sons, Ltd.; New York, E. P. Dutton and Co., [1906]. 184 pp. 15½ cm. L

1908

The Complete Poetical Works of James Thomson, ed. J. Logie Robertson. London, New York, Oxford University Press, 1908. xxiii, 516 pp. 19 cm. 8°. L

Thomson's Seasons, ed. Otto Zippel. Berlin, Mayer and Muller, 1908. 338 pp. 23½ cm. L

191-

The Poetical Works of James Thomson. New York, Crowell, [191–?], 479 pp. 19 cm. NNC

The Seasons, illus. Boston, Houghton, [191–?]. 80, 103, 89, 96 pp. 13½ cm. NNC

1927

The Seasons, illus. Jacquier. London, The Nonesuch Press, 1927. 198 pp. 27½ × 20 cm. 4°. L

1929

Winter. A Poem. [A facsimile of the first edition.] Oxford, Clarendon Press, 1929. 16 pp. fol. L

Not Dated

Thomson's Seasons and Castle of Indolence. London, J. F. Dove. Engraved for *Dove's English Classics*. xiv, 192 pp. 24°. EN

APPENDIX II

THE IDENTIFICATION OF A CRITIC

(a) ON NAMES AND DATES

IN 1777, when *Strictures Critical and Sentimental on Thomson's Seasons* was published, the author was identified as 'J. More' on the title page and 'John More' in the 'Dedication'. 'J. More' has undergone several transformations in bibliographical listing. The Library of Congress listed *Strictures* under 'More, John'—though it did not provide dates. The *British Museum* listed the volume under 'More, (John). *Essayist*', and in the James E. Tobin bibliography, *Eighteenth Century English Literature and Its Background* (New York, 1939), the author of *Strictures* was identified as 'More, Jacob'. In 1941, the index to the *Cambridge Bibliography* repeated the attribution to 'More, Jacob' and added the dates '1740–1793'.

Earlier bibliographies than Tobin and *CBEL*, however, cautiously repeated the initial entry. In *Bibliotheca Britannica* (Edinburgh, 1824) and *A Critical Dictionary of English Literature*, ed. S. Austin Allibone (Phila., 1897), the author of *Strictures* was listed as 'More, J.' and the *Monthly Review's* comment on *Strictures* by William Enfield did not attempt any further identification.

The christening of 'More, J.' as 'More, Jacob', made by A. H. Thompson in the bibliography to his article on Thomson in the *Cambridge History of English Literature, X* (1913), was, so far as I can discover, due to the assumption that 'More, J.' referred to the 'Roman Moore' or 'More', an Edinburgh painter and contemporary of John Moir, who was not the author of any book and did not provide any of the paintings or engravings for any editions of *The Seasons*. The *Cambridge Bibliography* merely provided the dates—taken from the *Dictionary of National Biography*—and thus seemed to reaffirm the attribution. But the basis for attribution—that his family name was sometimes spelled 'More', that his first initial was 'J.', that he came from Edinburgh and was a landscape painter—seems insufficient compared to the signature 'John More' which appears at the end of the 'Dedication' in *Strictures* and the abundant circumstantial evidence that relates the work of John More to that of John Moir.

The spelling of the Reverend John Moir's name had at least one variant, for *Bibliotheca Britannica* listed his works under 'Moire, John' and in one of the works, *Gleanings*, of which Moir was the author, the work in which he 'plagiarized' More's *Strictures*, there appeared a story about 'Serjeant More' in which Moir explained that the story was not a fiction and that 'the writer could assure the reader, that he had his intelligence from the mouth of one of the principal actors' (II, 22). The tale called 'Serjeant

More' at least hinted at the possibility that 'More' was a variant of the family name of the author.

The Reverend John Moir was the author of a volume of sermons called *Practical Discourses* which appeared in 1776 and, if we disregard *Strictures* in 1777, of *Female Tuition* and *Sermons* which appeared in 1784, and a two-volume collection of his writings called *Gleanings* in 1785. Other volumes appeared in subsequent years. In 1791, *One Thing Needful* and, according to the advertisement at the end of *Preventive Policy* (1796), there were at least three other publications available 'at his [the author's] House, No. 4, Newington Place, Surrey', *Hospitality* 'a Discourse occasioned by reading His Majesty's Letter in Behalf of the Emigrant Clergy, in St. Dionis, Back Church, May 26, 1793'; *Personal the best Pledge of Public Reform, addressed to Inferiors*, and *Embarrassments of a Clergyman with a numerous Family, and no Benefice to support them considered, in a Probation Sermon.*

John Moir does not appear in the *Dictionary of National Biography* nor is he listed in *CBEL*. His works are not discussed in any Scottish literary history which I have seen, and though reference to his *Gleanings* was made by Meyer H. Abrams, it was to a passage which also appeared in *Strictures*.

(b) 'STRICTURES' AND 'GLEANINGS'

The Reverend John Moir's *Gleanings*; or *Fugitive Pieces* in Two Volumes, was published in 1785 with the information, 'author of *Female Tuition*, and other literary performances' (advertisement). In the 'Preface' Moir declared, 'These *Gleanings* are the result of many years scribbling. Some of them have occasionally appeared in various periodical publications, and had no other attention, probably, than the trash with which they were consigned to oblivion; some were never before in print; two, *Gentleness of Mind*, and *Love and Joy*, are in great measure, borrowed from writers of known reputation; and all have received considerable corrections and improvements' (p. iii). The relation between *Strictures* and *Gleanings* exceeds any possible interpretation of 'borrowing'. Of the 279 pages of the *Strictures*, Moir reprinted either verbatim or in slightly revised form 125–30 pages. If one compares the statements regarding authorship made in the two volumes the conclusion seems very likely that 'More' and Moir were one and the same. Thus in a footnote in *Strictures* (p. 173) the author explained, 'The following *Ode to Politeness*, occasioned by the present popular system of education, has been printed but not published, and I hope the Reader will not be displeased with seeing it here. My pretensions to versification, however, are not so sanguine, as to subject me to much chagrin from its reprobation. . . . The truth is, it is nearly as good as I could make it; and though it should be thought very *bad*, it is at least not very long.' Under 'Verses on Various Subjects' in the second volume of *Gleanings*, Moir reprinted the poem, calling it 'Politeness' and with only two insignificant changes: 'O come, with meekness in thine eye' to 'Come then, with meekness in thine eye', and 'However choak'd with courtly whim' to 'However choak'd by courtly whim'.

In an earlier footnote in *Strictures*, the author wrote—in a not unusual disguise—'I have seen a manuscript poem called the *Season*, describing one of our summer *Watering Places*, from which the Author has indulged me with the following extract. So it is somewhat in the manner, though by no means an exact imitation of Thomson, I give it to the public merely as a curiosity' (p. 130 n.). The poem is reprinted in *Gleanings* (II, 152–5), but to it is added a stanza of fourteen lines, completely consistent with the lines which precede it, not only in thought but in verse structure. Thus the only two original poems in *Strictures* were reprinted in Moir's *Gleanings*.

But the material which was reprinted from the body of the *Strictures* was far more extensive than even these poems would lead one to believe. The selection in *Gleanings* called 'Genius of Poetry' was, with the omission of a footnote on 'Wit and Dullness' and with an occasional change of word, the reprint of the first pages of the chapter, 'On the Genius of Poetry'. The selection called 'Origin of Beauty or Grace' was, with minor revisions and the omission of a footnote, a reprint of pages 59–67 from the chapter, 'On Thomson's Powers of Description'. In *Gleanings*, Moir had a chapter called 'Thomson's Seasons' which was a reprint of the very long chapter in *Strictures* called 'Objections to the Seasons, considered'. More omitted the introductory page and reprinted pages 74–116. The selection of 'Originality' in *Gleanings* was, with slight revisions and omission of several paragraphs dealing with Thomson, and the footnote which contained 'Ode to Politeness' reprinted in volume II, a reprint of pages 168–80 of the chapter, 'On the Originality of the Seasons'. (Pages 181–7 of *Strictures* contain a long quote on Thomson from Warton's *Essay*.) This selection in *Gleanings* concluded with several passages taken from other parts of *Strictures* and included with revisions: pages 52–54 from 'On Thomson's Power of Description', followed by a paragraph from pages 51–52 and another from page 50. The selection in *Gleanings* called 'Sensibility' reprinted the beginning of the chapter called 'On the Pathetic of the Seasons', pages 188–94, and the selection 'Writing to the Heart' continued the chapter, with the addition of an introductory paragraph and minute revisions, from pages 194 to 197 followed by pages 241–2. This passage was then concluded by a selection from 'On the Use and Abuse of Criticism', pages 28–31. The chapter 'On the Use and Abuse of Criticism' was, according to the John More (in frontispiece) originally delivered 'to a private society of friends . . . and, though containing some bold expressions, is now published without any material alteration, rather as an apology for the Author's own manner, than any intentional attack on that of others'. Given this acknowledgement, it would surely seem dangerous, if not silly, for John Moir to have thanked his subscribers and worthy friends while perpetrating such an obvious hoax.

(c) THE RELATION OF 'STRICTURES' AND 'GLEANINGS' TO MOIR'S WRITINGS

Without engaging extensively in the question of the consistency of views between *Strictures* and Moir's works, it can be pointed out that the attitude to 'feeling', to 'system,' to 'discrimination', all appeared in Moir's *Practical Discourses*, printed the year preceding the publication of *Strictures*. Regarding 'discrimination', a key concept in *Strictures*, Moir wrote, 'Indeed the great and difficult art in this, as well as in most other things in life, is discrimination' (p. 188).

Gleanings, published in 1785, did contain selections from Moir's own writings. He included in it a long quotation from *Practical Discourses*, which he called 'Pulpit Eloquence', and he included two selections from *Female Tuition* published in 1784, 'Manly' and 'The Philosopher in Love'. A further demonstration of the argument for Moir's authorship appears in *Female Tuition*. That volume incorporated—pages 238–9—with slight revisions a footnote which appeared in *Strictures*, pages 62–63, dealing with the comparative sensibility of the male and female. The following paragraph from the *Strictures*, pp. 240–1, for example, was included slightly revised, in *Female Tuition*, pp. 226–7. I quote them as an example of Moir's practice. From *Strictures*:

> Of all those objects that work so powerfully on our natures, female distress is by much the most operative. This rouses all the heart, and touches the sympathy of men into action. The complaints of a woman, unless when defeated by some other feeling, procures immediate attention and instant relief. Indeed it is not in the masculine temper to treat them with indifference. We are often more solicitous about their welfare, than about our own, and there is hardly any man so barbarous as not to exhibit some striking proofs of generosity, when their subject is in question. The peculiar delicacy of their make, their exquisite sensibilities, their dependent conditions, the winning assiduities of their manners, and the settled propensity we discover to serve and protect them, give us a lasting and active concern in whatever relates to their pain or pleasure.

From *Female Tuition*:

> Among all the objects that powerfully affect our natures, female distress seems one of the greatest. This rouses all the heart, and touches the sympathy of men. The complaints of a woman, unless when defeated by some other feeling procure immediate attention and relief. It is not in the masculine temper to treat the sex with indifference. We are often more solicitous about their welfare than our own; and there is hardly any man so barbarous as not, occasionally at least, to exhibit some striking proofs of generosity at their instance. The peculiar delicacy of their make, their exquisite sensibilities, their dependent condition, the winning assiduities of their manners, and the invariable propensities we feel and discover to serve and protect them, give us a lasting and active concern in what relates to their pain and pleasure.

The final and, I trust, conclusive argument for Moir's authorship of the *Strictures* is the similarity of sentiments between *Discourses on Practical Subjects* [by John Moir, London, T. Cadell, 1776] and *Strictures* in 1777. Moir expressed these opinions before More did, and the closeness of language and idea argue that Moir who expressed them before the *Strictures* also expressed them in the *Strictures*. In addition to the sermonic style which appeared in *Strictures*, many of the particular premises were present in both works. Thus the *Discourses* developed the concept of enlightened sentiment (p. 180) which was repeated in the *Strictures* in the concept of the 'sympathetic *few*' (p. 1). The defence of 'enthusiasm' in the *Discourses*—'That noble spirit of Enthusiasm, so essential to excellence in arts, in science, in morals, will ever be considered as extravagant and romantic by the bulk of mankind' (p. 203 n.)—was repeated in similar terms in *Strictures*, p. 12 n.: 'Genius is a species of enthusiasm, which none but a genius comprehends . . . There is an ardour and pathos inseparable from its minutest exertions, which they [those not geniuses] do not understand because they do not feel, and which strike them only with an air of extravagance.' Moir in the *Discourses* suggested that great sensibility often led to weak constitutions and he repeated this idea in similar terms in *Strictures*, p. 192: 'The most exquisite sentiments, and the best feelings, are often found in conjunction with the weakest bodies.' In the *Discourses* he argued that women had more tender sensibilities than men (pp. 273–5) and this issue appeared again in *Strictures*, pp. 60–65. Even an argument such as the one that poetry should extend to all men, not merely the good, first appeared in the *Discourses* (pp. 178–9) and reappeared in *Strictures* (pp. 193–4).

These are only some of the less common ideas shared by both works. They are perhaps sufficient to establish that John More and John Moir are one and the same, and that 'John More' was indeed a variant spelling of John Moir.

INDEX OF NAMES

INDEX OF NAMES

INDEX OF SUBJECTS